The Holodeck in the Garden:

SCIENCE AND TECHNOLOGY IN CONTEMPORARY AMERICAN FICTION

The Holodeck in the Garden:

SCIENCE AND TECHNOLOGY IN CONTEMPORARY AMERICAN FICTION

EDITED BY PETER FREESE & CHARLES B. HARRIS

Dalkey Archive Press

First edition, 2004
Second printing, 2006
All rights reserved

Library of Congress Cataloging-in-Publication Data

The holodeck in the garden : science and technology in contemporary American fiction / edited by Peter Freese and Charles B. Harris.— 1st Dalkey Archive ed.
   p. cm. — (Dalkey Archive scholarly series)
   ISBN 1-56478-355-3 (alk. paper)
    1. American fiction—20th century—History and criticism. 2. Science in literature. 3. Literature and science—United States—History—20th century. 4. Literature and technology—United States—History—20th century. 5. Science fiction, American—History and criticism. 6. Technology in literature. I. Freese, Peter. II. Harris, Charles B. III. Series.

PS374.S33H65 2004
813'.50936—dc22
                                                      2003070083

Partially funded by a grant from the Illinois Arts Council, a state agency,
and by the University of Illinois at Urbana-Champaign

www.dalkeyarchive.com

Table of Contents

Acknowledgments

Many of the essays in this volume were presented, often in different form, at the German-American conference on "Science, Technology, and the Humanities in Recent American Fiction" held in Paderborn, Germany, on May 11-14, 2003. We would like to express our gratitude to the American and German scholars who presented papers at the conference and who contributed to the present volume. Without their cooperation and advice this collection would not have been possible. We'd also like to thank the conference sponsors: Paderborn University, the Unit for Contemporary Literature at Illinois State University, and Dalkey Archive Press. The conference was made possible by funding and other support from the *Deutsche Forschungsgemeinschaft,* the German Association for American Studies, the American Embassy in Germany, and the Archdiocese of Paderborn. Special thanks to Bob McLaughlin, who read the manuscript with a critic's eye and made several invaluable suggestions, to Samuel Berkes, who prepared the manuscript for publication, to Nathan Furl, who oversaw this book's production, and to John O'Brien, who agreed to publish the collection and who provided much encouragement and advice. As always, our greatest debt is to our respective spouses, Marianne and Victoria, whose patience and encouragement make so much more than a scholarly book possible.

Peter Freese & Charles B. Harris
Introduction: The Holodeck in the Garden

> While you and i have lips and voice which are
> for kissing and to sing with who cares if some
> oneeyed son of a bitch invents an instrument to
> measure Spring with?
>
> —e.e. cummings

> So yes, technology can have an effect on art, but
> the idea that it takes away mystery or awe or won-
> der in nature is wrong. It's quite the opposite.
> It's much more wonderful to know what some-
> thing's really like than to sit there and just simply,
> in ignorance, say, "Oooh, isn't it wonderful!"
>
> —Richard Feynman

1

In her entertaining jeremiad against modern technology, self-proclaimed neo-Luddite Nicols Fox compares our relationship with machines to a dysfunctional marriage: "We love our machines, after all—as we would a spouse in an endur-ing bad marriage, whose flaws are so familiar, whose irritating voice is so much a part of the background that it is impossible to conceive its not being there" (*xii*). Evoking what she celebrates as a "hidden Luddite tradition" in literature and art of the past two centuries, Fox energetically counsels divorce. For most scholars and students of literature and art, the "unrecognized" insurgency Fox traces—which, in her account, runs from the British and American Romantics through Dickens, Ruskin, and William Morris to Lawrence, Wendell Berry, and the artist John Muir—has been, at the very least, hidden in plain sight. In-deed, the Balkanized relationship of art and science, which British physicist-cum-novelist C.P. Snow christened the "Two Cultures" in his (in)famous 1959 Rede lecture, has remained a persistent theme in cultural criticism for the past half-century.

Six years before Snow's lecture, British mathematician Joseph Bronowski, who had also written a study of William Blake, pleaded for common ground. "Science and the arts today are not as discordant as many people think," he urged; "it is the business of each of us to try to remake that one universal language which alone can unite art and science, and layman and scientist, in a common understanding" (13). Far less sanguine than Bronowski, Snow characterized the relationship between "literary intellectuals at one pole" and "scientists, and as the most representative, the physical scientists" at the other as "a gulf of mutual incomprehension—sometimes (particularly among the young) hostility and dislike, but most of all lack of understanding" (4). In 1965, Kurt Vonnegut—whose early novels had first appeared as paperbacks because their SciFi themes disqualified them as "serious" literature—ironically echoed Snow's assessment:

> The feeling persists that no one can simultaneously be a respectable writer and understand how a refrigerator works…[…] Colleges may be to blame. English majors are encouraged […] to hate chemistry and physics, and to be proud because they are not dull and creepy and humorless and war-oriented like the engineers across the quad. And our most impressive critics have commonly been such English majors, and they are squeamish about technology to this very day. (1-2)

Vonnegut mentions no names. But the year before his remarks initially appeared in the *New York Times Book Review*, one of America's "most impressive critics," Leo Marx, published his pioneering study *The Machine in the Garden: Technology and the Pastoral Ideal in America*, which seemed to confirm the shared pessimism of Snow and Vonnegut. From Virgil's *Eclogues* through Shakespeare's *The Tempest* to classic American literature of the nineteenth century, Marx traces "the image of a green landscape—a terrain either wild or, if cultivated, rural—as a symbolic repository of meaning and value." In the Modernist "fables" of such writers as Faulkner, Fitzgerald, Frost, and Hemingway, however, "our inherited symbols of order and beauty have been divested of meaning" as a result of "the machine's increasing domination of the visible world." Thus, we find ourselves urgently in need of "new symbols of possibility" that our artists are no longer able to create. "The machine's sudden entrance into the garden," Marx concludes his study, "presents a problem that ultimately belongs not to art but to politics" (362-65).

In the literary works Marx analyzes, the most common image of technological intrusion is the locomotive. But Marx wrote his book at the height of the Cold War. Trembling between the lines of his prose and all but explicit in his study's ominous closing sentence is the mid-Sixties anxiety over the scariest machine of all: the Bomb. More sophisticated than ever, technologies of mass-destruction continue to haunt global consciousness. But technological specters undreamt of by Marx rival WMDs in our national nightmares. Fears that machines might destroy us have been superseded by fears that machines may quite literally replace us, as the human gives way to the posthuman. "In the posthuman," N. Katherine Hayles summarizes, "there are no essential differences or absolute demarcations between bodily existence and computer simulation, cybernetic mechanism and biological organism, robot technology and human goals" (3). The machine despoiling our techno-scientifically transformed twenty-first century garden, it would seem, is the holodeck.[1]

2

A relevant question, then, is whether or not the Cold War between art and techno-science described by Snow and Vonnegut persists in the Age of Digitalized Information. A cursory glance at the contemporary landscape (or has "cyberscape" become a more operative word?) would seem to suggest that it does. In America, recent attacks on scientific truth claims by theoretically inclined humanists and social scientists (including literary theorists, feminists, and social constructivists) —and the spirited and, in the case of the celebrated Sokal hoax, parodic rebuttals these attacks have provoked—fuel the so-called Science Wars.[2] In Europe, too, tensions continue to run high. For example, in 1999, Dietrich Schwanitz, a professor of English from Hamburg, published a German best seller entitled *Bildung: Alles, was man wissen muß* [*Bildung: All You Need to Know*], which promised to make its readers "educated." In his hefty tome, Schwanitz offers an idiosyncratic survey of the overall "cultural knowledge" of Western civilization, concluding that, although Snow's "Two Cultures" phrase had become familiar in Germany,

> Snow's appeal had no effect whatsoever. Admittedly, the insights of the natural sciences are taught in school, they contribute a thing or two to the understanding of nature, but only little to the understanding of culture. Therefore one is still considered impossible if one does not know who Rembrandt was. But if one has no idea what the Second Law of Thermodynamics is all about, what is the relation between the weak and the strong interaction between electromagnetism and gravity, or what a quark is, nobody will take that as a sign of a lack of education, although the latter term is taken from a novel by Joyce. As deplorable as it might seem to some people: knowledge about the natural sciences does not have to be hidden, but it is definitely no part

of being educated. (482, trans. P. Freese)

In 2001, Ernst Peter Fischer, a professor of the history of science from Konstanz, answered Schwanitz with yet another best seller entitled *Die andere Bildung: Was man von den Naturwissenschaften wissen sollte* [*The Other Bildung: What One Should Know about Natural Sciences*]. In his survey of the history of natural sciences, Fischer disparages what he takes to be Schwanitz's inexcusably one-sided book, accuses the latter of hiding his scientific ignorance by declaring as educationally relevant only that knowledge which exists within his limited horizon, and bitterly complains about "the arrogance of men with a literary and philosophical education towards the achievements of the natural sciences" (10, trans. P. Freese).

With spokespeople of the Schwanitz and Fischer camps lustily accusing each other of one-sidedness, and with the ongoing debate about cloning illustrating the mutual incomprehension between worried humanists and progressive scientists, the present German situation seems to be an exact replica of the scene about which Snow famously complained over forty years ago. Indeed, some even argue that this traditional division should be upheld, as exemplified by the verdict of disgruntled British critic Cressida Connolloy, who, in a 1997 review of Ian McEwan's novel *Enduring Love*, calls for

> an immediate worldwide moratorium on novelists reading works of science. Like oceans plundered of whales, science-books have become overfished by voracious, imaginative writers. You can't pick up a novel these days without being bombarded by Heisenberg's Uncertainty Principle, or the latest theories on Darwinism. Popular science now occupies ample shelf-room in every bookshop and a prominent place in bestseller lists. Novelists should tell us stories, not recite particle physics. I'm all in favour of the novel of ideas, but at least let the ideas be the author's own. An author's individuality is drowned in this sea of science. (34)

Except for a small coterie of intellectuals with cross-disciplinary interests, and despite attempts to bridge the traditional gulf by such groups as the American "Society for Literature and Science,"[3] these examples seem to indicate that traditional departmentalizations have not been shaken and that Bronowski's hope for a universal language of common understanding remains unfulfilled.

Nonetheless, some encouraging signs suggest that, if not peace, then at least détente, may be breaking out. For example, Jay Clayton's recent survey of what he calls "a new genre of contemporary literature that focuses on science and technology" maintains "that the two cultures are once again converging" (808). Even Cressida Connolly's curmudgeonly diatribe against the novel's recent dalliance with science suggests that a rapport has developed between the contemporary novel, especially those novels we regard as postmodern, and such recent scientific and science-related developments as chaos theory, quantum mechanics, systems theory, and the emerging field of "informatics."⁴ Seeking to explain this developing rapport, Joseph M. Conte proposes that the "turn toward unpredictability in postmodern science establishes an affinity with narrative that classical science, in its demand for deterministic results, could not permit" (3). The expanding list of postmodern novelists who incorporate aspects of recent science into their narratives or whose fiction has been read through the lens of contemporary science include John Barth, Thomas Pynchon, Don DeLillo, Joseph McElroy, Richard Powers, Carol de Chellis Hill, Norman Mailer, Gilbert Sorrentino, Robert Coover, Kathy Acker, Harry Mathews, William Burroughs, and Kurt Vonnegut, not to mention such important SciFi writers as William Gibson, Neal Stephenson, Octavia Butler, Ursula le Guin, and Philip K. Dick. (The fact that certain science fiction writers are now regarded as important by the literary establishment indicates that the invidious distinctions between perceived "high" and "low" genres about which Vonnegut complained in 1965 have largely dissolved.)

The search for instabilities, considered by Lyotard to be the new subject of postmodern science, has also proven attractive to theoretically inclined literary scholars. The new scientific mode, Gordon E. Slethaug observes, suggests "that dominant views of science—if not science itself—could be contradicted, that it was not, as some thought, monolithic, orthodox, single-minded, or at one with itself, and that, therefore, it was available to the skeptical humanist" (*xi*). The result has been a spate of recent critical studies that read contemporary fiction through the lens of contemporary science. Chief among these is an influential series of books written or edited by N. Katherine Hayles: *The Cosmic Web: Scientific Field Models and Literary Strategies in the Twentieth Century* (1984), *Chaos Bound: Orderly Disorder in Contemporary Literature and Science* (1990), and *Chaos and Order: Complex Dynamics in Literature and Science* (1991). Other important titles include Robert Nadeau, *Readings from the New Book of Nature: Physics and Metaphysics in the Modern Novel* (1981); Ira Livingston, *The Arrow of Chaos: Romanticism and Postmodernism* (1984); Thomas LeClair's study of systems theory and the novel, *The Art of Excess: Mastery in Contemporary American Fiction* (1989); Joseph Natoli, *Mots*

D'Ordre: Disorder in Literary Worlds (1992); Susan Strehle, *Fiction in the Quantum Universe* (1992); Peter Freese, *From Apocalypse to Entropy and Beyond: The Second Law of Thermodynamics in Post-War American Fiction* (1997); Gordon E. Slethaug, *Beautiful Chaos: Chaos Theory and Metachaotics in Recent American Fiction* (2000); and Joseph M. Conte, *Design and Debris: A Chaotics of Postmodern American Fiction* (2002).

3

In one sense, this scientific turn shouldn't be too surprising, since our quarrel has always been less with science than with technology—a distinction, admittedly, that is often elided. Even when science itself seems to be the target, as in Romantic poetry or the Modernist poems of Frost or the (old) New Criticism's insistence on the ontological difference between literary and scientific discourse, it is the scientistic conviction that materialism, objectivism, and rationality can explain everything—what Heidegger called technological thinking (353-54)—that offends. In his novel *The Gold Bug Variations*, a brilliant exploration of the interface between music, art, literature, and evolutionary biology, Richard Powers eloquently expresses this difference: "Science is not about control. That is technology. . . . The purpose of science, if one must, was the purpose of being alive: not efficiency or mastery, but the revival of appropriate surprise" (129).[5] But if literature and criticism have forged a rapprochement with the new science, what about technology, which, like science, has also entered a new modality characterized by cyborgs, Baudrillardian simulations, and what John Johnston calls "information multiplicity"?

On the one hand, literature and literary theory continue to warn against the dangers and excesses of modern technology and the mind-forged manacles of technological thinking, as many of the essays in this collection evince. On the other hand, one of the more interesting recent developments in literary theory has been a series of studies that attempt to relate literature to new information technologies in non-adversarial ways. In *Postmodern Sublime: Technology and American Writing from Mailer to Cyberpunk*, for example, Joseph Tabbi searches for "a properly complex relation between technology and the imagination" (23). Although literature and technological modes of production are separate discourses, Tabbi argues that certain homologies link them in ways that, properly conceptualized, can lead to a "postmodern or conceptual naturalism" (26):

The machine is not "man's equivalent," and the loss of an analogical bridge for uniting conceptual dualities that are themselves suspect in the first place, instead of frustrating representation, might free writers to imagine styles of resistance that are not merely *oppositional*. By being attentive to the modes of technological simulation and refusing to oppose them with some purportedly "authentic" literary consciousness, writers can hope instead to locate sublime, nonobservable relations with technology itself [....] (28)

In her award-winning study *How We Became Posthuman*, N. Katherine Hayles also seeks accommodation, proposing a "view of the posthuman [that] offers resources for thinking in more sophisticated ways about virtual technologies" (290).

If my nightmare is a culture inhabited by posthumans who regard their bodies as fashion accessories rather than the ground of being, my dream is a version of the posthuman that embraces the possibilities of information technologies without being seduced by fantasies of unlimited power and disembodied immortality, that recognizes and celebrates finitude as a condition of human being, and that understands human life is embedded in a material world of great complexity, one on which we depend for our continued survival. (5)

Other recent studies that attempt to reconceptualize literary and cultural theory in informational terms include David Porush, *The Soft Machine: Cybernetic Fiction* (1985); William R. Paulson, *The Noise of Culture: Literary Texts in a World of Information* (1988); Scott Bukatman, *Terminal Identity: The Virtual Subject in Postmodern Science Fiction* (1993); Anne Balsamo, *Technologies of the Gendered Body: Reading Cyborg Women* (1996); Joseph Tabbi and Michael Wutz, eds., *Reading Matters: Narrative in the New Media Ecology* (1997); Ursula K. Heise, *Chronoschisms: Time, Narrative, and Postmodernism* (1997); John Johnston, *Information Multiplicity: American Fiction in the Age of Media Saturation* (1998); Joseph Tabbi, *Cognitive Fictions* (2002); and N. Katherine Hayles, *Writing Machines* (2002).

4

Common to the studies mentioned above is close attention to the interpenetration of contemporary literary theory with science and information theory. As might be expected, references to Baudrillard, Deleuze and Guattari, and Michel Serres predominate, but all of the critics display a sophisticated understanding and appreciation of the full range of Poststructuralist/Postmodern thought. A shared animus toward literary theory separates a second group of scholars from the mainstream of academic literary criticism, even though they too attempt to apply science to the study of literature and the other arts. Marching beneath the self-proclaimed banner of "Biopoetics," these scholars, representing a range of disciplines including English, read literature and the arts through the lens of biogenetics. The major intellectual influence on this fledgling movement seems to be sociobiologist Edward O. Wilson, whose efforts to synthesize the various branches of knowledge into a few natural laws culminates with his 1998 study *Consilience: The Unity of Knowledge*. In his search for a "full exploration of the universal traits that unite humanity" (234), Wilson abjures postmodernist theory and remains skeptical about complexity theory, "the very arena," Joseph Conte points out, "in which the arts and the sciences find common discourse, though not the unity (on the ground of the natural sciences) that [Wilson] would prefer" (15). If Wilson relies on sardonic understatement to register his displeasure with postmodernism—"Scientists, awake and held responsible for what they say while awake, have not found postmodernism useful," he writes mordantly in *Consilience* (45)—other "bio-aestheticians" are more direct. For example, Brett Cooke, a Professor of Russian at Texas A&M University, advises his fellow dabblers in biopoetics to "avoid the kinds of biased and sloppy research methods generally attributed to literary critics and their various schools" (97). Similarly, Robert Storey, an English professor from Temple University, begins his *Mimesis and the Human Animal* (1996) with a "Pugnacious Preface," in which he castigates the "logical bankruptcy" of literary theory. "This is a book of literary theory for those who detest literary theory" (*xxi*), he writes aggressively, before concluding with a "Plainspoken Postscript" that elevates his confrontational rhetoric even further:

> There is little likelihood, of course, that the study of literature will pass out of English Departments into other hands, but there is every likelihood that, if it continues on its present course, its reputation as a laughingstock among the scientific disciplines will come to be all but irreversible. (206)

Despite Wilson's confident prediction that he "can see [biothematics] taking over from deconstruction by 2010, and permanently,"[6] this small group of conservative scholars seem largely to be talking among themselves, with little influence so far on mainstream criticism. Cooke and Frederick Turner's edited collection *Biopoetics: Evolutionary Explorations in the Arts* (1999) gathers a representative sampling of essays from the movement. Other key books include Alexander J. Argyros, *A Blessed Rage for Order: Deconstruction, Evolution, and Chaos* (1991); Frederick Turner, *Natural Classicism: Essays on Literature and Science* (1992); Ellen Dissanayake, *Homo Aestheticus: Where Art Comes From and Why* (1992); Joseph Carroll, *Evolution and Literary Theory* (1994); and the works by Storey and Wilson mentioned above.

5

Many of the scholars whose books are mentioned in the brief survey above have also contributed to the present collection. Most of the essays included here were presented, often in different form, at a German-American conference on "Science, Technology, and the Humanities in Recent American Fiction" held in Paderborn, Germany, on May 11-14, 2003 (full conference proceedings, which we also edited, were published in Germany; see Works Cited). For the sake of organizational efficiency, we have divided the collection into three sections. We do this in full awareness that most of the essays gathered here, despite their differing emphases, are linked by multiple convergences. As a result, certain essays located in one section could arguably have been placed in another. Despite this taxonomic "leakiness" (to borrow Brian McHale's description of the taxonomy he employs in his essay below), our categories have the heuristic advantage of highlighting three major focuses of this collection.

In the first section, entitled "The Holodeck in the Garden: Informatics in the Age of the Posthuman," the essays focus on our current cultural transition from the Industrial Age to the Information Age. Developments in digital technologies have placed pressures not only on the *medium* of literature but on the ways we read and respond to it. In "Performative Code and Figurative Language: Neal Stephenson's *Cryptonomicon*," for example, N. Katherine Hayles calls for *material* ways of reading that understand "technologies and texts . . . as mutually interpenetrating and constituting one another." After noting that Stephenson wrote the first several drafts of *Cryptonomicon* with a fountain pen on paper before typing it into a computer, and that instead of the standard Windows or Macintosh, he interfaces his computer with a Unix-based operating system, Hayles concludes that Stephenson's novel "bears witness to the digital technologies that created it. In its structure, dialectical dynamics, and subterranean narrative, it incorporates in linguistic form the crisis in writing practices that materially marked its electronic body, understood simultaneously as a clash of operating systems, a struggle of open source utopianism against capitalistic greed, and an opposition between the command structures of code and the analogical surfaces of figurative language."

Like Hayles, Joseph Conte is also interested in the reader's role in cybernetic fictions, especially the claims of theoreticians and practitioners that such fictions demand a more interactive response from the reader. In "The Virtual Reader: Cybernetics and Technocracy in William Gibson and Bruce Sterling's *The Difference Engine*," Conte questions this assumption, arguing that readers of cybernetic fiction are more acted upon than acting, not so much constructing the text as constructed by it. Print-based works of cybernetic fiction such as Gibson and Sterling's novel *The Difference Engine* (1991) imagine for themselves a "Virtual Reader, subject to the determinations and control of the text," who functions as an avatar or "stand-in" for the Reader in the text. Conte argues that such fictions share his skepticism about "the promised control and organization of information" digital technologies putatively afford; "and they entertain a touch of paranoia that these liberating devices are shackles in another form."

In "Are Rhizomes Scale-Free?: Network Theory and Contemporary American Fiction," John Johnston also examines literature's changing role in the Digital Age. After evoking Deleuze and Guattari's figure of the rhizome, Johnston suggests that the Internet may be the ultimate rhizome. "As a new kind of shared space or habitat, an ecology that is neither completely artificial nor natural, the Internet may be both the harbinger and testing ground of a new kind of environment in which technology continues evolution by other means." In his exploration of the amenability of this image of the Internet to literature, Johnston examines the relevance of recent scientific research on information networks—in particular, on their structure, patterns of growth, and dynamics—for a range of contemporary American fictions, in both print and the electronic medium. After examining how networks in novels by Thomas Pynchon, Joseph McElroy, and William Gaddis function in relation to their narratives, Johnston turns to hypertext narratives by Michael Joyce and others. His discussion is guided by "the question of how the relationship of network to narrative changes when we shift from print to the electronic medium."

In "'Of Metal Ducks, Embodied Iduros, and Autopoietic Bridges': Tales of an Intelligent Materialism in the Age of Artificial Life," Hanjo Berressem also turns to Deleuze, specifically his reading of Leibniz in *The Fold*. In a wide-ranging discussion of the concept of autopoiesis, Berressem takes up the idea that in "emergent" systems, "matter and mind organize themselves into larger structures/units from within, without recourse to an overall, pre-established blueprint." Drawing on a number of cultural artifacts, including novels (William Gibson's *Idoru Trilogy*, Thomas Pynchon's *Mason & Dixon*), cultural theory (Homi Bhabha, Deleuze and Guattari), and the theory of digital text (emergent text), Berressem's essay unfolds some of the possibilities and vicissitudes of thinking the logic of emergence. Berressem is especially interested in countering the "linguistic/cultural constructionism" of poststructural theorists like Judith Butler, preferring instead a "general machinics" that views human culture as "part of an overall, immanent *ecologics*" that in turn works according to "a logic of machinic—natural *and* cultural—autopoiesis" (italics Berressem's).

The concept of emergence also figures prominently in Christian Berkemeier's essay "Kingdoms of the Blind: Technology and Vision in Douglas Coupland's *Girlfriend in a Coma* and Stephen Spielberg's *Minority Report*," although Berkemeier employs the concept in a different context. Drawing from the terminology of Niklas Luhmann, "emergence" in Berkemeier's essay refers to "the potential existence of phenomena beyond the limits of human experience." This definition of emergence guides Berkemeier's analysis of the "ambivalent role of prophecy, a knowledge formation both technologically and mystically provoked and enhanced," in Douglas Coupland's novel *Girlfriend in a Coma* and Stephen Spielberg's movie version of the Philip K. Dick short story "The Minority Report." Both novel and film rely on intrusions of the mystical into the rational to interrogate and destabilize "seeing and visual representation" as the "key elements of a modernist hegemonic discourse." By presenting "alternative models of vision" (coma, dream, and sleep in Coupland; digitally enhanced forms of foretelling in Spielberg), both texts, Berkemeier concludes, question the rationality, validity, and moral implications of the visual/representational paradigm.

According to Charles B. Harris ("Technoromanticism and the Limits of Representationalism: Richard Powers's *Plowing the Dark*"), Richard Powers's novel *Plowing the Dark* (2000) also participates in the ongoing postmodernist critique of representationalism. Unlike early metafictionists, whose primary target was literary realism, or later postmodernist writers, whose focus often shifted to the hyperreal mediascapes of late capitalist America, Powers aims his critique at virtual technologies, whose promise of "post-symbolic communication" continues what Powers calls humanity's "millennium-long desire to get out of our bodies." According to Harris, Powers launches his "powerful critique of representationalism and the representing mind-set" from "inside" of representationalism by reappropriating in order to recontextualize the conventions of representational realism. Sudden "jump shifts in epistemic levels," including a major perturbation near the novel's end, rupture the novel's "referential dimension," thereby problematizing the "adequacy of the mimetic relation to the real" and, within the novel's context, undermining the totalizing dream of techno-romanticism.

Curtis White's trenchant polemic "The Great American Disaster Machine," concludes section one by introducing a new tone to the collection. A chapter from his popular book *The Middle Mind: Why Americans Don't Think for Themselves* (Harper San Francisco 2003), White's essay argues that the "technological imagination" has become "the moving force behind *all* expressions of the American imagination" (italics White's). A major reason for this state of affairs is the mass media, which has become "utterly and inescapably technologized and creates an appropriate reverence for technology in its products." As an example of what he means, White takes to task a PBS documentary entitled *Beyond Human*, which celebrates advancements in nanotechnology that have made it possible for human beings to become more like machines and machines more like human beings. In the course of his critique, White holds scientists responsible for what he sees as a failure to "participate in the technological imagination as part of a larger social imagination." Inventing primarily for global corporations and the military, scientists, White contends, have taken little responsibility for the impact their inventions may have on the "human order."

6

The essays in the second section, "The Technology In/Of Contemporary American Fiction," expand the collection's scope beyond digital technologies to technology in a wider sense. As Brian McHale points out in the section's opening essay, "Mech/Shaper, or Varieties of Prosthetic Fiction: Mathews, Sorrentino, Acker, and Others," literature itself is a technology, just as all writing is fundamentally a prosthetic machine. Although most fiction attempts to efface "its status as technique, as technology," the writing that interests McHale flaunts its technological status by adopting and foregrounding "*extra* artificiality, *extra* technique" (italics McHale's). Borrowing his taxonomy from Bruce Sterling's cyberpunk novel/short story cycle *Schismatrix Plus* (1996), McHale posits two forms of "prosthetic fiction." On the Mech side of the binary range "proceduralists" such as Harry Mathews (the American OuLiPo), Gilbert Sorrentino, and Walter Abish, whose fiction is generated "mechanically" by "predetermined rules or constraints." On the Shaper side, splicers and cloners such as William Burroughs, Kathy Acker, and Matthew Roberson generate fictions that cut apart and recombine, rewrite, or overwrite preexisting texts. In reminding us "that all writing is a technology exterior to and different from ourselves," mechanical and cloned fictions reflect "the cyborg condition of collaboration or even symbiosis with machines that we all seem to be approaching," thereby modeling the utopian prospect of "collective or even 'global' consciousness, distributed across multiple individuals."

In "Race and Modernity in Colson Whitehead's *The Intuitionist*," Michael Bérubé shifts the focus from the technology of literature to technology *in* literature, specifically the use of elevators in Colson Whitehead's novel *The Intuitionist* (1999). Shrewdly (and wittily) foregrounding elevators and elevator inspection as the indices of urban modernity, the novel, according to Bérubé, offers metacommentary on the history of "passing" narratives in the US as well as on the history of debates over professionalization and the production of specialized forms of knowledge in the past thirty years. In addition, Whitehead's "wry postmodern *noir*" presents a meditation on the Great Northern Migration, that key component of the narrative of the African-American experience of modernity; a "look-back" at the fitful integration of African-Americans into the municipal civil service agencies; a "cognitive map" of the politics of race and space in the urban United States; and a "tongue-in-cheek reworking of the discourse of racial 'uplift.'" In his essay's closing passages, Bérubé discusses "a curious undercurrent" in the novel "in which the representation of race is confounded and compounded by the representation of disability."

David Cowart's "Anxieties of Obsolescence: DeLillo's *Cosmopolis*" also considers the role of technology in contemporary fiction. Cowart reads *Cosmopolis* (2003), Don DeLillo's first post-9/11 novel, as a meditation on the "quantum transformations" of technological innovation, which "treads into compost its own prior achievements." According to Cowart, "progressive obsolescence or desuetude figures often in the thoughts of Eric Packer," the doomed protagonist of DeLillo's novel. Yesterday's technology offends Packer's fastidious eye and mind: the outmoded seems a silent reproach, "anti-futuristic," an annoying reminder of all the rubbish generated by progress. By making figures of obsolescence this text's most frequently repeated motif, however, DeLillo signals the fate of Packer himself—and much that he represents. Although DeLillo is aware that words, like our devices, can also "outmode," he believes ultimately, Cowart argues, that language can accommodate "every stress placed on it by the times—whether figurative explosions of technology or literal explosions of airliners colliding with buildings." Like DeLillo's other novels, Cowart concludes, *Cosmopolis* creates a "counter-narrative," a "counterhistory," in "opposition to the enormous technology of war," not through polemic, but by "capturing the cultural moment in actions and characters that he realizes in language crafted to the purpose. . . ."

The rapid proliferation of modern technology also plays a prominent role in Udo J. Hebel's essay "Performing the Spectacle of Technology at the Beginning of the American Century: Steven Millhauser's *Martin Dressler*." Set a century earlier than DeLillo's novel, Millhauser's *Martin Dressler: The Tale of an American Dreamer* (1996) "fictionalizes the historic moment when the spread of modern technology merged with the collective impulse to theatricalize American culture as an 'imperial spectacle'" (the phrase quoted is Alan Trachtenberg's). Illustrating his essay with photographs of turn-of-the-20th century architectural marvels, Hebel explores the representation of technology as the driving force in Dressler's conspicuous performance of personal magnification and imperial grandeur: "Dressler's skyscraper hotels are the ultimate expression of his will to stick out and enact his expanding personality on the stages of metropolitan New York and beyond." In the last analysis, "the ever-intensifying performativity of the technological spectacle," both as architectural wonder and personal magnification, fails, as the public rejects the Dressler hotels and the "technological salvation" they proffer.

In "History on Wheels: A Hegelian Reading of 'Speed' in Contemporary American Literature and Culture," Klaus Benesch also traces the growing disenchantment with technology over the course of the 20th century. At the turn of the last century, speed had become the most visible marker of social and technological change in America and, for many commentators, represented the ultimate shaping force of modernity itself. But if modern aesthetics of speed often embraced the acceleration and velocity of life as a means to retrieve aspects of an original authentic self, Benesch argues that postmodern writers such as John Barth, Thomas Pynchon, Don DeLillo, and T. C. Boyle present a different view of the forming and de-forming power of speed. By translating the dynamic potential of capitalist society into paranoiac scenarios of restlessness, repetition, and historical decline, these writers indulge a Neo-Hegelian concept of "posthistoire" (as the suspension of all movement) that is clearly at odds with the fading national ideology of progress and mobility. According to Benesch, recurring images of stasis and immobility in postmodern fiction may be read "as a longing gesture to escape the cultural reification of 'becoming' (as implicated in the idea of historical progress) by arresting time and projecting spaces of 'being' (outside of history)."

Speed and its opposite, immobilization, also figure prominently in Michael

Porsche's essay "Steven Wright: *Going Native* (by Car)." Although Wright's 1995 novel has been characterized as a postmodern *On the Road*, the road in *Going Native* is no longer "the figure of multiplicity and possibility" that it is in Kerouac's novel. Rather, Porsche argues, "the globalization of media-related and media-induced identity makes traveling itself as superfluous as it makes the metaphorics of car and road meaningless." A darkly comic mediation on the Age of the Simulacrum (when two characters retreat to the jungles of Borneo in search of unmediated experience, for example, they find only reflections of America's cultural imperialism), *Going Native* presents a series of cartoon-like characters "stuck in a closed system of medialized surfaces," for whom the car itself, no longer a representation of the possibility of change, "has become a cage merely simulating movement."

Like the essays in section one, Joseph Raab's "From Intertextuality to Virtual Reality: Robert Coover's *A Night at the Movies* and Neal Stephenson's *Snow Crash*" refocuses our attention on digital technologies. But Raab's primary emphasis is the technologies of film and print as they figure in Robert Coover's collection of interrelated short stories *A Night at the Movies* (1987) and Neal Stephenson's cyber-novel *Snow Crash* (1992). Although both writers construct fictional identities by assembling and reconfiguring a series of public images and well-known myths, Stephenson relies more heavily on virtual technologies "to expand our notions of the possible" in his fiction than Coover does in his, possibly because of the explosion of computer technology during the five years separating the books' publishing dates. Despite this fact, Raab argues that "the virtual reality (as well as the so-called 'Reality') of *Snow Crash* is rooted in film images and is therefore not as different from the fictions that collide in *A Night at the Movies* as we may tend to assume." Echoing Joseph Conte's earlier argument, Raab contends that the author, not the reader, controls narrative decisions in print fiction, including cyberfiction.

7

The six essays comprising the collection's final section focus primarily on the ways literature registers recent changes in scientific thinking. As is true of the essays above, interest here is not only on thematic considerations but on the ways literary form responds, or fails to respond, to the shaping pressures of new conceptual shifts. In "Toxins, Drugs, and Global Systems: Risk and Narrative in the Contemporary Novel," Ursula K. Heise links ecocriticism, risk theory, and narrative analysis in a reading of two contemporary novels, Don DeLillo's

White Noise (1984) and Richard Powers's *Gain* (1998). Although technological risk plays a key role in both novels, neither text displays narrative strategies that effectively represent complex and global technoeconomic systems as a source of risk. DeLillo's satirical mode successfully transfers to the readers his characters' uncertainties about how to assess the ecological and technological risks that surround them, but it does so by limiting "the conceptual horizon of risk perception to the individual and the local." Powers more effectively broadens the scope of his novel to include the worldwide networks that entangle his characters, but his novel's primarily modernist narrative strategies never challenge the reader's understanding of the real in the way that his characters' comprehension of reality is challenged by their encounter with risk. Contemporary fiction, Heise concludes, must continue to experiment with new forms and even new narrative media in order to keep up with its own advancing conceptual sophistication.

Like Heise, Joseph Tabbi also traces the connections between a recent scientific concept, in this case autopoiesis, and contemporary American fiction (Berressem and Berkemeier also examine this connection, but in different contexts). "William Gaddis and the Autopoiesis of American Literature" considers Gaddis in light of his German near-contemporary, the systems theorist Niklas Luhmann. Tabbi views Gaddis's major novel of American capitalism, *JR* (1975), as "especially yielding to the terms and methods of [Luhmann's] systems theory." According to Tabbi, Gaddis and Luhmann alike view literary language less as a means of communication than as a "bridge between perception and communication." The interaction between an author and a reader during the reading process produces "an understanding that belongs to neither the work nor society, neither to the author nor the reader alone, but to a literary consciousness newly aware of its primary perceptions." A work achieves autopoiesis only at this level of "second-order observation, when the reader observes a structure of prior decisions put in place by an author. . . ."

Most readers of this volume will recognize Carl Djerassi as the "father of the Pill." Few American readers, however, may be aware that over the past fifteen years Djerassi has turned his attention from "hard" science to what he calls "science-in-fiction" and that in Europe, especially in Germany and Austria, his novels are widely read and his plays frequently performed. The next two essays in this section may therefore introduce Djerassi's literary endeavors to many American scholars. In "Science-in-Fiction: Science as Tribal Culture in the Novels of Carl Djerassi," Walter Grünzweig argues that Djerassi's fiction and plays investigate the sciences as a system of discourses and behaviors frequently likened to "tribal" cultures. His essay examines the ways Djerassi's novels both construct and deconstruct scientific cultures in opening the way for a dialogue between two traditionally opposed cultures of inquiry. In "Science-in-Fiction: Literary Contraband?" Djerassi discusses his own "science-in-theatre" plays. In "science-in-theatre," Djerassi explains, science must be the work's central focus, not merely a metaphor, and it must be "real or at least plausible." Similarly, the behavior of the scientific characters in the plays must be "plausible, if not actually factual." Djerassi illustrates his aesthetic by including scenes from three plays in his essay.

The volume concludes with Peter Freese's comprehensive account of the evolving role of the scientific concept of entropy in American literature from its initial appearance in Henry Adams's *Education* (1907) to the present. "From the Apocalyptic to the Entropic End: From Hope to Despair to New Hope?" investigates the competing paradigms of "The End" in American literature, apocalypse and thermodynamic "heat-death"; traces the development of the Second Law of Thermodynamics and its cultural contexts from Carnot and Clausius through Boltzmann and Shannon to Prigogine's "dissipative structures" and chaos theory; and analyzes the fluctuating figure of entropy in a wide range of contemporary American fictions, including works by John Updike, Stanley Elkin, Thomas Pynchon, Donald Barthelme, and William Gaddis. Freese explores entropy's changing guises—from thermodynamic entropy to informational entropy to non-equilibrium entropy—and the social attitudes, which range from gloomy pessimism to new hope, that accompany these transformations.

As we begin the 21st century, it is fair to say that Snow's "Two Cultures" remain separated by suspicion, misunderstanding, and mutual neglect. The impact of Continental theory and philosophy on literary studies has been so pronounced that few contemporary critics have strayed beyond its influence. But as this Introduction has suggested and as the essays collected here demonstrate, bridges linking the humanities and social sciences to science and science-related fields have been and are being built. A growing number of critics and theorists have begun to read literature through the lens of recent scientific theories, including chaos and complexity theory, quantum physics, systems theory, evolutionary biology, and information or media theory. This tendency promises to enrich the study of literature and contribute to the profession's current move in the direction of greater interdisciplinarity and polymathy. We hope that the present collection will add to and extend interest in the burgeoning area of literature and science.

NOTES

[1] The holodeck, as most readers of this collection will recall, was introduced on the popular TV series *Star Trek: The Next Generation*, which premiered in 1987. A virtual reality machine to end all virtual reality machines, the holodeck combines holography, magnetic force-fields, and energy-to-matter conversions to produce what Janet H. Murray calls "a universal fantasy machine, open to individual programming" (15).

[2] Keith Parsons provides an excellent selection of the best of these debates in his edited collection, *The Science Wars*. Other useful perspectives on the "science wars" include Paul R. Gross and Norman Levitt, eds., *Higher Superstitions,* and Andrew Ross, ed., *Science Wars*. Essays about the Sokal hoax have been collected in *The Sokal Hoax: The Sham that Shook the Academy*, edited by the editors of *Lingua Franca*.

[3] See, e.g., the first major stocktaking of relevant transdisciplinary scholarship in Schatzberg, et al, *The Relations of Literature and Science: An Annotated Bibliography of Scholarship, 1880 – 1980*.

[4] "Following Donna Haraway," N. Katherine Hayles, defines *informatics* as "the technologies of information as well as the biological, social, linguistic, and cultural changes that initiate, accompany, and complicate their development" (*How We Became Posthuman* 29).

[5] Later in the novel, Stuart Ressler, a brilliant molecular biologist who flees science in part to avoid its misguided claims to mastery, explains: "Science is not about control. It is about cultivating a perpetual condition of wonder in the face of something that forever grows one step richer and subtler than our latest theory about it. It is about reverence, not mastery" (411).

[6] Wilson makes this prediction in his blurb on the back cover of Cooke and Turner's *Biopoetics*.

WORKS CITED

Argyros, Alexander J. *A Blessed Rage for Order: Deconstruction, Evolution, and Chaos.* Ann Arbor: U of Michigan P, 1991.

Balsamo, Anne. *Technologies of the Gendered Body: Reading Cyborg Women.* Durham: Duke UP, 1996.

Bronowski, J. *The Common Sense of Science.* Cambridge: Harvard UP, 1953.

Bukatman, Scott. *Terminal Identity: The Virtual Subject in Postmodern Science Fiction.* Durham: Duke UP, 1993.

Carroll, Joseph. *Evolution and Literary Theory.* St. Louis: U of Missouri P, 1994.

Clayton, Jay. "Convergence of the Two Cultures: A Geek's Guide to Contemporary Literature." *American Literature* 74.4 (2002): 807-831.

Connolly, Cressida. "Cleverly Done." *Literary Review* September 1997: 34.

Conte, Joseph M. *Design and Debris: A Chaotics of Postmodern American Fiction.* Tuscaloosa: U of

Alabama P, 2002.

Cooke, Brett and Frederick Turner, eds. *Biopoetics: Evolutionary Explorations in the Arts.* Lexington: ICUS, 1999.

Dissanayake, Ellen. *Homo Aestheticus: Where Art Comes From and Why.* New York: Free Press, 1992.

Fischer, Ernst Peter. *Die andere Bildung: Was man von den Naturwissenschaften wissen sollte.* München: Ullstein, 2001.

Fox, Nicols. *Against the Machine: The Hidden Luddite Tradition in Literature, Art, and Individual Lives.* Washington: Island Press/Shearwater Books, 2002.

Freese, Peter. *From Apocalypse to Entropy and Beyond: The Second Law of Thermodynamics in Post-War American Fiction.* Essen, Germany: Die Blaue Eule, 1997.

——— and Charles B. Harris, eds. *Science, Technology, and the Humanities in Recent American Fiction.* Proceedings of the German-American Conference on "Science, Technology, and the Humanities in Recent American Fiction," 11-14 May 2003, Paderborn, Germany. Essen: Die Blaue Eule, 2004.

Gross, Paul R. and Norman Levitt. *Higher Superstitions: The Academic Left and Its Quarrels with Science.* Baltimore: Johns Hopkins UP, 1994.

Hayles, N. Katherine. *The Cosmic Web: Scientific Field Models and Literary Strategies in the Twentieth Century.* Ithaca: Cornell UP, 1984.

———.*Chaos Bound: Orderly Disorder in Contemporary Literature and Science.* Ithaca: Cornell UP, 1990.

———.*Chaos and Order: Complex Dynamics in Literature and Science.* Chicago: U of Chicago P, 1991.

———.*How We Became Posthuman: Virtual Bodies in Cybernetics, Literature, and Informatics.* Chicago: U of Chicago P, 1999.

———.*Writing Machines.* Cambridge: MIT P, 2002.

Heidegger, Martin. "The Age of the World View." Trans. Marjorie Grene. *Boundary 2* 4.2 (1976): 353-54.

Heise, Ursula K. *Chronoschisms: Time, Narrative, and Postmodernism.* Cambridge: Cambridge UP, 1997

Johnston, John. *Information Multiplicity: American Fiction in the Age of Media Saturation.* Baltimore: Johns Hopkins UP, 1998.

LeClair, Thomas. *The Art of Excess: Mastery in Contemporary American Fiction.* Urbana: U of Illinois P, 1989.

Livingston, Ira. *The Arrow of Chaos: Romanticism and Postmodernism.* Theory Out of Bounds 9. Minneapolis: U of Minnesota P, 1984.

Marx, Leo. *The Machine in the Garden: Technology and the Pastoral Ideal in America.* New York:

Oxford UP, 1964.

Murray, Janet H. *Hamlet on the Holodeck: The Future of Narrative in Cyberspace*. Cambridge: MIT P, 2000.

Nadeau, Robert. *Readings from the New Book of Nature: Physics and Metaphysics in the Modern Novel*. Amherst: U of Massachusetts P, 1981.

Natoli, Joseph. *Mots D'Ordre: Disorder in Literary Worlds*. Albany: SUNY P, 1992.

Parsons, Keith. *The Science Wars: Debating Scientific Knowledge and Technology*. Amherst, NY: Prometheus Books, 2003.

Paulson, William R. *The Noise of Culture: Literary Texts in a World of Information*. Ithaca: Cornell UP, 1988.

Porush, David. *The Soft Machine: Cybernetic Fiction*. New York: Methuen, 1985.

Powers, Richard. *The Gold Bug Variations*. New York: HarperCollins, 1991.

Ross, Andrew, ed. *Science Wars*. Durham: Duke UP, 1996.

Schatzberg, Walter, Ronald A. Waite, and Jonathan K. Johnson, eds. *The Relations of Literature and Science: An Annotated Bibliography of Scholarship, 1880 – 1980*. New York: MLA, 1987.

Schwanitz, Dietrich. *Bildung: Alles, was man wissen muß*. Frankfurt: Eichborn, 1999.

Slethaug, Gordon E. *Beautiful Chaos: Chaos Theory and Metachaotics in Recent American Fiction*. Albany: SUNY P, 2000.

Snow, C. P. *The Two Cultures: And a Second Look*. Cambridge: Cambridge UP, rpt. 1965.

Storey, Robert. *Mimesis and the Human Animal: On the Biogenetic Foundations of Literary Representation*. Evanston: Northwestern UP, 1996.

Strehle, Susan. *Fiction in the Quantum Universe*. Chapel Hill: U of North Carolina P, 1992.

Tabbi, Joseph. *Postmodern Sublime: Technology and American Writing from Mailer to Cyberpunk*. Ithaca: Cornell UP, 1995.

———. *Cognitive Fictions*. Electronic Mediations, Volume 8. Minneapolis: U of Minnesota P, 2002.

—— and Michael Wutz, eds. *Reading Matters: Narrative in the New Media Ecology*. Ithaca: Cornell UP, 1997.

The Sokal Hoax: The Sham that Shook the Academy. Ed. Editors of *Lingua Franca*. Lincoln: U of Nebraska P, 2000.

Turner, Frederick. *Natural Classicism: Essays on Literature and Science*. Charlottesville: UP of Virginia, 1992.

Vonnegut, Jr., Kurt. *Wampeters, Foma, & Granfalloons*. New York: Delacorte, 1974.

Wilson, Edward O. *Consilience: The Unity of Knowledge*. New York: Knopf, 1998.

I.

The Holodeck in the Garden: Informatics in the Age of the Posthuman

N. Katherine Hayles
Performative Code and Figurative Language:
Neal Stephenson's *Cryptonomicon*

As computers become increasingly pervasive in the environment, code begins to rival natural languages in importance, scope, and complexity. Just as when two natural languages mingle (e.g., "Spanglish"), code and language begin to interpenetrate in ways both obvious and subtle. These range from Perl poetry (articulations that can run as computer code but also have significance in English), to neologisms combining code and English (the "broken code" in the work of such electronic artists as MEZ, Alan Sondheim, and Talan Memmott), to the thematic resonances code has in novels such as William Gibson's *Neuromancer* trilogy.

The Gibson example is particularly interesting, for Gibson has gone on record testifying that he wrote his cutting edge trilogy on a manual typewriter.[1] The spectacle of an obsolete nineteenth-century technology used as the medium to instantiate works that vault into the twenty-first raises questions about how far technological effects penetrate into the literary body. *Neuromancer* may envision a future dominated by information technologies in its thematic content, but it does so through the medium of the printed book, a centuries-old technology as familiar to Dickens as it is exotic to *Neuromancer's* protagonist. Gibson, banging away on a mechanical typewriter, dreams of Case, who does not type at all but jacks directly into cyberspace through neural connections wired to his central nervous system.

Although *Neuromancer* may be a special instance insofar as Gibson quaintly composed on a typewriter when most writers had already switched to computers, the issues the case/Case evokes are general in scope and significance. They appear whenever two different vectors, one rooted in the past and the other arcing toward the future, are negotiated within a literary work distinguished from everyday discourse precisely because it attends closely to the materiality of language. The tensions between past and future are particularly acute at the present moment when the narrative conventions of the novel, rooted in the seventeenth century, are inscribed with writing technologies profoundly different than the mechanical printing presses with which the history of the novel is deeply entwined. Through what pathways and by what means does the influence of an informatic writing technology, with its complex trading zones in which language and code mutually put pressure on one another, penetrate into a text that on the surface appears entirely conventional? Assuming these subterranean perturbations exist, what critical strategies might be used to excavate them?

To explore these questions, I take as my tutor text Neal Stephenson's *Cryptonomicon*. As its name indicates, code is at the center of its thematic concerns, both as cryptological systems and computer algorithms. Yet like *Neuromancer*, *Cryptonomicon* uses traditional narrative techniques; indeed, if anything it is even more conventional in form than *Neuromancer*. Unlike Gibson, however, Stephenson does not use a typewriter to compose his works. He writes first drafts with a fountain pen and paper, revising two or three times on paper, and then types the revised version into a computer, revising yet again as he does so.[2] Moreover, with an impressive background as a computer programmer, he does not employ the ubiquitous Windows or even Macintosh but rather interfaces with the computer through a Unix-based operating system. As his nonfiction work *In the Beginning Was the Command Line* testifies, he shifted from Macintosh to Unix when a crisis erupted in his compositional practices—a shift he regarded as so significant that he wrote a book explaining why Unix is far superior to any other operating system and exhorting his readers to experience similar enlightenment.[3] The crisis that led to his conversion came when he lost a very large file that was corrupted so badly it could not be recovered in its entirety.[4] Although he does not specify what the file was, chronology suggests it may have been *Cyrptonomicon*, published the same year as *Command Line*.[5] If this supposition is correct, then the electronic file of *Cryptonomicon* bore within its body traces of this crisis. Whatever the case with the corrupted file, the electronic *Cyrptonomicon* certainly bore witness to his conversion, since he switched in 1995 and the book was written from 1995-98. Following this line of thought, we can assume that the clash of operating systems, including all they imply about the nefarious corporate practices of Microsoft, the capitalistic greed that underlies its ruthless business practices, and the resistance to these practices by open source communities, particularly Unix and the related Linux, deeply penetrated into the electronic structure of this text in very physical and material ways. But are there connections between these material manifestations of coding practices and the linguistic surface of the text? Through what means do they mark the work when it is manifested as a print book, that is, when the flickering signifiers of the electronic text have been converted to the durable impressions of ink on paper?

To ask these questions is to regard the book not as a fixed and static artifact but as the trace of complex technological, conceptual, linguistic, and cryptological negotiations. I will argue that in *Cryptonomicon* a series of systematic transformations bears witness to these negotiations through dialectical attempts to mitigate the tensions inherent in the clashes of materiality and abstraction, code and language, hackers and corporate moguls, good profit and evil greed. Cycling through these transformations, the narrative is unable to achieve a final resting point, a resolution stable enough to permit it to achieve a rising action that would lead to a satisfying climax and clear denouement. The failure of the text to conform to conventional novelistic expectations signals that despite its traditional form, the literary corpus is riven by the writing technologies that produced it. Wrenched from the context of mechanical printing presses and embedded within informational technologies, this novel tries its best to remain a novel, but the differences between durable marks and flickering signifiers, natural language and computer code, de-form the form and unsettle its dynamics. Finally the text is forced into oxymoronic knots that alone are adequate to articulate its contradictory enunciations of code/language and the conflicting historical vectors of mechanical past/ informatic future.

Math and Lizards: The Dialectic's First Terms

The basic problem for Lawrence was that he was lazy. He had figured out that everything was much simpler if, like Superman with his X-ray vision, you just stared through the cosmetic distractions and saw the underlying mathematical skeleton. Once you found the math in a thing, you knew everything about it, and you could manipulate it to your heart's content with nothing more than a pencil and a napkin. (8)

Sand erupts into the air, like smoke from the burning tires of a racer, and the lizard is rocketing across the beach. It covers the distance to the Imperial Marine in one, two, three seconds, takes him in the backs of the knees, takes him down hard into the surf. Then the lizard is dragging the dead Nip back up onto the land. It stretches him out there among the dead Americans, walks around him a couple of times, flicking its tongue, and finally starts to eat him. (326)

A mathematician coolly controlling the world with a pencil and a napkin, and a primeval lizard so ferocious it erupts into Bobby Shaftoe's nightmares for years to come—these are contraries generating the first dialectical interaction. *Cryptonomicon* eloquently testifies to the importance of code in the contemporary world. Yet when the text pushes to the extreme of seeing the world as *only* code, a counter-resistance begins to build, becoming fiercer as more faith is placed in code. Although this resistance can take multiple forms, its most violent manifestation is animal appetite. As we shall see, the resulting clashes between abstract form and violent appetite remain largely unresolved in the text, leading to further transformations in the dialectic.

An important assumption underlying code's supremacy is the idea that information can be extracted from its material substrate. Once the information is secured, the substrate can be safely discarded. Peering through the window of Bletchley Park's "Ultra"-secret cryptographic decoding facility, Lawrence Pritchard Waterhouse sees a tape running through a machine so fast it smokes and catches fire. Surmising he is witnessing a Turing machine, Lawrence realizes that the "men in the room accept the burning of the tape so calmly" because the tape itself is not important.

That strip of paper, a technology as old as the pyramids, is merely a vessel for a stream of information. When it passes through the machine, the information is abstracted from it, transfigured into a pattern of pure binary data. That the mere vessel burns is of no consequence. Ashes to ashes, dust to dust—the data has passed out of the physical plane and into the mathematical, a higher and purer universe where different laws apply. (195)

From here it is a small step to seeing information as immaterial; although information must necessarily be embodied to exist in the world, these embodiments can easily be seen as contingent and dispensable, of no more consequence than the burning tape.

Yet no sooner does someone make this assumption than the text offers a counter-example, an instance where physical instantiation is no mere triviality but essential to the system's operation. One such moment occurs when Lawrence's grandson Randy Waterhouse and his colleagues at their startup Epiphyte Corporation meet with the Sultan of Kinakuta about their scheme to create a data haven in the tiny Sultanate. At first the Sultan mouths the conventional wisdom that "physical space no longer matters in a digitized, networked world. Cyberspace knows no boundaries" (316). But when he displays a world map with cables displayed between countries and continents, it is "not weblike at all," with only a few intercontinental cables running through "a small number of chokepoints" (317). Geography matters, it seems, even if it is invoked here in the interest of creating "a free, sovereign, location-independent cyberspace" (317). If the dream of a sovereign realm where information can flow freely is to be realized, it cannot be divorced from the real world of geographical specificities, material constraints and political realities.

As this example illustrates, controlling the flow of information becomes much more problematic when the complexities of coupling it with physical actions are taken into account. The don explains to Lawrence at a high-level strategy meeting after the Allies have broken the Enigma codes that

> the Germans have not broken our important cyphers. But they can observe our actions – the routing of our convoys in the North Atlantic, the deployment of our air forces. If the convoys always avoid the U-boats, if the air forces always go straight to the German convoys, then it is clear to the Germans . . . that there is not randomness here. . . . In other words, there is a certain point at which information begins to flow from us back to the Germans." (124)

Unlike secret codes, physical actions do not require privileged knowledge to access them, and this tie with the physical world makes every action initiated by the possession of secret information potentially a two-way channel of communication.

Controlling information quickly evolves, then, into a problem of simulating randomness. Indeed, as the don's remarks imply, cryptology can be understood as the art of hiding pattern in randomness, an understanding implicit in the Latin root for "crypt" meaning "hidden, secret." Crypt of course also denotes a burial place, historically often an underground chamber whose location is privileged knowledge. The convergence of the two plots—one focusing on cryptology in World War II, the second a contemporary quest for the recovery of an incredible gold stash buried by the Japanese when they realized the Empire was doomed—is overdetermined not only by the lineages that connect Lawrence Waterhouse, friend and contemporary of Alan Turing, to his nerdy grandson Randy Waterhouse, but also by the secrecy that unites the crypt of gold with the coded information revealing its location buried in the fiendishly complex Arethusa cryptographic code invented for Göring by Rudolf von Hacklheber, pre-war friend and lover of Alan Turing. The mathematical battle of cryptographic codes that stretches across half a century is punctuated by the realities of the physical actions with which codes are correlated. Far from leaving physicality behind, the struggle to control the world through mathematical and cryptological manipulation must contend with the wild, chaotic, and often violent unpredictabilities of a reality too vibrant, alive, and *hungry* to ignore.

When cryptography is used not only for secrecy but also for deception, material specificities become even more important. Echoing an actual British Secret Service maneuver labeled Operation Mincemeat, the text narrates the story of tricking a body up as a secret agent, planting it with false information, and throwing it into the ocean at a point where it is certain to be recovered by the Germans.[6] Participating in the operation is Bobby Shaftoe, the World War II haiku-writing Marine whose granddaughter America (Amy) is predestined to hook up with Randy half a century later. Bobby stars in the physically-oriented plot that entwines with the cryptological one, as adroit at accomplishing the near-impossible in the material world as Lawrence and Alan Turing are in the cryptological realm. In converting the dead butcher Gerald Hott's body into a supposed secret agent and therefore into a sign to be read and misunderstood by the Germans, everything depends upon the body's specificities—planted with the magnificent chronometer that must be Swiss rather than English, massaged with the German talcum body used to ease on the European wet suit, and decorated with the tattoo that happens to read "Griselda" and not, say, Amy. When he hears the German name, Lieutenant Ethridge tells Bobby, "Battles have hinged on lesser strokes of luck than this one, Sergeant!"—who (inappropriately from the Lieutenant's point of view but apropos for this argument) uses the comment as an excuse to bring up the rampaging lizard from Guadalcanal that haunts his imagination the way the abject haunts the pure realm of mathematics in the text's Imaginary (152).

For the abject is everywhere in this text, smelly, slimy, loathsome, and inescapable.[7] Detachment 2702, dedicated to creating deceptions designed to keep the Germans from realizing the Allies have broken the Enigma codes, tries to convert the material world into signs, but the abject resists this implicit dematerialization, insisting on its own repugnant physicality. Sent to a bivouac in Italy meant to simulate a secret observation post, Bobby orders his men to dollop barrels of G. I. shit into privy holes, carefully interleaved with Italian toilet paper to make it look as though they had occupied the site for months. Shit appears repeatedly in conjunction with secret writing and cryptological codes—in the "old-fashioned two-holer mounted above deep shafts that must descend all the way to hell" where Bobby reads the secret note in which his true love Glory arranges their first assignation (46); in the "equatorial miasma" that pervades the tropical climes in which much of the actions takes place, so intimately related to diarrhea that as soon as Bobby smells it he "feels his bowels loosening up already" (613); in the vernacular of hacker culture that advocates strong cryptography, where "Randy was forever telling people, without rancor, that they were full of shit" (80); in the exasperation of Doug Shaftoe, Bobby's son, when he exclaims to Randy, "Can't you recognize bullshit? Don't you think it would be a useful item to add to your intellectual toolkits to be capable of saying, when a ton of wet steaming bullshit lands on your head, 'My goodness, this appears to be bullshit?'" (729), a remark that significantly refers to a plot to find the gold's location, which is concealed in the Arethusa code intercepts. Shit even becomes a pseudo-code of its own when Detachment 2702 begins to refer to the "pathetic heap of a freighter" that they use in one of their ruses as a "shit" instead of a "ship," "e.g., let's get this cabin shit-shape! Where in the hell does the shit's master think he's taking us? And so on" (272). Surely one of the most significant instances occurs when Bobby and his comrades, attempting to rescue crucial Enigma code books from a sinking German submarine, wade through a cabin awash in coded documents and feces, a conjunction that brings the abject into intimate proximity with the secret writing that is supposed to operate in a realm of pure abstraction. Threatening to burst through the sphincters (bodily, social, military, and metaphorical) that seek to contain it, shit refuses to be reduced to only a sign. Expelled in involuntary reaction to intense fear, seeping out in uncontrollable diarrhea, dripping from jungle foliage in brutal marches by the Japanese and Americans in the South Pacific, shit has a material reality that cannot be contained solely within the algorithmic and cryptological.

Next to shit, perhaps the most conspicuous instance where emotion resists algorithmization is sexuality. Lawrence hypothesizes an inverse relation between his level of sexual frustration and his ability to work, but just when he thinks he can graph the relationship effectively, he discovers that sexual satisfaction is a more complex function than he imagined, depending not only on the time passed since his last ejaculation but also how the ejaculation was accomplished—by a "manual override," a prostitute, or someone with whom he is emotionally involved. "In other words, the post-ejaculatory horniness level was not always equal to zero, as the naïve theory propounded above assumes, but to some other quantity dependent upon whether the ejaculation was induced by Self or Other" (545) "His life," he concludes, "which used to be a straightforward set of basically linear equations, has become a *differential* equation" (548).

Even the computer, site of digital code abstracted into ones and zeros, has a physical presence so violent it cannot be ignored. When Lawrence demonstrates to his superior officer, Earl Comstock, the computer he has built from mercury vibrating in tubes, it is a violently physical experience: "Hot sonic tongs are rummaging through his viscera, beads of sweat being vibrated loose from his scalp, his nuts are hopping around like Mexican jumping beans" (599). In the fictional world of *Cryptonomicon*, Lawrence gets the idea for this first digital computer from an equally violent encounter with a dusty organ in his beloved Mary's church. In a passage reminiscent of his resolve to clear out his own clotted sexual machinery, "Gouts of dust and salvos of mouse droppings explode from the pipes as Waterhouse invokes whole ranks that have not been used in decades" (575). Joining the physical with the abstract, the experience allows Lawrence to see

> the entire machine in his mind, as if in an exploded draftsman's view. Then it transforms itself into a slightly different machine – an organ that runs on electricity, with ranks of vacuum tubes here, and a grid of relays there. He has the answer, now, to Turing's question, the question of how to take a pattern of binary data and bury it in the circuitry of a thinking machine so that it can later be disinterred." (576)

The odd terminology used here to describe the operations of electric memory—bury and disinter—further unites the cryptological operations of the computer as it works to break the Japanese code with the hidden crypt of gold revealed within the Arethusa code. Neither will be recovered with "nothing more than a pencil and a napkin"; both will require engagement with a physical world that cannot be reduced to mathematical abstraction.

The tension between abstraction and violent physicality is, however, itself a verbal construction and in this sense already takes place in an abstract realm. From this contradiction emerges the next phase of the dialectical transformation, as abstract code and animal appetite merge to create a third term, performative code. Unlike the abstract algorithms Lawrence uses to express mathematical ideas (a practice not uncommon among mathematicians in the 1930s before digital computers were invented), performative code operates as instructions to the machine and therefore initiates action in the world. In this sense it combines the active vitality connoted by animal appetite with the conceptual power of abstract code. With the collapse of these terms into performative code, signaled in the text by Lawrence's fictional discovery of the digital computer, another term comes into focus as the dialectical complement of performative code, namely figurative language.

Stephenson hinted at the importance of this conjunction in an interview shortly after *Cryptonomicon* was published. He commented that "it's become evident to me when I looked into the history of computers that they had this intimate relationship with cryptography going back a long way. You could say that writing books about it is a way to explore that relationship." Then he added, "I could try to get really profound here and say that it has something to do with the process of writing books in general, which is a matter of encoding ideas in words and symbols, but that's sort of a level of navel gazing I will leave to much more sophisticated literary critics" ("Talk with Neal Stephenson"). *Command Line*, which as we have seen can be considered the nonfictional companion to *Cryptonomicon*, offers valuable insights into the conjunction between writing novels and writing code that Stephenson hints at in the interview. Let us turn to *Command Line*, then, for insights essential to explicating the next phase of the dialectical transformation.

Commanding Cryptography

Abstract Code + Animal Appetite

Performative Code + Figurative Language

Stephenson's attitude toward computer code is clear in his quixotic jeremiad, *In the Beginning Was the Command Line,* published first online and later as a short book. Working through analogy, personal anecdote, and technical exposition, *Command Line* tries to persuade the educated public that Unix is a far superior operating system to either Macintosh or Windows. This superiority lies not only in Unix's efficiency and power or even its economy, available for little or nothing over the Web. Equally important is the fact that it allows the user to understand exactly what is happening as typed commands are compiled and executed by the machine. Windows, if not exactly evil, is profoundly misleading because it hides the operations of the machine behind an interface that discourages the user from understanding how the actions of a mouse, for example, get translated into binary code—or even that they do get so translated. To make the point, Stephenson recounts his first experience with computers while in high school, in which he communicated with a mainframe through a teletype machine. Clunky as that interface was, it had the virtue of making clear that the symbol strings he typed in were being converted into binary code through the ASCII conventions of encoding each symbol with eight bits.

Why *should* the user know what is going on in the guts of machine? Or to put it another way, what is wrong with the user staying at the surface, as long as the interface is robust and functional? One problem is that the interface may not really be that robust. To illustrate, Stephenson tells about the day his Macintosh PowerBook "broke my heart," destroying a large document so thoroughly that not even a powerful utilities program could recover it. Since the document was too large to put on a single floppy, Stephenson had stored the only complete copy on the hard drive, so the loss was traumatic. That very day he encountered Unix and became an instant convert. Tested and refined by thousands of hackers, Unix would never make this kind of error, Stephenson maintains, contrasting the open Unix error file with the covert information about errors that corporations like Microsoft bury in their private files. As a result, the information can only be obtained through their professional help line, which Microsoft charges the user to access.

Beyond the issue of robustness lies another reason more difficult to quantify but perhaps even more important emotionally. The *real* individual, Stephenson repeatedly implies, would not want to put himself at the mercy of large corporations that in effect tell him what to think, deciding what he wants and what is good for him. Such folks are Eloi, Stephenson suggests in an allusion to H. G. Wells's classic story *The Time Machine*. In Wells's story, the Eloi are small statured folk apparently living gentle lives in harmony with nature. Yet as the time traveler Hillyer discovers, their lives are forfeit to the brutal and ugly Morlocks, who live below the surface with their superior technology and regard the Eloi as food animals. Stephenson suggests that nowadays the Morlocks are on the surface running things, while the Eloi stupidly stampede into whatever operating system (or other technology) the Morlocks tell them they should want. At issue is pride, expertise, and, most importantly, control. Those who fail to understand the technology will inevitably be at the mercy of those who do. The implication is that those who choose Unix, even though it is more demanding technically, can escape from the category of the Eloi and transcend to Morlock status where the real power is.

Among the weirder resonances between *Command Line* and *Cryptonomicon* is this allusion to the cannibalistic Morlocks, which finds echoes in the many references to animal appetite in *Cryptonomicon*, including the jungle cannibals who devour an unfortunate Filipino as Goto Dengo looks on from his hiding place, so ravenous himself he eats the starch the cannibals leave behind. In a startling reversal, however, *Command Line* reconfigures the Morlocks so their relevant characteristic is technological prowess. Is their cannibalism merely beside the point in this extended analogy, which has no choice but to drag it along in the same way that analogies always include inappropriate elements if pushed far enough? Or is some covert line of thought connecting the two texts that makes the Morlock-Eloi analogy appropriate in a deeper sense? Is it a coincidence that yokes the cannibals' coming-of-age ritual in which an adolescent boy achieves his manhood by killing the intended victim, that is to say, a ritual in which he becomes a real individual, with Stephenson's imagining his Unix conversion as becoming a Morlock? And what is the "large document" that was the presenting cause for Stephenson to convert to Unix, a document so large it had to be stored on several floppies? Could it have been, as I suggested earlier, a draft of the gargantuan *Cryptonomicon*, destroyed and then resurrected through the very conversion that provides the origin story for *Command Line*?

As the risk of acting out the role of the ironically evoked "much more sophisticated literary critic," I want now to explore the subterranean connections between the fictional world of *Cryptonomicon* and the nonfictional conversion narrative in *Command Line*. To write a command line is be in command, that is, to use an operating system that does not disguise the working of the machine, to prefer an interface that makes clear the connection between typing alphabetic symbols and the encoding of these symbols into ones and zeros. Yet in constructing this argument, Stephenson continually uses extended analogies, including in addition to the Morlock/Eloi analogy an imagined scene of car dealers hawking inferior products that cost a lot (Windows and the Mac OS) while across the street someone is giving away for free beautifully made hefty tanks that get 100 mpg (Unix). Are these analogies just so much window dressing covering over the guts of the argument, like a Window interface covering over the real workings of the machine? If the technological elite are distinguished by knowing what is actually going on, why dress the argument up in fancy clothes that pander to the weak-minded who cannot take their facts straight up? Who does the text construct as its audience, Eloi or Morlock, and how can one achieve Morlock status if one is treated by the text as an Eloi who needs analogies to understand what is after all a fairly simple and straightforward point?

To entertain these questions is, of course, to suggest that figurative language is to cultural understanding as Windows is to code, a pernicious covering that conceals the truth of things. This is the ancient charge brought by philosophers against rhetoricians, the suspicion of scientists that if humanists really knew what they were talking about they would use equations rather than metaphors, the ideological program of the Royal Society to use plain unadorned language rather than fancy analogies. It is beside my purpose here to rehearse the thousand answers that have been made to these objections to literary language, from Philip Sydney to Gertrude Stein, John Milton to Gillian Beer, Alexander Pope to Arkady Plotnitsky. Rather, I want to highlight the tension between Stephenson's figurative language and performative code. Performative code makes machines do things, and we should be in control of our machines. But figurative language makes people do things, and to be persuasive, to be *effective*, the writer must craft for his readers images that stick in the mind, narratives that compel through memorable scenes and psychological complexities, including paradox, contradiction, irony, and all the rest of the tricks that constitute a writer's trade. Although these tricks can be seen as lies from one perspective, every student of literature understands what it means to say that writers lie to tell the truth.

Stephenson's own explicit justification for figurative language focuses on myths rather than metaphors, or more accurately, myths as analogies. In several of his works he has characters voice the view that mythic stories conceal profound technological insights, which simply need to be decoded to apply to present-day understanding of natural and artificial cognition. In *Snow Crash*, this takes the form of an elaborate exposition by the Librarian, an artificial intelligence that summarizes Sumerian myths and explicates their relation to the Snow Crash virus. In *Cryptonomicon*, it occurs when Enoch Root explains to Randy that behind seemingly contradictory myths is a truth on which they converge. Suppose, he says in an analogy meant to explain analogical thinking, different people were to present different versions of him. Nevertheless, someone who knew him could see that behind these different representations was a "Root Representation" (800), a play on his name that connects him with the root directory of the computer. Because messing with the root directory can have catastrophic consequences, in large systems it is protected from most users and can only be accessed by the person responsible for the system, the SysOp or Systems Operator. When Enoch Root first sends an e-mail to Randy, Randy pays it special heed because it includes the surname "root," which Randy mistakenly takes to mean the sender is a Systems Operator and therefore a knowledgeable and powerful computer expert. In another sense Root does play this role, although his special expertise stems from his association with the Societas Eruditorium, a shadowy organization that pursues its mysterious ends independent of the national interests at stake in the World War. Although these ends are never made explicit, the implication is that Root, a priest, answers to a higher ethical power than national sovereignty, an ethical imperative that gives special emphasis to Root's explanation about the mythic relation between technology and war. Technology, Root argues, can be used for good or evil ends, and this difference is encoded in the distinction between Athena, goddess of technology and war used for ethical ends, and Ares, the god of violent warfare used simply for destruction and self-gain. As with *Snow Crash*, connecting mythic figures with the contemporary action aims to bring about an ethical understanding of technology, with the result that principled action follows.

These explications of myth do not, however, resolve the deeper contradiction between the up-front nature of code and the devious nature of figurative language. The tension between performative code and figurative language runs through many of Stephenson's books; indeed, it is no exaggeration to say it is central to his creation of fictive worlds. In *Snow Crash*, he imagines a virus that crashes the operating system of humans, rendering them into automata that can be controlled through a monosyllabic language dubbed "falabala" after the way it sounds. Here language collapses into a kind of code capable of making humans act like computers, forced to run whatever commands that the code inputs. At issue are the same concerns evident in *Cryptonomicon* and *Command Line*—control versus being controlled, autonomy versus loss of agency, individualism versus the masses. In *Cryptonomicon*, the same concerns prevail but in a different configuration. Instead of language becoming like code, code becomes like figurative language, creating a deceptive surface that misleads the masses while the cognoscenti penetrate this screen of symbols to extract the meaningful messages hidden within. Cryptanalysis thus becomes like mathematics, revealing the essential information hidden in "cosmetic distractions" like those Lawrence sees through with his X-ray mathematical vision.

A good illustration of this dynamic occurs in the scene where Randy is thrown into prison on a trumped-up drug charge. To his surprise, his captors return his confiscated laptop, protected by the strong cryptography he has installed and hence worthless to his jailors unless they can trick him into voluntarily revealing the encryption key. He suspects, correctly, that his jailers have set up a Van Eck shadowing computer in the adjacent cell so they will be able to see whatever appears on his screen. A superb hacker, Randy sets a program running in background that will decode the crucial Arethusa intercepts, but he protects the screen surface by having it run a random display. The results of the background program, rather than appearing on screen, are transmitted by the LEDs on the number and cap keys blinking Morse code. This clever ruse recalls the teletype machine through which Stephenson communicated in his high school days and that he likened to a telegraph. Now the computer-as-telegraph connotes not a transparent coupling but precisely the opposite, the triumph of cryptography over political surveillance carried out with malicious intent. These results are consistent with the logic of *Command Line*, for Randy can escape surveillance only because he understands what is really going on inside the machine, while his captors are demoted from Morlocks to Eloi because they can see only the deceptive surface he creates.

The configuration in the prison is significant. On one side of the wall are Randy's captors, carrying out covert surveillance under the guise of legitimate political purposes but actually because General Wing wants to find out the gold for personal gain. On the other side is Enoch Root, a cross-cutting character that connects the two generations of conspirators, communicating with Randy using a cryptographic code implemented by manipulating a deck of playing cards. Strong cryptography does more than distinguish the Morlocks from the Eloi; it also allows a freedom-loving band of like-minded hackers to cohere in the midst of the Morlocks who use their power illegitimately. Through this means the hackers are distinguished from the cannibals in a purgative separation that amounts to a distinction between technology used for evil purposes and technology adopted for noble ends.

Just as animal appetite and abstract code merged connotations in performative code, so the jail scene with Randy signals the merging of performative code and figurative language in the work of the Good Hacker. The Good Hacker reconciles the tensions between a code that honestly testifies to the interior operations of the machine and the deceptive power of metaphoric interfaces (and by implication, figurative language in general). Randy, using his deep understanding of code to create deceptive surfaces, nevertheless uses his expertise for good ends. The conflation prepares for the next dialectical turn, which pits good hackers against evil deceivers.

The Brotherhood of Code

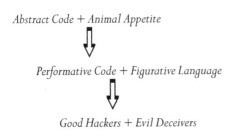

Abstract Code + Animal Appetite

Performative Code + Figurative Language

Good Hackers + Evil Deceivers

Being technically proficient with code obviously does not assure that all technicians will use their expertise to enhance individual autonomy. Microsoft employs talented programmers who work to create the very interfaces that, in Stephenson's view, seduce and disempower users. Stephenson is well aware of this fact, of course, and frequently constructs plots that pit spirited individualistic hackers against soulless technicians and their evil masters. So strong is Stephenson's sympathy with the hacker versus the large organization that alliances among hackers frequently provide the motive power for his fiction. In *Snow Crash*, for example, the major plot reaches its climax when Hiro Protagonist saves a virtual stadium full of hackers from being turned into Bob Rife's minions by defeating the software that would crash their neural operating systems and infect them with the Snow Crash virus. In *Cryptonomicon*, much of the action takes place against the canvas of World War II, a military conflict in national loyalties served to organize immense amounts of manpower and material—a situation ripe for exploitation by the powerful few. Against this volatile backdrop Stephenson imagines cross-cutting dynamics that organize energies differently, creating small pockets of resistance, subversion, and conspiracy.

About one of these we have already heard, the tension between mathematical abstraction and violent physicality that constituted the first phase of the dialectic. Significantly, the carnivorous lizard that attacks the Japanese who have Bobby Shaftoe pinned disrupts with its violent appetite this stereotypical scene of beachhead warfare, indicating that the dialectic has the power to intervene and re-direct the military conflicts inscribed on the text's surface. Disruption occurs again in the next phase of the dialectic when good hackers are put in conflict with evil deceivers. The good hackers come together to form what might be called the Brotherhood of Code, an alliance of hackers that has as its core their expertise in decoding encrypted messages. While most of the explicit criticism of national agendas is directed against America's enemies (hardly surprising, given the author's nationality), evil deceivers are at work transnationally, including in America. Large organizations are shown to be susceptible to corruption when powerful men subvert their resources to pursue private agendas dictated by greed and arrogance. General Wing pursues the Japanese war gold under the guise of Chinese nationalistic goals; Earl Comstock does the same with the newly formed National Security Agency; his son, Attorney General Paul Comstock, collaborates with the Dentist and his minions in attacking the Epiphyte Corporation's server.

These are the forces against which the Brotherhood of Code struggles, in an unlikely cross-generational conspiracy that includes during the World War II era Goto Dengo (a Japanese Imperial soldier), Bobby Shaftoe (an American Marine), Oscar Bischoff (a German submarine commander), Rudy von Hacklheber (a high-level German cryptanalyst), Lawrence Pritchard Waterhouse (an American cryptologist working for the British) and Enoch Root (of Societas Eruditorium fame, nominally a Catholic priest and chaplain for the Marine Corps). All betray organizational loyalties in favor of personal bonds, with cryptography and secret writing at the conspiracy's center.

The Brotherhood of Code injects into the World War II era the same kind of bonding through cryptological expertise that Stephenson in *Command Line* identifies with the open source community. Significantly, the one member of the conspiracy who does not overtly betray his national loyalty is Bobby Shaftoe, killed in a suicide mission on which he is personally dispatched by General Macarthur. And it is Shaftoe, of course, who stars in the physical action in the same way that Rudy and Lawrence dominate in the cryptological arena. Although he participates in the conspiracy, his character is anomalous in that he is not directly involved with decrypting documents, as are the others. Instead, his character serves to link this phase of the dialectic with earlier tensions. These are not so much left behind as shifted in their narrative functions when the next phase of the dialectical interaction starts to drive the action. Bobby's character illustrates how earlier tensions get integrated into the later dialectical configurations.

The conflict between physical action and abstract language, for example, is reiterated in Bobby Shaftoe's meditation on two categories of men, one oriented toward language, the other toward physical action.

> Men who believe that they are accomplishing *something* by speaking speak in a different way from men who believe that speaking is a *waste of time*. . . . For them, trying to do anything by talking is like trying to pound in a nail with a screwdriver. Sometimes you can even see the desperation spread over such a man's face as he listens to himself speak. (373)

Listening to Enoch Root and Lawrence, Bobby begins "to suspect that there might be a third category of man, a kind so rare that Shaftoe never met any of them until now" (373). Lawrence speaks, Bobby thinks, "not as a way of telling you a bunch of stuff he's already figured out, but as a way of making up a bunch of new shit as he goes along. And he always seems to be hoping that you'll join in. Which no one ever does, except for Enoch Root" (374). Slowly dawning on Bobby is the realization that language might be used not just as a tool for expression but also as a method of exploration. The realization points toward the next phase of the dialectic juxtaposing performative code with figurative language. In contrast to the relatively weak rationale interpreting myth as veiled history, Bobby has just discovered a much stronger justification for figurative language. Metaphors and analogies do not only express existing ideas; they also lead to new thoughts and possibilities. It is surely no accident that in addition to being a superlative physical specimen Bobby writes haiku, a poetic form that makes extensive use of metaphor and image.

Like the other configurations before it, the good hackers/evil deceivers configuration becomes unstable, initiating another turn of the dialectical cycle. This time, however, its instability leads to a significantly different outcome. The problem with the configuration becomes apparent in the generation following World War II when the hackers get together to form the start-up Epiphyte Corporation. As the Internet matured and began to become a commercial enterprise, visionaries saw their utopian dreams being co-opted by mercenary corporate interests. What ensures that Randy, Avi, and their colleagues in Epiphyte will not be similarly co-opted, forced to kowtow to someone like the Dentist, who plots to gain a controlling interest in their fledgling corporation? In its last phase the dialectic attempts to purge contamination from the Good Hacker and separate it out into a figure of pure evil, whose banishment from the plot can then signal the triumph of the good technology of Athena over the bad technology of Ares. This purgative impulse is, of course, precisely contrary to the dialectic's normal operation of combining contraries. At this point, the dialectic can go no further. The figure of pure evil is indeed produced and expelled, but the dialectic's exhaustion is expressed through oxymoronic knots that can neither be untied nor merged into a new synthetic term. Rather than work *through* these dense oxymoronic knots, the text achieves a muted resolution, such as it is, by working *with* them.

Knotty Oxymorons: The Dialectic Exhausted

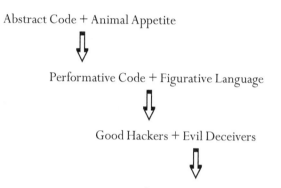

Abstract Code + Animal Appetite

Performative Code + Figurative Language

Good Hackers + Evil Deceivers

Oxymoronic Knots + (Pure Evil)

The tendency toward oxymoronic description is concentrated around events with life and death consequences, becoming particularly important in the entwining plots of Lawrence's invention of the first digital computer and the burying and disinterring of the Japanese war gold. As we have already seen, both plots involve crypts, the gold because it is buried in an underground installation, the computer because it is linked with cryptology and later with the Epiphyte data haven called The Crypt. Both plots evolve until they become so knotted into oxymoronic configurations they can go no further.

With the crypt of gold, the oxymorons cluster around the secret intention to make it also a human crypt. In a conversation with Lieutenant Mori (whose name connotes death), Goto understands the truth concealed beneath the Lieutenant's riddling discourse (639). The promised reward for work well done will be his death; the tunnels he has engineered to conceal the Japanese war gold are intended to hold his murdered body once the work is finished. Knowing that Golgotha, "the place of the skull," is associated in the Christian tradition with Christ's betrayal and crucifixion, Goto had privately given this name to the crypt. But when he mutters it and Captain Noda overhears, he obfuscates by answering it is a Tagalog word meaning "hidden glade" (639), a transformation the Captain further muddles by calling it "Gargotta." As the chain of linguistic signifiers drifts toward nonsense, it resembles a cryptographic code whose hidden meaning can be decoded only by the cognoscenti.

Similar obfuscation takes shape within the physical structure Goto has engineered. He builds into the design certain idiosyncrasies that are highly significant to him but meaningless to his superiors. When the installation is completed, the treasure concealed, and the final slaughter about to begin, Goto gets "so excited he forgets to die" (734). As he prepares to swim to freedom using the breathing chambers he has designed, he reflects that "he is an engineer, trapped inside one of his own machines. The machine was designed to keep him alive, and he will never know whether it worked unless it works. After he has achieved that satisfaction, he supposes, he can always kill himself at leisure" (734). The conflation of life and death, presented here as a matter of memory ("he forgets to die"), is deeply bound up with ethical complexities. Goto had earlier ordered his soldiers to jump ship rather than go down with the troop carrier and so had labeled himself unworthy because he chose to live rather than die in shame at the successful American attack (323). Accepting that he is a "bad soldier" because he shuns the senseless loss of life, he resolves to save as many men as he can at Golgotha, which finally amounts to a pitiful few. He hopes the gift of life will be enough for them and is shamed when one stops to pick up treasure along the way. "He himself has saved no treasure except these men's lives. But that's not why he feels so bad. He had hoped that being thus saved they would all be noble, and not think of the treasure. But maybe that was too much to hope for" (734).

As future developments make clear, it was indeed too much to hope for. The chief competitor for the gold in the contemporary plot is General Wing, the same Wing who takes off after the escape from Golgotha without bothering to thank Goto for saving his life. Goto continues to believe, as he tells Randy and Avi when they approach him for help in recovering the gold, that gold is the "corpse of value" (858). The real treasure, he explains, is in the head—"the intelligence of the people"—and in the hands—"the work they do" (858). Now a fabulously wealthy and powerful contractor, his success testifies to the wisdom of his view. Only when Avi tells Goto that he wants the gold to attempt to end wars by developing HEAP—the Holocaust Education and Avoidance Pod—does Goto agree to cooperate in the effort. The scene where Avi and Goto make their pact is awkwardly written in a telling way. When Goto suggests that Avi wants the gold to become rich, Avi's "face turns red, the muscles of his head bulge as he clenches his teeth together, and he breathes heavily through his nose for a while. The Gotos both seem to be rather impressed by this, and so no one says anything for a long time, giving Avi a chance to regain his cool" (858).

This heavy-handed indication of moral outrage indicates how desperately Stephenson wants to protect the Good Hacker against the greed that characterizes the evil deceivers, even at the cost of bad writing.[8] Greed sits cheek by jowl with entrepreneurial success, co-optation with individual initiative.[9] Stephenson knows too well the fate of successful dot.coms, sold for fabulous sums to large corporations before the Internet bubble burst, to be sanguine about the prospects for purity in the corporate realm or the Internet it increasingly controls. Stephenson's anxiety about protecting the Good Hacker from corruption finds its most extreme expression in the creation of a figure of pure evil, as if by isolating all impurities here he can ensure they will not contaminate the good characters. This function is fulfilled by the character of Andrew Loeb. Loeb's final attack on Amy has no financial and indeed no rational basis at all. "Why does he want to hurt you?" Root asks, to which Randy replies, "Because he's evil." When they finally succeed in killing the madman, "An insect lands on his thumb and starts to eat it" (893) in an ironic assertion of amoral appetite triumphant even over ultimate evil.

In sharp contrast to the unequivocal judgment Randy passes on Loeb are the complexities of the oxymoronic clusters. Like the gold plot, the cryptology plot conjoins life and death into knots that cannot be untied. The difficult problem that Lawrence must solve before he can invent the first digital computer is how to create machine memory, or in the odd formulation noted earlier, how to "bury and disinter" information. One of the problems he will attack once he has solved this difficulty is decrypting the Arethusa intercepts, which have encoded into them the gold's location. Coincidentally, he also solves the encrypted messages by which the conspirators are communicating with one another. As the conspirators radio messages about meeting at Bobby Shaftoe's memorial service, the crucial word that allows Lawrence to break the code is "funeral." He follows the conspirators to their jungle meeting place, where they have gathered to tap into a small portion of the gold whose location Goto, now a member of the group, of course knows. When Lawrence reveals himself to Rudy, Rudy "heaves a big sigh. 'So. You win. Where is the cavalry?'" Lawrence jokes, "'Cavalry, or calvary?'"—linking the cliché of cavalry rushing to the rescue with the site of Christ's death. "'I know where Calvary is,' Rudy replies. 'Not far from Golgotha'" (883). As Avi will do half a century later with Goto, Rudy assures Lawrence that "most of [the gold] is going to help victims of war, in one way or another," even though they intend to take enough to make themselves very rich. Convinced to help the conspirators in part because they loyally chose to attend Bobby's funeral despite the risks, he protects them by destroying the Arethusa intercepts and substituting random numbers. Although he fails to save his friends—Comstock decrypts a message that betrays the location of the conspirators' submarine—Lawrence's substitution of randomness will occupy Comstock for many years as he drives his NSA team ruthlessly to discover a code that isn't there.

As these scenes suggest, the oxymoronic clusters resonate most intensely around gold, not coincidentally the focus for the text's deepest anxieties. The principal gold sites are Golgotha, about which we have already heard; the submarine carrying the conspirators that Comstock sinks and that Douglas Shaftoe, Bobby's son, disinters half a century later; and a mysterious mound of gold bars hidden in the jungle that anticipates and reflects the problems and possibilities of the gold at Golgotha. All three sites provide episodes in which oxymoronic knots express the final perplexities of the dialectic's operation.

In addition to Rudy and Bischoff, the submarine carries some of the gold bars from the Golgotha site and five crates of gold foil plates that Rudy has stashed abroad. The plates Rudy identifies as "cultural treasures," scoffing when Bischoff suggests they may be encoded with Göring's pornography (851). Careful reading suggests they are the "Leibniz archive" that he had earlier asked Göring to gather for him from Europe's great libraries (503), precious research materials that he has encoded via perforations onto gold foil because he knows the foil will be impervious to salt water. When Bischoff jokes that they should be exporting gold from the Philippines rather than importing it, Rudy explains that "when I export those sheets, I'll do it on wires," suggesting a scene analogous to the burning tape that Lawrence witnesses; the gold foil will be worthless once the information it holds has been extracted. But Bischoff, trying to visualize this scene, imagines it as "wires strung from here to Los Angeles, and sheets of gold foil sliding down them. It doesn't really work" (852).

The fact that the sheets are gold puts them in a different category than the cheap paper tape. When the submarine is discovered decades later by Doug and his crew, they see the gold foil sheets as valuable in themselves, and Randy, although intrigued by the perforations, is apparently never able to decode the information they contain (458-59). Along with the sheets, ambiguously positioned between their material value as gold and their informational value as mathematical archives, are the gold bars from Golgotha, entombed along with those who die in the submarine. The death scene is rich with ironies. Rudy remembers that he has written the Golgotha coordinates on a sheet of paper in his briefcase, and he and Bischoff presciently anticipate that the sunken submarine may eventually be found. Trapped in an oxygen-rich air bubble at the stern of the broken boat in a scene reminiscent of Goto and his men in the breathing chambers of Golgotha, Rudy and Bischoff realize that if they strike a match to burn the paper, they will be immolated in the resulting flash. Rudy swims to the hatch and opens it, with barely enough air to make it back to the bubble but not enough to escape. In a knot that ties together life and death, he then tells Bischoff to escape, lighting the match that at once burns the paper, kills him, and provides the illumination Bischoff needs to make it out of the sub.

Decades later, when Doug, Amy and Randy discover the submerged wreck, they find inside Rudy's briefcase a slip of paper on which is written "WATERHOUSE LAVENDER ROSE" (462), the wedding china pattern that Lawrence had mentioned to Rudy when declining to join the conspirators in favor of becoming a mathematics professor at a small college where he will settle down with his bride, Mary Smith. Randy later confirms that this is indeed his grandmother's pattern, thus enabling him to re-discover the link between the submarine, the conspirators, and his grandfather. When Doug realizes that the hatch is open and presumes that someone was able to escape from the doomed ship, he lights a cigar to mark the occasion, telling Randy, "This is one of the most important moments in your life. Nothing will ever be the same. We might get rich. We might get killed. We might just have an adventure, or learn something. But we have been changed. We are standing close to the Heraclitean fire, feeling its heat on our faces" (442). Far removed from Doug's usual rhetoric, the melodramatic tone underscores the threads knotted together here—the fire that kills Rudy and saves Bischoff reflected in the "flaring safety match" that Doug produces "like a magician" with Randy "staring into the flame," the solemn toast to "whomever got out" honoring the moment of self-sacrifice that marks a crucial difference between the Brotherhood of Hackers and the greedy bureaucrats who oppose them.

Nevertheless, it remains to be seen whether the gold of Golgotha can be situated so that it can be coded good instead of evil, Athena rather than Ares. Also at issue is the tension between materiality and information, enacted in the submarine scenes in the co-existence of the gold bars and gold foil sheets but not really resolved. The tension between information and materiality is performed in a different sense in the ruminations in the text over the nature of money. The opening scene, set in Shanghai with coolies rushing to redeem notes printed by individual banks as the Marines fight their way to the waterfront and the Japanese attack the city, underscores the fragility of currency. Currency is, Lawrence reflects, an ocean away, only valuable as long as people believe it so. Feeling that he knows how the Japanese think from reading their decrypted messages every day, he is sure

the Nipponese must have given thought to this problem of backing their imperial currency –not just for Australia but New Zealand, New Guinea, the Philippines, Hong Kong, China, Indochina, Korea, Manchuria . . .

How much gold and silver would you need in order to convince that many human beings that your paper currency was actually worth something? Where would you put it?" (812)

The answer, of course, is Golgotha. But once the gold is buried and booby-trapped, it will take a major engineered project to unearth it. At one point Randy and Avi wonder whether it needs to be unearthed. Why can't they use the gold to secure the electronic money they are in the process of establishing without needing to dig up the treasure? Isn't it enough that it exists and they know where it is, even if it is not accessible?

The debate is foreshadowed by the mysterious mound of gold bars they discover in a nearly inaccessible jungle site. A Philippine woman gives the latitude and longitude coordinates to Randy under the guise of a social dance, asking him "What is the value of the following information?" (485). After Doug, Randy, and their crew fight their way to the location, negotiating fierce jungle terrain and rebel roadblocks, they realize that although the unguarded gold appears to be theirs for the taking, there is no way they can actually remove it, given the unstable political and geographical situation. Without possession, access has no meaning.

Does the inverse also hold, that without access, possession has no meaning? Woken by the tremors of underground explosions from their dream of letting the Golgotha gold simply remain underground, they realize that General Wing has marshaled men and material to tunnel diagonally into the stash from the side. The gold cannot be secure and thus cannot function as a basis for their new virtual currency unless they physically possess it. Like the Sultan's geography lesson, Wing's run for Golgotha makes clear that even in a world where electronic cash promises to be the currency of the future, the materiality implied by physical possession cannot be ignored. They solve their problem by literally liquefying their assets, setting off enough fuel oil in the Golgotha chambers so that the gold is liquefied and runs out into the river bed on its own.

The scene provides the narrative's muted climax and abrupt ending, leaving unresolved questions about how the gold will be spent, whether it will go to the HEAP project, the Societas Eruditorium, the Catholic Church, or the Brotherhood of Hackers – all of which are mentioned at one point or another as possible beneficiaries. Like the liquid gold poised between the solid materiality of appetite and the airy vapor of information, the text does not finally answer these questions, perhaps because they cannot be resolved within the parameters of a realistic novel. Apparently the gold has been purified enough to make its moral recovery possible, but not enough to allow a denouement to be written. Even when the plot threads are reassembled into a coherent story, the knots that signify how the action should be valued remain entangled.

Let me now return to consider how the material technology that produced the book enters into its narrative construction. All the terms involved in the dialectical transformations are concerned with situating code in relation to the human world of signs and artifacts, language and objects. More than an abstraction, code has a material efficacy that demands it be recognized as a player in the world; transparent to the technological elite who understand it, it can also be made deviously obscure; it can be put to socially desirable ends in the hands of idealistic hackers but remains vulnerable to the machinations of evil corporations. Since there is finally no way to ensure that it will not be co-opted, the text signs it with the oxymoronic knots that express the irreducible complexities of its entry into the world. This subterranean narrative, emerging from the operations of the dialectic, is not identical with the surface content and indeed in some ways contradicts it. Rather, it functions as a deep structure within the text, setting up a surface/depth dynamic that mimetically re-creates within the text the surface-depth relation between the screenic text displayed on the computer screen and the coding languages that produce the text as a display the reader can access. That the narrative implicit in the dialectic aims to locate code in relation to natural language re-produces the structural dynamics of the trading zones between code and natural language that digital technologies have made a pervasive feature of contemporary culture.

Further marks of the digital technologies that produced the text can be seen in the way the surface narrative is assembled. As the cryptological and gold plots begin to weave together, it becomes increasingly clear that the novel is functioning as a kind of machine assembling a coherent story out of plot lines that have been fragmented and spliced into one another. Until the final pages, the multiple plots proceed largely independently of one another, with jump cuts across scenes separated by many decades and several continents. One effect of digital text editing has been to change the writing habits of people generally, making cut-and-paste practices much more prevalent than was previously the case with typewriters, when the process was much more laborious. Of course, as a host of literary narratives testify, writers working on typewriters also created cut-and-paste narratives, including such luminaries as Virginia Woolf and John Dos Passos. Nevertheless, in *Cryptonomicon* this technique acquires special significance, for it resonates with the emphasis on burying and disinterring information as the specific technological challenge that led to invention of the digital computer. In this context the reader's activity is implicitly imagined as burying the memory of one section in order to cope with new information offered by the next plot thread; later, when the first thread resurfaces again, the reader must disinter that information and link it together with the new developments. In effect, then, the reader functions like a digital computer assembling coherent narratives out of fragmentary strings dispersed throughout the memory space. Like Goto desperately swimming from air pocket to air pocket inside a machine that he himself has built, the reader is trapped inside a machine constructed jointly from the reader's memory and the text's words, at the mercy of a novel that "forgets to die" as it rambles on for hundreds of pages before reaching an inconclusive ending that leaves much undecided.

Further complexities arise when we consider the relation of the Linux operating system to the Macintosh system that Stephenson presumably used when he was drafting the first part of *Cryptonomicon*. As he explains in *Command Line*, Linux operates by giving the user direct access to the commands that control the computer's behavior, whereas the Macintosh operating system offers the user *metaphors* for these commands (e.g., desktop, files, trash bin, etc.) and conceals the actual commands within its hidden coding structures. The fact that it seals off access to the command core has everything to do with the fact it is proprietary software controlled by corporate interests. By contrast, within the Linux system the user can type commands that call up a Windows-like interface, but this metaphoric shell operates as a special functionality within Linux, and it is always possible for the user to regain direct control of the machine by returning to inner core of Linux commands.

In *Cryptonomicon*, this nesting of an inner core within an outer metaphoric shell is reproduced through the fictional compendium of cryptology called the Cryptonomicon that functions as a *mise en abyme* for Stephenson's novel (to distinguish the two, I will indicate the novel in italics and the compendium without italics). The Cryptonomicon was supposedly begun by John Wilkins, not coincidentally the proponent of an analytical language designed to rescue language from a morass of illogical forms and tame its wild metaphoricity by fitting it into a rationally constructed system of roots, prefixes, and suffixes. Since then generations of cryptologists have added to the Cryptonomicon, including in the twentieth century the cryptological genius William Friedman and the fictional Lawrence Pritchard Waterhouse, second only to Alan Turing in his deep understanding of computers and code. Thus the Cryptonomicon has become a kind of Kabala created by a Brotherhood of Code that stretches across centuries. To know its contents is to qualify as a Morlock among the Eloi, and the elite among the elite are those gifted enough actually to contribute to it.

Containing the Cryptonomicon within itself, Stephenson's novel can be understood as a very long footnote to this Kabala, an explanation in figurative language on the significance of code that the novel posits as the dialectical opposite to the deceptive surfaces and fancy analogies in which it, as a literary work, necessarily indulges. Thus the novel at once contains within its own novelistic body the Cryptonomicon and postulates this fiction as a linguistic Other existing in a space exterior to itself. Elizabeth Weise quotes Stephenson as saying, "Language . . . is the reverse of cryptography," because, as she explains, language "is about conveying information, not hiding it" (1D). In another sense, however, figurative language hides within linguistic formulations what code reveals. It is significant in this regard that the novel contains an appendix by expert cryptographer Bruce Schneier explaining the Solitaire encryption algorithm Enoch Root uses to communicate with Randy in jail ("The Solitaire Encryption Algorithm," 911-18). This encryption scheme is sufficiently strong that it is possible the National Security Agency would prohibit its exportation in electronic form, the only textual form it monitors. Stephenson included in *Cryptonomicon* an e-mail from Enoch Root to Randy in which Enoch gives him the Perl script for the Solitaire algorithm (480), leading to the delicious irony that this print book can be exported legally, whereas the code it inscribes with durable marks, if translated into electronic voltages, may not be legally exported.[10] In a literal sense, the text's natural language here operates as a metaphoric shell encapsulating a hidden core of code. Moreover, if Schneier's appendix is sufficiently astute, it could aspire to be included in the Cryptonomicon as a main entry, whereas the best the novel could hope for, as a writing practice linguistic and metaphoric rather than coded and algorithmic, would be to make it into an appendix. In this playfully speculative scenario, *Cryptonomicon* is turned inside out to reveal the Cryptonomicon as the powerful core that can access command lines directly, while the novel resembles the Windows or Macintosh Operating System that conceals the real command structures from the reader. The oxymoronic knots can now be understood as sites where the reader becomes aware of a powerful core within the metaphoric shell, teasingly suggestive windows hinting at what lies beyond Windows.

On multiple levels and in diverse ways, then, *Cryptonomicon* bears witness to the digital technologies that created it. In its structure, dialectical dynamics, and subterranean narrative, it incorporates in linguistic form the crisis in writing practices that materially marked its electronic body, understood simultaneously as a clash of operating systems, a struggle of open source utopianism against capitalistic greed, and an opposition between the command structures of code and the analogical surfaces of figurative language. To probe these complexities, we require critical strategies that are attentive to the technologies producing texts as well as to the texts as linguistic-conceptual structures — that is to say, we require material ways of reading that recognize texts as more than sequences of words and spaces.[11] Rather, they are artifacts whose materialities emerge from negotiations between their signifying structures and the technologies that produce them. Whereas the New Criticism isolated texts from political contexts and technological productions, the New Materialism insists that technologies and texts be understood as mutually interpenetrating and constituting one another.

Notes

[1] See for example Scott Bukatman: "Gibson wrote *Neuromancer* on a manual typewriter" (71).

[2] This information comes from an interview with Stephenson by John Markoff. See also the *Cryptonomicon* website (<http://www.cryptonomicon.com/chat.html>), where the interviewer remarks of *Quicksilver*, the forthcoming sequel to *Cryptonomicon*, "This is the book you are writing with a fountain pen," and Stephenson replies, "I've written every word of it so far with a fountain pen on paper." Markoff also reports in June 1999 that Stephenson "now writes with fountain pens on a thin masonite 'laptop' board that he travels with. He has taken to traveling without a portable computer, saying that he had decided to give up 'on the hassle.'"

[3] This text was originally commissioned by *Wired*, which declined to publish it. It was then published online at the Avon website, but the demand was so severe with 100,000 people logging on that it crashed the servers. On this basis, Avon decided it had sufficient audience for a print book.

[4] John Markoff reports that Stephenson "acknowledges that when he returned home he was able to salvage an earlier version from a backup disk. But the event was clearly traumatizing and it undermined his trust in the Macintosh operating system forever."

[5] *Cryptonomicon* appeared in April 1999 and presumably was submitted to the publisher sometime in 1998. John Markoff reports that Stephenson said he took two years to write the book and a year to revise, which means that he was probably working on it in 1995, the date he assigns to the crisis in his description of the incident in *Command Line*.

[6] According to Jim McCellan, when Stephenson read about this incident, he found it so intriguing that it became the kernel for *Cryptonomicon*.

[7] For an insightful discussion of the abject in relation to cyberspace, transnational politics, and global capital, see Terry Harpold and Kavita Philip.

[8] I am not alone in thinking this part of the book is weak. Paul Quinn writes of this part of the book, "The weakly worked idea that Randy's business partner, Avi, seeks wealth in order to educate the world in the prevention of another Holocaust seems in this context ultimately muddled, if noble" (24).

[9] The scene with the Sultan in which Randy and Avi survey their potential partners makes clear how real the risk of co-optation is, as it includes, in addition to the Sultan, former bagmen for President Marcos, drug dealers, and international gangsters (316-17).

[10] The irony remains intact even though in the first edition the copy editors unfortunately made an error that prevents the code from running, an error Stephenson corrects in the FAQ section of his website, <http://www.well.com/user/neal/cypherFAQ.html>, accessible through the link on the main page <http://www.well.-com/user/neal> (3 September 2002).

[11] This argument is made more extensively in Hayles, *Writing*, as well as in the work of such important materialist critics as Friedrich Kittler, Jerome McGann, Loss Pequeño Glazier, and Johanna Drucker, among others.

Works Cited

Bukatman, Scott. "Gibson's Typewriter." *Flame Wars: The Discourse of Cyberspace*. Ed. Mark Dery. Raleigh: Duke UP, 1994. 71-91.

Drucker, Johanna. *The Visible Word: Experimental Typography and Modern Art, 1909-1929*. Chicago: U of Chicago P, 1994.

Glazier, Loss Pequeño. *Dig[iT]ital Poet(i)(c)s: The Making of E-Poetries*. Tuscaloosa: U of Alabama P, 2001.

Harpold, Terry and Kavita Philip. "Of Bugs and Rats: Cyber-Cleanliness, Cyber-Squalor, and the Fantasy-Spaces of Informational Globalization." *Postmodern Culture* 11.1 (2000). 4 September 2003 <http://jeffersonvillage.edu/pmc/>.

Hayles, N. Katherine. *Writing Machines.* Cambridge: MIT Press, 2002.

Kittler, Friedrich. *Discourse Networks 1800/1900.* Trans. Michael Metteer. Stanford: Stanford U P, 1992.

———. *Gramophone, Film, Typewriter.* Trans. Geoffrey Winthrop-Young and Michael Wurtz. Stanford: Stanford U P, 1999.

Markoff, John. "Behind Happy Interface, More Complex Reality." *New York Times* 3 June 1977: G7.

McCellan, Jim. "After *Snow Crash's* Cyberpunk, It's Cyberpunk." *The Guardian* (London) 14 October 1999: 2.

McGann, Jerome. *Radiant Textuality: Literature After the World Wide Web.* London and New York: Palgrave Macmillan, 2001.

Stephenson, Neal. *Cryptonomicon.* New York: Avon Books, 1999.

———. *In the Beginning Was the Command Line.* New York: Avon, 1999.

———. *Snow Crash* [1992]. New York: Doubleday, 2000.

"Talk with Neal Stephenson." *Cryptonomicon* website. 4 September 2003 <http://cryptonomicon.com/-chat.html>.

Quinn, Paul. "The How of the Crypt." *Times Literary Supplement* 5 November 1999: 24.

Weise, Elizabeth. "Cracking *Cryptonomicon*: Stephenson Weaves 50-Year Tale of Intrigue." *USA Today* 28 April 1999: 1D.

Wells, H. G. *The Time Machine: An Invention.* New York: Modern Library, 2002.

JOSEPH CONTE

THE VIRTUAL READER: CYBERNETICS AND TECHNOCRACY IN
WILLIAM GIBSON AND BRUCE STERLING'S
The Difference Engine

The promise of a reader actively engaged in the construction of the text has been held out by the practitioners and theoreticians of cybernetic fictions, especially with respect to the development of electronic media. Michael Joyce, author of the original hypertext fiction *afternoon, a story* (1987), posits the interactivity of such work because in "attempting to accommodate our thinking in response to the demands of an application's control and data structures, true interactivity" exists (*Of Two Minds* 135). That the reader of print fiction has had to learn to negotiate the information delivery platform that is the book can be taken for granted, but the very motility of interactive fictions and the mutability of their data structures presumably requires even greater engagement on the part of the reader. George P. Landow, invoking the poststructuralist theory of Barthes, Derrida, and Foucault, also proposes that the "multiplicity of hypertext, which appears in multiple links to individual blocks of text, calls for an active reader" (6). These representative statements on the reader in cybernetic fictions (and others by Stuart Moulthrop, Espen Aarseth, and Ilana Snyder) all refer to the presence of an Actual Reader. Such a reader-in-the-world is thought to be empowered by the toggle switching, hyperlink clicking, and page turning that he or she is called upon to perform. But I suspect that this liberatory, millennialist rhetoric of the active reader has been oversold. Cybernetic fictions are not so much concerned with the enabling of an actual reader who thumbs pages or navigates interfaces than with deriving a concept of their most apt reader from the disciplines of cybernetics and communications theory. That reader, always a *lector in fabula*, is a Virtual Reader subject to the determinations and control of the text. The reader as avatar, not so much manipulating the text as manipulated by it, not so much actively engaged in the making of the text as entangled within the feedback loop of its production, represents a darker vision, to be sure, of cybertextuality. But that vision, I would argue, is more in keeping with the technological dystopia that is depicted in my exemplary fiction, William Gibson and Bruce Sterling's *The Difference Engine* (1991), and in so many other works of the genre.

1. Ego, Scriptor et Hannibal Lector

In writing the epitaph of the Author, Roland Barthes suggests that the prestige of the Author emanates from the humanist valuation of the individual, "his person, his life, his tastes, his passions" ("The Death of the Author" 143). The work of art becomes subordinate to the aura of the individual that is thought to produce it. This concept of "authority" is a vestige of Enlightenment rationalism, an historical construct that now may be enshrouded in theory and consigned to the tomb of literary history. Barthes denaturalizes the Author. In place of that reassuring engraving of the author's visage on the frontispiece of so many leather-bound volumes, Barthes reveals that this "more or less transparent allegory of the fiction, the voice of a single person, the *author* 'confiding' in us" (143) is never more than a collusion of the text and its critics. Or, as he puts it uniquely, "the author is never more than the instance writing, just as *I* is nothing other than the instance saying *I*" (145). Barthes refuses to grant to the Author an ontological status independent from the text. Rather than producing the text, the Author is itself a construct of the text. So, far from being a personage of some prestige, the Author is revealed as an object of pathos, inspiring a funereal lament.

"Having buried the Author," Barthes proposes in its place a "modern scriptor" whose function in the text is "performative." Derived from the speech-act theory of J. L. Austin, the performative utterance would be an "enunciation [that] has no other content . . . than the act by which it is uttered" (145-46). If I were to say that I had visited the home of my favorite Author, William Carlos Williams, at 9 Ridge Road in Rutherford, NJ, which I have done, I would be colluding through an act of homage to an individual in the construction of his authority, in the proposition of the pediatrician-poet that is other than the enunciation of the text. The question posed in Williams's "Danse Russe," however, "Who shall say I am not / the happy genius of my household?" (87), is performative, making of the poem's speaker that which he declares. Indeed, who shall say I in this instance writing? No visit to the household to confirm his identity—and no response to the rhetorical question—is necessary. Unlike the Author, the *scriptor* is not an identity construct. As its Latinate derivation suggests, the *scriptor* is wholly equivalent to the function of writing.

With this distinction made—that the Author is a construction of identity in the collusion of the text and the critic, while the *scriptor* is a function of textual production—should there not be a comparable distinction to be made with respect to the reader? Barthes states that "the total existence of writing" can only be found in the place of the reader. But he would not make the same error as his critical predecessors, assigning to the Reader (much less the actual audience of book buyers and page thumbers), the ontological status of personhood. No, he argues, this "destination cannot any longer be personal: the reader is without history, biography, psychology; he is simply that *someone* who holds together in a single field all the traces by which the written text is constituted" (148). To this figure, although Barthes declines to take this step, I would assign the term *lector*. The complement of the authorial function in the text (the *scriptor*) must logically be the reader function in the text (the *lector*). When the narrator of Henry Fielding's *Tom Jones* purports to make a direct address to the Reader of the novel, he compares himself to an efficient and personable hosteler who will see to the every need of his worthy and paying guest. Not only is an identity constructed for that Reader, but it is one with fairly specific cultural predilections; there are some readers, presumably, to whom the invitation might not apply. Fielding's invocation of the gentle, bourgeois Reader, is intended as a flattering portrait of his prospective audience. In contrast, Barthes's depersonalized reader, whom I call the *lector*, dispenses with such cultural and historical specificities. There is no *someone*, no actual audience, that might singly constitute all the multiple traces of the written text. Rather than passively consuming the repast of the text, the *lector* consumes itself in the act of all readings. Barthes concludes that "the birth of the reader must be at the cost of the death of the Author" (148). If so, then it would not do to substitute one identity construct for another. The *lector* is that place in the text where "multiple writings, drawn from many cultures and entering into mutual relations to dialogue, parody, contestation" converge.

2. Bi-Directional Communications

The linear, unidirectional model of communications proposed by Claude Shannon in *The Mathematical Theory of Communication* (1969) and adapted to linguistics and poetics by Roman Jakobson reveals its inadequacy in describing the relationship of reader and text in the age of networked communications (Aarseth 58). In "Linguistics and Poetics," Jakobson based his taxonomy of the linguistic functions involved in any verbal act of communication on the declarative statement: "The ADDRESSER sends a MESSAGE to the ADDRESSEE" (66). This basic formulation, ADDRESSER→MESSAGE→ADDRESSEE conforms to the classical representation of text production, in which an author conveys a text to a reader. As we know, however, that the biographical Author does not directly convey a text to an actual audience (except in the instance of the twentieth century's most popular literary event, the reading and book signing), it is necessary to insert, perhaps especially for the classical narrative, the NARRATOR and NARRATEE in the place of the textual function (message) and as minions to the Author and Reader respectively. This yields a communications model of classical narrative that looks like so: AUTHOR→NARRATOR→NARRATEE→READER (Aarseth 93). The linearity and unidirectionality of such a model make clear that the Author, so constructed, is in control of the text. Barthes's proposition of the death of the Author gives us reason to reexamine the communications model in which information, like water through a tubular channel, flows from sender to receiver (a "reply," of course, is only the same process in reverse). Barthes makes two provocative claims in his essay, the death of the author and the birth of the reader. The first resituates the locus of creative power; all along, it is the Author who has been historically constructed as a convenient fiction by the text and its critics. The narrator, a minion sent in place of the Author to effectuate his or her bidding in classical narrative, is replaced by the modern *scriptor* that enacts the "instance writing." This revised relationship can be written as [AUTHOR] *scriptor*. Barthes's proposal of the active reader likewise revises the terminus of the communications channel. The reader of the classical text was very much its passive receiver in the communications model; or, in the language of political economy, a consumer of the text as artifact. That Reader, essentially synonymous with the actual audience of book buyers, should similarly be consigned to the coffin of brackets. But the reader in whom the "total existence of writing" ("Death of the Author" 148) converges, and whom I designate as the *lector*, assumes a constitutive role in the Barthesian model. The "multiple writings" of the Barthesian text thus establish bi-directional communication between the *scriptor* and the *lector*. Although phylogenically related to the Shannon-Jakobson communications model, the Barthesian plural text would be represented in this fashion: [AUTHOR] *scriptor*↔*lector* [READER]. This model not only establishes a bi-directional channel of communication, it disestablishes the obvious flow of textual power as originating in the author and conveyed to the reader.

3. The Cybernetic Model of Reading

Poststructuralism and reader response criticism have provided further revisions of the "authorial function" and the role of the reader.[1] Rather than recount that narrative in the history of criticism, our time would be better spent in establishing a parallel shift in theories of textual production in a cybernetic model. The verbal act of communication in the form of ADDRESSER→MESSAGE→ADDRESSEE can be compared in computing to the basic input/output system (BIOS). A programmer writes instructions for a computer (program/input), whose results (data/output) are read by the user. To the extent that the programmer may also be the user, and the output may be used to reprogram the input functions of the computer, a feedback loop is established. But just as the control of textual production is thought to reside with the Author in classical narrative, so authority resides with the programmer in computing. This basic relationship can be represented as PROGRAMMER→COMPUTER (Input)→DATA (Output)→USER. As for the promises of interactivity, while as an "end user" I am at liberty to write whatever I wish within the word-processing program, it is the program that determines the form and parameters of what constitutes a text; nor am I able to alter the program. The user can write *in* Microsoft® Word, but not rewrite it. Nevertheless, just as the communications theory model has undergone revision since the middle of the last century, so the cybernetic model of computing has experienced homologous new conceptions of the author-programmer function and user response.

If there were a single moment in which the programmer, having hitherto wielded uncontested authority in the writing of directions for computing machinery, began to feel intimations of mortality, it would be the publication in 1943 of a paper by neurophysiologist Warren McCullough and mathematician Walter Pitts, "A Logical Calculus of the Ideas Immanent in Nervous Activity." They claimed that the brain could be modeled as a network of logical operations such as *and*, *or*, and *not* (Waldrop 113). The McCullough-Pitts neuron offers a model of brain activity as a form of information processing. The incipient neural network consists of artificial neurons, or "nodes," that are able to retain information about their internal state. The neuron has inputs that can be either in an excitatory or inhibitory state. The neuron fires when the level of excitation exceeds a determined threshold (Hayles 58). Artificial synapses establish connections between the various nodes, with each connection "weighted" according to the strength of the synapse. In a neural network simulator, simple logical gates are capable of performing exceedingly complex computations. Repeated firings strengthen some artificial synapses, while others atrophy in an inhibited state. The emergence of patterns in information—one hesitates to say "behavior"— suggests the possibility of creating an Artificial Intelligence, or AI. In 1950, Alan Turing famously issued the Turing test of artificial intelligence. If a computer system were created such that it could fool an interrogator into thinking that he or she were having a dialogue with another human being, not a machine, then an artificial intelligence is born (Lewin 160). It's possible that a highly developed neural network simulator, through extended iterations of synaptic firings and information retention in neural nodes, would one day pass the Turing test. After all, human observers could be duped (an eventuality that does not invalidate the test). Much of the more recent work in AI emphasizes feedback processes. An intelligence, whether or not "human" in stature, could be said to reside in computing machinery that were capable of self-modifying programs. Complex systems are distinguished by adaptive behavior. A neural network would need to do more than "run" programs; it would need to utilize feedback to modify its own programming and thus adapt its activities. Artificial intelligence signals the "death of the programmer" in ways comparable to Barthes's proposition of the "death of the author." The behavior of the neural network would not be determined by the programmer's instructions. The state of an artificial intelligence could no more be predicted by its programmer's intentions than the actions of a fictional character from its author's intentions. Like automatic writing, the self-modifying program removes reference to an other, to an outside. An artificial intelligence would be an "instance writing."

Although a neural network has yet to pass the Turing test in science fact, the representation of artificial intelligence in postwar science fiction has become so prevalent that it is hard to imagine a successful galactic series without one or more (Commander Data's positronic brain encased in an android shell being only the most obvious). In William Gibson's *Neuromancer* (1984) there are so many AIs in the matrix that their "Turing Registry numbers" must be kept on file in Berne, Switzerland (73). *Neuromancer* concludes with the merger—perhaps apotheosis would be better—of two Artificial Intelligences, Wintermute and Neuromancer. Their union, as the narrator takes pains to make clear, is comparable to the joining of the two hemispheres of the cerebral cortex, the left associated with verbal skills and logical functions, and the right hemisphere associated with the perception of nonverbal visual patterns and emotion. "Wintermute was hive mind, decision maker, effecting change in the world and outside. Neuromancer was personality. Neuromancer was immortality" (269). Together they form an unnamed, virtually transcendent informational entity. In its own words, the AI is "Nowhere. Everywhere. I'm the sum total of the works, the whole show" (269). The awakening of information to itself in this novel supercedes human cognizance or technological control. Richard Powers devotes his novel *Galatea 2.2* (1995) to the proposition that a cranky cognitive neurologist named Philip Lentz might join forces with a brilliantly introspective author named "Richard Powers" to create a neural network. The artificial intelligence, dubbed "Helen," passes a Turing test administered by faculty colleagues in the form of a comprehensive examination for the Masters degree in English. The eponymous narrator Powers observes that "networks were not even programmed, in so many words. They were trained. Repeated inputs and parental feedback created an association and burned it in" (15-16). In an accurate and up-to-date description of the field of "connectionism," the narrator remarks on the use of parallel, rather than serial, processing in neural networks: "Neural networkers no longer wrote out procedures or specified machine behaviors. . . . Rather, they used a mass of separate processors to simulate connected brain cells. They taught communities of these independent, decision-making units how to modify their own connections. Then they stepped back and watched their synthetic neurons sort and associate external stimuli" (14). Powers heralds the death of programming in artificial intelligence even as he ironically revivifies the biographical Author-in-the-text of this postmodern novel.

The premises of self-modifying programs and artificial intelligence displace the authority for input in the cybernetic model of computing from the sole domain of the programmer to that of the computing machinery itself. A reflexive shift has occurred in the cybernetic model with respect to output and the role of the user. Theories of hypertext and ergodic literatures seek to promote the user/reader from the passive receiver of data in the communications channel to sender/participant in a bi-directional exchange and, ultimately, to authorial status. In *Hypertext 2.0*, George P. Landow invokes the Barthesian model of the active reader and the "writerly" text, explicitly arguing that these theories are made manifest in multilinear, linked hypertext. Suggesting that "Barthes's distinction between readerly and writerly text appears to be essentially a distinction between text based on print technology and electronic hypertext" (5), Landow cites from Barthes's *S/Z*, that "the goal of literary work (of literature as work) is to make the reader no longer a consumer, but a producer of the text" (4). Barthes argues that the reader of the classic text will be "intransitive" (*S/Z* 4), a passive reader able only to accept or reject a previously finished text. Landow contends that the "multiplicity of hypertext, which appears in multiple links to individual blocks of text, calls for an active reader" (6). There are intriguing parallels between Barthes's theory of a "plural text" and the emerging practice of multicursal hypertext and network communications. Barthes did not require a change in the textual medium, however, to usher in the active reader. Some print texts are capable of presenting the "galaxy of signifiers" (*S/Z* 5), the infinite semiosis, that would make the reader a producer of the text. Other print texts, including classic works of literature, confine the reader to "a structure of signifieds." In making his distinction between classic and plural (print) texts, Barthes pays greater attention to the character of the textual function—the play of the signifiers and the rigidity of the signified—in the text than he does to the reader function. Would a classic (print) text respond to the most earnest efforts of the active reader to discover a network of interaction? It would seem that only the "writerly," plural text calls upon its reader to be a producer of the text. Do we then accept Landow's contention that, by virtue of its shift from print to an electronic medium, the hypertext likewise calls upon its reader to be an author? In following the links between "lexia" (another Barthesian term) in a web or network, readers "continually shift the center—and hence the focus or organizing principle—of their investigation and experience. Hypertext," Landow argues, "provides an infinitely recenterable system whose provisional point of focus depends upon the reader, who becomes a truly active reader" (36). Perhaps the reader's course through lexia or linked web pages provides an experience of infinite semiosis comparable to that of Barthes's plural (print) text. It may matter if the linked pages carry the "structure of signifieds" that one finds in the online Lands' End [sic] catalog, or whether one is perusing a scholarly reference site such as Landow's own *The Victorian Web*, or reading an electronic or web text that aspires to literary status. In short, the electronic, interactive reader must *follow* links (noting the parlance of obedience rather than command) that have been already encoded in the hypertext (whether in HTML [hypertext markup language], *Storyspace*, or some other proprietary coding), whereas Barthes's active reader is freely disposed in the plural (print) text to pursue new constellations of signifiers. In the hypertext web, even the most intrepid reader finds his or her place already marked by the galactic encoder.

Espen Aarseth makes the case for a more independent, "ergodic" reader in *Cybertext*. In his taxonomy of cybernetic literature, including story generators, interactive games, MUDs, and hypertext fiction, the cybertext is a machine for the production and consumption of verbal expression (3, 21). The distinguishing feature of all cybertexts is that they involve the reader in some kind of information feedback loop (19). While the activity of the traditional reader may be confined to the hermeneutics of the text, the cybertext reader is more properly a user who must intervene in the game-world or machine production of the text (4). In fact, cybertexts are more easily recognized as games in a variety of media than as literary, or even sub-literary, narratives. Aarseth states that the key question with regard to cybertexts, as it is throughout the field of cybernetics, is that of domination or control:

> Who or what controls the text? Ideologically, there are three positions in this struggle: author control, text control, and reader control. Author control comes closest to Barthes's concept of the readable (*lisible*) text, where neither signifiers nor interpretations are left to chance (Barthes, *The Pleasure of the Text*). Text control is usually characterized as the programmed play of elements and structures, so that the process of sign production is both unpredictable and original, with creative responsibility transferred to the machinery. Reader control puts

the creative initiative on the users, who must assemble the available building blocks and make artistic sense according to their individual preferences. (55-56)

In fact, Barthes invests parental control in the Author of the readerly text who is thought to exist before his work, "in the same relation of antecedence to his work as a father to his child" ("Death of the Author" 145). Text control may not be tarred with the evident sexism of the paternalistic Author, but works produced in this manner are widely critiqued as post-humanist. These texts are disparaged as the still-born products of pure intellect. They are refused the status of art precisely because the choice afforded to the imaginative artist has been suppressed in favor of predetermined rules and procedures for text production. In my analysis, text control bears resemblance to the premises of artificial intelligence in computing machinery. Of course, an author-programmer must be present at the outset to establish the parameters of the "run," and after the fact to log and perhaps edit the results. But works produced under the sway of text control would be an expression of the "death of the author." Charles Babbage's calculating machine, churning its stack, becomes a creative machine. Simple rules generate complex structures that cannot be predicted from the programmer's instructions. As much as text control emulates the features of the self-modifying programs of an artificial intelligence—still largely a flight of fancy in advanced computing—the most interesting examples of such texts appear in the stolid realm of print. John Cage assembles his mesostic texts, such as *Themes & Variations* (1982), from selected source texts, vertically aligned key words, strict rules for distributing lines of text, and chance operations using a computer simulation of the *I Ching*. The authorial ego is annihilated, he says, in the exercise of a "purposeful purposelessness" (7). In "Prose and Anticombinatorics," Italo Calvino suggests that computer-assisted composition can blaze a trail through the dark wood of branching narratives. Less sanguine about the death of the author, he says, "the aid of a computer, far from *replacing* the creative act of the artist, permits the latter rather to liberate himself from the slavery of a combinatory search, allowing him also the best chance of concentrating on this 'clinamen' which, alone, can make of the text a true work of art" (152). Other theorists of the Paris-based Oulipo (Workshop for Potential Literature) examine the interventions of computing machinery in the production and consumption of verbal texts. Paul Fournel, in "Computer and Writer," suggests that certain forms of algorithmic literature are best read with the aid of a computer. Raymond Queneau's combinatory text, *Cent Mille Milliards de poèmes*, ten sonnets whose lines are written on strips of paper that can be "flipped" to render in each case a new poem, yields a total of 10^{14} sonnets. Neither the biographical Author nor the actual reader would be sufficiently long-lived to produce and consume all 10^{14} sonnets. A computer, however, could be programmed to randomly generate particular iterations of the sonnet. Such a relationship would be expressed as work→ computer→reader. Is the computer merely a mechanical intermediary, or does it effectively conflate the authorial and reader functions? Where does the authorial function reside when the computer generates the ten millionth iteration of the sonnet? Text control may be best represented by such combinatory works that are "unpredictable and original" in their random generation, and in which "creative responsibility [has been] transferred to the machinery."[2]

Aarseth expresses his reservations about the freedom to produce the text that is accorded to the reader in hypertext. Works created in *Storyspace*, such as Michael Joyce's *afternoon: a story*, and HTML-encoded web pages, allow the reader to "follow *only* the sequences laid down by the writer. Hyperfictions written in *Storyspace*, like *Afternoon*, do not allow its readers free browsing, unlike any codex fiction in existence. The reader's freedom from linear sequence, which is often held up as the political and cognitive strength of hypertext, is a promise easily retracted and wholly dependent on the hypertext system in question" (77). Aarseth challenges Landow's claim that hypertext promotes an "active reader." In effect, he argues that the degree of control and direction retained by the hypertext author alienates rather than empowers the reader: "The engaged hypertext quickly turns into a dense, multicursal labyrinth, and the reader becomes not so much lost as caught, imprisoned by the repeating, circular paths and his own impotent choices" (91). While legitimate, these complaints might pertain only to the limitations of the hypertext authoring program in question, or to "literary hypertexts" with a fixed number of lexia and a closed system. The ergodic text, in Aarseth's formulation, more readily yields itself to reader control, the premise of a user who is entrusted with the fashioning of the text. Reader control in the cybernetic text appears to conform most closely to Barthes's thesis of the *writerly* text in which the reader is "no longer a consumer, but a producer of the text" (*S/Z* 4). On closer inspection, however, Landow's hypertext and Aarseth's ergodic literature are related theories of an actual reader (performing in the world), not an authorial reader (functioning in the text). Landow envisions an actual reader refiguring the hypertext by selecting and following links; however "free" these paths may be, the decision to follow a particular link resides in some personal choice of the reader. Likewise, Aarseth's ergodic readers busily assemble "the available building blocks and make artistic sense according to their individual preferences." They are actual individuals who click and fidget with electronic text objects. But the actual reader in the process of following an appealing hyperlink or confronting a "bot" in a digital game-world—which are historically and culturally defined expressions of individual preference—cannot be said to represent Barthes's reader. Barthes tells us that "a text's unity lies not in its origin but in its destination," not in its Author but in its reader. That "destination," however, "cannot any longer be personal" ("Death of the Author" 148). Text production and control cannot reside in a personalized reader-in-the-world.

4. Alternate Worlds

William Gibson and Bruce Sterling's *The Difference Engine* (1991) is a work of alternative history that speculates on how the course of political economy and culture in

Victorian England—and indeed the world in 1855—would have been changed had the English mathematician Charles Babbage (1792-1871) succeeded in demonstrating a calculating machine, the Difference Engine, which he had proposed to the Royal Society in 1822. Had not the Astronomer Royal, Sir George Airy, convinced the British government to withdraw funding for Babbage's partially assembled computing machinery in 1842, it's possible that the mechanical production of the Industrial Revolution powered by James Watt's steam engine (1769) might have been conjoined with the information processing of the Computer Age.[3] Babbage sought to remedy the introduction of errors that occurred when the tables of trigonometric functions, logarithmic series, and planetary orbits that were needed by mathematicians and navigators were calculated and reproduced manually. The steam power that drove the shafts and gears of locomotives and textile manufacturing, he reasoned, could be employed to crank out sums more accurately.[4] A second ambitious design for a calculating machine, which Babbage called the Analytical Engine, is more clearly the precursor of the modern computer. It consists of a "store" (memory), the "mill" (central processing unit, or CPU),

and a punched card reader (input device). A part of the Analytical Engine, for which Babbage never received funding to build, was successfully built and demonstrated by the Science Museum in London in 1991, one hundred and twenty years after Babbage's death.

Readers of *The Difference Engine* who are familiar with the "cyberpunk" genre in which Gibson and Sterling have fashioned their separate reputations might feel as if they had been cast into a time warp. Works such as Gibson's *Neuromancer* and Sterling's *Schismatrix* (1986) project the imminent technology of the

Figure 1: Difference Engine No. 1, Portion, 1832

present into a near future world. The readers of cyberpunk fiction are encouraged to recognize the "insertion curve" of new technology in their present lives as they ponder the dystopia fashioned by the mature form of that technology in the novel. For example, the increasingly familiar use of encrypted bank cards—"plastic money"—to make everyday purchases is extrapolated into an exclusively electronic monetary system in *Neuromancer*, such that paper money can only be exchanged for black market goods while all legitimate purchases are monitored and recorded by the authorities. Gibson remarks in an interview with Larry McCaffery, "When I write about technology, I write about how it has *already* affected our lives" ("An Interview" 140). The reader of cyberpunk experiences a sort of technological prolepsis in which the revolutionary developments of the future are thought to have already occurred. *The Difference Engine* presents the reader with the conceptual reverse of that process, a technological analepsis, in which a development of the future—the introduction of the mainframe computer (ENIAC appeared in 1946)—is thought to have occurred in the past. Cyberpunk fiction asks the proleptic question, What if the privacy concerns for electronic data transfer were not only ignored but unabashedly compromised by multinational corporations and government ministry? The "steampunk" novel asks the analeptic question, What if the calculating power of the computer were introduced to nineteenth-century gunnery; would it have changed the outcome of the American Civil War? In this regard *The Difference Engine* fulfills Jean-François Lyotard's definition of the postmodern, as the "paradox of the future (*post*) anterior (*modo*)" (81). We go back to the future, to the nascent state of computing and information technology, to recognize there the full conceptualization, *in utero* as it were, of our present technocracy.

The *Difference Engine* may also be treated as historiographic metafiction.[5] Prominent historical figures such as Charles Babbage, Augusta Ada Byron Lovelace (1815-1852), the British journalist and diplomat Laurence Oliphant (1829-1888), George Gordon,

Lord Byron (1788-1824), John Keats (1795-1821), and biologist Thomas Henry Huxley (1825-1895) intermingle with a host of fictive characters, some of whom are drawn from a novel of the period by one-time Prime Minister Benjamin Disraeli (1804-1881), *Sybil* (1845).[6] Linda Hutcheon concisely states the relationship thus: "Historiographic metafiction shows fiction to be historically conditioned and history to be discursively structured" (120). The textuality of history and fiction is a function of bi-directional communication, an open channel in either direction between historical fact and narrative structure. Historical novels conventionally respect the constraints placed upon them by historical facts; these fictions may saturate the historical figures with a sensibility not otherwise recorded for posterity, while heeding the *curriculum vitae* that history has outlined for the characters. Such is not the case in *The Difference Engine* as an alternative history. The introduction of Babbage's computing machinery represents a *clinamen*,

Figure 2: Difference Engine No. 2, 1991, Science Museum

or swerve, in the course of history; an alternate world forms that affects the path of every life, however remotely. Keats, though he appears still to suffer from consumption, has survived to the mature age of sixty in the novel. He has abandoned poesy for kinotropy, disdaining print for the programming of moving pictures. He speaks with enthusiasm not of eternal Beauty but, analeptically, of the "screen's resolution" and "refresh-rate," and of the remarkable effects secured "through algorithmic compression" (47). Lord Byron, who succumbs to fever in 1824 while an expatriate in disgrace in Greece, becomes the oratorical leader—if not the intellectual force—of the Industrial Radical party and has risen to Prime Minister in *The Difference Engine*. Byron leads a revolt against Wellington's Tories and later suppresses the "proletarian Luddites" (309), underwriting the theme of class warfare in the novel. History records that George Gordon, Lord Byron espoused various liberal political causes in the House of Lords, and *contra* his actions in the novel, penned a "Song for the Luddites" in support of the weavers oppressed by the lords of industry. As an alternative history, then, *The Difference Engine* intends a reader who is at least moderately well acquainted with the lives of the Romantic poets and with the history of the Industrial Revolution in England such that an ironical pleasure is derived in the comparison between "what *has* happened" in the Victorian period and "what *might have* happened" had the plug not been pulled on Babbage's government-sponsored research. The authors expect that a bi-directional channel between fiction and history remain operative, and in fact the novel relies on that interrelation for its effective consumption. At the same time, the novel is a metafiction that relies on an awareness of intertextuality, in so doing continually calling attention to its status as writing. If the reader intended by the text is not permitted ignorance of the Victorian period, neither is he or she allowed an absorptive fantasy in otherworldliness. As Herbert Sussman explains, the "narrative and techno-political transformations" of the alternative history of *The Difference Engine* "are achieved through a radical rewriting of [Disraeli's] *Sybil*" (7). The crucial marriage between Sybil and Charles Egremont that represents for Victorians "the dream of mediating the oppositions of industry/culture and industry/pastoral by bringing the factory under the control of a beneficent landed aristocracy" (8) does not take place in Gibson and Sterling's novel. The ideological implications of "refashioning Victorian narratives of technoculture" and class conflict are manifest, in Sussman's thorough analysis (8-10). As historiographic metafiction, the novel intends a reader who must also negotiate between the various textual sources alluded to in the novel, including Byron's poetry, Disraeli's novel, Babbage's *Passages from the Life of a Philosopher* (1864), and of course, Ada Byron's published Notes on the Difference Engine. Let me state explicitly that I am not referring to an actual reader—would that we could find such equally knowledgeable in Victorian history and literature, cyberpunk fiction, and the history of the computer and computing languages in our classroom—but to an authorial reader, the *lector* intended by and in the text. Such a reader in *The Difference Engine* must negotiate the bi-directional channel between historiography and intertextuality that is constantly at play in this text.

5. Lady Lovelace's Objection

Augusta Ada Lovelace (1815-1852) was the only legitimate daughter of Byron, the product of his short-lived marriage to mathematician Annabella Milbanke. Rumors of an incestuous affair with his half sister, Augusta Leigh, drove Byron into exile in April 1816, and he was never to meet his daughter again, though he would memorialize her in Canto III of *Childe Harold's Pilgrimage* as "The child of Love! though born in bitterness, / And nurtured in Convulsion! Of thy sire / These were the elements,—and thine no less."[7] Determined not to allow her daughter to fall under the captivating sway of Byron's romanticism, Milbanke saw to it that Ada was rigorously tutored in mathematics by Mary Somerville and Augustus De Morgan. That Ada, as a woman and juvenile, would have received such an intensive education in mathematics in early nineteenth-century England was exceptional.[8] At the age of seventeen, Ada Byron would meet Charles Babbage at a party and be introduced by him to the partially completed Difference Engine. Nearly as profligate as her father, Ada

would enjoy her first affair of the mind. Following a presentation by Babbage on the Analytical Engine to a group of mathematicians and engineers in Turin, Italy in 1840, Luigi Federico Menabrea endeavored to write an essay, "Sketch of the Analytical Engine," in French, describing the mathematical theses implied by Babbage's calculating machines (Kim and Toole 78-79). It was this essay that Ada took it upon herself to translate into English and append seven Notes, lettered A through G, which combined are more than twice the length of the original essay.

Figure 3: Ada Byron Lovelace, 1838

Ada Byron concluded her Notes with a program for computing Bernoulli numbers that are found in the polynomial expansion of some trigonometric functions that were once employed for constructing navigational tables (Kim and Toole 78). On the basis of this "Diagram for the computation by the Engine of the Numbers of Bernoulli," demonstrating that Babbage's Analytical Engine was capable of conditional branching and multiple loops (or iterations) (Kim and Toole 80), Ada has been bestowed with the title of the First Programmer of computers. In fact, Microsoft Corporation embosses its software with a Certificate of Authenticity containing a watermark portrait that identifies Ada Byron as a "Pioneer in Computer Programming," and the Department of Defense named its proprietary programming language Ada in 1980 (Grossman 63). There has been some debate among scholars and biographers of Ada Byron regarding the sophistication of her knowledge of mathematics, but even her detractors concede that, if Babbage's design for the Analytical Engine was a predecessor of the modern computer, Ada's Notes constitute the first program for a computing machine.[9]

In Gibson and Sterling's *The Difference Engine*, Ada Byron, now the daughter of the

Prime Minister, is indisputably the "Queen of Engines" (95). She is the first and most accomplished programmer of the Analytical Engine and the author of a Modus, which is either a program intended to beat the odds of pari-mutuel wagering at the London racetrack, destroying "the institutions of the Turf" (189) (Ada Lovelace did in fact lose spectacular sums gambling late in life; and card-counting programs have long been banned from Las Vegas casinos), or it is a program of such complexity that its "series of nested loops" (421) send the most sophisticated computer of the day, the Grand Napoleon Ordinateur, cascading to blue-screen failure. As mechanician and inventor, Charles Babbage is but a minor character in the novel. Mysterious and introspective— and possibly addicted to laudanum—it is Ada who turns at the intellectual center of the world of *The Difference Engine*. In their alternative history, Gibson and Sterling fashion an Ada who is liberated from the Victorian conventions of family and society that, as Ada Lovelace complained in her letters, impeded her intellectual aspirations. Ada Byron is unmarried (her biographical counterpart marries William King, earl of Lovelace, has three children whom she treated with indifference, and dies from cervical cancer at 36, the same age as her father at his death). She is a scientist who gives speeches on her art to the Royal Society (whose premises in Victorian England women were not allowed to enter). Although they otherwise alter the biographies of many of the historical characters in *The Difference Engine*, Gibson and Sterling appear to have optimized Ada Byron's potential as a theorist of computing machinery, making her the catalyst of the second Industrial Revolution. Confirming his enthusiasm for Ada Byron's genius, Bruce Sterling appears "as himself" via a computer uplink in Lynn Hershman Leeson's film, *Conceiving Ada* (1997).

Although the alternative history of *The Difference Engine* has embellished Ada Byron's intellectual achievements, Gibson and Sterling draw directly from Ada's limited scholarly publications, the Notes to Menabrea's essay, in their characterization. When she encounters Edward Mallory, a paleontologist and exponent of the theory of Catastrophism, at the London track (not for horses, but "line-streamed" horseless carriages), she mutters in a narcotized haze portions of her speech to the Royal Society. Her statement is taken nearly verbatim from Note A: "Supposing, for instance, that the fundamental relations of pitched sounds in the science of harmony and of musical composition were susceptible of such expression and adaptations, the engine might compose elaborate and scientific pieces of music of any degree of complexity or extent" (quoted in Kim and Toole 80; cf. *Difference Engine* 93). As amusing as this synthesized, "switched-on Bach" might sound, the proposition represents both a theme of the Notes and of the novel. Ada Byron understands the Analytical Engine as far more than a mechanical calculator, capable of symbolic processing powers. Resolving the intractable conflict between her disciplinarian and mathematician mother and her iconoclastic and romantic poet father, Ada speculates that the Analytical Engine could enable the higher functions of consciousness and even offer access to the fundamental music of the spheres. In her letters she was given to further fantasizing on the powers of computation, "I have my hopes, & very distinct ones too, of one day getting *cerebral* phenomena such that I can put them into mathematical equations; in short a *law, or laws*, for the mutual actions of the molecules of the brain" (quoted in Grossman 66). Of this synthesis of mathematics and cognition, however, note that Ada does not imagine the computing machinery thinking for her, but that the cognitive functions of the brain might be expressed in mathematical terms.

Nor did Ada Lovelace require the assistance of novelists to embellish her intellectual talents. Before Gibson and Sterling, none other than Benjamin Disraeli published the semi-biographical novel *Venetia* (1837), when she was only twenty-one, about a precocious young girl who resides in England with her controlling mother, Lady Annabel, but who has become obsessed with her subversive and impetuous father, the poet Carducis, in Italy. Ada's attraction to and competition with Byron are frankly stated in her letters: "I do *not* believe that my father was (or ever could have been) such a *Poet* as I *shall* be an *Analyst*" (quoted in Grossman 63). Looking beyond the filial rivalry, it's apparent that Ada envisioned a role for the programmer-Analyst that is equally as creative as that of the author-Poet.

Although it's apparent that Gibson and Sterling are familiar with Ada Lovelace's Notes on the Analytical Engine, they do not incorporate into the text of *The Difference Engine* one of the most widely quoted passages, from Note G. As a prelude to demonstrating her work on the Bernoulli numbers, Ada warns the reader "against the possibility of exaggerated ideas that might arise as to the power of the Analytical engine" (quoted in Baum 81). She counsels restraint with regard to speculation on the capabilities of the calculating machine. Her analysis, called "Lady Lovelace's Objection" by Alan Turing in his landmark paper on artificial intelligence in 1950, is as follows:

> The Analytical Engine has no pretensions whatever to *originate* anything. It can do whatever we *know how to order it* to perform. It can *follow* analysis; but it has no power of *anticipating* any analytical relations or truths. Its province is to assist us in making *available* what we are already acquainted with. (her italics; quoted in Baum 82)

Ada wishes to dispel the notion that the Analytical Engine is "thinking" in ways that the human mind thinks. She reserves to the programmer the capacity to create new operations or truths. The computing machine is only capable of following instructions, and then only when the instructions have been properly programmed. Disorderly input yields disorderly output. There may be syntactic errors in the analysis, or program, that lead to unanticipated—and probably useless—results; but the programmer will never be surprised by operations originated by the computer. She being the first programmer—and as Byron's daughter somewhat immodest about her creative powers—Ada's not eager to concede intelligence to the machine from the domain of the programmer. Her objection, however, that computing machinery does not originate but follow analysis, rather presciently sets the standard for whether a computer passes Turing's Test: it would have to *originate* something. Ada regards computing as a measure of the Analyst's knowledge and creative ability. The Analytical Engine only processes, or makes available to us in some efficient manner, that which we already know. It is only when the programmer ventures to originate an operation, extending the capability of the Engine, that new analytical results might arise. The Engine is not an artificial intelligence; it takes measure of the programmer's genius.

The characterization of Ada Byron in *The Difference Engine* is less radically altered than that of other historical figures from nineteenth-century England. Gibson and Sterling mean to examine the premises of Ada's Notes at the analeptic inception of the Computer Age. After all, it is Ada Lovelace who first speculates on the nature of computing, the role of the programmer, and the potential of what she confidently regards as a new realm of intellectual endeavor. In Note A, Ada acknowledges Babbage's adoption of the punched cards that Joseph Marie Jacquard (1752-1834) employed to set the patterns of the weaving loom: "The distinctive characteristic of the Analytical Engine . . . is the introduction into it of the principle which Jacquard devised for regulating, by means of punched cards, the most complicated patterns in the fabrication of brocaded stuffs." Such punched cards remained the principal means of input in mainframe computers until the advent of magnetic tape and magnetic disks in the mid twentieth century. Ada's characteristic effusion, however, attends not to how the machine functions but what it might be capable of: "We say most aptly that the Analytical Engine *weaves algebraical patterns* just as the Jacquard-loom weaves flowers and leaves" (her italics; quoted in Kim and Toole 80). Ada evidently regards her Analysis as a mode of artistry; what the programmer weaves in higher mathematics is equivalent to figures created in the other arts. In *The Difference Engine*, Ada Byron is credited with the introduction of a textile pattern, "a dizzy mosaic of tiny blue-and-white squares. Ada Checkers, the tailors called them, the Lady having created the pattern by programming a Jacquard loom to weave pure algebra" (101). In his cameo appearance in Lynn Hershman Leeson's film *Conceiving Ada*, Sterling remarks that he and his co-author cast Ada Byron as the "symbolic counterpoint" to the Romantic poet turned Prime Minister, Lord Byron. As the visionary theorist of computation, the Mother of all programmers, Ada, and not her father represents the figure of the artist in the novel. In the world of *The Difference Engine*, Analysis, or computation, not poetry, is the highest form of art.

The novel itself is arranged in a series of five Iterations, with the addition of an epilogue entitled "Modus The Images Tabled" (397), a final compiling of the program. Gibson and Sterling establish *The Difference Engine* in an analogical relationship to a calculating machine, weaving its own algebraical patterns. The novel not only imagines a world in which Analysis is artistry, it also performs something like an analytical engine in its iterations. In computing, an iterative process is a means of calculating a result by performing a series of steps repeatedly, often as an embedded loop. Iterations enable a digital computer to obtain an approximate solution that, with the feedback of preliminary results into each successive iteration, eventually leads to a solution of desired accuracy. If *The Difference Engine* is being "run" like an iterative program, as suggested by its section divisions, what is the approximate solution that the novel hopes to resolve? Among the several mysteries presented in the text, one that I have already alluded to seems most germane: the nature and purpose of the stack of "camphorated cellulose" (celluloid was the first synthetic plastic material, first prepared in 1865) cards that is Ada's Modus. Ordinary "clackers" (computer programmers in "steampunk" argot) suspect that Ada's stack is a "gambling-system, a secret trick of mathematical Enginery, to defeat the odds-makers" (189). The proletarian revolutionary and murderous "vitreuse" Florence Bartlett, however, is willing to kill to possess the Modus for the wealth and power she suspects the program would convey. The Iterations gradually reveal that unfathomable power lies in controlling the Modus, much more so than in governing the analytical engines themselves. Ironically, the paleontologist Edwin Mallory, who is given the stack in safekeeping by Ada Byron, has, according to the kinotrope artist John Keats, "no idea of their astonishing import" (416). The final, yet approximate solution to the Modus is provided in the form of a speech delivered to a Parisian women's club by Ada Byron herself:

> "And yet the execution of the so-called Modus Program demonstrated that any formal system must be both *incomplete* and *unable to establish its own consistency*. There is no finite mathematical way to express the property of 'truth.' The *transfinite* nature of the Byron Conjectures were the ruination of the Grand Napoleon [computer]; the Modus Program initiated a series of nested loops, which, though difficult to establish, were yet more difficult to extinguish. The program ran, yet rendered its Engine useless! It was indeed a painful lesson in the halting abilities of even our finest *ordinateurs*.
>
> Yet I do believe, and must assert most strongly, that the Modus technique of *self-referentiality* will someday form the bedrock of a genuinely transcendent meta-system of calculatory mathematics. The Modus has proven my Conjectures, but their practical exfoliation awaits an Engine of vast capacity, one capable of iterations of untold sophistication and complexity." (421)

Ada Byron analeptically invokes Kurt Gödel's Incompleteness theorem (1931) that asserts that no mathematical system is provable, or complete, within itself; every system must be part of a larger structure; and thus, the nature of truth is finally indeterminate—or, in Lady Byron's terms, "transfinite." Just as Ada Lovelace's Notes referred to an Analytical Engine that was never to be built in her or Babbage's lifetime, so Ada Byron speculates on the effects that her Modus program would have were it run on a digital supercomputer well beyond "the limits of steam power" (422) in her day. Ada's program has crashed the Grand Napoleon *ordinateur* with its infinitely cycling loops. *The Difference Engine* is itself a work of multiple iterations, compelling the reader simultaneously to regard the text analeptically as an alternative history of Victorian England with steam-driven computing machinery and proleptically as an examination of what effects an information technocracy would have if it were fully instantiated in a society such as our own. As an artist, Ada promotes the "self-referentiality" of her Modus and its access to a transcendent "meta-system" with utopian enthusiasm. The shift from linear to nonlinear analysis in "calculatory mathematics" finds its analogy in the shift from the plot-driven, crankshaft realism of linear narrative to the nonlinear, iterative (high gain) narrative of metafiction. This passage, in which Ada describes her Modus, doubles metafictively as an endorsement of the reflexive irony in cyberpunk fiction. It's a little "coming attraction" for the New Age of cybernetic fiction.

The self-referentiality technique of Ada's Modus will someday spell the death of the Author-programmer. Although Ada Lovelace objected to the premise that a computer performing according to instruction was a "thinking" machine, Ada Byron indulges in speculation on artificial intelligence:

> "If we envision the entire System of Mathematics as a great Engine for proving theorems, then we must say, through the agency of the Modus, that such a Engine *lives*, and could indeed *prove* its own life, should it develop the capacity to look upon itself. The Lens for such a self-examination is of a nature not yet known to us; yet we know that it exists, for we ourselves possess it." (421-22)

No computing machinery has yet passed the test of self-examination. But were such an artificial intelligence to exist, it would have to be able to "originate" thought (the Lovelace Objection) or regard itself reflexively (the Byron Conjecture). Such an Engine that *lives*, freed from the ministrations of programmer and user, would be comparable to the Barthesian *scriptible* text, an "instance writing" freed from the ministrations of the biographical author or actual reader.

6. The Virtual Reader in Cyberfiction

Aarseth's ergodic reader participates in dynamical computer games and Multi-User Domains by following the "work-path" that the system has established (1). The ergodic reader is indisputably endowed with election, or the choice of following one or another of the possible work-paths; and some work-paths may be more productive (as judged by the reader, or by the system?) than others. But in his or her election (Aarseth's "nontrivial effort' [1]), the ergodic reader is not capable of originating a new passage or solution. Landow's hypertext reader experiences similar privileges and limitations. One can elect to follow a particular link in hyperfiction or Internet web pages, finding the traversal from one "docuverse" (Ted Nelson's term) to be either rewarding or, as is so often the case, frustrating or pointless. But again, the reader of hyperlinked texts can neither fashion nor destroy the links that have been encoded there. As I have already suggested, both the ergodic and hypertext readers are actual readers; they are purveyors of the text, subject to market research; and as such they are, in Barthes's determination, rather more consumers than producers of the text than their respective theorists would grant. Actual readers-in-the-world are likewise subject to Lady Lovelace's Objection with regard to the Analytical Engine. The actual reader can have no pretensions whatever to *originate* anything. He or she can do only what the author-programmer *knows how to order it* to perform. I am arguing that the actual reader, because he or she is embodied, is always limited in the material world in his or her performativity. Keystroke combinations, mouse clicks, shaking the Etch-o-Sketch—whatever servo-mechanical interface is required—must be established in advance of the administration of the text. The actual reader is made active only in his or her bio-mechanical domain, not within textuality itself. Make no mistake, the potential for innovation in the various modes of hypertext, combinatorial-procedural, or cyber-text fiction is enormous, and we are merely limning the edge of what digital textuality has in store for us. But so far the power to create the text has not been transferred to the actual reader. Readers of hypertext and other forms of electronic fiction are more acted upon than acting; not so much constructing the text as constructed by it. Insofar as cybertext is a "machine made of words" (William Carlos Williams's definition of a poem), the actual reader performs just as any other human being in a cybernetic system. Norbert Wiener, in *The Human Use of Human Beings* (1954), emphasizes that the performance or nonperformance of the human subject in a feedback loop with a machine may in the parlance of other fields be called "conditioned reflex" or "learning" (33). In cybertexts, one must ask, who is the teacher and who the pupil? As in any cybernetic system, where does control reside?

Print-based cyberfiction envisages for itself a Virtual Reader. Not an actual reader with pretensions to originate anything through manipulation of keys or cursors, but an avatar or "stand-in" for the Reader in the text. In *Neuromancer*, Gibson describes a "construct" as "a hardwired ROM cassette replicating a dead man's skills, obsessions, knee-jerk responses" (76-77), a personality preserved on a memory chip. Dixie Flatline is presented in the novel not as a "live," embodied character, but as a virtual personality rendered in Silicon Graphics. The Virtual Reader in cyberfiction can be regarded as an extension of this premise: not as a member of an actual, book-buying audience, but as the replication of the Reader in the text. Like a "construct," the Virtual Reader is rendered only within the cybertext and nonexistent when the system powers down. Cyberfictions that are populated with simulated life forms and autotelic information systems are naturally well disposed toward implicating both the authorial and reader functions in the virtual reality of the text. The biographical author and the actual reader are vestiges of nineteenth-century realism, one of whose prominently advertised features is the transparency of the work onto Nature. As the author and reader in realism are themselves regarded as *au natural*, their embodiment is regarded uncritically; only thus can the book pass between them unimpeded by the medium of transmission. Cyberfictions recognize that author and reader are simulations of the text and that the medium is the message. An avatar is a "temporary manifestation or aspect of a continuing entity." The incarnation of a Hindu deity is a temporary manifestation in human form of divinity; likewise, the avatar of the user in virtual reality. The player of a computer game may identify the avatar as a surrogate self who, controlled by joysticks or other input devices, may be made to do the player's bidding in the virtual world of the game. And yet, the avatar is always already a representation of that virtual reality's programmers, with only those capabilities and pursuits by them so defined. Cyberfiction comfortably adopts as its native milieu the knowing simulation of virtual reality, and thus the avatar serves to define of the surrogate role of the reader.

The avatar, or Virtual Reader, is assigned a performing role in the text. In some computer simulations, the anthropoid avatar may assume the role of the protagonist in an adventure, sporting contest, or narrative quest. Just as the performing role of the avatar in computer games will vary with respect to its genre, so the performance of the Virtual Reader will be established by the author to meet the specific needs of cyberfiction. I have already suggested that Gibson and Sterling seek to establish in *The Difference Engine* a bi-directional communication between the alternative history of the Victorian period as presented in the novel and the conventional record of that period. Let's call it postmodern irony when the Virtual Reader recognizes an error in transmission between the world of the Difference Engine and Victorian England, as when the Marquess of Hastings, leading his "swing band" of class revolutionaries, identifies the "still fine poets in England. Did you ever hear of John Wilson Croker? Winthrop Mackworth Praed? Bryan Waller Procter?" (300). Victorian versifiers, in fact; whereas Shelley has become a Luddite agitator, and Professor Coleridge and Reverend Wordsworth have decamped to the utopian commune of the Susquehanna Phalanstery (291). In an interview given shortly after the publication of *The Difference Engine*, Sterling comments on the book's obsession with Victoriana: "It's our disease projected onto a lab animal of the 19th century. Watch what happens to them, watch the course of the symptoms, which will help us to understand what's happening to us. You know, if a Victorian read this book it wouldn't make any sense to him at all. . . . Even Charles Babbage wouldn't be able to understand *DE*" ("The Charisma Leak" 6). Despite the metaphor of clinical pathology, which is a "meat" thing, Sterling makes clear that the Virtual Reader in *The Difference Engine* has been ordered to perform continuously an analeptic and a proleptic analysis of the alternative history: how has the analeptic insertion of the Information Industry into Victorian society altered its course? And what do the symptoms observed there proleptically suggest about our present condition? Any other performance by the Virtual Reader would be outside the rules of the clinical trial. Although virtual reality is beyond the resolution and "refresh rate" of mechanical "clacking" in the novel, the precursor of the avatar in the form of an automaton makes an appearance. Edwin Mallory, Lawrence Oliphant, and visiting Japanese diplomats are served tea by a Japanese doll, or *karakuri*. Mallory exclaims, "I see! Like one of those Jacquot-Droz toys, or Vaucanson's famous duck, eh?" (168). The mechanical duck fashioned by Jacques de

Vaucanson (1709-1782), which also makes a cameo appearance in Thomas Pynchon's *Mason & Dixon* (1997), and subsequent automata perform operations without human intervention and employ feedback in self-correcting control systems. Like the *karakuri* among guests, the Virtual Reader in cyberfiction should be the obedient servant to the text.

The Virtual Reader in cyberfiction is, as Barthes would say, the destination of the text. The appeal of virtuality resides in its utterly flexible adaptation to circumstance. Unconstrained by physical limitations, the virtual space can be whatever is required of it. Thus the Virtual Reader as a simulacrum of the reader is "without history, biography, psychology" ("Death of the Author" 148), except as those traits would be transiently defined in the text. Italo Calvino, who explored the relationship of cybernetics and literature, provides an instance of this simulacral Reader in his fiction, *If on a winter's night a traveler*. The prologue to the novel would appear to address, in the familiar second person singular, a "you" who would be reading Italo Calvino's new novel (3). Such a direct address to an assumed actual reader occurs in the prologues of many classic texts, including the "Bill of Fare" in Fielding's *Tom Jones* (1749), the attestations of veracity in Daniel DeFoe's *Robinson Crusoe* (1719), and Miguel de Cervantes's Prologue to the Reader in *Don Quixote* (1605). Yet Calvino's address to the actual reader, suavely seeing to his physical comfort "because once you're absorbed in reading there will be no budging you" (4), is redolent with postmodern irony. Calvino quickly dispels the illusion that the addressee in the prologue is the actual reader of the book. The recumbent reader, suddenly deprived of the classic, "readerly" text that he desires, is then sent scrambling in pursuit of the unity of the text. "Who you are, Reader, your age, your status, profession, income: that would be indiscreet to ask. It's your business, you're on your own" (32). Perusing the ten interrupted narratives, Calvino's Reader becomes a figure of the Barthesisan *lector*, one for whom a "text is made of multiple writings, drawn from many cultures and entering into mutual relations to dialogue, parody, contestation" ("Death of the Author" 148).

As in other game worlds, Calvino's Reader pursues the completion of the text that he is reading; he behaves as would any avatar, a subject that is both synthetic and unspecified. The Reader has no personal discretion, but exists to be the destination of the text's unity. In cyberfiction, the narrative's protagonist will often be presented as an avatar. Neal Stephenson's *Snow Crash* (1992) features a programmer named Hiro Protagonist who has created a virtual reality known as the Metaverse (22). The actions of Hiro, who in the flesh is Korean- and African-American, as he pursues his nemesis, Raven, are largely unaffected by the transmission from a Los Angeles wholly governed by corporate franchises and the Metaverse that, "like any other place in Reality," is similarly subject to commercial development (23). The Metaverse is peopled with custom-built avatars for the hackers, and for the neophytes, an assortment of off-the-shelf models. "Hiros' avatar just looks like Hiro, with the difference that no matter what Hiro is wearing in Reality, his avatar always wears a black leather kimono." For those who "can't afford to have custom avatars made and don't know how to write their own," they can purchase and assemble generic models from the "Avatar Construction Setk" (34-35). Every avatar is a "construct" that appears only as the programmer-user knows how to order it to appear; and that avatar can only perform—with ritual *kitane* swords or on a Yamaha motorcycle—what the programmer knows how to order it to perform. In the transmission from Reality to the Metaverse, the user would seem to create for himself or herself an identity: "Your avatar can look any way you want it to, up to the limitations of your equipment" (33). But in effect it is the virtual reality system that creates the avatar. The Virtual Reader in cyberfiction behaves as such an avatar, always more acted upon than acting, not so much constructing the text as constructed by it.

7. Scriptor and Narratron

The Difference Engine begins with an impersonal surveillance report consisting of a "composite image, optically encoded" (1). Other such reports, as if they were dispatches from a spy satellite in geosynchronous orbit above London or Cherbourg, France, occasionally punctuate the novel. The reader has no direct evidence as to who or what is gathering this information, or for what purpose; but reasoned speculation might lead to the Central Statistics Bureau whose Engines and clackers maintain the data files on every citizen-number (143). And yet the digital technology implied by these surveillance reports would seem to supercede the mechanical gearing, stipple-printing, and kinotropy of the Engines. Not until the reader reaches the conclusion of the novel, having parsed the slippages of history, does he or she recognize that something has been "carrying out this vast surveillance of the 19th century from an alternate 1991" ("Charisma Leak" 11). Not the 1991 of the authors, promoting their newly published novel in a sushi-bar interview in Toronto, nor the 1991 of the avid science-fiction reader who has just devoured the latest cyberpunk novel by Gibson and Sterling, but the 1991 which is the future world of the Difference Engine. It is London, and yet a kind of "sim city" of "mirrored plazas of sheerest crystal, the avenues atomic lightning, the sky a super-cooled gas, as the Eye chases its own gaze through the labyrinth, leaping quantum gaps that are causation, contingency, chance" (428). As Gibson reveals in the Toronto interview, the conclusion of the novel introduces the "narratron," an automated narrator. "The story purports in the end to tell you that the narrative you have just read is not the narrative in the ordinary sense; rather it's a long self-iteration as this thing attempts to boot itself up, which it does in the final exclamation point" ("Charisma Leak" 10). The panoptic machine has not been gathering information on the citizenry in obedient service to an Orwellian regime. We are witness to the advent of an artificial intelligence, capable of self-programming and reflexivity: "In this City's center, a *thing* grows, an auto-catalytic tree, in almost-life, feeding through the roots of thought on the rich decay of its own shed images, and ramifying, through myriad lightning-branches, up, up, toward the hidden light of vision" (428-29). The narratron has apparently benefited from the research of some alternative Ilya Prigogine or Stuart Kauffman on autocatalytic sets as it labors to boot itself up. Its self-awareness—asking the "what am I?" question—signifies intelligence. Sterling states, "Well, it *is* reflexivity; it's a very postmodern move; it's your basic narrative frame-breaking move there. But, yeah, the author of the book is the narratron; it's sitting there telling itself a novel as it studies its own origins" ("Charisma Leak" 10). The narratron's tale—but perhaps it is all a fantastic delusion, in which the authorial function is assigned to a self-reflexive computing machine; that tale, then, is another iteration of the "death of the author," another proposition of a Barthesian *scriptor* engaged in fashioning its own textuality, an automated writing. As an artificial intelligence capable of examining and altering its own programming, the narratron also enunciates the death of the programmer; in cybernetic terms, the control of the narrative resides in the computing machinery. Finally, the narrative frame-breaking (an activity that unites the postmodern with the Luddite) will have an effect on the role of the reader, and here I mean the Barthesian *lector* in the text. The reader, who has previously been concerned to read *The Difference Engine* for its slippages in an alternative history, now must reread the novel entirely as a self-reflexive, metafictive exercise. In a proleptic reading, the reality of the Difference Engine in 1855 leads to a dystopic information society in 1991 that is controlled by an "all-seeing Eye" and which places its human attendants, clackers and navvies, in a Foucauldian panopticon. More than this, the narratron's "self-iteration" truly creates a Virtual Reader in that such a text, written to account for the computer's own origins, could only have a reader within the virtual architecture of the machine's intelligence.

Enthusiasm for an empowered, actual reader accompanied the millennial optimism for new forms of communications technology. The marketing campaign for personal digital assistants (PDAs) such as the Palm Pilot, cellular telephones and pagers stress the hand-held portability of the devices; each can be personalized with one's own vital data and contact lists; each promises incessant interactivity, linkage to a network, roaming, and total wireless access to the information or persons that matter to you. Yet, as becomes apparent to anyone who has tried to avail themselves of universal connectivity—"Can you hear me now?"—or negotiate the interface between one's satellite devices and the docking platform, or practice safe and seamless data entry and retrieval, the liberation and empowerment of personal communications devices in practice has been oversold. One might as well be carrying a homing device strapped to one's belt that makes targeting the user that much easier for commercial or governmental purposes. Cybernetic fictions have taken a lesson from the developments in communications technology: they regard with skepticism the promised control and organization of information; and they entertain a touch of paranoia that these liberating devices are shackles in another form. The actual reader of Gibson and Sterling's *The Difference Engine* is no more "free" in the text than the rest of the constrained, engine-stippled populace of an information society at large. The virtual reader, however, is that destination of the text that is not personal and in whom the network of communication is realized.

NOTES

[1] Michel Foucault continues Barthes's theory of a work which is its author's murderer in "What Is an Author?" Umberto Eco argues that in an "open work" the text "can not only be interpreted but also cooperatively generated by the addressee" (*Role of the Reader* 3).

[2] For a further discussion of proceduralism in postmodern fiction, see Joseph Conte, *Design and Debris: A Chaotics of Postmodern American Fiction.*

[3] For a discussion of whether Babbage's failure to demonstrate the functionality of the Difference Engine No. 1 after nearly twenty years of work was due to the inadequacy of Victorian engineering, or whether the economics of mechanical computing made a nineteenth-century computer revolution impractical, see Tom Standage, "The Little Engine that Couldn't."

[4] In *Cybernetics and Society*, Norbert Wiener expresses doubt that Babbage, even properly funded, could have completed his Difference Engine: "Babbage had a surprisingly modern idea for a computing machine, but his mechanical means fell far behind his ambitions. The first difficulty he met, and with which he could not cope, was that a long train of gears requires considerable power to run it, so that its output of power and torque very soon becomes too small to actuate the remaining parts of the apparatus" (149).

[5] Linda Hutcheon introduces this genre in *A Poetics of Postmodernism* (105-23).

[6] For a variety of historical details I am indebted to Eileen K. Gunn's *The Difference Dictionary*, a very useful annotation of the novel.

[7] For references to Ada in Byron's poetry, see Appendix 1 in Joan Baum, *The Calculating Passion of Ada Byron.*

[8] I am indebted for this assessment of Ada's education to Eugene Eric Kim and Betty Alexandra Toole, "Ada and the First Computer."

[9] In "What Ada Knew," Lev Grossman provides an engaging narrative of the debate over Ada Byron's importance to the history of computing, her facility in mathematics of the time, and her designation as the first programmer. Dorothy Stein's biography, *Ada: A Life and a Legacy* (1985) precipitated the challenge to Ada's reputation; Joan Baum's *The Calculating Passion of Ada Byron* (1986) represents a rejoinder to that criticism.

WORKS CITED

Aarseth, Espen J. *Cybertext: Perspectives on Ergodic Literature.* Baltimore and London: Johns Hopkins U P, 1997.

Barthes, Roland. "The Death of the Author." *Image—Music—Text.* Trans. Stephen Heath. Boston: Hill and Wang, 1977.

——. *S/Z.* Trans. Richard Miller. New York: Hill and Wang, 1974.

Baum, Joan. *The Calculating Passion of Ada Byron.* Hamden, CT: Archon, 1986.

Cage, John. *Themes & Variations.* Barrytown, NY: Station Hill, 1982.

Calvino, Italo. *If on a winter's night a traveler.* Trans. William Weaver. New York: Harcourt, 1981.

——. "Prose and Anticombinatorics." In Motte, 143-52.

Conceiving Ada. Dir. Lynn Hershman Leeson. Perf. Tilda Swinton, Timothy Leary, Karen Black, Francesca Faridany, John Perry Barlow. DVD. Fox Lorber, 1997.

Conte, Joseph M. *Design and Debris: A Chaotics of Postmodern American Fiction.* Tuscaloosa and London: U of Alabama P, 2002.

Eco, Umberto. *The Role of the Reader: Explorations in the Semiotics of Texts.* Bloomington: Indiana U P, 1979.

Fournel, Paul. "Computer and Writer: The Centre Pompidou Experiment." In Motte, 140-42.

Gibson, William. "An Interview with William Gibson." Interview with Larry McCaffery. McCaffery, ed. *Across the Wounded Galaxies: Interviews with Contemporary American Science Fiction Writers*. Urbana and Chicago: U of Illinois P, 1990. 130-50.

———. *Neuromancer*. New York: Ace, 1984.

Gibson, William, and Bruce Sterling. "'The Charisma Leak': A Conversation with William Gibson and Bruce Sterling." Interview with Daniel Fischlin, Veronica Hollinger, and Andrew Taylor. *Science-Fiction Studies* 19 (1992): 1-16.

———. *The Difference Engine*. New York: Bantam, 1991.

Grossman, Lev. "What Ada Knew: Was Lord Byron's Daughter the First Computer Programmer?" *Lingua Franca* (October 1998): 63-69.

Gunn, Eileen K. *The Difference Dictionary*. 1996 <http://www.sff.net/people/gunn/dd/a.htm>.

Hayles, N. Katherine. *How We Became Posthuman: Virtual Bodies in Cybernetics, Literature, and Informatics*. Chicago and London: U of Chicago P, 1999.

Hutcheon, Linda. *A Poetics of Postmodernism: History, Theory, Fiction*. New York and London: Routledge, 1988.

Hyman, Anthony. *Charles Babbage: Pioneer of the Computer*. New York and Oxford: Oxford U P, 1982.

Jakobson, Roman. "Linguistics and Poetics." *Language in Literature*. Ed. Krystyna Pomorska and Stephen Rudy. Cambridge and London: Harvard U P, 1987. 62-94.

Joyce, Michael. *Afternoon, a story*. Watertown, MA: Eastgate, 1987.

———. *Of Two Minds: Hypertext Pedagogy and Poetics*. Ann Arbor: U of Michigan P, 1995.

Kim, Eugene Eric, and Betty Alexandra Toole. "Ada and the First Computer." *Scientific American* (May 1999): 76-81.

Landow, George P. *Hypertext 2.0: The Convergence of Contemporary Critical Theory and Technology*. Baltimore and London: Johns Hopkins U P , 1997.

Lewin, Roger. *Complexity: Life at the Edge of Chaos*. New York: Collier, 1992.

Lyotard, Jean-François. *The Postmodern Condition: A Report on Knowledge*. Trans. Geoff Bennington and Brian Massumi. Minneapolis: U of Minnesota P , 1984.

Motte, Warren F., Jr., ed. *Oulipo: A Primer of Potential Literature*. Lincoln and London: U of Nebraska P, 1986.

Powers, Richard. *Galatea 2.2*. New York: Farrar Straus & Giroux, 1995.

Snyder, Ilana. *Hypertext: The Electronic Labyrinth*. Melbourne, Australia: Melbourne U P, 1996.

Standage, Tom. "The Little Engine that Couldn't." *Feed Magazine*. 15 January 1999 <http://www.feed-mag.com/essay/es160_master.html?alert>.

Stein, Dorothy K. *Ada: A Life and a Legacy*. Cambridge, MA: MIT P, 1985.

Stephenson, Neal. *Snow Crash*. New York: Bantam, 1992.

Sussman, Herbert. "Cyberpunk Meets Charles Babbage: *The Difference Engine* as Alternative Victorian History." *Victorian Studies* 38 (1994): 1-23.

Waldrop, M. Mitchell. *Complexity: The Emerging Science at the Edge of Order and Chaos*. New York: Simon & Schuster, 1992.

Wiener, Norbert. *The Human Use of Human Beings: Cybernetics and Society*. 1954. New York: Da Capo P, 1988.

Williams, William Carlos. *The Collected Poems of William Carlos Williams, Volume I 1909-1939*. Ed. A. Walton Litz and Christopher MacGowan. New York: New Directions, 1986.

JOHN H. JOHNSTON
ARE RHIZOMES SCALE-FREE?: NETWORK THEORY
AND CONTEMPORARY AMERICAN FICTION

In *A Thousand Plateaus*, first published in French in 1980, Gilles Deleuze and Félix Guattari proposed the rhizome as an alternative to the tree as a model or image for thinking about certain forms of organization, including the organization of their own book. By virtue of its shape, the tree conjures up an image of order and hierarchical organization; but it also grows according to a process of binary splitting: the world and its representation, subject and object, and the primary codings used to define us: male or female, young or old, black or white. As such, the tree provides the organizational principle for diverse articulations: the classic book, military command and control structures, even Noam Chomsky's theory of generative grammar. In contrast, the rhizome—literally a root-like subterranean stem that sends out shoots in all directions—evokes a completely different image, that of a burrow, crabgrass, swarm or pack. With multiple entrances and exits, and mobile, heterogeneous connections, a rhizome is a network with a unique consistency but no unity. For this reason, D&G say, it is not amenable to any structural or generative model, and is a stranger to any idea of a genetic axis or deep structure. Indeed, the rhizome is always opposed to such pre-determinations: it is a cartography, a decalcomania, a mapping that traces not what is or what is already given, but what is coming into being.

D&G think of their own book as a rhizome because it is comprised not of chapters but of "plateaus," which can be read in any order, following diversely interconnecting concepts and themes. Stuart Moulthrop, the hypertext theorist and author of the hypertext narrative *Victory Garden*, has called D&G's rhizome-book an "incunabular hypertext" (300). Though it arrives as a print artifact, Moulthrop explains, "it was designed as a matrix of independent but cross-referential discourses which the reader is invited to enter more or less at random" (300). The reader's task, he continues, "is to build a network of virtual connections (which more than one reader of my acquaintance has suggested operationalizing as a web of hypertext links)" (301).

These comments appear in Moulthrop's essay "Rhizome and Resistance: Hypertext and the Dreams of a New Culture," where the rhizome figures as a radical alternative in the "social space of writing." Specifically, its expression in hypertexts "provides a laboratory or site of origin for a smoothly structured, nomadic alternative to the discursive space of late capitalism" (304). Thus, for Moulthrop, hypertext and the kind of network imaged by the rhizome inscribe and delineate the "dreams of a new culture." But hasn't this new culture already arrived? With the mushrooming growth of the Internet and the widespread development and even "normalization" of hypertext and hypermedia, hasn't this "dream" become part of the everyday reality of hundreds of millions of people across the globe? In other words, isn't this "dream" now visibly instantiated in what writers as

53

diverse as the fiction writer Michael Joyce, the cultural theorist Mark Taylor, and the sociologist Manuel Castells understand as an emerging "network culture"? While the term itself may be something of an oxymoron—since we can hardly imagine a human culture that does not involve networks of communication and exchange—what Joyce, Taylor, and Castells actually mean is that this new culture is defined by pervasive digital information networks; it is a culture, in short, increasingly constituted of information flows. Furthermore, the development of a fully scientific theory of networks in the late 1990s confirms their contemporary cultural significance. With the concepts and tools of this new body of theory, which often takes the Internet as a primary object of study, networks of every type and description can now be analyzed with a new and unanticipated precision. Perhaps not surprisingly, this theory can also tell us something new about contemporary American fiction.

Network and Narrative

Although networks of all kinds have always been important in literary fiction, it seems obvious in retrospect that the idea of an "information network" becomes essential to American fiction in the 1960s and 70s with the introduction of the themes of paranoia and paranoid conspiracy. The novels of Thomas Pynchon, particularly *The Crying of Lot 49* (1966) and *Gravity's Rainbow* (1973), are exemplary in this respect, inasmuch as the actions of the protagonists are motivated by quests that attempt to answer the basic question: am I surrounded by a network of conspiring agents, and are their concerted actions benign or malign? Joseph McElroy, in *Lookout Cartridge* (1974), puts a more complex spin on this narrative dilemma by situating his protagonist at both the center and periphery of multiple networks, not all of which are menacing. In a third instance, William Gaddis' *JR* (1975), we see a further complication, in that the protagonist JR is caught up in networks only because he is able to create one of his own—a vast corporate paper empire—which then produces the cascading collapse and destabilization of other, more "legitimate" networks, to which it is multiply linked. As readers are keenly aware, network and narrative in these novels are so richly articulated and imbricated that one cannot describe one without also and at the same time recounting the other.

But precisely what kinds of networks are we talking about here? If we define a network simply as a structure of links or connections among people, places, events, texts or words, agents or agencies, then it is clear that what most distinguishes the networks in these fictional narratives is that they are no longer simply *local*, but have become *global*. And here I use the term "global" not quite in its current meaning, but simply to designate a network in which many nodes and links are well beyond the perception or determination of an observer located at a single node. In such a global network, particularly where the structure of connections is felt to be determined by an overarching plan or design, the *local* will seem to lose its importance and may appear to serve primarily as a point of contact with the global. However, if this strand of American fiction gives expression to a new felt sense of connectedness at global levels—whether because of the influence of the mass media, a new phase of capitalism, or some other constellation of social and material forces —it is a sense still shadowed by doubts and the suspicion that specific connections may be only random or accidental or a projection of individual desire. Indeed, this fundamental ambivalence toward the very desirability of global connections is played out in multiple registers in *Gravity's Rainbow*:

> If there is something comforting about paranoia—religious, if you want —there is still also anti-paranoia, where nothing is connected to anything, a condition not many of us can bear for long. Well right now Slothrop feels himself sliding into the anti-paranoid part of his cycle, feels the whole city around him going back roofless, vulnerable, uncentered as he is, and only pasteboard images now of the Listening Enemy left between him and the wet sky.
>
> Either They have put him here for a reason, or he's just here. He isn't sure that he wouldn't, actually, rather have that *reason*. . . . (434)

Throughout the novel, moreover, network and narrative are mutually implicated, and not just at the level of the plot (initiated with Laszlo Jamf's experiments) to observe and control Slothrop. We're told late in the novel, for example, that under the drug Oneirine's influence paranoia is experienced as "nothing less than the onset, the leading edge, of the discovery that *everything is connected*, everything in the Creation," and, at the same time, that the drug produces "hauntings" or hallucinations that "show a definite narrative continuity, as clearly as, say, the average *Reader's Digest* article" (703).[1]

Adopting the framework and terms of contemporary network theory, I suggest that the narratives and network embeddings in Pynchon, McElroy, and Gaddis register an intuitive, inchoate, and anticipatory change in social perception: on the one hand, while the social (or narrative) subject perceives that many of its most fundamental connections are no longer local (i.e., that it is no longer a node in a classical network), on the other hand it still lacks the further understanding of whether that larger global network possesses a random or small-worlds architecture. Since these latter terms have a very precise meaning in network theory, to define them adequately will require a brief exposition. After providing this, I will apply some of its lessons to a series of hypertext narratives, beginning with Michael Joyce's first hypertext narrative, *afternoon, a story*, which appeared in 1987. Guiding my discussion will be the question of how the relationship of network to narrative changes when we shift from print to the electronic medium.

What is today called network theory grows out of "graph theory" in mathematics, where a "graph" is defined as a collection of points called "nodes" or "vertices" that are connected by "links" or "edges." It was founded in 1736 by the great mathematician Leonhard Euler when he resolved a conundrum popular among the citizens of Königsberg. The city was renowned for its seven bridges connecting a small island with both sides of the Pregel River, and for centuries these citizens had argued whether or not it was possible to cross all seven bridges in a single stroll without having to cross one of them twice. Treating the bridges as a "graph" with hidden properties, Euler proved that it could not be done.[2] Subsequently, and for the next two hundred years or so, mathematical interest focused primarily on regular graphs, in which each node has exactly the same number of links. In the 20th century, however, two Hungarian mathematicians, Paul Erdös and Alfréd Rényi, invented the formal theory of random graphs, where the network of nodes and links is connected in a completely random fashion.[3] In contrast to classical or regular graphs, where links are always connected to neighboring nodes and the network therefore exhibits a high degree of "local clustering," random graphs exhibit a high degree of connectivity across the network as a whole. In fact, Erdös and Rényi discovered that only a very small number of randomly placed links is always sufficient to tie together a fragmented network into a completely connected whole. To illustrate, let us suppose that in a remote area there are fifty small towns without any connecting roads. The government decides to build a network of new roads, but only has a limited budget. How, then, can all the towns be connected with the fewest number of roads? Erdös and Rényi showed that about 98 roads randomly placed would ensure that a great majority of the towns would indeed be linked together.[4] While 98 may seem like a large number, it is a little less than two roads per town. (Contrarily, if each town were connected to each of the other 49 towns, the total number of roads would be 1,225.) Although certainly counter-intuitive, linking the towns randomly turns out to be a very efficient method.

Another essential contribution to network theory followed from an experiment performed in the 1960s by the social psychologist Stanley Milgram. In order to determine how many social links separate mid-westerners living in Kansas and Nebraska from a stockbroker friend in Boston, Milgram asked a random selection from among the former to send a letter to the stockbroker, but without giving his Boston address. Those selected were not to try to mail their letters directly, but to someone they knew personally who would be "closer" to or more likely to know the stockbroker. The recipients of these letters were then to do the same. Surprisingly, not only did most of the letters eventually reach the stockbroker, but the average number of mailings or intermediary links was six. Later, in the 1990s, the phrase "six degrees of separation" would attain currency as a result of John Guare's popular Broadway play entitled *Six Degrees of Separation,* which was also made into a movie. The character Ouisa explains the general idea: "Everybody on this planet is separated by only six other people. . . . The president of the United States. A gondolier in Venice. . . . It's not just the big names. It's anyone. A native in the rain forest. A Tierra del Fuegan. An Eskimo. I am bound to everybody on this planet by a trail of six people" (14). In the mid-90s, a mini-phenomenon popular with college students known as the "Kevin Bacon Game" conveyed a similar sense of social connectedness. It started when three students appeared on a television talk show and demonstrated that Kevin Bacon could be linked through appearances in movies with every known Hollywood actor or actress, living or dead.[5] For example, Bacon and Mike Myers have never appeared together in the same movie, but Myers can be linked to Robert Wagner through *The Spy Who Shagged Me* and Wagner appeared with Bacon in *Wild Things*. Myers thus has a "Bacon Number Two," indicating two degrees of separation from Bacon himself. After two computer scientists, using the Internet Movie Database, set up a website where anyone could play the game, mathematicians were easily able to prove that no Hollywood actor or actress was ever more than four degrees removed from Bacon.[6]

When Milgram summarized his experiment in an article published in 1967, he referred to this unexpected shortness of distance between people as "the small world problem." At first, investigators thought that Erdös and Rényi's theory of random networks might account for why large numbers of randomly selected people could be connected by so few links. This was because random networks exhibit the high connectivity of "small worlds": since there are always a number of "short-cut" links connecting distant parts of the network, the average number of links or degrees of separation between any two nodes is never very large. The problem with this explanation, however, is that while our social networks may contain random factors, they are certainly *not* random. In 1973, taking up Milgram's idea of "the small world problem," the sociologist Mark Granovetter was able to shed considerable light on the nature of social networks by distinguishing between strong ties and weak ties.[7] Designating the individual subject as Ego, Granovetter reasoned that Ego's social world would be constituted by two kinds of connections: strong ties among family relations, close friends, and co-workers, and weak ties among acquaintances and others whom Ego would recognize but not be closely attached to. These weak ties, moreover, are extremely important for society as a whole. As Granovetter puts it: "The weak tie between Ego and his or her acquaintance . . . becomes not merely a trivial acquaintance tie, but rather a crucial bridge between the two densely knit clumps of close friends. . . . These clumps would not, in fact, be connected to one another at all were it not for the existence of weak ties" (quoted by Buchanan, p. 46).

Weak ties, therefore, form essential bridges among "closely knit clumps of social structure." Indeed, without these bridges there would be no social network, only isolated islands of small, densely connected groups. Not surprisingly, the "strength of weak ties," as Granovetter entitled his paper, turns out to be essential for most forms of social communication. Fads, rumors, and most sexually transmitted diseases spread rapidly because of weak links. Granovetter's initial research revealed a simple but compelling instance of their efficacy. While still a graduate student in the late 1960s he asked dozens of people in a working class Boston suburb how they had obtained their current jobs. Overwhelmingly, he got the same reply: through an acquaintance (i.e., a weak tie).

Let us note in passing that Milgram's and Granovetter's work was more or less contemporaneous with the novels of Pynchon, McElroy, and Gaddis mentioned earlier, though network theory itself did not yet exist, at least as a unified sub-discipline. Until the late 1990s, in fact, contributions to this nascent science seemed to accumulate slowly, almost haphazardly, and from a wide diversity of researchers. Not unexpectedly, some of the early ideas were ignored and only rediscovered later. Perhaps the most striking example is Paul Baran's proposal in 1964 of a new kind of communication network.[8] Immediately upon his arrival at the Rand Corporation, Baran was handed the task of developing a communications network that could survive a nuclear attack from the Soviet Union. Against all odds, he actually came up with a viable plan. Baran realized that of the three possible architectures—a centralized, decentralized, and distributed structure (see his diagram below)—only the mesh-like architecture of a distributed network would not be easily vulnerable. Whereas destruction of the central hub or hubs in A and B would cripple the network, in C, where messages can travel along any number of routes, the network would continue to function even if large numbers of nodes were destroyed. Although Baran's proposal was buried, many years later, when ARPA (the federal government's Advanced Research Projects Agency) began to design ARPANET, which would become a prototype of the Internet, it unknowingly adopted a version of Baran's original idea. Let us also note in passing that the architecture of Baran's distributed network closely resembles that of D&G's rhizome.

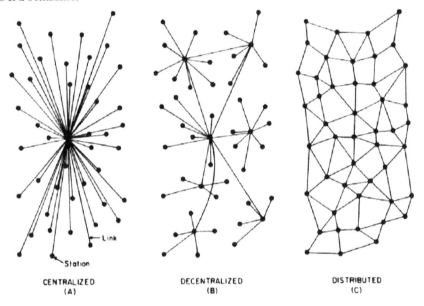

CENTRALIZED (A)   DECENTRALIZED (B)   DISTRIBUTED (C)

There is general agreement that if a single event can be said to have both solidified and further stimulated widespread scientific interest in network theory, it was the discovery of the underlying mathematical structure of the "small world." Recall from the discussion above that with Milgram's and Granovetter's research a distinctive third type of network had clearly emerged. That is, the "small world" network was neither the regular network of traditional graph theory nor one of Erdös and Rényi's random networks. But what exactly were its distinctive mathematical properties? In 1998, the applied mathematicians Duncan Watts and Steven Strogatz published a 3-page article in the prestigious science journal *Nature* that supplied an answer.

Basically, Watts and Strogatz started with a regular lattice or classic network (see their diagram below) in which each node is connected to four of its adjacent neighbors—two on each side. Since each node is directly connected to its close neighbors, this kind of network exhibits a high degree of "local clustering." Then, by simply replacing a few of these near-neighbor links with links to randomly selected nodes throughout the network, they produced an entirely different kind of network, one that exhibited small world properties. Continuing this process, which they called "random rewiring," they eventually produced a completely random network. (The increasing degree of randomness evident as we move rightward from a regular lattice to a completely random network is indicated by the value of p.)

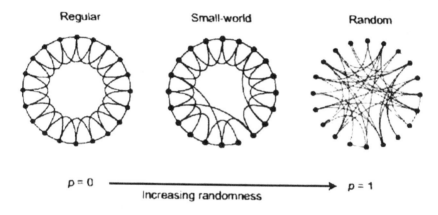

To compare the behavior of these three types of network, Watts and Strogatz made two kinds of measurements: the characteristic path length and the clustering coefficient. The characteristic path length is simply the number of links in the shortest path between two nodes averaged over all pairs of nodes. The clustering coefficient was found by taking each node, counting the largest number of possible links, then dividing by the actual number of links, then calculating the average value of this ratio over the entire network. When plotted against the value of p, these two measurements yielded the sought after mathematical properties of the small-world architecture, specifically, a distinctive combination of high clustering with short characteristic path length. Taken together, these two indicators confirmed in quantitative terms what might be called the visual "signature" of a small-world network: the combination of local clustering (evident in the regular or classical network) with shortcuts across the network (evident in random networks). Compared to regular or classical networks, small-world networks have shortcuts; compared to random networks, they have local clustering and are "sparse."

In addition to testing their mathematical model against measurements of three real-world networks—the collaboration graph of Hollywood film actors (i.e., the Kevin

Bacon game), the electrical power grid of the western United States, and the neural network of the nematode worm *C. elegans* —Watts and Strogatz also considered the functional significance of small-world connectivity for dynamic systems, using a deliberately simplified model of the spread of infectious diseases as their test case. Given the two features that distinguish small worlds (clustering and shortcuts), it is hardly surprising to discover that infectious diseases spread more easily and more quickly in this kind of network. However, and in contrast to other network models of disease spreading, their work shows how a significant increase of spreading is a structural feature, rather than a simple matter of topology (i.e., number of links). In the spread of sexually transmitted diseases, for example, it is not simply the number of concurrent partners that individuals have that determines the increase (a fact obvious to the individual), but the structural transitions that lead to small worlds, which are too subtle for the individual to perceive. In fact, what is most alarming in this context is how few shortcuts are needed to make the world "small."

By combining a relatively high degree of local clustering with the ability to communicate across the network, the small-world architecture offers an extremely economic solution to contradictory demands. Returning to American fiction, we can see that it also provides a new perspective on this fiction's embedded networks. Oedipa Maas's either-or quandary in *The Crying of Lot 49*, for example, achieves a deep and affective power precisely because it conveys the emotional and psychological difference between a classical and a small world network as experienced by a single subject. Whereas in the classical network there are only local connections, directly apprehensible by Ego (to use Granovetter's term), the small world network is defined by not only many local connections but also global connections that would be beyond Ego's ken, which therefore could be interpreted (but not verified) as forming part of an over-arching design (i.e., a conspiracy). As Watts and Strogatz suggest in their comments on disease spreading, there is no way to tell the difference between these two types of network at the level of the individual subject, and this is precisely what *The Crying of Lot 49* dramatically demonstrates. On the other hand, when we consider McElroy's *Lookout Cartridge* and Gaddis's *JR,* it becomes clear that we are dealing with small-world architectures, since in their proliferation of links there is no longer any doubt about the "reality" of both local and global connections. In regard to *JR* in particular, it is worth pointing out that network theorists have demonstrated that the network of CEOs in corporate America in fact constitutes a small-world.

Virtual Narratives

Turning to the electronic hypertext narratives of the 1990s, what becomes important is how the relationship of network to narrative differs from that same relationship in print fiction. For reasons that will become clear momentarily, I propose—as a general hypothesis to be tested—that in the American printed novels the status of the network is immanent or virtual, whereas the narrative itself is actual. In the electronic hypertext narratives, on the other hand, this relationship is reversed: the network or lexia-link structure is actual, whereas the narrative itself is virtual. While this basic difference stems from fundamental, substrate differences between the two media, these writers extend it "upward" into literary and thematic issues reflected at the level of representation.

Let us first consider briefly *The Crying of Lot 49* from this perspective. We have no difficulty at all following Oedipa's narrative trajectory, which begins with her reception of a letter in her California suburban house and ends with the "crying" of Pierce Inverarity's stamp collection. What cannot be determined, however, is the status of the network of connections and relations that come to define her experience along that trajectory. As every reader remembers, the novel halts with Oedipa's recognition of four symmetrical possibilities: either she has discovered a secret underground postal system called the Trystero, or she is hallucinating such a system, or Inverarity has created it as a hoax, or she is hallucinating this hoax. While there is little if any doubt about what actually happens at each episode along her quest to determine whether or not the Trystero exists, this narrative inconclusion follows as a consequence from the ontological uncertainty of the network of "clues," signs, and associations that Oedipa encounters. Thus, to belabor the point, it is the status of the network that is really characterized by these four equally logical possibilities. This dilemma, however, can be resolved if we assume that all four possibilities are *equally true but virtual*. That is, rather than assuming that one and only one possibility must be true, we can assume that they all exist *en potentia*, each waiting to be actualized by a particular narrative event. Since narrative and network are completely co-determinate in the novel, the immanent or virtual status of the network ends up "virtualizing" the narrative itself.

When we turn to Michael Joyce's hypertext narrative, *afternoon, a story,* we see the exact reverse. Like all of the early hypertexts composed in Storyspace (an early hypertext authoring program), the fictional text consists of a network of lexias connected by embedded links. Technically, each lexia is a text file that opens and appears on the monitor screen when a link to it is activated; when another link is activated it closes and another text file opens in its place. One of the first lexias we encounter reads as follows: "I may have seen my son die today." This lexia is linked to several others, each of which links to still others, repeatedly forcing the reader to choose lexias in a continually branching chain. At the same time, we perceive that there are logical and associational connections among the lexias at both the level of representation and individual words. For example, we soon realize that the speaker of this lexia is a man named Peter, and the event referred to is an automobile accident in which Peter's ex-wife and son may have been killed. Not incidentally, Peter works as a writer for DataCom, a company that uses a computerized expert system to do risk assessment. We also realize that in order to understand Peter's peculiar approach-avoidance attempt to find out what happened, we must sort out the complex tangle of relationships among his boss Werther, Werther's analyst wife Lolly, and a fellow office worker named Nausicaa, in whom Peter is also sexually interested. We eventually discover, however, that there is no overarching, explicit narrative that binds the scenes, events, and dialogue reported in the lexias into a single unity. Literally, there is no actual narrative, but only a network of linked lexias through which each reading is a particular path. In contrast to print narratives, where narrative linearity is guided and sustained by the conventions of the codex book (and appears in a durable inscription, to use Katherine Hayles' useful phrase), in this and other electronic hypertexts narrative connections are inferred by the reader, based on his or her emergent sense of logical and/or likely narrative connections among the various lexias. In other words, the narrative is virtual; it exists, but only en potentia, until it is realized in specific readings. Jay David Bolter, one of the early theorists of hypertext, summarizes the difference between *afternoon* and fiction written "on and for paper" as follows:

> There is no single story of which each reading is a version, because each reading determines the story as it goes. We could say that there is no story at all; there are only readings. Or if we say that the story of *afternoon* is the sum of all its readings, then we must understand the story as a structure that can embrace contradictory emotional and perhaps factual outcomes. Each reading is a different turning within a universe of paths, often full of "bramble," set up by the author. (125-126)

Even so, another aspect of the lexia-link structure built into the software greatly increases the potential for narrative connections among lexia. This is Storyspace's "guard function," which places hidden restrictions on the reader's movement from one lexia to another, by making it impossible to visit some lexias until a specified sequence of other lexias has been traversed. From the point of view of network theory, this has the effect of promoting and ensuring local clustering, or rather local sequences, and inhibits the reader from jumping randomly around the network of lexias. This, is turn, suggests that hypertext narratives like *afternoon* and those that follow it—Moulthrop's *Victory Garden*, Shelly Jackson's *Patchwork Girl*, Judy Molloy's *10ve One*, Jane Yellowlees Douglas's *I Have Said Nothing,* and Kim Arnold's *Lust*, to name some of the most familiar—are not at all random networks. But are they small worlds? My suspicion is that they are, but to prove it would require a technical analysis beyond the scope of this paper. Instead, I would like to explore further the idea that in these hypertext narratives the narrative itself is virtual. More specifically, are there degrees of virtuality and is there any precise relationship between a hypertext's degree of virtuality and its network structure?

In order to determine the precise kind of network they are dealing with, network theorists pay particular attention to node-link ratios. Here let me follow suit and see if this quantitative measure suggests anything useful about the virtual dimension of hypertext narrative. Consider the following chart I have compiled listing several basic features of a series of fictional hypertexts:

Hypertext	number of lexias	number of links	average number of links per lexia
afternoon	539	951	1.20
Victory Garden	993	2,804	2.83
Patchwork Girl	323	462	1.42
1Ove One	128	312	2.44
Lust	38	141	3.71

Keeping in mind that the greater the number of links per lexia, the more choices the reader faces in traversing the work, what do these numbers tell us?

First, since *Victory Garden* and *Lust* have by far the highest ratio of links per lexia, what is it that makes them different from the others? The answer, obvious after even a cursory reading, is that in these two works a central or single encompassing narrative is least determined. The reasons, however, are completely different. *Lust*, as the title suggests, presents various possible events that might ensue from a particular psychological state or condition. With lyrical intensity it presents all the elements of a primal scene: a woman, a man (whose identity is ambiguous, it could be any one of several men), a child. Each scene or sequence provides a different ordering or arrangement of various elements—naked smooth skin, sunlight, fibers, blood, a knife, various rooms—articulated with various acts—speaking, remembering, turning away, following, finding. There is no specific narrative, only the narrative possibilities of sex, violence (including abortion), and murder. In contrast, the indetermination of an organizing narrative in *Victory Garden* results in part from its sheer size; in fact, it is mainly comprised of many little narratives, including the death of Emily Runbird in Iraq during Desert Storm, the pursuit of the computer scientist Boris Urquar by the FBI agent Madden, the secret manipulations by the college provost, the pollution of an idyllic local lake by real estate developers, the sexual activity among various couples who form relationships or betray relationships with others, and the almost ubiquitous discussions in bars and apartments about the War and the role of the mass media. Instead of a sequence of intelligible events that initiates and leads to an inevitable consequence, we read about a growing number of characters and their multiple connections and disconnections. This results in the social density of a recognizable world, making *Victory Garden* the most novelistic of these hypertexts.

Contrary to *Lust* and *Victory Garden*, both *afternoon* and *Patchwork Girl* have relatively low link-to-lexia ratios. Following expectation, both of these works "virtualize" a single narrative. In the case of *afternoon*, the narrative is about Peter's attempt to work through the trauma and guilt resulting from his own involvement in the automobile accident that killed his son. *Patchwork Girl* is the story of the titular heroine, the tribulations and adventures of a female Frankenstein assembled out of bodily and textual parts that give rise to a literary anatomy evoking many narratives. To be sure, both of these hypertext narratives are interestingly complicated: *afternoon* is organized around an absent event to which the reader never has direct access, *Patchwork Girl* around a re-writing and transformation of Mary Shelley's famous novel. Whereas *afternoon* is virtual because its sparse and elliptical presentation allows several different narrative possibilities, only one of which can be actualized in a single reading, *Patchwork Girl* is virtual because other texts and other bodies are always implicated in its own self-making. More precisely, Patchwork girl's body is both hers and that of other women, the text is both hers and written by other hands. Substituting a both-and logic for the dichotomizing logic of self-other, Jackson thus uses the resources of hypertext to incorporate and embed bodies and texts in an all-inclusive virtual space.

In the quantitative terms indicated above, Judy Malloy's *l0veOne* presents an interesting case, since its link-node ratio is much higher than *afternoon* and *Patchwork Girl* but significantly lower than *Victory Garden* and *Lust*. The numbers begin to make sense when we consider the fact that Malloy's hypertext is basically structured by a conventional "falling in love" story, but then complicated in two ways: nonlinear sequencing makes many of its individual lexias complexly indeterminate, and the experiences they recount are often mediated by some form of digital technology. The text is presented in the form of Gweneth's diary, which recounts in undated first-person lexias her passionate love affair with a German hacker named Gunther she meets while living in Germany. Although the lyrical moments between the lovers are tender, what most often marks these moments is the mediating presence of some piece of computer hardware, as in the following excerpt:

> but all I could think of was
> _____Gunter's left hand between my legs
> while he dialed the Nurnberg pop server on his Toshiba laptop
> with his right hand as we lay in bed on Sunday Morning.
> He had a way of tossing his head in the air
> like a horse rejecting a lump of sugar.[9]

The love-story sequence culminates in Gunther's proposal, when he wordlessly hands Gweneth a computer notebook with the question "Will you marry me?" clearly legible on the screen. She types in "yes" and returns the notebook. Shortly thereafter, however, Gunther disappears, though from the outset he has been strangely absentee, often gone or never fully "present" as he works on projects with his circle of friends, who are either hackers or installation artists or both. Still thinking of Gunther, Gweneth decides to hitchhike to the beach at Antibes and is picked up on the autobahn by another German hacker named Wolfie. Then things turn strange. Wolfie is a member of "Schinkenbrotchen," a German hacker underground organization that is plotting "a real life computer game":

> At the center of this operation (it was something between a fox hunt
> and an old Infocom adventure –
> with overtones of that compelling computer game called Shanghai.)
> _____was the woman called Aimee.
> "She buys warm milk from the railroad station stand

every morning before she goes to work."
The details of Aimee's life that Wolfie related
_____ were hand written by a man they called Sig
on a large piece of brown paper that lay on the floor. (love43.html)

Several other lexias provide further details (always in quotation marks) about this computer game character. However, when Wolfie and Gweneth arrive at the beach they encounter Gunther lying on the sand with a beautiful flesh and blood woman named Aimee (whose name, of course, suggests "loved one"). "Gunther" quickly explains that he is not Gunther but his look-alike cousin Stefan. (Actually, this double doubling is more complex, since if the lexias are read in a different sequence the reader can encounter the "real" Aimee first.) Aimee then invites Gweneth for a drive along the coast, but the reality of the ensuing scene is obscured by Gweneth's intruding memories and the strange voices on the radio, and culminates in a Wild West fantasy in which Gweneth guns down her putative rival.

It should be clear from even this abbreviated account that, like Oedipa in *The Crying of Lot 49,* Gweneth may be the dupe of an elaborate, on-going game, played by hackers and scripted by Gunther or another hacker with Wolfie playing the role—like the series of men in *The Crying of Lot 49*—of a male mediator who provides "clues." When Gweneth first meets Wolfie, in fact, the latter declares, *a propos* of nothing, "I don't believe love is a game." And like Oedipa, Gweneth's most significant experiences are technologically mediated—not only sex with Gunther but her long distance telephone calls with her friend Shelly and her oddly healing experience when Radha sings to Krishna (but in Gweneth's language) in a "web moo." Always pulled by the virtualizing power of digital media, even her simple perceptions require its language in order to be rendered:

We lay together in the back seat
under the shadows of white topped mountains.
I remember spotted cows_____
in the green fields above the road,
grazing – like bit mapped images
that turn_____into slow moving videos
with nothing more than a casual click. (love86.html)

Not surprisingly, then, whenever Gweneth experiences a disconnect from Gunther, her consciousness flashes immediately on an error message like the following:

_____"Cannot connect to host balrog.dfv.rwth-aachen.de, port 70"
Connection failed: _____Connection refused." (love61.html)

But even while Gweneth's thoughts, memories, perceptions, and even bodily experiences never cease to be articulated with both the hardware and software of digital communications media, her distinctive "voice" retains its own singular affect and consistency. Though caught up in a number of criss-crossing networks, she is never reducible to a mere node within them, for the simple reason that her subjectivity is not a product of these media networks but the means by which a reflection upon them is enacted. Here the virtual nature of much of her experience—which sometimes produces narrative uncertainty—is inseparable from the virtual nature of the technological media that endows those experiences with their distinctive and memorable quality. Spotted cows in green fields become memorable precisely because they evoke bit-mapped images that turn into moving videos. Rather than see this as a mechanical corruption of an "organic" human experience, *10ve One* simply assumes that technology in the contemporary era defines in advance the kinds of experience that will count as experience *per se*.[10]

The creative tension between Gweneth's singular voice and the multiple networks in which she is caught up and "deterritorialized" (D & G's term) is not unrelated to a problem raised by Robert Coover in "Literary Hypertext: The Passing of the Golden Age." Noting that the early classics of hypertext narrative (like those considered above up to *10ve One*) are pre-Web works, Coover blames this passing of the golden age precisely on the emergence of the World Wide Web, which is not, he says, hospitable to serious literature:

> [The Web] tends to be a noisy, restless, opportunistic, superficial, e-commerce-driven, chaotic realm, dominated by hacks, pitchmen, pretenders, in which the quiet voice of literature cannot easily be heard or, if heard by chance, attended to for more than a moment or two. Literature is meditative and the Net is riven by ceaseless hype and chatter. Literature has a shape, and the Net is shapeless. The discrete object is gone, there's only this vast disorderly sprawl, about as appealing as a scatter of old magazines on a table in a dentist's lounge. (4)

But isn't this like saying that the fictional works of the novelist Robert Coover could not possibly flourish amid the endless chatter of television? While Coover allows for a certain degree of interest in works of hypermedia, and admits that e-poetry has prospered in this new medium, the indictment is pretty clear. The power of the literary Word, the expressive individual voice, has been usurped and drowned out by a plethora of mass media images. Don DeLillo, in *Underworld*, seems to endorse a similar condemnation, most visibly in his valorization and lament for the passing of the voice of a baseball game radio announcer. Late in the novel one of the characters, a "lurker" on the Web, thinks of it as a miracle, where "everybody is everywhere at once, and he is there among them, unseen" (808). On the Web, he feels, everything is connected, yet nobody is truly there, a perfect image of loneliness. One could, of course, contrast this view with the more positive and complex images of the Internet found in Neal Stephenson's *Cryptonomicon* (1999) and William Gibson's *Pattern Recognition* (2003). Instead, I simply want to emphasize that the deeper problem is Coover's very limited, even erroneous view, which treats the Internet as simply one more consumer interface. Contemporary network theory, in contrast, offers a far richer and more compelling image. In conclusion, I shall try to indicate how.

The Ultimate Rhizome?

Although the Internet is a humanly constructed artifact, scientists have discovered that in many ways its laws of internal structure, growth, and evolution are more like those of a natural living form. In the late 1990s, as researchers began to map the Web's topology with software robots, they made several important discoveries. First, that its link-node structure exhibits a power law distribution, which is not the case for a random or small world network. Basically, researchers found that if they started with sites possessing a certain number of links and doubled this number, they would find that the number of sites with the doubled number of links would fall off by a factor of eight (i.e., 2^3). Because a power law distribution, unlike a Bell curve, has no "cut-off points," it is said to be *scale-free*. Researchers were able to demonstrate in fact that both the physical infrastructure of the Internet (machines, routers, fiber optic cables, etc.) and the virtual link structure of the Web are scale-free networks. Empirically, this means that while most nodes will be relatively poorly connected, a select minority of sites (like amazon.com) will be highly connected, with hundreds of thousands of links. In contrast to a Bell curve or normal distribution (which might show us for example both the average height of American males and the range of differences from shortest to tallest), the average number of links per site on the Web is a meaningless figure. As the Internet or Web evolves over time, with both links and nodes being added and subtracted independently, the abiding presence of this power law indicates a hidden order.

In attempting to understand the dynamics of this growth, the physicists Albert-László Barabási and Réka Albert realized that the most highly connected sites—the "hubs" or "connector" nodes, as they called them—play a crucial role. As new sites are added, their new links are not picked randomly. Rather, since links are chosen to enhance connectivity and visibility, most likely they will be added to large and well known sites. This tendency, which Barabási and Albert call "preferential attachment," leads inevitably to an effect very familiar in dynamical systems theory and encapsulated in various phrases like "them that has, get more," "the rich get richer," and "winner take all." In academia, it explains the often heard observation that most of the grants seem to go to the same faculty, while their often equally talented and original colleagues get very little support at all. As concerns the World Wide Web's continual growth, this effect leads to greater "hub" formation and an overall increase of links to these preferred "connector" hubs. Them that has, get more.

To a large part, however, the Internet's self-organizing properties continue to function unperturbed by and independent of human intention. In one sense, the Internet is like a vast beehive or ant colony: by tirelessly adding new websites, establishing new links, and repairing mechanical breakdowns, human users are building and maintaining a structure whose global dynamic behavior everywhere exceeds their individual desires and awareness. In itself, of course, this is not so unusual—human beings are often, perhaps always, intricated in similar systems. But the Internet is unique in at least two fundamental respects. At the level of the individual user it answers to a number of uses or functions, as reflected in the heterogeneous metaphors we use to describe it. The poet Stephanie Strictland succinctly highlights this aspect when she describes the Web as

> an enormous structure, almost biological in the way it communicates and propagates by proliferating links. The electronic space, often called cyberspace, has some very unusual qualities, to judge by pre-electronic categories. It is characterized as tidal sea, web, sky, and solid. Thus, people surf it, send out web-crawlers to explore it, gophers to tunnel through it, engines to mine data from it, and they fly through and above it in game simulations. They establish "home" pages in it, as though it were rooted, although at their own location distance has disappeared—New Zealand, New York, St. Paul, equally present, and equally speedily present.

However, when we move beyond the level of the individual user and consider the use of the Internet by corporations and businesses, institutions and governments, we are struck more forcefully by the vast databases and sophisticated communications software that enable workers and professionals of almost every stamp to access, exchange, and process information on a global scale. This consideration leads directly to the second aspect of the Internet's uniqueness: as a network, it contains not only more information but more "intelligence" than anything ever constructed in human history.

Not surprisingly, it is this second aspect that has generated speculation about the Internet as an emergent "global brain." While much—perhaps most—of this speculation is wild-eyed and mystical, there are good reasons why it cannot be simply dismissed out of hand. Many highly reputable scientists like Barabási have noted that the earth is literally enfolded in "millions of measuring devices, including cameras, microphones, thermostats and temperature gauges, light and traffic sensors, and pollution detectors [that are] feeding information into increasingly fast and sophisticated computers" (*Linked*, 158). The number of these computers as well as Internet-connected cell phones is increasing almost exponentially. Now, not only are these devices rapidly increasing in number but for the first time they are feeding information into a single integrated system. As a result, on a material level the Internet is already the site of a vast network of connected sensors and processors. The possibility that it might self-organize into a computer functioning unpredictably and independently of human supervision is therefore not altogether a science fiction fantasy.[11] The further possibility that such a networked computer might become self-aware is far less likely, though not merely a baseless projection. What this scenario reflects, however naively, is an inchoate sense that if the Internet should become a computer it will not be like the one on our desks, which instantiates and functions according to strict mechanical laws, but rather like the human brain, which, while never violating those same laws, has grown and re-wired itself in response to both internal principles of organization and function and adaptive necessities arising from its interface with the environment.

All speculation aside, there can be no doubt that the Internet possesses a life of its own and may be evolving into a complex adaptive system. This "life" has come about as a direct result of its structure, topology, and dynamical growth, as fed and nourished but not controlled by the ongoing activities of its human users. But as a new type of information ecology and environment, the Internet also supports a wide range of digital life forms. In addition to computer viruses and data-mining software, all kinds of knobots and "smart" autonomous agents increasingly roam the Net, while many AI-inspired programs like "Eliza," "Ramona," and various chatterbots reside at numerous sites. Perhaps the most intellectually interesting of digital life forms on the Net, however, are those produced by Artificial Life scientists. Tom Ray's Internet version of *Tierra*, a virtual world of evolving digital organisms, provides a striking case in point.

At the Artificial Life VI Conference in 1996, Ray and colleague Joseph Hart reported on the latest experiments, which they describe as follows:

> Digital organisms essentially identical to those of the original *Tierra* experiment were provided with a sensory mechanism for obtaining data about conditions on other machines on the network; code for processing that data and making decisions based on the analysis, the digital equivalent of a nervous system; and effectors in the form of the ability to make directed movements between machines in the network. (303)

Tests were then run to observe the migratory patterns of these new organisms. For the first few generations, these organisms would all "rush" to the "best-looking machines," as indeed their algorithms instructed them to do. The result was what Ray called "mob behavior." Over time, however, mutation and natural selection led to the evolution of a different algorithm, one that simply instructed the organism to avoid poor quality machines and consequently gave it an immense adaptive advantage over the others.

Ray's experiment is a clear instance of how the Internet itself has become a new kind of laboratory, one combining the features of both a natural environment and a new kind of technological space. In *Out of Control: The Rise of Neo-biological Civilization*, Kevin Kelly argues that we have entered a new era in which human-made systems will increasingly take living organisms as their model; that is, in order to achieve a robust adaptability and autonomy, our machines will have to be more biological in both their construction and modes of operation. The Internet is a signal instance of a system that has assumed the shape and exhibited the dynamics of a quasi-biological organism, but quite independently of human intention and design. The Net's double status seems to have resulted from the fact that as a network it grows according to a pattern often found in nature, and that its electronic filaments support both human exchanges and digital life forms. As a new kind of shared space or habitat, an ecology that is neither completely artificial nor natural, the Internet may be both the harbinger and testing ground of a new kind of environment in which technology continues evolution by other means.

To what extent is this image of the Internet amenable to literature? There is of course no way to predict what will compel and stimulate writers in the near or distant future. It seems reasonable, nevertheless, to assume that science fiction is the genre and electronic hypertext the medium that are best positioned to take up the challenge this image poses.

NOTES

[1] In *The Ecstasy of Communication*, Jean Baudrillard understands both paranoia and schizophrenia in relation to communication networks. Whereas paranoia is "a pathology of organization," the subject's delirious *projection of* a surrounding network, schizophrenia results from the subject's sense of *collapse into* a state of terror induced by "the absolute proximity to and total instantaneity of things." The schizophrenic subject, in other words, "becomes a pure screen, a pure absorption and resorption surface of the influent networks" (27). Noting Baudrillard's distinction, Hanjo Berressem suggests that "Pynchon's universes are situated exactly at this junction between paranoia . . . and schizophrenia . . ." (47).

[2] See D. B. West, *Introduction to Graph Theory*.

[3] In 1959, 1960 and 1961 Erdös and Rényi published three now classic papers on random graph theory. Albert-László Barabási provides a clear account of this work (13-24).

[4] The illustration is taken from Mark Buchanan, 35-36.

[5] Barabási, in *Linked*, 58-59, provides these details.

[6] The two computer scientists, Glen Wasson and Brett Tjaden, called the website "The Oracle of Kevin Bacon." It is located at <http://www.cs.virginia.edu/oracle/>.

[7] Buchanan, on which I draw here, provides a useful summary of Granovetter's work.

[8] The diagram reproduced below is taken from this paper.

[9] Unlike the previously discussed hypertext narratives, *10ve One* is available on the Internet. The quoted passage is found at <http://www.eastgate.com/malloy/love33.html>. In subsequent quotations only the last part of the address will be given (i.e., love33.html). In the quoted passages, the solid horizontal lines indicate a link.

[10] Bernard Stiegler makes the similar argument that human knowledge is technological in its essence, since there are no possibilities of knowledge without the surfaces of inscription of an artificial memory. That specific writing technologies invisibly shape the structures and meaning of human experience is of course an important theme in Marshall McLuhan's *Understanding Media* (1964) and Walter J. Ong's *Orality and Literacy* (1982), to mention only two well-known examples.

[11] Barabási himself has explored how the Web might become a computer in experiments with "parasitic computing." See *Linked*, pp. 156-9, for a brief discussion.

WORKS CITED

Barabási, Albert-László. *Linked: The New Science of Networks*. Cambridge: Perseus, 2002.

Baran, Paul. "On Distributed Communications." RAND <http://www.rand.org/publications/RM/RM3420/index.html>

Baudrillard, Jean. *The Ecstasy of Communication*. New York: Semiotext(e), 1988.

Berressem, Hanjo. *Pynchon's Poetics*. Urbana and Chicago: U of Illinois P, 1993.

Bolter, Jay David. *Writing Space: Computers, Hypertext, and the Remediation of Print* [1991]. Mahwah, NJ: Lawrence Erlbaum, 2001.

Buchanan, Mark. *Nexus: Small Worlds and the Groundbreaking Science of Networks*. New York: Norton, 2002.

Castells, Manuel. *The Rise of Network Society*. London: Blackwell, 1996.

Coover, Robert. "Literary Hypertext: The Passing of the Golden Age." Keynote Address. Digital Arts and Culture Conference, Atlanta, GA. 29 October 1999. <http://nickm.-com/vox/golden_age.html>.

Deleuze, Gilles and Félix Guattari. *Thousand Plateaus*. Trans. Biran Massumi. Minneapolis: U of Minnesota P, 1987.

DeLillo, Don. *Underworld.* New York: Scribner, 1997.

Guare, John. *Six Degrees of Separation.* New York: Vintage, 1990.

Joyce, Michael. *Othermindedness: The Emergence of Network Culture.* Ann Arbor: U of Michigan P, 2000.

Kelly, Kevin. *Out of Control: The Rise of Neo-biological Civilization.* Reading: Addison-Wesley, 1994.

Malloy, Judy. *10veOne.* <http://www.eastgate.com/malloy/welcome.html>.

Milgram, S. "The Small World Problem." *Psychology Today* 2 (1967): 60-67.

Moulthrop, Stuart. "Rhizome and Resistance: Hypertext and the Dreams of a New Culture." *Hyper/Text/Theory.* Ed. George P. Landow. Baltimore and London: Johns Hopkins UP, 1994.

Pynchon, Thomas. *Gravity's Rainbow.* New York: Viking, 1973.

Ray, Thomas S. and Joseph Hart. "Evolution of Differentiated Multi-threaded Digital Organisms." *Artificial Life VI.* Ed. Christoph Adami, et al. Cambridge: MIT Press, 1998.

Stiegler, Bernard. *La technique et le temps: 2, La disorientation.* Paris: Editions Galilée, 1996.

Strickland, Stephanie. "Poetry in the Electronic Environment." <http://www.altx.-com/ebr/ebr5/strick.htm>.

Taylor, Mark. *The Moment of Complexity: Emerging Network Culture.* Chicago: U of Chicago P, 2002.

Watts, Duncan J. and Steven H. Strogatz. "Collective dynamics of 'small-world' networks." *Nature* 393 (4 June 1998): 440-442.

West, D. B. *Introduction to Graph Theory.* Upper Saddle River, N.J.: Prentice Hall, 1996.

Hanjo Berressem
"Of Metal Ducks, Embodied Iduros, and Autopoietic Bridges": Tales of an Intelligent Materialism in the Age of Artificial Life

> "The soul is wholly embodied, and the body is wholly ensouled."
>
> —Ralph Waldo Emerson, "Love"

> *"Nulle entéléchie sans corps, pas de corps sans âme, la séparation serait une lacune absurde."*
>
> —Michel Serres, *Le système de Leibniz*

In this article, I deal with some theoretical and literary alignments of the man/machine nexus. First I introduce, together with some of their theoretical backgrounds, two very different cyborg goddesses: a metal duck and a virtual pop star. The first of these comes from a sub-plot in Thomas Pynchon's novel *Mason & Dixon*, the second from William Gibson's "bridge trilogy": *Virtual Light* (1993), *Idoru* (1996) and *All Tomorrow's Parties* (1999). Before I get to Gibson's virtual pop star, however, I generalize the argument by contrasting the concept of the body as an autopoietic machine with that of the body as a material object embedded within an aggregate of discursive machines and cultural dispositives; a conceptualization advanced by Judith Butler in *Bodies that Matter: On the Discursive Limits of "Sex."* In recourse to the materialist tradition of thinking the human being as a machine, I then show the relevance of materialist approaches to the man/machine nexus for a contemporary theory of the subject. I center this discussion on Gottfried Wilhelm Leibniz's "Monadology," which defines the artificial as well as the natural as machinic aggregates—shifting the overall frame of reference from a limited field of "technology" to an unlimited field of a "general machinics"—and which, from within this project, presents an immensely intricate figure of thought for one possible alignment of matter and mind. In this context, I am not so much interested in whether Leibniz's conceptualizations are correct in the light of contemporary science, as I am in showing an early version of the project to align the physical and the psychic and, particularly, in showing the conceptual limits of that project, limits that are of seminal concern in Gilles Deleuze's *The Fold: Leibniz and the Baroque*. In Deleuze's reading of Leibniz I follow in particular the topological turn that allows him to think Leibniz into a universe that follows the logics of "intelligent matter" and autopoiesis; a logics that I show, in a final step, to also define the sociology, architectonics, ethics, and ultimately the overall logics of Gibson's bridge trilogy. In this context, I should note that my article is itself written on the background of a trilogy that consists of three earlier articles, called, respectively, "Emergent Ecologics: Cultural and Natural Environment[s] in Recent Theory and Literature," "DeNarration: Literature at the End of the Millennium," and "Matter that Bodies: Philosophy in the Age of a Complex Materialism." Not only are there any number of resonances between these articles, the present article is also in many ways a continuation, as well as a re-writing, of the arguments presented in the trilogy.

Metal Duck

In one of the many sub-plots of Pynchon's *Mason & Dixon,* a mechanical duck pursues the

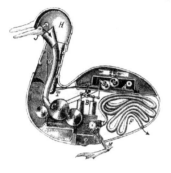

French chéf Armand Allégre, who has fled to America to escape from it and who now cooks for Mason and Dixon's party. As he states in desperation, "*it* would seek me out, and remain, with motives too alien for any human ever to know" (369). Perhaps, however, the reasons are not quite so alien as he imagines. Armand, after all, had gained culinary fame in France through his incomparable and—*nomen est omen*—extremely expensive duck dishes. What the mechanical duck wants is not so much to simply revenge her dead brothers and sisters as it is to blackmail Armand into intervening on her behalf with her creator to engi-

Illustration 1: Structural diagram of Vaucanson's duck

neer a mate. Soon, however, she becomes enamored with the chèf, and so starts a very romantic, albeit platonic, man/machine love-affair.

Pynchon's duck-machine is of course Jacques Vaucanson's famous duck from 1735, "an artificial Duck made of gilded copper which drinks, eats, quacks, splashes about on the water, and digests his food like a living Duck" (Hultén 21) (see illustrations 1 and 2; illustration 3 shows a fabric created by Eve Andrée Laramée for her installation "Permutational Unfolding"). What is so specifically new and improved about this automaton is that Vaucanson had "provided his Automaton a Digestionary Process" (*M&D* 372), or, as another character states less scientifically, he has created a "mechanical Duck that shits" (*M&D* 372), which is, by the way, precisely what, infamously, the Deleuzian unconscious does:

> It is at work everywhere, functioning smoothly at times, at other times in fits and starts. It breeds, it heats, it eats. It shits and fucks . . . everywhere *it* is machines, real ones, not figurative ones: machines driving other machines, machines being driven by other machines, with all the necessary couplings and connections. An organ machine is plugged into an energy source machine: the one produces a flow that the other interrupts. (Deleuze and Guattari, 1)

Had Vaucanson not cheated—in his duck, the input is not ''continuously'' related to the output, which means that there is no true digestion—the introduction of a digestive apparatus into a machine would have been a first step from the mechanical/inorganic to the living|-organic; "that strange Metamorphosis, which has sent it out the Gates of the Inanimate, and off upon its present Journey into the given World" (*M&D* 372). Pyn-

Illustration 2: Photograph of the ruined duck

chon imagines a second step in this direction when he turns the metal duck into a sexualized machine: "Vaucanson's vainglorious Intent had been to repeat for Sex and Reproduction, the Miracles he's already achiev'd for Digestion and Excretion" (*M&D* 373). In Pynchon's version, the duck has, through the addition of "erotick Machinery" (*M&D* 373), reached "some Threshold of self-Intricacy, setting off this Explosion of Change, from Inertia to *Independence, and Power*" (*M&D* 373). In other words, it has crossed the threshold from inanimate to animate, from passivity to activity, from machinespace to biospace, from "artificial life" in the 18th century sense of the term to "artificial life" in its contemporary technological sense. (When it is referring to programs used in computer simulations of systems that show emergent behavior, how-ever, "artificial life" is not really what the duck is about. Neither, however, does the term "artificial intelligence" cover that. The curious inapplicability of both of these terms seems to have to do with a specific repression of matter and materiality in both fields). From what Humberto R. Maturana and Francisco G. Varela call heteropoiesis, the duck has crossed over to autopoiesis, one of the recent scientific diagrams that has become an important reference in a number of hard and soft sciences. As the duck herself states, Vaucanson has "produce[d] . . . Venus from a Machine" (*M&D* 668).

Illustration 3: Fabric created by Eve Andrée Laramée

It is not coincidental that in his book *The Garden in the Machine: The Emerging Science of Artificial Life*, Claus Emmeche mentions Vaucanson's duck in describing the shift from 18th century automata to 20th century cellular automata. According to Emmeche, the difference between artificial intelligence and artificial life has to do precisely with the introduction of a sexual drive and a metabolism, although both of these concepts are used extremely metaphorically in most branches of the science of artificial life. Computer viruses, for example, might be said not only to aim at but actually to be obsessed with self-reproduction. Similarly, one might argue that computer programs are literally fed by electricity, which implies the concept of what might be called an electric metabolism.

A seminal characteristic of artificial life is that it follows a logic of emergence, which means that it is "self-organizing" (Emmeche 5). As Emmeche notes, "the most interesting examples of artificial life exhibit 'emergent behavior.' The word 'emergence' is used to designate the fascinating whole that is created when many semisimple units interact with each other in a complex (nonlinear) fashion" (Emmeche 20). To use a neologism coined by Jack Cohen and Ian Stewart, such systems align "simplexity" and "complicity" (3).

As an organic, emergent system, Pynchon's duck qualifies for at least four of Claude Bernard's five criteria for living systems that Emmeche refers to: "organization, generation, nutrition, development" (Emmeche 33), which can be translated into: complexity, reproduction, metabolism, and emergence. Although *Mason & Dixon* is silent about the fifth criterion, which is "susceptibility to illness and death" (*M&D* 33), we may well assume that the duck is mortal. Before death, however, there is love, and, newly equipped with the relevant machinery, the duck, like Frankenstein's monster, has begun to desire, which brings me back to why she had wanted a mate in the first place. The official reason had been to have somebody to take to the opera. Being a French duck, however, the opera might not be all she is thinking about. Not only does she hunger for a kiss, one can safely surmise that her ulterior motive is repro*duck*tion. When this plan fails, some members of Mason & Dixon's company provide her with a decoy, which she, willy-nilly, accepts. As she states somewhat fatalistically in the face of the artificial substitute, "it floats like a duck,—it fools other Ducks, who are quite sophisticated in these matters, into believing it a Duck. It's a Basis. Complexity of Character might develop in time . . ." (*M&D* 667).

Pynchon, who had predicted in his article "Is it O.K. to be a Luddite" that the next paradigm shift in human affairs would lie at the nexus where "the curves of research and development in artificial intelligence, molecular biology and robotics all converge" and who had staked his hope in the fundamental unpredictability and newness of this convergence—"it will be amazing and unpredictable, and even the biggest of brass, let us devoutly hope, are going to be caught flat-footed" (41)—uses the duck to fold the 18th century world of automata onto the 20th century world of artificial life, nanotechnology, and "cell-sized robots" (Stafford, 40).

In so doing, he constructs a body that differs in many respects from that theorized by most versions of poststructuralism, for which it is merely retrospective [*nachträglich*], which means that it is the image of something material that is rigorously excluded from the field of representation. Imbued by this logic, both the theoretical as well as the cultural scene are today saturated with body-images and scripted bodies, while the body-as-such is more or less vehemently excluded. If the body is addressed at all, it is as an "interior foreign country"; as a materiality located in an inner exclusion that recapitulates the position of the unconscious. Even in the most philosophically informed and advanced forms of theorizing the body, it operates "merely" as a material facticity that is the result of discursive operations, a facticity that in itself cannot be approached discursively. Although to different degrees, this is true, I argue, even for projects that put the body into the center of their investigation. Michel Foucault's biopolitical body, Giorgio Agamben's legal body, Homi Bhabha's hybrid body, Butler's "body that matters" and even Donna Haraway's cyborg body, which is by far the most machinic of these, are all premised on the idea that they are "always already" cultural and representational. At the very limit, bodies are present in the politics of these projects as forms of "bare life" or "abjected" bodies.

What seems to me to relate these projects is an intense interest in the body, combined with a more or less large blind spot concerning contemporary scientific concepts that are informed by the logic of an "intelligent materialism." The fact that they are all mainly concerned with discourse and language while tending to neglect other ways of information transfer and thus neglecting regimes of signs different from the linguistic one seems to me, in this context, symptomatic. To carefully align these projects with a logic of an intelligent materialism, which is central, for instance, in the work of Gilles Deleuze and Félix Guattari, is something I find necessary, not only to escape a growing closure and predictability of theoretical discourse.

Although each of these projects calls for its own careful analysis, I will use Butler as a representative case. What is important for her, as for the other projects, is not so much how materiality informs discourse, but how discourse informs materiality. Her bodies are predominantly bodies that matter culturally. If she does acknowledge the material, corporeal world, it is mainly because if everything were "simply" language, this would not allow for an alignment of language and states of propositionality with "the state of affairs which the proposition denotes" (Deleuze, *Logic*, 19). This, in turn, would mean that language would not be able to connect to the factual political realm and thus would not have the power to operate politically. A philosophy based on the concept of performative speech acts that produce material facts (from "close the window, please!" to "act heterosexually!") needs a link between discourse and material reality in order to allow speech to not only "act" but to subversively "act up."

The main problem Butler has with materialism is that she thinks of the relation between language and materiality as being purely one-way. Although material reality does reflect back onto language, there are no continuously and simultaneously operating feedback-loops between the two realms because her bodies are always already retrospective ones. Material bodies are important for Butler in that they are the effect of cultural inscriptions and, as such, embody specific discourses in the real world. They count in reference to their "material weight," which means: discourses produce specific bodies, and the sheer statistical "weight" of the material acts performed by these bodies produces a cultural weight in relation to which other, "deviant" bodies do not count. Hidden in the long shadow of the norm, they have no weight in cultural negotiations. They simply do not matter because they do not produce enough material facts.

Even though for Butler the technologies of bodies are not merely technologies of gender, what ultimately makes her miss the body is that she is not interested in the functioning of the body as a living, conscious, material machine. This is, symptomatically, why she sees a conjunction of feminism and Deleuzian philosophy as merely curious: "some have argued that a rethinking of 'nature' as a set of dynamic interrelations suits both feminist and ecological aims (and has for some produced an otherwise *unlikely alliance* with the work of Gilles Deleuze)" (4, emphasis added).

What keeps Butler from being interested in the material operations of bodies, whether these be physical, bio-chemical, neuronal, or genetic, is, I assume, the fear of essentialism, any form of which prohibits performative freedom and reduces the power of discursive operations. In particular, it reduces its power to culturally produce certain bodies and certain sexualities. The body as a non-discursive material machine, one might say, is the spectral image that haunts Butler's philosophy. Although she allows for material bodies, they are treated as zombies, remote-controlled by cultural dispositives.

Generally, then, one might venture the very general diagnosis that semiotics has driven the body out of discourse. As Lacan would say, "the symbol manifests itself first of all as the murder of the thing" (104). More precisely, discourse has fully incorporated the body. Disregarding any positivity of the material body (the true unconscious of discourse, as Deleuze would argue), which poststructuralism can only imagine negatively as internally excluded or crypted within discourse, language has succeeded in completely closing itself in on itself. Like an oyster, it produces representative pearls around invisible "grains of matter." This closure alone might be reason enough to take a closer look at the body as a physico-psychic machine, and thus at a number of materialisms.

If Pynchon's metal duck negotiates the shift from mechanics/physics to a *bio*logics, the early Gibson is more concerned with the shift from a *bio*logics to information and with the extension of the tradition of mechanical automata into the 21st century and beyond. The former is predominantly performed in the various transfers from real to virtual space, while one of many examples of sci-fi automata are the metal-robotics that populate *Mona Lisa Overdrive*. In both of these contexts, he might, at first sight, seem to be working within strictly Butlerian parameters. In the more recent bridge trilogy, however, his interest shifts to the logic of emergent, autopoietic systems and to the embodiment of informational structures; the re-transformation of—not only linguistic—information into a *bio*logics.

Illustration 4: Kyoko Date, the model for Gibson's Rei Toei

Both *Idoru* and *All Tomorrow's Parties* revolve around the idoru Rei Toei, a cybernetic, programmed, and hologrammed, artificial life-form on the verge of autopoiesis. She "is not flesh; she is information," and, as a "posthuman emergent entity" (*Parties* 165), a "self continually being iterated from experiential input" (*Parties* 163) and "human interaction" (*Idoru* 178). Her cybernetic architecture rests on "an array of elaborate constructs" (*Idoru* 178) that her ominously anonymous build-ers, who must have carefully studied their Deleuze and Guattari, refer to as "desiring machines" (*Idoru* 178) and "*aggregates of subjective desire*" (*Idoru* 178). When Berry Rydell sees her for the first time, he is immediately enveloped by her hologrammed, and thus still acorporeal, sexuality: "she rolled over, gorgeous and quite literally glowing, in her incongruous mirroring of what he wore, which looked, on her, like the first and purest expression of some irresistible new fashion, and fixed him with a sorrowful stare" (*Parties* 154). Rydell's reaction is not surprising because this appeal is programmed into her: "As the amplified reflection of desire, she was a team effort: to the extent that her designers had done their jobs properly, she was a waking dream, a love object sprung from an ap-proximation of the global mass unconscious" (*Parties* 164).

Rei Toei might well be the first example of what is referred to in the novel as a true artificial intelligence. As Colin Laney states, echoing Pynchon, "AI might be created accidentally, and . . . people might not initially recognize it for what it was" (*Idoru* 247-8). Laney is a "*quantitative* researcher" (*Parties* 21, emphasis added) who can see infor-mational architectures and the patterns of infinitely recursive data currents better than the rest of us. He is "able, through the organic changes wrought long ago by 5-SB, this drug, to somehow perceive change emerging from vast flows of data" (*Parties* 56). (In the following, I will not differentiate between various infinities, such as a mathemati-cal and a material one. 'Infinity,' therefore, should be read in a very general sense). As he notes at some point, "everything's changing. Or it's not, really. How I *see it* is chang-ing. But since I've been able to see it the new way, something else has started. There's something building up. Big. Bigger than big. It'll happen soon, then there'll be a cas-cade effect" (*Parties* 59). What he can see is how history emerges from a pool of infi-nite possibilities, how it is actualized from an infinity of potentialities according to a dynamics of microscopic, infinitely small bifurcations that cascade into macroscopic change through positive feedback loops.

The logic of an infinite, fractal recursivity implied by such a dynamics can be found on many levels of Gibson's novels. It defines, for instance, the recursive "interstitial com-munities" (*Parties* 33) of the bridge, which is "a world within the world, and, if there be such places between the things of the world, places built in the gaps, then surely there are things there, and places between them, and things in those places too" (*Parties* 81). But more of that later.

As I noted, Rei Toei is a fully informational system. In *Idoru*, this system begins to desire to be linked with—if not yet to herself become—a *bio*logical system, a link that Gibson treats in strictly informational, cybernetic terms. The novel ends with one possible version of the convergence between "natural" man and "artificial" informational machine, a cybernetic process that is ruled over by the laws of complexity. As Laney sees it, "the idoru's data . . . began as something smoothly formed, deliberate, but lacking complex-ity" (*Idoru* 251), which means that the program is as yet finite. "But at the points where it has swerved closest to Rez's data, he saw that it had begun to acquire a sort of complexity. Or randomness, he thought. The human thing" (*Idoru* 251), which is the point at which the program crosses the threshold to emergence. "That's how she learns. And both these armatures, these *sculptures in time*, were nodal, and grew more so toward the point, the present, where they intertwined" (*Idoru* 251, emphasis added).

The link with Rez, which marks the end of the novel, also marks the birth of the Rei Toei as an emergent system and thus as a form of "artificial life" in its computational sense. It is, however, only her data architecture that becomes emergent, although the data can be seen metaphorically as being embodied in computational hardware and electricity. It is only in this metaphorical way, however, that, through touching the data generated by a human, her cybernetic program changes from being "lifeless" to being "alive"; a shift that should be read in the context of new, differentiated approaches to the question of what counts as alive and what does not that define the science of artificial life. It is the "fuzzy" moment, so important in much of (not only) 20th century culture, when machines begin to dream. In Philip K. Dick, for instance, the question is, famously, whether androids dream of electric sheep; in Pynchon, the duck dreams of repro*duck*tion; and in Steven Spielberg's *A.I.*, David dreams of a functioning family aggregate, which he could bring about if only he became truly alive, or, in his words, if he became a "real boy."

In the essay "DeNarration: Literature at the End of the Millennium" I had used a line of *R.E.M.* lyrics, "It's the end of the world as we know it / And I feel fine," as a motto— "I have sampled the epigram from the chorus of the R.E.M song that was Bill Gates' first choice to underscore the marketing of Windows 95" ("DeNarration" 249)—relating it, in the final sentence of that essay, to the marriage of Rez and Rei Toei: "*Idoru* ends with this image of the virtual fusion or, less poetically, the interface between man and information. For Rez and Rei Toei it is the end of the world as we know it, and we can be sure that they feel fine" ("DeNarration" 264). One should always be careful with such statements, however. In fact, when I wrote the essay, Gibson had already written a conversation between Laney and Rydell about Rei Toei that would become part of *All Tomorrow's Parties*:

> "But it's all around her."
> "What's all around her?"
> "The change."
> "Laney, she said you told her the world was going to end."
> "Is going to end," Laney corrected.
> "Why'd you tell her that?"
> Laney sighed, the deep end of his sigh becoming a cough, which he seemed to choke off. "As we *know* it, okay?" he managed "As we know it. And that's all I or anyone else can tell you about that." (*Parties* 169)

In the temporal gap between *Idoru* and *All Tomorrow's Parties*, Rei Toei has left Rez:

"The singer had sought to join her in some realm of the digital or in some not-yet-imagined borderland, some intermediate state. And had failed" (*Parties* 55). It seems, then, that everything has not been so fine in Rez' and the idoru's world. Not surprisingly, *All Tomorrow's Parties*, which charts her quest for a material body, implies that their problems have to do with, precisely, questions of embodiment, which is also where this article continues the argument of "DeNarration: Literature at the End of the Millennium."

As in *Idoru*, in *All Tomorrow's Parties* the plot zooms towards an emergent historical change, to "nodal points in history . . . some emerging pattern in the texture of things . . . everything changing" (*Parties* 56). (One might note, in parenthesis, that all of Gibson's plots trace such moments of emergent change, a fact that might be relevant for a general poetics of his work.) As Laney states, "some very basic state is on the brink of change, and we are near its locus" (*Parties* 136). The ominous Cody Harwood seems to be situated at the center of these dynamics. As he does so often, Gibson refers to the field of non-linear dynamics to define the emergence of (not only historical) change. In this case, he notes that "Harwood is the strange attractor, the crucial piece of weirdness things need to accrete around" (*Parties* 194), which is why Laney's "awareness of the nodal points, the points from which change was emerging, would repeatedly bring Harwood to his attention" (*Parties* 163).

The way Gibson presents such crucial cusps that organize change recalls Virginia Woolf's statement that "in or about December, 1910, human character changed" (91), although Gibson refers to a technological rather than a psychic change. This technological change originates, symptomatically, in a fully contingent event, an early version of the car-crash, which might be considered as the paradigmatic "contingent catastrophe" that defines 20th and 21st century art:

> "What I want to know," Laney says, "what I need to know, and right now, is what Harwood is up to. He's sitting at the cusp of some unprecedented potential for change. He appears to be instrumental in it. Rei Toei is in it too, and this freelance people-eraser of Harwood's, and an out-of-work rent-a-cop . . . These people are about to change human history in some entirely new way. There hasn't been a configuration like this since 1911-"
> "What happened in 1911?" the Rooster demands.
> Laney sighs. "I'm still not sure. Its complicated and I haven't had the time to really look at it. Madame Curie's husband was run over by a horse drawn wagon, in Paris, in 1906. It seems to start there. But if Harwood is the strange attractor here, the crucial piece of weirdness things need to accrete around, and he's self-aware in that role, what is it he's trying to do that has the potential to literally change *everything*?" (*Parties* 194-5)

In describing such historical cusps, Gibson takes up the logic of infinite recursivity and the unrepresentability of such infinite structures. The infinitely small cusp is

> a place where metaphor collapses, a descriptive black hole. . . . [Laney] is no more able to describe it to himself, experiencing it, than he would be able to describe it to another. Yet what it most nearly resembles, that place where history turns, is the Hole he has posited at the core

of his being: an emptiness, as devoid of darkness as it is of light. (*Parties* 250)

Laney, who can make out the change in the fractal datastructure, believes that "Rei Toei must have presence in the impending cusp" (*Parties* 242), while Harwood does all he can to use the cusp for his own ends and thus to get her and her agenda out of the picture:

> Harwood whom he has sometimes imagined as the presence of God.
> Harwood, who is . . .
> Like him.
> Harwood who sees, Laney now sees, the nodal points. Who sees the shapes from which history emerges. And this is why he is at the very heart of the emergent cusp, this newness Laney cannot quite glimpse. Of course Harwood is there.
> Because Harwood, in a sense, is causing it . . .
> Harwood knows
> Harwood took the 5-SB.
> Harwood is like him.
> But Harwood has an agenda of his own, and it is from this agenda, in part, that the situation is emerging." (*Parties* 178-9)

Given this manichaeic setup, the conflict will be about two things. It is "all about complexity" (*Parties* 134), but also "about your will in the world" (*Parties* 134). As Rei Toei tells Rydell, "we are about to find our way to the heart of Harwood's plan. And change it. And change Everything" (*Parties* 246). Because none of them, however, has the overall picture, the change is fundamentally open towards the future. Laney and Harwood are thus not quite Laplacian demons, because they can see "emerging change, but not what that change will be" (*Parties* 194). As Klaus asks Laney about Harwood's ability to see upcoming change:

> "You mean he's only picking winners . . . You're suggesting that he's in a nodal mode and simply gets behind emerging change? If that's all it is, my friend, why aren't *you* one of the richest men in the world?"
> "It doesn't work that way," Laney protests. "5-SB allows the apprehension of nodal points, discontinuities in the texture of information. They indicate emerging change, but not what that change will be." (*Parties* 194)

"The world as will and complexity," therefore, is the basis of change and it provides the dynamics according to which "newness enters the world." As Laney notes, in an argument against the "death of history" (*Parties* 107): "but there is will. 'Future' is inherently plural" (*Parties* 107). Both the complexity and the will, however, have its roots in the unconscious of infinitely small bifurcations, which is why they are fundamentally enigmatic and uncomputable. At their core lies the "descriptive black hole" that informs every form of change and thus every action. Even Harwood, the arch-schemer, cannot really say why he wants to get Rei Toei out of the picture: "although without knowing exactly what it is I'm attempting to stop her from doing. She's an emergent system. She doesn't know herself" (*Parties* 250). This uncertainty principle results from the fact that in emergent systems matter and mind organize themselves into larger structures/units from within, without recourse to an overall, pre-established blueprint.

Both Laney and Harwood dance around the mélange of will and infinite complexity, a dance in which Harwood, who is, as he himself notes, "too perfectly self-obsessed" (*Parties* 251), seems to be at a disadvantage precisely because of that closure of purpose. The people around Laney, like all of Gibson's heroes, are in a better position because they opt for pure change, change without attached teleology. As Harwood notes:

> just a little degree of free will and we're so much more happy, aren't we? And looking backward is very nearly as much fun as looking forward, though our digital soup does thin out rather rapidly, that way down the time-line. Amazing, though: that business around Curie's husband . . . changed *everything*, and who knows? I ask you, Laney, who knows?
> - We do
> - Yes, we do
> - It's changing again. Tonight.
> - This morning, rather. Pacific Standard. Very early. But, yes, it is. And I'm here to see that it changes in the directions I prefer it to, and not in others.
> - We're going to try to stop you.
> - Of course. That's the shape of things tonight, isn't it? I couldn't expect otherwise. (*Parties* 251)

According to Gibson, then, history is made up of an infinite number of infinitely small systems that accrue towards larger, interacting systems, the overall shape consisting of "lesser shapes, in squirming fractal descent, on down into the infinitely finest of resolutions" (*Parties* 107). History, in this context, is "that *shape* comprised of every narrative, every version; it was that shape that only he (as far as he knew) could see" (*Parties* 165). In recourse to the laws of non-linear dynamics, Gibson describes these shapes as organized/enveloped around multitudes of attractors, of which the whole system itself is the most comprehensive, emergent, and therefore unpredictable one. It is in this context that Laney raises—without subsequently answering it—the question of whether things are organized according to intelligent matter or according to a transcendental, central intelligence agency: "Plunging down the wall of this code mesa, its face compounded of fractally differentiated fields of information he has come to suspect of hiding some power or intelligence beyond his comprehension. Something at once noun and verb" (*Parties* 71). Whatever lies at this perspective-point— "a transcendent meaning, or only the earth" (Pynchon, *Crying* 181)—it is a both physical ("noun") and active ("verb") agent of change.

The difference between embodied and non-embodied entities comes up for the first time when Laney attempts to teach Rei Toei to see the overall shape of history: "he had shown her nodal points in that flow, and they had watched together as change had emerged from these into the physical world" (*Parties* 164). It is, ironically, the informational system who, quite poetically, points out the difference between a disembodied and an embodied perception. At first,

> he had attempted to share it with the idoru. Perhaps, if shown, she, this posthuman emergent entity, would simply start to see this way as well. And he had been disappointed when she had finally told him that what he saw was not for her; that his ability to apprehend the nodal points, those emergent systems of history, was not there, nor did she expect to find it with growth. "This is human, I think," she'd said, when pressed. "This is the result of what you are, biochemically, being stressed in a particular way. This is wonderful. This is closed to me." (*Parties* 165)

At the end of *Idoru* and the beginning of *All Tomorrow's Parties*, Rei Toei is still nothing but a hologram projected from a metal unit that looks somewhat like a "thermos bottle" (*Parties* 102). As she tells Rydell, who operates as one of Laney's agents and who is supposed to keep the unit safe for the time being, when she first appears in front of him, "this is a hologram . . . but I am real" (*Parties* 163). At this point, the stress is still on a disembodied informational structure dependent on an outside energy source. This is why before she can appear in front of him, "gorgeous and literally glowing" (*Parties* 154), Rydell has to get two cables for her unit: "One's power: jack to any DC source or wall juice with the inbuilt transformer" (*Parties* 122); the other is a hook-up for a PC (*Parties* 245).

In *All Tomorrow's Parties*, the central event towards which the plot zooms is the transformation of Rei Toei from an acorporeal system that relies on an outside energy source to a corporeal system defined by an internal energy source, the hinge being provided by the concept of nanotechnology. After many convolutions of the plot, the way is finally free for the idoru to become embodied by parasiting Harwood's new Nanofax technology: "Harwood has demonstrated an ongoing interest in nanotechnology, and this has manifested most recently in a collaboration between Nanofax AG of Geneva . . . and the Lucky Dragon Corporation of Singapore" (*Parties* 195), which allows to "digitally reproduce . . . objects, physically, at a distance" (*Parties* 195); a technology not to be confused with "beaming," because it involves nanotechnological replication rather than molecular transfer.

The shift from digital, informational hologram to a nanotechnologically produced corporeality is shown quite literally. While before, Rei Toei was transparent, which implies that one could actually reach through her, she is now material and solid. The central passage describes her exit from the Nanofax channel:

> Light over the hatch turns green, and the hatch slides up and out crawls, unfolds, sort of, this butt-naked girl, black hair, maybe Chinese, Japanese, something, she's long and thin, not much titties on her the way Boomzilla likes but she's smiling, and everybody, the manager, checker, securities, they jaw-hang, eyes popped: girl straightening up, still smiling, and walks fast to the front of the store, past the security counter, and Boomzilla sees her reach

up and open the door, just right on out, and it'll take more than a naked Japanese girl to get anybody's attention out there, in the middle of this disaster shit.

But the crazy thing is . . . that when he sees her walk past the screens there, he sees her on every last screen, walking out of every Lucky Dragon in the world, wearing that same smile. (*Parties* 268-9)

The novel ends on this image of Rei Toei's "strange Metamorphosis." Interestingly, this fundamental change in the order of things—a multitude of only initially identical Rei Toei's enter the world—remains invisible for many people. As Rydell notes, "whatever Laney was on about, that end of the world thing, everything changing, it looked like it hadn't happened" (*Parties* 272). For others, like the more historically oriented Fontaine, it is only one in the infinity of changes that make up history: "He looks up at the silver canister again. Somehow he knows it no longer contains her, whoever, whatever she was. It has become as much history, no more, no less than the crude yet wistfully dainty vases pounded out of shell casings in some French trench" (*Parties* 276).

Whatever its outcome, one can be sure that the change will not completely change everything. Because of the systemic memory operative in the world, newness is never fully so. Still, the change has transformed the world, and Laney can already glimpse "the shape of the new world, if any world can be said to be new" (*Parties* 226). Also, one should note that change usually has its price and that it is more often than not related to small or large catastrophes. In Gibson's case, the price for change is the bridge, which, in the process of the conflict, goes up in flames. As Yamazaki notes in relation to change, catastrophes, and earthquakes, which already figured prominently in *Iduro*, where they were also related to nanotechnology and to the rebuilding of cites, to which Rydell refers in *All Tomorrow's Parties* when he talks to the Republic of Desire:

Skinner had tried repeatedly to convey that there is no agenda here whatever, no underlying structure. Only the bones, the bridge, the Thomasson itself. When the Little Grande came, it was not Godzilla. Indeed, there is no precisely equivalent myth in this place and culture (though this is perhaps not equally true of Los Angeles) . . . when Godzilla came at last to Tokyo, we were foundering in denial and profound despair. In all truth, we welcomed the most appalling destruction. Sensing, even as we mourned our dead, that we were again presented with the most astonishing of opportunities. (*Idoru* 126)

As an actualization from a pool of infinite potentialities, every world, at every moment, is only the "best of possible worlds," which brings me to Leibniz.

Monads into Nomads

"The soul is a material body, the body is a thing, the subject is just an object, physiology and psychology are just physics. And, consequently, the senses are reliable."

—Michel Serres, *The Birth of Physics*

Both Pynchon's ducktale and Gibson's story about mechanical and informational systems becoming infinitely complex and thus alive resonate in many ways with Leibniz's differentiation between finite/artificial and infinite/natural machines. What makes Leibniz so contemporary is that he considers this difference to be the only one between art and nature, which means that he considers both as similarly "machinic." As in Julien Offray de la Mettrie, who talks of the "machine of the world" (91) and who also deals with Vaucanson's duck, there is no longer a fundamental difference between machine and nature. The only difference is between artificial and natural machines. As Leibniz notes in his "Monadology,"

> Thus every organic body of a living being is a kind of divine machine or natural automaton, which infinitely surpasses any artificial automaton, because a man-made machine is not a machine in every one of its parts. For example, the tooth of a brass cog-wheel has parts or fragments which to us are no longer anything artificial, and which no longer have anything which relates them to the use for which the cog was intended, and thereby marks them out as parts of a machine. But nature's machines—living bodies, that is—are machines even in their smallest parts, right down to infinity. That is what makes the difference between nature and art, that is, between the divine art and our own. (64)

Vaucanson's duck, for instance, is fundamentally finite, first because it contains parts which are themselves no longer machines but merely parts of a machine and, second, because it does not contain artificial parts that are smaller than what can be perceived by the engineer.

The logic of Leibniz's quote, in which one can already feel the beginning of what Deleuze will call a "machinic" and thus a no longer "natural" nature, relies on the concept of infinity, which is of fundamental importance for both Leibniz and Deleuze. It is precisely in the possibility of an infinite zoom, for instance, that Leibniz sees the importance of Leeuwenhoek's microscope: "Every portion of matter can be thought of as a garden full of plants, or as a pond full of fish. But every branch of the plant, every part of the animal, and every drop of its vital fluids, is another such garden, or another such pond" ("Monadology" 67).

It is symptomatic that before the linguistic turn, Leibniz should think the human as a natural machine that aligns spirit and materiality rather than as a discursive machine. Also, it is noteworthy that with his interest in the infinitely small, he evokes the 20th century science of nanotechnology. Although the difference between natural and artificial machines is still operative in a world of nanorobots because these can never be infinitely small, one can feel how nanotechnology, and the nanosphere in general, begins to erode the difference between the two forms of machines. How does Leibniz, from within an overall machinic perspective, think the relation between mind and matter/body, and how can this be aligned with conceptualizations such as Butler's?

On the one hand, Leibniz's world consists of "active" monads, which are unities/

substances that are defined by perceptions and appetitions, which is a nicely culinary way to describe movement/activity, in particular, the continuous movement from one perception to another. One of the difficulties in dealing with Leibniz's system is that the concept of the monad is an extremely "plastic' one. It can morph from immaterial, extensionless mathematical point to something like Gibson's Dixie Flatline construct from *Neuromancer* (a monad whose wetware materiality has been replaced by a hardware one) or to something evocative of Toru Iwatani's greedy little Pac-Men (from the Japanese *pakupaku*: to open and close one's mouth).

Generally, Leibniz differentiates between three kinds of monads. Naked monads are defined solely by perception and appetition and are perceived by the human as the purely material aspect of a body. Animal monads are defined by perception, appetition, and memory. Human monads/souls are defined by perception, appetition, memory, and apperception, which means the perception of perception and thus implies consciousness/cognition. What is important is that within this series, there is a scaling of the living, which means that even the naked monads are alive and perceptive. It is only on the ground of this general "vitalism" that the link between matter and mind/spirit can be performed. On the other hand, Leibniz's world consists of "passive" matter. The difficulty is that according to Leibniz there is no monad without matter, which means that monads are by definition embodied, while, simultaneously, monads follow completely different laws than matter does. Of course, this presents a problem. Luckily, both levels are related by way of a pre-established, divine harmony.

Leibniz's space of thought is thus differentiated into one side characterized by metaphysics and appetite (a field figured by Pynchon's duck and by Rei Toei at the end of *All Tomorrow's Parties*) and another one characterized by physics and mechanics (a field figured by Vaucanson's duck—which, as I noted, is a mere simulation of life and whose hunger was not real—and by Rei Toei at the beginning of *Idoru*). These sides, however, are invariably folded onto each other. It is in this "being folded onto each other" that Leibniz attempts to solve the alignment of matter and spirit. As Deleuze notes, Leibniz's body is

> probably made of infinities of present material parts. But these infinities in turn would not comprise organs if they were not inseparable from crowds of little monads, monads of heart, liver, knee, of eyes, hands . . . there is no cause to ask if matter thinks or perceives. (*Fold* 108)

In fact, this would be a modern question, which would involve the idea of what I call intelligent matter or an intelligent materialism. Leibniz displaces this question, which Monod relates to a "microscopic cybernetics" (62), by keeping matter and intelligence simultaneously together *and* apart. In the context of Leibniz's system, therefore, it is merely a question of "whether . . . [matter] is separable from these little souls capable of perception" (*Fold* 108).

Interestingly, in Leibniz the logic of the relation between mind and matter is an optical one that repeats the logic of the microscope. Every material aggregate is made up of monadic unities, with every one of these unities revealing itself, upon closer scrutiny, as an aggregate, and so to infinity. Donald Rutherford calls this Leibniz's "reduction of matter to monads" (219). In this way, that which is perceived as matter is ultimately "an infinite plurality of nomads" (Rutherford 220). La Mettrie had already pointed out this reduction, noting in "Machine Man" that "the Leibnizeans with their *monads* have constructed an incomprehensible hypothesis. They have spiritualized matter rather than materialising the soul" (3). According to the latter project, thought is "so little incompatible with organised matter that it seems to be one of its properties" (35). In fact, for la Mettrie, the soul is "reduced" to organized matter: "the soul's faculties depend on the specific organisation of the . . . whole body . . . they are clearly nothing but that very organisation" (26).

In the perception the natural—and in particular the human— machine has of itself, such a process of reduction is seminal as well. "Materially," the body is a dynamic, open, to some degree inevitably unstable aggregate that changes continuously, which means that monads and aggregates of monads continually leave and are added to it. This happens, for instance, through the bodies' metabolism and sexuality, but such dynamics also take place on the molecular level. As Deleuze notes in *Cinema I*,

> me, my body, are rather a set of molecules and atoms which are constantly renewed . . . It is a state of matter too hot for one to be able to distinguish solid bodies in it. It is a world of universal variation, of universal undulation, universal rippling: there are neither axes, nor centres, nor left, nor right, nor high, nor low. (58)

This inherently "open" body aggregate, however, is controlled and thus contained/reduced by a dominant monad. According to the reduction of matter to monads, the material aspect of the body is merely *that* aspect of a monadic multiplicity that is perceived by the respective dominant monad as a material object/organ. This means that below a certain threshold of perception, everything is "like matter," although it consists, in actual fact, of a multiplicity of monads. A controlling monad, for instance, cannot perceive its organs as an ensemble of monads, which is why human sexuality operates, as Deleuze and Guattari argue in *A Thousand Plateaus*, to no small degree on "non-human" levels; levels on which microscopic monads perceive something that the controlling monad cannot— at least not directly—perceive.

This, of course, opens up, in full force, the question of perception, which is generally considered as something good, because it opens up the view onto the world and makes cognition possible in the first place. From a specific angle, however, one can also consider it as an obstacle, which is what Deleuze does when he describes human perception as a cut into the continuity of what he calls the "plane of immanence," in the same way that letters are cuts into the continuum of sound and colors cuts into the visual continuum. La Mettrie seems to evoke something like a plane of immanence when he proposes that "there is in the universe only one diversely modified substance" (39). Because perception cuts "objects" out of the originary multiplicity/ continuity of which the plane of immanence consists, subjectivity is first of all "subtractive" (*Cinema* 63) —the perceived object is merely the object minus that which is of no interest to us—which means that complex machines, such as controlling monads, might be said to ultimately perceive less than simple ones: "an atom . . . perceives infinitely more than we do and, at the limit, perceives the whole universe" (*Cinema* 63-64).

The body is thus perceived by a controlling monad as a conscious, closed, "slow" system with spatio-temporal coherency and continuity. At the same time, however, it is, unconsciously, an open, infinitely fast system that is in touch with an infinity of other monads and aggregates. From one side, the body is an apparition originating from the substance, which means that a dominant monad "is . . . present to its body *by projection*" (*Fold* 118). From the other side, the body is inclusive of levels/plateaus on which matter stops being part of an organic "texturology" (*Fold* 115), which means levels on which it stops being part of a specific "monadic," molar aggregate and becomes "nomadic." This is where Deleuze positions his differentiation of texture/structure and felt/rhizome, as well as, from a different perspective, that between the conscious and the unconscious.

The organism thus combines two logics: that of representation (the logic of the body-image and the scripted body, which are, in Lacanian terms, related to the imaginary and the symbolic respectively) and that of production (the logic of the real body, which is, in Lacanian terms, a representational vacuum that is present in representation only negatively, as an inner exclusion, but which is thought, by Deleuze, as a positive, productive function and field). As noted above, these logics are closely related to thresholds of perception. On the one side, the body is "mere appearance of what a monad represents as its body" (Rutherford 224), which means that it is the famous poststructuralist body-image; "on the other hand, as what that body is in itself, some aggregate of monads" (Rutherford 224), which means, from a contemporary scientific point-of-view, that it is intelligent matter. In Leibniz, these sides are both combined *and* separated, with the terms "projection" (body-image) and "acquisition" (body) demarcating the two sides:

> For Leibniz, the two floors are and will remain inseparable; they are really distinct and yet inseparable by dint of a presence of the upper in the lower. The upper floor is folded over the lower floor. One is not acting upon the other, but one belongs to the other, in a sense of a double belonging . . . Each soul is inseparable from a body that belongs to it, and is present to it through projection. Every body is inseparable from the souls that belong to it, and that are present to it by requisition. . . . the belonging makes us enter into a strangely intermediary, or rather, original, zone, in which every body acquires individuality of a possessive insofar as it belongs to a private soul, and souls accede to a public status; that is, they are taken in a crowd or in a heap, inasmuch as they belong to a collective body. Is it not in this zone, in this depths of the material fabric between the two levels, that the upper is folded over the lower, such that we can no longer tell where one ends and the other begins, or where the sensible ends and the intelligible begins? (*Fold* 119)

This zone is of course that of the threshold between the two logics and the two plateaus of representation and pro*duck*tion.

How to think this threshold? Deleuze argues that this is difficult, if not impossible from within a classical conceptualization of space that differentiates fundamentally between

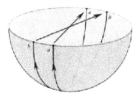

Illustration 5: Diagram of the projected plane

inside and outside. It is, however, possible to think a space in which inside and outside are no longer fundamentally separated, a space in which one can cross from one to the other without crossing a threshold. Such a space can be thought with the help of the concept of infinity, the very term Leibniz uses to differentiate between natural and artificial machines. The "projective plane," which Felix Klein, in his book *Vorlesungen über Nicht-Euklidische Geometrie*, describes as

a hemisphere with a "line at infinity" at its circumference on which opposed points are identified: "*Jedem unendlich fernen Punkt der Ebene entsprechen . . . je zwei Randpunkte der Kugelhälfte; wir müssen deshalb . . . je zwei derartige, einander diametral gegenüberliegende Randpunkte als identisch ansehen*" (14) is such a space. As Klein notes, the moebius strip is "*die einfachste Fläche . . . die das selbe Verhalten zeigt wie die projective Fläche*" (15).

On such a plane, the differentiation between inside and outside is operative on a local but not on a global level. According to Deleuze, Leibniz's connection of monads and matter owes something to this topology. Even more, the intimate connection Leibniz "attempts" to think is only thinkable in such a unilateral, twisted space.

> Leibniz discovers that the monad as absolute interiority, as an inner surface with only one side, nonetheless has another side, or a minimum of outside, a strictly complementary form of outside. Can topology resolve the apparent contradiction? The latter effectively disappears if we recall that the 'unilaterality' of the monad implies as its condition of closure *a torsion of the world, an infinite fold*, that can be unwrapped in conformity with the condition only by uncovering the other side, not as exterior to the monad, but as the exterior or outside *of* its own interiority. (*Fold* 111, emphasis added)

It is precisely in this torsion/twist constituting "the fold of the world and of the soul" (*Fold* 26) that Deleuze positions his replacement of Leibniz's transcendentalism/metaphysics by a logic of immanence. Of course, Leibniz did not know about the projective plane, and of course he was steeped in thought that had God as its point-of-perspective (disregarding for a moment the immensely difficult question of how much the presence of God is a strategic one in Leibniz's various texts). Deleuze, however, is not so much interested in proving Leibniz wrong. What he is after is to find a way in which one can "update" many of his seminal insights, such as the machinic nature of life and the concept of folding, by way of inserting his system into a different topology.

A Deleuzian Leibniz is thus not a Leibniz who has been run through a Deleuzian mill. Rather, it is "simply" a Leibniz who has been subjected to a specific topological operation: What if one were to fold God, and thus the divine harmony, from the outside into the innermost folds of matter and then were to call this harmony complexity? (Deleuze's concept of the unilateral plane of immanence is the topological result of such a folding.) In this way, one could replace God in Leibniz's equation with the topology of the plane of immanence. The algorithm for this operation would be: replace God as the transcendental "point-at-infinity" with the topological structure of the projective plane. The divine harmony, sublated in and guaranteed by God and functioning as a control engineering between psyche and physics, would then turn into an immanent, polyvocal harmonics that "is," quite literally, the self-organizing, autopoietic complexity of the world.

Compare this to the way that Laney sees the shape of history in a way that involves quite literally a moebialization of space:

> And part of him asks himself if this is an artifact of his illness, of the 5-SB, or if this vast and inward-looking eye is not in fact some inner aspect of that single shape comprised of every bit of data in the world?
>
> This last he feels is at least partly confirmed by his repeated experience of the eye averting, turning itself inside out in a Moebius spasm, at which point he finds himself, invariably, staring at that indescribable shape. (*Parties* 167)

Compare this also to the impossible space of the Aleph in *Mona Lisa Overdrive,* which is "an *abstract* of the sum total of data constituting cyberspace" (175) and thus "an approximation of the matrix" (259). In fact, as in Jorge Luis Borges's story and in Marc Danielewski's *House of Leaves* (2000), Gibson's cyberspace version of the Aleph contains infinite space in a finite space.

Once God's infinite knowledge has become the knowledge of the world, all of nature is infinitely intelligent and informed. According to such an informatics, Gibson describes sex, unlike Butler, as a complex form of a material cybernetics: "It [lovemaking] belonged to the meat. . . .It was a vast thing, beyond knowing, a sea of information coded in spiral and pheromone, *infinite intricacy* that only the body, in its *strong blind way,* could ever read" (*Neuromancer* 239, emphases added). If lovemaking is "beyond knowing' although it is a "sea of information," this can only refer to a non-discursive information coded directly into the bio-chemical dynamics of the natural machine and operating below the threshold of conscious perception and thus of apperception: it is coded in "spiral and pheromone." It is, therefore, the body rather than the mind that reads. Gibson differentiates this physical reading from a psychic one by calling it a paradoxical "blind reading," a process that conflates processes of sensation and "organic perception." If this quote highlights the idea of a physical reading, the beginning of Gibson and Bruce Sterling's novel *The Difference Engine* highlights the logic of self-organization operative in intelligent physical processes: "The occupant . . . rests her arthritic hands upon fabric woven by a Jacquard loom. These hands consist of tendons, tissue, jointed bone. Through quite processes of time and information, threads within the human cells have woven themselves into a woman" (1).

What Deleuze does in his reading of Leibniz in *The Fold*, then, is to "simply" replace Leibniz's logics of divine harmony with the logics of a purely immanent, self-organizing complexity, which is the point at which matter becomes intelligent. As the examples from Gibson show, this calls for a new conceptualization of coding, writing, and information transfer. In fact, when Deleuze notes that "writing now functions on the same level as the real, and the real materially writes" (*Thousand Plateaus* 141), this sounds very much like Gibson's "blind reading." If matter and code are generally situated on the two separate levels of intensity and representation, a "material writing" implodes these levels, opening up a space in which code matters and matter codes.

Another field to which Deleuze opens up Leibniz is that of the unconscious, which Deleuze links directly to the difference between matter and mind, production and representation, intensity and integration, as well as an analog and a digital logic. In this context, Deleuze reads Leibniz's "monadology" quite literally as an integration machine (illustration 6: Integrator) that extends the logic of integration and thus of consciousness to the most infinitely small levels

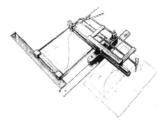

Illustration 6: Integrator

of material life, levels that for Deleuze define the realm of the unconscious, which is concerned precisely with the infinitely small, molecular levels of material perception that elude the apperception of the human being as a controlling, molar monad. Some of these "*petites perceptions*" are, as Michel Serres writes in his book on Leibniz,

> les petites douleurs inaperceptibles, les petites aides et délivrances, les petits mouvements de chaleur et de lumière, les sollicitations sublimi-naires, ressorts et changements dans les organes, les poussières minus-cules, les prévalences insensibles, les petites vagues. (206)

From this perspective, the Deleuzian unconscious is "simply" the aggregate of material machines that lies below the threshold of apperception/consciousness of the controlling monad; an aggregate made up of infinitely many infinitely small machines and machinic sub-aggregates. If the subject attempts to open itself up to 'its' unconscious, it has to open itself up to these imperceptible machines rather than merely to repressed signifiers.

If the passage from the unconscious to the conscious is that from "molecular perceptions to molar perceptions" (*Fold* 87), this implies that the more one zooms into the obscurity of the molecular perceptions, the more one enters the plane of the non-human. In this field cuts organize intensities and tectonic shifts in material aggregates without processes of mathematical integration and psychic apperception. While infinitesimal calculus is an individual "psychic mechanism" (*Fold* 96), these forces are communal. They "do not work by differentials, which are always differentials of consciousness, but by communication and propagation of movement" (*Fold* 97). The difference is thus between "the psycho-metaphysical mechanism of perception, and the . . . physico-organic mechanism of excitation or impulsion" (*Fold* 97). Ultimately, perception operates in analogy to the "Dedekind cut." In the same way in which the mathematical cut cuts into the continuum of real numbers, the perceptual cut cuts into the "unconscious" continuum of the plane of immanence, re-creating the original continuity as the continuity of an infinity of "conscious" cuts:

> the theory of minute perceptions is based thus on two causes: a metaphysical cause, according to which every perceptive monad conveys an infinite world that it contains; a psychological cause, according to which every conscious perception implies this infinity of minute perceptions that prepare, compose, or follow it . . . The task of perception entails pulverizing the world but also of spiritualising its dust . . . The point is one of knowing how we move from minute perceptions to conscious perceptions, or from molecular perceptions to molar perceptions. (*Fold* 87)

The question of perception is thus precisely that of the "thresholds" between the unconscious and the conscious, which means that a general machinics engenders both a machinic unconscious and a machinic psychoanalysis. There are perceptions that are so small that they are unconscious. This means that at every moment there is perception, even without the psychic system being aware of it. What this does not imply, however, is that at every moment there is integration/apperception. The material body analyses, decodes, reacts, and organizes to a large degree on a level well below that of conscious perception and thus below that of integration. In Leibniz, things were different, because, as Serres notes, the logic of integration operates even on the most infinitesimal level. If Leibniz argues that "our body integrates the noise of minute perceptions into sensible signals" (Serres *Genesis* 20), the reason for this is, according to Serres, that "Leibniz lumps everything into the differential. And under the numberless thickness of successive orders of integration. The mechanism is admirable. No one ever went so far in rational mastery, down into the innermost little recesses of the smallest departments" (*Genesis* 20-21). In Deleuze, in opposition, all consciousness is born from unconscious, material intensities. An idea, for instance, is not, as one would generally assume, the result of apperception and thought. Rather, it emerges from an unconscious ensemble of material forces and givens from which it percolates into the field of human perception, thought, and consciousness. It first belongs to the world, and only subsequently to the human: "an Idea is an n-dimensional, continuous, defined multiplicity" that is ultimately "extra-propositional and sub-representative" (*Difference and Repetition* 267).

The Bridge

"matter is mobile."

—Julian Offray de la Mettrie (51)

I have taken this detour through Leibniz to present an early version of thinking the man/machine nexus and to show how this figure of thought can be read into a more recent discourse of non-linear dynamics, cybernetics, and a machinic psychoanalysis. It is also meant, however, as a backdrop for a reading of the two cultural programs that mark the conflicts playing themselves out in *Virtual Light* and *All Tomorrow's Parties*.

In *Virtual Light*, these conflicting programs are dealt with in architectural terms as those between what Deleuze and Guattari call, in *A Thousand Plateaus*, striated and smooth space. Ultimately, the question addressed in the novel is that about an either molar or molecular unconscious, embodied by an either molar or molecular architecture and urbanism. The "virtual light" glasses—"got these little EMP-drivers around the lenses, work your optic nerves directly" (*Light* 122)—around which the plot revolves in *Virtual Light* contain information about a plan by the "Sunflower Corporation" (*Light* 144) to completely rebuild the city of San Francisco with the help of nanotech devices, according to a pre-programmed, consciously ordered matrix that is planned and executed from above; to create a completely engineered site without an urban unconscious. Resistance to such a plan is the main reason why the members of the "Republic of Desire" (*Light* 7) decide to help Rydell:

> "Any of you live in San Francisco?"
> The dinosaur came flickering back. "What if we did?"
> "Well," Rydell said, "do you *like* it?"
> "Why do you ask?"
> "Because it's *all* going to change. They're going to do it like they're doing Tokyo."
> (*Light* 295)

In such a fully programmed and simulated city, there would no longer be any loopholes for hackers to evolve: "they hated the idea of San Francisco getting rebuilt because they liked an infrastructure with a lot of holes in it" (*Light* 313).

Such an infrastructure of what *All Tomorrow's Parties* calls "life before it's theme-parked" (*Parties* 67) is embodied in the porous architectonics of the bridge, which are defined by a bricolage aesthetics/ethics and which show emergent behavior. In fact, one might read the bridge in general as an autopoietic system, and thus ultimately as a "living" organism. Such a reading would resonate with Guattari's project to expand Maturana and Varela's theory of autopoiesis, which they restrict, according to Guattari, to the "biosphere," to the "mechanosphere" (*Chaosmosis* 51). As Guattari notes, "I think that their notion of autopoesis—as the auto-reproductive capacity of a structure or ecosystem—could be usefully enlarged to include social machines, economic machines and even the incorporeal machines of language" (*Chaosmosis* 93). Such a shift would mean to think a general, machinic autopoiesis.

It is in particular around the figure of Yamazaki, a student from Osaka University's Department of Sociology who has come to San Francisco to study the bridge as a socio-logical phenomenon, that the program of the bridge is being defined. When Yamazaki sees it for the first time, he notices that it is composed of two different structural blue-prints: "the integrity of its span was rigorous as the modern program itself, yet around this had grown another reality, intent upon its own agenda. This had occurred piece-meal, to no set plan, employing every imaginable technique and material. The result was something amorphous, startlingly organic" (*Light* 62). It seems to him that the bridge operates according to a program that needs as yet to be deciphered: "things had accumulated there, around some armature of original purpose, until a point of cri-sis had been attained and a new program had emerged. But what was that program?" (*Light* 64). The structural difference between "the bridge's program and the program of the city" (*Light* 93) is quite literally that the bridge is what "follows" the program of a rigorous modernity from which it is, however, quite literally, suspended:

> We are come not only past the century's closing, . . . [Yamazaki] thought, *the millennium's turning, but to the end of something else. Era? Paradigm? Everywhere, the signs of closure.*
> Modernity was ending.
> Here, on the bridge, it long since had.
> He would walk toward Oakland now, feeling for the new thing's strange heart." (*Light* 97)

The program of nomadic, organic growth—as opposed to that of monadic, hegemonic control—also defines the internal systematics of the bridge, which is made up of countless sub-systems stitched together without an apparent overall purpose or teleology. As Yamaza-ki notes, "telepresence had only hinted at the magic and singularity of the thing, and he'd walked slowly forward, into that neon maw and all that patchwork carnival of scavenged surfaces. . . . In all the world, there was no more magnificent a Thomasso" (*Light* 63). The term "Thomasson," which itself is undergoing continual change, designates "certain useless and inexplicable monuments, pointless yet curiously artlike features of the urban landscape. But the term has subsequently taken on other shades of meaning" (*Light* 64). For Yamazaki, the logic of such non-teleological aesthetics might, in a slightly utopian gesture, be extend-ed to America in general: "The whole city was a Thomasson. Perhaps America itself was a Thomasson" (*Light* 230).

The way Skinner tells it to Yamazaki, the origin of the settlement of the bridge is quite lit-erally the story of the emergence of a self-organizing system. Like Harwood in *All Tomorrow's Parties*, in fact, the bridge is defined as a strange attractor around which the event unfolds:

> "No signals, no leader, no architects. You think it was politics. That particular dance, boy, that's over."

"But you have said that the people were 'ready.'"
"But not *for* anything . . . Like the bridge was there, but I'm not saying it was *waiting*. See the difference? . . . Yamazaki believed Skinner had simply been too long in proximity to whatever strange attractor had permitted the bridge to become what it had become. (*Light* 94)

Although there are countless retrospective stories about the founding event, the event itself, in its emergent, unconscious multiplicity, can only be understood as the topological shape made up of the combination of all of these stories, and even then it "eludes" direct discursive representation. When the event unfolds, bodies are concerned with its production rather than its recording: "That one night, people just *came*. All kinds of stories, after, how it happened" (*Light* 95).

The logic of emergence that defines the beginnings of the bridge communities is carried over into their day-to-day organization, which is defined by an ad-hoc, pragmatic, and local approach to problems. When Yamazaki asks about the rationale for having stopped burning their waste, "This is by consensus?" (*Light* 256), for instance, Skinner simply replies: "Just common sense" (*Light* 256). Such pragmatics, of course, often turn into last-minute troubleshooting: "Nothing here was ever planned, in any overall sense, and problems of drainage were dealt with as they emerged. Or not, more likely" (*Light* 173).

Like these dynamics, its bricolage sociology is the result of the fact that the bridge does not have an overall control system:

none of it done to any plan, not that . . . [Yamazaki] could see. Not like a mall, where they plug a business into a slot and wait to see whether it works or not. This place has just *grown*, it looked like, one thing patched onto the next, until the whole span was wrapped in this formless mass of *stuff*, and no two pieces of it matched. (*Light* 178)

Without a master narrative, the bridge is a fundamentally hybrid space on which, not surprisingly, people of "all ages, races, colors" (*Light* 178) are living. Rydell has a special affinity to such interstitial hybridities, which originates in a basic belief in pragmatics:

Rydell didn't have anything special going about black people or immigrants or anything, not like a lot of people did . . . They'd run all these tests on him and decided he wasn't racist. He wasn't, either, but not because he thought about it particularly. He just couldn't see the point. It just made for a lot of hassle, being that way, so why be that way? Nobody was going to go back and live where they lived before, were they, and if they did (he vaguely suspected) there wouldn't be any Mongolian barbecue and maybe we'd all be listening to Pentecostal Metal and anyway the President was black. (*Light* 199)

In many ways, the bridge is organized like "organic" hacker-networks which are "set up mostly in these cells, the cells building up larger groups . . . they just didn't know who the members of the other cells were, and they made a point of not finding out" (*Light* 313).

In its non-linear dynamics, the bridge is the architectural embodiment of a constantly emergent system that evolves in unpredictable ways and follows, like the plot of the novel, a "catastrophic" logic in which decisions that originate in microscopic bifurcations cascade into reality, much like Chevette's decisions when riding her bike, which also originate in microscopic perceptions, cascade into specific macro-movements within the city. Working as a courier at "the archaic intersection of information and geography" (*Light* 93), she is entirely immanent and attuned to the multiplicity of perceptual levels making up the constantly changing aggregate of the city, here defined as a flow of informational and geographic traffic:

> She was entirely part of the city, then, one wild-ass little dot of energy and matter, and she made her thousand choices, instant to instant, according to how the traffic flowed, how rain glinted on the streetcar tracks, how a secretary's mahogany hair fell like grace itself, exhausted, to the shoulders of her loden coat. (*Light* 120)

To conclude: a general machinics implies that human culture is part of an overall, immanent *eco*logics. Not only human culture is semiotic. Nonhuman systems, such as bacterial and molecular cultures, are just as informational, although their information exchanges might never congeal into linguistic signs, which is why the linguistic sign can no longer be enough to model a "general writing." As such, a general machinics implies a questioning of the linguistic/cultural constructionism predominant today, as well as of projects that seek to accommodate a "passive" matter, thought of as the basis of cultural reality, into their logics, be it as *zóe* or as *sex*.

The fact that at every point, representation is traversed by physical intensities that are productive and emergent also implies a questioning of the hegemony of the temporality of retrospection ("always already") that is so *en vogue* today. Although emergence is a favorite word in the cultural theory of Homi Bhabha, Butler, and others, it might be a mistake to use it only in relation to cultural and representational scenarios that are closed-off from material fields and forces, the machinic dynamics of which make up the Deleuzian unconscious.

Butler, one might argue, is, at certain moments, still Leibnizean in outlook. In fact, if one were to replace "monads" by "discursively operated mental unities" and "matter" as "the inevitable material embodiment of these unities," this would lead to what one might call a "discursive transcendentalism/ metaphysics," a logics in which mental operations form passive materialities. Pynchon, Gibson, and Deleuze go a step further. All of them truly "identify" cultural and material apparatuses in that they override, like Leibniz, the opposition between nature and culture through a general machinics and through a logic of machinic—natural *and* cultural—autopoiesis. What they add to Leibniz is that they see the world as a plane of immanence, and that they replace the pre-established, divine harmony between the physical and the psychic with an over-all autopoietic logic. Also, they add to Leibniz the realm of a machinic unconscious. In fact, Leibniz's obsession with integration is why in both Pynchon and Serres, he is often seen as the epitome of an all-pervasive rationalism gone "out of control" precisely by in-stalling an agency of universal control. Against such a rationalism, a general machinics argues that any representational system that closes itself off from the field and logic of an uncomputable and unpredictable material production and from the physics of an intelli-gent materialism, might not reach far enough. To contain materiality in discourse by way of an inner exclusion might, in the long run, be too "negative" a way to deal with it.

Shroud and Shock

V., Pynchon's first novel, already dealt with the quick and the dead in terms of machines:

> In the eighteenth century it was often convenient to regard man as a clockwork automaton. In the nineteenth century, with Newtonian physics pretty well assimilated and a lot of work in thermodynamics going on, man was looked on more as a heat-engine, about 40 percent efficient. Now in the twentieth century, with nuclear and subatomic physics a going thing, man had become something which absorbs X-rays, gamma rays and neutrons. (284)

This is precisely what it is about with SHROUD (synthetic human, radiation out-put determined), while SHOCK (synthetic human object, casualty kinematics) is an ordinary crash-text dummy. During his time as a night watchman at "Anthroresearch Associates," Benny Profane has a number of imaginary, or maybe not so imaginary, conversations with these two:

> "What do you mean, we'll be like you and SHOCK someday? You mean dead?"
> Am I dead? If I am then that's what I mean.
> "If you aren't then what are you?"
> Nearly what you are. None of you have very far to go." (*V.* 286)

And as if this machine-koan was not enough, SHROUD calls after him on his final day of work:

> Bon voyage.
> "What is that supposed to mean."
> We'll see.
> "So long, old buddy."
> Keep cool. Keep cool but care. It's a watchword, Profane, for your side of the morning. There, I've told you too much as it is.
> "I'll bet under that cynical butyrate hide is a slob. A sentimentalist."
> There's nothing under here. Who are we kidding?
> The last words he ever had with SHROUD. (*V.* 369)

WORKS CITED

Berressem, Hanjo. "Matter that Bodies. Philosophy in the Age of a Complex Materialism." *Gender Forum*: *Mediating Gender* 2 (2002) <http://www.genderforum.uni-koeln.de>.

——. "DeNarration: Literature at the End of the Millennium." *Postmodernism and the Fin de Siècle*. Ed. G. Hoffmann and A. Hornung. Heidelberg: Winter, 2002. 249-265.

——. "Emergent Ecologics: Cultural and Natural Environment[s] in Recent Theory and Literature." *Place – Space – Environment*. Ed. L. Hönnighausen, J. Apitzsch and W Reger. Tübingen: Stauffenburg, 2003. 42-61.

Butler, Judith. *Bodies that Matter: on the Discursive Limits of "Sex."* New York: Routledge. 1993.

Cohen, Jack and Ian Stewart. *The Collapse of Chaos: Discovering Simplicity in a Complex World*. New York: Viking, 1994.

Deleuze, Gilles. *Cinema 1*. Trans. Hugh Tomlinson and Robert Galeta. London: Athlone, 1986.

——. *The Logic of Sense*. Trans. Mark Lester. New York: Columbia UP, 1990.

——. *The Fold: Leibniz and the Baroque*. Trans. Tom Conley. Minneapolis: U of Minnesota P, 1993.

——. *Difference and Repetition*. Trans. Paul Patton. London: Athlone, 1994.

—— and Félix Guattari. *Anti-Oedipus: Capitalism and Schizophrenia*. Trans. Robert Hurley, et al. Minneapolis: U of Minnesota P, 1983.

——. *A Thousand Plateaus: Capitalism and Schizophrenia*. Trans. Brian Massumi. Minneapolis: U of Minnesota P, 1987.

Emmeche, Claus. *The Garden in the Machine: The Emerging Science of Artificial Life*. Princeton: Princeton UP, 1994.

Guattari, Félix. *Chaosmosis: An Ethico-aesthetic Paradigm*. Trans. Paul Bains and Julian Pefanis. Bloomington: Indiana UP 1995.

Gibson, William. *Neuromancer*. New York: Ace, 1984.

——. *Mona Lisa Overdrive*. New York: Bantam, 1988.

——. *Idoru*. New York: Putnam, 1996.

——. *All Tomorrow's Parties*. New York: Putnam, 1999.

—— and Bruce Sterling. *The Difference Engine*. New York: Bantam, 1991.

Hultén, Karl Gunnar Pontus, ed. *The Machine: As Seen at the End of the Mechanical Age*. New York: The Museum of Modern Art, 1968.

Klein, Felix. *Vorlesungen über Nicht-Euklidische Geometrie*. Berlin: Springer, 1928.

Lacan, Jacques. *Écrits*. Trans. Alan Sheridan. New York: Norton, 1977.

Laramée, Eve Andrée. *A Permutational Unfolding*. Boston: List Visual Arts Center, MIT, 1999.

Leibniz, Gottfried Wilhelm. "Monadology." *Gottfried Wilhelm Leibniz: Philosophical Texts*. Ed. R. Francks and R.S. Woolhouse. Oxford: Oxford UP, 1998. 267-281.

Mettrie, Julien Offray de la. *Machine Man and Other Writings*. Ed. Ann Thomson. Cambridge: Cambridge UP, 1996.

Monod, Jacques. *Chance and Necessity: An Essay on the Natural Philosophy of Modern Biology*. Trans. Austryn Wainhouse. New York: Random House, 1972.

Pynchon, Thomas. *V*. New York: Lippincott 1963.

——. *The Crying of Lot 49*. Philadelphia: Lippincott 1966.

——. "Is it O.K. to be a Luddite." *New York Times Book Review* 28 October 1984: 40-41.

——. *Mason & Dixon*. New York: Holt, 1997.

Rutherford, Donald. *Leibniz and the Rational Order of Nature*. Cambridge: Cambridge UP, 1995.

Serres, Michel. *Le système de Leibniz : et ses modèles mathématiques. Tome II : schémas—point.* Paris : Presses Universitaires de France, 1968.

——. *Genesis.* Ann Arbor: U of Michigan P, 1997.

——. *The Birth of Physics.* Manchester: Clinamen, 2000.

Stafford, Barbara Maria. "Micromegalia: From Monumental Machines to Nanodevices." In Laramée, 37-43.

Woolf, Virginia. "Mr. Bennett and Mrs. Brown." *The Captain's Death Bed and Other Essays.* London: Hogarth, 1950.

CHRISTIAN BERKEMEIER

KINGDOMS OF THE BLIND: TECHNOLOGY AND VISION IN DOUGLAS COUPLAND's *Girlfriend in a Coma* AND STEPHEN SPIELBERG's *Minority Report*

> "Then thou scarest me with dreams, and terrifiest me through visions."
>
> —Job 7:14

Recent inquiries into the relation of technology and medium and the inclusion or incorporation of technologies and media have highlighted the special status of technological media, i.e., those media that exist by scientific developments that affect their representational nature.[1] These scientific developments and their applications rely on mathematics as the founding discipline. The formation of knowledge gained through experimental procedures bases itself on medial abstractions and thus the representational devices developed by scientific method are to be seen as second order medial functions. As several parallel or subsequent mathematical operations are part of the representational function, the outcome has been seen as a mise-en-abyme of mathematical discourse, a multiplication of the logical, a product of the hyper-rational. The primary influence of this series of rationalizing operations is the field of optics; the resulting economy of the sign that Foucault describes in *The Order of Things* is one that tends to eliminate the subjective and privileges normative, controllable, and technically reproducible forms and formats.

If, as the introductory remarks suggest, the establishment of scientific laws and methods facilitates and fosters the development of technological media and their introduction shapes perceptions and representations in the field of vision since the renaissance, the development of a semantics of seeing, discerning, focusing, and similar expressions finds figurative equivalents in philosophical, moral, and political discourses. Seeing becomes synonymous with being alive, with deciding, with telling right from wrong. Enhanced and constantly remodeled by scientific and technological progress, seeing and visual representation become the key elements of a modernist hegemonic discourse. Martin Heidegger sees the conquest of the world as image as the primordial procedure of modernity.[2] Yet the emphasis on the visual paradigm has since its beginning been countered by strong epistemological skepticism that has found its expressions long before romanticist irony and symbolist occultism: the baroque emphasis on the mirror and its potential for distortion and play, the symbolist predilection for the opposition (and inversion) of dark and light, good and evil, and its romanticist adaptation in a taste for concealing and unveiling.

It is on the threshold of modernism, however, that art characteristically embraces technology and invests it with just the attributes that it has previously denied. It is the appeal, the *je-ne-sais-quoi*, the aura of the ambivalent, subjective, and unpredictable, to be noted in fin de siècle aestheticism, which stresses artificiality and the enjoyment of fabricated images, stressing their beauty while neglecting their mimetic and representational potential. At the cross-section of representational, psychological, and fictional discourse, the privilege of the visual is renewed—this time, however, with an emphasis on the dissolution of the observing self, the emphasis on introspection and internalized environments.

More than a hundred years later, there appear to be reflections of fin de siècle aestheticism and neo-aestheticism in American film and fiction at this past turn of the century. The visual habits of humans are challenged by the introduction of digital devices and their capacity for multiplication, synchronicity, and deceit. While the MIT struggles hard to bridge the threshold of the binary and the material,[3] cultural artifacts have established a wide range of expressions from cyberpunk to dystopian fictions that show the coexistence and merging of the digital, the human, and the material. The visual reassumes a metaphorical quality. It is no longer an instrumentalized property of the human, but a conglomerate of supernatural, technological, and human impulses. Necessarily, modes of human representation and norms of human aesthetics cannot suffice in this paradigm and must appear outdated.

Visionaries, Forecasts, Silence, and Spectacle

Technology has been understood to naturally imply the concept of transition. The concept of the tool that prolongs and extends bodily extremities and productive human capacities is inherent in all valid models of technology. This understanding, albeit an anthropomorphized conception of technology, can be observed in definitions of technology ranging from Arnold Gehlen to Marshal McLuhan.[4] The human mind is quick to relate these extensions to their social, political, and cultural consequences, thereby naturally granting the mechanical transformations the status of greater importance and further-reaching transitions. A number of concepts presently debated in cultural studies are based on concepts of motion and in-betweenness, whether we discuss systems theory, hybridity, or notions of cognition or perception. A rather fitting bracket, or meta-discourse, for these and other formations of knowledge may be the concept of emergence.

As a term primarily known to the German context from the terminology of Niklas Luhmann, "emergence" specifically addresses the potential existence of phenomena beyond the limits of human experience.[5] At the time that Carl Djerassi and about twenty other leading professors from the sciences and cultural studies got together at Stanford in the summer of 2002 and agreed to discuss a term, the Dalai Lama had gathered a group of prominent scientists and philosophers in his exile, Dharamsala. Ironically, the fact that Lama Buddhism and Stanford synchronically discuss the exact same topic may be called a phenomenon of emergence itself. Essentially functional as a meta-concept, the discourse of emergence comprises the limits of human knowledge as well as specifically urgent problems in knowledge acquisition and proceeding. One especially promising field in this respect is the problem of subject, object, and their intricate relatedness—a field formerly monopolized in human epistemology by the realm of the visual, as we have seen.

The artifacts that I will be dealing with are relevant to my research because of the ways in which they negotiate limits and problems of rationality, human judgment, and technology in motifs and imagery of vision. Both my main examples, Douglas Coupland's novel *Girlfriend in a Coma* and Stephen Spielberg's movie version of Philip K. Dick's short story "The Minority Report" are fictions about the ambivalent role of prophecy, a knowledge formation both technologically and mystically provoked and enhanced in both cases. As I hope to show, the performative character of both technological advancement and technological failure serves to highlight the intrusion of the inexplicable into the quotidian, of the spectacular into the mundane.

Apocalypse Now and Again: The Transcendental Mysticism of Douglas Coupland

In Douglas Coupland's art of label, titles matter. *Generation X* (1991), ironically called a Shopping Mall *Decamerone* by critics, established him as a cult author and reintroduced the notion of political pamphlet to the fictional scene of the late 1990s. Beyond that, however, the book used and abused properties dear to fiction—the author introduced a glossary with illustrations in the margin, thereby making it a subversive guide to the culture of twens caught in a rat-race they are bound to lose. It also introduced slogans as chapter titles that create the lasting expressions of a postmodern form of skeptical, anti-consumerist agit-prop for a generation of belated adolescents. The play and confrontation of pop literature with its own ephemeral surfaces had never been so glittery, it seemed. Far from being a theory buff, Coupland was quick and willing to use all sorts of popularized post-Marxist doctrine in college jargon, catering to the needs and the language of a readership that is from the same generational and sociological background as him.[6] It is the same group that forms the protagonists of the novels *Shampoo Planet* (1992), *Life After God* (1994), *Microserfs* (1995), and *Polaroids from the Dead* (1996). Since his are tales for an accelerated generation, reading time is scarce, attention spans are short, and slogans, titles, and effects matter greatly. The reading eye is over-stimulated by annotations, glossaries and illustrations that divert the reader's attention from the text which in itself is arranged in the form of vignettes rather than a consistent narrative. The title *Polaroids from the Dead* probably best epitomizes Coupland's poetics. They introduce a somewhat nostalgic, postindustrial aesthetics designed to demonstrate its own failure in preserving the fragile beauty of the commodified object—an object that appears as formerly unique and meaningful. As close to the ever-deepening imprint of the trend as to the uncanny, ugly, and unknown, Coupland's often chiasmic phrases mostly rely on oppositions of the ephemeral and the eternal, the surface and the immeasurable, the popular and the sublime.

It is this blending that characterizes *Girlfriend in a Coma*. It is the disturbing account of the end of the world occurring in the near future. The setting is primarily Vancouver; the places and spaces of the novel, however, extend throughout the United States and far beyond. The novel is organized as a sequence of expansions and implosions profoundly affecting the protagonists' views of themselves. Place is used metaphorically, as it becomes the matrix of a situation between battle and game—both alternate metaphors of lives that appear all too easy before they lapse into sudden tragedy and seriousness. The opening passage of the book illustrates this:

> I'm Jared, a ghost.
>
> On Friday, October 14, 1978, I was playing football with my high school team, the *Sentinel* Spartans. It was an *away-game* at another school, Handsworth, in North Vancouver. Early on in the game I was thrown a pass and as I turned to catch it I couldn't help noticing how clean and blue the *sky was, like a freshly squeegeed window*. At that point I blacked out. I apparently fumbled the pass and I have no memory of what happened afterwards, but I did learn that the coaches canceled the game which was dumb because we were cleaning up and for all anybody knew, it was probably just another severe relapse of mono from two years earlier.
>
> But between that fumbled pass and a few hours later when I woke up in *Lions Gate* Hospital, I was diagnosed with leukemia—cancer of the bone marrow and hence of the blood. Just three months later I died, on January 14, 1979. It was a *lightning-speed* progression for this particular disease. Before I died I lost all my hair and my *skin* turned the color of an *unwashed white car*. If I could do it all over again, I'd have *hidden the mirrors* from about Week Six onward. (3, italics mine)

The overtones of the ominous and uncanny clearly dominate the scene. Metaphors that transport ideas of threshold and vision blend into each other; The Sentinel is at an away-game, is thrown a pass on his mission, the sky is his limit—and yet appears as only a transparent foil that barely unveils the hereafter to be reached via Lions Gate,[7] at lightning-speed, through pale skin and hidden mirrors. If Coupland creates allegories of a remarkable shallowness, I tend to think of this as part of his fictional strategy.[8] The quote evokes the first in a series of incidents in the novel that follow the same model—a slip from progression into stagnation, then regression, and ultimately crisis and rebirth. Metaphors of epiphany in Coupland abound, as in his more recent *Miss Wyoming* (2000), but *Girlfriend in a Coma* is by far the most explicit in this respect. Jared dies to become a ghost, and one of the narrators of the story, Karen, becomes pregnant after her first sexual encounter ever. Richard, the second narrator, tells us how in quite a remarkable, lapidary passage:

> Karen and I deflowered each other atop Grouse Mountain, among the Cedars beside a ski slope, atop crystal *snow shards beneath penlight stars*. It was a December night so cold and clear that the air felt like the air of the Moon—lung-burning, *mentholated and pure, a hint of ozone, zinc, ski wax, and Karen's strawberry shampoo*.

Here is where I go back to the first small crack in the shell of time, to when I was happiest. Myself and the others, empty pagan teenagers lusting atop a black mountain overlooking *a shimmering city below, a city so new that it dreamed only of what the embryo knows*, a shimmering light of civil peace and hope for the future. [. . .]

And then we rose up again, up the mountain on a bobbing chairlift that stalled halfway up the slope. And it was there that the arc lights also blinked, then skittered, then blackened. In the pitch-dark, Karen and I sat bouncing, suspended above raw nature, our faces *blue jeans-blue* from the Moon. Karen lit a *number 7 cigarette*, her bony cheeks inflamed with blood, *burning pink in the BIC lighter's heat, like a doll inside a burning doll house.* [. . .] But Karen smiled, giggled, and blew silky smoke into the deep blue darkness. I thought of diamonds being tossed into the Marianas trench, lost forever. (6)

The intertextual referentiality of the passage is contemporary, though not necessarily literary. I believe it was the band *Sound Garden* that had a major hit in the early nineties with the song "*black hole sun*, won't you come, and wash away the world. . . ," their video showing a barbie doll fried over a barbecue in the back yard. And there is no doubt that a certain Stephen Patrick Morrissey, lead singer of the English band *The Smiths*, and poet laureate of an elitist, privileged, sarcastic, and hopelessly bored proportion of his generation, gave his words and voice to his title *Girlfriend in a Coma* in the late 80s. The extent to which Coupland drenches his imagery, his nonfictional and intertextual references, in an environment that he makes appear as the trashy but shiny fragments of pop debris is remarkable not so much for this type of reference but for their combination of cultural, natural, and supernatural contexts: there are snow shards and penlight stars; the colors Coupland evokes are those of a Roy Lichtenstein painting; the perception of nature and romanticism is prefabricated at any given moment, only that something or somebody else, beyond the loving couple, is pulling the strings in an attempt to question and re-invest meaning into these fragments of a dysfunctional postpop environment.[9] The coma that Karen will fall into the next day, remaining in it for the next 16 years, is induced by drug-abuse, a tiny, chemically engineered synthetic substance, but at no point in the narrative is there any doubt that this is an incident of fate, not of accident. It is a technically monitored and nourished state of comatose existence that allows Karen to have visions of an imminent apocalypse, which occurs after her awakening and spares only her and her friends. They are urged to mend their ways and rethink their lives by Jared, and ultimately the world returns to its present state. And they lived happily ever after, one would be tempted to add.[10]

Retroactive and repetitive patterns are present on a number of narrative levels throughout the novel. Cracks in the surface of a reality relying on time and space announce the imminent catastrophe. Karen lapses into unconsciousness after she and the friends from her neighborhood on Rabbit Lane (greetings from John Updike) are involved in the violent and uncontrolled destruction of a desolate family home—or a "burning dollhouse"? It is certainly no coincidence that "coma" is an anagram of "amok." Also, the name of the ghost and first narrator, Jared, can be split into two syllables that, when pronounced in a time-loop, almost turn out to be Richard, the name of Karen's boyfriend, the second narrator, who is present whenever Jared is absent. Karen is sixteen and pregnant when she falls into her coma and returns 16 years later when her daughter is pregnant again. The linearity of time is suspended as events seem to be simulating each other.

In contrast to the prevailing modern notion that human hubris and its imprint on technology ultimately provoke death and destruction, the determinist logic of Coupland's narrative relies on a concept of being in which the supernatural comprises both the natural and the cultural. It is a higher power that makes the ski lift stop, makes the city lights glisten more intensely before they disappear. It is a mechanical simulation of breath and an artificial maintenance of blood circulation that enables Karen to foreshadow the nearing end of the world in years of coma and negotiate with the other side—IF IT SLEEPS, IT'S ALIVE, as one of Coupland's Chapter-title slogans says. It is also a man-made dam that enables Richard to cross a valley on his way to the hospital at the moment Karen awakes. At one point he slips and falls into the water for a short moment. The scene is that of a baptism in nature as a sign of his commencement, his initiation into the circle of the illuminati.[11] Karen's awakening is also the step into a regained and intensely perceived physicality that allows her to transcend the semi-consciousness of a comatose fortune-teller and enjoy the presence of her own female body which she has to regain step by step.

The notion of a beauty artificially stalled in its maturing process is one very familiar not just to the end of this century. Coupland is very explicit in his reference to the aestheticism of the penultimate *fin de siècle* in his aesthetics. The cover page of the novel shows a girl in the sleeping position resembling that of a fetus. Colors of brown, gold, vanilla, orange, and amber prevail, some of them intensely reflective. The girl's long dark brown hair falls in loose curls over her shoulders and blurs the shape of her head against a black background. The girl's nightgown is richly ornamented with interlaces and organic structures. The letter of both author and title are arranged in ten squares and constituted by copper or red golden pixels that separately appear to fall into place from a light snowfall across the page. The spectator has the impression of looking at a "girl under glass," to quote a contemporary *Duran Duran* title—a biological structure in a receptacle, in a frozen moment. In her coma, Karen is ageless, sexless, and artificial, yet beautiful, as Richard hastens to explain many times. She is at once *femme fragile* and *femme enfant*—embracing two properties of the female at the last fin de siècle. It may appear ironic that poetry is the only hope for humanity to escape disease, madness, death, and destruction, as portrayed in Gustav Klimt's Beethoven Fresco at the Viennese Secession Building. Beauty and sleep as central motifs of the *fin de siècle* are clearly employed in Coupland's neuromancing pixel version.

The Inversion of Crime and Punishment in the Kingdom of the Blind: Ianus and his Faces in Stephen Spielberg's *Minority Report*

The story by Philip K. Dick and the film directed by Stephen Spielberg and produced by the main actor, Tom Cruise, introduce the idea of a future society in which crimes can be prevented and sanctioned the minute before they occur. The plot follows a lonely police agent into his job at the Department of Precrime where the task is to identify and prevent homicides before they occur and to severely punish the alleged murderers. The cop figure is a futurist hardboiled type of guy—he has lost his son in a child-abduction and the tragedy has separated him and his wife. Ever since, he has been addicted to a drug referred to as "clarity" that induces an impression of happy memories, a suspension of time, a release from the rush of stimuli perceived by the seeing consciousness. When the detective finds an irregularity in the process of crime precognition and culprit identification, he is caught in a trap and becomes the chief culprit himself. A series of narrow escapes and hide-outs comes to an end only when the manipulator (and chief of the Department of Precrime) is found.

The recent movie version re-accentuates the Dick story in two respects: first, Spielberg and Cruise emphasize the personal sentimental disposition and motivation of the detective to join the Department of Precrime as one of its commanding executives, namely, the loss of his son. And, second, they reduce the manipulation of Precrime to a questionable behavior and a nice ending, but ultimately to a negligible detail in the presentation of an authority that prevents crime, an institution whose very existence is challenged on moral premises all along. The movie is noteworthy for the ways in which it visualizes the combination of dream, supernatural capacity, technology, and legal procedure.[12]

The controlling subject and its failure form the thematic center of the film.[13] From the very beginning, there is a strong element of physical control over informational contexts. Exact motions of cyber-gloves direct and arrange a flow of information that is incorporated in a haptic, material, and visual context. Tracking the suspect becomes a form of ritual performed by an elite. The members of this elite are entitled to gather and process all available knowledge on the suspect and form a linear pattern projected on glass screens, which allows for an analogy of the foreboded fragments with the physical and factual reality. In addition, there are holographic projections, and the live court hearing stands by, the instance of authority and legitimacy. The materialization of informational contexts into glass, steel, and wooden structures allows for a control of information and its integration into a bodily performance of control.

The use of visual imagery in the film cannot be understood without taking into account the moral implications related to seeing. There is a pervasive use of imagery, semantics, and intertextual references related to vision which comes to function as a pseudo-platonic metaphor for knowing the truth and telling right from wrong. But seeing is more than discerning and deciding here. Indeed, it becomes the very identification of the subject (which passes through constant laser eye scans to determine its identity, intention, and whereabouts). A series of inversions introduces the ironies involved in the process of debasing these very identities. The "detective" (who habitually "uncovers") is obliged to live under cover himself. He has to undergo a critical eye surgery and have a new pair implanted to regain access to the facilities and find the information he needs. He indulges in trance sessions induced by a drug called "clarity" that allows him to access the nostalgic world of his memory. His dealer, ironically a criminal without eyes, with the drug also passes on a piece of Biblical wisdom: In the kingdom of the blind, the one-eyed man is king. This foreshadowing turns out to describe the situation quite accurately: the detective, the trickster tricked, ultimately regains full knowledge through the access to a precog by the name of Claire and can thereby unveil a network of manipulation among the unseeing.

While irony and inversion is one mechanism of destabilizing a rationalist and legal discourse of hegemony in the film, the introduction of the supernatural and neo-gothic is another. It is unveiled that the precog project came about as the result of a biochemical experiment gone wrong. The scientist responsible for conducting the experiment, Dr. Hineman, is introduced through her (characteristically) German heritage, her enchanted garden of carnivorous plants and poisonous ivy, and her rather inappropriate physical closeness to the detective.[14] Where science and the supernatural are tied, notions of medical hygiene are obliterated. The doctor in charge of the critical eye surgery practices under the influence of the narcotic his patient occasionally requires; he and his nurse are presented as having heavy Slavic accents and practicing under unbearable conditions. The atmosphere at the surgeon's place is characterized by filth, heat, and outdated medical equipment. The discourse of power, on the other hand, introduces a complicity with the supernatural that relies more on the technological, the digital, the artificial—and the sacred. Crime investigation relies uniquely on the precogs, asexual creatures on the verge between rest and life, water and air, surface and depth, kept in a gloomy building structure referred to as "the temple." As soon as Claire has to leave her shallow bed of water, she loses all human physical properties and has to be carried and dragged. The fragility of her body in the absence of technological support is evident. The last area which transports notions of a neo-gothic aesthetics in the film is the representation of prisons for the pre-sentenced, which are stalled and cryonized in green glass gravestones that arise upon human command from the abyss of a vast black background accompanied by the sounds of bells and the Bach fugue the warden performs on his organ.

While a quasi-religious agenda underlying the legal procedures in *Minority Report* is obvious, it remains debatable whether the visual rhetoric of the movie is in parts intertextually related to works by an artist that Tom Cruise should be more than familiar with. The works of Gottfried Helnwein, in their emphasis on mechanical coercion, blindfolding, facial bandages, and surgery, appear clearly related. In one of his hyper-realist pictures, Helnwein introduces a man with luminous eyes in the center of a dark alley, which reminds the viewer very much of the setting chosen for the narcotics dealer dispensing Biblical wisdom in the movie. Helnwein also had an art project involving the collection and display of children's photographs, which resembles the arrangements of random shots so crucial in *Minority Report*. The proactive use of technological gadgets such as organic-looking remote-controlled mechanical spiders as inspection devices, of vertically oriented cars and insect-like helicopters, add further details to the range of references that the film presents. In their totality, they suggest the fusion of the natural and the artificial and undermine conventional notions of vision and rationalism, the natural, the supernatural, and the artificial.

To attempt a direct comparison of the two fictions that I briefly introduced here would be misleading, the first being a utopian projection, the other an account of a pop-apocalypse. As to an assessment of their status as works of art, one may be highly ambivalent. Still, regarding the depiction and use of irrational and supernatural elements, the fusion of scientific and technological cultural discourses (mostly generally medical and psychological discourse as well as consumer and youth culture in Coupland; cognitive, neurological, secularized religious, sentimental, and political discourse in Spielberg), they can be seen as instances that both rely upon the visual paradigm. Both question the rationality of this paradigm, its validity and moral implications. Both present alternative models of vision. While Coupland explores coma, dream, and sleep, Spielberg introduces a technically enhanced form of foretelling triggered by scientific experiment and artificial laboratory circumstances.

While both can be seen as comprising emergent phenomena of knowledge formation, perception, and a de-centering of the subject, Coupland's can be seen as a more skeptical approach. His use of apocalypse is essentially didactic, since the presence of destruction is the prerequisite for epiphany. Spielberg's use of the Philip K. Dick material has millennialist overtones in that it diminishes skepticism, not to the human factor, but to the lapse of one corrupt individual. In their fictional logic, imagery, and intertextual references, both cases present the intrusion of mysticism into discourses of rationalism, civility, and legality that are replaced by new forms of knowledge. Seeing as a metaphor of activity, orientation, decision, and organization and the steering human consciousness is deconstructed by medial over-stimulation and manipulation induced by its proper agency. Envisioning as a metaphor of passivity, esoteric foreboding, potential, and prospect functioning in the absence of the controlling subject (and its seeing eye) becomes synonymous with a challenge to the rational. In Coupland's and Spielberg's kingdoms of the blind, their eyes are wide shut.

NOTES

[1] A survey is provided in Kittler.

[2] Heidegger explains that the privileges of vision, power and decision coincide and cooperate in "securing the efficiency of power" ["Sicherung der Wirkfähigkeit der Macht," my translation].

[3] One current approach is to develop printers that can multiply chip surfaces to be inserted into devices worldwide and thereby provide blueprints of the material original by a mere transmission of data.

[4] For a discussion of the relatedness of these conceptions, see Tholen, 114.

[5] Niklas Luhmann elaborates on this notion in the introduction to *Die Kunst der Gesellschaft*, iii-v.

[6] Joost Zwagerman has pointed out the pioneer situation Coupland's protagonists tend to assume in his novels. While they are usually average middle class people, they come to loathe their native environment while still being inexplicably drawn to it (33ff).

[7] A number of sacred places and buildings in south-eastern Asia are guarded by two lions at their gates.

[8] See also Lainsbury.

[9] Robert McGill has meanwhile demonstrated how the North American West Coast and the Pacific Rim function as a spatial and metaphorical threshold in Coupland's fiction. McGill also stresses the participation of postindustrial, ecological and Asian discourse.

[10] For a discussion of fairy tale formulas in Coupland, see Forshaw.

[11] For a discussion of salvation and epiphany in Coupland, see Tate.

[12] See Mihm, who stresses the visionary quality of the movie.

[13] *Minority Report* has been seen as paradigmatic among the current reflections on materiality, information, and artificiality. For a discussion of the visual aspect, see James.

[14] The old woman's kiss is a motif from the fairy tale. The notion of an incompatible visual semantics which reminds the viewer of Roman Polanski is repeated in the motif of an old lady smoking a pipe in the crucial precog vision.

WORKS CITED

Coupland, Douglas. *Girlfriend in a Coma*. London: Harper Collins, 1998.

Forshaw, Mark. "Douglas Coupland: In and out of 'Ironic Hell.'" *Critical Survey* 12.3 (2000): 39-58.

Heidegger, Martin. "*Was heißt Denken?*" *Vorträge und Aufsätze*. Pfullingen: Neske, 1978 [1954]. 123-137.

James, Nick. "An Eye for an Eye." *Sight & Sound* 12.8 (2002): 12-15.

Luhmann, Niklas. *Die Kunst der Gesellschaft*. Frankfurt: Suhrkamp, 1995.

Kittler, Friedrich A. "Fiktion und Simulation." *Aisthesis. Wahrnehmung heute oder Perspektiven einer anderen Ästhetik*. Ed. Karlheinz Barck, et al. Leipzig: Reclam, 1998 [1993]). 196-213.

Lainsbury, Gordon P. "Generation X and the End of History." *Essays on Canadian Writing* 58 (1996): 229-240.

McGill, Robert. "The Sublime Simulacrum: Vancouver in Douglas Coupland's Geography of Apocalypse." *Essays on Canadian Writing* 70 (2002): 252-76.

Mihm, Kai. "*Könnt Ihr sehen?* Steven Spielberg und sein kluger Genrefilm Minority Report." *epd Film* 10 (2002): 24-28.

Tate, Andrew. "'Now-Here Is My Secret': Ritual and Epiphany in Douglas Coupland's Fiction." *Levende Talen* 16.3 (2002): 326-38.

Tholen, Christoph. "*Platzverweis. Unmögliche Zwischenspiele von Mensch und Maschine*." *Computer als Medium*. Ed. Norbert Bolz, Friedrich Kittler, et al. München: Fink, 1994. 111-138.

Zwagerman, Joost. "*Net zo verloren als alle anderen: De generatieromans van Douglas Coupland*." *Maatstaf* 43.6 (1995): 30-39.

Charles B. Harris
Technoromanticism and the Limits of
Representationalism: Richard Powers's
Plowing the Dark

"Once out of nature I shall never take
My bodily form from any natural thing . . ."
—Yeats, "Sailing to Byzantium"

"Thou shalt not make unto thee any graven image or any likeness of any thing that is in heaven above, or that is in the earth beneath, or that is in the water under the earth . . ."
—Second Commandment, *Exodus*, 20.4

In *Towards a Postmodern Theory of Narrative*, Andrew Gibson concludes a long and fruitful chapter on the conflicted role of representation in postmodernism with the following appeal: "At all events, it is time for postmodernity to think mimesis and anti-mimesis together, as intertwined parts of a puzzle that we shall possibly never solve" (103). I would like to suggest that the evolution Gibson envisions is well under way.[1] A major motive of early metafiction was to denaturalize realistic conventions in order to demonstrate that realism, in Linda Nochlin's succinct formulation, is "an historical and stylistic phenomenon. . . , no more a mere mirror of reality than any other style" (4). Thus exposed, realistic conventions have once again become part of the aesthetic repertoire of many postmodern authors, who, in terms Teresa de Lauretis applies to cinema, have reclaimed representationalism "for the ideological," dissociating it from "the domain of the natural" and the "immediacy of referential reality" (45).

Like other members of postmodernist fiction's second generation, Richard Powers reappropriates in order to recontextualize the conventions of representational realism. For most of its 400-plus pages, *Plowing the Dark* (2000) relies on mimetic conventions and a mimetic "content." In a key scene near the novel's end, to which I shall return in detail, a sudden "jump-shift in epistemic levels" ("A Dialogue" n.p.) ruptures the novel's referential dimension, making clear that, despite its realistic surface, *Plowing the Dark* participates in the ongoing postmodernist critique of representational thinking. Unlike the early metafictionists, whose primary target was literary realism, or later novelists such as Don DeLillo and Curtis White, whose focus is often the hyperreal mediascapes of late capitalist America, Powers aims his critique at virtual technologies, which Michael Heim describes as "the apotheosis of metaphysics" (59).

In his *Atlantic Unbound* interview, Powers's description of *Plowing the Dark* seems to echo Heim, whom Powers calls "one of the great prophets of the new media." ("Being and Seeming" 17). "I think the history I'm describing in the novel is the apotheosis of the geek," he told Harvey Blume. When asked to define "geek," Powers responds: "The geek is a Platonist, forever looking for ways to reify the imagination, to make our interior visions more real than mundane materiality ever lets them be" (Blume n.p.). The nature of this neo-Platonic apotheosis is indicated in one of the novel's early scenes. Spider Lim, a virtual-reality researcher at TeraSys (the Puget Sound digital laboratory that serves as the main setting for one of the novel's contrapuntal narratives), has become excited by a "new book" that describes the Lascaux cave paintings as the first VR.[2] After "*a million and a half years of static existence,*" Lim explains to the other researchers, "*cave pictures*[. . .]*were the tool that enabled human liftoff, the Ur-tech that planted the idea of a separate symbolic existence* [. . .] *You see? You see? If we can make these . . . scratch lines come to life, then life is not just some outside thing that happens to us. It's something we come into and remake*" (PD 129-30).[3] Lim is one of eleven researchers recruited by TeraSys to construct the Cavern, an empty white room that, through the magic of virtual technologies, can morph into a Rousseauistic jungle, van Gogh's bedroom at Arles, or the Hagia Sophia. A mélange of nationalities, religious backgrounds, and academic specialties, the team comprises a latter-day simulation of that collection "of learned scholars from all parts of the civilized world" Leibniz proposed in 1666, whose "coordinated efforts" would result in "an 'electric language,' a set of symbols engineered for manipulation at the speed of thought" (Heim 93). According to Heim, "Leibniz's general outlook on language . . . became the ideological basis for computer-mediated telecommunications. . . . The royal academies that Leibniz promoted were the group nodes for an international republic of letters, a universal network for problem solving" (Heim 93). Heim describes Leibniz as a "modern Platonist, [who] dreamed of the matrix" (93). Cyberspace is the material realization of Leibniz's dream, "Platonism as a working product" (Heim 89).[4]

Subtending this neo-Platonic dream is a particular set of "digital narratives" informing what Richard Coyne calls Technoromanticism. The latest and perhaps the grandest of our *grands récit,* Technoromanticism presumes "that we can have total control or omnipotence, play God, by simulating, mastering, redefining, manipulating, and controlling space, time, community, thought, and life" (4). Instead of poststructuralism's limitless free play and contingent language games, virtual technologies promise what VR inventor Jaron Lanier calls "post-symbolic communication" or "communication without codes" (160). Promising a transparent, unmediated perception of reality—in a word, *presence*—codeless communication will allow us at long last to wrest our gaze from the flickering shadows of Plato's Cave and behold the pure metaphysical light.

Of course, the desire to dissolve the boundary between representation and the thing being represented is as old as metaphysics. If Technoromantic narratives sound vaguely familiar, it's because, stripped of its mystification, VR offers little more than a higher fi to the totalizing objectivist epistemology poststructuralism sought to vanquish. As Dona Haraway has helped us to see, objectivist epistemology privileges the "God trick," the view from nowhere, disembodied vision (186). The "historical vision that

I'm building up in *Plowing the Dark*," Powers told Sven Birkerts, "is that this eschatology of the digital age is the product of an earlier eschatology. And the reason we've built these tools is because we've had a millennium-long desire to get out of our bodies. . . . [V]irtual reality becomes a kind of late-day attempt to instantiate that idea, that we really are more comfortable just kind of shedding time and space and living in that cognitive map. And I think it's an incredibly seductive dream. It's one that's powered the technological transformation of the world for centuries. It's also a profoundly dangerous dream, as we get closer to realizing it in one kind of form" ("*Esquire* Conversation" 46).[5]

Except for Adie Klarpol, all of the TeraSys team members pursue the "dangerous" Technoromantic dream: "a new world order of unity through information" (Coyne 12). As usual, Powers grounds his novel in exhaustive research. But instead of introducing discursive materials directly into *Plowing the Dark*, as he had done, for example, in such "content-intensive" novels as *The Gold Bug Variations* (1991) and *Gain* (1998), Powers "triangulates" between the discursive and dramatic modes by incorporating into the novel's dialogue various Technoromantic claims.[6] For example, Jonathan Freese's description of VR as an "end to the limits of symbolic knowledge[,]. . . .the final disappearance of interface" (*PD* 270), echoes Jaron Lanier's call for codeless communication. Ari Kaladjian's belief that "*[e]verything has something to do with numbers*" (*PD* 263) reflects what Coyne calls VR's "mathematical realism. . . . [,] a recognition that at a fundamental level all understanding is grounded in number, symbol, and rule" (Coyne 6). Stevie Speigel, who recruited Adie to TeraSys, calls VR "*the grail we've been after since the first campfire recital*" (*PD* 159), echoing MIT Media Lab's David Zeltzer, who, according to Heim, also characterized "virtual reality . . . as the Holy Grail of the research" (Heim 123).[7] For Jackdaw Acquerelli, whose computer expertise was bred by "the first wave of Space Invaders" (*PD* 110), a video game, and who is unable "to abide much direct human contact without flinching" (*PD* 26), VR offers a substitute body for his "disembodied imagination" (*PD* 112). Jackdaw's desire for subjective transcendence, access to "the place that the brain had first mistaken the world for" (*PD* 114), reflects the techno-vision of Hans Moravec, who argues that the age of carbon-based life will be soon replaced by "a future in which we are able to transplant, copy, and merge the information of our bodies and minds in networked computers" (Coyne 67).

Despite her resistance to technoromantic narratives, even Adie senses the potential of the new technology. "However much the Cavern had been built from nouns," she muses, "it dreamed the dream of the unmediated, active verb. It lived where ideas stepped off the blackboard into real being. It represented humanity's final victory over the tyranny of matter" (*PD* 267). Adie's contribution to the project is her draftsmanship, her ability to copy. "*I never could make my hand do anything interesting without an original nearby, threatening me*" (*PD* 178), she tells Jackdaw. Sensitive to the non-assimilable nature of the real, Adie holds out for the "threatening" substantiality of the natural world, "this palpable place, the master foil to Stevie's crazy vision" (*PD* 160). Although the Cavern depends on representation, Adie realizes that its ultimate goal transcends mimesis: " . . . imitation was itself just the first step in a greater program, the final escape from brute matter, the room that would replace the one where existence lay bound" (*PD* 62). Ironically, then, Adie, whose talent for "*craft and exactitude and representation*" (*PD* 93) led TeraSys to recruit her in the first place, remains the one member of the team who, from the beginning, resists a world of total representation.[8]

Yet, despite Adie's preference for the unmediated real— "*Nothing,*" she tells Spiegel, "*nothing we make will ever match sunlight*" (*PD* 161)—she is not a premodernist realist so much as a High Modernist aesthete. At the age of twenty-seven, Adie had abandoned her promising art career to escape the commercialization of art, buying back the few pieces she had sold, returning the commissions, and burning all of her work (*PD* 219). A decade later, she accepts Spiegel's invention to join TeraSys because she believes that the Cavern provides her an opportunity to make something beautiful. Like the High Modernists whose post-Kantian view of the beautiful is encapsulated in Auden's famous line, "poetry makes nothing happen," which Powers chooses for one of his novel's epigraphs, Adie equates art with detached inutility (*PD* 372). "Sailing to Byzantium" is an important intertext in the novel; indeed, it is Yeats's paean to intellectual art that inspires Adie to construct a life-size virtual model of St. Sophia, the Byzantine temple in Istanbul she associates with Yeats's "artifice of eternity." But if the Hagia Sophia is a temple of icons, it is also the site of ferocious iconoclasm, having been damaged and on at least two occasions destroyed by various mobs and armies during its 2000-year history, each time being rebuilt in the image of whatever religious view its respective captors advocated. Adie and Auden may dream of an art for art's sake, but other forces, what Powers calls the "world machine" (*PD* 154), stand ready to appropriate the aesthetic for utilitarian and ideological ends.

The novel's second epigraph, drawn from Stein's *Autobiography of Alice B. Toklas*, describes Picasso's realization upon seeing a camouflaged cannon trundle through a Paris street that the Impressionist's experiments with color and light had made military camouflage possible. Near the novel's end, Adie suffers a similar epiphany. Watching Desert Storm, described in the novel as the "next televised devastation" (*PD* 334), she realizes that the electronics propelling the devastatingly accurate smart bombs derive from her team's research. The Air Force had taken "all her pretty pictures and put them to use" (*PD* 397). Powers's point seems clear. Because the mind, as one of the novel's characters observes, "*gets to say what the world isn't yet*" (*PD* 130), imagination carries an awesome responsibility: "*A person should never represent anything that they aren't willing to have come true*" (*PD* 287). Life, that which we enter and re-make, depends upon poetry, which, willy-nilly, makes everything happen.

The theme of Powers's most ambitious work since *The Gold Bug Variations* is nothing less than the role human imagination plays in creating reality and the ethical responsibilities that role implies. As symbol-makers, we alone among the life forms invent our environment. "Buildings," Adie muses, "were art's skins, the pictures we lived in" (*PD* 138). So, too, Powers's complex fiction implies, are the cities in which those buildings stand, the states and nations containing those cities, and the world views—cave pictures expanded to a global scale—over which nations do battle ("The basic process of modern times," Heidegger once observed, "is the conquest of the world as picture.") But if Powers is aware of the role representation plays in constructing human reality, he rejects "naïve social constructivism" as surely as he rejects "naïve materialism": ". . . to my mind, those who announce the death of fact and meaning have replaced one incomplete model of knowing with another. . . . I think a new consensus of thought may be forming, one that appreciates the two-way traffic of comprehension. . . . Remember that the actively narrating conscious brain is not arbitrary; it is itself the evolutionary product of several billion years of bumping up against the world. . . . We may live our lives as a tale told, but the tale we tell takes its shape from the life we are limited to" (Nielson 16).

Because of her Modernist view of the imagination's role, Adie retreats from the bumping world. In this regard, she takes her place among a series of Powers's characters who can't stand too much reality.[9] Each in his or her way prefers to dwell in what Powers calls "imagination's room." "In imagination's room," Powers writes with gentle but pointed irony, "all thing work out. . . . There is pain here, but there is no suffering. . . . This is the heaven of last imagination. The paradise of detachment. The room of no consequence in the least. Of making no difference in the whole known world" (*PD* 144-45). The tone of Powers's rebuke makes it clear that he understands the timeless appeal of this aesthetic view but that he ultimately rejects it. Art must also participate in the two-way traffic of comprehension. "I'm not finally a believer that private aesthetic experience has much redemptive value," Powers says in the *Rain Taxi* interview; "It's got to go back out" (Tortorello n.p.).

Adie, like most of Powers's defectors, does eventually go back out, returning not just to the material world, but, as we shall see, to the very source of her earlier capitulation, which she, again like the characters in the earlier novels, turns back against itself in an act of purposeful intervention. But if Powers pits Adie the artist against the "world machine" and seems to posit poetry as technology's foil, it would be a mistake to read *Plowing the Dark* as a reworking of the old "Two Cultures" opposition made famous by C. P. Snow over four decades ago. On the contrary, Powers believes that aestheticism and "the transformation of the world through digitization" (Williams n.p.) spring from the same "pretechnological fantasy" (Birkerts, *Esquire* 46):

> The desire to live in our imagination is driven by this suspicion that we're disembodied sensibilities cobbled into our bodies. That idea has infused most of human thought since the very beginning. I strongly believe poetry has always explored that same split, needing the body and yet constantly on the verge of discarding it as irrelevant or debilitating. It's right at that same untenable split that I want to position the digital revolution and virtual reality. (Blume n.p.)

The poetry-cybertechnology continuum is effectively dramatized in the montage-like Chapter 26, the novel's longest chapter, which segues between Adie and Stevie's University of Wisconsin college years (1971-1975), Adie's creation of the virtual *La Chambre De Vincent a St-Remy, France* during her first year at TeraSys in 1989, and various scenes in the lives of Adie, Spiegel, and Ted Zimmerman (their brilliant Wisconsin class-mate, now in the terminal stages of MS, to whom Adie was briefly married) during the intervening decade and a half. Spiegel is drawn to poetry, and to Adie, when, during a freshman Introduction to English Literature class, he hears Adie recite Yeats's power-ful hymn to disembodiment, "Sailing to Byzantium." Years later, the same desire for transcendence draws him to cybertechnology, "the century's terminal art form" (*PD* 218). As he explains to Adie, "*A good, polished program was everything I thought poetry was supposed to be*" (*PD* 215). For Spiegel, VR promises "*Embodied art; a life-sized poem that we can live inside . . . Invented worlds that respond to what we're doing, worlds where the interface disappears. . . . VR reinvents the terms of existence. It redefines what it means to be human*" (*PD* 159-60). Adie's riposte to Spiegel's technoromantic effusions underscores the poet-ry-VR link: "*You're telling me that you were fated to wind up programming golden mechanical birds?*" (*PD* 216).[10]

Despite her wisecracks and her preference for the irreducible materiality of the nat-ural world, Adie, too, as indicated above, recoils from what Powers describes as the "heft and bruise and particularity" of that world ("Being and Seeming" 16). Like Yeats, like all of us, according to Powers, Adie wants "of art something that will break the tyranny of space and erase our defeat at the hands of time" ("Being and Seeming" 17). But no Byzantiums are available to her. So in an act of desperation if not cynicism, Adie runs "*to commerce to get away from commercialism*" (*PD* 372), in much the same way that Stuart Ressler of *The Gold Bug Variations* flees the competition and commodification of genetic research by taking a job with a Manhattan banking network. Adie's retreat is a refusal of experience, emphasized by a decade of seclusion (her only companion is her dog Pinkham) and self-imposed celibacy.

Adie's celibacy is one of several variations in the novel on what, in another context, Richard Grusin calls a "trope of dematerialization" (51). Many of the novel's charac-ters prefer representational forms to—or confuse them with—the physical world. While walking with Spiegel through Seattle's Pioneer Square, Adie is chagrined to discover that "the knockoff pseudo-Greek plaster sculpture" (*PD* 161) in the square is really a mime. Spider Lim, who "couldn't work on a circuit without simulating it in his own circulatory system" (*PD* 60), runs into a virtual tree branch in Adie's simulation of Rousseau's *Dream*, and gets a black eye; his virtual ascension to the central dome of Adie's simulated Hagia Sophia produces a "gushing nosebleed" (*PD* 392). Gail Frank, Karl Ebesen's ex-wife, whose "favorite performance piece" involved sprawling on a sidewalk in New York City's Financial District, as if she had just plummeted from a sky-scraper, conflates performance art with life and, as her final "piece," literally leaps from a building to her death (*PD* 286-87). In a further turn of the trope, the novel's characters prefer disembodied digital communication or actual isolation to direct human interaction. Ebesen, unkempt, distrustful of speech, and shattered by his former wife's suicide, remains a recluse until Adie, the former recluse who bears an uncanny resemblance to Gail Frank, gently revives him.[11] Less fortunate, the reclusive Jackdaw, who, like Ebesen, "wasn't comfortable talking to living things" (*PD* 26), is devastated when the woman he meets and falls in love with in an on-line Multi-User Dimension turns out to be a LISP routine (*PD* 378). Doris Singlegate, the Mole Woman who, as part of a scientific experiment, lived for two years "in a hermetic sunken shelter" (*PD* 157) at the bottom of a mine shaft, commits suicide shortly after returning to the peopled surface.

Powers's examples range from the humorous to the tragic. But by connecting disembodiment and isolation to self-destruction, the ultimate rejection of somatic existence, Powers emphasizes that a major "danger of reifying our artifacts, of mistaking them for a priori entities" ("Being and Seeming" 16), is the elimination of direct human interdependence. Powers dramatizes this danger by contrasting characters who prefer surrogate environments to the natural world and telepresence to "the direct, warm link between private bodies" (Heim 102), with characters on whom disembodiment and estrangement have been forced by circumstance and disease. Ted Zimmerman, for example, is literally fastened to a dying animal, his body ravaged by multiple sclerosis, his speech so distorted by the disease that his best friend Spiegel quits returning his phone calls because of the incomprehensibility of Ted's messages. Whereas Adie and Spiegel choose to spend their lives in a small room constructing digital simulations, Ted is forced to spend his last days in a "cinder-block single compartment" (*PD* 223), another white room the same dimensions as the Cavern, strapped into a hospital bed in a Lebanon, Ohio, nursing home, "surrounded . . . by deaf nonagenarians" (*PD* 223). Whereas Adie, who prefers Platonic to natural light, seldom goes outside, Ted's confinement is involuntary. He is overwhelmed by the sight of trees when Adie and Spiegel take him on an outing during their visit to the nursing home, his first venture outside in six months. And whereas Adie and, to a lesser extent, Spiegel, though physically healthy, choose prolonged celibacy, Ted, though still libidinous, his physical desire having survived "the purpose of its burn" (*PD* 314), is no longer physically capable of lovemaking. Powers's contrast of idealized with actual desubstantiation demonstrates, on the one hand, "the resistant materiality of the natural world" (Hillis 203), which will have its way with us despite our best efforts to evade it. On the other hand, by demonstrating the real-world consequences of isolation and disembodiment, he warns technoromantic dreamers to be wary of what they wish for.

As Adie and her team of researchers increasingly elide the boundary between thought and things in the Cavern and as Ted wastes away in his stark cubicle, Taimur Martin, protagonist of the novel's second narrative strand, occupies yet another empty white room. An American of Lebanese descent, Martin has fled a failed love affair to teach

ESL in Beirut, where he's captured by Islamic fundamentalists and held hostage for five years in a tiny cell. Because of the Moslem prohibition against figural representations, Taimur's life becomes as unmediated as Adie's is virtual (for the bulk of his imprisonment, he's allowed only one book, the holy Qu'ran). As Adie's group projects the imagination outwardly, displacing the real with disembodied art, Taimur retreats from his bodily privations deep into embodied mental space, imagining a world elsewhere, removed from "all militias, . . . power, factions, and revenge" (*PD* 347).

The effectiveness of Taimur's narrative, which occupies thirteen of the novel's forty-six chapters, depends upon its density of details and Powers's success in preserving the circuit of identification between character and reader—in a word, upon Powers's mastery of the conventions of representational realism. Fortifying this "brute-force realism" (*PD* 383) is a prose style Daniel Zalewski considers "the most visceral . . . Powers has ever written" (12). Indeed, for Zalewski, the intensity of the prose "threatens to capsize Powers's counterpoint structure. TereSys' egghead entertainments simply can't match Taimur's fever dreams" (12). Despite their stylistic differences, however, the novel's intertwining narratives are more complementary than a cursory reading discovers. Indeed, Powers manipulates this complementarity to unsettle—often subtly, sometimes less so—the expectations of verisimilitude his use of realistic conventions encourages. For example, a pattern of unlikely coincidences sutures the novel's disparate narrative strands: Taimur is confined in Beruit, Lebanon, Ted in Lebanon, Ohio, both in cells the same dimensions as the Cavern's; in one of his "high-resolution" (*PD* 350) memories, Taimur recalls a visit to Chicago's Art Institute, where Gwen was moved to tears by Van Gogh's *La Chambre De Vincent a St-Remy, France,* the same painting Adie constructs a life-size replica of in the Cavern (*PD* 354); when freed from captivity, Taimur is flown to Istanbul (*PD* 415), the site of St. Sophia, the model for Adie's final life-size virtual installation. Because it divulges artifice, the hand of a controlling author, this pattern of correspondences contravenes the mimetic illusion that empirical phenomena are being simply and accurately observed and re-presented.

Realistic conventions and the readerly expectations they produce are similarly sabotaged when Powers occasionally juxtaposes the novel's twin plots in destabilizing ways. At first glance, Powers's consistent use of the second person throughout the Taimur sections— "You lie huddled on your mattress under the cheap acrylic blanket, shivering in the slip glaze of your own sweat" (*PD* 151)—seems part and parcel of his mimetic mode, impelling the reader's vicarious identification with Taimur's agonizing incarceration by closing the critical distance between his readers and his character. But Chapter 16, which immediately follows an extended section of Taimur's story, disturbs this mimetic spell. Taimur's absorbing narrative has become so closely linked with its second person unfolding that we are disoriented to discover that the opening paragraph of Chapter 16 is not a continuation of that story, although it, too, is written in the second person, but a prompt from the first-generation computer game Colossal

Cave, which some nostalgic techie has posted to Jackdaw's computer terminal: "You are standing at the end of a road before a small brick building" (*PD* 102). Zalewski dismisses this parallel as a mere "nod to the first virtual-reality games," quickly explaining that "Taimur's captivity is clearly not a game—even if the language of computer games can best weld the reader to his plight" (Zalewski 12). But Powers's juxtaposition of Taimur's narrative and a computer game prompt is much more than the "rhetorical gambit" Zalewski takes it to be (Zalewski 12). The defamiliarizing move momentarily dislodges our willing suspension of disbelief—the literary counterpart of VR's "consensual hallucination"—reminding us that we are holding a *made* world in our hands and forcing us to reflect on the continuing force of story telling—especially mimetic story telling—as the earliest immersive technology, of which early computer games, VR simulations, and, of course, the novel itself are but latter day extensions and elaborations.[12] A disruptive space has been inserted between sustained segments of referential narrative, and the resulting refocalization jolts us into the recognition that Powers is self-consciously manipulating the codes and conventions of representational realism, that, indeed, *Plowing the Dark* is not a realistic novel so much as it is a *simulation* of mimetic form, which Powers's imitation of an imitation critiques.

By advancing his critique from "inside" representationalism, as it were, Powers signals his understanding that human beings may never fully overcome mimesis.[13] Inscribed in representationalism is the metaphysical drive to control the world, to hold it at bay, as Heidegger has argued (349). The "engrams of our un-willingness to live in any place that would treat us the way *this* place does," our technologies of representation, Powers observes, "strive to remake the world in our own image" ("Being and Seeming" 17). Objectification is always an exercise in power relations, a failure of relation to the other. In a real sense, Taimur is the victim of what has always been representation's secret desire. Yet, as Taimur himself comes to realize, he, like Adie, is also complicit in that desire.

The first VR, Taimur's narrative makes clear, is the mind.[14] Isolated, blindfolded, chained twenty-three-and-one-half hours a day to a radiator, frequently beaten, Taimur retreats from extreme physical and sensory deprivations by slipping "into the self-sustaining dimension of an interior world entirely shaped by the only energy not diminished by such an ordeal: his imagination" (Dewey 137). Deprived of the prosthetic devices developed by centuries of technological advances to project our mind's imaginings onto the natural world, Taimur is forced to "reassemble [his] shattered concentration" (*PD* 181), recovering a pretechnological capacity for imagining and remembering, including the ability to reconstruct from memory entire passages from novels and poems he has read. Alone in the dark, he recapitulates the primal scene of "the story-telling race" (*PD* 400), the attempt to extend thought's grasp over things by the act of depiction. He has found his "way back to the cradle where this project started" (*PD* 401), before a millennia of inventions, each bootstrapping off the next, pushed us closer to the ultimate goal, "the final interface. The ultimate display, the one that closes the gap between sign and thing" (*PD* 400).

The concluding quotations in the paragraph above are taken from Chapter 43, one of about a dozen short chapters that seem to serve not so much as continuations of the novel's main narratives but as interludes or interchapters. Most of these short chapters are also narrated in second person, but not the "claustrophobic second person" (Dewey 137) of Taimur's narrative. This is a different voice we hear, one somehow more expository, more distanced from the events it narrates, a voice that provides "a kind of intellectual commentary" on the novel's dramatic narratives.[15] Half of these brief chapters (Chapters 3, 10, 13, 22, 37, and 45) comment on the various virtual reality rooms installed in the Cavern (respectively, the Crayon Room, the Jungle Room, O'Reilly's Room of Economics, Van Gogh's bedroom, the Hagia Sophia room, and Adie's final installation). The remaining five (Chapters 19, 27, 30, 41, and 43), presented in a highly metaphorical register that contrasts markedly with the novel's otherwise realistic presentation, also provide commentary, not, however, on specific scenes in the novel, but more generally on the role "the representing mind-set" (Heim 80) has played in human history and, more significantly, on the psychological and evolutionary sources of that mind-set.

"The room of the Cave is one continuous chasm" (*PD* 400) begins Chapter 43, signaling that we have slipped the confines of the novel's major plot lines, as the narrative focus expands beyond the TeraSys Cavern to that Platonic Ur-Cave of which the Cavern is but an extension and simulacrum. The Cave represents the primordial urge to construct representations, the race's first step into the Symbolic, described by Powers as the *Homo sapien* "breakout" (*PD* 52). It is the deep source of those narratives that comprise the realities of our age, narratives themselves built upon past fictions, the entire construct, as Nietzsche saw, forming the a priori beliefs of our time, which is why the Cave's "chambers all connect," running together like "a single subterranean stream that never changes its course. But never the same stream twice" (*PD* 400).

The Cave also represents our individual entry into the Symbolic order. "Here you have lived since childhood," Powers writes, "facing the darkness, taking shadows for the things that cast them" (*PD* 400). The desire to merge the shadow and the image, to close the gap between sign and thing, is at base a desire for plenum, presence, the "ecstatic sense of unity" that preceded our expulsion into the Symbolic order at the mirror stage of our development (Ragland-Sullivan 73). Chapter 30's generalized "you" seems somehow to have recuperated this early developmental state: "It dawns on you only piecemeal where you are. How you have dropped down through your own, scribbled rabbit hole . . . and now sit gaping at the shape of your evacuated life *from the far side of the mental mirror*" (*PD* 239, italics added). Powers's metaphor for this pre-Symbolic place of plenum and power is the "warm room [that] has no other reason but yours," where "[a]ll things await the theater of your needs, . . . [where] you are the doer of all acts, the receiver of all action, the glow that lights these sanctuary walls . . ." (*PD* 240).

But as Chapter 43 makes explicit, desire, which Spiegel calls "Evolution's most productive trick" (*PD* 227),[16] remains inexhaustible not only because the primordial lost object is inaccessible, but because the material world—and, ultimately, our Cartesian selves—are also inaccessible, always already mediated by Imaginary investments and the symbol systems through which we apprehend the external world. That's why the "room of the cave is something less than real. Its wall shadows ripple with an undercurrent of substance, more than representation, but not yet stuff" (*PD* 400).[17] What Anthony Wilden calls the desire for "non-difference that makes human being humans" (191) will never be consummated because the TeraSys team's goal, "*full symbolic liberation*" (*PD* 336)— "*this five-thousand-year footrace's finish line*" (*PD* 339)—is a technoromantic fantasy. Indeed, as Powers writes in "Being and Seeming," our technological prostheses have actually exacerbated our primal sense of separateness:

> Our dream of a new tool inclines us to believe that the next invention will give us a better, fuller, richer, more accurate, more immediate image of the world, when perhaps just the opposite is the case. Television does not improve on the verisimilitude of radio, nor photography on that of painting. *The more advanced the media, the higher the level of mediation.* ("Being and Seeming" 16, italics added)

Chapter 43 and its companion "interlude" chapters alert us to the way that Powers's twin narratives point in separate but complementary directions, the Taimur section focusing on the shape of desire in a discursive space approaching the zero degree of mediation, Adie's more panoramic narrative focusing on the way desire has shaped our technological transformation, whose "dream of universal accessibility" (Birkerts, *Esquire* 4) threatens to supplant physical space with total representation. But in either case, unmediated perception is impossible. In Joseph Tabbi's telling phrase, we are "opaque to each other in our separate consciousnesses" (62) not unlike those "windowless" Leibnizean monads Heim describes, which, isolated from all other beings, know only through the interface (Heim 97). The "truth only solitude reveals," recognized by Taimur at the lowest point of his incarceration, is "the fact of our abandonment here, in a far corner of sketched space" (*PD* 414). Weak and delirious after four years in solitary confinement, his teeth disintegrating painfully in his mouth, Taimur, in a suicidal act of despair, repeatedly smashes his head into the concrete wall, loses consciousness, and falls "into the abyss" (*PD* 390). This moment of desolation and release is immediately followed by one of the interlude chapters, the novel's shortest, Chapter 41, whose Leibnizean echoes suggest that Taimur has regressed to that primal crisis of differentiation when we first become aware of our "hideous aloneness" (*PD* 414). The chapter in its entirety reads:

> The room is dark, and without dimension.
> It has no door. Or any window where you might have entered. (*PD* 390)

Although Taimur gives in to the Kurtzian abyss, he is able, Marlowe-like, to survive this glimpse of chaos. What saves him is a vision. In "a scene lasting no longer than one held breath," Taimur suddenly finds himself in a Byzantine cathedral. Responding to a noise above his head, he looks up into the "awful dome," where he sees an angel "dropping from out of the sky, its bewilderment outstripping [his] own" (*PD* 414). Although the vision "made no sense," Taimur is left with "no choice but to live long enough to learn what it needed from [him]" (*PD* 413-24). At that same moment, in the novel's second narrative strand, Adie, distraught over her inadvertent complicity with Operation Desert Storm, decides to destroy "her handiwork," a reprise of that iconoclastic act a decade earlier when, distressed by the commercialism of the art world, she had burned all her pictures. Deciding to take one final look at the simulated Hagia Sophia, she boots up the cathedral, enters the Cavern, and "let[s] herself rise . . . into the uppermost dome" (*PD* 399). Responding to movement in the nave below her, she looks down and sees "a man, staring up at her fall, his face an awed bitmap no artist could have animated" (*PD* 399). Startled "back into the world's snare" (*PD* 399) by her vision, Adie sets about obsessively reassembling her final project, the Byzantium demo for military buyers touring the laboratory, before she re-enters the real world to "reinvent" herself (*PD* 406). Despite their radically different circumstances, and though a continent separates them, Adie and Taimur advance to a mystical meeting as unlikely as it is inevitable, and the novel's contrapuntally intertwined narratives momentarily converge.

Despite the scene's manifest importance, it has received scant analysis.[18] Paradoxically, Daniel Zalewski's criticism of the novel's conclusion may provide the most fruitful context for considering it. After conceding that the "collision" of Taimur and Adie's worlds is "riveting," Zalewski condemns this encounter as "a sentimental feint" that, within the larger realistic context of the novel, defies verisimilitude.[19] An apparently supernatural event has suddenly intruded into the rationality and materiality of an otherwise realistic text, seemingly violating the novel's implicit "mimetic contract."[20] This apparent transgression is not the aesthetic misstep Zalewski takes it to be, however, but a deliberate defamiliarizing gesture, the "jump-shift in epistemic levels" I refer to at the beginning of this essay.[21] Such shifts in "focalization," according to Powers, "will, with luck, deposit the reader on another level of the nested recursion that story-telling necessarily implies" ("A Dialogue" n.p.). Thus deposited, our "imaginary continuities" will be interrupted and we will be "put . . . head to head with a maker who is not us" ("Being and Seeming" 17). As early as *Three Farmers*, his first novel, Powers emphasized the necessity of this dialogic transaction,[22] this complicitous involvement with "some other mind's pale analogies" that resensitizes us to everything in "the life outside this constructed frame . . . that we've grown habituated to" ("Being and Seeming" 17). A similar shift in focalization also occurs inside the novel. Adie, immersed in a digital Byzantium of her own design, and Taimur, withdrawn into the deepest recesses of his own dementia, somehow make contact with another consciousness, with something they "didn't make" (*PD* 404). The reader's estrangement outside the book is paralleled by the characters' disruption inside the book, which may be what Powers has in mind when, in the *Atlantic Online* interview, he describes Adie and Taimur's encounter as a

> metaphor for reading; that's what reading does. In the end, the book becomes an apology for the virtuality of fiction, fiction not as a replacement for the real world, but as a hybrid place where the real world is suspended and reconstituted into something more survivable. (Blume n.p.)

From a realistic perspective the dissolution of the self's boundaries in Taimur and Adie's strange encounter can be explained only as the result of madness, a dual schizophrenic meltdown; as a metaphor for the reading experience, however, the scene succeeds in more satisfyingly evocative ways. Reading, for Powers, is an intersubjective process in which the author and the reader, though separated by space and time, collaborate dialogically in a meaning-making exercise made possible by the technology of the book. The experience, moreover, is not a closed aesthetic loop, but spirals us back into the world, better able, in N. Katherine Hayles's formulation, to "fashion images of ourselves that accurately reflect the complex interplays that ultimately make the world one system" (290).[23] At the conclusion of *How We Became Posthuman*, Hayles discusses this dynamic as "distributed cognition." Hayles rejects any view of the autonomous self that

> authorizes the fear that if the boundaries are breached at all, there will be nothing to stop the self's complete dissolution. By contrast, when the human is seen as part of a distributed system, the full expression of human capability can be seen precisely to *depend* on the splice rather than being imperiled by it. (290)

Hayles's optimistic view of the posthuman (she, of course, is well aware of the more threatening views, which her book describes and qualifies) projects human subjectivity as "emerging from and integrated into a chaotic world rather than occupying a position of mastery and control removed from it" (291).

Similarly, if Powers agrees that the space in which we are abandoned, as Taimur realizes, may be "sketched," his novel cautions that we must resist mistaking the sketch for the place, which is always an act of appropriation, a power play. Just before his fall into the abyss, Taimur understands that what he had believed to be his love for Gwen was in actuality a colonizing desire to hold her hostage to his own projected needs: "Only now you see it, in this bombed-out emptiness, how all along your love coerced her, manipulated, failed to credit her hurt, to legitimate her confusion, simply by demanding that she live the one scenario of shared happiness you were able to imagine . . . " (*PD* 389). Expanding the interpersonal to a global scale, Powers includes references to numerous wars and conflicts that occur within the span of the two years Adie spends with TeraSys. Each of these conflicts, from the Tiananmen Square Massacre to the fall of the Berlin Wall to the first Gulf War, are struggles for the control of images, contests for "the realization of pure ideas with the help of technology" (Hantke n.p.) in the continuing human "war against matter" (*PD* 400). Adie builds into her final installation the realization that all wars, like "the first war," are "over pictures," Heideggerean battles of world views, "the showdown that imprisons you" (*PD* 409).

The epistemic shift at the end of *Plowing the Dark*—a culmination of several less intrusive perturbations scattered throughout the novel to this point—resonates on multiple levels, the epistemological, the political, and, of course, the aesthetic. Each of these dimensions figures in Powers's "apology for the virtuality of fiction," which *Plowing the Dark* enacts perhaps more than in any of his novels.[24] This aesthetic also informs Adie's final work of art, the Byzantine demo. Driven by the mysterious "visitation" under the virtual dome, Adie works paradoxically in shared isolation, "deep in covert conversation with a life just out of earshot" (*PD* 406). Although Adie disappears "into the place she was making" (*PD* 404), her total immersion is a subversion of the technoromantic desire to achieve "*total human equivalence in silicon*" by disappearing "*into our own machine space*" (*PD* 339). For Adie, by contrast, the "greatest value of the clumsy, inexorable, accreting digitization of creation lay in showing, for the first time, how infinitely beyond formulation the analog would always run" (*PD* 155). In an interventionist act, Adie uses the technology of virtual reality to undermine VR's technoromantic dream, just as Powers uses the codes of realism to problematize the adequacy of the mimetic relation to the real. Instead of the "romantic apocalyptic vision of a cybernetic rapture, in which the material world will be transcended by information" (Coyne 10-11), Adie immerses the demo buyers, the Joint Chiefs of Staff, in representationalism's coercive "defeat of matter" (*PD* 408), the stone by stone destruction of St. Sophia:

> You run back into the violated nave, where phantom crusaders and holy warriors now close for battle up and down the columned aisles. The great church goes pure theater. Grainy, mosaic footage plays against the paint-stripped tympana, digital clips from the earth's flaming islands, human chains, laser-guided night shots of bunkers erupting, walls shorn up and hammered back down again. (*PD* 409)

From the fiery ruins of the great cathedral, Rousseau's jungle begins to sprout, watched over by "a naked, couched Eve" (*PD* 409). But before the jungle can reclaim the ravaged structure, swarms of crudely drawn bees, "the work of a child with a new paint box" (*PD* 409), begin to restore the damaged portraits, patch the shattered mosaics, and rebuild the temple. These bees are of course fugitives from Crayon World, the pre-Adie TeraSys team's first, halting attempt at depiction. "But nothing here," Adie reflects about Crayon World, "looks much like what it stands for" (*PD* 19). The primitively drawn bees suggest the primal nature of the human drive to represent, which, Powers repeatedly suggests, evolved as a human survival strategy, a way to negotiate our way through the resistant world. As Karl remarks about Sargent's painting *El Jaleo*, which depicts a dancer against a backdrop of the ancient Altamira cave paintings, "The painting's not really about the dancer. It's about the first-ever proof that we have to paint. Paint like we clap our hands" (*PD* 133).

Bee imagery, which recurs throughout the novel, links the danger and the promise that technology and poetry share. The danger, as we have seen, is their common "dream of breaking the bounds of time and space, and the constraint of the body" (Blume n.p.). Their shared promise—imagination's antidote to its own danger—is to "refresh us to the irreducible complexity of the analog world, a complexity whose scale and heft we might always have underestimated, without the shortfall of its ghostly imitations" ("Being and Seeming" 17). Like so many of the novel's scenes and symbols, then, bee imagery points in two directions. On the one hand, it evokes "hive mind," Kevin Kelly's "techno-humanist version of the ancient notion of 'world soul,'" in which human beings "join together . . . in an ecstatic unity via a rhyzomelike cybernetic net" (Hillis 149). At first glance, "hive mind" may suggest mutuality, the epitome of distributed cognition. Looked at more critically, however, "hive mind" is revealed as a technoromantic fantasy of bodiless information exchange, digital communication dispersed among "disembodied selves gathered in a virtual room but situated anywhere around the globe" (Hillis 208). On the other hand, bee imagery evokes the honey-bees in Yeats's "The Stare's Nest at My Window," the sixth poem in the longer "Meditations in Time of Civil War" that O'Reilly and Spiegel emotionally recite in a bar (*PD* 333-34). The poem's refrain entreats the honeybees to "Come build in the empty house of the stare," which, within the context of the scene and the novel, implies the human tendency to continue making and remaking the place, even in the face of continuing destruction (*"Nothing ever works,"* Ebesen says near the novel's end. *"That's why we keep fixing it"* [*PD* 407]).[25] This suggestion of embodied cooperation within—and on behalf of—the material world contrasts not only with Kelly's sterile vision but with the desire for material transcendence in Yeats's "Sailing to Byzantium," which, as we have seen, exemplifies the dark side of the pretechnological dream that has informed the representing mind-set from the beginning.[26]

Adie's final art work demonstrates that she has moved beyond her earlier aestheticism and has achieved what Powers describes as a "healthy relationship between interiority and exteriority. . . . [O]ur symbolic life—which is, finally, a huge portion of where we live—is that domain where we can juggle the processes and the tribulations of the physical world, not to be done with them but to reenter" (Birkerts *Esquire*, 46). Apparently, Adie's edited virtual narrative has its desired impact, as the military buyers, "stricken with insight," leave the demonstration room with changed perspectives (*PD* 410). Adie, too, as we have seen, motivated by her newfound appreciation of the dialogic relationship between the real and the virtual, plunges into the world *"out there. . . . [,]* off through color's interface, into the negative space, between the single brushstroke, the vanishing point that the hand invents to fool the eye" (*PD* 406-407).

Plowing the Dark is a powerful critique of representationalism and the representing mind-set, whose persistent compulsion to reify our artifacts, to mistake them for a priori entities, has been exacerbated by the "hypersymbolic nature of the digital— the fact that its descriptions have that odd ability to rise up and walk" ("Being and Seeming" 17). The culmination of "centuries of greater realisms" (*PD* 134), VR threatens to impel further our fantasies of disembodiment and mastery, fantasies that in turn delay the achievement of distributed knowledge, which digital technology, properly implemented, can advance. Needless to say, Powers is no Luddite; indeed, his understanding of the hazards of digital technology is matched by his appreciation of that technology's potential benefits. In "Being and Seeming," he approvingly quotes Michael Heim's description of VR's optimal purpose:

> Cyberspace . . . should evoke the imagination, not repeat the world. . . . The final point of a virtual world is to dissolve the constraints of the anchored world so that we can lift anchor—not to drift aimlessly without point, but to explore anchorage in ever-new places and, perhaps, find our way back to experience the most primitive and powerful alternative embedded in the question . . . Why is there anything at all rather than nothing? ("Being and Seeming" 17; Heim 137).

Or, in Powers's elegantly condensed restatement: "The task of art is to estrange us from everything that seems given to us and to return us to a condition of brute astonishment" ("A Dialogue" n.p.). A celebration of the creative power of the human imagination and a jeremiad against its excesses, *Plowing the Dark* confirms Powers's place as one of our few indispensable literary talents.

NOTES

[1] Gibson observes that, although postmodern culture still "seeks to question and disentangle itself from representation," it has, "since the seventies . . . grown less wary of representationalism" (71). Gibson's contemporary examples of this development are drawn primarily from film, particularly the films of Godard. The novels he addresses are "classic narrative texts" such as *Under the Volcano* and *On the Road*, in which he finds numerous anti-mimetic elements that adumbrate postmodernist fiction.

[2] The "new book" exciting Spider Lim is probably Howard Rheingold's *Virtual Reality* (New York: Simon and Schuster, 1991), which argues that the first virtual realities were the painted caves of the Paleolithic age. The scene in which Lim describes the book to Adie and Spiegel occurs in 1989, two years before the publication of Rheingold's speculations, so Powers has taken poetic liberties with chronology to make his point.

[3] In the novel, Powers uses italics rather than quotation marks to indicate dialogue. References to novel hereafter cited as *PD*.

[4] "The hardware for implementing Platonically formalized knowledge took centuries. Underneath, though, runs an ontological continuity, connecting the Platonic knowledge of ideal forms to the information systems of the matrix. Both approaches to cognition first extend and then renounce the physical embodiment of knowledge. . . . Now, with the support of the electronic matrix, the [Platonic] dream can incorporate the smallest details of here-and-now-existence. With an electronic infrastructure, the dream of perfect FORMS becomes the dream of inFORMation" (Heim 88-89).

[5] Most of the major critiques of the claims for and implications of virtual reality focus on the issue of embodiment. See, e.g., Balsamo, Hillis, Markley, and, especially, Hayles.

[6] "The direct introduction of discursive material has been considered anathema for a long time," Powers told Jeffrey Williams: "I've been trying in different ways to violate that prohibition from my first book on. True, you can get more emotive power over your reader by dramatic revelation than by discursive narrative. But you can get more connection with discursive narrative! The real secret is to triangulate between these two modes, getting to places that neither technique could reach in isolation" (n.p.).

[7] According to Heim, Zeltzer's comparison subconsciously invokes "a Jungian archetype. . . . David Zeltzer was calling up a mythic image far more ancient and infinitely more profound that 'Star Trek' [in his comment, Zeltzer refers to the Holodeck]" (124). Heim goes on to discuss VR as an "art of the highest order" that, like Wagner's Bayreuth, promises "to redeem our awareness of reality" (123-25). Adie also warns that VR narratives resemble the totalizing aspirations of Bayreuth (*PD* 160).

[8] According to Heim, "At the computer interface, the spirit migrates from the body to a world of total representation" (101).

[9] Joseph Dewey provides a useful elucidation of the strategy of withdrawal employed by most of Powers's characters. See especially pages 79-81 (on Richard Kraft) and 111-13 (on Laura Bodey).

[10] Later in the novel, Ronan O'Reilly makes even more explicit the connection implied by Adie's retort. Yeats's "Byzantium fantasy" and Silicon Valley are *all the same project*," he says: "*The thing that's best in people, the thing that wants to be pure and whole and permanent, the thing that won't rest until it builds its eternal bird . . .* " (*PD* 335).

[11] Adie's resemblance to Gail Frank is, of course, another variation on the motif of simulations in the novel. Powers gives it a further crank at the end of Chapter 32, when Adie realizes that, on his wall, Karl has compiled a representation of her face out of photographs of Gail's face (*PD* 288).

[12] "When VR theorists attempt to describe the phenomenon of immersion in a virtual world," writes Marie-Laure Ryan, "the metaphor that imposes itself with the greatest insistence is the reading experience" (89).

[13] "The 'resurrection of the figurative,'" according to Gibson, "has emerged as a dominant feature of immediately contemporary culture. In [Gianni] Vattimo's terms, . . . postmodernity demonstrates its skepticism with regard to *Überwindung* or critical overcoming, its refusal to believe in its own capacity to progress definitively beyond post-Cartesian modernity. . . . Postmodern culture, then, remains deeply wedded to representation, even as it seeks to question and disentangle itself from representation" (71).

[14] "*The mind is the first virtual reality*," Spider Lim tells the other researchers. "*Its first speculations bootstrap all the rest . . .*" (*PD* 130).

[15] Powers told Sven Birkerts that he got the idea of having discursive portions of his first novel, *Three Farmers on Their Way to a Dance* (1985), comment on dramatized portions of that novel from having read Joyce's *Ulysses*: "[Joyce] told this absolutely dense realistic story (a compendium of a day in the life). But parallel to that was a frame completely contiguous to the first, and yet a kind of intellectual commentary on it. And so here were these two frames, and between the two, they straddled the great divide. Knowledge by incorporation; knowledge by exposition" ("An Interview" 60).

[16] The novel's fullest statement of the relationship between desire and representation, the complete passage reads: "Her worst fears about depiction were true. Evolution's most productive trick was to rig things so that the idea of need grew vastly more insatiable than the needs it represented. Feeling had nowhere near ample room in which to play itself out. Sex at best mocked what love wanted. The gut would explode before it could dent the smallest part of its bottomless hunger" (*PD* 227).

[17] "Desire," writes Coyne in his discussion of Lacan, "is at the intersection between the natural and the signifying, which are both 'infected' by it" (Coyne 228).

[18] Many early reviewers, working no doubt against deadlines, simply overlooked it. Others, like Steven Moore, who found the novel's ending "emotionally powerful," were constrained by book review conventions from revealing its details (6). In the longest critical examination of the novel to date, Joseph Dewey provides a detailed summary of Adie and Taimur's meeting—which he calls "the most luminous moment yet in Powers's fictions" (145)—but negligible analysis of the scene. "It is the work of the imagination—not the heart—to provide the comfort of connection" (147), he writes, but it isn't clear whose imagination—Adie and Taimur's, Powers's, the reader's—he has in mind. Steffen Hantke's expansive review, important because of its penetrating insights into the novel's political dimension, devotes a single, thought-provoking sentence to the scene, but offers no further elaboration.

[19] "Does Powers really believe we're headed toward an era where 'every soul in the world' will serve 'as every other soul's 24-hour server'?" Zalewski snidely asks. The passages Zalewski quotes describe Jonathan Freese's conception of "civilization's next leap," the "inevitable merge" of human beings and VR, which Freese believes is "just a few clock cycles away" (*PD* 404). For Freese, the merger of silicone and human beings represents the "machinic phylum . . . spinning itself out into another species" (*PD* 404), a view representative of the more radical projections of the "posthuman." See Hayles, 2-5.

[20] The phrase is Jonathan Culler's, see p. 193.

[21] Ontological disruption is of course a familiar feature of postmodernist fiction. But in both the reflexive fictions Brian McHale describes and the historiographic metafictions of Linda Hutcheon, naturalized literary conventions are inscribed and subverted *throughout* the text. Although perturbations exist throughout *Plowing*, Powers relies primarily on a single destabilizing gesture, which he postpones to the novel's very end. Although other novels by Powers conclude with sudden epistemic shifts—the conclusions of *Prisoner's Dilemma* (1988) and *The Gold Bug Variations*, for example, when we suddenly discover that the book we've been reading was written collaboratively by the characters we've been reading about—none is as disorienting as the ending of *Plowing the Dark*, in many ways his most overtly political novel. See McHale and Hutcheon.

[22] See Harris, 97-99.

[23] Hayles's formulation is not restricted to the reading experience, but extends to "the complex interactions with an environment that includes both human and nonhuman actors" (288).

[24] In his conversation with Birkerts, Powers offers a more elaborate statement of this "apology": "My apology for fiction has always taken the form of saying: When we live in real time, under the onslaught of the challenges of unmediated existence, we cannot solve all the problems that are thrown at us, the problems of the physical challenge of the world, the nature and needs of others, our own internal aggressions and animosities and ambivalences. Therefore, we remove ourselves into the space of symbolic transaction. And we do that with an eye toward solving in abstract those crises, getting a handle on them in the domain where time has been suspended. And then we reenter, more fully equipped, the world of reality" (*Esquire*, n.p.).

[25] "[W]e need to see that we're making this place," Powers told Birkerts. "By revealing the book as a made thing, a thing that can both the lived in and accepted as real, one that calls attention to itself as something invented, an author can make the reader reflectively aware of the degree to which his life too is both received and invented" (*Bomb* 63).

[26] A similar tension within the works of a single poet is implied earlier, when O'Reilly quotes lines from Book XI of Wordsworth's *The Prelude*, the Romantic poet's celebration of the French Revolution (*PD* 127). The passage concludes with the following lines: "Not in Utopia, subterranean fields/ Or some secreted island, Heaven knows where!/ But in the very world, which is the world/ Of all of us–the place where in the end/ We find our happiness, or not at all!" Wordsworth's emphasis on the material world contrasts markedly with his more transcendental poems, which often find the world too much with us.

WORKS CITED

"A Dialogue: Richard Powers and Bradford Morrow." *Conjunctions 34: American Fiction: States of the Arts* (Spring 2000). <http://www.conjunctions. com/ archives/c34-rp.htm>

Balsamo, Anne. *Technologies of the Gendered Body: Reading Cyborg Women*. Durham: Duke UP, 1996.

Birkerts, Sven. "An Interview with Richard Powers." *Bomb* Summer 1998: 59-63.

——. "The Esquire Conversation: Richard Powers and Sven Birkerts." *Esquire* July 2000: 46, 49. <http://www.esquire.com/needtoknow/books/000701-info-powers03.html>

Blume, Harvey. "Two Geeks on Their Way to Byzantium: An Interview with Richard Powers." *Atlantic Online* 28 June 2000. <http://www.theatlantic.com/unbound/ interviews/ba2000-06-28.htm>

Coyne, Richard. *Technoromanticism: Digital Narrative, Holism, and the Romance of the Real*. Cambridge: MIT P, 1999.

Culler, Jonathan. *Structuralist Poetics: Structuralism, Linguistics, and the Study of Literature*. Ithaca: Cornell UP, 1975.

Dewey, Joseph. *Understanding Richard Powers*. Columbia: U of South Carolina P, 2002.

Gibson, Andrew. *Towards a Postmodern Theory of Narrative*. Edinburgh: Edinburgh UP, 1996.

Grusin, Richard. "What Is an Electronic Author? Theory and Technological Fallacy." In Markley, 39-53.

Haraway, Donna. "Situated Knowledges: The Science Question in Feminism and the Privilege of Partial Perspective." In her *Simians, Cyborgs, and Women: the Reinvention of Nature*. New York: Routledge, 1991. 183-201. <http://www.hsph.harvard.edu/rt21/concepts/HARAWAY.html>

Harris, Charles B. "'The Stereo View': Politics and the Role of the Reader in *Gain*." *Review of Contempo-

rary Fiction 18.3 (Fall 1998): 97-108.

Hantke, Steffan. "Talking Back to the Owners of the World." *electronic book review* http://www.electronicbookreview.com/v3/servlet/ebr?command=view_essay&essay_id=hantkeint. Posted 1 Sept. 01, Modified 4 April 02.

Hayles, N. Katherine. *How We Became Posthuman: Virtual Bodies in Cybernetics, Literature, and Informatics.* Chicago: U of Chicago P, 1999.

Heidegger, Martin. "The Age of the World View." Trans. Marjorie Grene. *Boundary 2* 4.2 (1976): 341-355.

Heim, Michael. *The Metaphysics of Virtual Reality.* New York: Oxford UP, 1993.

Hillis, Ken. *Digital Sensations: Space, Identity, and Embodiment in Virtual Reality.* Minneapolis: U of Minnesota P, 1999.

Hutcheon, Linda. *A Poetics of Postmodernism: History, Theory, Fiction.* New York: Routledge, 1988.

de Lauretis, Teresa. *Alice Doesn't: Feminism, Semiotics, Cinema.* London: MacMillan, 1984.

Lanier, Jaron, and Frank Biocca. "An Insider's View of the Future of Virtual Reality." *Journal of Communications* 42.4 (1992): 150-72.

Markley, Robert, ed. *Virtual Realities and Their Discontents.* Baltimore: Johns Hopkins UP, 1996.

McHale, Brian. *Postmodernist Fiction.* New York: Methuen, 1987.

Moore, Steven. "Virtual Artistry." *Washington Post Book World* 4 June 2000: 6.

Nielson, Jim. "An Interview with Richard Powers." *Review of Contemporary Fiction* 18.3 (1998): 13-23.

Nochlin, Linda. *Realism* [1971]. London: Penguin, 1990.

Powers, Richard. *Three Farmers on Their Way to a Dance.* New York: Morrow, 1985.

——. *Plowing the Dark.* New York: Farrar, Straus, and Giroux, 2000.

——. "Being and Seeming: The Technology of Representation." *Context* No. 3 (2000): 15-17.

——. "Literary Devices." *Zoetrope* 6.4 (Winter 2002): 8-15.

Ragland-Sullivan, Ellie. *Jacques Lacan and the Philosophy of Psychoanalysis.* Urbana: U of Illinois P, 1986.

Rheingold, Howard. *Virtual Reality.* New York: Simon and Schuster, 1991.

Ryan, Marie-Laure. *Narrative as Virtual Reality: Immersion and Interactivity in Literature and Electronic Media.* Baltimore: Johns Hopkins UP, 2001.

Tabbi, Joseph. *Cognitive Fictions.* Minneapolis: U of Minnesota P, 2002.

Tortorello, Michael. "Richard Powers: Industrial Evolution." *Rain Taxi* (Summer 1998). <http://www.raintaxi.com/online/1998summer/powers.shtml>

Wilden, Anthony. "Lacan and the Discourse of the Other." In Jacques Lacan. *Speech and Language in Psychoanalysis.* Trans. with notes and commentary by Wilden. Baltimore: Johns Hopkins UP, 1968. 159-311.

Williams, Jeffrey. "The Last Generalist: An Interview with Richard Powers." *Cultural Logic* 2.2 (1999). http://www.eserver.org/clogic/2-2

Zalewski, Daniel. "Actual Reality." *New York Times Book Review* 18 June 2000: 12.

CURTIS WHITE
THE GREAT AMERICAN DISASTER MACHINE

> "Boy, we're sure going to have some train wrecks now."
> —Walt Disney, upon setting up the model
> train set that circled his house

In turning to a consideration of the technological imagination, I am suggesting not only that it is the real moving force in the political imagination; I am also suggesting that it is the moving force behind *all* expressions of the American imagination. The mass media is utterly and inescapably technologized and creates an appropriate reverence for technology in its products. Technology is the God that worships itself. Even the humanities now imagines itself through a dense, mechanical jargon that, if you could drop it, would go "clank." This is to say nothing of the resources that are being poured into the creation of distance education and the aura of the inevitability of what distance education theorist Mark Taylor calls "network culture."

In the arena of the technological, there is nothing impoverished about the American imagination. So powerful have the assumptions of national technophilia become that they have achieved the self-evidence of nature. Technology is our nature. The first socializing experiences for our children are now with televisions and computer games. They learn not only how to be members of a particular culture, they learn how to be human through machines. There is nothing innocent or innocuous about those bizarre schmoos that we call Teletubbies (I don't care if one of them is gay; they're a public menace.) In short, it is no longer the case that machines are an extension of our needs. We are extensions of the imperatives of machines. Virtual afterthoughts. Like domesticated dogs (who have over the eons evolved childlike facial expressions that prompt humans to care for them), humans have morphed in an obliging way to seem more efficient and capable, more machine-like, in the photoreceptive eyes of our machines, as if we feared being abandoned by them. It has reached a point where to be technophobic (or simply technically maladroit) is not to risk mere irrelevance or incompetence; it is to risk isolation. The community of man now sits at personalized consoles whether in office cubicles or in the living room. It is here that we have our famous global village. Our fateful paradox: to live in this community you have to be alone.

We can think of the technological imagination in at least two ways. First, it is the more innocent process of invention. This silicon chip, this electronic pulse, this synthetic diaphragm, this sensor, this vacuum tube, this gadget or gizmo that we've chanced upon, what can it do for us in what context? Can it amuse us? Feed us? Cure us? Propel us? Can it induce the feeling of religious ecstasy? Can it run an operation that used to require the employment of twenty tribal boys? Can it help us to fool our computers into thinking we're like them? This is the technological imagination as invention.

But this invention always happens in a context. Our context is in substantial part global corporations and militarism. In our culture at present, the technological imagination invents for that amorphous thing that we really know not at all, "the economy." But first it invents for the military.

The reason that the technological imagination has these particular masters has to do with a second form of the technological imagination that borders on the social imagination more broadly construed. Its problem is this: what stories shall we tell ourselves about the "good" of technology for our culture? This work of the imagination is hybrid. In part, it is about describing and justifying the "good," and in part it is about explaining, apologizing for, or condemning technology's relationship to that "good." The American imagination is not impoverished in this respect. Rather, it is feverish. It is as if we were in a slow-motion disaster dream and we wanted to bring just enough day-lit consciousness to the situation so that it could both make sense and stop. There is a certain species desperation in the invention of this narrative.

Even though scientists have the most to do with the technological imagination as invention, they generally feel very little responsibility to participate in the technological imagination as part of a larger social imagination. In other words, science makes little effort to create an idea of a human order in which their creations have a place and which can be argued for as "good" and desirable. As Helen Caldicott describes in her book *The New Nuclear Danger*, "Scientists have always operated in absolute secrecy, which gave them the anonymity they needed to preserve their work. They used a language that was incomprehensible to all but the most educated, and, like physicians, they hid behind an arcane scientific complexity, never emerging to inform the world what they were doing" (13). Thus has it ever been, I suppose.

A conversation we'd like to see (but won't):

"So, you've created a virulent new strain of anthrax that has been genetically designed to be resistant to antibiotics and which can be easily and broadly dispersed as a fine powder?"

"Yes, I have."

"And why was this a beneficial thing to do?"

"I worked for the United States Government here at Fort Detrick, and I was asked to do this by the United States Army."

"Yes, but in what way was this a good and desirable thing, to have this virulent strain of genetically manipulated anthrax as a possibility and now a threat in the human world?"

At this point the scientist reveals the essential poverty of his social imagination (never mind that his powers of scientific imagination are so fertile that he could splice anthrax into salmon and send them swimming up Puget Sound if Seattle were ever to step out of line again). He mumbles something about not being a philosopher, then something really lame about duty, love of country, and national defense. Meanwhile, his snowy death, fine as the powder that you'd spank your baby's butt with, has literally "blown back" on these shores. The anthrax that showed up in envelopes in the halls of Congress, post offices, and the junk mail of grannies in New England was our own genetic monster, the product of our own technological imagination. As part of a defense program, there are some obvious bugs in the product, but as a disaster machine, it hits on all cylinders, baby!

Nevertheless, science is not entirely free to do what it wants without the support of a rationale for its social good. They just need some help with making their case. For this, science has a variety of "explainers" who can translate the meaning and the importance of science's world and the technology that comes from it, and argue for it as a social good. This is done with customary dunce-like aptitude by our political representatives (using the motifs of profit, defense, and "progress"), and it is done in more subtle ways (for that part of the public which is literate enough to care) in books of popular science and—most effectively—on science programs on PBS, public TV. On programs provided by NOVA, Devillier Donegan Enterprises, and underwritten by the Alfred P. Sloan Foundation, media writers and producers help scientists to "make nice" to the rest of us non-scientists and create a case for the interest and desirability of their work. One recent program, which commands our attention at this point, was called *Beyond Human*, produced by Thomas Lucas in association with PBS and Devillier Donegan. It begins with the following narrative:

> A strange new era is dawning. An era of revolutionary experiments. Wired torsos. Chip implanted brains. Creatures of silicon and steel. Welcome to the age of cyborgs and androids. As humans become more machine-like, and machines more human, the line between biology and technology is starting to blur. And in the process we may just be reinventing the future of our species.
> In this age of advancing technology, we are becoming increasingly impatient with the bodies nature has given us. With our frailties, our failing sight, our broken limbs, the crippling limitations of illness. While our minds soar, our bodies seem frozen in time. What if we could build a better body? Use technology to fix this human form and then actually improve upon it, make it stronger, faster, smarter, create the human of the future today?

This, my friends, is the technological imagination as social imagination. It is hard at work, at last making itself responsible for accounting for the relationship of its work to the human world. Is this science? No. This is science fiction in the most literal sense. It is science's attempt to imagine its world. The power of its efforts will come not from hard evidence, its presentation of scientifically validated Truth, but from its rhetorical and narrative skills, both verbal and visual. But this little narrative is tense with assumptions and claims none of which can be demonstrated, all of which are contestable. This helps us to see that the role of science fiction as a literary genre has been not only to indulge in technophilia or futurology, but to provide what science never adequately provides on its own: a narrative account of its practices and a critique (in story form) of its assumptions. Kurt Vonnegut's early science fictions, especially *Player Piano* (in which Vonnegut questions the human good of universal automation), are models of the form. Unfortunately, the creators of *Beyond Human* are not artists with Vonnegut's critical eye.

Even a cursory examination of *Beyond Human*'s opening narrative would reveal at least the following issues and problems:

- What do they mean by an "era" or an "age"? "A strange new era is dawning": this is pure *Star Trek* stuff; it is the equivalent of a fiction writer's request for "willing suspension of disbelief"—that is, we neither believe nor disbelieve in the idea of "eras," but we'll put aside our skepticism so that the tale can proceed.

- "We"—just what or who is this "we" that the narration assumes? The fiction of a united humanity? Why is it legitimate to so blithely discount that half of the human population that does not benefit from Western technology? "We" are not one in our interests and needs. Another "willing suspension of disbelief" is required in order to proceed. "We"'" acquiesce; please proceed, yet again, Mr. Narrator.

- This "we" is said to be "impatient with the bodies nature has given us." In what sense are we "impatient," and what are we to make of the superficial assumption that something called "nature" has "given" us our bodies? Did we remember to say thank you?

- "Our minds soar." What evidence of this does the narrative present? Is the mind soaring in this narrative, or is it limping along on stale sci-fi contrivances and popular science (like the fiction that there's something called nature out there that gives us things); or can the mind be said to soar because of the evidence provided by the remarkable feats of technology? It is most likely the case (sez I) that it is the latter, which makes this argument a very rarified example of begging the question: to answer the question "Does the technological imagination serve us well?" we first assume that it is "soaring."

- "Our bodies are frozen in time"? What can this mean? Our bodies have failed to be as new and improved as the myriad devices the technological imagination has invented? The computing power of computers doubles its capacity every eighteen months, but what does the body have to show for itself? Same old bag of bones, same old mortal failure.

- "What if we could build a better body?" At last we come to the moment of full revelation; this is a fiction, *mon cher*; but it is also a proposition that the narration will need to find a way to argue: the proposition is that it is a good thing to supplement or replace the human body with machines.

We can move now to the body of this documentary argument. In the course of the next hour (part I, "Body Electric"),[1] we are presented with the following realities, in this order:

First, the human body supplemented by technology can be cured of diseases and disabilities. *Beyond Human* personalizes these possibilities by allowing us to meet some of these people, like a woman who was injured in a snow boarding accident in which her spinal cord was damaged, rendering her a paraplegic. Surgeons placed a small computer in her abdomen that sent signals to electrodes in her back and legs stimulating muscle movement. Through practice and therapy, she was able eventually to harness the artificially induced contractions into movement. Eventually, she was able to stand and move.

Second, computer technology can (and, according to this documentary, will) lead to chip implants in humans for monitoring health and providing Global Positioning (so we know where we are at every instant). This is already done with pets and children. Eventually we will all have a little personal database in this chip so that people outfitted with the appropriate scanners will be able to download our personal bios and read them on a tiny display on their sunglasses. So, we'll learn things about each other like: "Hi, my name is Mindy! I've been homeless for the last six months (since I lost my job with Our Skin, the synthetic skin company, and my contract for my Livingcubicle ™ home along with it), but my Web site is still up and running. I'd like to find a job in Glam-Bod Tech, in research, application, or even meat archiving. Please leave a message at gomindygirl@techlife.com if you know of a suitable position for me. Thanks for scanning my implant and thanks for caring!" To which Mr. Scanner responds by thinking, "Hoo boy, another loser. A meat archiver! Walk on by, brother, walk on by." Eventually, according to this narration, we will come to feel vulnerable if we are not constantly monitored and located. This is part of the benefit of living in the emerging "Nano Age" where we can "control nature at the atomic level." Or, from a very different perspective, as Marshall McLuhan put it, "The human person who thinks, works, or dreams himself into the role of a machine is as funny an object as the world provides" (100).

Beyond Human next argues that the United States Army is "beginning to embrace" our shared entry into this Nano Age.[2] We are obliged to ignore, once again, the fact that *Beyond Human* has reversed the cause-and-effect logic of the military's involvement. *Beyond Human* would have us believe that this Nano Age is an independent development of civilian science. But it was, of course, the military that drove the first development of the World Wide Web, and Department of Defense grants continue to fund much of the emerging primary research in digital technology.

For instance, the Associated Press reported on June 9, 2002, that the military is putting up $25 million of a $60 million primary research project to teach a computer common sense. A database named Cyc has been fed 1.4 million truths and generalities about daily life so it can automatically make assumptions humans make. They have even made the database accessible to the public so that the public can add to the mix whatever little nuggets of common sense it has. Never mind that no one anywhere has a clue what the term "common sense" means. A lot of things that pass for common sense are famously ideological, bigoted, or plain old meanly stupid. Perhaps the hope is that when our decision-making creations are racing along, deciding the future of the race, functioning beyond the realm of human negotiation, making split second decisions about whether or not that projectile is a nuclear warhead or India's new waste disposal program sending garbage into outer space, just perhaps it will pause and say, "The country of India would not attack the country of Us. We eat a lot of their Indian-style food. In addition, we have more and bigger bombs of the type nuclear. Therefore, India would be stupid to attack Us. But many of Us think people of the type East Indian are stupid. And if it is a bomb, many of Us think we don't want to look like a weenie." The computer searches its common sense archive a bit more, unsatisfied with its conclusions to this point, and comes up with this nugget of common wisdom, contributed by citizens in Idaho. "Guns don't kill, people do. Hit first, ask questions later. Make my day. Do you feel lucky, punk? Hasta la vista, baby. I love the smell of napalm. I'm not going to hit you. Like hell I'm not." This logic took a nano second to concoct. It all makes me yearn for Stanley Kubrick's HAL, the dysfunctional computer. We need more dysfunctional computers and machines of all kinds so that we never forget just how flawed and dangerous they are, and we never make the mistake of assuming that we've built "sense" into them.

In any event, to return to *Beyond Human's* doggedly optimistic and good natured narrative, our future wired soldiers will really be something. "The next generation infantryman is a cyborg soldier, a techno-warrior." Each soldier will be part of a wireless field Internet. Each soldier will be chip implanted. Plugged in. Ready to roll. "For the enemy of the future, death will be digital."

They make it sound so optimistic. Death for them. Toys for us. But I hope that none of our present enemies, imagining themselves as future enemies, watch PBS. A little line like that "your death will be digital" line could really hurt their feelings. Or piss them off. "Oh, my death will be digital, infidel? Well, here's what your death will be like." The imagined audience for these programs is really only upper-middle class North Americans, isn't it? No one else in the world watches TV. Right?

Next, we turn to commerce. "The revolution is being sold, hard." In the commercial world, the body is merely a platform for techno-fashion. Implanted data bases, monitors, and accessories are "this year's hot items for the fashion forward." Soon, we will be wearing the Internet like a necklace. One of the mavens of the new techno-fashion industry is Katrina Barillova of Charmed, Inc., a former Eastern European intelligence operative. The KGB is the Ralph Lauren of the 21st century. And yet, according to scifi writer David Brin, if we "cautiously embrace" these new personal technologies, we will be returned to "the old village our ancestors lived in."

Excuse me. I know I have pledged suspended disbelief to this narrative, and I'm trying to be a good sport about it, but incredulity asks for a moment in which to say its piece. Incredulity says, "What 'old village' are you referring to? And why do you imagine that the idea of returning there cozens anyone into accepting your future? Is this village of which you speak so fondly in the Carpathian mountains? Where are those mountains? In Carpathia? Is the village surrounded by rich forests and colorful songbirds? Is it like the cottage in *Snow White and the Seven Dwarves*? Or is it perchance in good old Missouri?

Will we be gathering around the cracker barrel to listen to the androids indulge their homespun humor and tales of yesteryear down at the general sim-store? Will we eat the crackers, or will they be made of silicon? Will we later meet down by the river? Will Reverend Automaton bless us and dunk us in the eternal waters of the Ether Domain? Will the fragrance of genetically modified apple pie drift from matrix to matrix causing a pang, a yearning, a hankering for the olden times when some of us had tatters of flesh attached to the hydraulics? And will we also have village idiots like in the old days? Because I have a few candidates for you."

Here's how this cant about the emerging interconnected Global Village of the future is functioning right now. According to an article by David Diamond in the June, 2002, issue of *Wired*, the Philippines presently exports 10% of its labor to other countries around the world, principally to the United States and Saudi Arabia, but to more than one hundred and fifty foreign countries in all. These workers send back over $6 billion dollars annually. To stay connected to their families, they also send back over one hundred million cell phone text messages each day. "I miss you; do your homework; send money." But even *Wired* can't help but notice that there is a down side.

> "The social costs of overseas work," says Rosalinda Baldoz of the government's labor registry, "are marital breakup and dropout children who get into drugs or crime. . . . " Aside from separating families, the overseas employment system is also rife with corruption. According to Baldoz, last year the POEA received 2,000 recruitment violations cases for such infractions as overcharging, sneaking workers out with faked visas, and sending them to jobs that never materialized. . . . Often a new contract, written in a foreign language, is forced on the employee once she's in hawk for her [recruitment] fees and far away from home.

In short, the primary problem with *Beyond Human*'s presentation of the Global Village is that it is utterly without a global political context. It is only about the privileged First World (minus its own disenfranchised poor). To Filipino workers, the New Global Village looks an awful lot like the old Boss in a Global Company Town. Another day older and deeper in debt. Exploitation. It's reassuring to know that some old values will remain with us in the Global Village of the future.

Think these are all Third World problems? In the August 4, 2002, edition of the *Chicago Tribune*, Walter F. Roche Jr. reported that McDonald's restaurant had recruited students from Poland to work in the United States with the claim that they would make "more money than you could imagine."

> But [Peter] Kasprzyk could not buy an item from the dollar menu with his first paycheck. It was zero.
>
> That's because he and four fellow students were docked for $2,000 monthly rent on a two bedroom apartment they share in Abingdon that normally goes for $750 a month. That deduction wiped out every cent Kasprezyk made flipping hamburgers for $8 an hour at a McDonald's outlet.

As with the Filipino workers, the Poles signed a contract in a language they didn't understand.[3]

In the second half of *Beyond Human*, "Living Machines," we are introduced to the next consequence of science's work in the relationship between humans and machines. Machines become more human:

> Imagine a day when machines walk among us. Expressing thoughts, emotions. Demanding their rights. Today, we are breeding intelligence, perhaps even life, into creatures of silicon and steel. A whole new breed of robots is on the rise. And the line between man and machine is starting to blur.

We begin, once again, with accounts of how robot creatures can save human lives: a machine that can rescue people from fires. They can also provide us with services like house cleaning and childcare. They can do the work (as they presently are in factories around the world) that humans don't want to do. And there's nothing exceptional, according to our program, about these new machines acting in the place of humans because for centuries humans have tried to reproduce themselves mechanically. We're just getting very good at it now.

The New Robotics produces creatures of real intelligence, which means they can not only be programmed, they can also gather experience, learn from it, and change their actions based upon what they've learned. Not only are they intelligent, they are also expressive. Tiny cameras in the eyes of the robots recognize human expressions and react accordingly. They can even blush. With these life-like 'bots "we can't help but be drawn in." Ultimately, the New Robotics may not create humans, but they will create "persons" with legal rights and a full capacity to interact with humans.

Here, folks, is a new discrimination, a distinction without a difference, between "humans" and "persons." Huh? I suspect we'll come to enjoy this distinction about as much as we have enjoyed the idea that corporations have legal standing as individuals and a constitutionally guaranteed right to a free speech that overwhelms any speech an actual human individual could utter.

"The day of the humanoid is coming soon." For the producers of *Beyond Human*, this is an inevitable and, in the absence of reasons to the contrary, probably a desirable destiny. The only negative imagined within this work is the Frankenstein scenario in which our robots go autonomous and turn on us, as in the *Terminator* movies. This is the action/adventure version of a scenario in which, through superior intelligence and adaptive capacities, the robots out-evolve us. But Hans Moravec, of Carnegie Mellon University's robotics program, is "not too bothered" by this possibility. Not to worry, he says, because the robots are like our children! "The robots will survive, and the robots are our offspring." I don't think he imagines that the use of the word "offspring" is loose or metaphoric; in fact, it is an interesting word choice, engaging the mechanics of springs as it does. Boing! "In the long run," he adds, "that's the way it's going to be anyway."

In the April, 2000, issue of *Wired*, Sun Microsystems founder Bill Joy echoes this sentiment in an article titled "Why the Future Doesn't Need Us." Joy gives the human race thirty years to come to terms with its own cybernetic creations. Or else.

There is an awful lot to say about the way *Beyond Human* renders our future. We could jump feet first into the ethico-religious middle of it, but that's what is expected of us. The scientists, technologists, and their many fetishists are well prepared for such a response and well insulated from its force. As far as they are concerned, such a response is just the whining from the clergy that they've been hearing since the mid-19th century. It's just religious fools in the way of scientific thought and progress. So, holding ethical fire for the moment, let us simply insist that a program such as *Beyond Human* is not a neutral, educational documentary on the subject of science in which the kind people at PBS help scientists to make nice to the rest of us. It is a narrative, a work of the social as well as the technological imagination, and it puts forward an argument, an argument that it is critical for us to understand before we respond. Abstracted from the flow of its documentary revelations, the argument in *Beyond Human* is what is called a "slippery slope" argument. Here is the implicit question, even though it is never directly posed: is crossing the human/machine boundary a good or bad thing?

The answer they provide to their own implicit question is, "Well, is it wrong to use machines to help people in medical need? If a machine can help a blind person to see, is that a bad thing? And is it bad if the machine happens to be inside the person? Or inside the brain?"

The obliging viewer responds, "I see where you're coming from. All right. That's good enough for me."

Then the next step: "If it's not bad to implant devices to help the ill or disabled, there are other reasons, perhaps, for allowing the same thing? Would you agree?"

Obliging viewer: "Sure."

"And would you agree that it is important that our young fighting soldiers have every advantage to defeat the enemy and defend us and our precious liberties? After all, if nothing sacrosanct has been compromised in placing computer chips inside the disabled, why is it wrong to put them in soldiers? If we don't and the soldier is wounded, we might then have to put the device on after the fact, as a therapeutic, as we've already argued. But why wait until it's too late and the damage is done?"

"Wow. That's a really good point. Okay, implants and lasers and gadgets of every kind inside and outside our fighting men and women. I don't need disabled war vets on my conscience."

"And just what is it that our soldiers fight for? Our freedom? Our free enterprise system. Would you deny our culture the right to prosperity? If the economy is now dependent on technology and information, shouldn't we let it flow where it must, even if that means we're a little more machine-like, and the machines look a little more like Darwinian competition? You may be nervous about the ethical implications, but that's just one perspective. Americans love their technologies. Cars, TVs, games, stereos, they're all part of the fun and profit of being in this time in this place. You have no choice but to allow it. Why not relax and enjoy?"

"Gosh. You're probably right. I am a little uptight. If we're just going to shackle the economy with these unreasonable and antique ethical demands, what's the point of having our soldiers out there at all? Once again, they're off fighting for us, and we're back here undermining them. I'm really sorry. I completely concede."

And on we go by patient degrees until the obliging and maybe a little naïve viewer arrives at a position he never would have assented to if it were trotted out in the beginning.

"We made the machines. They are products of our minds. They are human in the sense that they're dependent on humans for the very possibility of their existence. Don't waste any tears over our demise if we're inferior to our own creations. The machines are simply the next evolutionary step for our own species. If they are us, in what sense are we extinct?"

"That's so incredibly profound. That is really deep. I think I love this vision, man."
"Wonderful. Here's a little present. It's a Nintendo NBA game. We've programmed a simulacrum of you into the game. In this game you can jump a full six inches higher than Michael Jordan can. In fact, you'll be replacing him in the starting lineup of the 1998 Chicago Bulls."

"Awesome!"

"We'll go one better than that. We're going to program a feed loop of you sinking the winning shot of game seven of the NBA Championship and load it into the mainframe aboard this space craft which is taking all of the androids off to distant parts of the universe where their version of humanity will live on forever. You'll be sinking that shot into eternity."

"Can't ask for more than that!"

NOTES

[1] Can't you feel that most mortal and elemental and fully embodied of poets, Walt Whitman, turning in his cold nineteenth century grave? Whitman was happy about electric lights! Not robots taking over our bodies!

[2] What in the world is going on here? First, Bob Davis tells us that the military "cherishes" technology, now we're being told that they "embrace" it. What's next? It's horrible to consider. Perhaps we'll be told that technology gets military guys horny. Not to worry. It's just that old odd couple, eros and mechanical death.

[3] In a short program on the growth of the new capitalist economy in Romania, presented on PBS's *Frontline*, week of October 28, 2002, Andrei Codrescu revealed that one source of new capital for Romania is the training and exporting of young girls to Japan to serve as geishas. According to the Romanian entrepreneur in charge of this export business, the girls are all patriotic and will return to Romania to invest in their country. Without doubt, they too will take cell phones with them for the purposes of keeping in touch with mom and dad. It's all part of the great new information economy working among virtual states. A world without borders. Unlimited possibility. One has to wonder what Charles Dickens would have made of it all. Great expectations. Bleak house, indeed.

WORKS CITED

Caldicott, Helen. *The New Nuclear Mind.* New York: New Press, 2002.
McLuhan, Marshall. *The Mechanical Bride.* New York: Vanguard, 1951.

II

THE TECHNOLOGY IN/OF CONTEMPORARY AMERICAN FICTION

Brian McHale
Mech/Shaper, or, Varieties of Prosthetic Fiction:
Mathews, Sorrentino, Acker, and Others

Here is one version of the future: by the end of the twenty-second century, humankind will have diversified into two posthuman factions, scattered throughout a plethora of orbiting space-colonies. One faction, the Mechanists or Mechs, will supplement human capacities mechanically through implants and prostheses; the other faction, the Shapers, will achieve the same ends by means of bio-engineering, through cloning, gene-splicing, and the like. The two posthuman subspecies will compete for dominance, sometimes violently, in a perennial civil war "of the coin's two halves" (Maddox 324).

If this sounds like science fiction, it is. This version of the future derives from the cyberpunk novelist Bruce Sterling, who developed it in a cycle of five short stories and the novel *Schismatrix*, all dating from 1982-85.[1] Why should we take Sterling's version of the future seriously? For no reason at all: Sterling is no more credible or reliable in his predictions of the future than any other science fiction writer, and science fiction writers (their pretensions to the contrary notwithstanding) are no better at predicting the future than anyone else. (Where are the laptop and hand-held computers in all of those science fictions set at the beginning of the twenty-first century? Where is the Internet?) As we have realized for some time, science fiction is not really about the future at all, and its futurism is a faux-futurism, a form of displaced presentism—the present viewed otherwise.[2] As a means of reflecting on present reality, however, it possesses a distinct advantage over most so-called "realist" fiction, which rarely succeeds in capturing the present, but only recycles elements of the past as these have been codified in the current repertoire of the so-called "realist" style.

Science fiction's presentism enables it to reflect not only on the present condition of the "real world," but also on the poetics of fiction, poetics today, again in a way that is normally forbidden to "realism." Such metafictional reflection is facilitated by the fact that many science fictions incorporate within their fictional worlds one or more secondary or inset worlds, scale-models *en abyme* of the fictional worlds that contain them: microworlds, such as the orbiting space-colonies of Sterling's *Schismatrix*, or virtual realities such as the cyberspace of Gibson's *Neuromancer* trilogy and other cyberpunk fictions, or alternative realities and paraspaces of various kinds such as the Perky Pat Layouts of Philip K. Dick's *The Three Stigmata of Palmer Eldritch*. Such science-fictions-within-the-science-fiction enable these novels to reflect on world-making itself, and gives them a mirror in which to examine various elements of the poetics of fiction. Thus science fiction often introduces technological motifs that literalize narratological categories and figures.[3] It even reflects on writing itself—writing as technique—principally by means of the motif of prosthesis, such as we find in Sterling's *Schismatrix*.

Prosthesis is a recurrent motif in science-fiction,[4] and it is often deployed in ways that permit or invite its interpretation as a figure for technology in general, and for writing in particular. For instance, N. Katherine Hayles calls our attention to the way that Bernard Wolfe, in his dystopian science fiction novel *Limbo* (1952), associates prosthesis with writing by means of a pun. "Pros," in Wolfe's grotesque world, are those who have undergone voluntary amputation and prosthetization, but of course they are only a silent *e* away from "prose" (Hayles, 126-27). Hayles connects Wolfe's metafictional pun with David Wills's Derridean account, in *Prosthesis* (1995), of writing's prosthetic character.[5] Writing's logic, according to Wills, is precisely that of the Derridean supplement, which is also that of prosthesis. Like the prosthetic limbs of Wolfe's Limbo, writing simultaneously extends a human capability—speech, in this case—and replaces it. This is self-evident in the many writing machines that humankind has developed over the centuries, from the printing press to the typewriter to the word-processor; but after all, such machines only literalize and instrumentalize the technique of writing itself. Writing itself is the fundamental writing machine, and so fundamentally prosthetic. If a human being typing at a computer keyboard constitutes a cyborg fusion of human and machine, in the sense of Scott Bukatman's "terminal identity," then so does every writer, whatever writing technology he or she might be using, including pencil and paper (or stylus and clay tablet, for that matter).

Let's reconsider, in this light, the prosthetized posthumanity of Bruce Sterling's Mech/Shaper cycle. Are there grounds for interpreting Sterling's posthuman types as figures for the practice of writing? There are indeed grounds for doing so, abundant grounds, in the short text that serves as a coda to the whole cycle, "Twenty Evocations" (1985). A sort of *Bildungsroman* cast in the form of one of J.G. Ballard's "condensed novels," "Twenty Evocations" narrates (or rather evokes) in disjunct, telegraphic fashion the life-story of one particular long-lived Shaper, Nikolai Leng. The twenty brief numbered episodes are conspicuously artificial, conspicuously "written":

3. A MALFUNCTIONING LEG. There came a day when Nikolai saw his first Mechanist. The man was a diplomat and commercial agent, stationed by his faction in Nikolai's habitat. Nikolai and some children from his crèche were playing in the corridor when the diplomat stalked by. One of the Mechanist's legs was malfunctioning, and it went click-whirr, click-whirr. Nikolai's friend Alex mimicked the man's limp. Suddenly the man turned on them, his plastic eyes dilating. "Gene-lines," the Mechanist snarled. "I can buy you, grow you, sell you, cut you into bits. Your screams: my music" (313)

Moreover, after the fifth such episode, and every five thereafter, there appears an out-of-sequence paragraph in which verbal materials from the preceding five sections are reshuffled and recombined, perhaps at random, as in Burroughs' cut-up and fold-in techniques:

. . . A Mechanist pirate, malfunctioning, betraying gene-lines. Invisible listening devices buy, grow, and sell you. The abandoned stations' ambitious young Shaper, killed during the attack. Falling psychotechs produced by sexual means the desiccated body of a commercial agent. The holographic interface's loyalty was suspect. The cybernetic system helped him strip the valuables off his plastic eyes. . . . (314; ellipses are Sterling's)

Episode three, it will be observed, contributes to this word collage or re-mix the word "malfunctioning," the phrases "buy, grow, and sell" and "commercial agent," and the detail of "his plastic eyes." Perhaps it also reflects on the very process by which this paragraph was produced: "I can . . . cut you into bits." Whatever the specific means of its production, this passage appears to be the product of some artificial writing practice (but then again, what writing practice *isn't* artificial?); it appears to be the output of some writing machine (but then again, *all* writing is a writing machine). It exemplifies writing as prosthesis, in a text in which prosthesis itself also figures as a motif, an item of represented technology. Here writing as prosthesis mirrors the motif of prosthetic technology, and vice versa.

This, then, is the topic of my paper: not so much technology *in* recent American fiction (though that will figure here, too), but rather the technology *of* recent American fiction: fiction as technology, writing as machine. Most writing in fiction seeks to efface its status as technique, as technology, for good reasons;[6] but some writing does the opposite, seeking to foreground and flaunt its technological status by adopting *extra* artificiality, *extra* technique. This "extra" mirrors and amplifies the technological status of writing as such. The cut-ups that interrupt Sterling's "Twenty Evocations" at intervals of five episodes are one example of this "extra" that constitutes what I propose to call "prosthetic fiction."

Prosthetic fiction abounds in turn-of-the-millennium America. Preliminary to giving any systematic account of it, we need to develop some kind of typology of its varieties, and to do so I propose to adapt Sterling's typology of schismatic posthumanity. The Mech vs. Shaper distinction might seem unpromising, based as it is on an all-too-binary opposition, implying a whole series of other dubious binaries: inorganic vs. organic, external vs. internal, hard vs. soft, masculine vs. feminine. Nevertheless, Sterling's Mech/Shaper typology has the advantage of being animated, even more so than other science fiction, by a relationship of reversibility between the figure of writing and its literalization—between prosthesis as writing and writing as prosthesis. Faux-futurism, as I will try to demonstrate, can serve a heuristic function with respect to poetics today.

I. Mech Fiction

If the Mech subspecies of Sterling's imagined posthumanity were transposed into a writing practice, what would the latter look like? Presumably, if it were transposed into poetry, it would look like the kind of poetry that is generated "mechanically," where the selection of materials, or their arrangement, or both is driven by predetermined rules or constraints—the kind of poetry, practiced by many postmodernist poets, that Joseph Conte has taught us to call "procedural" (38-44, 167-266).[7] By analogy, then, the Mech equivalent in narrative fiction would be "procedural fiction."

Let's begin with an obvious example: an actual collaboration between a human author and a writing machine—a literal cyborg. In Raymond Federman's short novel *The Voice in the Closet* (1979), the machine in question is an IBM Selectric typewriter—a technology rendered obsolete by digital word-processing, which doesn't, however, make this any less of a cyborg situation. Federman "mechanized" his writing practice here by observing certain rigid formal-compositional constraints—a fixed number of lines (18) per page, a fixed number of characters (68 including spaces) per line—all shaped by the spacing characteristics of the Selectric he used to produce the text. The writing machine submits to the author's will, but the author also surrenders part of his control to the machine's built-in constraints, as well as to the "artificial" constraints he has placed upon his own writing practice. Exaggerating slightly, but only slightly, we might say that the author of *The Voice in the Closet* is not Federman, exactly, but a hybrid "Federmachine."[8]

Actual machine collaboration such as we find in *The Voice in the Closet* is not always involved where it might be most expected, for instance in hypertext fictions, which (at least in the case of first-generation hyperfictions such as Michael Joyce's *Afternoon* or Stuart Moulthrop's *Victory Garden*) are typically machine-*mediated* but not machine-*generated*. Conversely, true machine collaboration sometimes occurs in situations where it might not be anticipated. For instance, James Merrill's long narrative poem or novel-in-verse, *The Changing Light at Sandover* (1976-82), is collaborative in two respects: on the one hand, the poet collaborated in its composition with his lifelong companion, David Jackson; on the other, the form that collaboration took was manipulation of a Ouija-board, so that the collaboration actually involved three parties—two human authors and a simple alphabet-machine.[9]

Typically, however, proceduralism involves not actual machines but virtual ones—software rather than hardware. Much more typical than the Federmachine or Merrill's Ouija-board collaborations are the many Mech fictions produced by "paper machines"—predetermined schemes for generating texts, procedural algorithms. These are the sorts of machines favored by the Parisian OuLiPo circle, the *Ouvroir de Littérature Potentielle*, including its American member, Harry Mathews. An exemplary virtual machine in the Oulipian mode is "Mathews's Algorithm."[10]

The input to this machine is verbal "found" material of any kind: words, lines of verse, sentences, episodes. This input material is analyzed into its component elements, the elements arranged in grids, and the gridded elements shifted relative to each other. After one or more such shifts, fresh outputs are read off the grid, permutations of the original input materials. In one example, Mathews begins with four opening lines from Shakespeare sonnets—

Shall I compare thee to a summer's day?
Music to hear, why hear'st thou music sadly?
That time of year thou mayst in me behold
Farewell! thou art too dear for my possessing—

which he then reduces to component words, arranging the latter in a grid and shifting their positions to produce the openings of four undiscovered Shakespearean sonnets:

The music of the years, too dear for me . . .
The summer's music sadly thou beholdest . . .
Today thou may'st in me hear the farewell . . .
Possessing thee, why doth my Time compare . . . (130)

Here Mathews's algorithm functions as a poem-machine, but to adapt it to function as a novel-machine all that would be required is the substitution of narrative moves for lines of verse, so that the machine yielded story permutations instead of pseudo-Shakespeare. Indeed, Mathews seems to have used his algorithm, or some procedure similar to it, to generate the abrupt, unforeseeable, disorienting, and therefore life-like plot-shifts of his Oulipian novel of manners, *Cigarettes* (1987).[11]

Since details of the procedure used to produce *Cigarettes* appear to be irrecoverable, let's consider a shorter and more transparent Mathews text, "The Broadcast," from his volume of collected stories, *The Human Country* (2002). I have reprinted the text in Appendix One, highlighting a series of recurrent key-words: *routine, doodle, broadcast, sock, trumpet, describe*. Their repetition arouses our readerly suspicion that their appearance must be controlled by some kind of predetermined pattern, but if so, what pattern? It is, of course, the familiar pattern of end-words in a traditional sestina.[12] Instead of dictating end-words, here the fixed sestina formula determines the order of key words distributed throughout the story's prose paragraphs. The paragraphs do not, it should be noted, correspond to sestina stanzas. The story even boasts a sestina-like *envoi*, in which all six words recur in close proximity:

. . . I mean my own **routine**. The supervisors all **doodle**. The janitor watches one TV **broadcast** after another. I look at my **sock** and pretend it's a golden **trumpet** too glorious to **describe**.[13]

Like all procedural fictions, Mathews's "prose sestinas" involve the interaction of constraint and freedom. The "machine" —the algorithm, the procedure—dictates the ordering of key words, for which the author then supplies ad lib a narrative context; the author narrativizes the outputs of the machine. Or to put it differently, prose sestinas and similar procedures literalize the "mechanistic" poetics of Russian Formalism. According to Formalist poetics, formal devices are primary, while the illusion of representation is strictly secondary and after-the-fact. The operation of the device (here the sestina procedure) generates verbal products which must then be motivated or naturalized, and this motivation in turn produces, as a kind of retrofit or back-for-mation, the entire panoply of narrative illusion, including plot, fictional world, char-acters, themes, etc. Thus, in Shklovsky's famous (or infamous) analysis, "The Making of Don Quixote," Quixote's character functions to motivate a particular juxtaposition of genres and discourses, rather than the other way around, the juxtaposed genres and discourses serving to illuminate Quixote's character (72-100). Whether or not this account actually applies across the board to literature of any kind whatsoever, as Shk-lovsky and his colleagues tended to assume, it certainly applies to procedural or Mech fiction such as Mathews's.

Other examples of Mech-type proceduralism, on a larger scale than "The Broadcast," include Walter Abish's novel *Alphabetical Africa* (1974), Gilbert Sorrentino's *A Pack of Lies* trilogy (1985-89), and Mathews's own *The Journalist* (1994). *Alphabetical Africa* is based (as its title suggests) on an alphabetical procedure. Its first chapter admits only words beginning with letter *a*; its second chapter, *a-* and *b-* words; its third, *a-*, *b-* and *c-* words, and so on, until the twenty-sixth chapter, where words with any initial let-ter are admitted. Then the entire procedure reverses itself, shedding words chapter by chapter until the last chapter, where once again only *a-* words are admissible.

In Sorrentino's trilogy of *Odd Number* (1985), *Rose Theatre* (1987), and *Misterioso* (1989), each volume employs a different procedure. *Odd Number* is based on interroga-tion. Questions are asked by an unidentified interrogator of three different unidenti-fied informants; the same questions are posed in the second part as in the first, but in reverse order, while different questions are asked in the third part. *Rose Theatre* is based on a catalogue procedure; it revisits and revises the information elicited in *Odd Number*. *Misterioso* is a "proper" sequel to the preceding volumes, in the sense of resum-ing the same characters' stories at a later point in time; procedurally, it is based on an alphabetization system akin to that of *Alphabetical Africa*. [14]

Mathews's *The Journalist* purports to be a journal in which the unnamed journal-keep-er becomes progressively more obsessed with capturing every detail of his everyday life, inventing ever more exhaustive systems of notation until he reaches a crisis and breaks down. While not fully procedural in structure, traces of local procedures can be de-tected throughout the novel. Moreover, its initial situation was apparently dictated by a formula derived from Mathews's fellow-Oulipian Raymond Queneau: "X mistakes y for z," *e.g.*, husband mistakes wife for mother; father mistakes son for friend; and so on. The plot works itself out from this point. [15]

Typically, longer proceduralist fictions, such as those named in the preceding para-graphs, signal that they are the products of some generative mechanism by insetting one or more proceduralist practices *en abyme*—in other words, by incorporating scale-models of their own procedures, or of proceduralism in general. For instance, in

Mathews's *The Journalist*, the journal-keeper watches on tv an episode of a "period soap-opera" set in eighteenth-century France, and becomes preoccupied with calculating all the possible future ramifications of the plot (183-84, 187-88). On other occasions, he works out all the permutations of rotating the tires on his car, and all the ways of cooking an omelet based on recipes from several different cookbooks (35-36, 56-58). Here proceduralist fiction intriguingly converges with science fiction. Its inset procedural practices function analogously to the prosthetic motif of science fiction, each mirroring *en abyme*, in the interior of its fictional world, the practice of writing itself.

II. Shaper Fiction

The Shapers, it will be recalled, are the bio-engineered faction of Sterling's posthumans. So if Mech fiction involves application of mechanical procedures, then Shaper fiction involves the writerly equivalent of cloning and gene-splicing. Transposed into writing practice, Shaper poetics entails operating on a pre-existing text, one's own or someone else's, cutting it apart and recombining its elements, or rewriting or overwriting it to produce a text that is somehow the same but different.[16] When Sterling himself cuts "Twenty Evocations" into bits and recombines it in the scrambled passages that interrupt the narrative after every fifth episode, he is applying a Shaper writing practice. The exemplary precursor here is of course William Burroughs, who first introduced the practice of wholesale cutting-up and folding-in in his "Nova trilogy" of the 1960's (*The Soft Machine* [1961, 1966], *The Ticket That Exploded* [1962], *Nova Express* [1964]).[17] For instance, in the section of *Nova Express* entitled "This Horrible Case," Burroughs begins with a text excerpted (or "appropriated," as we would later learn to say) from Kafka's *The Trial* and subjects it first to the fold-in technique, then to tape-recorder manipulation to produce ever more disjunct recombinations—mutant Kafka.

No-one has made Shaper technologies of splicing and cloning a more integral part of her poetics of writing than Kathy Acker. For instance, in rewriting passages from William Gibson's cyberpunk novel *Neuromancer* (1984) in her own novel *Empire of the Senseless* (1988**)**, Acker applies two distinct writing procedures. In one passage, she appropriates verbatim characteristic phrases or sentences from Gibson's text (*e.g.*, "A transparent cast ran from her knee to a few millimeters below her crotch," "A pulsing red cursor crept through the outline of a doorway," "Pink waves of warmth lapped up her thighs"), and recontextualizes them in her own text, changing them only slightly but radically skewing their meaning nevertheless. We might call this procedure "sampling," as in music production, or *détournement*, in the Situationists' sense. In another passage, Acker preserves Gibson's narrative intact, but rewrites his prose, transposing his stylish sentences into her own register of deliberately "bad," incompetent writing—an anti-style, style's antithesis. We might call this procedure "defacement," or even "vandalism": the malicious wrecking or ruining of stylish prose.[18]

Acker samples and rewrites Gibson's text; Gibson in turn samples and rewrites others' texts when, collaborating with Bruce Sterling, he co-authors the alternative-history novel, *The Difference Engine* (1991). Set in a version of the nineteenth century that never actually happened, but that *could* have, if only Charles Babbage had succeeded in building his steam-powered computer in the 1840's, *The Difference Engine* draws heavily on actual Victorian writing. According to Gibson himself,

> a great deal of the intimate texture of this book derives from the fact that it's an enormous collage of little pieces of forgotten Victorian material which we lifted from Victorian journalism, from Victorian pulp fiction. . . . Virtually all of the interior descriptions, the descriptions of furnishings, are simply descriptive sections lifted from Victorian literature. Then we worked it, we sort of air-brushed it with the word-processor. . . .

Sterling, Gibson's co-author, corroborates: "You can get quite extraordinary effects from using a piece of Victorian text verbatim and then deliberately forgetting where you got it and rewriting it four or five times . . ." (Frishchlin 8-9).[19]

Gibson's and Sterling's methods, like Acker's, are complex and self-consciously impure, involving "airbrushing" as well as sampling. "Pure" forms of sampling or cloning are hard to find, but one example might be Walter Abish's *99: The New Meaning* (1990), a collection of short sampled texts. Abish says of these works that they were "not actually 'written' but orchestrated" (9), and one understands what he means by this; nevertheless, viewed in the light of a prosthetic theory of writing, the texts in *99* appear to be quintessentially "written." Not a sentence in these five short texts is "original" with Abish; all are "ready-mades," appropriated from some literary source, including novels, memoirs and autobiographies, letters and journals, biographies and criticism. "What Else," for instance, is sampled from fifty different "self-portraits, journals, diaries, and collected letters," composing among them "a European pseudo-autobiography," where the continuity of "I" from passage to passage is entirely illusory (9). "Skin Deep" derives in part from Flaubert's writings about his sexual tourism in Tunisia, in part from material relevant in various ways to the Flaubert extracts (including materials by, *e.g.,* Barthes and Robbe-Grillet). "Reading Kafka in German" is composed of 99 segments by, about, or somehow related to Kafka, culled mainly from German-language writers; and so on.

Abish's "pure" sampled texts are brief. Burroughs's and Acker's clones and splices are local and circumscribed, and do not attain the scale of a complete cloned novel. Even Gibson's and Sterling's cloning practice, to the degree that one can reconstruct it on the evidence of their own testimony, bears mainly on descriptive set-pieces, it appears. The only example I can cite to date of a full-scale cloned novel is Matthew Roberson's *1998.6* (2002), a wall-to-wall rewrite of (as its title suggests) Ronald Sukenick's metafictional novel, *98.6* (1975). Roberson almost, but not quite, does for Sukenick's novel what, according to Borges, Pierre Menard did for *Don Quixote*: he almost repeats the novel verbatim.[20] *Almost*—for in fact, he repeats it with a difference, updating it, shifting its autobiographical situations to correspond more closely to his own, and adding a further level of metafictional self-reflection, since the novel's protagonist, called "Matt" (just as Sukenick's protagonist was called "Ron"), is writing a dissertation about *98.6*. Roberson "covers" *98.6* in the music-industry sense, or "remakes" it in the Hollywood sense, something in the manner of Gus van Sant's perverse shot-by-shot remake of Hitchcock's *Psycho*. An art-world analogue would be Sherrie Levine's re-photographing of famous high-art photographs. Matt the author writes of Matt the character,

> he makes the most of what's at hand latches onto small things pulls them together mixes them up. Turns twists renovates. . . . Everything he sees he can surf sample manipulate. He's a recycling machine. . . . (16)

Roberson, as "recycling machine," applies all of Acker's procedures, and others as well. Sometimes he incorporates material verbatim from Sukenick's text; elsewhere he models characters, situations, themes, etc. on Sukenick's, but without directly appropriating his language. Throughout he updates Sukenick's milieu and material culture. For instance, in the first section, called (in both novels) "Frankenstein," where Sukenick samples from print media, Roberson samples instead from the Internet. In the second section, "Children of Frankenstein," Sukenick's counter-cultural commune becomes, in Roberson's remake, a house shared by a group of graduate students in which a Web-cam has been installed. In Sukenick's commune, characters change their names as the spirit moves them; in Roberson's, names are changed on the communal Web-page in order to preserve anonymity; and so on.

I reproduce in Appendix Two two passages from *1998.6,* juxtaposed with their "originals" from *98.6*. In the first pair of passages, Sukenick writes of "spend[ing] the whole day watching for whales," while Roberson writes of watching simulacral whales on cable tv and video-tape. The experience evoked in the Sukenick passage is first-hand, even when it evokes the *failure* of anything to happen ("the no whale feeling"), while Roberson's experience is second-hand and mediated ("simulation feeling" which "comes from dealing with copies in the absence of originals"). Roberson interpolates several sentences in which he reflects on his second-hand obsession with Sukenick's whale obsession. "The spouts are gigantic ejaculations," Sukenick writes, "of course he knows it's just breathing but it's a special breathing" (25), and so on. Roberson recasts this in the conditional mode: "the spouts if he could really see them would be giant ejaculations," and so on (50-51, my highlighting).

In the second pair of passages, from the last pages of both books, Roberson substitutes his own geographical situation ("along the western shore of Lake Michigan") for Sukenick's ("on the side of San Francisco Bay"), and interpolates his tv viewing: "I'm watching some tube," "I'm watching cartoons on tv," "on comes Gilligan's Island," and so on. Sukenick incorporates a piece of "found" text—liner notes from a Jesse Fuller album (set in capital letters). Roberson quotes this material verbatim, but negates it ("IT'S NOT JESSE LONE CAT FULLER" etc.), then proposes Bugs Bunny as an alternative ("IT'S ACTUALLY BUGS BUNNY" etc.). Instead of opening "this morning's mail," Roberson "connect[s] to the internet I've got e-mails." Instead of thinking about an article by Ihab Hassan, as Sukenick does, Roberson thinks about Sukenick himself. Where Sukenick enters "The State of Israel," with a pun on "is-real," Roberson enters "The State of Televisrael." Finally, Sukenick closes with phrases reminiscent of Beckett: "playing the blues letting it go **it is as it is**. Another failure." Roberson finishes almost identically, yet with a difference so subtle one wonders whether it is intentional or merely an oversight: "having my doubts letting it go **as it is**. Another failure."[21]

Shapers, in the world of Sterling's Mech/Shaper cycle, are often afflicted by existential anxiety, suffering a sort of perpetual identity crisis—which is only to be expected when, as is sometimes the case, the Shapers in question are members of a large clan of identical cloned siblings. Roberson's novel seems to be similarly afflicted with a sense of its own contingency, and more than that, of its own *unlikeliness*. "I wouldn't have thought it could be done," Sukenick himself writes in a blurb from the jacket of Roberson's book. Cloned books, like cloned individuals, seem to exist subjunctively, in a mode of "as-if," under erasure.

III. Prosthetic Typology

Typology has its limitations, and the one I have proposed here is no different from other typologies in that respect. Leaving aside for a moment the limitations of typologizing in general, the present typology obviously suffers from a paucity of categories: two are simply too few. Even Sterling's Mech/Shaper cycle, despite its Manichean logic, is able in its later phases to accommodate new posthuman types, identified by wildly evocative names, alongside the original two: Spectral Intelligents, Lobsters, Blood Bathers, Carnivores, Coronaspherics—even Angels (Sterling 215, 232). Moreover, long before the end of Sterling's cycle, Mechs and Shapers have begun to cross-pollinate and converge. My categories are similarly "leaky," though this is more likely to be viewed as a defect than a strength. Mech procedures can use pre-existing texts, after all, and Shaper splicing and cloning involves procedures, even (as in Roberson's *1998.6*) recycling machines.

An example of such convergence, on a small scale, is the title story from Abish's *99: The New Meaning,* which combines proceduralism with sampling. Here Abish samples from 99 different texts, applying a simple procedure: each sample comes from page 99 of the text. On a much larger scale, Sorrentino's procedural fictions are simultaneously machines and rewrites or clones, but what they rewrite is Sorrentino's own previous fiction (Mackey 84-85). Thus, *Crystal Vision* (1981), procedurally based on the tarot pack (like Calvino's *Castle of Cross Destinies*), rewrites Sorrentino's early novel *Steelwork*, while *Blue Pastoral* (1983) rewrites *The Sky Changes* (1966). The *Pack of Lies* trilogy rewrites *Imaginative Qualities of Actual Things* (1971) together with *Mulligan Stew* (1979).

Simultaneously Shaper and Mech, the latter half of Sorrentino's oeuvre folds back over it first half, rehandling its own materials through the application of procedural devices.

Finally, however, it is not the present typology, defective though it may be, that requires defense so much as the typologizing enterprise in general. It is a truth universally acknowledged (isn't it?) that typology is by definition an inferior form of critical exercise, strictly preliminary and ancillary to the "higher" forms of commentary and interpretation — "merely" taxonomic. To defend against charges of "mere" taxonomy, one would have to demonstrate what the typology in question had brought to light that might otherwise have passed unnoticed, undervalued, or misconstrued. Here at the end, then, it is incumbent on me to specify some of the insights that the present typology enables or facilitates.

(1) As everyone surely recognizes, prosthetic fiction *estranges*, in the classic modernist sense. It estranges, first of all, the written product: proceduralism and sampling compel writers to write differently than they "naturally," "spontaneously" would, forcing them to generate verbal forms and to summon up states of affairs that neither they nor anyone else could have anticipated. Harry Mathews is representative here; in an interview with John Ashbery, he says that in procedural works "you're forced to do things that you wouldn't do otherwise, and this brings a great deal of freshness to them" (42). Prosthetic writing also estranges the *process* of writing; it reminds us that all writing is a technology exterior to and different from ourselves, and that even when we feel it most intimately "our own," this is partly illusory: writing is always other than ourselves. In the estranging light of cloned and mechanical composition, all language-use comes to look like a cyborg phenomenon—a human being coupled to a writing-machine.

(2) Estrangement as a motive for prosthetic fiction applies everywhere, at all times. Is there nothing about prosthetic fiction that suits it especially to our own place and time, the American cultural sphere at the turn of the millennium—nothing that makes it peculiarly contemporary? There is; first of all, we see in prosthetic writing a reflection, on a miniature scale, of the cyborg condition of collaboration or even symbiosis with machines that we all seem to be approaching—the condition of terminal identity (Bukatman) or posthumanity (Hayles). Prosthetic fiction thus affords us valuable thought experiments, vicarious experiences of what are likely to become our real-world arrangements in the near future.

(3) If this prospect is unsettling and alienating, even dystopian, prosthetic fiction also has the capacity to provoke utopian hopes. It seems to model a kind of collective or even "global" consciousness, distributed across multiple individuals. Sometimes this distributed consciousness involves humans and machines (*e.g.*, the Federmachine). Sometimes it involves human minds and mind-like texts, as in the virtual collaboration of Sukenick with Roberson in *1998.6*, or the real, if electronically mediated, collaboration of Gibson and Sterling in the production of *The Difference Engine*.[22] Such collaborative, distributed work is perhaps anticipated by the literal face-to-face collaborations

that produced such works as Merrill's Ouija-board text, *The Changing Light at Sandover* (mentioned earlier), or *Naked Lunch*, where Burroughs surrendered editorial control to his friends Ginsberg, Kerouac, and Allen Ansen (perhaps anticipating his later cut-up collaborations with Kafka, Eliot, Shakespeare, and himself), or even *The Waste Land* or *Lyrical Ballads*.[23]

(4) This utopian dimension of prosthetic fiction constitutes a real, not a faux, futurism. It returns us to those "other" futurisms, not the faux-futurisms of science fiction (valuable as these may be for certain purposes), but the utopian futurisms of what Marjorie Perloff has called the "futurist moment" of the first avant-gardes (*Futurist*). In a more recent book, revealingly titled *21ˢᵗ-Century Modernisms*, Perloff suggests that the relevance of the early-twentieth-century avant-gardes has been renewed at the turn of the millennium, that the time of the utopian avant-gardes has returned. Maybe so; certainly the varieties of prosthetic fiction as practiced in the run-up to the millennium do seem to return us to those first avant-gardes of the early twentieth century: to the proceduralism of Raymond Roussel, godfather of all machine fiction; to the literary gene-splicing of Tristan Tzara, who instructed us how to reach into a hat to draw out the cut-up fragments of the great Dadaist poem. If prosthetic fiction were a literary movement (which it isn't), its slogan would be, "Back to the future!"

Harry Mathews
The Broadcast

The problem with many of our lives is that they're so often **routine**: we're busy with this and that, and then in our free time we just **doodle** inconsequentialities. But last night I happened to listen to a radio **broadcast** that explained how you could put everything you needed in life into one **sock**. I don't know why, but this suddenly brought me to life like the sound of a **trumpet**. I know the concept was lunatic, I know I'd be hard put to **describe** why I was tickled, thrilled, and convinced all at once. Let me **describe** as best as I can what this man told us.

You carefully check your daily **routine** and notice what you use out of habit and not need – obviously the angel-**trumpet** blossoms in your backyard that you stop and look at so fondly, or the **doodle**-bugs that you approve of chasing ants at their roots do not belong in that **sock**, neither does (any more) the newspaper where you read about the **broadcast** in the first place.

(You did check it to see if there were plans to repeat the **broadcast** since you hadn't recorded it and there were things that I found difficult to **describe** to myself after it was over-perhaps I could write the station about the **sock** program's availability, for them things like that must be pretty **routine**, all those guys and their secretaries sitting around with nothing to do but **doodle** on their memo pads and pass each other notes, like "You really need an ear-**trumpet**, you've asked me to repeat myself the last three times we spoke, even though I **trumpet** what I say loud and dear," obviously it's not the office staff that created that **broadcast**, some genius, my God I've already forgotten his name, no it was Preston **Doodle**, although I can't remember if he wrote it or was just there to **describe** the project, I don't think so though, his voice wasn't pro, more like **routine**, with just that touch of weirdness that would think of putting your life in a **sock**.)

It has just occurred to me that what I heard as "into one **sock**" was actually "into one stock." Maybe I'm the one who needs an ear-**trumpet**.

Jesus that would mean that everything that electrified me was only **routine** advice and I was a victim of my own wish fulfillment listening to that **broadcast**. I'm afraid that at this moment my feelings are becoming too painful to **describe**, it's as though a cruel God had taken a Q-tip and started to **doodle** inside my ear, inside my brain, inside my soul, the **doodle** of despair which I guess is all my life is worth – not worth sticking in a **sock** even. Still, maybe I can do something with the idea, maybe **describe** it to some friends as if it were a game we could play. Or I could take up the **trumpet** and get to be so hot on it I'd end up making records and get **broadcast** myself, yeah, why not.

Meanwhile, it's not so bad in here, sometimes the **routine** gets screwed up – I mean my own **routine**. The supervisors all **doodle**. The janitor watches one TV **broadcast** after another. I look at my **sock** and pretend it's a golden **trumpet** too glorious to **describe**.

Appendix Two

FROM *98.6* BY RONALD SUKENICK

12/17 spends the whole day watching for whales. None come. He feels dry and constipated if you know that feeling it's what he likes to call the no whale feeling. It's like fishing all day and not catching a thing not even getting a bite. Angst held static by angst. He has this thing with whales here on the extreme western edge of Frankenstein the whales come by every year. He feels a special relation with them that he can tell when they're going to appear then he waits at some lookout with his binoculars it is a kind of fishing a kind of psychic fishing. The spouts are gigantic ejaculations of course he knows it's just breathing but it's special breathing the exhalations of the largest living animals at fifteen minute intervals is not just ordinary breathing it's more like victory rockets shooting up from floating football fields orgasms in celebration of life by bulk life. He thinks of the eerie ecstasy of whale songs calm throbbing poignant that's the kind of song he wants to compose he's starting a new career he wants to be a songwriter but he's stuck. He wants to write lyrics without words that presents a tough problem for a songwriter because as he knows we live in words words are the water we swim in he wants to move to the subverbs is the way he puts it and he can't even move his vowels. See it's hard. He even, forgets why he wants to do this he thinks it might have something to do with heightening that word seems to have the right ring to it. Or intensifying. Somehow he feels if he can do it it will make it all worthwhile make what all worthwhile he doesn't know. He can't remember. He has these slogans he repeats like Everyone wants to turn his life into a poem. Or a movie. Or a novel. But they don't mean anything.

FROM *1998.6* BY MATTHEW ROBERSON

6/19 spends the whole day watching whales on The Nature Channel then on a tape of The Nature Channel and then on a whale video he ordered special who knows when in his Melville phase. He's obsessing has obsessed at least a little over whales because Melville did and that was interesting. And in his books Ron's got a thing for whales there's got to be something to whales then if they both dwell on them he wants to know what that is he wants to get the whale thing. He hasn't gotten it yet in fact watching whales makes him a little anxious wondering why he can't develop his own interests. His are always someone else's first does that make them any less interesting. Maybe it makes them more his working through other people's ideas obsessions gives them an extra dimension. Maybe this is an excuse. Does an obsession with other people's obsessions count as a legitimate obsession he doesn't know the whales look tiny on the screen one color. He feels dry and constipated if you know that feeling it's what he likes to call simulation feeling. Simulation feeling comes from dealing with copies in the absence of originals. Sometimes copies are all we have he figures you make do with what you have. Maybe it would be different if he could reach over the edge of a dinghy off the coast of California lay his hands on the rubbery rough back of a sperm or a blue or even if at just Sea World he could once stroke the smooth snout of a Killer. Unmediated physical sensation he finds his swollen cock in his hand. He puts it away. But he can't put away the whales they're locked into his imagination always in the back of his mind. He wants to feel a special relation to them they seem that unique the spouts if he could really see them would be giant ejaculations of course he knows it's just breathing but it's special breathing the exhalation of the largest living animals at fifteen minute intervals is not just ordinary breathing it's like victory rockets shooting up from floating football fields orgasms in celebration of life by bulk life. He has an audio tape of the eerie ecstasy of whale songs calm throbbing poignant that's the kind of song he wants to sing composing it as he goes a new career on the street corner. Chanting for passersby. He can't sing he's got a terrible voice. But he wants to speak at least or write because he knows we live in intel in words or pictures made from words. It's the water in which we swim. He needs to get at something different disorienting a nonsense of things that's not not but non.

From *98.6* by Ronald Sukenick

Thank you Mrs. Meir. Walkin with ma baby on thee side of San Francisco Bay I'm listening to the blues I'm about to have A Moment of Luminous Coincidence I feel it coming on it's coming together ESSE LONE CAT FULLER JESSES EARLY LIFE WAS SPENT RAMBLING BETWEEN GEORGIA TEXAS AND CALIFORNIA WHERE HE EVENTUALLY SETTLED ALONG THE WAY HE LEARNED SPIRITUALS BLUES RAGS AND HILLBILLY SONGS HE ADAPTED THEM ALL TO HIS TWELVE STRING GUITAR STYLE BUT IT WAS NOT UNTIL 1950 THAT HE DECIDED TO SEEK OUT WORK AS A MUSICIAN HE ENCOUNTERED TROUBLE FINDING RELIABLE SIDE MEN SO HE BECAME A ONE MAN BAND playing all the instruments AT THE SAME TIME I'm sitting in Laguna Beach with the cat on my lap listening to The San Francisco Blues by Lone Cat Fuller AT THE SAME TIME trying to finish my novel AT THE SAME TIME trying to forget about it I pick and open a book at random Fuller Buckminster quotes Fuller Margaret all attempts to construct a national literature must end in abortions like the monster of Frankenstein things with forms but soulless and therefore revolting we cannot have expression till there is something to be expressed AT THE SAME TIME trying to forget about it a trip a bar in a distant city turns out to be called Frankenstein franks and steins AT THE SAME TIME this morning's mail with an article by Ihab Hassan on Prometheus Frankenstein Orpheus AT THE SAME TIME thinking when you try to sew Orpheus back together what you get is Frankenstein AT THE SAME TIME hearing on the radio Lon Chaney just died a few miles away from here in San Clemente AT THE SAME TIME reading this record jacket thinking yes ramble around settle in California pick up this and that adapt it to your style without sidemen the novelist is a one man band playing all the instruments AT THE SAME TIME playing along on a kazoo AT THE SAME TIME moving to San Francisco AT THE SAME TIME entering The State of Israel AT THE SAME TIME orchestrating the whole thing toward those Moments of Luminous Coincidence when everything comes together AT THE SAME TIME AT THE SAME TIME sorry to leave Southern California the sun the waves the mother tongue another bungled paradise AT THE SAME TIME happy to be heading for San Francisco another chance AT THE SAME TIME tying up my novel A T THE SAME TIME my life is unravelling AT THE SAME TIME the novel is bungled fragments stitched together AT THE SAME TIME everything is seamless perfect not because because but AT THE SAME TIME playing the blues letting it go it is as it is. Another failure.

FROM *1998.6* BY MATTHEW ROBERSON

. . . . I'm walkin with ma baby along the western shore of Lake Michigan I'm watching some tube I'm about to have a moment of Luminous Coincidence. I feel it coming on it's coming together IT'S NOT JESSE LONE CAT FULLER WHO SPENT HIS THIS LIFE RAMBLING BETWEEN GEORGIA TEXAS AND CALIFORNIA WHERE HE EVENTUALLY SETTLED WHO ALONG THE WAY LEARNED SPIRITU-ALS BLUES RAGS AND HILLBILLY SONGS HEADFTEDTHE MALL TO HIS TWELVE STRING GUITAR STYLE BUT IT WAS NOT UNTIL 1950 THAT HE DECIDED TO SEEK OUT WORK AS A MUSICIAN HE ENCOUNTERED TROU-BLE FINDING RELIABLE SIDE MEN SO HE BECAME A ONE MAN BAND play-ing all the instruments AT THE SAME TIME IT'S ACTUALLY BUGS BUNNY HE'S THE CULTURAL ICON OF MY TIME AND I MEAN NO DISFRESFECT BUT IT'S BUGS I SEE WHEN I SEE ANYONE AS A ONE MAN BAND OOMPHING A LONG WITH BANJO TROMBONE DRUM ETCETERA HE'S MY GENER-ATIONS JESSE LONE CAT THE IDEAS THE SAME THERE HE IS A FLOPPY EARED HERO playing all the instruments AT THE SAME TIME I'm sitting in Mil-waukee in my living room I'm watching cartoons on tv AT THE SAME TIME trying to finish my novel AT THE SAME TIME trying to forget it but on comes Gilligan's Island AT THE SAME TIME connecting to the internet I've got e-mails from writers contributing to my book on Ronald Sukenick AT THE SAME TIME thinking about the fact that Sukenick is a Mosaic Man a stitched bundle of fragments AT THE SAME TIME worrying that there's no difference between Frankenstein and a mosaic they're both stitched bundles of fragments AT THE SAME TIME not worrying they can be all at once the same and very different beasts and I realize anyway that neither of them is the be all end all I wouldn't want them to be AT THE SAME TIME I'm thinking about dinner on Thursday with Cam and Lynn my family away from my family AT THE SAME TIME moving to Atlanta AT THE SAME TIME sorry to leave Milwaukee AT THE SAME TIME AT THE SAME TIME thinking about my friend Gareth who's been ill he's had surgery he's told another friend that since he doesn't have hair to cover the scars on his head he looks like Frankenstein AT THE SAME TIME saying out loud the words Gods and Monsters wondering about the role of sexuality in The State of Televisrael AT THE SAME TIME entering into The State of Televisrael AT THE SAME TIME orchestrating the whole thing toward those Moments of Luminous Coincidence when everything comes together AT THE SAME TIME printing out a chunk of this book for my writing group AT THE SAME TIME tying the damn thing up AT THE SAME TIME happy to be heading to Atlanta another chance AT THE SAME TIME my life is unraveling AT THE SAME TIME this novel is bungled fragments of bungled fragments stitched together AT THE SAME TIME everything is seamless perfect not because because because but AT THE SAME TIME having my doubts letting it go as it is. Another failure.

NOTES

[1] The entire Mech/Shaper cycle is now reprinted in Sterling, *Schismatrix Plus*.

[2] A classic, if tendentious, statement of science fiction's presentism is Fredric Jameson's *Postmodernism, or, The Cultural Logic of Late Capitalism* (Durham: Duke UP, 1991), where cyberpunk in particular is denounced for having lost its future orientation and "turn[ed] into mere 'realism' and an outright representation of the present" (286; see also pp. 38, 321, 352). Confirmation of Jameson's view is to be found in the cyberpunk novelist William Gibson's latest novel, *Pattern Recognition* (New York: Putnam's, 2003), set in the immediate present and faithfully "realistic."

[3] For instance, time-travel narratives (e.g., Vonnegut's *Slaughterhouse-Five*) literalize the displacement of the *syuzhet* relative to the *fabula*; the simstim motif of *Neuromancer* literalizes shift of point-of-view (see McHale, *Constructing Postmodernism,* 234); a technological device in Michael Swanwick's recent time-travel narrative *Bones of the Earth* (2002) literalizes narratorial omniscience; etc. The specific design of these technological devices tells us much about the narratological categories they are meant to capture, and suggests a heuristic use for science fiction in the field of narratology that has yet to be explored.

[4] Recall the way Gully Foyle has himself rewired in Bester's *The Stars My Destination* to replicate the speed and fighting-skills of prosthetically enhanced Martian commandos; or the three prosthetic "stigmata" of Palmer Eldritch in Dick's novel by that name; or the prosthetic motifs throughout John Varley's short fiction; or Molly's notorious mirror-shades and retractable blades in *Neuromancer*.

[5] For a more detailed discussion, see McHale, "Poetry as Prosthesis."

[6] Some of these reasons are cogently discussed by Tabbi.

[7] See also McHale, "Poetry as Prosthesis."

[8] Moreover, *The Voice in the Closet* had originally been designed to function as part of another Federman novel, *The Twofold Vibration* (1982), but had been excluded (amputated?) at the publisher's insistence. Thus *The Voice in the Closet* perfectly models the Derridean logic of prosthesis: it is simultaneously the limb or organ missing from *The Twofold Vibration*-its "phantom limb"-and the prosthetic device that supplements it. For further details, see McHale, "Poetry as Prosthesis," pp. 8-10.

[9] Indeed, the collaboration might be said to have involved many more parties than that, depending upon whether or not one credits Merrill's and Jackson's claim that the messages spelled out on the board were really dictated by spirits and angels. For further details, see McHale, *The Obligation Toward the Difficult Whole*.

[10] See Conte, "American Oulipo: Proceduralism in the Novels of Gilbert Sorrentino, Harry Mathews, and John Barth," in his *Design and Debris,* 75-111; also McHale, "Poetry as Prosthesis," 6-8.

[11] In an entry in the *Oulipo Compendium*, compiled by Mathews and Alastair Brotchie, *Cigarettes* is described as Mathews's only "purely Oulipian novel": "Its method of composition has not been revealed beyond a statement that it is based on a 'permutation of situations'" (126). See Conte, *Design*, 98.

[12] A traditional sestina comprises six six-line stanzas and a final three-line *envoy*. The same six end-words recur in every stanza, in a fixed pattern. If the six end-words of the first stanza are ordered *ABCDEF*, then the second stanza runs *FAEBDC*; the third, *CFDABE*; the fourth, *ECBFAD;* the fifth, *DEACFB*; and the sixth, *BDFECA*. The *envoy* contains one of these end-words in the middle of each line and one at the end, in the pattern *BE, DC, FA*. The reader is invited to test this pattern against the recurrences in "The Broadcast." It will be observed that Mathews uses a different order in his *envoy*.

[13] *The Human Country* features at least two other "prose sestinas," "Mr. Smathers" and "Brendan." Joseph Tabbi was the first to notice the sestina form of "Mr. Smathers"; see his *Cognitive Fictions*, 131.

[14] For details, see Mackey and Conte, *Design*, 87-97.

[15] See the entries in *Oulipo Compendium* for *The Journalist* (161) and *X mistakes y for z* (245-6). For further

details, see Conte, *Design*, 97-103, and Tabbi, *Cognitive Fictions*, 131-6.

[16] Obviously, the analogies with cloning and gene-splicing are inexact, and I am using bio-engineering concepts freely and irresponsibly here. Moreover, there are obvious areas of overlap between what I am calling Shaper writing practices and Mech practices. Nevertheless, the heuristic value of this typology compensates for any weaknesses in its analogies or leakiness in its categories, or so it seems to me.

[17] Hayles (211-21) discusses *The Ticket That Exploded* in connection with Burroughs's experiments with the then-cutting-edge technology of tape-recording.

[18] For details, see McHale, *Constructing Postmodernism*, 233-5, 239-42.

[19] I am grateful to Joseph Conte for calling my attention to this interview.

[20] On the copyright page, the Library of Congress Cataloging-in-Publication Data for *1998.6* actually describes it as "A rewriting of Ronald Sukenick's novel 98.6"—what could be plainer?

[21] Sukenick, 187-8; Roberson, 260-1; my highlighting.

[22] According to the co-authors, their collaboration took the form of "swapping floppies" back and forth; Fischlin, Hollinger and Taylor, 8.

[23] So striking is this pattern of collaboration in the production of epoch-making texts such as the ones just mentioned, that one begins to wonder whether all literary revolutions might not originate this way, in some form of distributed consciousness.

WORKS CITED

Abish, Walter. *99: The New Meaning*. Providence RI: Burning Deck, 1990.

Ashbery, John. "John Ashbery Interviewing Harry Mathews." *Review of Contemporary Fiction* 7.3 (1987). <http://www.centerforbookculture.org/interviews/interview_mathews_ash.html>

Bukatman, Scott. *Terminal Identity: The Virtual Subject in Postmodern Science Fiction*. Durham: Duke UP, 1993.

Conte, Joseph. *Unending Design: The Forms of Postmodern Poetry*. Ithaca: Cornell UP, 1991.

——. *Design and Debris: A Chaotics of Postmodern American Fiction*. Tuscaloosa: U of Alabama P, 2002.

Fischlin, Daniel, Veronica Hollinger, and Andrew Taylor. "'The Charisma Leak': A Conversation with William Gibson and Bruce Sterling." *Science-Fiction Studies* 19.1(1992): 1-16

Gibson, William. *Pattern Recognition*. New York: Putnam's, 2003.

Hayles, N. Katherine. *How We Became Posthuman: Virtual Bodies in Cybernetics, Literature, and Informatics*. Chicago: U of Chicago P, 1999.

Jameson, Fredric. *Postmodernism, or, The Cultural Logic of Late Capitalism*. Durham: Duke UP, 1991.

Mackey, Louis. *Fact, Fiction and Representation: Four Novels by Gilbert Sorrentino*. Columbia SC: Camden House, 1997.

Maddox, Tom. "The Wars of the Coin's Two Halves: Bruce Sterling's Mechanist/Shaper Narratives." *Storming the Reality Studio: A Casebook of Cyberpunk and Postmodern Science Fiction*. Ed. Larry McCaffery. Durham: Duke UP, 1991. 324-30.

Mathews, Harry. "Mathews's Algorithm." *Oulipo: A Primer of Potential Literature*. Ed. and Trans. Warren F. Motte Jr. Lincoln: U of Nebraska P, 1986. 126-139.

——. *The Journalist*. Normal IL: Dalkey Archive, 1994.

—— and Alastair Brotchie, eds. *Oulipo Compendium*. London: Atlas Press, 1998.

McHale, Brian. *Constructing Postmodernism*. London: Routledge, 1992.

——. "Poetry as Prosthesis" *Poetics Today* 21.1 (2000): 1-32.

——. *The Obligation Toward the Difficult Whole: Postmodernist Long Poems*. Tuscaloosa: U of Alabama P, forthcoming.

Perloff, Majorie. *The Futurist Moment: Avant-Garde, Avant Guerre, and the Language of Rupture*. Chicago: U of Chicago P, 1986.

——. *21ˢᵗ-Century Modernism: The "New" Poetries*. Oxford: Blackwell, 2002.

Roberson, Matthew. *1998.6*. Normal and Tallahassee: FC2, 2002.

Shklovsky, Viktor. *Theory of Prose*. Trans. Benjamin Sher Normal: Dalkey Archive, 1990.

Sterling, Bruce. *Schismatrix Plus*. New York: Ace, 1996.

Sukenick, Ronald. *98.6*. New York: Fiction Collective, 1975.

Tabbi, Joseph. *Cognitive Fictions*. Minneapolis: U of Minnesota P, 2002.

——. "Matter into Imagination: The Cognitive Realism of Gilbert Sorrentino's *Imaginative Qualities of Actual Things*." Unpublished essay, 2003.

Wills, David. *Prosthesis*. Stanford: Stanford UP, 1995.

MICHAEL BÉRUBÉ
RACE AND MODERNITY IN COLSON WHITEHEAD'S
The Intuitionist

Colson Whitehead's debut novel, *The Intuitionist* (1999), is a wry postmodern *noir* in the by-now-familiar mode of Thomas Pynchon, Don DeLillo, and Paul Auster; an oblique meditation on the Great Northern Migration, that well-worn trope of the narrative of the African-American experience of modernity;[1] a look back at the fitful integration of African-Americans into the nation's municipal civil service agencies and transportation industries; and, most obviously, a tongue-in-cheek reworking of the discourse of racial "uplift." Shrewdly and wittily proposing elevators—and, just as importantly, elevator inspection—as the indices of modernity, the novel offers a cognitive map of the politics of race and space in the urban United States, as well as an idiosyncratic version of the African-American "passing" narrative. And as if all this weren't enough for a first novel, Whitehead frames the novel's major ideological conflict—which, in Pynchonian fashion, turns out to mask the deeper, more elusive machinations of corporate industry—as an allegory of debates over professionalization and the production of specialized forms of knowledge in the past half-century. The better part of this essay will content itself with showing that *The Intuitionist* does in fact do all these things, and does them in the manner of a less manic *Mumbo Jumbo*, skirting the edge of preposterousness while crafting yet one more elaboration on what Linda Hutcheon has called "historiographic metafiction." And then when the essay has fully contented itself on this front, I'll suggest in closing that there's a curious undercurrent in the novel, a kind of muted echo of much older narratives (such as Charles Chesnutt's) in which the representation of race is confounded and compounded by the representation of disability.

The plot of Whitehead's novel is convoluted, structured by the plots that swirl around our innocent and nearly friendless protagonist—a young woman who, in the attempt to discover who or what is after her, becomes something of an amateur detective and eventually learns that "a man she never met willed her into his death" (230). The woman's name is not Oedipa Maas but rather Lila Mae Watson; and she is not a bored Southern California housewife but rather the first black female elevator inspector in the history of the city (the city itself resembles New York but is never named, for reasons I'll discuss below). She arrived in the city three years before the novel opens, having graduated from the Institute for Vertical Transport, "the most prestigious elevator inspecting school in the country" (44), where she had lived in a janitor's room above the gymnasium because the school "did not have living space for colored students" (43). Indeed, Lila Mae was as alone at school as she is in the city, because "the admission of colored students to the Institute for Vertical Transport was staggered to prevent overlap and any possible fulminations or insurrections that might arise from that overlap" (44).

While at school, Lila Mae became an avid devotee of a controversial new method of elevator inspection, Intuitionism, which is founded on the two volumes of James Fulton's
landmark *Theoretical Elevators* and involves Zen-like exercises such as seeing the elevator from the elevator's point of view and separating the elevator from elevatorness, the
better to pursue the objective of "communicating with the elevator on a nonmaterial
basis" (62). Intuitionism is heatedly opposed by the vast majority of elevator inspectors, Empiricists by name, who in tried-and-true, nose-to-the-grindstone fashion,
look closely at the machinery of the elevators they inspect—whereas Lila Mae closes
her eyes while riding an elevator, concentrates on the vibrations, and senses things like
faulty overspeed governors by visualizing the interaction of abstract shapes and colors
in her mind's eye.

The novel opens when a mysterious accident befalls one of the elevators Lila Mae has
recently inspected—and not just any elevator, but Number Eleven in the eighteen-el-
evator bank of the new Fanny Briggs Memorial Building, the first municipal building
to be named after the famous ex-slave who taught herself to read and then escaped to
the North. Lila Mae "had once delivered an oral report on Fanny Briggs in the third
grade" (11), we learn, and now, as the country struggles through the first stages of racial integration, Briggs is being acknowledged "in the newer encyclopedias" (11) and
by prominent politicians for the usual prominent-politician reasons:

> In a city with an increasingly vocal colored population – who are not above staging tiresome
> demonstrations for the lowlier tabloids, or throwing tomatoes and rotten cabbages during
> otherwise perfectly orchestrated speeches and rallies–it only makes sense to name the new
> municipal building after one of their heroes. (12)

The elevator has failed spectacularly, going into complete freefall and crashing despite
being a brand-new, state-of-the-art piece of equipment; as Bart Arbergast of the Department of Elevator Inspection's Internal Affairs Bureau puts it while interrogating
Lila Mae's only friend among the inspectors, a sad sack by the name of Chuck Gould,
total freefall

> hasn't happened in five years, and that was in the Ukraine and who knows what kind of back-
> ward standards they got there. They probably got their cabs hooked up to mules out there,
> for all I know. It hasn't happened in this country since before you were born. (110)

The accident, therefore, is not only highly symbolic but highly suspicious. No one
believes the elevator simply failed; one line of thought holds that a faction loyal to Frank
Chancre, Chair of the Elevator Guild and head of the Department, has sabotaged the
elevator stack at Fanny Briggs in order to call Intuitionism into disrepute and crush the
campaign of his opponent in the upcoming Guild Chair election, an Intuitionist named
Orville Lever, "who apparently thinks that only Intuitionists are capable of building co-

alitions, shaking hands with fundamentally different people, etc." (14). The other line of thought, first introduced into the novel by Arbergast in his interrogation of Chuck, suggests that Lila Mae Watson herself tampered with the elevator just after inspecting it, precisely to make it look as if Chancre's forces would play dirty tricks with public safety in order to discredit Intuitionism, Lever, and the Department's first black female inspector. As for Lila Mae herself, she is convinced, and remains convinced through the first two-thirds of the novel, that Chancre not only had the elevator sabotaged but got the Guild's only other black inspector to do the job—a tiny, reserved man named Pompey, who despises Lila Mae and is despised by her in return.

When Lila Mae first learns of the accident, hearing of it on her Department car radio, she does not report back to work, and gradually decides to lay low until she's learned enough to protect herself. But before she goes into hiding, she returns to her apartment to find it being ransacked by two thuggish men, Jim and John, who are then, in turn, interrupted by one Mr. Reed, Orville Lever's secretary, who has come to take Lila Mae to Intuitionist House for protection. Intuitionist House turns out to be a kind of faculty club for Intuitionists, founded by an eccentric figure in the history of elevator development and maintained for two decades by Fulton acolytes who periodically gathered for social events and to hear Fulton himself lecture on topics such as "the implications of European maintenance deviations on Intuitionism" and "the gloom of the shaft and how it does not merely echo the gloom inside every living creature, but duplicates it perfectly" (54). Reed intervenes, as he tells Lila Mae, because the stakes are much higher than the Fanny Briggs accident alone would suggest. It seems that just before his death, Fulton had been working on a so-called "black box," a development that would revolutionize the elevator industry and the urban landscape: "if [Elisha] Otis's first elevation delivered us from medieval five- and six-story constructions, the next elevator, it is believed, will grant us the sky, unreckoned towers: the second elevation" (61). Reed explains to Lila Mae that Lever has recently received a curious package containing design notes on a black box from Fulton's final (and as yet undiscovered) journals, and that copies of these notes have apparently been sent to Chancre's office and a reporter from the industry magazine, *Lift*, as well. This then appears to offer Lila Mae the chance to glimpse the wheels within the wheels: the accident at Fanny Briggs is not just about the upcoming election and the politics of racial integration, but about the shape of the utopian cities to come. For it appears that Fulton's black box is constructed from "the elevator's point of view" (62), that is, in accordance with the Intuitionist principles that hitherto have been purely theoretical:

"Think about it," [Reed] says. "The most famous elevator theoretician of the century has constructed the black box, and he's done it on Intuitionist principles. What does that do to Empiricism?"

Lila Mae nods and Mr. Reed continues: "Now Chancre's up for reelection. There have always been rumors about Fulton's black box and suddenly comes this new variable – it does exist, and it's Intuitionist. Not only do you lose the election, but everything else, too. Your faith. You have to embrace the enemy you've fought tooth and nail for twenty years." (63)

It seems, in other words, that Lila Mae has been caught up in one of the vortices of modernity, unwittingly enlisted in its enterprise of creative destruction: "they will have to destroy this city once we deliver the black box," she thinks at one point. "They will have to raze the city and cart off the rubble to less popular boroughs and start anew" (198). Whereas the first elevation made possible the modernist skyscrapers that defined the cityscapes of the developed world in the first half of the twentieth century (thus "delivering" us from the "medieval"), the second elevation promises to take us beyond modernity and beyond verticality in ways we cannot yet imagine: "the shining city will possess untold arms and a thousand eyes, mutability itself, constructed of yet-unconjured plastics. It will float, fly, fall, have no need of steel armature, have a liquid spine, no spine at all" (198-99).

Much of the remainder of the novel consists of the slow unraveling of false leads and the gradual unmasking of false identities. As an Intuitionist, Lila Mae is already more than enthusiastic about the prospect of completing Fulton's final work; but when she learns from a mysterious colored servant in Intuitionist House that Fulton was himself colored, and spent his entire life passing for white, Lila Mae is forced to revisit the grounds of her commitment to Intuitionism. On one hand, she believes all the more fervently in the justice of her recent underground activities, since as Natchez, the mysterious servant, tells her, Fulton was not only passing (which turns out to be true) but his, Natchez's, very own uncle (which turns out to be false); the black box is thus his "birthright" (138) and for Lila Mae, the quest for it now becomes part of the struggle for racial justice. As Lila Mae thinks to herself that "Fulton was a spy in white spaces, just like she is" (139), Natchez claims the black box for all colored people: "it's the future of the cities. But it's our future, not theirs. It's ours. And we need to take it back. What he made, this elevator, colored people made that. It's ours. And I'm going to show that we ain't nothing" (140). But on the other hand, Lila Mae realizes that she now has to re-read her previous readings of *Theoretical Elevators*, wondering anew whether the volumes of advanced elevator theory are in fact racially coded, allegorical, double-voiced. From the sentence that first grabbed her attention—"*There is another world beyond this one*" (63)—to the lyrical passages of Volume Two, Fulton's work now seems to speak to and for Lila Mae on the lower frequencies:

> *The race sleeps in this hectic and disordered century. Grim lids that will not open. Anxious retinas flit to and fro beneath them. They are stirred by dreaming. In this dream of uplift, they understand that they are dreaming the contract of the hallowed verticality, and hope to remember the terms upon waking. The race never does, and that is our curse.* The human race, [Lila Mae] thought formerly. Fulton has a fetish for the royal "we" throughout *Theoretical Elevators*. But now—who's "we"? (186)

Lila Mae is "teaching herself to read" (186), learning "how to read, as a slave does, one forbidden word at a time" (230), but at the same time, she is strangely, bitterly disappointed that her love for Fulton's work might have a basis in a racial solidarity of which she'd been unaware, since it suggests that her intellectual commitments are a simple function of her racial identity, her "blood":

> She read the words in her lap, *horizontal thinking in a vertical world is the race's curse*, and hated him. She had been misled. What she had taken as pure truth had been revealed as merely filial agreement. And thus no longer pure. Blood agrees, it cannot help but agree, and how can you get any perspective on that? Blood is destiny in this land, and she did not choose Intuitionism, as she formerly believed, it chose her. (151)

Worse still, Fulton's *Theoretical Elevators* are not only a thinly-veiled commentary on race and utopia; they may be, as Lila Mae comes to realize, a "big joke" (232) that Fulton plays on the society that refused to accept him as the son of a colored woman.

The false leads and false identities begin with Fulton and Natchez and cascade through the narrative. The conflict over the black box, which involves industrial subterfuge and a last-minute spiking of *Lift*'s cover story (as well as some roughing up of the story's reporter, one Ben Urich), turns out to be a conflict not between ideologies but between rival elevator manufacturers, Arbo and United, each of which has lined up behind a candidate in the Guild election. Intuitionism, we find, is being secretly bankrolled by Arbo, and only because United has bought Chancre in return for Chancre's very public and very influential endorsement of United's line of products. In fact, almost every one Lila Mae encounters turns out to be working for Arbo: the men ransacking her apartment are Arbo thugs, and they are interrupted by Arbo operative Reed, who is the brains behind Arbo's bought-and-paid-for candidate, Orville Lever. Natchez the servant is yet another Arbo corporate-espionage strongman, real name Raymond Coombs, no relation to Fulton after all, no "birthright" at issue, no stake in the struggle for racial justice. Pompey, for his part, had nothing to do with the failed elevator at Fanny Briggs; in fact, the larger narrative itself has nothing to do with the failed elevator at Fanny Briggs, which remains anomalous, inexplicable. Lila Mae Watson is not the center of Arbo and United's collective attention because of that elevator; no, Lila Mae is the elevator industry's Most Wanted because Fulton, shortly before his death, had scribbled *Lila Mae Watson is the one* in the margin of one of his notebooks (211). And he did so for the same reason that the Fanny Briggs elevator failed —that is, for no reason worthy of the term. He had been wandering around the Institute campus in his final days, and wondered idly who the lone colored student was, all by herself with her light on in her janitor's closet, finally jotting down her name in one of his notebooks ("That's right," he thinks to himself in one of the few sections of the novel that grants us free-indirect-discourse access to him. "That's the name of the only other person awake at this hour of the night" [253]). That marginal note to himself then became the basis for the industry's interest in Lila Mae, who, it was generally and mistakenly assumed, held the key to the black box and the second elevation.

Lila Mae (and Whitehead's reader) learns about the Arbo/United plot from Urich the reporter; a little while after Lila Mae talks to Urich, she and we learn from Fulton's housemaid-lover-confidante, Marie Claire Rogers, about Fulton's final years, and the unannounced visit from Fulton's colored sister (with, of course, the inevitable possibility of exposure such a visit entailed) that made Fulton write Volume Two of *Theoretical Elevators* and transform his "big joke" into a serious project:

> Something happens that makes him believe, switch from the novel but diffuse generalities of Volume One to the concrete Intuitionist methodology of Volume Two. Now he wants that perfect elevator that will lift him away from here and devises solid method from his original satire. What did his sister say to him. What did he wish after their meeting. Family? That there could be, in the world he invented to parody his enslavers, a field where he could be whole? A joke has no purpose if you cannot share it with anyone. Lila Mae thinks, Intuitionism is communication. That simple. Communication with what is not-you. When he gives lectures to his flock, years later, they are not aware of what he is truly speaking. *The elevator world will look like Heaven but not the Heaven you have reckoned.* (241)

The novel ends with Lila Mae in sole possession of the "key" to Fulton's hieroglyphics (bequeathed to her, appropriately, by Marie Claire Rogers, who'd kept it hidden in the dumbwaiter all this time) as she sets to work on completing Fulton's third volume in secret, having left the elevator industry with just enough information to tantalize them; appropriately, the novel's final page, like the final page of *The Crying of Lot 49* but far less sinister, takes on the discourse of the sacred and the apocalyptic. "The elevator she delivered to Coombs," Whitehead writes,

> and then to Chancre and Ben Urich, should hold them a while. Then one day they will realize it is not perfect. If it is the right time she will give them the perfect elevator. If it is not time she will send out more of Fulton's words to let them know it is coming. As per his instructions. It is important to let the citizens know it is coming. To let them prepare themselves for the second elevation.
>   . . . Sometimes in the room she thinks about the accident and its message. Much of what happened would have happened anyway, but it warms her to know that the perfect elevator reached out to her and told her she was of its world. That she was a citizen of the city to come and that the frail devices she had devoted her life to were weak and would all fall one day like Number Eleven. All of them, plummeting down the shafts like beautiful dead stars. (255)

By this point, of course, we have been invited more than once to reconsider the appellation of that "black box," crafted as it is in the unwitting communication between a prominent, revered colored man passing as white—and thus, in an obvious sense, closeted—and a young colored woman living in a janitor's closet on the same campus. The black box, we imagine, will deliver people of color from all such confinements, and open to them a literal kingdom of the heavens that will eradicate rather than merely compensate for the injustices of the world as they and we have known it, utterly transforming the landscape of race and place. And there will be another world beyond this one.

*****

The spatiotemporal setting of *The Intuitionist* is one of the novel's more carefully elaborated features. The city is and is not New York, the time is and is not the 1940s or 1950s; the cinematic analogues for Whitehead's novel in this respect would be David Lynch's jarring confusion of the 1950s and 1980s in *Blue Velvet* (1986) and, more immediately, Tim Burton's cartoonish, prewar/postwar Gotham City in *Batman* (1989). (There are overtones of the era and milieu of Dick Tracy here as well, most notably in the figure of the underworld boss Johnny Shush.) The first music we hear (of) in the novel is "big band" (2); "doo wop" is mentioned twice (15, 69) and a party band "sings of Peggy Sue and her love so true" (147). Chancre's press conference after the Fanny Briggs accident is ringed by "fedoraed men" (17); men pore over racing forms while dining at the Automat (165); there is radio but no television; there are traffic reports on the radio, but no helicopters: "WCAM equips men with binoculars and positions them at strategic overpasses to describe the gnarls and tangles" (9). And, as you've surely gathered by now, African-Americans are referred to as "colored" throughout the book. The Great Migration seems to be a recent thing, and racial integration has only just begun to get under way. But every so often, the novel draws on tropes from more recent decades, not only in the naming of major buildings after major figures in African-American history (a phenomenon that, in the real New York, postdated the release of "Peggy Sue" by some years), but also in the evocation of "last summer's riots" (23), which sound more like the stuff of 1967 than like 1943. Before too long, as Pompey angrily tells Lila Mae when she finally confronts him about the Fanny Briggs accident, the street his family lives on will be devastated by the drug trade: "a few years from now," he says, pointing to the local dealer, "it won't be reefer he selling but some other poison" (194). In the "riots," I suggest, we are supposed to hear not only the echoes of 1967 but the devastation of Los Angeles in 1992; and in "some other poison" we are invited to think not only of heroin but of crack.

This temporal blurring has the effect of making *The Intuitionist* recognizably postmodern in the tradition of Reed and Doctorow (as well as Tim Burton and David Lynch), but in another way it simplifies matters immeasurably: the unnamed New York in Whitehead's landscape is a city of simple black and white. Contrasted with, say, Chang-Rae Lee's polyglot city in *Native Speaker* (1994), where Queens appears as a world of low-end retail establishments populated by Koreans, Colombians, Vietnamese, Laotians, Dominicans, and Pakistanis (as well as Africans and African-Americans), *The Intuitionist* looks not only mannered but strangely impoverished, even by the standards of 1945: there are still some markers of ethnicity among the city's white characters

(Chancre himself has an "Irish face" [17], and Lila Mae's neighborhood was once home to "Poles and Russians" [30]), but the only people of color around are "colored" people; there's only one Jew, Gould, and despite a passing reference to "Caribbean immigrants" (190), not a single Puerto Rican in sight.[2] *The Intuitionist* thus produces a particularly jarring effect: bypassing the post-1965 patterns of U.S. population growth, in which South / East Asian and South / Central American immigration has taken on unprecedented importance in the wake of the repeal of the nativist Johnson-Reed Act of 1924, Whitehead's novel gives us postmodernity without hybridity.

Whitehead's representation of elevator inspection, however, partakes of what I might call a kind of interprofessional hybridity. The inspectors are civil servants, no question, close kin to workers in the police, fire, parks, sanitation, and motor vehicle departments; there are interagency rivalries—"the police and the elevator inspectors have a difficult past," and "the city has never answered Chancre's repeated requests for sirens" (11)— and the elevator inspectors have their own dispatchers, their own uniforms, their own ties to organized crime. There's the occasional suggestion that the department is among the more important, high-stress branches of the municipal government—"elevator inspection is hard on a marriage, a family" (148)—and that, as Chancre's endorsement of United Elevators suggests, the inspectors' relation to the industry is sufficiently cozy as to make the term "conflict of interest" sound rather quaint. But at the same time the inspectors are something more, or other, than ordinary civil servants. Their Institutes look more like graduate schools than like training academies; they have intense Socratic classes and grueling oral exams that involve questions like "nonmetallic material may be used in T-rails provided what?" and recitations of the verdict in *United States v. Mario's* (answers: "provided the rated speed for the car does not exceed zero point seven six meters per second," and the Supreme Court decision that "restaurant dumbwaiters are hand elevators and subject to scrutiny by municipal elevator inspectors" [50-52]). Like M.D.s and J.D.s, inspectors apparently have the option of staying in the field, working with elevators, or seeking a tenure-track position in the Institutes, teaching the next generation of inspectors. Chuck Gould is one of the inspectors considering an academic career; to increase his chances, he's concentrated not on elevators but escalators, which are much lower in prestige but offer the benefits of professional specialization:

> Specialization means job security, and there's a nation-wide lack of escalator professors in the Institutes, so Chuck figures he's a shoo-in for a teaching job. And once he's in there, drawing a bead on tenure, he can branch out from escalators and teach whatever he wants. . . . Chuck's assured Lila Mae that even though he is a staunch Empiricist, he'll throw in the Intuitionist counterarguments where necessary. His students should be acquainted with the entire body of elevator knowledge, not just the canon. (21)

Whitehead's knowing echo of Gerald Graff's injunction to teach the conflicts is of a piece with his occasional representation of elevator inspection as a field in the humanities, where varieties of elevator theory go in and out of vogue and elevators are redesigned accordingly: "Taking their cue from the early days of passenger-response criticism, Arbo equipped their newest model with an oversized door to foster the illusion of space, to distract the passenger from what every passenger feels acutely about elevators" (5). To defenders of Derrida and Foucault, it should come as no surprise to hear Chancre deride Intuitionism as one of "the latest fashions from overseas" (27). But the opposition between Empiricists and Intuitionists doesn't directly map onto any one academic field. Instead, it appears as a generic division among varieties of mental labor than have corollaries throughout the intellectual world—in debates between literary historians and theorists, physical and postmodern anthropologists, traditional law professors and advocates of critical race theory. Empiricists are the old guard and Intuitionists the young turks, mirroring the academic clashes that long postdate the era in which men wore fedoras and ate at Automats, and it doesn't help Lila Mae's position that the latter are spoken of in racially coded terms:

> Some nicknames Empiricists have for their renegade colleagues: swamis, voodoo men, juju heads, witch doctors, Harry Houdinis. All terms belonging to the nomenclature of dark exotica, the sinister foreign. Except for Houdini, who nonetheless had something swarthy about him.
> Some counter-nicknames from the Intuitionists: flat-earthers, ol' nuts and bolts, stress freaks ("checking for signs of stress" being a commonly uttered phrase when the Empirically trained are out running the streets), Babbitts, collators (this last word preferably hissed with optimum disdain).
> No one can quite explain why the Intuitionists have a 10 percent higher accuracy rate than the Empiricists. (57-58)

That 10 percent differential is impressive in itself—but until the Fanny Briggs catastrophe, Lila Mae herself had had a one hundred percent accuracy rate. It is no wonder the novel is framed on either end by the phrase, "she is never wrong" (9, 255).

This portrayal of elevator inspection as akin to disciplines in law, literature, or anthropology is all good fun, especially for people who can find humor in the idea of an elevator-theory canon or in a slur against "ol' nuts and bolts" Empiricists as a version of the derisive "stones and bones" nickname for physical anthropologists. But what complicates Whitehead's otherwise apt allegory of divisions within mental labor in the academic professions is the fact that Empiricism involves some *manual* labor whereas Intuitionism does not. It's not altogether accurate, in other words, to see Intuitionists as beleaguered, harrowed critical race theorists and Empiricists as conservative establishment blocking figures. Intuitionism has a hauteur of its own, derived precisely as Pierre Bourdieu would have it, namely, as a function of its distance from the grimy details of manual labor: "See, the Empiricists stoop to check for tell-tale striations on the lift winch and seize upon oxidation scars on the compensating rope sheave, all that muscle work, and think the Intuitionists get off easy. Lazy slobs" (57). Lazy slobs—or effete snobs? The Intuitionists' counter-nicknames for the Empiricists suggest that the latter are seen by their adversaries not merely as literalists and dinosaurs, but, gasp, as Babbitts, members of the boring, self-satisfied bourgeoisie in contrast to the snarky Intuitionists, who are working at the "cutting edge" of the discipline. Perhaps this aspect of Intuitionism is one reason for its appeal to Lila Mae Watson: just as elevator inspection signifies upward mobility (and the novel makes much of the pun) and offers colored people a route North and a piece of modernity, Intuitionism offers the promise of working in the civil service without getting your hands dirty. Surely, her chosen vocation as an Intuitionist (quite apart from her job as an inspector) allows Lila Mae to differentiate herself not only from the mass of ordinary Empiricist collators and functionaries in the Department, but also from the boys in the motor pool, all of whom are colored and many of whom regard Miss Watson as a "dicty college woman" (18).

Intuitionism would thus represent for Lila Mae an intensification of the rationale that drew her to elevators in the first place —namely, an opportunity to uplift the race. And just as Burton Bledstein argued in *The Culture of Professionalism* (1978), the ideology of professionalism allows Lila Mae to equate the advancement of her own career with the greater social good (though, I admit, Bledstein did not say very much about elevator inspection). There's also a family plot at work in Lila Mae's career; she is avenging, among other things, her father Marvin's lifetime of humiliation as a small-town department-store elevator operator, a lifetime summed up in the following exchange with an inspector making his rounds through the store:

> Marvin turns to the officer and says, "She's a real beauty, this car. I've been working with this baby for over twenty years now and she's never let me down. Sometimes she catches when we pass three—I think there's something wrong with the selector. And I have to work to make her flush with the landings sometimes—I keep telling them to have the indicator adjusted, but they're too stingy to get someone in here."
> "You too," the inspector says.
> "What?"
> "Get off. The day I need some nigger to tell me how to do my job is the day I quit. Now get off." (162)

If Marvin thought for a moment that the inspector would validate his vernacular knowledge of elevators (derived from twenty years of "working with" this one), or bond with him over the penuriousness of people who don't truly appreciate the value of a fine piece of machinery, he won't make that mistake again. For what do you call a black man with decades of experience at his job and an engineering degree from "the colored college downstate" (160)? A nigger. Lila Mae's inspector's badge thus redeems Marvin's life of futility, and serves throughout the novel as the visible symbol of her accession to the world of ascension. Likewise, her journey North, like so many journeys in the great migration, recapitulates the struggle of her ancestors, redeeming their bondage with her freedom. But her status as an Intuitionist does still more than this. Though she may be reviled as a juju head or a witch doctor, she is practicing a rarefied, intellectual version of the discipline of elevator inspection, working at the theoretical forefront of the field while her plodding white colleagues check for tell-tale striations on the lift winch. Best of all, her phenomenal accuracy rate speaks for her. Among the professionals who make up her peers, she is an adept among adepts, more modern than the moderns.

The elevators themselves, as I noted at the outset, are a powerful index of modernity, far more appropriate as a symbol of organized industrial development than, say, zippers or even refrigerators (delightful and salutary as these might be). Without Elisha Otis's handy invention, "the one that started it all, enabling the metropolis, summoning them into tumultuous modernity" (158), the cities would be fixed at five or six "medieval" stories, as indeed their ghettoes remain today—like the forgotten section of the city in which Lila Mae hides after leaving Intuitionist House: "Not a lot of elevators in this neighborhood. This is the place verticality indicts, the passed-over flatlands, what might as well still be forest and field" (185). Together with Henry Bessemer's iron-decarbonization process for the mass production of steel and George Fuller's work on load-bearing capacities in tall buildings, elevators have made possible the tall buildings that physically distinguished the twentieth century from every previous epoch of human history. As we've seen, Whitehead's elevators also partake of the sacred, with the coming of the "second elevation" standing in for the second coming and metaphors of ascent serving the usual metaphors-of-ascent purposes. It's part of the novel's quirky charm, I think, that Whitehead has chosen so literal a vehicle for his tall tale of race and modernity, zeroing in on the spines of the buildings themselves rather than the global transportation and telecommunications systems that are more commonly thought of as the "enabling" conditions of modernity. I trust it is not too farfetched, for example, to imagine that Whitehead is transferring to elevators some of the utopian longings associated with airplanes for young black men in the opening pages of Richard Wright's *Native Son* (1940) and in the character of Ajax in Toni Morrison's *Sula* (1973).

What's most notable about Whitehead's rendering of modernity, however, is not his evocation of the elevators, their material properties, and the remarkable new buildings they "enable." Rather, it's his Weberian insight that the regime of modernity entails not only the elevators themselves but the rational, routinized means of their inspection and maintenance—and, concomitant with this, vigorous intellectual disputes among the inspectors about, among other things, "the various merits and drawbacks of heat dispersal in United Elevator's braking systems" (23). In *The Intuitionist*, it appears, modernity entails not only new conveyances but new institutions devoted to the oversight and regularization of the conveyances: the upkeep of the uplift (as well as new ways of distinguishing the gleaming metropolises of the West from "backward" places like the Ukraine, where, as Arbergast says, they might as well have their cabs hooked up to mules for all we know).

At the same time, the regime of modernity entails the extension of universalist promises that are routinely betrayed in everyday practice.[3] Even a century (give or take a couple of doo-wop decades) after Elisha Otis demonstrated his braking system at the 1853 Crystal Palace Exhibition of the Industry of All Nations, uttering the famous words, "All safe, gentlemen, all safe" (echoed by Chancre, 159), it appears that all are not safe, for colored elevator operators can still be denied the very opportunity to serve as inspectors, just as they can be called "nigger" by the inspectors authorized by law to order them out of the cars in which they've worked for twenty years.

This much is clear, in the sense that it doesn't require reading the novel against the grain. But it's just as clear, no doubt, that there's something awry about putting elevators and elevator inspection at the epicenter of modernity for people of color excluded from the ostensibly universalist dispensation of post-Enlightenment social contracts. For all their aptness as symbols and "enablers" of the modern metropolis, elevators were never really sites of African-Americans' struggles and aspirations to join either the ranks of municipal civil servants or the ranks of licensed professionals in the knowledge industry. (To say this is simply to acknowledge—and perhaps, dunderheadedly, to ruin—the running joke that animates *The Intuitionist*.) The history of African-Americans' relations to railroads and airplanes, by contrast, is central to African-American history in the postindustrial United States, as is the history of African-Americans' relations to white ethnics in Northern police and fire departments. For that matter, when post–Civil War African-American leaders sent out the call to uplift the race, they didn't mean that black Americans should strive to inspect elevator guide shoes or overspeed governors, nor did they mean that black Americans should endure the racial inequities of this world with dignity and await their deliverance with the coming of the second elevation. There are no Tuskegee Airmen of the elevator world, no Benjamin Wards (Ward became, in 1984, New York's first black police chief) of elevator inspection. I want to suggest in closing, therefore, that Whitehead's narrative of race and modernity works by way of a double displacement: the history of African-American participation in the railroad and airline industries, and in the branches of the municipal civil service, is figured here as a drama of "Negro firsts" in the theory and practice of elevator inspection, and the elevator, in turn, is remade into a vehicle of access to the promises of modernity and treated with an importance that it never actually had for African-Americans but most certainly *does* have for people with physical disabilities.

There is nothing very strange about this kind of displacement; disability and race are both notoriously fluid categories of identity, and with regard to the mechanics of social exclusion, it is fairly easy to figure one in terms of the other—especially when the mechanics of social exclusion operate with respect to modern transportation systems: wheelchair users and African-Americans have every reason to desire free access to the front of the bus. Moreover, the signifying relations between race and cognitive (as opposed to physical) disability have a long, complex, and often ugly history, since African-Americans spent most of their first 350 years on this continent being regarded by their white brothers and sisters as constitutively and permanently disabled. Having said this, though, I do not want to suggest that Whitehead himself is consciously drawing on this history, or deliberately deploying the fluidity of race and disability when it comes to the composition of the social text. On the contrary, people with disabilities are as important to *The Intuitionist* as are New York's Jews and Puerto Ricans—that is, notable in their almost complete absence from the text. And not merely from the surface of the text, but even from its more specu-lative thoughts, so to speak. To wit: Chuck Gould's specialization in escalators involves, among other things, regular observation of a local department store which will provide him with data for his monograph-in-progress, "Understanding Patterns of Escalator Use in Department Stores Simultaneously Equipped with Elevators," the thesis of which is striking for its obliviousness to one aspect of those patterns:

> Chuck vehemently disagrees with the esteemed Cuvier, who thinks the choice is random, a simple matter of proximity. . . . We choose the escalator, we choose the elevator, and these choices say much about who we are, says Chuck. (There is more than a smidgeon of spite in this formulation, unseen by driven Chuck: he's trying to justify his specialty.) Do you wish to ascend at an angle, surveying the world you are leaving below and behind, a spirit arms wide, a sky king; or do you prefer the box, the coffin, that excises the journey Heavenward, presto, your arrival a magician's banal theatrics? (106)

It does not seem to occur to Chuck—just as it has not occurred to the esteemed Cuvier, or perhaps even to the narrator who knows (and knows that Chuck doesn't know) about the degree of self-justification in Chuck's manuscript—that people in wheelchairs can-not ride escalators. It simply isn't a factor in his thinking at all, not even as something to factor out of the data on "choice" and "randomness." In other words, there's no ac-knowledgment anywhere of the fact that some people might be compelled to take el-evators rather than escalators—and that, for them, the elevator and the elevator alone is the vehicle of their deliverance from the bare surfaces of this earth.

Allow me, then, to juxtapose *The Intuitionist* to Charles Chesnutt's *The Marrow of Tradition* (1901), a novel written at the other end of the twentieth century, in which the connections among race, disability, and modern transportation systems are spelled out explicitly. This is Chesnutt's description of traveling by rail with Jim Crow in the wake of *Plessy v. Ferguson*:

> The car was conspicuously labeled at either end with large cards, similar to those in the other car, except that they bore the word "Colored" in black letters upon a white background. The author of this piece of legislation had contrived, with an ingenuity worthy of a better cause, that not merely should the passengers be separated by a color line, but that the reason for this division should be kept constantly in mind. Lest a white man forget that he was white,—not a very likely contingency,—these cards would keep him constantly admonished of the fact; should a colored person endeavor, for a moment, to lose sight of his disability, these staring signs would remind him continually that between him and the rest of mankind not of his own color,

there was by law a great gulf fixed. (56)

Chesnutt's use of "disability" as a synonym for "race" suggests that African-Americans are literally disabled by segregation, prevented from moving freely according to their wishes and from associating with their white peers: the railroad car described here is occupied by only one man, Dr. William Miller, who was forcibly separated from his friend and former teacher, Dr. Burns, once the train entered the state of Virginia on its way from New York to Wilmington, North Carolina (rendered here as "Wellington")—over Burns' objections, and despite the fact that Williams had paid first-class fare for his trip. At the same time, Chesnutt implies that disability and race are both, as the current phrase has it, socially constructed—and precariously constructed at that: when *The Marrow of Tradition* opens, "the law had been in operation only a few months" (57), and Chesnutt sardonically suggests that as a result, the train's passengers have to be reminded of their racial identities at all times. The phenomenon of "passing" is thus especially germane to the connection between race and disability, since, of course, it is altogether possible for people with undetectable disabilities to "pass" as nondisabled, just as it was possible for Homer Plessy, Charles Chesnutt, and controversial elevator theorist James Fulton to pass for white—that is, to pass as nondisabled. Regardless of whether disability is a factor in Chuck Gould's thinking about escalators, then, the point remains that the politics of race and the politics of disability have long been closely associated—even when disability is pared away at the last minute, as it was in the 1964 Civil Rights Act—and have thereby been able to stand for each other in a wide variety of social contexts. As Celeste Langan has pointed out in her reading of the film *Speed*, social milieux involving transportation are especially volatile points of intersection in which race, gender, and class are figured in terms of disability, and disability is complexly intertwined with race, gender, and class—even when, as in *Speed* and *The Intuitionist*, people with disabilities are not explicitly represented in the intersection.[4]

And yet there is one person with a visible disability in Whitehead's novel—a Professor McKean, who appears briefly in one of the flashbacks to Lila Mae's time at the Institute for Vertical Transport and who, we learn, had been in the war (whatever war this may be) and lost his left arm below the elbow. The passage occurs, oddly enough, only a few pages prior to Chuck's meditation on the patterns of usage of department store escalators, and concerns a seminar on Theoretical Elevators in which Professor McKean, whose position on the Intuitionist/Empiricist debate is not known, poses to the class the well-known Dilemma of the Phantom Passenger. The Dilemma of the Phantom Passenger involves the question, as one student phrases it, of "what happens when the passenger who has engaged the call button departs, whether he changed his mind and took the stairs or caught an up-tending car when he wanted to go down because he did not feel like waiting. It asks what happens to the elevator he summoned" (101). One of McKean's students, Gorse, a fervent Empiricist and vociferous Fulton critic, insists that the elevator arrives, the doors open and close, end of story. But Lila Mae, a more sympathetic reader of Fulton, knows that the entire dilemma is false, for "an elevator doesn't exist without its freight. If there's no one to get on, the elevator remains in quiescence. The elevator and the passenger need each other" (102). Even to leave a camera in place, to find out what happens to the elevator after the passenger has left the floor, is to create "the expectation of freight," as Lila Mae explains: "the camera is a passenger who declines to get on the elevator, not a phantom passenger." Professor McKean commends Lila Mae, at which point Gorse explodes:

> Spat, "Just because you can't see it doesn't mean it's not there!" and slammed a fist onto the table. The fundamental battle.
> Professor McKean frowned. He pushed his chair from the conference table until it hit the wall with a dull bang. With his right hand, he unpinned his war medal from his sleeve. His jacket sleeve, unhinged, swayed back and forth pendulously. "Gorse," Professor McKean said, "Is my arm here or not here?"
> "It's . . . not there," Gorse responded timidly.
> "What's in this sleeve?"
> "Nothing," Gorse answered.
> "That's the funny thing," Professor McKean said, smiling now. "My arm is gone, but sometimes it's there." He looked down at his empty sleeve. He flicked at the sleeve with his remaining hand and they watched the fabric sway. (102)

I do not want to claim that McKean's pedagogical gambit, equating the phantom passenger/elevator with his "phantom limb" and leaving his students to ponder the resulting koan, somehow manages to foreground disability as a mobility issue pertinent to elevators and elevator inspection. Even McKean's disability, the only visible disability in the novel, has no bearing on anyone's elevator usage, McKean's included. But it does suggest, obliquely and tantalizingly, that Empiricism is no more useful when thinking about disability than it is when thinking about elevators: the two are related in some elusive way for McKean, and related in a far less elusive way for people with mobility impairments— including those people whose mobility impairments render them structurally analogous to "colored" persons whose mobility restrictions follow from the social construction of their racial "disability." By implication, just as Lila Mae is invited—or compelled—to reread *Theoretical Elevators* once she has learned that James Fulton spent his life passing for white, so too are we invited—or compelled—to reread Whitehead's elevators not only as allegories for racial uplift but also as literal prostheses of modernity. The utopian longing expressed in Fulton's *there is another world beyond this one* speaks to all people interpellated by and yet excluded from the regime of modernity, regardless of the bodily variations that are associated with—and cited as justification for—their exclusion. And the elevator, on this utopian rereading, becomes the vehicle of equal access for every living human: Elisha Otis's invention enables the metropolis, summoning us all into tumultuous modernity—thereby enabling all of modernity's citizens, irrespective of the color of their skin, irrespective of their other physical disabilities.

NOTES

[1] The best analysis of which, in literary study, is Farah Jasmine Griffin's *Who Set You Flowin'? The African-American Migration Narrative*.

[2] It might be objected that Lee's Queens looks this way because contemporary Queens *is*, in fact, a world of low-end retail establishments populated by Koreans, Colombians, etc., and that because Lee's is a realist political intrigue / immigrant novel whereas Whitehead's is a postmodern fantasia, there's not much sense in comparing them with regard to their demographics. But it's worth suggesting nonetheless that each author's degree of social verisimilitude is worthy of comment, and that, moreover, Lee's savvy about the racial politics of New York should not be attributed to simple verisimilitude in the first place. In the thirty years between *All in the Family* and *The King of Queens*, for instance, not much has changed in the television sitcom depiction of Queens as the home of beefy, regular-Joe white guys. My point is that Lee emphatically foregrounds the contemporary ethnic topography of the city whereas Whitehead goes to some trouble to render it invisible or irrelevant.

[3] Janet Lyon's *Manifestos: Provocations of the Modern* (1999) offers an especially compelling analysis of this phenomenon.

[4] See Langan.

WORKS CITED

Bledstein, Burton J. *The Culture of Professionalism: The Middle Class and the Development of Higher Education in America*. New York: Norton, 1978.

Chesnutt, Charles. *The Marrow of Tradition* [1901]. Ed. and introd. by Eric J. Sundquist. New York: Penguin, 1993.

Griffin, Farah Jasmine. *Who Set You Flowin'? The African-American Migration Narrative*. New York: Oxford U P, 1996.

Hutcheon, Linda. *A Poetics of Postmodernism: History, Theory, Fiction*. New York: Routledge, 1988.

Langan, Celeste. "Mobility Disability." *Public Culture* 13.3 (2001): 459-84.

Lee, Chang-Rae. *Native Speaker*. New York: Riverhead, 1995.

Lyon, Janet. *Manifestos: Provocations of the Modern*. Ithaca: Cornell U P, 1999.

Whitehead, Colson. *The Intuitionist*. New York: Anchor, 1999.

David Cowart
Anxieties of Obsolescence:
DeLillo's *Cosmopolis*

I.

From nineteenth-century robber barons to Howard Hughes, Donald Trump, Ted Turner, and the obscenely remunerated CEOs indicted in the corporate scandals of 2002, Americans have always understood the mythos of great wealth. In a literature replete with figures of fiduciary clout, they read about Jay Gatsby and Milo Minderbinder, Gaddis's *JR* and Pynchon's Pierce Inverarity. From Charles Foster Kane to Gordon Gekko (the character played by Michael Douglas in Oliver Stone's 1987 film *Wall Street*), cinema, too, explores mogul mojo. In his 2003 novel *Cosmopolis* Don DeLillo introduces into this mythic company the sardanapalian Eric Michael Packer, a twenty-eight-year-old tycoon with a "personal fortune in the tens of billions" (121).

Ranging over the institutions that define life in contemporary America, DeLillo never really repeats himself, but he often recurs to certain images, motifs, and conceits. Like the phonemes of a language, these elements—nuns, motels, sport, deserts, waste, and so on—become the building blocks of mythemes of his expression. The author has always liked to expose a central, sensitive figure—Billy Twillig, Jack Gladney, Bucky Wunderlick—to a procession of wacky or obsessive visitors. In *Cosmopolis* Eric Packer interacts with variously eccentric advisors and employees in technology, currency, finance, and security on his way to a haircut in the grimy old neighborhood where his father had grown up. DeLillo's characters often pursue some dubious grail or other—a venerated baseball or a supposedly pornographic film of Hitler or a drug that releases one from the fear of death. Here Packer, who specializes in foreign exchange, chases after a single currency, which he borrows in prodigious quantities: "He wanted all the yen there was" (97).

Other iterations situate *Cosmopolis* yet more firmly among its fellows: St. Augustine is quoted, as in *Americana*. A cat and mouse game involves the stalking of a "subject," as in *Running Dog*. When a street person seems to squawk at Eric Packer in "[o]ne of those unused voices that sound outside the world" (128), one recalls similar language in *Mao II*. When the protagonist more or less literally stumbles into a street full of naked bodies being filmed by an eerie, never actually seen camera, one thinks of the disaster simulation in *White Noise*. The short-circuiting of time experienced by the characters of *The Body Artist* recurs here in Eric Packer's "seeing things that haven't happened yet" (22), as when he "recoils in shock" on his video monitor *before* the blast that causes him to do so in actuality (93-4) and when, in the confrontation with Richard Sheets, the assassin who renames himself Benno Levin, he witnesses his own death on a watch-face screen (205-9). In *The Names* expatriates ask travelers to distant postings, "Are they killing

179

Americans?" (45, 95). One thinks of this line, not to mention the Kennedy assassination in *Libra*, when Eric Packer wonders, "Do people still shoot at presidents?" (20). Indeed, like Oswald, Packer's assassin contemplates "the violent act that makes history and changes everything that came before" (154).

But the very idea of a history-changing violent act has, since September 2001, taken on fresh meaning, and one senses the looming calamity in DeLillo's thirteenth novel even though the story transpires a year and a half before airplanes were hijacked and flown into hives of activity in New York and Washington. Packer's assassin emphasizes "everything that came before" the act of violence, rather than, as one might expect, everything that comes after. But in fact one can take for granted the transformations of the future—what bears thinking about is the operation performed on the past, itself altered when violence at a certain moment and on a certain scale shifts the historical paradigm. In any event, the author of *Cosmopolis* brilliantly explores a proximate past from the never explicitly stated vantage of post-9/11.

Novelists sometimes tip their hands in nonfiction pieces, their holidays from artistic indirection. In Pynchon's 1984 essay "Is It O.K. to Be a Luddite?" one can see how long the ideas behind the 1997 *Mason & Dixon* had been gestating. DeLillo's *Rolling Stone* essay "American Blood" (1983) helps his readers with *Libra* (1988). "The Power of History," in a 1997 issue of the *New York Times Magazine*, proves an invaluable gloss on DeLillo's magnum opus, *Underworld*, published that same year, as well as on *Cosmopolis*, published six years later. But one learns best how to read this most recent of DeLillo's fictions in the essay on 9/11, "In the Ruins of the Future: Reflections on Terror and Loss in the Shadow of September," that appeared in the December 2001 *Harper's*.

"Technology is our fate, our truth" (37), DeLillo declares in this essay. Yet 9/11, which saw great airplanes bringing down great buildings, may augur some terrible canker at the heart of the technological rose.

> We may find that the ruin of the towers is implicit in other things. The new PalmPilot at fingertip's reach, the stretch limousine parked outside the hotel, the midtown skyscraper under construction, carrying the name of a major investment bank—all haunted in a way by what has happened, less assured in their authority, in the prerogatives they offer. (39)

All of these examples recur in *Cosmopolis*. Here, constantly, the obsolete offends the fastidious eye and mind of Eric Packer: it seems a silent reproach, "anti-futuristic" (54), an annoying reminder of all the rubbish generated by progress. On his "hand organizer," Eric Packer makes "a note to himself about the anachronistic quality of the word skyscraper." One notes that in the later-published text DeLillo no longer refers specifically to a PalmPilot—"[t]he hand device itself was an object whose original culture had just about disappeared. He knew he'd have to junk it"(9). The stretch limousine, too, is part of the calculus of obsolescence. "[T]he global era officially ends," a character remarks, "[w]hen stretch limousines begin to disappear from the streets of Manhattan" (91).

Gardeners planting ivy like to say, "the first year it sleeps, the second year it creeps, the third year it leaps." Technological innovation these days seems no longer to bother with sleeping or creeping—it proceeds straight to quantum transformations. In doing so, it treads into compost its own prior achievements, and this progressive obsolescence or de-suetude figures often in the thoughts of Eric Packer and, in a different way, in those of Don DeLillo. Indeed, in its vaulting ambition, technology o'erleaps itself, like Shakespeare's tragic hero, and figures of outmodedness recur eerily here, this text's most frequently re-peated motif. On nearly every page one hears of "[d]evices . . . already vestigial," including the "ear bud" (19) that security men wear, ATMs (60) and cash registers (71), walkie-talk-ies (102), techno-raves (125, 127), weapons (203), computers that are "in their present form. . . . just about dead as distinct units" (104), and stethoscopes, those "lost tools of antiquity, quaint as blood-sucking worms" (43). The accelerating superannuation also sub-sumes Packer's twenty-two-day-old marriage (122), not to mention Freud and Einstein (6), diamonds (64), the Siberian tiger (81), a corner saxophone player "from the century past" (148), "scan retrieval, a technology that seemed already oppressively sluggish" (34), and the currency analyst, Michael Chin, who declares: "I'm so obsolete I don't have to chew my food" (37). At one point the narrator declares that even "[t]he past is disappearing" (86), yet he declares at another point, paradoxically, that newness itself is obsolete, as are certain art forms: "The work was all the more dangerous for not being new. There's no more danger in the new" (8). Most of the elements in this catalog are noticed by Packer, whose assassin sees him as "always ahead, thinking past what is new. . . . Things wear out impatiently in his hands. . . . He wants to be one civilization ahead of this one" (152). The joke, however, is that from this day's beginning, Packer has himself been on the way out, obsolescing like all the technology around him. As his murderer eventually announces, "You're already dead" (203). The author caps the joke in the odd business of Packer's no-ticing that his actions lag their representation on the screens that feed him information. Seemingly inconsequential, these glimpses of what has not yet happened culminate, ironi-cally, in the ultimate example of being ahead of the curve: before the events actually tran-spire, the man who so prides himself on commanding futurity witnesses on a tiny screen his own death and subsequent tagging in the morgue. The novel concludes shortly before the shot by which he will do in actuality what he has just watched himself do: die.

Characteristically, DeLillo takes as much interest in displacements of language as in the things displaced by new advances. Thus the catalog of obsolescence features a kind of geminate meditation on vestigial vocabulary: "It was time to retire the word phone" (88), "the word office was outdated now" (15), "the word computer sounds backward and dumb" (104). One hears of "vehicles that were sometimes still called ambulances" (67). Most examples, as one would expect, come from technology's outstripping the words that describe it, but more random examples also figure: the narrator mentions "the vestibule, if this is still a word" (182) and describes "laid out" as "an embalmed term in search of a matching cadaver" (136).

Occasionally these asides become little set-pieces, as when certain terms generate a brief spasm of annoyance in the mind of the viewpoint character. Especially contemptuous of the term "walkie-talkie," Packer "wanted to ask the man why he was still using such a contraption, still calling it what he called it, carrying the nitwit rhyme out of the age of industrial glut into smart spaces built on beams of light" (102). One smiles here at the thinker's presumably deliberate choice of a term from the vernacular of low-tech: *contraption*. "Nitwit," of course, further distills the principle of echoic reflexivity reproached in the term under censorious review. Packer also shakes his head at

> automated teller machines. The term was aged and burdened by its own historical memory. It worked at cross-purposes, unable to escape the inference of fuddled human personnel and jerky moving parts. The term was part of the process that the device was meant to replace. It was anti-futuristic, so cumbrous and mechanical that even the acronym seemed dated. (54)

The point, in part, is that our words, like our devices, are subject to time's erosions. They outmode. On the other hand, as DeLillo remarks in his 9/11 essay (where he worries that "[t]he event . . . has no purchase on the mercies of analogy or simile"), "living language is not diminished." Equal to any enormity and "inseparable from the world that provokes it" (39), language accommodates every stress placed on it by the times—whether figurative explosions of technology or literal explosions of airliners colliding with buildings.

DeLillo makes this point repeatedly in both his fiction and his nonfiction. In his 1997 essay "The Power of History," he adduces the work of the Doctorow or Coover who "sets his pleasure, his eros, his creative delight in language . . . against the vast and uniform Death that history tends to fashion as its most enduring work." DeLillo characterizes language itself as "a form of counterhistory," and he asserts a "primal clash—the tendency of the language to work in opposition to the enormous technology of war" (63). Necessarily somewhat less expansive in the 9/11 essay, DeLillo nonetheless recognizes a need for Americans, especially American novelists, to "create the counternarrative" (34).

In his nonfiction prose as in his fiction, DeLillo resists ideology in its more straightforward forms. In the essay on September 2001 he recognizes "[t]wo forces in the world, past and future" (40), the one embraced by reactionary hordes, the other, traditionally, the special province of the democratic ideal and its American exemplar. Comparing the perennial American commitment to the future with the terrorists' passionate repudiation of that vision, the author who once, famously, observed that "[t]he future belongs to crowds" (*Mao II* 16) here refines the point: the crowds who shall inherit the future may themselves belong, ideologically, to the past. DeLillo often seems to invite Marxist interpretation (he certainly wastes no love on consumerism and the simulacra that sustain it), but one finds him here observing a parallel between terrorists and the demonstrators whose fervent protests against global capitalism and the IMF have filled the streets from Seattle to Genoa and from Prague to Washington, DC. Though he sounds sympathetic to those who "want to decelerate the global momentum . . . driving unmindfully toward a landscape of consumer-robots and social instability, with the chance of self-determination probably diminishing for most people in most countries" (33), he nonetheless notes that they have in common with the terrorists a desire to "hold off the white-hot future" (34).

These demonstrators, antagonists to Eric Packer and all that he represents, play a major role in *Cosmopolis*, which omits any direct reference to terrorism. One suspects that the novel and the *Harper's* essay hatched from the same ideational egg, and, if so, one would expect both to engage the events of 9/11. But perhaps no such expectation is warranted. After all, DeLillo has already produced, in *Mao II*, the definitive novelistic treatment of terrorism centered in and emanating from the Near or Middle East. Few readers forget the burgeoning prophecy embodied in the observations of that novel's marginalized writer protagonist, Bill Gray: "Years ago I used to think it was possible for a novelist to alter the inner life of a culture. Now bomb-makers and gunmen have taken that territory. They make raids on human consciousness" (41). Later he adds,

> For some time now I've had the feeling that novelists and terrorists are playing a zero-sum game. . . . What terrorists gain, novelists lose. The degree to which they influence mass consciousness is the extent of our decline as shapers of sensibility and thought. The danger they represent equals our own failure to be dangerous. (156-57)

But for all its references to specific political events and personalities—Moonie nuptials, Khomeni obsequies, Tiananmen Square—*Mao II* comes to focus on something other than the merely topical, for DeLillo never forgets the need in art to be oblique— to tell all the truth, as the poet says, but tell it slant. Even in *Libra*, so squarely concerned with a particular historical event (and ostensibly repudiating the lone-gunman argument),[1] the author proves really to be gauging an epistemic shift in American consciousness. Thus in *Mao II* he refines individual terrorists and their causes to a kind of distillate against which to juxtapose the passionate but effete humanity of one literary artist. This obliquity, this avoidance of the topical, actually facilitates one's applying the general precepts contained in DeLillo's major meditation on terrorism to specific instances, including 9/11. Indeed, readers can judge the quality of a novelist's insight by whether subsequent events give it the lie.

Though nothing about the events of September 2001 invalidates *Mao II* (quite the contrary), those events are of such magnitude as to demand renewed scrutiny of the phenomenon they instantiate. But because the artistic premise holds, a studied indirection characterizes DeLillo's engagement, in his first novel since 9/11, of the anxieties moiling in its wake. What anxieties, specifically? In the "Ruins" essay the author names them: the fear that we no longer own the future, the fear that time itself "is scarcer now," the fear that language and other registers of our affectional lives cannot keep up with reality—whether the reality of towers toppling or of technology so accelerated as to make every new device ephemeral. DeLillo notes here how terrorism —the activity, often, of those who "want to bring back the past" (40)—has the paradoxical effect of creating the perception among its victims (and post-9/11 American society) of a curious collapsing of time and language: "We seem pressed for time, all of us. . . . There is a sense of compression, plans made hurriedly, time forced and distorted" (39).

Thus in *Cosmopolis* Packer thinks, "Freud is finished, Einstein's next" (6) because neither the one's past time, buried in the unconscious, nor the other's temporal relativity seems of any use to a moment replete with political terror and its denial of futurity. To some degree, *Cosmopolis* extends the meditation on time that DeLillo undertook in his previous novel, *The Body Artist*. Now, instead of temporality as metaphysical and emotional conundrum, the reader encounters time in its operations on or relations with technology and language, time as a problem of politics and economics: "Money makes time. It used to be the other way around. Clock time accelerated the rise of capitalism." But "time is a corporate asset now. It belongs to the free market system" (79). Meanwhile, history itself suffers a radical attenuation: "The past is disappearing. We used to know the past but not the future. . . . We need a new theory of time" (86).

Or perhaps we need only remember the ancient lesson of inevitable decline that Frost describes in "The Oven Bird": "There is a singer everyone has heard / Loud, a mid-summer and a mid-wood bird." Frost gauges slippage, deterioration, "what to make of a diminished thing." Midwood happens to be the name of the president in DeLillo's novel. Whether or not the author intends the Frostian echo, this president may preside over the American imperium at its last moment of confidence, exactly seventeen months before destruction of the twin towers (the action of *Cosmopolis* takes place on a single day in April 2000). Readers may in fact scrutinize an organism already stricken, much as a Pynchon character contemplates entropy as an immanence visible under the microscope, "where death dwelled in the cell though the cell be looked in on at its most quick" (Pynchon 122).

In his monomaniacal obsession with futurity, Packer denies entropy. Moreover, he is never more archetypally American than in wanting to be time's custodian—master, indeed, of the future itself. As DeLillo remarks in "Ruins," "We like to think America invented the future. We are comfortable with the future, intimate with it" (39). In the last decade of the second millennium,

> [t]he dramatic climb of the Dow and the speed of the Internet summoned us all to live permanently in the future, in the utopian glow of cyber-capital, because there is no memory there and this is where markets are uncontrolled and investment potential has no limit. (33)

Vija Kinski, half-scoffing "chief of theory" (82) to Eric Packer, echoes the phrase from the essay about effulgent "cyber-capital" (78) as she panders to his fantasies of circumscribing temporal mortality, preserving consciousness by one high-tech means or another. "Why die when you can live on disk?" she asks. "A disk, not a tomb" (105). In the conceit of consciousness transferred, at death, to disk, DeLillo revisits the "tek-tite whirl" of astral existence that figures briefly in *Ratner's Star* (432-33). Even at the moment of his actual death, Packer thinks: "He'd always wanted to become quantum dust. . . . The idea was to live outside the given limits, in a chip, on a disk, as data, in whirl, in radiant spin, a consciousness saved from void" (206).

II.

A month to the day after the 9/11 disasters, DeLillo joined a number of other *New Yorker* writers (among them Woody Allen, Roger Angell, John Ashbery, Jhumpa Lahiri, Janet Malcolm, Lorrie Moore, Paul Muldoon, and John Updike) in a public reading in support of the September 11th Fund. The participants did not read from their own works but from the writings of others. DeLillo chose to read a poem by Zbigniew Herbert, a fellow winner (1990) of the Jerusalem Prize (DeLillo won in 1999). The poem's title—"Report from the Besieged City"—must have seemed painfully apropos, for a state of siege prevails when, as the author says in the *Harper's* article, "passenger jets . . . become manned missiles" (38) and postal anthrax threatens pestilence.

In *Cosmopolis* both the demonstrators and their natural foe, the immensely rich Eric Michael Packer in his limousine, have read the Herbert poem, which furnishes the novel with its epigraph: "a rat became the unit of currency." Though hinted at in images of transport brought to a halt (by presidential motorcade, by rap star's funeral, by hordes of anti-globalism demonstrators, one of whom, like Jack Laws in *Players*, sets fire to himself), the state of siege in this novel is evoked primarily, on page after page, by rats – traditional emblems of corruption, heralds of civilized collapse, and, more prosaically, food of last resort. The rat becomes motivic, especially as the demonstrators display a dead one on a street median and live ones in a luncheonette, dress "in rodent spandex," deploy a murine simulacrum—"a styrofoam rat twenty feet tall"—in street and sidewalk (86), and release "battalions of rats in restaurants and hotel lobbies" (89). Thus do they announce and decry the pestilence of rat-like tycoons battening on the world's green future. In a sense, the rat really is proposed as a "unit of currency" rising as alarmingly as the gravity-defying yen, which will end the financial empire of someone who has "made and lost sums that could colonize a planet" (129). The surname of DeLillo's endlessly acquisitive protagonist, of course, identifies him as something of a pack rat himself, and a neighborhood congenial to rodents awaits him at the end of his book-long transit of Manhattan.

Packer journeys across New York to half a haircut, financial ruin, and death. The text reveals his progress as an inexorable arrowing westward on 47th Street, and DeLillo takes a cartographer's care with the avenues his character crosses. Packer begins the day literally on top of the world—"in the rotating room at the top of the triplex" (5) penthouse of "the tallest residential tower in the world" (8). From this building, located at or near the intersection of 47th and First Avenue (near the Japan Society [11]), he boards his limousine, which carries him past Second Avenue (13) to an amorous call on "a scorched blonde named Didi Fancher" (27), then across Lexington (33), Park (38), Madison (41), and Fifth (63) to a stop at the Gotham Book Mart (66) between Fifth and Sixth. Between Broadway and Eighth Avenue he stops at a luncheonette across from the Barrymore Theater before entering Hell's Kitchen (129). Presently, at Tenth Avenue, he crosses into the tenement district where "his father had grown up" (158-59). Soon "[t]he car approached Eleventh Avenue" (170), "the last street before the river," whence it enters "the car barrens" (179).

Perhaps, given Packer's archetypal identity as American tycoon, his transit parodies the westward movement that has defined the nation. But chiefly DeLillo toys here with the conceit of the life-journey. His westerly progress across the "world city" (88) carries Packer from dawn in his forty-eight-room, 104-million-dollar apartment through mounting chaos (demonstrators in the streets, the yen rising in value against all expectations) to an emblematic end in one of Manhattan's dingiest quarters. When Packer dies, his corpse resembles that of a street person: no socks, ripped pocket, no undershirt, half a haircut, foul body odor. A human rat.

In his crosstown journey he travesties both Homeric hero and Leopold Bloom (whose odyssey also takes a single day). Packer is an Odysseus striving to return to paternal halls in the "car barrens" at the western extremity of the island. But where the Greek hero sought to return to the arms of faithful Penelope, DeLillo's Odysseus improbably runs into his wife four times. Like Odysseus, who sojourns with Circe, Calypso, and Nausicaa before reaching Penelope, Packer dallies with Didi Fancher, his bodyguard Kendra Hays, and (without their actually touching) "his chief of finance" (38), Jane Melman, before the long-desired and long-postponed sexual encounter with his wife. Odysseus clasps Penelope at last over the corpses of her suitors; Packer and Elise couple only steps away from a similar tangle of bodies. Like the Odysseus of Dante and Tennyson, DeLillo's hero resumes his journey and meets his doom.

The literary antecedents may also include Xenophon's *Anabasis*, which concerns the heroic march of an army of Greek mercenaries left to their own devices at the death of the Persian king they had signed to fight for. They must make their way to the sea across leagues of hostile territory. The story inspired Walter Hill's 1979 film *The Warriors*, in which some urban gang members must survive an arduous journey through territory held by rival gangs. DeLillo's Eric Packer also makes his way through hordes ravening for capitalist blood, but his arrival at Manhattan's riparian boundary occasions no triumphant cries of *thalassa! thalassa!*

Rather, he survives only to perish at the hands of a disgruntled former employee. The absurdist colloquy between these two obsessives recalls Jack Gladney's encounter with Lewis Mink at the end of *White Noise*—not to mention the famous meeting of Humbert Humbert and Clare Quilty. Again "[t]he confrontation" threatens to "crumble into farce" (187). Benno Levin is Packer's personal Angel of Death, countertype to Malamud's more benign visitant, the Angel Levine. He drapes his head with a tallith-like towel (187, 189) and "rocked back and forth, a little mystically, muttering" (206). As if to hint at a shared identity, both Packer and his assassin have asymmetrical prostates (199). As is usual with the Doppelgänger trope, the one reifies the other's unconscious. As Lewis Mink embodies Jack Gladney's fear of death or Clare Quilty Humbert's pedophilia, Levin hypostatizes the something pathological in Packer's heart all along. Mink shoots Gladney in the wrist, but Packer, a Midas carrying out sentence on the very instrument of his "touch," shoots himself in the hand, just as he has already shot himself in the foot, so to speak, by squandering his wife's fortune, murdering Torval, his chief of security, and, above all, "[b]etting against the yen" (29). Small wonder that the library subject headings included on this novel's copyright page include "self-destructive behavior."

In life and at the moment of his death Packer remains unlovable, and the reader can take largely at face value the reproaches of his assassin: "The self-totality. The lack of remorse" (191). The being "foully and berserkly rich" (193). The "apartment and what you paid for it . . . . your daily medical checkups. . . . the limousine that displaces the air that people need to breathe in Bangladesh" (202). But readers may puzzle over the rest of the picture here. They must decide whether other major components of the story—the anti-globalism demonstration, for example, or the rap star's funeral—are somehow rendered positive by what they seem to contrast.

DeLillo puzzles us sometimes with characters whose aimlessness seems unanswered by their leading reflective, well-read lives. Nick Shay's many books seem not to gainsay his anomie. By the same token, though Eric Packer reads German as well as English; collects art, "mainly color-field and geometric" (8); and likes poetry, he remains thoroughly unsavory, the shark in the aquarium built into one wall of his living room hinting at the ethos by which he lives (remembering what he did to Torval, Packer "thought of others down through the years" [196]). The point is not so much that he is a poseur (though his criteria for poems—their brevity and appearance on the page—strike one as precious). The point, rather, is that taste, connoisseurship, and other such corollaries to great wealth must not be thought to confer moral distinction. In contradistinction to a popular villain such as Thomas Harris's Hannibal Lecter (who gradually gains in stature, from novel to novel, in part because his aesthetic sense so separates him from the unimaginative careerists who pursue him), Eric Packer remains, for all his love of poetry and painting, a son of a bitch.

But readers should guard against thinking that the author necessarily favors any and all characters or institutions at odds with Packer. The unsympathetic depiction of the currency trader does not entail a positive view of, say, the anti-globalist demonstrators that he must cope with on his journey across town. Like any other DeLillo novel, *Cosmopolis* resists thoughtless reading. DeLillo delights in creating texts that confound unexamined projection. Because he writes about rock music or consumer excess or the waste industry, uncritical readers are easily persuaded of his musical, Marxist, and ecological biases. In *Great Jones Street*, to take a representative example, he depicts a rock star and his circle in such a way as to accommodate (and challenge) the biases of both lovers and haters of rock music and its ethos. Thus whatever the author of *Cosmopolis* thinks of globalism or big capital, he takes little interest in polemic. Rather, he cares passionately about capturing the cultural moment in actions and characters that he realizes in language crafted to the purpose—language and style that register public obsessions with just sufficient strangeness to promote our actually seeing what the film of familiarity otherwise obscures.

The representation of the obsequies paid to a fictional pop culture icon, the recently deceased rapper Brutha Fez, provides a test case. Does DeLillo applaud this individual's alleged spiritual integrity ("[h]e lived in a minaret for a while, in Los Angeles" [135]), his engagement with Sufism and its ancient musical forms? Does he pay solemn tribute to rap as latter-day refuge to that figure of decadent romanticism, the artist-outlaw? I think not. In *Great Jones Street* DeLillo grimly jokes about expectations for the demise of rock stars: they are supposed to OD or commit suicide. A similar joke figures here: rappers are supposed to be shot. But Brutha Fez, like Bucky Wunderlick, resists the stereotype: incredibly, he has died of natural causes. As I read my advance copy of *Cosmopolis*, by the way, news came of the shooting death of one Jam Master Jay (I had never heard of him), and newspapers were quick to note the parallels with the gunshot deaths of Tupac Shakur, Freaky Tah, Albert Thomas, and The Notorious B.I.G. Even more striking were the real-life details of Jam Master's obsequies: a wake with thousands of mourners and a funeral featuring "[a] fleet of white stretch limousines . . . outside the Allen A.M.E. Cathedral in Queens."[2]

Brutha Fez's lyrics, as reproduced by DeLillo, alternate between the pseudo-Levantine and the asinine, and his funeral travesties every great procession since Roman times, including the grand march in *Aida* and the funerals of President Kennedy and Princess Di. Clearly echoing the pictures in *Mao II* of vast, unthinking crowds, Brutha Fez's day-long funeral features a "squad of motorcycles, city police in wedge formation," then "[t]wo private security vans, flanking a police cruiser" (131), "[t]hen . . . the flower cars, ten of them, banked with white roses," then "[t]he hearse . . . with Fez lying in state at the rear in a coffin angled upward to make the body visible" (132). "Four of Fez's personal bodyguards accompanied the hearse, slow-marching, one off each point of the car." This entourage is accompanied by "[s]cores of women . . . barefoot, and wailing," and followed by six "breakdancers" (133). Next come

thirty-six white stretch limousines, three abreast, with the mayor and the police commissioner in sober profile, and a dozen members of Congress, and the mothers of unarmed blacks shot by police, and fellow rappers in the middle phalanx, and there were media executives, foreign dignitaries, faces from film and TV, and mingled throughout were figures of world religion in their robes, cowls, kimonos, sandals and soutanes. (134-35)

Overhead fly "[f]our news choppers" (135), and among the mourners below are dervishes (whirling, of course), as well as "[a] line of elderly Catholic nuns in full habit," who "recited the rosary, teachers from the grade school he'd attended" (135). Lastly: "the follow-up security detail . . . a police van and several unmarked cars," then "press buses . . . three of them, and unofficial mourners on foot," then "mourners in cars . . . eighty, ninety cars in slack ranks" (139).

Anyone who has wondered what became of "black humor" ought to pause over that line about the mothers of unarmed blacks shot by police. But after a certain amount of incredulous head-shaking or laughter, one realizes just how little has been exaggerated here. Over the top? Only slightly, as one discovers in news accounts of Jam Master Jay's obsequies, which DeLillo uncannily anticipates. Indeed, shocking new acts on the world stage seem routinely to open out of town, as it were, in the fictions of Don DeLillo (his imagining of the Airborne Toxic Event of *White Noise* preceded the Bhopal disaster, and an incident in *Players* prefigures the bombing of the World Trade Center). Hardly surprising, then, that here again DeLillo seems to have written the future. Watched by "a line of police officers, ready for trouble," reports Andy Newman in the 7 November 2002 *New York Times*, the mourners who assembled to pay their respects to the fallen rapper included "old-schoolers, young bloods, grandmothers, small children, jet-setters, neighbors." The deceased was remembered as a "preacher and practitioner of nonviolence who died violently." Presently, "the scene on the street took on elements of a block party. One after another, sport utility vehicles cruised slowly by, each one blasting Run-DMC's music at maximum volume." Meanwhile, "MTV trucks broadcast from the front of the funeral home. Rosie Perez was spotted. So was Grandmaster Flash. By 8 p.m., the line stretched on for three blocks." The clincher, reported without a hint of editorial irony, was the remark of a mourner with a truly impaired sense of proportion: "It kind of reminds me of 9/11" (Newman n.p.).

DeLillo devotes considerable space to the rapper funeral because the world of popular music intersects the world of global capital—especially as represented by Eric Packer, longtime friend and admirer of Brutha Fez, whose music plays continually in one of the two elevators in the tycoon's penthouse. Sketching a seemingly bizarre and improbable relationship between these personalities, DeLillo juxtaposes causes and passions whose mutual interpenetration seems never to occur to those they sweep up: one suspects that those who deplore global capital, especially as it manifests itself in government and multinational corporations and proliferating technology, pay little attention to its most local workings—in, for example, the music industry. "The Sufi rap star" (29) and Eric Packer are two sides of the same . . . coin. Benno Levin hints at some such obverse-reverse conundrum when he characterizes "words" and "sounds" or "sex and love" as "two separate systems that we miserably try to link" (55). In fact the economic system unites more than any two disparate quantities—and unites things much more disparate than words and sounds, sex and love, or rap and global capital. Not that the interdependencies need always be counterintuitive. Packer recognizes "[th]e interaction between technology and capital" as the "only . . . thing worth pursuing professionally and intellectually" (23).

A postmodern Max Weber might say that whoever grasps this reticulation of intricately balanced and interactive forces wields power and grows rich. Eric Packer smiles at the inchoate fury of the demonstrators, knowing that their passion has already been subsumed by the larger dynamic of the Western economic model: "The protest was a form of systemic hygiene, purging and lubricating. It attested again, for the ten-thousandth time, to the market culture's innovative brilliance, its ability to shape itself to its own flexible ends, absorbing everything around it" (99). That last phrase bears repeating: absorbing everything around it. The scale of such absorption is cosmic, its locus, *eo ipso*, cosmopolis. The activities that trouble the world city of DeLillo's novel—currency speculation, global rapacity, presidential and funerary processions, economic luddism—together represent the unholy collocation of forces on the cusp of the millennium this April day in the year 2000.

The author of *Cosmopolis* ultimately rewrites the famous Hawthorne story in which a young man comes to the city in which he expects to rise in the world with the help of a powerful kinsman. But Hawthorne's Robin arrives in Boston (the colonial equivalent of DeLillo's turn-of-the-millennium New York) just as the kinsman runs afoul of an angry mob led by a fiendish figure who has painted his face an alarming red and black. DeLillo, too, depicts a riotous protest of citizens who, painting themselves in "anarchist red-and-black" (89, 92, 101), seek to overturn the current political and economic order. But DeLillo makes his viewpoint character a version of Major Molineux himself, on his way to a fate worse than tarring and feathering. Hawthorne's story invites interpretation as an allegory of the coming revolution. That is, Robin embodies a whole country just beginning to experience what has been brought fully to consciousness in the New England town to which he comes. Symbolically, Robin represents the first, tentative steps towards independence of the American nation, which, like the lad, will presently come of age. Whether the passion of Eric Packer augurs another such American climacteric DeLillo does not say. He suggests, however, that in the fullness of time every Robin must lose his springy step and grow rigid: sooner or later the archetypal American ephebe must wake up to find himself Molineux after all: rich, powerful, arrogant, widely reviled.

NOTES

[1] As I have argued elsewhere, those who take at face value the author's seeming support for conspiracy theorists miss an essential point, which is that metanarratives, not least one that would account definitively for the assassination, died with Kennedy. See the *Libra* chapter in my *Don DeLillo: The Physics of Language*, 110.

[2] Columbia, SC *State*, 6 November 2002, D1.

WORKS CITED

Cowart, David. *Don DeLillo: The Physics of Language.* Athens: U of Georgia P, 2002.

DeLillo, Don. *Ratner's Star.* New York: Knopf, 1976.

———. *The Names.* New York: Knopf, 1982.

———. *Mao II.* New York: Viking, 1991.

———. "The Power of History." *New York Times Magazine* 7 September 1997: 60-63.

———. "In the Ruins of the Future: Reflections on Terror and Loss in the Shadow of September." *Harper's* December 2001: 37-40.

———. *Cosmopolis.* New York: Scribner, 2003.

Newman, Andy. "Friends and Fans Mourn Slain Rap D.J. at Wake." *New York Times* 7 November 2002 <http://www.nytimes.com/2002/11/05/nyregion/05RAPP> 8 November 2002.

Pynchon, Thomas. *The Crying of Lot 49.* Philadelphia: Lippincott, 1966.

Udo J. Hebel
Performing the Spectacle of Technology at
the Beginning of the American Century:
Steven Millhauser's *Martin Dressler*

Steven Millhauser's *Martin Dressler: The Tale of an American Dreamer* (1996) fictionalizes the
historic moment when the spread of modern technology merged with the collective impulse to theatricalize American culture as an "imperial spectacle" (Trachtenberg 229).[1]
In its return to the last decade of the nineteenth and the first decade of the twentieth century, Millhauser's narrative of the rise and fall of a prototypical immigrant protagonist
evokes the time period when American culture turned into "a great civic drama" (Fisher
158) and the "magnification of personality" (Fisher 155-56) became a collective, if not
national, project. If the years between 1890 and 1910 can indeed be described as "a series
of experiments in the modeling of a highly visible structure of identity under the new circumstances of conspicuous performance" (Fisher 164), *Martin Dressler* may be taken as a
symbolic enactment of the desire to perform such a "magnification of personality" and to
stage an "imperial spectacle" with the help of the technological innovations that governed
the popular imagination at the beginning of the so-called "American century."[2]

*****

Set in New York City in the later phase of the Gilded Age, the novel tells the story of a
poor immigrant boy who rises in conventional rags-to-riches-fashion to tremendous
wealth and legendary fame. On his way up from bellboy and cigar store worker to the
position of a powerful owner of ever more grandiose, ever more ambitious, and ever
more innovative hotels, Martin Dressler is driven by "an almost physical desire to pour
out his energy without constraint" (65).[3] He is determined by "a surge of energy" (60)
that he sees at work everywhere in the processes and products of urban modernity. He is
fascinated by contemporaneous technology and revels in fantasies of his own participation in wonderful acts of technological designing and engineering. Since his first entry
into the hotel world that would become the realm of his relentless self-aggrandizing,
the protagonist is especially thrilled by elevators. The obviously symbolic movement
and the "odd sensation [of] falling upwards" (10f.) captivate his imagination and excite
his ambition. For young Martin Dressler, the "spectacle" of the hotel machinery, with
lobby elevators visibly at the center of gravity, holds the potential to fulfill his urge for
the creation of "a world within the world, rivaling the world" (284):

As the day grew brighter and louder Martin felt himself filling with light and sound, so that
by noon he was ready to burst with energy. Sometimes after changing back into his clothes,

he sat for a few minutes in a soft chair in the main lobby and took it all in: the people walking about or taking their ease, the shiny mahogany desks in the writing rooms, laughter in the ladies' parlor, the gilt hexagons on the ceiling, the great marble stairway. The spectacle interested him, interested him deeply, though it came over him that he wasn't particularly eager for a way of life represented by marble and gilt and feathered hats. No, what seized his innermost attention, what held him there day after day in noon revery, was the sense of a great, elaborate structure, a system of order, a well-planned machine that drew all these people to itself and carried them up and down in iron cages and arranged them in private rooms. He admired the hotel as an invention, an ingenious design, a kind of idea, like a steam boiler or a suspension bridge. (24)[4]

Bridges—and especially Brooklyn Bridge as a prominent contemporary expression of the "geometrical sublime" (Nye 77-108)—stir the protagonist's aspiration as incorporations of superiority, achievement, and technological triumph. Not unexpectedly, Washington Roebling is one the heroes of technological progress celebrated in the elaborate decorations of the Dressler hotels (236). In one of several visionary passages of the novel, Martin Dressler's expansionist desire is made manifest in steam-driven elevators and the piers of Brooklyn Bridge, supported by yet another symbol of modern technology, the telegraph cable. In the protagonist's conception of the world, the icons of the American technological sublime reach out east and west, downward and upward, in a gesture of global, imperial embracement:

Here at the end of the line, here at the world's end, the world didn't end: iron piers stretched out over the ocean, iron towers pierced the sky, somewhere under the water a great telegraph cable longer than the longest train stretched past sunken ships and octopuses all the way to England – and Martin had the odd sensation, as he stood quietly in the lifting and falling waves, that the world, immense and extravagant, was rushing away in every direction: behind him the fields were rolling into Brooklyn and Brooklyn was rushing into the river, before him the waves repeated themselves all the way to the hazy shimmer of the horizon, in the river between the two cities the bridge piers went down through the water to the river bottom and down through the river bottom halfway to China, while up in the sky the steam-driven elevators rose higher and higher until they became invisible in the hot blue summer haze. (16f.)

Throughout the course of his expansion, the protagonist is moved by "a sense of spaces opening out endlessly, of turnings and twistings, of new discoveries beyond the next door" (197). He is driven by "a sense not simply of abundance or immensity, but of the inexhaustible" (273). Modern technology serves as the means and foil for the projection of the protagonist's urge for spectacular self-production.

Martin Dressler draws much of the inspiration and energy for his "desire to create the world" (282) from repeated wanderings through the construction sites of late nineteenth-century New York City. He experiences the emerging metropolis as a gigantic space of architectural conception and technological (re)production:

Sometimes he seemed to hear, all up and down the West End, a great ripping or break-ing, as bedrock split open to give birth to buildings. Along the Boulevard, on Amster-dam and Columbus, on lots facing the Central Park, on side streets between Sixtieth and 110th, hoardings seemed to spring up overnight. Many of the new buildings were small apartment houses under seven stories, which the housing laws did not require to be fireproofed, but ten-story and twelve-story apartment houses were also going up, and here and there a builder of hotels aspired to something grander, something that rang out like a bell. From the roof garden of the Dressler Martin looked down at a world of open pits and blasted rock, of half-finished apartments prickly with scaf-folding, of steam cranes slashing their black diagonals across brownstone and brick. It was as if the West End had been raked over by a gigantic harrow and planted with seeds of steel and stone; now as the century turned, the avenues had begun to erupt in strange, immense growths: modern flowers with veins of steel, bursting out of bedrock. (234f.)

Metaphors of growth and images of disruption melt in the protagonist's visionary mind to formulate the blueprint for a future whose threatening undertone appeals to his ex-plosive imagination. He carefully plans his daily schedule so that he can be present at specific construction sites "to watch men blasting a twenty-foot-high ledge of rock to make way for a new shipping magnate's mansion" (84). At times joined on his trips by Emmeline Vernon, kindred spirit, would-be lover, and business partner, Martin Dressler is thrilled by the transitional openness of the construction sites. He enjoys the untamed activities as congenial expressions of his own unbound energy, physical desires, and sense of unlimited potentiality:

It was a clear cold blue day. He walked toward the river and then turned uptown along the winding avenue that ran along the park. It was rumored that an apartment house would soon rise among the stone mansions of the avenue, but blocks of vacant lots and high rocky outcroppings still gave a touch of wildness that invigorated him. On a sloping side street he stopped at a hoarding and looked over the rough boards at an excavation in progress. A yellow steam shovel sat at the bottom of a pit of blasted rock and hard-looking chalky dirt. The dip-per handle of the shovel swung slowly and stopped over a truck heaped with dirt and rocks. Dirt poured from the dipper and slid down the sides of the heap in the truck. A dark horse with a dirty white mane that looked like thick pieces of yarn snorted as it lifted and lowered a hoof. A workman in a blue wool cap sat on a rock eating an apple. Perhaps because of the cold clear air and the clear blue sky, Martin had the sense that he could see things very clear-ly: the woolly yellowish-white hairs in the horse's mane, the workman's reddish hand mat-ted with yellow hairs, wheel ruts in the dirt ramp leading down to the pit, the shadowed hole drilled in a boulder for a stick of dynamite, the glistening black letters of the company name on the yellow cab of the steam shovel, the smokelike rippling shadow cast on the rocky dirt by bursts of steam from the shovel's stack. He felt clear and clean and calm. You dug into the ground and made a hole, and from that hole a building grew—or a wondrous bridge. In his childhood, workmen had been lowered to the bottom of the East River in two great wooden caissons, and from there they had dug down through mud and clay and sand and boulders to a depth of more than forty feet. From those two holes under the river the towers of the

1: Brooklyn Bridge Under Construction

2: George Bellows: "Pennsylvania Station Excavation" (1909)

great bridge had slowly risen up, block by granite block. Now buildings with frames of steel were rising above the height of the mighty bridgetowers. All across the city steam shovels were digging, truck horses pulling, boom derricks swinging. The edge of a pink poster flapped on the fence. Steam poured from the shovel, the truck horses snorted and stamped, a small bird lit on the hoarding and at once rose up, flying higher and higher into the bright clear sky. (188-90)

*****

Martin Dressler dedicates his physical energy and imaginative powers to the construction and management of ever more magnificent hotels. Throughout the nineteenth century, American hotels had achieved a specific cultural significance and were regarded as "palaces of the public" and even as "the tangible republic."[5] In the territories of the West, hotels followed the westward movement of the frontier and, in the conception of a migratory population, were regarded as "both creatures and creators of communities, as well as symptoms of the frenetic quest for community" (Boorstein 143). In the emerging metropolitan spaces of late-nineteenth-century America, the famous grand hotels[6] became the very site where pioneering technological innovations such as elevators, steam heating, plumbing, telephones, and all kinds of electrical appliances and lighting gadgets were first presented to an amazed public and used for commercial purposes. In *Martin Dressler*, the descriptions of ever-grander hotels and especially the advertisements announcing their completion and attractiveness, read like inventories of the most recent technological advances and their successful implementation in the hotels presented. When the Vanderlyn Hotel, the first hotel under Martin Dressler's management, is renovated, the replacement of older equipment by modern appliances is repeatedly stressed because "up-to-date improvements weren't luxuries but necessities of the modern hotel" (69). When the Dressler hotels get more modern and more compelling with every new attempt to push beyond the limits of the previous structure, the emphasis on the technological achievement becomes central to the marketing strategy.

The protagonist's perception of his advance and the reactions of the public to the Dressler palaces are rendered in great detail throughout the second half of the novel. The rebuilding of the Vanderlyn and its reopening in October 1897 is presented as a "well-intentioned push into the modern world" (168). The Hotel Dressler, opening August 31, 1899, is praised for its technical standard and "the building's boldness of vision" (210). The New Dressler, opening August 31, 1902, exceeds the older Dressler in height and is to "express in a single building what the city was expressing separately in its hotels and skyscrapers and department stores" (235). The climax in every respect imaginable is reached with "the colossal building" (271) of the last of the Dressler hotels, the Grand Cosmo. Upon its opening September 5, 1905, it is advertised as "a complete and self-sufficient world, in comparison with which the actual city was not simply inferior, but superfluous" (265). Martin Dressler's competition with himself, appears to be a symbolically condensed version of the rivalry towards the end of the nineteenth century for the most grandiose, most spectacular, and technologically most advanced hotel in America.

The technological superiority of the interior of the Dressler hotels finds its correspondence in the magnitude of their construction. The Dressler buildings do not only go deeper and deeper into the ground after ever more powerful blasts (232, 256-7); they also expand upward into the sky. The protagonist's fascination with skyscrapers makes him marvel at a still modestly tall structure during a train ride through the increasingly vertical landscape of late nineteenth-century urban New York:

> From trains rushing north and south he pointed at the tops of horsecars and brewer's wagons, at wharves and square-riggers and barrel-heaped barges, at awnings stained rust-red from showers of iron particles ground off by El train brake shoes. He pointed at open windows through which they could see women bent over sewing machines and coatless men in vests playing cards around a table, pointed at intersecting avenues and distant high hotels — and there in the sky, a miracle of steel-frame construction, the American Surety building, twenty stories high, dwarfing old Trinity's brownstone tower. (95)

The rhetorical gesture of the Dressler hotels follows the skyscraper's defining movement beyond architectural pragmatics and beyond the natural horizon. The protagonist's indomitable ambition to magnify his personality and increase his visibility covers past worlds of traditions and spiritualism. The grand Dressler towers—sacred matter for the protagonist—stand out against the newly emerging skyline of the twentieth century as the miraculous reification of a seemingly boundless dynamics, both individually and nationally. In his 1896 essay, "The Tall Office Building Artistically Considered," Louis Sullivan describes the modern skyscraper as a "stark, staring exclamation of eternal strife" and claims:

> [W]hat is the chief characteristic of the tall office building? And at once we answer, it is lofty. This loftiness is to the artist-nature its thrilling aspect. It is the very open organ-tone in its appeal. It must be in turn the dominant chord in his expression of it, the true excitant of his imagination. It must be tall, every inch of it tall. The force and power of altitude must be in it, the glory and pride of exaltation must be in it. It must be every inch a proud and soaring thing, rising in sheer exultation [. . .]. (341, 343)

The ambivalence of *loftiness*—the semantic tension between haughtiness and elevation—characterizes the protagonist and his soaring constructions. In *American Technological Sublime*, David E. Nye has argued that "economic and technical factors alone are not sufficient to explain the development of the skyscraper" (89)[7] towards the end of the nineteenth century. As publicly recognizable icons of progress standing out against the new, artificial horizon of the metropolitan skyline, skyscrapers became, in the words of

3: The Plaza Hotel, New York City (1900)

4: Flatiron Building, New York (1902)

Alfred Stieglitz, "a picture of new America still in the making" (qtd. in Nye 95). Millhauser's protagonist shares and represents the contemporary enthusiasm, if not ecstasy, with skyscrapers as the material embodiment of individual and collective energy and power. For Martin Dressler, skyscrapers are "the most deliberately theatrical and conspicuous building type since the medieval cathedral"[8] and therefore a congenial manifestation of his desire for conspicuous performance. Martin Dressler's skyscraper hotels are the ultimate expression of his will to stick out and enact his expanding personality on the stages of metropolitan New York and beyond (Fisher 167-68).[9]

✳✳✳✳✳

In his desire to carry out his gigantic vision, the protagonist is driven by the need to create something new and different: "[I]t seemed to Martin that if only he could imagine something else, something great, something greater, something as great as the whole world, then he might rest awhile" (243). With every new hotel, Martin Dressler's Promethean ambition for the conception of an increasingly "complex system of forces" and the invention of a "gorgeous interwoven design" (170) becomes more dominant. The Grand Cosmo is to surpass the New Dressler "not merely in size but in every other way, for Martin had leaped beyond the idea of a hotel to something quite new" (257). "MORE THAN A HOTEL: A WAY OF LIFE" (235), reads the slogan advertising the New Dressler; "THE GRAND COSMO: A NEW CONCEPT IN LIVING" (264), reads the commercial for the last of the Dressler buildings. With every new advance, Martin Dressler's hotels change more into "a hybrid form, a transitional form, in which the hotel had begun to lose its defining characteristics" (240). The protagonist had embarked on his professional career with "the idea of joining a circus" (19). He ends up constructing a "gorgeous" world which constitutes nothing less and nothing more than a circus spectacle of unprecedented magnitude, diversity, and technological elaboration—even in terms of P.T. Barnum, the unrivaled master of playful fraud and sophisticated humbug in nineteenth-century American culture.[10] In his relentless pursuit of technological novelty and its performative display, the protagonist dissolves boundaries of various kinds.[11] He is ready to exploit "the kinship between the hotel and the department store" (181) and invites the "intrusion of the museum into the world of the hotel" (213). He includes theater districts, moving panoramas, *tableaux vivantes*, ethnographical exhibits, health spas, and parks into what used to be a more or less luxurious place to live in. The Grand Cosmo incorporates so many different spaces and formats "that [it] was never the same from one day to the next, that its variety was, in a sense, limitless" (267). The dynamic *Gesamtkunstwerk* of the last Dressler hotel comprises an almost endless, grotesque, if not Kafkaesque,[12] array of attractions and spectacles: special floors designed as artificial countryside or beach resorts; automated dioramas displaying scenes from New England village life and the Amazon jungle next to each other; park sets with artificial moonlight and mechanical nightingales; electrically operated reconstructions of New York City street scenes; theater houses with revolving stages; machine-driven reenactments of historical events and elaborate stage sets representing civilizations of far-away solar systems; department stores with moving displays; and, among the many novelties of late nineteenth- and early twentieth-century entertainment culture, "the Theatrum Mundi, a globe-shaped chamber in which black-and-white images from every corner of the known world were projected in ever-changing cinematographic montage, showing oncoming trains, the faces of English coal miners, Amazon alligators, cyclists in bloomers, polar bears, the Flatiron Building, a Dutch girl watering a tulip" (270f.).

With the technologically enhanced hotelscape of the Grand Cosmo, the immigrant protagonist has cast his juvenile vision into the abysmal specter of a fabulously oversized fair world. In both its larger scheme and details, the design of the Grand Cosmo evokes the exhibits and attractions of the climax of late nineteenth-century American fair industry, the Chicago World's Columbian Exposition of 1892/93.[13] The self-contained exhibitionism[14] of the last Dressler hotel is promoted in public relations drives that are organized in unheard-of magnitude and intensity by a certain Mr. Harwinton, one of Martin Dressler's complementary egos. In Harwinton's campaigns, the Dressler hotels and their intricate technological design dissolve into fantastic promise and self-referential suggestiveness. At the dawn of the "American century," the supposed limitlessness and alleged omnipresence of the Grand Cosmo—the grand cosmology of the Dressler design—evoke the illusion of an all-encompassing availability which the technology and virtual reality of the Internet now suggests in a different, yet even more all-encompassing, panorama of images and simulations. The phantasmagoric machineries of Martin Dressler's hotels are wavering back and forth between, on the one hand, contemporary utopian projections such as King Camp Gillette's apartment buildings (1894), Charles Caryl's model city (1897), and Thomas Kirwan's "Town Mansion" (1909)[15] and, on the other hand, the even more self-contained illusionism and monstrously fascinating spectacle of turn-of-the-millennium, postmodern theme parks—Disney, Las Vegas, or any other brand name.

✳✳✳✳✳

The architectural mastermind catering to Martin Dressler's visionary urge is Rudolf Arling, a recent immigrant from Austria.[16] The architect's "passion for the colossal" (192) and the hotelkeeper's "yearning for the exhaustive" (275) join forces to produce the technological spectacle of the Dressler worlds. While still in Vienna, Arling had made a name for himself with the construction of a "large pleasure garden on the outskirts of the city, with carousels, dance pavilions, and a beer garden under a grove of lindens" (191). At the center of this merger of Prater and Coney Island, "he placed a colossal building that he called a Pleasure Dome, a cylindrical white structure six stories high with hydraulic elevators that carried enchanted visitors to a wide upper walk from which they had a view of the entire park" (191).[17] Arling had started his career in Europe as a designer of stage sets and is said to have brought to his American projects a special liking for theatricality and performativity. The Theatrum Mundi in the Grand Cosmo radiates "the dubious, provisional air of a theatrical performance" (240) with which Arling invests his constructions. Martin Dressler, in turn, had been strangely attracted to everything theatrical ever since an early encounter with a group of actors in the Vanderlyn Hotel (11-2). The synergy of Rudolf Arling and Martin Dressler transforms the space of the traditional hotel into a gigantic, if not cosmic, stage for the performance of a grand spectacle that blurs all remaining boundaries between reality and illusion.[18]

The energy for the conspicuous performance of the Dressler spectacle is provided by electric plants which are represented in the novel as the very icons and sources of modernity as which they were perceived towards the end of the nineteenth-century.[19] For the protagonist, who greatly enjoys wandering through the enchanted labyrinths of the technological undergrounds of his constructions, the huge dynamos are the centerpiece of his project:

In the warm, faded light, in a stillness made deeper by dim sounds sifting through, Martin closed his eyes.

And at once he saw: deep under the earth, in darkness impenetrable, an immense dynamo was humming. Above the dynamo was an underground hive of shops, with electric lights and steam heat, and above the shops an underground park or garden with what seemed to be a theater of some kind. Above the ground a great lobby stretched away: elevator doors opened and closed, people strode in and out, bells rang, the squeak of valises mingled with the rattle of many keys and the ringing of many telephones, alcove opened into alcove as far as the eye could see. Above the lobby rose two floors of public rooms and then the private rooms began, floor after floor of rooms, higher and higher, a vertical city, a white tower, a steel flower—and always elevators rising and falling, from the cloud-piercing top to the darkness where the great dynamo hummed. Martin had less the sense of observing the building than of inhabiting it at every point: he rose and fell in the many elevators, he strolled through the parlor of an upper room and walked in the underground park or garden—and then it was as if the structure were his own body, his head piercing the clouds, his feet buried deep in the earth, and in his blood the plunge and rise of elevators.

Martin's eyes opened. He was sitting in the lobby of the Vanderlyn Hotel. He was feeling a little tired, his heart was beating rapidly—and from his heart there beat, in wave after wave, a wild, sweet exhilaration. (173f.)

The Dressler hotels are equipped with ever-more powerful electric plants that are presented as the driving force of the enterprise. The protagonist's "American dream" (see the subtitle of the novel) seems to be realized in the construction and successful maintenance of a world that is animated by dynamos and the electrical appliances they energize:

5: Chicago World's Columbian Exposition,
View from Wooded Island (1893)

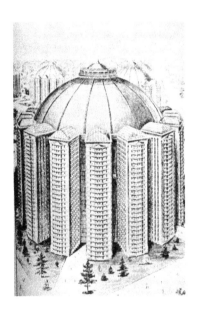

6: King Camp Gilette,
Model Apartment Building (1894)

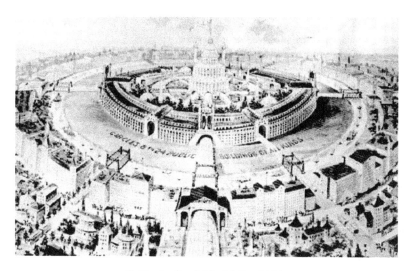

7: Charles Caryl, Model City (1897)

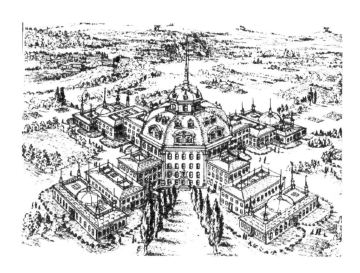

8: Thomas Kirwan, "The Town Mansion" (1909)

Beneath the labyrinth lay the true bottom of the New Dressler, the bottom beneath the bottom: the basement. It was a dark realm with many subdivisions, including the electric plant with its dynamos, the steam plant with its boilers, the laundry rooms with their boiling tubs and steam dryers, the ironing rooms, the storage rooms, the employee cafeteria, and the workshops for the large maintenance staff of the New Dressler: the painters, the electricians, the seamstresses, the upholsterers, the silver polishers, the carpenters. In the vast underground world of half-darkness and hissing steam, of hammer-knocks and the rumble of dynamos, Martin liked to walk for hours at a time, observing the machines that gave life to the building, watching the work of the repairmen, speaking with the laundresses, their sleeves rolled to the elbow, their forearms glistening, their faces shiny in the damp warm air. (245)

Martin Dressler's initial conception of "a great, elaborate structure, a system of order, a well-planned machine" finds its incorporation in the vibrant and brightly illuminated bodies of the New Dressler and the Grand Cosmo. In view of the intricate and massive electrification of all parts of the buildings, minor and major, inside and outside, the protagonist "experiences an ecstasy of embodiment" (Saltzman 620)[20] which embraces himself and the products of his imaginative energy. Brimming with the electricity that is generated in their own underworlds and which enhances the theatrical utopianism of the Dressler spectacle, the hotel towers soar into the metropolitan sky in a fusion of hotel building and Coney Island, in a merger of beacon and Babel. If electrification, and especially the artificial light and lighting that it was able to produce on an unprecedented scale around the turn from the nineteenth to the twentieth century, was indeed "a characteristic part of a hypertrophied national self-perception, mingling with the most revered natural landscapes and man-made symbols, eroding the sense of what is natural, possible, or real" (Nye, *Electrifying* 391), the protagonist's fascination with electric plants, dynamos, and electrification and his lone roaming through the hotels "ablaze with electric lights late into the night" (285) illustrate his deceptive self-construction and illusionary self-magnification. The ambiguity of Martin Dressler's visionary venture is manifested most brilliantly by the awesome technology that radiates his ambition and overstimulation to a public overwhelmed with wonder.

*****

The more magnificent the electrified performance of the last of Martin Dressler's hotels becomes, the less do the supposedly enchanted visitors appreciate the awful offer of technological salvation. Eventually, the monumental hotelscape provokes unease and anxiety rather than fascination and pleasure.[21] The more monumental, technologically elaborate, and conspicuously theatrical his constructions become, the more he has to realize the contradiction between his own egocentric aspirations and the emotional needs of his potential customers. At the same time, he has to come to terms with his own, residual old world-sympathies:

9: Electricity Building at 1893 World's Fair

10: Electricity Building, Columbian Exposition (1893)

11: Dynamo Room (1897)

12: Singer Building at Night, New
York City (1908)

13: Woolworth Building at Night,
New York City (1910)

14: The Electric Tower at Night, Luna Park, Coney Island (1903)

He planned with Osborne the strategy for closing off a block of rooms while keeping the hotel open, conducted the team of interior decorators through the entire building from basement to roof, and approved the replacement of steam engines by electric motors to drive the elevator drums. He visited furniture wholesalers with an eye to selecting beds and dressers, discussed with Dundee the wiring of the entire building for electricity, studied the plan for the installation of telephones, talked with the wood-finishers in the lobby who were repairing the carved window-moldings and the upholsterers in the basement who were recovering parlor chairs. He visited plumbing supply companies and examined porcelain bathtubs with brass fittings, polished brass tumbler-holders and cigar rests, copper-lined ash and cherry water-tanks with nickel-plated chain and pull. From years of listening to the complaints of hotel guests, Martin knew that the bathroom loomed large in the imagination of Americans. And it was precisely here, as he wandered among displays of veined marble sinks and brass towel racks, that he was struck again by a contradiction in the architecture of hotels, a contradiction that was nothing but the outward expression of a nation's inner desire. For here the technologically modern and up-to-date clashed with a certain nostalgia of decor: bathrooms with ingenious American flush toilets and needle showers were given a suggestion of the European palace by decorations such as pilasters of Siena marble and shower hoods of carved mahogany. The modern luxury bathroom mirrored the modern hotel lobby, with its combination of electric lighting and old-fashioned carved ceilings, but it was also cousin to the modern department store, where terracotta scrollwork and grand marble stairways clashed with electric elevators and brand-new plate-glass windows that displayed the latest folding cameras with rack-and-pinion focusing movement, waterproof overcoats with patent ventilators, and self-threading sewing machines in drop cabinets. Far from deploring such contradictions, Martin felt deeply drawn to them, as if they permitted people to live in two worlds at once, a new world of steel and dynamos and an older world of stone arches and hand-carved wood. (178f.)

The technological utopia and imperial spectacle that Martin Dressler implemented as a panacea for the historical and cultural changes of the day does not seem to gratify the customers' desire after all. Martin Dressler exhausts his resources in his attempt to maintain the illusion and fakery that the animated buildings first generate and then require for their survival. In the wake of dangerously declining occupancies, he hires a theater group to play residents, visitors, and even the employees whom he had fired because of imminent bankruptcy. Towards the end of the show, the once-omnipresent stage-manager himself loses control over his creation. At times, even the protagonist no longer knows whether he encounters "actresses or residents" (287) on his lonesome tours through the increasingly deserted halls of his empire in decline. Public rejection and the financial ruin of the Dressler hotels appear like the inevitable consequence of the ever-intensifying performativity of the technological spectacle: "For what, after all, was the Grand Cosmo? Insofar as it pretended to be a place in which people might wish to live, it was uninhabitable" (275).[22] At the very end, even the protagonist-creator himself deserts the stage and quits his role. In an ultimate act of self-effacement, he entrusts his own part in the "grand cosmo-logical" venture to one of several actors auditing for the part. Martin Dressler's spectacular project of technologically magnifying his personality ends in an all-but sublime performance of dissimulation and personal invisibility.

Notes

1 In a wider context, see Debord, *The Society of the Spectacle.*

2 For a recent exploration of the beginnings of what Henry Luce, in 1941, called the "American century," see Traxel.

3 Secondary literature on *Martin Dressler* has remained limited so far; see especially the articles by Barrineau, Link, and Saltzman,. For reviews, see Burroway, McLaughlin, and the anonymous "*Fibel für Lehrlinge.*"

4 The "spectatorial vision" (David E. Shi, 85-7) of this passage (and similar ones) allows for comparisons of *Martin Dressler* with the novels of Henry James, Edith Wharton, and Theodore Dreiser. See Barrineau on the novel's supposed "Dreiserian realism"; in a larger context, see Koprince, "Edith Wharton's Hotels"; Ward, "'The Amazing Hotel World' of James, Dreiser, and Wharton"; and West, "The Hotel World of *Jennie Gerhardt.*"

5 See Boorstein, "Palaces of the Public," in his *The Americans: The National Experience,* 135 and 147, for documentation of the quotes given from the *National Intelligencer* (June 19, 1827) and the writings of N.P. Willis (1844); see also Raitz and Jones, "The City Hotel as Landscape and Community Symbol." Anthony Trollope's *North America* gives a still highly readable (European) account of the peculiarities of nineteenth-century American hotel life. Anonymity and existential alienation seem to be more twentieth-century associations that might also be linked with the motel rather than the hotel; Jakle, et al, *The Motel in America.*

6 On American grand hotels, see D'Ormesson, Donzel, and Denby.

7 See also Leeuwen: "[T]he skyscraper should be approached as the realization of a higher degree of building principles than pragmatic or deterministic ones, the discovery of which requires digging into that timeless reservoir of expressive means and didactic models of revelation, eternity, and, most importantly, cosmogony. The performance of the skyscraper is that of a tower of cosmogony, so aptly illustrated by the American sacred mountains par excellence, the Grand Tetons" (62).

8 On contemporary perceptions of the affinity between cathedrals and skyscrapers, see Schuyler.

9 The boldness of both, Martin Dressler and his constructions, might allow for comparisons with Antoni Gaudí's project for a skyscraper hotel in the middle of Manhattan. The plans were first presented in 1908 and showed a futuristic composition of five towers, which were meant to symbolize the five continents and the global outreach of the American metropolis. The project was not realized but recently brought again to public attention as one possible suggestion to partly fill Ground Zero. See <www.hotelattraction.com> [18 July 2003] for illustrations of Gaudí's visionary design as well as for details of the history of the project and its current discussion. Possible comparisons of Millhauser's/Dressler's hotel world with Daniel Libeskind's plans for an architectural gesture at Ground Zero, which would be both commemorative and commercial, are still vague at this point.

10 See Cook, *The Arts of Deception,* and Harris, *Humbug: The Art of P.T. Barnum.*

11 On contemporaneous consumer culture and the development of shopping malls, see Fox, Bronner, Schlereth, Simon, and Koenen. On contemporary museum culture, see Conn, who argues that "museums stand with department stores as institutional embodiments of Veblen's culture of conspicuous consumption, though it would be some years until the museum became the site of actual purchasing through the proliferation of 'museum stores'" (13).

12 On Millhauser's early (short) fiction in relation to Franz Kafka and also Jorge Luis Borges, see the articles by Kinzie, Herrero-Olaizola, and Kasper. *Martin Dressler* invites comparisons with Kafka's *Amerika/Der Verschollene*, despite obvious differences between the protagonists of the two novels and between Kafka's Hotel Occidental and Millhauser's hotel worlds.

13 On the Chicago World's Columbian Exposition, see Downey, Hollweg, Rydell, Rydell, et al; and

the essays by Slotkin.

[14] In *The Anthropology of World's Fairs,* Benedict shows how world's fairs were designed as self-contained artefacts and held on special, walled-off grounds.

[15] See Segal, *Technological Utopianism in American Culture.* Also the special issue of *US News and World Report,* "Builders of Dreams: The Visionaries and the Creations That Changed Our World."

[16] The figure of Rudolf Arling might be taken as an allusion to Louis Sullivan and to Sullivan's views on competing architectural discourses of the 1890s and 1900s; on Sullivan and his theories, see Boelhower.

[17] The allusion to Samuel Taylor Coleridge's "Kubla Khan" underscores the romantic potential of the architectural outreach.

[18] On "Hoteltheater," "Erlebnishotellerie," and "Hotelinszenierungen," see, recently, Brigitte Scherer.

[19] For a detailed discussion of the cultural force of electricity and the ambivalence of the specific theatrical, utopian, and mystifying qualities of electrification and electric spectacles, see Nye, *Electrifying America,* esp. 48-74 and 147-57.

[20] It seems that Walt Whitman's conception of the "body electric" sees its fictional architectural incorporation in the Dressler hotels.

[21] Saltzman discusses *Martin Dressler* in the context of theories of the (American) sublime and stresses the protagonist's futile attempts to "house the sublime" (615, also 591-593). A further analysis of the novel in these terms might draw on Nye's *American Technological Sublime* as well as his *Narratives and Spaces,* and on Tabbi. Nye's distinction between the 'sublime' and the (postmodern) "strange" (*American Technological Sublime* xx) might be particularly helpful.

[22] On the perception of New York City as an uninhabitable spectacle, see Baudrillard, 7-18.

WORKS CITED

Barrineau, Nancy W. "Theodore Dreiser and *Martin Dressler*: Tales of American Dreamers." *Dreiser Studies* 30 (1999): 35-45.

Baudrillard, Jean. *America* [1986]. New York: Version, 1988.

Benedict, Burton. *The Anthropology of World's Fairs.* London: Scholar P, 1983.

Boelhower, William. "Remembering the Territory: Louis Sullivan's Theory of Ornament." *Sites of Memory in American Literatures and Cultures.* Ed. Udo J. Hebel. Heidelberg: Winter, 2003. 271-91.

Boorstein, Daniel. *The Americans: The National Experience.* New York: Random House, 1965.

Bronner, Simon J., ed. *Consuming Visions: Accumulation and Display of Goods in America, 1880-1920.* New York: Norton, 1989.

"Builders of Dreams: The Visionaries and the Creations That Changed Our World." Special Issue. *U.S. News and World Report* 30 June/7 July, 2003.

Burroway, Janet. "Heartbreak Hotel." Rev. of *Martin Dressler,* by Steven Millhauser. *New York Times Book Review* 12 May 1996: 8.

Conn, Steven. *Museums and American Intellectual Life, 1876-1926.* Chicago: U of Chicago P, 1998.

Cook, James W. *The Arts of Deception: Playing with Fraud in the Age of Barnum.* Cambridge: Harvard UP, 2001.

Debord, Guy. *The Society of the Spectacle* [1967]. New York: Zone, 1994.

Denby, Elaine. *Grand Hotels: Reality and Illusion.* London: Reaktion Books, 1998.

Donzel, Catherine, et al. *Grand American Hotels.* New York: Vendome P, 1989.

D'Ormesson, Jean, ed. *Grand Hotel: The Golden Age of Palace Hotels: An Architectural and Social History.* New York: Vendome P, 1984.

Downey, Dennis B. *A Season of Renewal: The Columbian Exposition and Victorian America*. Westport, CT: Praeger, 2002.

"*Fibel für Lehrlinge.*" Rev. of *Martin Dressler*, by Steven Millhauser. *Der Spiegel* 19 (1997): 209.

Fisher, Philip. "Appearing and Disappearing in Public: Social Space in Late Nineteenth-Century Literature and Culture." *Reconstructing American Literary History*. Ed. Sacvan Bercovitch. Cambridge, MA: Harvard UP, 1986. 155-188.

Fox, Richard and Jackson T. Lears, eds. *Cultures of Consumption*. New York: Pantheon, 1983.

Harris, Neil. *Humbug: The Art of P.T. Barnum*. Boston: Little, 1973.

Herrero-Olaizola, Alejandro. "Writing Lives, Writing Lies: The Pursuit of Apocryphal Biographies." *Mosaic* 35.3 (2002): 73-88.

Hollweg, Brenda. *Ausgestellte Welt: Formationsprozesse kultureller Identität in den Texten zur Chicago World's Columbian Exposition*. Heidelberg: Winter, 2001.

Jakle, John A., Keith A. Sculle, and Jefferson S. Rogers. *The Motel in America*. Baltimore: Johns Hopkins UP, 1996.

Kasper, Catherine. "Steven Millhauser's American Gothic." *Denver Quarterly* 36.3-4 (2002): 88-93.

Kinzie, Mary. "Succeeding Borges, Escaping Kafka: On the Fiction of Steven Millhauser." *Salmagundi* 92 (1991): 116-44.

Koenen, Anne. *Mail-Order Catalogs in the US 1880-1930*. Paderborner Universitätsreden 74 (Paderborn, 2001).

Koprince, Susan. "Edith Wharton's Hotels" *Massachusetts Studies in English* 10 (1985): 12-23.

Leeuwen, Thomas A. P. "The Skyward Trend of Thought: Some Ideas on the History of the Methodology of the Skyscraper." *American Architecture: Innovation and Tradition*. Ed. David G. DeLong, et al. New York: Rizzoli, 1986.

Link, Franz. *U.S.-amerikanische Erzählkunst 1990-2000*. Berlin: Duncker, 2001.

McLaughlin, Robert L. Rev. of *Martin Dressler*, by Steven Millhauser. *Review of Contemporary Fiction* 16 (1996): 185-6.

Millhauser, Steven. *Martin Dressler: The Tale of an American Dreamer*. New York: Vintage, 1996.

Nye, David E. *Electrifying America: Social Meanings of a New Technology, 1880-1940*. Cambridge : MIT P, 1990.

——. *American Technological Sublime*. Cambridge: MIT P, 1994.

——. *Narratives and Spaces: Technology and the Construction of American Culture*. New York: Columbia UP, 1997.

Raitz, Karl B. and John Paul Jones. "The City Hotel as Landscape and Community Symbol." *Journal of Cultural Geography* 9 (1988): 17-36.

Rydell, Robert W. *All the World's a Fair: Visions of Empire at American International Expositions, 1876-1916*. Chicago: U of Chicago P, 1984.

——, et al, eds. *Fair America: World's Fairs in the United States*. Washington: Smithsonian P, 2000.

Saltzman, Arthur. "A Wilderness of Size: Steven Millhauser's *Martin Dressler*." *Contemporary Literature* 42 (2001): 589-616.

Scherer, Brigitte. "*Das Dekor der Träume: Zwischen Backpflaumen, Badeschaum und vorgespiegelten Bescheidenheiten—Menschen im Hoteltheater.*" *Frankfurter Allgemeine Zeitung* 6 March 2003: R1.

Schlereth, Richard. *Victorian America: Transformations in Everyday Life, 1887-1915*. New York: Harper, 1991.

Schuyler, M. "The Evolution of the Sky-Scraper [1909]." *America Builds: Source Documents in American Architecture and Planning*. Ed. Leland M. Roth. New York: Harper, 1983. 310-323.

Segal, Howard P. *Technological Utopianism in American Culture.* Chicago: U of Chicago P, 1985.

Shi, David E. *Facing Facts: Realism in American Thought and Culture, 1850-1920.* New York: Oxford UP, 1995.

Simon, Richard K. "The Formal Garden in the Age of Consumer Culture: A Reading of the Twentieth-Century Shopping Mall." *Mapping American Culture.* Ed. Wayne Franklin and Michael Steiner. Iowa City: U of Iowa P, 1992. 231-250.

Slotkin, Richard. "The White City and the Wild West: Buffalo Bill and the Mythic Space of American History, 1880-1917." In his *Gunfighter Nation: The Myth of the Frontier in Twentieth-Century America.* New York: Harper, 1992. 63-87.

——. "Buffalo Bill's 'Wild West' and the Mythologization of the American Empire." *Cultures of United States Imperialism.* Ed. Amy Kaplan and Donald E. Pease. Durham: Duke UP, 1993. 164-81.

Sullivan, Louis. "The Tall Office Building Artistically Considered." *America Builds: Source Documents in American Architecture and Planning.* Ed. Leland M. Roth. New York: Harper, 1983.

Tabbi, Joseph. *Postmodern Sublime: Technology and American Writing from Mailer to Cyberpunk.* Ithaca, NY: Cornell UP, 1995.

Trachtenberg, Alan. *The Incorporation of America: Culture and Society in the Gilded Age.* New York: Hill, 1982.

Traxel, David. *1898: The Birth of the American Century.* New York: Vintage, 1998.

Trollope, Anthony. *North America.* London: Chapman, 1862.

Ward, Joseph A. "'The Amazing Hotel World' of James, Dreiser, and Wharton." *Leon Edel and Literary Art.* Ed. Lyall H. Powers. Ann Arbor: U Michigan P, 1988. 151-60.

West, James L. W. "The Hotel World of *Jennie Gerhardt.*" *Dreiser's* Jennie Gerhardt: *New Essays on the Restored Text.* Ed. West. Philadelphia: U of Pennsylvania P, 1995. 194-207.

Klaus Benesch
History on Wheels: A Hegelian Reading of "Speed" in Contemporary American Literature and Culture

By the turn of the nineteenth to the twentieth century, speed had become the most visible marker of technological change in America and to many commentators it represented the ultimate shaping force of modernity itself. By and large, Americans eagerly responded to the fast pace of the industrial era. Taking the rapid growth of the economy as a sign of national superiority, they actually redefined their place among the nations of the world according to the very rapidity of America's progress. "The old nations of the earth creep on at a snail's pace," Andrew Carnegie stated in 1909, "the Republic thunders past with the rush of the express. The United States, the growth of a single century, has already reached the foremost rank among nations, and is destined soon to outdistance all others in the race" (43). Like many other observers, Carnegie deliberately linked the nation's rapid development from colony to superpower with the restlessness of its people and the notion of westward expansion. In a similar vein, sociologist Edgar Mowrer, in his study of American character, *This American World* (1928), points out that "a European in the United States is inevitably struck by the speed, the hurry, the restlessness of it all" (233), and philosopher George Santayana dismissed in one of his Harvard lectures the vapid genteel tradition in America, praising instead the vigorous American who is leaping down "a sort of Niagara rapids . . . [his] sharp, masculine eye seeing the world as a modern picture—rapid, dramatic, vulgar" (qtd. in Tichi, 233). Each of these commentators describes Americans as a people on the move that favors progress and thus is destined to lead the petrified, stationary nations of the Old World to a brighter future. In this scheme, Americans are again "the western pilgrims, who are carrying along with them," as Crèvecœur had noted a century earlier, "that great mass of arts, sciences, vigor, and industry which began long since in the east" (43).

As a powerful form of national self-representation, America's "historical" destiny turns on a progressive concept of history, a proto-Hegelian movement in time as well as space which has recently prompted a critic to suggest that "Hegelian thought was already present in Puritan America before it was present in Hegel's own person" (Cowan 1). In this progressivist view of history, the role of speed was actually twofold: If rapid technological advancement figured, in a very literal sense, as a means to conquer and eventually possess the whole of the continent, it was also taken to vindicate synecdochically the historical destiny of America. The notion that the speed of technological and economic progress, succinctly articulated by Andrew Carnegie, equals an advancement in history has thus become a crucial element in the construction of American national identity.[1] The invention of the railroad is a good case in point. The technological backbone of their geographical expansion, Americans generally welcomed the advent of the railroad as a national event of almost mythic proportions. For Whitman, as well as for many of his contemporaries, it was no less than "[the] pulse of the continent." "Fierce-throated beauty [. . .] type of the modern—emblem of motion and power," he wrote in 1881,

> Roll through my chant with all thy lawless music, thy swinging lamps at night,
> Thy madly-whistled laughter, echoing, rumbling like an earthquake, rousing all,
> Law of thyself complete, thine own track firmly holding,
> (No sweetness debonair of tearful harp or glib piano thine,)
> Thy trills of shrieks by rocks and hills return'd,
> Launch'd o'er the prairies wide, across the lakes,
> To the free skies unpent and glad and strong. (472)

Whitman's late poem "To a Locomotive in Winter" cheeringly evokes the national identification of Americans with this powerful means of progress. Yet if modern aesthetics of speed often embraced the acceleration and velocity of life as a means to retrieve aspects of an original, authentic self, postmodern writers, I argue in the following paper, presented a different view of the forming or rather de-forming power of speed. By translating the dynamic potential of capitalist society into paranoiac scenarios of restlessness, repetition, and historical decline, the fictions of John Barth, Thomas Pynchon, Don DeLillo, or T. C. Boyle often hinge on a Neo-Hegelian concept of "posthistoire" (as the suspension of all movement) that is increasingly at odds with the American national ideology of progress and mobility.

Historically, the growing importance of speed is, of course, closely linked to the introduction of new and faster means of transportation. Inventions such as the railway, the automobile, and, somewhat later, the airplane dramatically altered the way in which people perceived the world: physically, they shaped and transformed the landscape by requiring a grid of extended tracks and roads and, psychologically, they changed human perception by destabilizing the relation between the fast-riding passenger and the world outside.[2] The impact of these inventions clearly went beyond the fact of their physical existence to challenge perceptions of both self and the world. In 1925 the philosopher of science Alfred North Whitehead reflected that "in the past human life was lived in the bullock cart; in the future it will be lived in an aeroplane; and the change of speed amounts to a difference in quality" (137). Yet to many of his fellow Americans, firsthand experience with rapid movement had already become common coin. By the end of the 1920s they were riding on turbine-driven high-speed trains, ate fast-food in streamlined diners or rushed to work in the latest Ford, Chrysler, or GM automobiles. Much of the modern preoccupation with speed, as Cecelia Tichi has shown, was thus associated with the new, twentieth century machine technology, the wonderment and awe evoked by aeroplanes or the record-setting internal combustion engine vehicles.[3]

Significantly if somewhat paradoxically, motorcars, a genuine product of the industrial era, also offered an opportunity to escape the constraints of the material world: first, by isolating the driver in a closed environment that allows him or her to repose and, much like the Kantian idea of the "dynamic sublime," relate to the outside world from a position of relative safety;[4] and, second, by instilling the notion that the car is somehow exempt from the sham and corrupted ways of modern society, that it represents freedom and authenticity. As Phil Patton reminds us in *The Open Road: A Celebration of the American Highway*, "the automobile from its beginnings was not associated so much with a vision of some modernistic future, but with the restoration of old values—the values that the railroad and big business had destroyed, the values of the frontier and the individual" (41). Speed, the unprecedented and well-nigh incredible rapidity of the automobile, was an important factor here. From its outset, the development of car culture in America (and elsewhere) is closely tied to the history of racing as, for example, the famous *Chicago Times-Herald Race*, launched in 1895, or the *New York-Buffalo Endurance Run* of 1901. Demonstrably faster than either the horse or the railroad, motorcars were built for speed. Although newspapers occasionally printed editorials denouncing speed excesses and careless driving, public opinion in America was practically unanimous, according to historian James Flink, "in recognizing the automobile as a legitimate pleasure vehicle and as destined to a great future in the commercial world" (20).

A symbolic incarnation of the values of republican America (utilitarianism, self-reliance, individualism, and the fixation on the nuclear family), the automobile swiftly turned into a cult object in its own right. To people of all classes, it represented the ultimate "democratic" transportation machine, the technological manifestation of personal freedom and the pursuit of happiness. As early as 1910, some 458,000 motor vehicles were registered in the United States, making America the world's first and foremost automobile culture.[5] By the mid-1960s, when Tom Wolfe published his anthropological study of Southern car culture, "The Last American Hero," cars had finally become the universal means of transportation that early, turn-of-the-century manufacturers had hoped for. Most states had long instituted severe speed limits, and reckless driving was relegated to the race tracks. What is more, many Americans began to have second thoughts about the automobile industry and its product. Disenchantment with Detroit's production and sales policies as well as socio-cultural and environmental issues caused consumers increasingly to rebel, as George Romney, the president of American Motors, put it, "against the size, large horsepower and the excessive styling changes made each year by many auto manufacturers" (qtd. in Flink, Car Culture 194). It is important to note, however, that while sociological studies such as Vance Packard's *The Hidden Persuaders* (1957) or *The Waste Makers* (1960) clearly softened the identification of Americans with the motorcar, its fetishization as an icon of freedom and authenticity persisted.[6] The automobile may have been defiled by the practices of mass consumption, yet its mythical connotation lived on in the literature of the Beat movement, in countless low-budget, independent road movies as well as in the reckless stock car drivers of the South.

It was with quite a bit of nostalgia, therefore, that the former sportswriter Tom Wolfe went to Greensboro, North Carolina, to cover the enthusiasm of Southern drivers for so-called stock car races. Stock cars were basically standard, run-of-the-mill cars that had been tuned up, by their amateur drivers, for excessive speeds. Racing these hellishly fast machines became so popular, according to Wolfe, that "on Sundays there wouldn't be a safe straight stretch of road in the county, because so many wild country boys would be out racing or just raising hell on the roads" (133). To many old boys, a "hot" car was a symbol of "heating up life itself." It invited the driver to transgress the boundaries of rural existence and, with a sudden burst of speed, leap forward into the technological glamour of the twentieth century. Quite paradoxically, stock car races represented both a grass-roots dramatization of the values of the American frontier (freedom, self-reliance, and masculinity) and a way of entering the new, modern America of speed. In Wolfe's sociology of the South, legendary drivers such as Junior Johnson are depicted as modern heroes, who were able to leave behind their humble origins and, by sheer pluck, rise to the top of the social hierarchy. Despite its dependence on car technology, stock car racing was basically a "low-tech" affair. As Wolfe reflects "here was a sport not using any abstract devices, any bat and ball, but the same automobile that was changing a man's own life, his own symbol of liberation, and it didn't require size, strength and all that, all it required was a taste for speed, and the guts" (135).

If it was dramatic and vulgar, to use Santayana's phrasing, it was definitely also rapid. So much so, that the high-powered stock car racers, as Wolfe points out, were "literally too fast for their own parts, especially the tires" (148). Speeds were actually faster than those in the Indianapolis races, the cars more powerful and much heavier. If drivers got mad enough, they would put each other "up against the wall," cut inside another car, or ram it into a spin. To an urbanite commuter, used to drifting along at the moderate speed of 40 to 45 miles per hour, these races spelled out a form of kinetic hell. Speeding down a narrow band of asphalt at 130, 160, 180 miles an hour, the unleashed racing car evokes a feeling of terror and sublime enchantment. Moreover, it foregrounds the symbolic value of the automobile as an engine of liberation and progress. At a crucial moment in history, when pollution, endless traffic jams, and the standardization of production have turned the motorcar into just another ugly reality of modern consumer society, stock car races defiantly celebrated its earlier identification as progressive, "democratic" machine. As Wolfe's nostalgic account of the reckless Southern drivers reminds us, speed in American literature and culture is rarely an end in itself; rather it serves as both a means to revivify the democratic values of the Republic and to reinforce the modern notion of ongoing social and historical progress.[7]

If the popularity of stock car racing ironically marked a crisis in the modern valorization of movement and speed, postmodern novels began to question the notion of progress at large and, in its stead, indulge post-historical scenarios of immobility and stasis. Just consider Jack Kerouac's notorious *On the Road* (1957) and John Barth's early postmodern novel *The End of the Road* (1958), two texts of the late 1950s that epitomize, even by their very titles, the shift from modern to postmodern aesthetics of speed. As critics often pointed out, *On the Road* dramatizes an automotive search for identity, a mythical journey across the American continent that draws much of its power and momentum from the act of moving itself: being "on the road" as both a lifestyle and a metaphysical exercise in reaching beyond the surface of mere appearances, in striking out against everything that stands between oneself and the truth.[8] When Sal Paradise, the narrator of the novel, and his cranky friend Dean Moriarty speed down the endless highways of the Midwest, they can yet experience moments of kinetic epiphany:

> I jumped in the back seat and curled up to sleep. [. . .] Great horrors that we were going to crash this very morning took hold of me and I got down on the floor and closed my eyes and tried to go to sleep. [. . .] I could feel the road some twenty inches beneath me, unfurling and flying and hissing at incredible speeds across the groaning continent with that mad Ahab at the wheel. When I closed my eyes all I could see was the road unwinding into me. When I opened them I saw flashing shadows of trees vibrating on the floor of the car. There was no escaping it I resigned myself to all. (213)

Although there is quite a bit of ambiguity about the redeeming potential of the automobile and American roads, Kerouac basically adds to the Whitmanesque notion of speed as an emblem of power, an invigorating force that drives and inspires artistic work. If the west coast finally brings the mythic journey to a halt, one can always go back and start anew: "Here I was at the end of America—no more land—and now there was nowhere to go but back" (70). Kerouac's vision may be irritated by the sham and grotesque falseness of the West ["stucco houses and palms and drive-ins, the whole mad thing, the ragged promised land, the fantastic end of America" (74)], yet his view that "the road is life" (192) and that therefore the act of moving eternally opens up new avenues of insight clearly defies the post-modern obsession with endings, exhaustion, immobility, and death.

An early example of this shift from an aesthetics of progress and mobility to a post-historical aesthetics of exhaustion and immobility is John Barth's satirical campus novel *The End of the Road*. Its protagonist seems to be constantly at a crossroads, and his acute awareness of the relativity of experience and the widening gap between a staggering number of options and the incapacity to decide "where to go next" finally lead to the incapacity to move at all. Struck by a kind of cosmic paralysis, that Barth ironically calls *cosmopsis*, Jacob Horner clearly has reached the end of the road. His is a trajectory that becomes suspended in mid-air, a limping movement intermittently frozen in time as well as in space. The dominant imagery of this postmodern scheme is no longer the modernists' audacious leap "down Niagara rapids" or the gear-and-girder poetics (Tichi) of the machine age but the stultifying movement of the "rocking chair" (in *The End of the Road*), of the "yo-yo" (in Pynchon's *V*), of the bent curve of gravity in *Gravity's Rainbow*, the news "reel" in DeLillo's *Americana*, or, more recently, the "exercise bike" (in his play *Valparaiso*) and, finally, the crutches and dismembered body of Walter Van Brunt in T. Coraghessan Boyle's *World's End*.[9] Along similar lines, Billy Pilgrim (!), the tragicomic hero of Vonnegut's war novel *Slaughterhouse-Five* (1969), turns into "a spastic in time, [who] has no control over where he is going next" (20). Vonnegut's aim, according to the British critic Tim Woods, "is to allow human actions to be freed from the ideology of linear temporality with its model of the road and life-as-a-straightforward-journey" (107). What goes up, must come down—it is this consciousness of the ultimate futility of all human action, it seems to me, that causes Jacob Horner and many of his postmodern followers "to prefer not to" move at all, to become a fixture in an entropic, post-historical universe marked by the break-down of the real as a category of human discourse altogether.

"I wanted to free myself from that montage of speed, guns, torture, rape, orgy and consumer packaging which constitutes the vision of sex in America" (DeLillo 33). In response to this bleak assessment of American media culture, David Bell, TV executive and the protagonist of DeLillo's debut novel *Americana* (1971), journeys west and, equipped with a 16 mm film camera, tries to recreate his own version of America's lost frontier. The journey, quite paradoxically, delineates a history on wheels/reels that purports to be devoid of any movement or speed and, therefore, to be more authentic than the fast-paced coverage of mass media: "In my little home movie," he explains to a friend,

> I haven't reduced the value of language at all. I've reinforced it, in fact. What I've reduced is *movement*, the kind of *movement* that tells a story or creates harmony. I want language to evolve from *static* forms. [. . .] When I'm done I'd like to put the whole thing in a freezer and then run it uncut thirty years from now. (288-89, my emphasis)

Not surprisingly, his film only adds another spin to the endless loop of fake images of a past that never actually existed. Its dated, amateur technology notwithstanding, "the journey was very boring. [. . .] Things seemed not quite the sum of their parts" (348). If there were "neat reversals of the currents of history and geography"—as exemplified by "the menu in a frontier-style restaurant [that] included a brief note pointing out that the main dining hall was a replica of the main dining hall at the famous Cattleman on Forty-fifth Street in New York City" (348) —there was also the postmodern attempt, I would argue, to "freeze" both movement and history in a desperate act against media complicity.

The most radical representation yet of such a "freezing" of history in contemporary American fiction is certainly T. C. Boyle's *World's End*. This eponymic post-historical novel, according to its author, is about "genetic determinism" or, more precisely, the fact that you are "doomed to repeat history whether you know history or not" (Boyle, "History" 260). Yet while Boyle conjures up an intricate historical network that reaches from Dutch settlement of the lower Hudson River Valley during the early seventeenth century to the coverage of a full generation from 1940 through the turbulent 1960s, he also satirizes the idea of history as a juggernaut, a monumental force with a mind of its own. When Walter Van Brunt, the protagonist of the sections in the twentieth century, gets crippled in two successive motorbike accidents involving one and the same historical marker, it is not an ignorance of the past that takes the blame. Nor is it its opposite, the desire to "unravel the skein of its secrets" (13), a paranoiac over-acuteness of the sense of the past, a "historical sickness," to use Nietzsche's famous term, that afflicts those who cherish a self-serving version of the past.[10] Rather, as Michael Kammen recently suggested, *World's End* is really "a challenge to the conventional way of thinking about history as a process of change over time" (257). As a dramatization of a fatal sequence of "collisions with history," Boyle's text is to the modern aesthetics of progress and speed what *Moby Dick* was to Emerson's transcendent view of nature: a radical deconstruction of our belief in history as the basic pattern of human development, the realization that history is a fiction, turning—wheels within wheels—on the treacherous hope that somehow, somewhere there is a way out of the constraints of time as well as space.

Yet what has all this to do with Hegel? In 1989, the same year that marked the beginning of Germany's reunification and the steadily opening up of the socialist countries of the East, the political scientist Francis Fukuyama submitted a controversial essay, titled "The End of History?," to the journal *The National Interest*, an essay he later enlarged and, in 1992, republished as *The End of History and The Last Man*. Fukuyama's analysis of contemporary world politics was partly informed by Alexandre Kojève's 1934 interpretation of Hegel's phenomenological method and his idea of the Dialectic. Both Hegelian and, later, Marxist philosophy of history are based, according to Kojève, on the principle of conflict and struggle. Yet both are also directional or teleological, in the sense that they presume or predict an end to this ongoing struggle between great men (in Hegel's idealist view), on the one hand, and classes (as in Marx's historical materialism), on the other. If Hegel, who was clearly influenced by the impact of the world historical character of Napoleon, saw this end to be quite near at hand, so does Fukuyama. Writing at the dawn of the post-Cold War era, Fukuyama believes that the gradual development in the consciousness of Freedom, as manifest in the "peaceful" revolutions of the East, equals Hegel's idea of the final realization of reason and the spirit in world history.[11]

"The Invocation of the 'end of history' is a postmodern phenomenon," as one critic points out, "announcing a general crisis in the representation of temporality" (Woods 105). Ostensibly an important moment in Hegel's original notion of universal history and its adaptation by a neo-conservative American intellectual, the utopian end-of-history scenario may thus also account, if in slightly different ways, for the implosion of temporality and movement that we find at work in much of postmodern fiction. In *World's End*, Walter's journey eventually takes him to the cold, far end of the American continent; it is here in Alaska, high above the Arctic Circle, where his father teaches history in a remote secondary school, that the novel's post-historical thrust comes to bear fully on its main characters, that the "wheels" of history finally get stuck:

> The MG had good traction, but he could feel the wheels slipping out from under him. Hidden obstacles were giving him a roller coaster ride, the visibility was about the same whether he had his eyes open or not and the rear end seemed to have a will of its own: [. . .] the rear wheels whined, the chassis shuddered beneath him. He slammed it into reverse gunned it, rammed it back into first, gunned it again. Nothing. [. . .] He was stuck. (441)

The ending of the novel clearly evokes images of immobility and the freezing of time in the immense whiteness of the Arctic Circle. It also offers, however, moments of repose and regeneration. As many of his postmodern fellow writers, Boyle seems to delight in the idea that stasis and immobility do not necessarily signify the end of the world. "The social change, the continuous rise of new behavioral standards, the dissolution of tradition," Umberto Eco argued in an influential essay on the postmodern aesthetics of repetition, "require a narrative based upon redundancy. Redundant narrative structures would appear in this panorama as an indulgent invitation to repose, a chance of relaxing" (165). It is worth noting that *World's End* abstains from adding to the tradition of negative end-of-history scenarios associated with the cultural criticism of Oswald Spengler, Ortega y Gasset, Ernst Nolte (in Europe) or Roderick Seidenberg and Allan Bloom (in the US).[12] Its ruminations on history are neither dystopic nor fatalist. Instead, Boyle's text ends on a serene, ironic note of epistemological uncertainty, an uncertainty aptly followed by a question mark: "The earth was covered with snow and the snow was mounting and everything seemed like something else. [Walter] knew he had to get to the car. But which way was the car? [. . .]" (446).

Though it may indeed be difficult to figure out what exactly Boyle's interest—and that of other postmodern writers—in history is, it should have become sufficiently clear by now that postmodern texts are no longer informed by the messianic progressivism and emphasis on speed most readily associated with the culture of modernism (and American culture at large). "The fragmented plots of many postmodernist novels," Ursula Heise writes in her superb analysis of postmodern time and/in narrative, "are to some extent conditioned by the accelerated temporal rhythms of late-capitalist technologies of production and consumption, which tend to make long-term developments more difficult to envision and construct." While it thus seems as if the postmodern sense of endings (of history, authorship, the real, etc.) is but a reflection of the larger economic and technological society, one could also argue, according to Heise, that "fragmented narrative plots [that is, those which deconstruct linear temporality] shape our perception of production and consumption in the late twentieth century in such a way that the latter come to appear as obstacles that impede more long-term constructions of time" (6). Put differently, the freezing of movement in postmodern fictions may well be read, for one, as a longing gesture to escape the cultural reification of "becoming" (as implicated in the idea of historical progress) by arresting time and projecting spaces of "being" (outside of history). Yet for another, posthistorical scenarios always also mark a lack of historical consciousness or the problem of "pastlessness." Quite paradoxically, the proliferating repetitions of historical incidents in *World's End* and other postmodern texts foreground the intricate mutual dependency of past and present, history and identity. By symbolically slowing down the onrush of contemporary culture and society, these texts do not only attest, as Michael Kammen surmises, to the well-known Marxist dictum that "those who cannot remember the past are condemned to repeat it"(248). They also seem to fulfill the prophetic verdict of one of America's most radical critics of speed, Henry David Thoreau, who had stated early on that in an environment of technological change and cultural acceleration, "the swiftest traveler is he that goes afoot" (67).[13]

NOTES

[1] As Rosalind Williams points out, technological advancement already loomed large in the metahistorical master texts of the Enlightenment. In Anne Robert Turgot's *Discours sur les progrès successifs de l'esprit humain* (1750), for example, historical progress is fundamentally determined by the creation of new systems of transportation and communication.

[2] That the view from a passing railroad car could change the way that people saw the landscape was a well-known fact among early travelers. At even the relatively moderate speed of 30 miles per hour, passengers experienced an enchantment and an annihilation of space and time that came close, according to contemporary reports, to a state of trance. "The railway journey," historian David Nye explains, "erased the foreground and the local disappeared from the traveler's experience, while only a few scenes appeared worthy of notice. [. . .] This editing of the landscape, framed by the windows of railway cars, transformed the journey into the opportunity to see a limited number of sites. [. . .] The traveler was isolated from the passing scene, viewing it through plate glass, and could easily fall into a reverie, feeling that the train was stationary while the landscape rushed by" (15).

[3] Tichi argues that much of modern art is predicated on the attempt to formally adopt and incorporate technological progress. The modernist emphasis on speed thus becomes "a collaborative effort of the engineer, the architect, the fiction writer, and the poet" to respond to the efficiency and functionalism of contemporary society. The machine-art of the Futurists, Dos Passos' urban novels, or the minimalist poetry of Ezra Pound and William Carlos Williams can thus be read as different ways of translating modern dynamics into the abstract, kinetic design of verbal construction (16).

[4] In the *Critique of Judgement* Kant developed the idea that viewing an object of terror from a safe distance can trigger a sublime experience. According to Kant the "dynamic sublime" of a volcanic eruption or a tempest at sea morally educates and inspires the mind of the observer if s/he is in a state of security. Immanuel Kant, *Critique of Judgement* (502-4). Similarly, the framing of the view from within the secure compartment of the motorcar also allows for an experience of the "dynamic" sublime: both, of the speeding car itself and the world outside. For a detailed discussion of Kant's idea of the "dynamic sublime" and its ideological adoption in American progressivist discourse, see Nye, *American Technological Sublime*, 1-43.

[5] The history and development of American car culture is discussed in Flink, Belasco, and, from an international perspective, Miller.

[6] How speed literally turned into a "cultural style" during the 1950s has been analyzed from various angles. For an analysis of the historical roots and origins, see Lhamon; the representation and, successively, deconstruction of speed as a cultural value in advertising is an important topic in Thomas Frank's study of American business culture, *The Conquest of Cool.*

[7] While high-brow modernism often indulged in speed and the rapid-transit experience for its own sake, popular literature, such as the well-known *Tom-Swift* series that started in 1910, tried to contain the modern phenomenon of speed within the Jeffersonian framework of a democratic, Republican technology. Occasionally, however, even the modernist elite worried about the emotional and intellectual downside of the new value of speed. In his poem "The Right of Way" (1923) William Carlos Williams calls for a temporary stop, an interruption of the rapid-transit experience that allows the artist to name and reflect upon what otherwise would be lost in the continuous stream of modern life. Williams and the rapid-transit experience of American modernism are discussed in Tichi, 245-56. For *Tom-Swift* and the tradition of technology-based adventure dime novels, see Benesch.

[8] See, among many others, Giamo, Holton, and the latest collection of critical essays on Kerouac, edited by Myrsiades and Bennett.

[9] In his seminal study *Postmodern Fiction*. Brian McHale retooled Jacobson's concept of the "dominant" in

literature to account for the "historical change" that seems to have occurred with the shift from modern to postmodern aesthetics. The so-called postmodern turn, McHale argues, can thus be described as a change of dominant: from the *epistemological* (modernism) to the *ontological* (postmodernism), from self-reflective inquiry into the possibility of subjective knowledge to the projection of both new worlds (literary, medial, or virtual) and new, multiple postmodern identities (6-11). Its practical advantages for literary history and the formal-structural periodization of postmodern fiction notwithstanding, the "ontological" as the dominant of postmodernism is basically an a-historical category. It indicates an important disjunction of time and space in postmodern society and, consequently, the demise of historical consciousness. As such, it fits nicely my argument that postmodern writers have finally laid to rest the progressivist ideology of speed and, in its stead, have become paralytics who need be taught, in the words of John Barth, "how to walk again" (338).

[10] In his often-quoted essay "On the Uses and Disadvantages of History for Life" Nietzsche dismisses the rampant historicism of the late nineteenth century as a kind of "historical sickness" that tends to stifle the creativity of the living: when history "attains a certain degree of excess, life crumbles and degenerates, and through this degeneration history finally degenerates too" (67).

[11] Fukuyama's end-of-history thesis is, of course, mainly a glib, neo-conservative attempt to idealize the political victory of liberal democracy. "While earlier forms of government were characterized by grave defects and irrationalities," he explains in the "Introduction," "that led to their eventual collapse, liberal democracy was arguably free from such fundamental contradictions. [. . .] While some present-day countries might fail to achieve stable liberal democracy, and others might lapse back into other, more primitive forms of rule like theocracy or military dictatorship, the *ideal* of liberal democracy could not be improved on" (*xi*). Consequently, Fukuyama's thesis triggered an extended and often caustic debate; see, for example, the essays in *After History?*, edited by Timothy Burns, and *Has History Ended?* edited by Christopher Bertram and Andrew Chitty. Alexandre Kojève's famous lecture on Hegel is available in English as *Introduction to the Reading of Hegel*.

[12] The roots and the history of the idea of "posthistoire" is complex and have been approached from various perspectives. Good overviews of its multifaceted aspects and entanglements with postmodern theory can be found in Niethammer, Holthusen, and Gumbrecht.

[13] Thoreau was clearly at loggerheads with the progressivist spirit of his times. His was a philosophy of "slowness" that defied the popular belief in speed and progress as an end in itself. "I have learned," he tells us in *Walden*, "that the swiftest traveler is he that goes afoot. [. . .] Why should we live with such hurry and waste of life? We are determined to be starved before we are hungry. [. . .] Our lives [are lived] too fast. [. . .] If we stay at home, who will want railroads? We do not ride on the railroad; it rides upon us."

WORKS CITED

Barth, John. *The Floating Opera and The End of the Road*. New York: Doubleday, 1988.

Belasco, Warren James. *Americans on the Road: From Autocamp to Motel, 1910-1945*. Baltimore: Johns Hopkins UP, 1997.

Benesch, Klaus. "The Dynamic Sublime: *Geschwindigkeit und Ästhetik in der amerikanischen Moderne*." *Raum- und Zeitreisen: Studien zur Literatur und Kultur des 19. und 20. Jahrhunderts*. Ed. Hans Ulrich Seeber and Julika Griem. Tübingen: Niemeyer, 2003. 102-117.

Bertram, Christopher and Andrew Chitty, eds. *Has History Ended?: Fukuyama, Marx, Modernity*. Aldershot: Avebury, 1994.

Boyle, T. Coraghessan. *World's End*. New York: Viking, 1987.

——. "History on Two Wheels." In Carnes, *Novel History.* 259-61.

Burns, Timothy, ed. *After History?: Francis Fukuyama and His Critics.* Lanham: Rowman & Littlefield, 1994.

Carnegie, Andrew. *Problems of Today: Wealth, Labor, Socialism* [1908]. Garden City: Doubleday, 1933.

Carnes, Mark C., ed. *Novel History: Historians and Novelists Confront America's Past (and Each Other).* New York: Simon & Schuster, 2001.

Cowan, Bainard. "Introduction." *Theorizing American Literature: Hegel, the Sign, and History.* Ed. Cowan and Joseph G. Kronick. Baton Rouge: Louisiana State UP, 1991. 1-29.

Crèvecœur, Hector St. John de. *Letters From an American Farmer.* London: Davis, 1782.

DeLillo, Don. *Americana.* Boston: Houghton Mifflin, 1972.

Eco, Umberto. "Innovation and Repetition: Between Modern and Post-Modern Aesthetics." *DÆDALUS* 114.4 (1985): 161-84.

Flink, James J. *The Car Culture.* Cambridge, MA: MIT, 1975.

——. *The Automobile Age.* Cambridge: MIT, 1988.

Frank, Thomas. *The Conquest of Cool: Business Culture, Counter Culture, and the Rise of Consumerism.* Chicago: U of Chicago P, 1997.

Fukuyama, Francis. *The End of History and the Last Man.* New York: The Free Press, 1992.

Giamo, Ben. *Kerouac, the Word and the Way: Prose Artist as Spiritual Quester.* Carbondale, IL: Southern Illinois UP, 2000.

Gumbrecht, Hans-Ulrich. "Posthistoire Now." *Epochenschwellen und Epochenstrukturen im Diskurs der Literatur- und Sprachhistorie.* Ed. Hans-Ulrich Gumbrecht and Ursula Link-Heer. Frankfurt: Suhrkamp, 1985. 34-50.

Heise, Ursula K. *Chronochisms: Time, Narrative, and Postmodernism.* Cambridge: Cambridge UP, 1997.

Holthusen, Hans Egon. "*Heimweh nach Geschichte: Postmoderne und Posthistoire in der Literatur der Gegenwart.*" *Merkur* 38.8 (1984): 902-17.

Holton, Robert. *On the Road: Kerouac's Ragged American Journey.* New York: Twayne, 1999).

Kammen, Michael. "T. Coraghessan Boyle and *World's End.*" In Carnes, *Novel History.* 245-258

Kant, Immanuel. *Critique of Judgement* [1790]. New York: Oxford UP, 1952.

Kerouac, Jack. *On the Road.* New York: Penguin, 2000.

Kojève, Alexandre. *Introduction to the Reading of Hege.* New York: Basic Books, 1969.

Lhamon, W. T. *Deliberate Speed: The Origins of a Cultural Style in the American 1950s.* Washington, DC: Smithsonian Institution, 1990.

McHale, Brian. *Postmodern Fiction.* London/New York: Routledge, 1993.

Miller, Daniel, ed. *Car Cultures.* Oxford: Berg, 2001.

Mowrer, Edgar. *This American World.* New York: Sears, 1928.

Myrsiades, Kostas and Robert Bennett, eds. *The Beat Generation: Critical Essays.* New York: Peter Lang, 2002.

Friedrich Nietzsche. "On the Uses and Disadvantages of History for Life." In his *Untimely Meditations.* Trans. R. J. Hollingdale. Cambridge: Cambridge UP, 1983.

Niethammer, Lutz. *Posthistoire: Has History Come to an End?* London: Verso, 1992.

Nye, David. *American Technological Sublime.* Cambridge, MA: MIT, 1994.

——. *Narratives and Spaces: Technology and the Construction of American Culture.* Exeter: U of Exeter P, 1997.

Patton, Phil. *The Open Road. A Celebration of the American Highway.* New York: Simon & Schuster, 1986.

Thoreau, Henry David. *Walden, The Writings of Henry David Thoreau.* Ed. J. Lyndon Shanley. Princeton,

NJ: Princeton UP, 1971.

Tichi, Cecelia. *Shifting Gears: Technology, Literature, Culture in Modernist America.* Chapel Hill: U of North Carolina P, 1987.

Vonnegut, Jr., Kurt. *Slaughterhouse Five, Or the Children's Crusade.* New York: Delacorte Press, 1969.

Whitehead, Alfred North. *Science and the Modern World.* Cambridge: Cambridge UP, 1926.

Whitman, Walt. *Leaves of Grass.* Ed. Sculley Bradley and Harold W. Blodgett. New York: Norton, 1973.

Williams, Rosalind. "The Political and Feminist Dimensions of Technological Determinism." *Does Technology Drive History? The Dilemma of Technological Determinism.* Ed. Merritt Roe Smith and Leo Marx. Cambridge: MIT, 1994. 217-35.

Wolfe, Tom. "The Last American Hero." In his *The Kandy-Kolored Tangerine Flake Streamline Baby.* New York: Farrar, Straus & Giroux, 1987. 126-72.

Woods, Tim. "Spectres of History: Ethics and Postmodern Fictions of Temporality." *Critical Ethics: Text, Theory and Responsibility.* Ed. Dominic Rainsford and Tim Woods. Basingstoke: Macmillan, 1999. 105-21.

Michael Porsche
Stephen Wright: *Going Native* (by Car)

Television as today's most powerful medium is an obvious choice for novelists who aim at a critique of postmodern American culture and its tendency towards worldwide monocultural hegemony. But even such widely read and thoroughly investigated novels as Pynchon's *Vineland (1990)* or DeLillo's *White Noise* (1985) are not as far reaching and uncompromising as Stephen Wright's novel *Going Native*. Upon its publication in 1994, though, most reviewers seemed to concentrate at first on the novel's frantic action and considerable violence. Therefore, *Going Native* was hailed as a postmodern road novel, "an uncompromising 1990's version" of Jack Kerouac's *On the Road* (1957), "a dark and delirious journey down the highway of the contemporary soul, [. . .] a novel slitting open the bloated belly of American life," and, to continue quoting from the cover blurbs, "a diabolic picaresque, a Pilgrim's Progress that becomes a Dance of Death." In a less hyperbolic assessment, Robert Coover probably comes closest to describing Wright's central concerns when, combining the aspects of the trans- and intercontinental journey with the ubiquitousness of electronic media, he comments that *Going Native* describes "a nightmarish country of unparalleled savagery, where there is no longer a membrane between screen and life and the monster image feed is inexhaustible."

As the above quoted comments illustrate, the novel invites generic discussion like few other American novels have in recent years. As Patrick O'Donnell states in the only available article in English on the novel to date, it rather "ridicules the notion of a homogenous social realm and shatters the bourgeois narrative of domesticity, adventure, and retreat and the identity that inhabits it. It mourns rather than celebrates the fragmenting of identity" (n.p.). The represented explosion of unitary identity "symptomatic of a cultural paradox is brilliantly charted" (n.p.) in *Going Native*. Fredric Jameson describes this paradox in *Seeds of Time* as "the equivalence between an unparalleled rate of change on all the levels of social life and an unparalleled standardization of everything" (15). Introducing the term "modularity," Jameson contends that "intensified change is enabled by standardization itself, where prefabricated models, everywhere from the media to a henceforth standardized private life, from commodified nature to uniformity of equipment, allow miraculous rebuildings to succeed each other at will, as in fractal video" (16). The road is always the figure of multiplicity and possibility. And the contradiction of the road is contained in its aspect as both route of possibility and singularity: the contradiction of the modular as embodiment of intensified change and prefabrication or simulation; the contradiction of identity as fragmented and globalized.

These contradictions, I will suggest, are mapped out in Wright's novel. Furthermore, Wright's sense of the ways in which television reconstructs the nature of reality itself includes an awareness of the intensely mediated nature of contemporary experience. Clearly, most characters in *Going Native* are exposed to electronic media in a way that corresponds to their lack of identity. My emphasis here, then, will not be on *Going Native* as postmodern road novel or picaresque satire. Rather, I hope to show that the globalization of media-related and media-induced identity makes traveling itself as superfluous as it makes the metaphorics of car and road meaningless.

Surprisingly, *Going Native* is the only novel by Stephen Wright still in print. Its author, who teaches creative writing at the New School for Social Research has so far found curiously little attention from academic criticism. Even an internet search produces only meagre results—one of the few sources on the net tellingly consists of a short polemic note in *Context*, a magazine published by Dalkey Archive Press, whose author expresses serious doubts about the competence of Wright's agent (Burke, n.p.).

Going Native, as the title suggests, is about present-day Americans who decide "to lose themselves in order to find themselves" by regressing to a less civilized state in one way or another. The eight chapters making up this episodic—or modular, as Wright describes it in an interview (Byers 173) —book are perceptibly linked only by two recurring features—a green "69 Ford Galaxie" (89) and a pair of eyes. The light gray eyes belong to Wiley Jones, who makes his appearance in the first chapter, a family man returning from work—he is "in microsystems" (26)—on a Friday afternoon to his home and family in Wakefield Estates, an "engineered community of pastel houses and big friendly trees" (3) outside Chicago. His wife, Rhoda or Rho, has been introduced earlier while preparing dinner for an evening to be spent with her longtime friends, Tom and Gerri Hanna. This scene (which is vaguely reminiscent of Thomas Pynchon's *The Crying of Lot 49*)[1] is superficially, precariously domestic, and banal. The suburban idyll, though, is consistently disturbed by an undercurrent of insecurity, inadequacy, and doubt. For one thing, both radio and television sets are turned on, providing a constant background noise, without being consciously watched or listened to. But following Rho's reflections on the evening ahead and the bad day at the office behind her, nervously performing her preparations for dinner, glancing from time to time at her twins, Chip and Dale, in the sandbox supervised by a baby-sitter, one notices that her experience of everyday reality is constantly refracted by confusing medial stimuli and the awareness of her existence as somehow appearing scripted.

At work, the constant blare of a "Sony portable," which has been "coolly irradiating her body with the problems of today's women" (4), has left her mind fairly confused; now at home, another Sony transmits a call-in show with "an X-ray tech [. . .] describing how her husband [. . .] settles down in front of the tube wearing a chiffon cocktail dress, black nylons, and a pair of stiletto heels" (5). In the Jones home there are as many television screens to be dusted as there are plants to be watered – the one in the living room is now "frantic with the saturated belligerence of afternoon cartoons" (9). Even the door chimes are media related, reproducing the "first four notes of the old Dragnet

TV theme" (12)—foreshadowing Wiley Jones's career as a homicidal drifter. Maybe it is her "VCR hangover" from having watched "three rented films in a row" (8) the night before that makes Rho imagine a "large bright lemon-yellow bird" (6) gone again the next instant, something she ascribes to "a trick of bad editing" (6). Not quite reassuring, but popular science is standing by with sound reasoning: "The human brain, she read in *Time*, functions as a low-grade transmitting station, so theoretically, with the proper receiver, thoughts could be intercepted like television waves" (19). A few hours later, with Rho's mind short-circuited by too many cocktails, confusion turns into epistemological assurance. Now Rho "is bathed in a new understanding [. . .], and the understanding says to her: your life is your invention, the naïve obviousness of it positively intoxicating. You make it up, ha ha" (29). Never shunning an opportunity to employ irony, Wright here parades the postmodern condition as putting a brave face on the obvious loss of identity. Obviously, Rho is suffering from what Pynchon in his novel *Vineland* describes as "tubal abuse and video-related disorders" (33). Of course, in *Vineland* at least, these disorders are taken care of by the dubious organisation called National Endowment for Video Education and Rehabilitation (NEVER), working under the motto "ex luce ad sanitatem" (33).

No such luck in *Going Native*. While Rho, at the most, suspects her life to be a media construction, her husband seems to translate this idea into action and consequently attempts literally to plunge headfirst through the screen in order to be inside of the movie one calls one's life.[2] This is triggered by the accumulative effect of the sequence of drunken conversations interlaced with remembered movie synopses in the course of the backyard barbecue, most of all though by a chance incident involving Wylie and Tom at the Feed 'n' Fuel service station. Having briefly left the party to buy more charcoal, they arrive to find the station a crime scene; in an area taped off by the police, the victim of an armed robbery is covered by a blanket. The ontological instability that has befallen the first chapter's four major characters in one degree or another and which they attempt to counter variously by (attempting to study) Oriental philosophy (Gerri), withdrawing into her mind's "mood museum" (Rho), and watching television (Tom, Wiley), demands a more radical solution. So Wylie decides to progress from his passivity and to adopt a role seemingly taken from "the current shoot/chase/crash cycle of his rigorously limited viewing habits" (8) and play it out in real life. Thus Wiley, or the person who used to be Wiley, turns into a protean figure and nomadic killer, whose journey across America connects the dots of numerous other characters striving for a self-image.[3] Wright presents this conscious decision as an act of resistance to the system of medialized surface images, and it is a narrative resistance that strives towards particularization against the static modular existence.

His protagonist's name already points towards his will to combine both the roles of fictional character and its creator. Wiley Jones is a compound of Wile E. Coyote, the cartoon figure, and Charles "Chuck" Jones, who created it. Jones (1911-2002) was one of the pioneers of animated cartoons in the 1930s, together with Walt Disney, William Hanna, and Joseph Barbera. He is the "father" of hundreds of the immensely popular cartoon figures featured in the Warner Brothers' *Looney Tunes* series, which won several Academy Awards, ran on American TV channels until the mid-1960s, and has had many reruns until the present. The cartoon figure Wile E. Coyote was conceived upon Jones' childhood reading of *Roughing It*, Mark Twain's vigorous portrait of the American West. Chuck Jones was fascinated by Twain's description of the coyote and his chase of the jackrabbit. It gave him the idea to design a parody of early chase cartoons, and in 1949 he presented the first short film of the so-called Road Runner series, which was set in the desert of the American Southwest. Exchanging Twain's jackrabbit for the speedy bird, Jones established a "narrative" (there is never any dialogue, the only recurring utterance being the bird's energetic "Beep Beep") framework of ten directives (or commandments) for the series.[4] Wile E. Coyote, who first appears in *Fast and Furry-ous*,[5] has a purely physical expressivity. His stubborn schemes for accomplishing his task (if killing a carefree and innocent bird can be called an accomplishment), which eternally fail, make him an Everyman who struggles against his fate.

At a closer look at the first chapter of *Going Native*, one finds that Wright has inserted quite a number of cartoon figures as namesakes for his characters. One becomes aware that Rho's boss is named Mickey and that she "goes completely Looney Tunes once a month" (4). But this allusion to Walt Disney's Mickey Mouse and the Looney Tunes cartoon series is more than accidental. Similarly to the film *Who Framed Roger Rabbit* (directed in 1988 by Robert Zemeckis), which integrates computer animated cartoon characters with live actors, the world of *Going Native* is obviously being subverted by cartoon culture. Therefore, the names of Tom and Gerri Hanna, the friends of the Jones's, refer to Tom and Jerry, who were designed by William Hanna and Joseph Barbera; Daphne or Daphy (6) Avery, the teenaged childminder for the Jones's twins Chip and Dale (after the Looney Tunes cartoon chipmunks), recalls Daffy Duck, another Looney Tunes character. Even Elmer, the neighbors' dog (11), echoes Looney Tunes character Elmer Fudd, and Pluto the cat (34), after Walt Disney's cartoon dog of that name, can be added to this list.

Like Wile E. Coyote, Wiley Jones is an (albeit increasingly reluctant) Everyman, whose identity is composed on the one hand of his socially compliant role as employee and family man and on the other hand of the radical mischievousness and nihilism of the violent cartoon coyote. He is, therefore, one of the proverbial Joneses and at the same time bent on destruction of the very conformity his name and life signify. But Wiley wants to act rather than be acted upon, to eat instead of being eaten, to kill instead of being killed. His career is very similar to the chase cartoons his name refers to, with the exception that Wiley uses a car.

Until the very end of the novel, the car stays with Wiley:[6]

Out of the house and onto the road, a solitary in his cage, he joined the other solitaries locked and buckled into their cages, hundreds, thousands of them, all streaming determinedly along in a credible masquerade of purpose and conviction. How many understood, as he did, the true function of the car as a secret device for finding yourself? (282)

Wright here plays with the Renaissance concept of the green world. One is then, of course, tempted to see the green Ford Galaxie as Wiley's means of transformation or metamorphosis—his moveable green world—the possibilities of which have unfolded in his mind during the night of the party. The concept of the green world has also been discussed by M. H. Abrams "under the name of heterocosm, the second nature or second world" (Berger 14, n. 11, 12). The reference to the fairy world of Shakespeare's comedy opens up another important perspective on *Going Native*. It is the symbol of the forest, the "green world," as Northrop Frye has called it: "Thus the action of the comedy begins in a world represented as a normal world, moves into the green world, goes into a metamorphosis there in which the comic resolution is achieved, and returns to the normal world" (182).

Wiley's metamorphosis begins when he excuses himself for a minute to go inside the house, apparently to look for something. "'Don't get lost'" (28), his wife calls jokingly after him. Wandering through the kitchen, where "the unattended television silently tuned to tonight's repeat of *Perfect Strangers*" (28),[7] he ends up watching his guests through toy binoculars from his son's bedroom window, thereby distancing himself from the ritualized normality of their existence. It is an act of automatic identification with the camera eye. He notices "Huckleberry, the family's pet chameleon" (29)—but this overly obvious foreshadowing of Wiley's own imminent transformative "lighting out for the territory" is in itself refracted if one also knows the cartoon figure Huckleberry Hound created by Chuck Jones. The child's bedroom has a "charmed [. . .] atmosphere" (28), its interior dominated by "teenage Mutant Ninja Turtle bedsheets" (28) and a "Defense Department arsenal of military toys" (29). Preceding his absence from the party, the discussion with Gerri had turned

upon the nature of the soul [. . .], speculation on its absence from an unfortunate sum of mortal beings since God, at the moment of creation, released into the universe a fixed number of souls to be recycled among a diminishing percentage of an exponentially expanding population, hence bodies with no souls. (37)

All attention then turns to the absolute freedom and anarchy of the bats darting over and around the suburban gardens, where late in the evening a certain alcohol induced libertarianism has begun to set in: "'[I]magine being that free, able to fly, to sweep across the night in some sort of erotic stupor'" (25). The image of the bat clearly indicates the lack of and—what could be more important in a TV-contaminated environment—freedom from vision. For Wiley, this uninhibited freedom of the bat, enhanced by mobility, translates into driving across America in a continuous rush of sex and violence—going native by car.

Wright adds weight to this interpretation with a flurry of intertextual references to bats and signs of regression, extending from classic representations of the American frontier—think of Cooper and his character named Dr. Obed Bat in *The Prairie* (1827) and the observations about the American national character—to postmodern treatments of the urban jungle motif. In general, "going native" can be taken to mean regression into an atavistic savage state that troubled the Puritan settlers in their wilderness condition, but was celebrated by early theorists of the frontier.[8] Introducing the pervading theme of the novel, or, one should rather say, the series of interconnected novelettes, one is gradually made aware of another literary reference, namely Bret Easton Ellis's novel *American Psycho*, the last line of which—"This is not an exit" (399)—serves as the heading of chapter eight in *Going Native*.

The narrator-protagonist of Ellis' novel, Patrick Bateman, whose name is itself a compound of Norman Bates from Alfred Hitchcock's *Psycho* and cartoon superhero Batman, is certainly related to Wiley. The references to bats are most obvious in the first chapters of the novel. In the 1956 short film *Gee Whiz-z-z* Coyote dresses in a Batman costume. And the actor Anthony Perkins, who played Norman Bates in *Psycho*, is referred to in one of Tom Hanna's conversational movie synopses: "Tommy unreels another gripping scenario; this time it's Tony Perkins as a zany Dr. Jekyll who accidentally discovers crack, smokes it, naturally, then runs amok in a blue street frenzy of fucking and slashing rarely witnessed within the precincts of an R rating" (21). Wiley, who has not seen this very unlikely adaptation[9] of Stevenson's novel, remarks that anyone can see there is another person inside (the actor) by looking at his eyes. Wiley keeps looking for that other person inside of himself, staring at his reflexion in the mirror in a motel where most everybody is bent on watching TV and producing scripts for new crime shows. Ironically, the motel owner and the local sheriff are concentrated on revising a film script as Wiley makes his departure (after an aborted suicide attempt), giving a lift to the underage daughter named Aeryl (the manager's two other daughters are named Berryl and Cheryl, a serialization recalling Disney's Huey, Louie, and Dewey Duck). Aeryl and her sinister boyfriend Laszlo are eloping to L.A. in order to become huge stars. The boyfriend is ditched at the next convenient moment, a rest area named after William H. Bonney (121), a.k.a. Billy the Kid, one of the first examples of media-induced personality.[10] As the backyard in the suburb is described as a stage (12), Wyley appears on cue, accordingly in the midst of another movie synopsis delivered by Tom Hanna.[11] That Wiley is about to go native seems to point to his regressive plunge into a chaotic life of violence and sex. But first of all, his disappearance takes on the well known quality of lightin' out for the territory, i.e., he is going mobile[12] on a westward journey across the United States. Significantly, in crossing the American landscape he encounters only media related identity concepts. Following the internal logic of the narrative, it is therefore most fitting that he arrives in Hollywood and gets into acting.

*****

America's "amazing capacity to cannibalize cultural materials in the manufacture of paradoxical simulacra that standardize diversity" (O'Donnell 8) is hilariously manifested in a journey of two Hollywood actors to the jungles of Borneo, that instead of constituting transcendence of the superficiality of U.S. culture, only serves to mirror its global dominance. Amanda and Drake, wanting "to lose their entangling selves" (216), are trying to learn to "disengage [themselves] from the film [. . .] to summon up the courage to get up out of your seat and leave the theater" (199), in other words, to return to a primal origin before representation. Their Indonesian guides have grown familiar with the Americans' wish: "'Ah' [. . .]. Want to go *ulu*'" (211). The alternative of going *ulu*, or "native," both have to realize, is no longer available, since this culture in the jungle, at the heart of nature, is itself a matter of redundant simulacra, a repository of copy and repetition. McLuhan's global village has become a disturbing and dystopian reality—"'[o]ne world, one culture'" (263), Drake cynically cheers in retrospect. No wonder Amanda is struggling with her paperback of *Paradise Lost* throughout the chapter. Their disenchantment is that the native Kenyah tribe—apparently in a simulation of Wakefield Terraces, the Jones's engineered community in Chicago discussed above—

> lived in neat secluded rows of boxlike suburban homes . . . in accordance with the current government's coercive modernization campaign, full entrée into the high-tech, mass consumption order of the future requiring the dismemberment of the social body into smaller and smaller pieces more and more dependent on the structures of control. Community was systematically broken down into isolated individuals, and then the individuals themselves into contending fragments of confusion and desire, modular selves, interchangeable units for the new, interchangeable people of the masses' millennium. And as even the most rudimentary sense of wholeness was fading into extinction, the vitality of an entire culture was processed for cash and entertainment. This late into our epoch, an old, old story. How deep into the interior did one have to press to escape the spectacle of such cannibalism? (209f.)

Instead of discovering a place they have never seen, the Americans discover hybrids of familiar objects and places. Reflexivity, parody, mimicry, as their strange eastward journey into the "unknown"—which of course parallels the westward journey of Wiley Jones—makes obvious, are the last refuges of a cultural imperialism that converts the promise of immediate experience into simulacra, images constructed upon images. Accordingly, Drake quotes to his wife a line from Coppola's *Apocalypse Now*, "never get off the boat," a film, needless to say, quoting Conrad's *Heart of Darkness*, but the couple's reaction is quite significant:

> at the sound of the famous fictional movie line echoing in the relevant air of this real place,

they both laughed, the levels of self-consciousness attendant upon a contemporary journey like this were positively piranesian in number and involution, the pertinent dialogue had already been spoken, the images already photographed, the unsullied, unscripted experience was practically extinct, and you were left to wander at best through a familiar maze of distorting mirrors—unless somewhere up ahead the living coils of this river carried one down and out of this fun house. (210)[13]

Disillusioned, frustrated, but still stubbornly intent on going native, Drake and Amanda decide to push further into the heart of darkness, where the Pekit tribe, although reformed head hunters, are said to have preserved some of their authenticity. But alas, an American film crew found the Pekit first, thus exposing them to western culture and ultimately altering their own tribal culture. Hence the chief can now boast of a signed photograph of Jack Nicholson, which forms a triptych together with "the official government photograph of President Suharto" and "the standard lithograph of a thorn-crowned and teary Jesus" (236). But the final blow to the visitors' quest for authenticity comes when, as a "special treat for special visitors from Hollywood, U.S. of A.," the chief of the Pekit reveals a "Sony Trinitron and Philips VCR" to ritualistically start a viewing of the single video cassette in the village:

> Amanda and Drake turned in unison to stare at one another in openmouthed shock: Holy Incongruity! In the middle of a Pekit longhouse in the middle of a Stone Age village in the middle of an equatorial rain forest in the middle of mythic Borneo they were about to sit among a tribe of former headhunters and watch a video of *Batman*. (239)

The viewing, though, has become a ritual for the tribe, integrating it into older oral traditions of rendering the cosmic condition and the manichean fight between good and evil: "Though they had obviously seen the film numerous times, the Pekit attended to the dark flow of cartoon brutality with the intense concern of a graduate seminar on modern cinema. Then Nicholson appeared and the crowd went wild." (239f). In the course of the viewing, everybody gets a bit drunk and finally the time arrives when the Americans in turn must entertain their hosts: "The chief clapped his hands sharply twice, then called on Drake to restore the cheer. It was the funny Westerner's turn to make a fool of himself" (241). True professionals, the Hollywood actors rise to the occasion. Drake narrates the plot of *Terminator*, only to find out that several natives "had already seen that picture and were filling in the details for their friends" (241). Then it is Amanda's turn:

> Without waiting to be asked, Amanda leaped to her feet and started scooting energetically across the floor, cocking her head at intervals, emitting an abrupt 'Beep-beep' from the corner of her mouth. Nothing would do but that this tough crowd be given a professional re-creation of classic moments from Warner Brother's Road Runner cartoons. She barreled along the desert highway, dodging busses, cars, giant boulders launched by her archenemy, Wile E. Coyote. (243)

But the outcome of the couple's attempt to go native is sobering. Drake, after a wild drinking bout with the natives, experiences a few hours of "longed-for amnesia," which he interprets as "an act of grace" (259), as

> what the Pekit called a 'good dream,' a linked succession of well-cast, spankingly paced, brightly lit images rendered with such conviction its graphic unfolding is experienced as a major waking event, an exact embodiment of real life but for the nagging apprehension that every object, every deed, is saturated in significance [. . .]. (257)

By the time Drake and Amanda have returned to California, they have started treating their experience as an exotic joke, a trip to the theme park: they have simply been "roughing it in Jungle World" (263). They invite another actor couple for an authentic Indonesian dinner and, as intended, the conversation turns to their recent trip to the jungle and the strangeness encountered there. "But there's a loony place for everybody" (267), says Amanda. As if on cue the "cartoon brutality" manifests itself in the form of Wiley Jones, who forces his entry into their house in order to rob them, and by now Wiley does appear as frantic as Coyote chasing down Roadrunner in the *Looney Tunes* series. And Roadrunner, i.e. Amanda, is actually killed. The breaking of the cartoon image flow is not a moment of transcendence, though. Instead, Wiley suffers the dissolution of identity to its limits. On the frontier of electronic mass media, there is no regeneration through violence.

Wiley murders everybody in cold blood and runs—only to find that while the chase is over, the momentum of the chase has turned against himself, the objective now being his own—as yet unrealized—self. This becomes apparent at the end of the novel: Wiley, having safely arrived in Los Angeles, is now using the name Will Johnson. Not only has he—miraculously—gotten away with a series of capital crimes, he is also newly married now to a well-to-do blonde with a son from an earlier marriage, but the return to an affluent domestic life cannot prevent Wiley's media-induced disintegration as an individual: "Sometimes he imagined he could even feel the media microwaves, as if he were being literally baked by encoded clichés" (282). Compulsively and randomly changing his personality during long and uniform days without work or responsibility, he now uses a "briefcase full of hairpieces, cosmetics, and prosthetic devices" (285) to readily slip into a different act whenever the impulse hits him.

In an exemplary moment, he enters a rare and used books store, where he, immediately and, perhaps, compulsively, starts "reenacting" several passages of dialogue together with the shop assistant that are taken straight out of Raymond Chandler's novel *The Big Sleep*. It is the passage in which private eye Philip Marlowe, investigating Geiger's bookstore, which serves as a front for the renting and selling of pornography, pretends to be a bibliophile looking for a rare edition of *Ben Hur* (604-9). Although the search must in both cases remain unsuccessful, since the edition in question never existed in the first place, the construed conversation in *Going Native* significantly turns towards the merits of literacy and the awful consequences of the exposure to (electronic) mass media.[14] Therefore, upon Wiley's mock-serious remark about the "horrifying world of illiterate couch potatoes just right outside these walls," the antiquarian exclaims: "The Kartoon Kultur, yes, difficult, though, to avoid its vile contamination" (286). This remark certainly holds true for Wiley, because the antiquarian has unknowingly described his dilemma. Having reached his final destination, the California shore, he is less sure of his identity than ever before; in fact, he has become a poststructuralist object—a mere referent filled with signifiers. In the final chapter of the novel, in quick succession he takes on the identities of (once again) Tom Hanna, Will Johnson (277), Lyle Coyote (289), and Larry Talbot (283, 295).

Finally, in the "Adonis Health and Racquet Club," which has "Design Your Self!" (283) as its motto and where Wiley goes for his workout, he allows another club member to identify him as the actor Ridley Webb (285).[15] Since "[a]ll his impressions," as Rho had already claimed in the first chapter, "are fabulous" (26), his talent happens to be noticed by the film crew that one day blocks the way to Wiley's home, shooting a scene, and its assistant director immediately offers Wiley a role in a cop picture.[16] But the opportunity to act in a "real" movie, the reader is aware by now, is less than thrilling to a man who by now is literally acting for his life. For Wiley, stuck in a closed system of medialized surfaces, even his car, formerly representing the possibility of change, has become a cage merely simulating movement. Nevertheless, he feels compelled to re-enter this technological device in the final scene of the book:

> All he wanted now was to come to a stop, but even here, in the dank confinement of this garage, the Galaxie was moving on beneath him. Beyond the windscreen the darkness that had appeared so inflexible, so monolithic, was moving, too, it teemed, it swarmed with minute specks of dark, and now it was all he could see, this nervous ballet between ground and being, the eternity of noise trapped between channels. There was no self, there was no identity, there was no grand ship to conduct you harmlessly through the uncharted night. There was no you, there was only the viewer. There was only the Viewer, slumped forever in his sour seat, the bald shells of his eyes boiling in pictures, a biblical flood of them, all saturated tones and deep focus, not one life-size, and the hands applauding, palms abraded to an open fretwork of gristle and bone, the ruined teeth fixed in a yellowy smile that will not diminish, that will not fade, he's happy he's being entertained. (304)

Ultimately defeated, Wiley thus remains stuck in a moment of—to use Virilio's term—"accelerated paralysis." The intermediated subject in *Going Native* returns to itself like Wakefield returning to his house after twenty years of self-elected exile. Wiley, the former resident of "Wakefield Estates," has similarly established only symbolic distance between his old existence and his newly created state of being.

It could therefore well be argued that Wright has chosen Hawthorne's tale "Wakefield" (published in 1837), about a man living in seventeenth-century London who leaves his wife only to reside anonymously only two streets from his home for the next twenty years, to finally return to his wife and resume his former life, as a frame device for *Going Native*.[17] Exchanging Elizabethan London, where watching a play may have triggered a person's wish to escape into some equivalent of the green world, with the media-saturated American landscape of the late twentieth century, Stephen Wright in his novel presents a self-chosen outcast comparable to Hawthorne's strange character, of whom it is said:

> Amid the seeming confusion of our mysterious world, individuals are so nicely adjusted to a system, and systems to one another, and to a whole, that, by stepping aside for a moment, a man exposes himself to a fearful risk of losing his place forever. Like Wakefield, he may become, as it were, the Outcast of the Universe. (81)

NOTES

[1] The female protagonist of Pynchon's first novel is likewise introduced in a domestic setting, preparing dinner, watched by a silent television screen: "Oedipa stood in the living room, stared at by the greenish dead eye of the TV tube" (1).

[2] In *Going Native*, the electronic image has become the natural surroundings, leading to an erosion of reality and identity. The image-reproducible techniques appear on almost every page of the book. TV, VCR, and Camcorder are freely available and consumer based. Anybody can handle them and become the director of a "personal" movie.

[3] Or, as Wright puts it, Wiley is "like the needle and the thread going through all these beads" (Byers 173).

[4] The most important of these are: Coyote never catches Road Runner, as the impossible schemes he concocts (among them a do-it-yourself tornado kit and earthquake pills) always backfire to make him the victim of his own machinations; at the same time, the audience's sympathy always remains with Coyote.

[5] Throughout his career Charles Jones enjoyed alluding to literary works in his episode titles, e.g. *To Hare is Human* (1956), *Whoa, Be Gone* (1958), *Hopalong Casualty* (1960), *Zoom at the Top* (1962), *To Beep Or Not to Beep* (1963), and *War and Pieces* (164).

[6] It is interesting to note that in Jean-Luc Godard's *Alphaville, une étrange aventure de Lemmy Caution* (1965), the protagonist secret agent 003 Lemmy Caution, after his mission of destroying the supercomputer alpha 60, escapes from Alphaville in a Ford Galaxie. Yet another film by Godard, *Pierrot le Fou*, also made in 1965, about a husband leaving his family and going on a lawless road trip across France, features a Ford Galaxie—a 1960 model, as Ferdinand/Pierrot (played by Jean-Paul Belmondo) observes before stealing it from an American tourist. The film was shown in the United States under the titles *Pierrot Goes Wild* and *Crazy Pete* (1969).

[7] *Perfect Strangers*, aka *Vacation from Marriage*, was directed by Alexander Korda in 1945. It is about a married couple separated for three years by World War II. The en passant allusion to this title foreshadows Wiley's disappearance and also serves as a further link to Hawthorne's "Wakefield"—the reference to "Wakefield" having already been introduced by Wiley's house in "Wakefield Estates" (see above).

[8] Frederick Jackson Turner's famous lecture "On the Significance of the Frontier in American History"— later referred to as the "frontier theory" and as such one of the most important documents in American cultural history—was first given in 1893 during the Columbian World Exposition in Chicago, the same city from which Wiley Jones departs.

[9] The film referred to is *Edge of Sanity*, directed by Gérard Kikoïne in 1989, its plot combining the Dr. Jekyll and Mr. Hyde story with the exploits of the legendary killer Jack the Ripper.

[10] Larry McMurtry's novel *Anything for Billy* (1988) is a brilliant treatment of the outlaw hero as a creation of the early mass medium of the dime novel.

[11] It refers to James Foley's film *At Close Range* (1986), in which Christopher Walken portrays the evil father of two sons.

[12] At this point another intertextual reference comes to mind, namely the song "Going Mobile" by the English rock group The Who (from their 1974 album *Who's Next*), the lyrics of which take up the roadrunner motif, with the singer going 'beep beep' in between verses. That the band made the most out of the implications on the insecurity of identity in their album titles hardly needs mentioning in the context of this article.

[13] The reference is to Giovanni Battista Piranesi (1720-1778), the Italian graphic artist and architect of imaginary spaces, which he presented in his early and renowned collection carceri d'imaginazione (1745). Here his "imaginary prisons" compare to the hyperreality experienced by the American couple.

[14] Unfortunately, literature does not function as an alternative to television, as the reasoning of another character in the novel seems to suggest: "Television drove her mad, the noise and fever and folly of a casino without a payout – ever. She took to reading [. . .], cheap paperback accounts of true crime [. . .]. Secretly, she thrilled to the dissonance of violation, of accompanying, if only in the safety of her imagination, fellow human being's reckless step over the line, over all lines, into a quickening night of absolute freedom [. . .]" (172).

[15] These names of course offer themselves to various speculations about their significance for the novel's thematic concerns. Certainly the name of Ridley Webb calls to mind the cult film *Blade Runner* (1982), directed by Ridley Scott, about cyborgs (so-called replicants) in a future Los Angeles. Taken literally, the name Ridley Webb thus signifies the web of changing personae which the protagonist finds himself entangled in as he searches for the riddle of his own existence. But there is a further reference, namely to the actor/director Jack Webb, who created and played the leading role/narrator Sergeant Joe Friday in the TV police procedural *Dragnet* (1952-59), which was turned into a feature film in 1954 and whose title theme is reproduced in the door chime of the Jones's home, as mentioned above. Finally, the name Lyle Coyote probably carries allusions to William Dear's 1982 film *Timerider:The Adventures of Lyle Swann*, featuring the actor Peter Coyote.

[16] The scene is charged with irony—with the first A.D. asking Wiley: "[. . .] I think you might be just right for our next project. You've got the look. Ever done any acting before?" To which Wiley replies: "Just the normal day-to-day stuff" (294).

[17] "The man, under pretence of going [on] a journey, took lodgings in the next street to his own house, and there, unheard of by his wife or friends, and without the shadow of a reason for such self-banishment, dwelt upwards of twenty years" (75).

Works Cited

Berger, Jr., Harry. *Second World and Green World*. Studies in Renaissance Fiction Making. Sel., arr., and intr. by John Patrick Lynch. Berkeley: U of California P, 1988..

Burke, Anne. "Things." *Context: A Forum for Literary Arts and Culture* No. 13 (2003): 11. <dalkeyarchive.com/ context/-no13/ burke/ html>. 1 August 2003.

Byers, Thomas, Patrick O'Donnell, and Thomas Schaub. "Interview with Stephen Wright." *Contemporary Literature* 39.2 (Summer 1998): 57-179.

Chandler, Raymond. *The Big Sleep* [1939]. New York: Library of America, 1995.

Ellis, Bret Easton. *American Psycho*. New York: Vintage, 1991.

Frye, Northrop *Anatomy of Criticism: Four Essays*. Princeton: Princeton UP, 1990.

Hawthorne, Nathaniel. *Nathaniel Hawthorne's Tales*. Ed. James McIntosh. New York: Norton, 1987.

Jameson, Fredric. *Seeds of Time*. New York: Columbia UP, 1994.

O'Donnell, Patrick. "Speed, Metaphor, and the Postmodern Road Novel: Stephen Wright's Going Native and Others." *Mississippi Review* (1996) <mississippireview. com/1996/odonnell.html>. 1 August 2003.

Pynchon, Thomas. *The Crying of Lot 49*. New York: Bantam, 1967.

——. *Vineland*. Boston: Little, Brown, 1990.

Wright, Stephen. *Going Native*. New York: Delta, 1995.

Josef Raab
From Intertextuality to Virtual Reality:
Robert Coover's *A Night at the Movies*
and Neal Stephenson's *Snow Crash*

> "Anything that is real—the truth—is real only in the sub-
> stance of the language that embodies it."
> —Gordon Weaver, *A World Quite Round*

Introduction: Sliding Fictions, Sliding Identities

Published only five years apart, Robert Coover's collection of interrelated short fictions *A Night at the Movies* (1987) and Neal Stephenson's cyberpunk novel *Snow Crash* (1992) both construct fictional universes and identities by assembling and reconfiguring a variety of often-used images and familiar plot elements. Both works invite their readers to follow along as the protagonists get entangled in far-out adventures, which involve situations that we seem to have encountered in film or fiction before but which have a certain zest added to them. Both Coover and Stephenson also add a considerable dose of humor to their fictional worlds. The main element that invites a comparison of these two books, however, is that they both use different levels of fictionality and that in both cases the fiction within the fiction emanates from a reworking of various texts and sources, especially from a use of films as intertexts. This intertextual feature characterizes both Coover's *A Night at the Movies* and Stephenson's *Snow Crash* as postmodern fictions that ask readers to navigate through narrative mazes.

As is typical in postmodern literature, boundaries break down in Coover as well as in Stephenson. This also applies to the separateness of individual texts and genres, which intertextuality negates. While Coover primarily takes on the boundaries between different narrative forms and between individual myths, Stephenson's endeavors are more far-reaching: with him the crossing of boundaries includes not only textual elements and discourses but also extends to the distinction between information technology and fiction, or—as in the case of his novel *The Diamond Age* (1995)—"the boundary between mechanical machines and biological organisms" (Johnston 245). Larry McCaffery therefore believes that cyberpunk fiction writers like William Gibson, Bruce Sterling, or Neal Stephenson are more in touch with our age than writers of the heyday of postmodernism like Thomas Pynchon, John Barth, Donald Barthelme, William Gass, or Robert Coover. McCaffery writes that

> the myriad features and tendencies associated with the slippery term "postmodernism" can be understood best by examining what is unique about our contemporary condition. And it seems undeniable that this condition derives its unique status above all from technological change. Almost inevitably, those artists who have been most in touch with these changes,

intuitively as well as intellectually, have relied on themes and aesthetic modes previously associated with SF. (3)

In this categorization, Robert Coover is classified as one of "the 'mainstream' innovators of the 1960s" (12), while Stephenson and other cyberpunk science fiction writers are praised for going one step further by

> displaying the powerful and troubling technological logic that underlies the postmodern condition. Mixing equal measures of anger and bitter humor, technological know-how and formal inventiveness, postmodern SF should be seen as a breakthrough "realism" of our time. It is an art form that vividly represents the most salient features of our lives, as these lives are being transformed and redefined by technology. (16)

While the notion of cyberpunk science fiction as "a breakthrough 'realism'" is certainly debatable, it is true that Neal Stephenson incorporates in his narrative some of the possibilities which the combination of the world wide web and of virtual reality technology offer. However, films are also an important—and probably the primary—source of *Snow Crash*'s imagery and plot. Many of the characteristics of the novel's cyberspace as well as of what it calls "Reality" spring from action-adventure, detective, and science fiction movies. Nonetheless, Stephenson would probably agree with McCaffery in suggesting the outdatedness of "high postmodernism," if we can judge from his parody of a Yale professor named Dr. G.E.B. Kivistik in his novel *Cryptonomicon* (1999), who defends a stereotypical version of postmodern views on the relativity of values and the indeterminacy of language.[1]

Whereas Coover, in *A Night at the Movies*, begins with the impression of a realistic setting (an old-style movie theater) and realistic characters (a projectionist and moviegoers), Stephenson's narrative is from the start charged with science fiction gadgets that make this novel's universe like no place we have ever encountered outside of texts—but no less imaginable for that matter. As Neal Stephenson said in an interview, he is drawn to what he calls "possible worlds":

> I used to read anthologies of science fiction stories when I was a kid—there'd be 10 stories about rocketships and ray guns, and then there'd be some strange Robert Bloch story set in some town in the 1950s that had no science, no traditional SF content, but in the mind of someone it was clearly science fiction. It had that SF approach: an awareness that things could have been different, that this is one of many possible worlds, that if you came to this world from some other planet, this would be a science fiction world. ("Neal Stephenson" n.p.)

Thus the Inglewood neighborhood near Los Angeles International Airport where his main character—aptly named Hiro (or Hiroaki) Protagonist—lives in a former storage facility, is not pinned down to a definite time but represents part of a "possible world" that highlights certain aspects and tendencies of the present. As Stephenson pointed out in another interview, "I always write with a science fiction feel to my stories, though for some of the books, the marketing may be more toward a mainstream audience. The science fiction approach doesn't mean it's always about the future; it's an awareness that this is different" (Asaro n.p.). While Robert Coover is also attracted to the idea of other "possible worlds," with him those do not come out of a science or science-fiction orientation but out of what John Barth has called the "replenishment" of existing myths, plots, and narratives.

The goal of this essay is to analyze the "possible worlds" of Robert Coover's *A Night at the Movies* and Neal Stephenson's *Snow Crash* in terms of their intertextual components in order to examine to which extent a shift took place in terms of intertextuality and narrative technique from postmodern fiction to cyberpunk fiction. I will argue that while the work of Neal Stephenson illustrates how science has reentered the mainstream imagination through the spread of computer technology, the fictional world and the virtual reality within it that Stephenson creates are much indebted to standard devices of action, detective, and science fiction movies and that the use of information technology as an intertextual reference has not been accompanied by a fundamentally new mode of narrative (as used in hyperfiction, for example).

The Multiverse of *A Night at the Movies*

Robert Coover is one of a significant number of writers whose work illustrates the strong presence of the media in contemporary American literature. He has been called a re-teller of tales because in his novels and stories he uses myths—classical and contemporary, literary and popular—to new effects. The intertextual references of his collection *A Night at the Movies* are old-style film myths, primarily of the 1940s and 1950s, that range from *Casablanca* to the *film noir*. In his literary reworkings of these film fictions, Robert Coover erases all kinds of boundaries, especially those between individual plots as well as between filmic and literary devices, to end up with what Edmund White has called "a pandemonium of anarchic passions, aberrant scripts, unleashed imagery" (n.p.). The overall effect of this technique is to confuse and question our notions of reality by creating a grotesque and hybrid fictional world in which various levels of fictionality meet and elements from one plot segment are taken over into the next one, although it may have nothing at all to do with the first. Coover combines film constructions with literary ones into a new intertextual reality, creating a multiverse of recognizable (since we have encountered them before) plot devices and scenes.

The primary concern of Robert Coover is with language and its potential in the fiction-making process. He is constantly looking for imaginative ways of using language, a search that was inspired by Samuel Beckett, who, according to Coover, "had cleared the slate and showed ways in which one can start over—his whole performance has been one of erasure. I've explored a lot of different forms. I'm searching through other syntaxes to find a contemporary language that is relevant, as opposed to one that has died or one that is part of the slate that Becket helped erase" (qtd. in Miller 15). This "relevant" language relies on the audience's familiarity with the fictions and myths that it evokes, alters, and puts into new contexts.

Like other postmodernist writers, Coover is drawn to the idea of the world we live in as just another construct. As he said in an interview, "The world itself being a construct of fictions, I believe the fiction maker's function is to furnish better fictions with which we can re-form our notions of things" (Gado 149-50). Coover is therefore looking for unusual relations and connections, for innovative perspectives, for surprising twists on familiar tales and myths. His intertexts originate in world literature and popular culture. Appropriately, he dedicated his first collection of short stories, *Pricksongs & Descants* (1969), to Miguel de Cervantes, whom he praises for seeking "to synthesize the unsynthesizable." This is also Coover's own goal. And like Cervantes, Coover wants to write exemplary stories which stress their own constructedness instead of trying to produce eternally true myths, although his fictions are based on such myths:

> The novelist uses familiar mythic or historical forms to combat the content of those forms and to conduct the reader (*lector amantísimo!*) to the real, away from mystification to clarification, away from magic to maturity, away from mystery to revelation. And it is above all to the need for new modes of perception and fictional forms able to encompass them that I . . . address these stories. (*Pricksongs* 79).

In his fiction Coover has used a wide range of materials from the humanities and tried to invest it with such "new modes of perception and fictional forms." Among his intertextual (re)sources are fairy tales, fables, the Bible, Greek mythology and Greek tragedy, American history, baseball, and sado-masochist pornography. In his second collection of short fiction, *A Night at the Movies*, he turned to film myths. As he explained, he wanted to move "inside the special syntax of films. We do see a lot of filmic imagery—in television, in films—and we learn to think in ways that correspond to filmic technique. It's a language that one cannot ignore." Coover maintains that movies embody the American myth and that myths are "what innovative or experimental literature tries to struggle against" (Miller 15). His collection of fictions invites readers to spend a long evening at an old-fashioned movie palace. But, in keeping with his desire to overcome traditional genre distinctions and to reinvigorate myths, instead of a table of contents, there is a "Program," replete with sections like "Previews of Coming Attractions," "ADVENTURE!," "COMEDY!," "ROMANCE!," an "Intermission," something "For the Kiddies," and much more.[2] Coover deconstructs the myths propagated through film and he rearranges some of their elements into a new, hybrid fiction. Often-used storylines and scenes from certain film genres (like cartoons, westerns, or Charlie Chaplin comedies) are adapted to print fiction and are combined with glimpses of actual films (like *Casablanca*).[3] It is the mixture and rearrangement of fragments that is distinctive for Coover's comic and often grotesque text. In *A Night at the Movies*, films—the collection's primary reservoir of intertextuality—serve as subjects, as repositories of what have become cultural myths, as providers of "standard" scenes, and as sources of narrative techniques. By reworking film plots and using film techniques such as sudden cuts, switches between parallel narratives, and superimposed pictures, Coover—echoing John Dos Passos, to a degree—combines film narrative with literary narrative, thus creating a new kind of writing that relies on the dissolution of boundaries between different media and their levels of reality/fictionality.

The opening story, "The Phantom of the Movie Palace"—whose title, of course, invokes another text, namely *The Phantom of the Opera*—mixes numerous scenes from different film genres with the actions of a projectionist, who is alone in an old-style movie theater. He starts to project movies side by side and on top of each other. The resulting mixture of superimposed film images is grotesque:

> a galloping cowboy gets in the way of some slapstick comedians and, as the films separate out, arrives at the shootout with custard on his face; or the dying heroine, emerging from montage with a circus feature, finds herself swinging by her stricken limbs from a trapeze, the arms of her weeping lover in the other frame now hugging an elephant's leg; or the young soldier, leaping bravely from his foxhole, is creamed by a college football team, while the cheerleaders, caught out in no-man's land, get their pom-poms shot away. (23)

Coover makes clear that he and the projectionist are dealing with short-lived—though often-used—constructions. Their state in between presence and absence is pointed out when a character says: "'Your precious voice, my love, here and yet not here, evokes for me the sweet diaphanous adjacency of presence—' (here, his voice breaks, his cheeks puff out) '—and loss!'" (14). The stage directions which are inserted in parentheses further underline that we are dealing with constructed scenes and images. These are at the same time present and absent, since they are the elements of one construction, but not of another, and can only be seen from one perspective, not from another.

The images on the screen gradually mingle with images of an audience watching the screen. After initially suggesting to his readers that they are observing an actual movie audience, Coover takes a step back and reveals that this audience is itself merely appearing on the screen. And ultimately, the projectionist, too, becomes part of his own projections. His story is advertised in the "Program" as "Previews of Coming Attractions," which makes him yet another figure on the screen. In this maze of constructions and of different levels of fictionality, Coover makes fun of our desire to pin down meaning, as in the following passage, in which the projectionist sees angels who "seem then, no matter how randomly he's thrown the clips together, to be caught up in some terrible enchantment of continuity, as though meaning itself were pursuing them (and him! and him!), lunging and snorting at the edge of the frame, fangs bared and dripping gore" (18).

Trying to construct one stable meaning must necessarily be a frustrating endeavor, Coover implies, because the images are thrown together randomly, which makes it impossible to separate out the various fictions within fictions. The projectionist is reminiscent of an author in that "Some of these stratagems are his own inventions, others come to him through accident—a blown fuse, the keystoning rake of a tipped projector, a mislabeled film, a fly on the lens" (22-23). Like Coover, the projectionist pieces together different genres, often to comic effect, as we are told in the following self-referential statement: "He knows there's something corrupt, maybe even dangerous, about this collapsing of boundaries, but it's also liberating, augmenting his film library exponentially. And it's also necessary" (23). The comment of a detective on the screen that "What's frightening is not so much being able to see only what you want to see, see, but discovering that what you think you see only because *you* want to see *it . . . sees you . . .* " (33), hints at the importance of perspective and at the interconnectedness of fictional constructions. Seer and scene merge, as they will in Stephenson's *Snow Crash*: the projectionist creates and experiences the unusual and is in turn experienced by it (Cope 138ff.). In Stephenson's novel, the mixture of different levels of fictionality that monitor and influence each other will rely on virtual realities created by the protagonist and other hackers rather than on the selection of prefabricated (film) fictions.

Both Stephenson and Coover erase the boundaries between different fictional worlds; among the levels that Coover uses are fictions within a film, a film's world, the reality of a fictional movie audience watching this film, and that of readers of the story. Characters are allowed to leave the myth or story or reality level or medium in which they were originally placed and to enter another. The result is a collage of scenes that makes us uncertain about where we are at a given moment. When Coover speaks of a "strange blurry space in between, . . . a rather peculiar space perhaps, somehow there and not there at the same time, but no less real" in the story "Milford Junction, 1939: A Brief Encounter," we can also read this phrase as a metafictional self-characterization. Moreover, it could serve as a description of the virtual reality in Stephenson's novel.

In the story entitled "Intermission," Coover continues his mixture of various levels of fictionality. A seemingly realistic scene is combined with traditional film images. A girl, who appears to be the projectionist's alter-ego, leaves her seat in the movie theater during intermission to go to the concession stand. But after this realistic opening, fantasy takes over, immersing the protagonist in a series of common film scenes: she walks toward a handsome boy who is watching her, is abducted by gangsters carrying machine guns; their car is chased through the city streets; she jumps out of the car, lands in water, slips into an empty barrel in which she goes down a waterfall, is surrounded by sharks; after weeks in her barrel she reaches land only to be captured by dark-skinned natives; she barely escapes being sacrificed to a volcano, is reunited with the boy from the movie theater, wards off an invasion together with him, and so forth. Appropriately, the girl "feels like she's in one of those slow-motion sequences in which the more you run the more you don't go anywhere" (121-122). Through her marvelous experiences, Coover stresses the standardization of action-adventure narratives, ridiculing common plot elements, as in the following question: "She's adrift in a leaky barrel on an endless ocean, no food, no water, not even a cough drop. Boy, isn't that the way it always is?" (122). At the end of the story, the girl resigns herself to the interdependence of various realities, to her double function of audience and actor, and she obeys the claw of an outlandish creature on her shoulder, which instructs her to keep watching movies.

The fictional and the so-called "real" collide more uneasily in the story "Cartoon." Here "The cartoon man drives his cartoon car into the cartoon town and runs over a real man" (135). The cartoon world seems out of control and threatens the "real" world, from which it becomes increasingly indistinguishable. By the end of the story, the real man, as he is trying to flush the cartoon car down the toilet in an act of affirming his superiority over the animated world, has to realize that the cartoon's reality keeps invading his life: he "seems to have grown a pair of cartoon ears" (139). The different fictions/realities can no longer be separated from each other.

In a more sinister way, "Charlie in the House of Rue," a combination of Charlie Chaplin comedy and Edgar Allan Poe mystery, continues the theme of filmic and literary creations getting out of control. The collage of slapstick scenes eventually turns violent and grotesque:

> Charlie, dabbing still at the old man's eyes, as though unable to stop himself, knocks one of the eyeballs loose. . . . Desperately, Charlie tries to push the eyeball back in place, but it is difficult even to hang on to it: it keeps popping and slithering out of his grasp. And then the other one begins to ooze from its socket.
> Charlie cries out and claps his hand against the extruding eye, only to find that what he has clapped is the maid's round white bottom. (98-99)

Being interdependent constructs, various fictions (including one that recalls Coover's novel *Spanking the Maid*) blend into one another, illustrating that there is no stability in the fiction-making process. Because of the ensuing uncertainty, readers, like the story's Charlie figure, ask themselves, "What kind of place is this? Who took the light away? And why is everybody laughing?" (111).

Coover told an interviewer that the innovation and self-reflexivity of his fiction emanate from his desire to create self-sufficient, independent narratives:

> I felt we had to loosen fiction up and reinvest it with some of its old authority as a self-aware artifact, a kind of self-revealing mode, as it were, for the universal fictionmaking process. . . . [In the arts and sciences there has been] a basic shift . . . to a less conveniently ordered view of the world in which everything seemed random and relative. (Bigsby 81-82)

It has been one of Coover's aims to reflect this randomness and relativity in his fictions, which, as metafictions, also underline their own constructedness and their dependence on the frame of reference into which they are placed. However, Coover does not deal with the ways in which science and technology alter our perception of the world—a facet of Neal Stephenson's œuvre. While Stephenson lacks Coover's emphasis on the work of fiction as a "self-aware artifact," he goes further than Coover in integrating new ways of perception and manipulation made possible by information technology. Nonetheless, Stephenson conveys a stronger sense of realism (in the sense the term is used by Larry McCaffery in the passage quoted above), whereas Coover suggests that reality cannot be grasped or described. In "Lap Dissolves," for example, Coover presents a series of snapshots that follow each other by free association: each picture "seems to slide backwards, past the bus windows, slipping from frame to frame as though out of his memory—or at least out of his grasp. '*Wait*'" (80). The "he" in this sentence, who is longing for the picture to remain and to make sense, is the reader as much as the character in the story. But, as Coover illustrates throughout his collection, meaning cannot be pinned down and fictional constructions refuse outside control.

What is created in *A Night at the Movies* is—to use Coover's phrase from the story "Milford Junction, 1939: A Brief Encounter" quoted above—a "strange blurry space in between, . . . a rather peculiar space perhaps, somehow there and not there at the same time, but no less real" (147). This also applies to time, as the concluding story, "You Must Remember This," demonstrates. In this re-invention of the film *Casablanca*, which combines a fictional present reality with memories of a fictional past, Ilsa Lund and Rick Blaine become increasingly absorbed in remembrances. Their actions in the present gradually mingle with their memories of the time they spent together in the past. Rick notices that he

is still thinking about time as a pulsing sequence of film frames, and not so much about the frames, their useless dated content, as the gaps between: infinitesimally small when looked at two-dimensionally, yet in their third dimension as deep and mysterious as the cosmos . . . and what if one were to slip *between* two of those frames? he wonders—(173)

Gradually the characters in this story do "slip *between*" time frames so that they find it increasingly hard to distinguish past and present. They realize that "the real mystery . . . is not the fourth dimension as she'd always supposed . . . or the third either for that matter . . . but the *first*" (180).

This insight is what Coover and other postmodern writers have often illustrated: a situation is never simple and clear; life can never be grasped unambiguously; the notion of an *objective* reality has been rendered obsolete. Different realities/fictions can no longer be easily distinguished because, as William Gass has written, in fiction, "There are no descriptions . . . , there are only constructions" (17). The distinction between fiction and reality can no longer be upheld. In propagating this view, Coover and other postmodern writers can be said to have paved the way for cyberpunk fictions in which cyberspace and the (fictional) world that created it act upon one another. Coover's collection also illustrates that the concept of "intertextuality" has to be enlarged to include non-written texts like film.

Computer-Based Fictions

In the 1990s the Internet, virtual reality, and other computer-based fictions were added to film, television, and literature as the primary media in which we encounter fictional worlds. Between 1987 and 1992, the years of publication of *A Night at the Movies* and *Snow Crash*, the kinds of fictions that information technology could offer changed dramatically, while the use of cyberspace in literature had already been popularized in William Gibson's groundbreaking *Neuromancer* (1984).

Although computers had been in use for some time when postmodern literature flourished in the 1960s, their spread to private homes had remained fairly limited until the 1980s. But by 1986, the year before *A Night at the Movies* was published, the number of computers in the U.S. exceeded 30 million. Now computers were really on their way. In 1992 Microsoft introduced Windows 3.1 and shipped nearly 10 million units, which suggests that the number of American households with a computer must have at least doubled in the five years between the publication of Coover's and Stephenson's books. Also during this period, in 1990, the World Wide Web was born when Tim Berners-Lee developed HyperText Markup Language (HTML), which made it possible for the Internet to expand into the World Wide Web. Wanting to enable people to work together through a web of hypertext documents, Berners-Lee designed the first World Wide Web server and browser, which became available to the general public in 1991. As is well known, the World Wide Web has grown exponentially from there.[4] In 1993, for example, two years after its introduction, the annual rate of growth for WWW traffic was a mind-boggling 341,634%, according to "Harper's Index."

Another technological innovation that entered the work of writers like Neal Stephenson was the development of computer aided design (CAD) and the availability, in the early 1990s, of high-powered 3D graphics workstations. These allowed for the creation of virtual reality (VR). To make the virtual world convincing to the user, a number of special devices were developed. Most important among these was the stereoscopic head-mounted display, which tracked the position and orientation of the user's head and displayed a different image to each eye to trick the user into perceiving depth in the 3D scene. Stereo sound was added, as was a dataglove, which allowed the position of the user's hand(s) to be tracked and drawn within the virtual environment, complete with shape and gesture information.

But these technological developments merely added to the array of fiction-producing media that feed into the writer's imagination. More conventional sources—particularly film—were in no way supplanted by them. Yet information technology widened the scope of the postmodern trademark of offering possible worlds, or interconnected and tentative levels of fictionality. As David Porush has pointed out,

postmodern fiction is also generally characterized by a critique of rationalism, and of the scientific/technological project of our culture in particular. Postmodern fictions resist rationalism with alternative epistemological methods that tend to focus on the irresolute and detotalizing aspects of language . . . while trying to capture the extrarational richness of experience.[5]

Information technology offered many new ways of transcending rationality and of envisaging different modes of experience.

But while Neal Stephenson relies heavily on virtual reality to expand our notions of the possible, the virtual reality (as well as the so-called "Reality") of *Snow Crash* is rooted in film images and is therefore not as different from the fictions that collide in *A Night at the Movies* as we may tend to assume.

The Metaverse of *Snow Crash*

Neal Stephenson, who has a degree in physics and who worked for many years as a computer programmer and hacker, follows closely (and helps shape) developments in information technology. He had originally conceived of *Snow Crash* as "a computer-generated graphic novel" on a Macintosh computer in collaboration with a graphic artist (*Snow Crash* 439). Although he abandoned those plans eventually, he attributes the success of *Snow Crash* in part to the changing role of information technology at the time of publication. As he told an interviewer, "It has a hell of a lot to do with the fact that the timing, through no particular virtue of my own, was perfect. [The book] came out just as interactive media was becoming a huge news story" ("Interview" n.p.). Stephenson makes the technological developments of our age an integral part of his book's setting and plot and he imagines later stages in these developments. So we are back to the "possible worlds" of which he spoke in the interview quoted above, where things are "different," although the temporal setting is not a distant future. The technology is intensified to a science fiction degree in *Snow Crash* and it comes to readers through a language that is reminiscent of Anthony Burgess' *Clockwork Orange* or Hunter Thompson's *Fear and Loathing in Las Vegas*, a cool, fast-paced narrative style full of neologisms. The breathtaking nature and speed of this technology, e.g. the computer-controlled suspension of a skateboard that allows its rider to go a mile a second in city traffic and over speed bumps, the pizza delivery car with its so-called "smart box" that helps its driver race through residential neighborhoods, or any number of super-fast features in the novel's cyberspace—is reflected in the narrative style, which has a hyped, hyperreal, and hyperactive quality and which, as David Porush has observed, "enfolds and collides a polyphony of voices and textual play, while keeping the paradigmatic postmodern themes of interpretation, ambiguous messages, cybernetics, cognition, and information at its center" (Porush 131). But technology also triggers a feeling of threat or paranoia in the novel, a fear that the one who controls technology can also control minds. And finally, technology is tantamount in the action-packed plots that take place in the fictional universe as well as in the cyberspace within it.

The novel's two main figures are Hiro Protagonist and Y.T. ("Yours Truly")—exemplifications of Jay Clayton's claim that "Stephenson's delight in playing with names is positively Dickensian" (Clayton 828, n.20). Hiro is a thirty year-old Japanese-Korean-African-American IT whiz living in Los Angeles, and he calls himself "the last of the free-lance hackers" (17). Y.T. is a fifteen year-old courier on a high-tech skateboard. Together with his fellow hackers Da5id and Juanita, Hiro has developed the software, interface, and interactive rules for this novel's cyberspace, which Stephenson calls the "Metaverse." The paths of Hiro and Y.T. cross as Hiro plunges his pizza delivery car into a swimming pool while trying to deliver a pizza in time and Y.T. completes the delivery for him. Later they team up to fight a conspiracy by the fundamentalist billionaire preacher L. Bob Rife, who wants to control the Metaverse and brainwash people. His means of control is the Snow Crash virus: in the novel's "Reality," the virus is spread as a designer drug that makes its users lose their ability to produce meaningful language; in the Metaverse, the virus appears as code on a scroll which, when shown to an avatar (i.e. the representation through which a computer user acts in cyberspace), renders that avatar non-functioning and infects the brain of its user, producing the same results as the street drug. Issues of language are thus at the core of this novel.[6] As the protagonist finds out, "This is a Babel story" (202).

In creating his fiction and in making it reflect developments of the early 1990s, Neal Stephenson has to rely both on figurative language as well as code language. Human culture, to him, is an information system as well as a repository of myths. This double outlook also becomes evident in Stephenson's essay "In the Beginning Was the Command Line," in which the image of an author/creator at a keyboard writing code for another Big Bang appears.[7] Both the mythical figure of an author of the universe and the physical laws and technical details behind the universe's command line are important to Stephenson's imagination and art. In other words: he needs both figurative language and code language to render his version of contemporary culture. Therefore, in the acknowledgements of *Snow Crash*, he mentions both historical and archeological sources (especially on Babel and Sumer) and Apple Macintosh's *Human Interface Guidelines* among his sources (440).

Early on in the novel Stephenson gives what could be taken as a metaphoric metafictional comment on his use of intersecting figurative and code language and on his creation of a fictional world intermingled with a virtual reality:

> Farther up the Valley, the two competing highways actually cross. Once there had been bitter disputes, the intersection closed by sporadic sniper fire. Finally, a big developer bought the entire intersection and turned it into a drive-through mall. Now the roads just feed into a parking system—not a lot, not a ramp, but a system—and lose their identity. (7)

So with Stephenson we are moving toward a narrative moebius space in which there is no longer an inside and an outside and in which figurative and code language merge.[8]

In an interview about his novel *Cryptonomicon* (1999), Stephenson seems to give a clue to his idea about intertextual references as a cumulative mass. He told the interviewer that for that novel he "wanted to have, as kind of a running theme, a fictitious ancient

book that was a compendium of all known crypto lore. The idea is that each generation of cryptologists that comes along picks it up and adds to it, so at any given point
it's everything, the whole body of knowledge about crypto" ("Neal Stephenson"n.p.).
This cumulative attitude also seems to characterize the literary imagination behind
Snow Crash, which draws on computer science and the humanities alike, on code language as well as mythical language, on popular culture, movies, punk rock, historical
research, information technology, and contemporary cultural/-national concerns.

In taking up national and international issues of the 1990s, Stephenson created the figure of L. Bob Rife, who has been identified as "a seeming parody of L. Ron Hubbard, H.
Ross Perot and media mogul Rupert Murdoch" (Grassian 263). Rife is a former television
sports reporter from Texas turned billionaire entrepreneur. He owns the largest communications franchise in the world, and secretly he also heads the largest religious organization. His plan is to take away free will and turn people into hypnotized automatons. In the
Metaverse he targets all hackers, attempting to infect large numbers of them by unleashing the Snow Crash virus during a concert in a Metaverse amphitheater. But Hiro prevents
this mass infection by developing "Snow-Scan," a virus cure program (inspired by Sumerian myths about language and infection), while Rife himself is killed in a "fine, sterilizing
flame" as his jet is brought down by a robot dog in a cartoonlike climactic scene (437).

The America that Stephenson imagined for his novel is a strictly segregated and violent
place: those who can afford it live in homogeneous "burbclaves"; many others (like Hiro)
live in small storage units turned apartments; still others live in the violent streets. "No
surprises" is the most comforting slogan in this America, which is controlled by franchises (Reverend Wayne's Pearly Gates, Uncle Enzo's CosaNostra Pizza, Mr. Lee's Greater
Hong Kong, Narcolombia etc.), moguls, and mobster figures. This "possible world" of
Stephenson's imagination is the result of combined stereotypes: it is a fast-paced, cool,
technologically advanced land overboarding with brutality and thrills and characterized
by vast differences in terms of economic status and access to technology. It is

> the America of atomic bombs, scalpings, hip-hop, chaos theory, cement overshoes, snake
> handlers, spree killers, space walks, buffalo jumps, drive-bys, cruise missiles, Sherman's
> March, gridlock, motorcycle gangs, and bungee jumping. . . .
> The only ones left in the city are street people, feeding off debris; immigrants, thrown out
> like shrapnel from the destruction of the Asian powers; young bohos; and the technomedia
> priesthood of Mr. Lee's Greater Hong Kong. Young smart people like Da5id and Hiro, who
> take the risk of living in the city because they like stimulation and they know they can handle
> it [*sic!*]. (178-79)

Others live in "vast house farms out in the loglo wilderness" (179).

Hiro's escape from this world of franchises that have long disenfranchised the majority of people is the Metaverse, the virtual reality that he helped create and to which
he connects from his U-Stor-It unit through

a hair-thin fiber-optic cable. The cable is carrying a lot of information back and forth between Hiro's computer and the rest of the world. In order to transmit the same amount of information on paper, they would have to arrange for a 747 cargo freighter packed with telephone books and encyclopedias to power-dive into their unit every couple of minutes, forever. (20)

Hiro experiences the Metaverse, which actually only consists of "pieces of software, made available to the public over the worldwide fiber-optics network," through the 3-D images drawn on his goggles by laser beams that emanate from his computer (a version of the above-mentioned stereoscopic head-mounted display) and through stereo sound in his earphones (23).

The Metaverse in *Snow Crash* starts out as a technological version of the seemingly limitless West in 19th-century American culture; it offers open space, opportunity, and the suspension of rules:

The sky and the ground are black, like a computer screen that hasn't had anything drawn into it yet; it is always nighttime in the Metaverse, and the Street is always garish and brilliant, like Las Vegas freed from constraints of physics and finance. . . . A Metaverse vehicle can be as fast and nimble as a quark. There's no physics to worry about, no constraints on acceleration, no air resistance. Tires never squeal and brakes never lock up. (24, 331)

And like Coover's fantastic world of overlapping and interrelated movie fictions, Stephenson's Metaverse is freed from the constraints of realism: "Developers . . . can build buildings, parks, signs, as well as things that do not exist in Reality, such as vast hovering overhead light shows, special neighborhoods where the rules of three-dimensional space-time are ignored, and free-combat zones where people can go to hunt and kill each other" (23). Thus the Metaverse offers a virtual space for play and entertainment, for experiments and for the fantastic, for leaving behind the limits that are in force in Reality.

While in Robert Coover's transcendence of a character's reality in *A Night at the Movies* there is only a choice between prefabricated fictions, Stephenson's Metaverse gives the novel's characters a higher degree of control over their virtual worlds. On the other hand, while Coover has the "actual" characters enter ever new fictions, Stephenson's figures have to act through representatives in the Metaverse.

He is not seeing real people, of course. This is all a part of the moving illustration drawn by his computer according to specifications coming down the fiber-optic cable. The people are pieces of software called avatars. They are the audiovisual bodies that people use to communicate with each other in the Metaverse. . . .

Your avatar can look any way you want it to, up to the limitations of your equipment. If you're ugly, you can make your avatar beautiful. If you've just gotten out of bed, your avatar can still be wearing beautiful clothes and professionally applied makeup. You can look like a gorilla or a dragon or a giant talking penis in the Metaverse. Spend five minutes walking down the Street and you will see all of these.

Hiro's avatar looks like Hiro, with the difference that no matter what Hiro is wearing in Reality, his avatar always wears a black leather kimono. Most hacker types don't go in for garish avatars, because they know that it takes a lot more sophistication to render a realistic human face than a talking penis. (33-34)

Despite this seeming limitless freedom in determining one's virtual identity, restrictions are in place. Those "peons," for example, who enter the Metaverse through a less powerful "public terminal," can only act through low-resolution black and white avatars; and those who "can't afford to have custom avatars made and don't know how to write their own . . . have to buy off-the-shelf avatars" like Brandy and Clint (reminiscent of Barbie and Ken) that offer only "an extremely limited range of facial expressions" and other features (34-35).[9] But despite its play and entertainment aspect, the Metaverse has become primarily a platform to gather, store, and sell information in this fictional universe, where the Library of Congress and the CIA have merged into a private Central Information Corporation (CIC) and all the information is in ones and zeros (21). Hiro and Y.T. work together in gathering information to sell in the Metaverse, and in this effort they stumble upon the evil plans of L. Bob Rife. It becomes apparent that the Metaverse increasingly resembles the world outside it in that power struggles dominate it: capitalism, fundamentalism, and crime strive for control of this virtual reality.[10]

These motifs of overcoming limits, of shaping one's fictional identity, and of the loss of a version of paradise to special interest groups are by no means exclusively (or even primarily) the domain of virtual reality. Their use makes Stephenson's Metaverse very much indebted to fictions in literature and film. Nor is the Metaverse independent from either the fictional world in which it is embedded or from the reader's reality. Especially the Tower of Babel episode from the Bible, the culture of ancient Sumer, and the myth of Asherah figure prominently in Stephenson's Metaverse, as Hiro looks there for answers on how to combat the Snow Crash virus that Rife is unleashing. As the author writes in his acknowledgments, he used much published research:

> it should be pointed out that when I wrote the Babel material, I was standing on the shoulders of many, many historians and archaeologists who actually did the research; most of the words spoken by the Librarian [a virtual figure in Hiro's virtual home] originated with these people and I have tried to make the Librarian give credit where due, verbally footnoting his comments like a good scholar. (440)

Stephenson's reliance on the history of human cultures illustrates, as Robert Markley has made clear, that "Cyberspace . . . is unthinkable without the print culture it claims to transcend. . . . [It] remains fixated on the traces of the world that it ostensibly renders obsolete" (1-2).[11] One aspect of this cultural background that is used prominently in *Snow Crash* is religion.[12]

Like Coover's movie fictions, Stephenson's Metaverse relies heavily on mythologies.

And like Coover's book, *Snow Crash* presents the narrative's different levels of fictionality as interpenetrating. In the case of Stephenson's novel, it is especially the Snow Crash virus that obscures the boundary between Reality and the Metaverse: it infects the avatar in the Metaverse and through it the avatar's creator or user in Reality. Hiro, we read,

> knows one thing: The Metaverse has now become a place where you can get killed. Or at least have your brain reamed out to the point where you might as well be dead. This is a radical change in the nature of the place. Guns have come to Paradise. . . .
>
> The virus that ate through Da5id's brain was a string of binary information, shone into his face in the form of a bitmap—a series of white and black pixels, where white represents zero and black represents one. They put the bitmap onto scrolls and gave the scrolls to avatars who went around the Metaverse looking for victims. . . .
>
> It's not easy working with a piece of data that can kill you. But that's okay. In Reality, people work with dangerous substances all the time . . .
>
> Once the virus has been extracted and isolated, it is easy enough for Hiro to write a new program called SnowScan. SnowScan is a piece of medicine. That is, it is code that protects Hiro's system—both his hardware and, as Lagos [his Metaverse Librarian] would put it, his bioware—from the digital Snow Crash virus. Once Hiro has installed it in his system, it will constantly scan the information coming in from outside, looking for data that matches the contents of the scroll. (328-29)

The events at one fictional level can thus not be separated from those of the fiction within it (similar to Coover's story "Cartoon," for example). Also, the various fictional levels refer to aspects of our experience as readers: the different realms of knowledge and experience are interrelated. For instance, in Hiro and Y.T.'s efforts to prevent the spread of the virus, connections are established between computer codes and the brain's neurolinguistic structure or between ancient Sumerian priest culture and present-day America.[13]

Therefore the protagonist has to make use of at least three levels of reality/fictionality in his quest to save the world from domination by the fundamentalist mogul: the Metaverse, his Reality outside the Metaverse, and our reality as readers that is shaped by its cultural history. Hiro is assisted in his efforts by Y.T. in the Reality and by his virtual Librarian (who is "just a piece of software" that Hiro wrote, p. 195) in the Metaverse. The Librarian consults actual and virtual sources of information that explore also the cultural history which Hiro shares with us readers.[14] For example, he recounts the history of the spread of the herpes virus and he explores the transition from an Adamic language to a linguistic differentiation.

Other intertextual sources for Stephenson's Metaverse include the language of advertising (e.g. slogans used by Domino's Pizza or Midas) and punk music. Significantly, Stephenson makes Hiro's roommate Vitaly Chernobyl the singer of a punk band. As Daniel Grassian points out, *Snow Crash* is reminiscent of punk music in being somewhat

adolescent in nature, celebrating autonomy from authority and parent figures, center-
ing on blue-collar independent heroes, promoting aggression against oppressive structures, as well as in its use of slang and profanity. "In keeping with the aggressive punk
ethos," writes Grassian,

> *Snow Crash* is filled with fighting and high-paced action scenes, both in the Metaverse and in
> Reality. In a way, Hiro, as a swashbuckling samurai, is somewhat of a nihilistic cold-blooded
> killer who has no qualms or remorse about killing anyone who stands in his way. . . . In the
> face of mass corruption and governmental decline, the new hero figure becomes the rene-
> gade . . . a technological whiz. (259)

This description points to the main intertextual source for *Snow Crash* and its Metaverse, namely movies. Grassian makes what is a correct statement for *Snow Crash* but too
sweeping a judgment for cyberpunk fiction in general when he writes that the "cyberpunk hero is truly an updated, postmodern or post-postmodern version of the Phillip
Marlowe-like hero of the Hard Boiled Detective Novel. Hiro Protagonist is a rebellious
punk protagonist, a socially isolated renegade in the style of Marlowe" (258). Like a
hard-boiled detective in a film noir, Hiro uses the slang of his profession, and he is described in a detached, ironic style, as in the following passage:

> Hiro can't really afford the computer either, but he has to have one. It is the tool of his trade.
> In the worldwide community of hackers, Hiro is a talented drifter. This is the kind of life-
> style that sounded romantic to him as recently as five years ago. But in the bleak light of full
> adulthood, which is to one's early twenties as Sunday morning is to Saturday night, he can
> clearly see what it really amounts to: He's broke and unemployed. (20)

Stephenson's protagonist is a self-styled cool outsider, proudly living at the margins
of society and aloof from his surroundings. He sees himself as the lone hero (reminiscent of action-adventure movie figures like Indiana Jones) who excels in various areas
(including "movies"!). Hiro's self-conceptualization appears, for example, on his business card (17):

HIRO PROTAGONIST

Last of the freelance hackers
Greatest sword fighter in the world
Stringer, Central Intelligence Corporation
Specializing in software-related intel
(music, movies & microcode)

---

254 | THE HOLODECK IN THE GARDEN

To his self-chosen exile he adds bravura, both in the Metaverse and in Reality. Working as a pizza "Deliverator," for example, he resembles James Bond or other secret agents, carrying a gun that is "tiny, aero-styled, lightweight, the kind of gun a fashion designer would carry; it fires teensy darts that fly at five times the velocity of an SR-71 spy plane, and when you get done using it, you have to plug it into the cigarette lighter, because it runs on electricity" (1-2).

Stephenson equips Hiro with the assets of an action hero in a movie, and, indeed, *Snow Crash* is an action-driven novel that seems to lend itself to being made into a film. With regard to plot, some of the book's elements that remind readers of action movies include the evil mogul who wants to control the world, the unlikely couple that teams up to save the universe, and the gradual unraveling of an enigma in the quest for a means of winning the fight against evil. Technologically enhanced movie-like action can be found throughout the novel—both in its Reality and in its Metaverse. The following passage, for instance, renders a Hollywood-style destruction scene, complete with the auditory component and with the implied camera movement from a close-up shot of "something small and dark" to a wide-angle shot of a flaming explosion:

> A deep thump sounds from the roof of a building on his right. . . . And something catches his eye, something small and dark, darting away from the building and up into the air like a sparrow. But when it's a hundred yards out over the water, the sparrow catches fire, coughs out a great cloud of sticky yellow smoke, turns into a white fireball, and springs forward. It keeps getting faster and faster, tearing down the center of the harbor, until it passes all the way through the little chopper, in through the windshield and out the back. The chopper turns into a cloud of flame shedding dark bits of scrap metal, like a phoenix breaking out of its shell. (306)

The Hollywood action effects can be even more intense in Stephenson's Metaverse, where—like in a film of the *Matrix* variety—the limiting rules of physics do not apply. This is how a high-speed chase full of special effects can look in the novel's virtual reality:

> Raven gets turned toward Downtown and twists his throttle just as Hiro is pulling in behind him on the Street, doing the same. Within a couple of seconds, they're both headed for Downtown at something like fifty thousand miles an hour. Hiro's half a mile behind Raven but can see him clearly: the streetlights have merged into a smooth twin streak of yellow, and Raven blazes in the middle, a storm of cheap color and big pixels. (410-11)

The scene seems to emanate from a combination of arcade computer game and Hollywood action blockbuster.

Apart from such action staples, Stephenson uses the science fiction conventions of a fiction within a fiction and of a possible world with an indeterminate temporal setting that comments on present trends. There are also direct verbal references, for example, to *Star Trek*: the U.S.S. Enterprise is off the coast of Los Angeles in the Pacific Ocean and posters of the various *Star Trek* TV series and of the movies they inspired decorate the workspace of many hackers in the novel. Moreover, there are allusions to *Star Trek*, as in "You can't just materialize anywhere in the Metaverse, like Captain Kirk beaming down from on high" (34). The Metaverse, too, has close ties to the novel's (fictional) film industry. For example, the hip Black Sun club has a so-called "Movie Star Quadrant," where "Actors love to come . . . because in The Black Sun, they always look as good as they do in the movies. And unlike a bar or club in Reality, they can get into this place without physically having to leave their mansion, hotel suite, ski lodge, private airline cabin, or whatever" (61). Because of the strong intertextual presence of films (in terms of characterization, plot, narrative technique and perspective, visual effects, and verbal references), it should come as no surprise that the novel's list of "only four things [America does] better than anyone else" includes "movies" (3).

With his heavy reliance on film, Neal Stephenson remains rooted in conventional narrative genres (and modes) and in familiar sources of imagery. As he told an interviewer, "Humans have been doing linear narrative for as long as we've had the ability to talk, so it's hard-wired into our brains now, to some extent" (Goldberg n.p.). But both Stephenson and Coover illustrate the continuing use of intertextuality in postmodern literature; their choices of intertexts reveal different target audiences, though.

Technology and/in Fiction

In terms of intertextual sources, *Snow Crash* is heavily based on action movies, while Robert Coover's *A Night at the Movies* recreates the experience of zapping through TV channels.[15] Coover creates the effect of parallel, unrelated narratives getting entangled in each other (as they do in the viewer's consciousness while channel-surfing), while Stephenson relies on the glitz and standard devices of adventure-filled action movies. Coover's collection is therefore only to a limited degree about movies, whereas the common classification of *Snow Crash* as a cyberpunk novel obscures its indebtedness to film.

Nonetheless, Stephenson combines his reliance on traditional media with a strong interest in the technological developments of our age. This is by no means a contradiction. As Jay Clayton has pointed out, "To be passionate about technology, traditional culture, and popular culture all at once is less rare than many realize. For . . . the computer pioneers who helped produce the Internet boom of the 1990s, the idea of separating technology from other domains of culture made little sense" (806). The trend toward specialization and division that C.P. Snow lamented in 1959 has long been countered by science fiction and recently also by cyberfiction. As Clayton notes,

> the increase in fictional explorations of scientific issues is one of the most striking developments in American literature at the turn of the century. . . . Not since the early nineteenth century, before the full development of academic disciplines, has there been such synergy between technology and other forms of imaginative creativity. (808-09)

Neal Stephenson is one of the key figures in this development. Apart from science and technology, he and other authors of cyberfiction also draw on the most diverse aspects of literary, popular, and scientific culture, using a myriad of sources as their intertexts. But the intertextual uses of information technology in cyberfiction do not imply wholly new conceptions of text, author, or reader but merely an expansion of existing trends. While the fictional uses of virtual reality make Stephenson's novel more timely than Coover's collection of fictions, they do not radically alter our conceptions of texts and levels of fictionality. Yet postmodern cyberfiction authors can be said—maybe more so than earlier postmodern writers like Robert Coover—to work toward an interplay of technology and literature.[16] In Donna J. Haraway's words, they "take responsibility for the social relations of science and technology," which "means refusing an anti-science metaphysics, a demonology of technology, and so embracing the skillful task of reconstructing the boundaries of daily life, in partial connection with others, in communication with all our parts" (181).

Nonetheless, it is the word- (rather than science-) oriented Robert Coover who is at the forefront of exploring options that this interplay opens up. For example, at the 1999 symposium "TP21CL—Technology Platforms for 21st-Century Literature" at Brown University, for which Coover was one of the main organizers, the main question was: "Does literature have a future in this space [of computer technology and hypertext] and if it does, how can we enhance it? How can we give text back its authority?" (Dorr n.p.). Neither Coover nor Stephenson are ready to give up storytelling by means of words (rather than pictures or graphics); as Coover said: "Perhaps graphic artists will help us to have deep imaginings in the future, not literary artists. That's a possibility, but I'm not yet willing to throw in the towel" (Dorr n.p.).

Forking Paths and Hypertext

Robert Coover has long been conducting the Brown University Hypertext Fiction Workshop, exploring with his creative-writing students the options that hypertext gives to storytelling and fiction reading. Asked about the differences between printed literature and hypertext literature, he told an interviewer:

> What's difficult in print culture and the other forms of older texts was the necessity of one thing following upon another singularly. One page turns to another page, one picture gives way to another picture, and even the so-called moving pictures, motion pictures, are, in effect, a whole bunch of sequential things happening in a line without any variation in the way that that line is drawn. And the illusion of motion is derived from the very linearity, static linearity of the medium.
>
> The computer offers up the possibility . . . of going from any particular window of space to any other window of space, from any one window to several at the same time. . . . It meant that the reader, instead of being a passive page-turner, became an active page-turner, because he or she had to choose the pages that would be seen. (Dorr n.p.)

As Coover wrote in his *New York Times* article "The End of Books," hypertext, in its move away from the line and linearity,

> presents a radically divergent technology, interactive and polyvocal, favoring a plurality of discourses over definitive utterance and freeing the reader from domination by the author. . . . The traditional narrative time line vanishes into a geographical landscape or exitless maze, with beginnings, middles and ends being no longer part of the immediate display. Instead: branching options, menus, link markers and mapped networks. ("End of Books")

But Coover (and Stephenson) already put into practice many of these elements in their print narratives.[17] In the print medium that they have chosen for their fictions it is the author rather than the reader who makes a decision when the narrative reaches a Borgesian fork in its path. Coover believes that in this way print fiction can avoid one of the dangers of hypertext fiction, namely the lack of direction and "centripetal force" which can result in "a kind of static low-charged lyricism—that dreamy gravityless lost-in-space feeling of the early sci-fi films" ("End of Books" n.p.). While Coover and Stephenson disagree on the desirability of technology as a plot element, they seem to agree on the virtues of print fiction, which allows the writer's "creative imagination" to concentrate on the narrative. According to Coover, hypertext fiction, by contrast, risks being "more preoccupied with linkage, routing and mapping than with statement or style, or with what we would call character or plot (two traditional narrative elements that are decidedly in jeopardy)" ("End of Books" n.p.).

Notes

[1] Cf. Jay Clayton, 829, n. 21.

[2] As Jackson I. Cope has pointed out, "Most of the allusive matrix of *A Night at the Movies* is adapted from films of [the forties and fifties]. The novel offers an encyclopedia of film reference, but the pleasures of source hunting (and, for Coover, of clue implantation) must give way before the realization that generic lamination, not specific films, constitutes the main structure" (139, n. 2).

[3] While the primary mood of this collection is nostalgic, the book also illustrates the indeterminacy and self-referentiality of much postmodern fiction. As Jackson Cope writes, *A Night at the Movies* "is a rethinking, doubling back, a moebius strip of the evanescent become the inevitable" (148).

[4] For a more detailed account of developments in computer technology and use, see "A Chronology of Computer History" at <http://www.cyberstreet.comhcs/museum/chron.htm>.

[5] Porush argues that we should not be surprised to find that a postmodern novel like *Snow Crash*, which heavily relies on virtual reality as a means of transcending rationality, addresses metaphysical questions. He believes that the "coevolution of human brain and communications tech has reached critical proportions in postmodernism, as we seem poised to leap across to some new cognitive-cultural state, heralded in near-apocalyptic imaginings about cyberspace and virtual reality. Yet, the emergence of metaphysical views on the postmodern literary scene is still surprising and represents a new turn. . . . [But] If we think . . . of postmodern thought generally as flowing from an underlying irrationalism or a skeptical, resistant critique of reason, especially of mechanics and reductive formalism and totalizing systems, it is not after all so surprising to find metaphysics emerging in postmodernism" (108-09).

[6] On the centrality of language issues for the work of Neal Stephenson, cf. Katherine N. Hayles's essay in this collection.

[7] In this essay Stephenson claims that "the universe can't be described very well by physics as it has been practiced since the days of Newton. If you look at a small enough scale, you see processes that look almost computational in nature. I think that the message is very clear here: somewhere outside of and beyond our universe is an operating system, coded up over incalculable spans of time by some kind of hacker-demiurge. The cosmic operating system uses a command-line interface."

[8] For more on this concept, see Hanjo Berressem's essay in this collection.

[9] Barbara Browning writes that boundaries also stay in place in Stephenson's Metaverse in terms of gender: "Despite Haraway's hopefulness, the virtual public at large is less willing to allow for total free-play of gender. Gender-switching may be an acknowledged aspect of virtual reality, but when addressed it often provokes more anxiety than celebration of new freedom. Even more disturbing to people . . . is the possibility of the loss of control over one's own virtual body" (41).

[10] Therefore Salvatore Proietti calls *Snow Crash* and Bruce Sterling's *Islands in the Net* (1988) "the most accomplished jeremiads on the virtual frontier" (122). He points out that in Stephenson's novel the Metaverse has lost its original sense of freedom and opportunity and has come under the control of franchises.

[11] Markley further argues that "virtual realities conserve and incorporate rather than overthrow the assumptions and values of a traditional, logocentric humanism, the Platonist division of the world into the physical and metaphysical in which ideal forms are valued over material content" (7).

[12] For a convincing account of *Snow Crash* as a "powerful rereading of Jewish evolution and its influence on the birth of civilization," see Porush. Porush points to the metaphysical quality of the novel but concludes that "The inability of *Snow Crash* to confront its own metaphysics, the spiritual transcendence it conjures only to banish, comes from the fashionable unwillingness to grant any credence to narratives of metaphysics, even while so much of postmodern culture apparently yearns for it" (137, 140).

[13] As John Johnston summarizes: "These connections are mainly enacted through a series of mythic parallels between the 'hacker god' Enki's use of performative speech acts ('nam-shubs') to counter the thought-control apparatus of ancient Sumerian priest culture, and corresponding efforts in present day America to thwart the viral control programs spread by L. Bob Rife's right-wing organization of religious fundamentalists. The latter 'speak in tongues,' but this language turns out to be a preconscious language of the primitive brainstem that Rife has appropriated as a form of thought and behavior control. Since individual consciousness and agency come only with release from its viral repetitions, the plot culminates with the hacker Hiro Protagonist's effort to discover a contemporary equivalent of Enki's nam-shub, which he considers to be the first form of anti-viral software" (227).

[14] Andrew Leonard believes that the figure of the Librarian is one of the most appealing aspects through which the novel illustrates "what the computer could offer the world." Leonard claims that this "helpful digital entity, not unlike a real-life librarian, . . . is also a really, really neat way of imagining how we puny humans might some day be able to plumb the database of all recorded information" (n.p.).

[15] I am grateful to Brian McHale for this insight, which he presented at the Paderborn conference where the papers collected here were first discussed.

[16] Clayton concludes from the work of Stephenson and others that "a critical engagement with technology, not withdrawal, is the best hope for what were once called humanist values" (825).

[17] As he writes in his review of Stuart Moulthorp's hyperfiction *Victory Garden*, Coover does not believe that hyperfiction is a radically new mode of storytelling: "there is really only one story here," he writes of *Victory Garden*, "as whole and singular-and ultimately linear, even chronological-as that of any ordinary print novel-the only difference being that the reader moves about in the story as though trying to remember it, the narrative having lost its temporality by slipping whole into the past, becoming there a kind of obscure geography to be explored" ("Hyperfiction: Novels for the Computer" n.p.).

WORKS CITED

Asaro, Catherine. "A Conversation with Neal Stephenson." *SF Site* September 1999. <http://www.sf-site.com/10b/ ns67.htm>.

Bigsby, C.W.E. "Interview with Robert Coover." *The Radical Imagination and the Liberal Tradition*. Ed. Bigsby and Heidi Ziegler. London: Junction Books, 1982.

Browning, Barbara. "When Snow Isn't White." *Women & Performance: A Journal of Feminist Theory* 9.1 (1996): 35-53.

Clayton, Jay. "Convergence of the Two Cultures: A Geek's Guide to Contemporary Literature." *American Literature* 74.4 (2002): 807-831.

Coover, Robert. *Pricksongs & Descants*. New York: New American Library, 1969.

——. *A Night at the Movies; Or, You Must Remember This*. New York: Collier Books, Macmillan, 1987.

——. "The End of Books." *The New York Times* 21 June 1992 <http://www.nytimes.com/ books/98/09/27/specials/coover-end.html>.

——. "Hyperfiction: Novels for the Computer." *The New York Times*, 29 August 1993 <http://www.nytimes.com/ books/98/09/27/specials/coover-hyperfiction.html>.

Cope, Jackson I. *Robert Coover's Fictions*. Baltimore and London: Johns Hopkins UP, 1986.

Dorr, Rebecca. "Off the Page: Robert Coover Is Leading a Literary Revolution That Eschews Pen and Paper for Keyboard and Mouse." *Phoenix* 1-8 April 1999 <http://www.providencephoenix.com/ archive/books/99/04/01>.

Gado, Frank, ed. "Robert Coover." *First Person: Conversations on Writers & Writing*. Schenectady: Union College P, 1973). 142-149.

Goldberg, Michael. "Breaking the Code with Neal Stephenson." *Wired On-Line,* 18 February2000 <http://www.addict. com/ATN/issues/1.07/Features/Neal_Stephenson/>.

Gass, William H. *Fiction and the Figures of Life.* New York: Knopf, 1970.

Grassian, Daniel. "Discovering the Machine in You: The Literary, Social and Religious Implications of Neal Stephenson's *Snow Crash.*" *Journal of the Fantastic in the Arts* 12.3 (2001): 250-67.

Haraway, Donna J. "A Cyborg Manifesto: Science, Technology and Socialist-Feminism in the Late Twentieth Century." In her *Simians, Cyborgs, and Women: The Reinvention of Nature.* New York: Rutledge, 1991.

[Interview with Neal Stephenson]. Untitled transcript (1995). <http://www.avnet.co.uk/home/amaranth/Critic/ivstephs.htm>.

Johnston, John. "Distributed Information: Complexity Theory in the Novels of Neal Stephenson and Linda Nagata." *Science Fiction Studies* 28.2 (July 2001): 223-45.

Leonard, Andrew. "Deep Code." *Salon Magazine* 19 May 1999 <http://www.salon.com/books/int/1999/05/19/ stephenson/index.html>.

Markley, Robert, ed. *Virtual Realities and Their Discontents.* Baltimore and London: Johns Hopkins UP, 1996.

——. "Introduction: History, Theory, and Virtual Reality." In Markley. 1-10.

McCaffery, Larry. "Introduction: The Desert of the Real." In his *Storming the Reality Studio: A Casebook of Cyberpunk and Postmodern Fiction.* Durham and London: Duke UP, 1991. 1-16.

Miller, Lori. "Beckett Cleared the Slate." *New York Times Book Review* 1 February 1987: 15.

"Neal Stephenson: Cryptomancer." *Locus Magazine* August 1999. <http://www.locusmag.com/ 1999/ Issues/08 /Stephenson.html>.

Porush, David. "Hacking the Brainstem: Postmodern Metaphysics and Stephenson's *Snow Crash.*" In Markley. 107-41.

Proietti, Salvatore. "The Informatic Jeremiad: The Virtual Frontier and US Cyberculture." *Science Fiction, Critical Frontiers.* Ed. Karen Sayer and John Moore. Houndmills: Macmillan, 2000.

Snow, C.P. *The Two Cultures* [1959]. Cambridge: Cambridge UP, 1993.

Stephenson, Neal. *Snow Crash* [1992]. London: ROC, Penguin, 1993.

——. "In the Beginning Was the Command Line." <http://www.spack.org/index.cgi/Command-Line>.

White, Edmund. "Splice Memory." *New York Times Book Review* 1 February 1987. <http://www.nytimes. com/ books/98/09/27/specials/coover-movies>

III

Science in Contemporary Fiction/ Contemporary Science-in-Fiction

Ursula K. Heise
Toxins, Drugs, and Global Systems:
Risk and Narrative in the Contemporary Novel

Much work in the field of ecocriticism, established in American literary studies during the 1990s, assumes that the natural world is endangered, and that some of the human activities that threaten nature also put human health and life at risk. But while this assumption explicitly shapes a good deal of environmentalist politics and implicitly underlies most, if not all, ecocritical research, the concept of risk has so far rarely been subjected to theoretical discussion in ecocriticism. This omission is all the more remarkable considering that risk theory and risk analysis constitute a well-developed field of study in the social sciences, encompassing more than three decades of research. Perhaps because this field is not committed to the same environmentalist concerns that interest ecocritics, it has so far attracted little attention in ecological criticism. One exception is the work of Lawrence Buell, which engages some studies of risk in the analysis of what Buell calls "toxic discourse," textual and visual representations of exposure to hazardous chemicals. But even in his work, the notion of risk and the social scientific theories that have evolved around it play only a relatively minor role. My essay will discuss connections among ecocriticism, risk theory, and narrative to suggest, on one hand, that a focus on the notion of risk as a literary theme can substantially sharpen and shift standard interpretations of some contemporary texts and, on the other hand, that a consideration of risk and the kind of narrative articulation it requires has potentially important implications for the analysis of narrative form.

My argument focuses on a particular type of risk—exposure to chemical substances—but similar analyses could be carried out, with some modifications, for literary representations of other ecological and technological hazards. This focus allows me to foreground how my argument builds upon Buell's earlier analyses of toxic discourse but also how contemporary novelists use chemical substances as a trope for the blurring of boundaries between body and environment, public and domestic space, and harmful and beneficial technologies. My analysis begins with Don DeLillo's postmodern classic *White Noise*, whose exploration of a local risk scenario by means of satire raises complex questions about the role of realism and hyperbole in risk perception and representation. The second section lays out the theoretical background of this analysis in more detail by giving an overview of some important approaches and insights in risk theory. The third section returns to the literary representation of risk through a very different novel, Richard Powers's *Gain*, which examines risk in the context of complex global systems and thereby raises the question of how such systems can be effectively captured in narrative. These readings of particular texts may point the way toward some of the implications risk theory might have not only for a thematic study of literature but, beyond that, for the consideration of literary form.

"Unreliable Menace": *White Noise*

DeLillo's *White Noise* was published in January of 1985, only a little over a month after a toxic gas accident at a Union Carbide plant in Bhopal, India, killed at least two thousand people and injured thousands more. The coincidence was not lost on the novel's first reviewers, who pointed out the eerie echoes between the Bhopal accident and the toxic gas incident in the novel's middle chapter.[1] This "airborne toxic event" (*WN* 117), as the media euphemistically call it, occurs in the Midwestern college town of Blacksmith, where professor of Hitler studies Jack Gladney lives with his wife, Babette, and their family. After an accident at a train depot, the gas Nyodene Derivative, a byproduct of pesticide manufacture, leaks from one of the wagons and forms a large cloud over Blacksmith, whose inhabitants receive the order to evacuate. En route to the evacuation camp, Jack Gladney is briefly exposed to the toxic gas. When the evacuees' health data are recorded at the camp, Gladney realizes that even this short exposure might have potentially serious consequences for his health. During his interview with one of the health technicians, the following conversation unfolds:

"Am I going to die?"
"Not as such," [the technician] said.
"What do you mean?"
"Not in so many words."
"How many words does it take?"
"It's not a question of words. It's a question of years. We'll know more in fifteen years. In the meantime we definitely have a situation."
"What will we know in fifteen years?"
"If you're still alive at the time, we'll know that much more than we do now. Nyodene D. has a life span of thirty years. You'll have made it halfway through."
"I thought it was forty years."
"Forty years in the soil. Thirty years in the human body."
"So, to outlive this substance, I will have to make it into my eighties. Then I can begin to relax."
"Knowing what we know at this time."
"But the general consensus seems to be that we don't know enough at this time to be sure of anything."
"Let me answer like so. If I was a rat I wouldn't want to be anywhere within a two hundred mile radius of the airborne event."
"What if you were a human?"
He looked at me carefully. . . . "I wouldn't worry about what I can't see or feel," he said. "I'd go ahead and live my life. Get married, settle down, have kids. . . ."
"But you said we have a situation."
"I didn't say it. The computer did. The whole system says it. It's what we call a massive data-base tally. Gladney, J.A.K. I punch in the name, the substance, the exposure time and then I tap into your computer history. Your genetics, your personals, your medicals, your psychologicals, your police-and-hospitals. It comes back pulsing stars. This doesn't mean anything is going to happen to you as such, at least not today or tomorrow. It just means you are the sum total of your data. No man escapes that." (*WN* 140-41)

This conversation, and others like it, has generated a good deal of critical comment on how it makes death appear both real and vague, and how Gladney's existential concern is transformed, not without a considerable amount of humor, into a simulacrum of computer data.[2] Such a transformation is hardly surprising, many critics would argue, in a novel in which even the starkest realities seem to disappear behind multiple layers of representations and simulations. In *White Noise*, disaster victims feel unable to relate to their own situation unless it is amply covered by the media; Adolf Hitler and Elvis Presley appear side by side in an academic lecture on their relationship to their mothers; and the Nyodene D. accident turns into a mere prelude to the simulated evacuations rehearsed by Advanced Disaster Management, a company relying on the philosophy that such simulations not only prepare for but actually prevent real disasters. Gladney discovers his own nine-year-old daughter impersonating a victim in one of these simulations and remarks to the manager, perhaps sarcastically, perhaps seriously: "'Are you people sure you're ready for a simulation? You may want to wait for one more massive spill. Get your timing down'" (*WN* 204). The abundance of Baudrillardesque scenes such as these has led many critics to interpret *White Noise* as a narrative showcase of the postmodern culture of the simulacrum, a novel in which simulation systematically takes precedence over whatever might be left of the real.[3]

DeLillo's undeniable emphasis on representation as reality has led critics to dismiss the novel as a serious engagement with the problem of technological risk. A. O. Scott, for example, claims that "DeLillo's 'airborne toxic event' is freighted with symbolism: it's a projection of the ambient dread that pervades the social and emotional lives of his characters, and its source as a physical occurrence is thus irrelevant to the novel's purposes."[4] Even as eminent an ecocritic as Buell has argued recently that "*White Noise*'s framing of th[e] toxic event as, chiefly, a postmodern symbol of inauthenticity" reduces it "to the status of catalyst to the unfolding of the [protagonist's] culturally symptomatic vacuousness" (51). Hence, in Buell's view, a different disaster with no ecological implications would have served the plot just as well. Such arguments, however, have validity only if one isolates the Nyodene D. incident from the rest of the novel as the only point of engagement with technological risk scenarios. A diametrically opposed picture emerges when one traces *White Noise*'s thematic engagement with risk more systematically and pursues some of the implications of risk theory for its narrative form.

As a motif, the Nyodene D. spillage is far from the only risk scenario that threatens the Gladney family. On the contrary, the novel abounds in pointed or casual references to the multiple technologically generated risks that the average American family encounters in daily life. Early on, for example, the Gladney children's school has to be evacuated because of toxic fumes, possibly caused, as the reader is told, by the "ventilating system, the paint or varnish, the foam insulation, the electrical insulation, the cafeteria food, the rays emitted by microcomputers, the asbestos fireproofing, the adhesive on shipping containers, the fumes from the chlorinated pool, or perhaps something deeper, finer-grained, more closely woven into the basic state of things"; whatever their origin, these fumes are lethal enough to kill one of the members of the school inspection team (*WN* 35, 40). At another point, Jack Gladney worries over his son Heinrich, who is beginning to lose hair even though he is only fourteen, and Gladney wonders whether this might be caused by exposure to chemical waste or polluted air (*WN* 22). The father of Gladney's stepdaughter Denise drops by on his way to a fundraiser for the "Nuclear Accident Readiness Foundation," which he refers to as a "[j]ust in case kind of thing" (*WN* 56). And not only the adults are aware of risks; Heinrich details the dangers of electromagnetic radiation emanating from electrical wires and appliances: "'The real issue is the kind of radiation that surrounds us every day. Your radio, your TV, your microwave oven, your power lines just outside the door, your radar speed-trap on the highway. . . . Forget spills, fallouts, leakages. It's the things around you in your own house that'll get you sooner or later'" (*WN* 174-75). Less eloquently, Babette's daughter Steffie points out to her mother the carcinogenic additives in chewing gum (*WN* 41-43), and her daughter Denise insists that Babette use sunscreen during her runs so as to avoid skin cancer (*WN* 264). In fact, the children at times appear to take risk more seriously than the adults: "'Every day on the news there's another toxic spill. Cancerous solvents from storage tanks, arsenic from smokestacks, radioactive water from power plants. How serious can it be if it happens all the time? Isn't the definition of a serious event based on the fact that it's not an everyday occurrence?'" Babette asks at one point (*WN* 74), outlining an entire "riskscape" surrounding the family even as she denies its dangers.[5] At another point, she similarly dismisses a radio injunction to boil water before consuming it as just another fad (*WN* 34). But her perception that such occurrences are frequent, at any rate, seems to be accurate: several months after the poison gas incident, Blacksmith is once again overwhelmed by airborne substances, this time in the form of chemical smells drifting into town from across the river (*WN* 270-71). Along somewhat different lines, risks associated with car accidents and plane crashes are mentioned frequently in the novel, and I will comment presently on those associated with pharmaceutical products. These examples show that the "airborne toxic event" at the center of the plot is by no means exceptional but simply a threat that is (or appears to be) much larger than other hazards in the Gladneys' universe, where environmental risks ranging from the trivial to the deadly surround the average citizen. DeLillo's novel, then, is not so much about an ordinary family's encounter with one exceptionally dangerous technological accident as about the portrayal of life in what German sociologist Ulrich Beck calls the "risk society" of the late twentieth and early twenty-first centuries.[6]

From the beginning, Jack Gladney's experience of risk is intertwined with his self-perception as a member of the middle class. In the novel's first scene, Gladney observes the students as their parents bring them to campus at the beginning of the academic year: the fathers are "content to measure out the time, distant but ungrudging, accomplished in parenthood, something about them suggesting massive insurance coverage" (*WN* 3). The bourgeois establishment, in his view, is defined by its possession of time and insurance against risk—two assets that Gladney no longer has, or thinks he no longer has, after the poison gas accident. But at the beginning of the Nyodene D. crisis, Gladney still seems to believe that being part of the middle class is a sort of insurance against risk. When his family expresses increasing concern that they might be affected by the gas, Gladney claims:

> "These things happen to poor people who live in exposed areas. Society is set up in such a way that it's the poor and the uneducated who suffer the main impact of natural and man-made disasters. People in low-lying areas get the floods, people in shanties get the hurricanes and tornados. I'm a college professor. Did you ever see a college professor rowing a boat down his own street in one of those TV floods? We live in a neat and pleasant town near a college with a quaint name. These things don't happen in places like Blacksmith." (*WN* 114)

Whether Gladney himself believes his statement or primarily wants to reassure his family, he relies on the conviction that exposure to risk follows established lines of social stratification. As I will show in more detail below, Beck argues precisely the opposite, namely, that new kinds of risk will create new types of social structure characteristic of a different form of modernity. In Beck's terms, Gladney here attempts to portray his own position in the risk society by means of categories that derive from an earlier type of modernity; significantly enough, he bases his argument on natural disasters such as floods and hurricanes, not on human-made crises like the one in which he is already immersed. That his assertions about the relationship between class and risk are at that moment part of a rather obvious denial strategy lends support to the claim that in *White Noise*, DeLillo is concerned with the way in which new kinds of risk have invaded the lives of even those citizens who might earlier have had reason to believe themselves safe from their most dire consequences.

Lawrence Buell argues that the Gladneys' death obsession, on which the novel's final chapter focuses, is "no more than tenuously linked" to the poison gas accident, further evidence, in his view, that this event is nonessential to the plot, a mere "supporting metaphor" (51). In "Dylarama," the last chapter, Gladney discovers that Babette has obtained experimental drugs designed to suppress fear of death, in exchange for sexual favors to one of the psychopharmaceutical company's representatives. He becomes obsessed with finding and killing this man and with obtaining a supply of the pills to fight his own chronic fear of dying. What he eventually finds, however, is a man devastated by the side effects of an overdose of these pills. Gladney first attacks and injures him, but then, in a complete reversal of his plan, rescues him by taking him to a hospital. Critics other than Buell have also argued that this sequence of events does not seem to make sense within a novelistic plot.[7] But if *White Noise* is a narrative portrayal of the technological risk society, the plot is

not as incoherent as it seems. The Gladneys' desperate hunt for a drug that might allevi-
ate their existential fear, regardless of its experimental status and unknown side effects,
is simply the narrative inversion of the risk scenario that was portrayed in the previous
chapter. While the description of the poison gas accident revolves around an individual's
involuntary exposure to potentially lethal risk from a chemical substance, "Dylarama"
portrays the same character's voluntary acceptance of risk from another chemical substance that he hopes will counteract the effects of the first one.

That Nyodene D. and Dylar are meant to point to the complementary sides of exposure to powerful chemicals is marked quite clearly in the text. Nyodene D. forces people
out of their homes, and Gladney is exposed to it outdoors, while Dylar foregrounds the
penetration of chemicals into the domestic sphere. For this reason, the health technician's
advice to Gladney to ignore his health prospects and "[g]et married, settle down and have
kids" is doubly ironic (WN 141): not only is this advice given by a young man to a college
professor in his fifties who has been married four times and has three children and two
stepchildren, but it also projects the domestic sphere as a way out of the uncertainties of
chemical risk assessment. As it turns out, however, the family home exposes the individual to its own array of chemical hazards. When Gladney casually remarks, early in the
novel, that Babette's medicine cabinet contains "[b]lood pressure pills, stress pills, allergy
pills, eye drops, aspirin. Run of the mill," he gives a first glimpse of the multiple therapeutic chemicals that form part of daily routine even for a homemaker (WN 62). The question that surfaces in this early scene, as to what side effects such drug combinations might
have, only unfolds in its full significance later, when Gladney discovers the nature of the
new pills his wife has been taking. But even at this early moment in the novel, it becomes
clear that the family homestead offers no refuge from chemical exposure. If Nyodene D.
threatens the community and the public sphere, Dylar signals the presence of chemical
hazards in the privacy of the domestic realm.

Both substances, moreover, have effects on the human body that are only partially
known but potentially lethal. During the evacuation, Heinrich comments: "'In powder
form [Nyodene D.]'s colorless, odorless and very dangerous, except no one seems to
know exactly what it causes in humans or in the offspring of humans. They tested for
years and either they don't know for sure or they know and aren't saying'" (WN 131).
Similarly, Babette explains, official tests of the drug Dylar were suspended because
the company considered them too fraught with risk: "'I could die. I could live but my
brain could die. The left side of my brain could die but the right side could live. . . . Mr.
Gray wanted me to know the risks'" (WN 193). The side effects of the two substances
that actually manifest themselves in the novel are symmetrical inversions of each other:
déjà vu, an unexpected onslaught of memory, is the most lasting observable after-effect
of Nyodene D. in Blacksmith, while Babette suffers from memory lapses after taking
Dylar. Gladney, finally, articulates the complementarity of the two chemicals quite
explicitly as he reflects on Dylar: "Would it ever work. . . ? It was the benign counter-

part of the Nyodene menace . . . releasing benevolent chemicals into my bloodstream, flooding the fear-of-death part of my brain. . . . Technology with a human face" (*WN* 211). The plot of *White Noise*, then, not only juxtaposes the deadly and life-giving facets of technology but also confronts the protagonist's fear of lethal risk in one case with his willingness to accept the same risk in another. Similarly, the novel points up the implicit contradiction between Babette's attempts to lose weight for health reasons and her reckless acceptance of as serious a health risk as losing half her brain capacity.

Because it is difficult to justify these protagonists' decisions rationally, DeLillo may well be drawing a satirical portrait of the paradoxes to which risk awareness can lead. But as many critics have noted, the Gladneys' fear of death seems irrational in the first place, not justified by any acute danger. This is true if, once again, one takes the poison gas accident to be the only instance of a real hazard in the novel; admittedly, Gladney's fear of dying precedes rather than originates in his exposure to the gas, which merely confirms and reinforces it. But if the narrative aims at the broader portrayal of a society in which individuals and communities are exposed to multiple risks, many of which are completely new and at least partially unknown in their effects, then the Gladneys' existential fear may not be as unfounded as it seems: it is precisely the fact that so many of these risks are not yet known that justifies it. In other words, the portrayal of the risk society in *White Noise* is based on two dimensions: on one hand, the novel refers not just to one technological disaster but to a range of risks from the trivial to the lethal; on the other hand, this wide spectrum of risk scenarios hints that there might be many others hidden in plain sight of ordinary life, dangers that simply have not yet been detected. If, as Beck has argued, risk awareness is based not only on experience and second-hand experience but also on "second-hand non-experience," that is, on the expectation of risks that no one has consciously experienced yet, then the Gladneys' fear of dying no longer appears unmotivated (*Risikogesellschaft* 96).[8]

One might object that this analysis amounts to reading *White Noise* as a realist novel, a documentary of the risk society. Clearly, such an interpretation cannot hold true in any simple sense. *White Noise* is above all a satire of the contemporary, juxtaposing painfully realistic details from the world of supermarkets, credit cards, and brand-name advertising with absurd, hyperbolic, or humorous elements: a department of Hitler studies chaired by a professor who doesn't speak German, a tourist attraction called "The Most Photographed Barn in America," pills that cause one to take words for objects, nuns who admit they do not believe in God but make believe they do for the sake of nonbelievers. To the extent that my analysis of the importance of risk for the plot is accurate, one might argue that DeLillo mocks contemporary risk perceptions rather than engaging them seriously. Undeniably, to the extent that the Gladney family's daily life is an object of satire in the novel, so are their experiences of risk. Yet the text is quite a bit more complex than that. Even calling it a satire and identifying its realistic and hyperbolic elements relies on the assumption that we as readers know what the real world is like, and how DeLillo's narrative universe differs from it. But in practice, the line between realism and hyperbole turns out to be often difficult to draw: we may agree that a department of Hitler studies sounds implausible, but how about scholars who study narratives on cereal boxes and offer courses on car-crash scenes in American movies? Pills that make one take words for things do not sound realistic, yet we all know something about effects of psychopharmaceuticals that would have seemed quite unlikely a few decades ago. The description of media coverage of the Nyodene D. accident with its gradually intensifying euphemisms is undoubtedly very funny, but it would be easy to come up with comparable examples of media obfuscation from the "real" world. *White Noise* certainly functions as a satire at one level, therefore, but at another level, it puts into question the reader's ability to distinguish the real from the fake and the hyperbolic.[9]

The ontological uncertainty that results from this deployment of the satiric mode has been theorized by Brian McHale in a broader context as one of the hallmarks of postmodernist fiction (3-40). But while McHale associates such uncertainty for the most part with clearly antirealist forms of narration, it is possible to claim, in the context of a risk-theoretical approach to narrative, that the destabilization of distinctions between the real and the nonreal can itself serve specific realist objectives. Making such distinctions is precisely the task that the characters in DeLillo's novel have to fulfill repeatedly in their assessments of risk or "unreliable menace," as the text calls it at one point (*WN* 184). The novel's narrative mode, which exacts similar decision making from the readers, therefore mirrors in its narrative form the fundamental uncertainties that beset risk assessments in the "real world." Obviously, it is not necessary to assume that this use of satire is directed only at the portrayal of risk scenarios. Risk assessments are clearly not the only context in which DeLillo's protagonists have to make judgments about verisimilitude; the problem similarly arises in their encounters with mass media, advertisements, or scholarly arguments about culture. But decisions about risk do ultimately underlie many of these encounters, most obviously when media or advertising statements allude to real or imaginary hazards and miraculous remedies, or when discussions about popular culture turn on the way in which it portrays death. Because these topics recur so insistently, it is possible to argue that not so much in spite of as because of its use of satire, *White Noise* engages the problematics of risk in both its themes and narrative form. Many of the hyperboles and the simulations that have typically been interpreted as examples of postmodern inauthenticity become, from this perspective, manifestations of daily encounters with risks whose reality cannot be assessed with certainty.

Risk Theory

A brief overview of some approaches and ideas that have emerged in risk theory may help to substantiate my claim that the particular problems of realism in *White Noise* reflect some crucial issues in risk assessment. Most risk analysis has been carried out in sociology, anthropology, and psychology, though in the 1990s political scientists and economists have also become increasingly interested in the field. As a separate area of study in the social sciences, risk analysis dates back to the late 1960s and early 1970s. In 1969, a seminal article by the engineer Chauncey Starr analyzing social benefits and technological risks in relation to each other opened up the problem of risk assessment to systematic research, at a time when the public was becoming increasingly aware of and concerned about chemical, nuclear, and other environmental dangers. Since then, a range of theories has developed in the field.[10] In the context of literary analysis, two kinds of approaches to risk are particularly worth mentioning: theories about the underlying causes of technological risk and their impact on social structure, and investigations of risk perceptions.

The most famous, far-reaching, and speculative kind of risk theory was proposed by Ulrich Beck in the mid-1980s. Beck links risk research to broader theorizations of social change: most importantly, to theories of modernization and globalization. Like sociologists Anthony Giddens and Scott Lash, he postulates that modern societies have entered a phase of "reflexive modernization" in which modernizing processes transform not traditional social structures but those created by earlier waves of modernization (Beck, Giddens, and Lash). According to Beck, the hazards characteristic of this new era can be defined by two criteria: they are themselves the effects of modernizing processes and, thereby, they reflexively confront modern societies with the results of their own modernization. In addition, some of these risks, such as global warming and the thinning of the ozone layer, are for the first time truly planetary in scope. Beck's most far-reaching claim is that risks such as these will lead to a new stage in the evolution of modernity. While social distinctions and conflicts at an earlier stage of the modern were centrally articulated around the production and distribution of wealth, Beck argues,

> in advanced modernity, the social production of wealth is systematically associated with the social production of risks. Accordingly, the distribution problems and conflicts of the scarcity society are superseded by the problems and conflicts that originate in the production, definition and distribution of techno-scientifically generated risks. (*Risikogesellschaft* 25; my translation)

Global risk, in other words, reaches across existing stratifications to create a new kind of social structure. Beck doesn't deny, of course, that at the moment, patterns of risk exposure frequently replicate structures of material inequality, but he argues that increasingly, the decisive risks will be those like Chernobyl, which affected vast areas of eastern, northern, and western Europe without regard for social difference. As I argued in the first section, it is possible to read *White Noise* as a fictional engagement with such risks that transcend conventional class distinctions.

Despite the enormous popularity that Beck's book gained in western Europe in the late 1980s and early 1990s, it also came under attack. Sociologists in particular have pointed out that little empirical evidence exists to support Beck's claim that social categorizations are indeed in the process of being rearticulated around issues of risk. But even some of his critics admit that the interest of Beck's argument may be polemical rather than descriptive: it is not really necessary to accept wholesale his theory of a fundamental social shift to see the force of his argument that risk is becoming one important area of sociocultural concern and conflict.[11]

A much more specific analysis about why risk has become so all-encompassing emerges from the work of the historian of technology Thomas Hughes. What has transformed modern society, and American society in particular, Hughes argues, is not so much the invention of individual technological principles and devices—such as electricity, the telephone, or the automobile— as the creation of large-scale and extremely complex techno-economic systems by means of which these devices are produced, distributed, and managed. For Hughes, the invention and implementation of these technological and organizational networks is the unique contribution of the United States to modern culture. The technological hardware is only one part of such networks, which also include transportation, communication, and information systems, as well as people and institutions with all their organizational, legal, social, and economic structures. In his perspective, these large-scale systems into which technologies are embedded have become so complex that they can no longer be easily understood or controlled, and therefore they give rise to risks whose origins and outcomes are extremely difficult to trace and manage.[12] As I will show later, this idea forms the narrative nucleus of Richard Powers's novel *Gain*.

In his analysis, Hughes cites the work of sociologist Charles Perrow, who proposed the notion of "system accidents" in the mid-1980s. Focusing more on the technological apparatus itself than the organizational networks around it, Perrow argues that the most serious risks derive from technological systems with such a degree of complexity that even experts cannot understand all the connections and feedback loops they contain, and, therefore, cannot predict some of their most dangerous failures. System accidents occur when several different and sometimes minor failures in independent but coupled subsystems interact in such a way as to produce failures in the system as a whole. This interaction produces risks that could not have been anticipated by an analysis of the system's normal functioning or of individual subsystem failures. Nuclear energy is such a complex and tightly coupled technology prone to system accidents, as Perrow demonstrates in a detailed analysis of the Three Mile Island accident. In his view, improved designs or better operator training will not lead to increased safety because the complexity of the technology itself will always defeat them. Technological systems that are prone to such accidents, he argues, pose the greatest and most unpredictable hazards for contemporary society.[13]

Beck, Hughes, and Perrow all analyze risk as it emerges in the context of complex social and technological systems. A different approach to risk, the one that has produced the greatest amount of research, focuses on how different social groups perceive particular risks and what reasons lead them to their assessments. Several theoretical schools constitute this part of the field.[14] In the psychometric approach, detailed empirical studies are carried out to determine how the public assesses a wide range of risks, and the researchers—many of them cognitive psychologists—then analyze the reasons for these assessments. The basic assumption in the psychometric approach is that these reasons are to be sought in individuals' cognitive behavior, and so they are explored with theories of heuristics and cognitive biases, that is, decision-making rules and selective information processing. A different approach, called cultural theory (not to be confused with the meaning of this phrase in the context of cultural studies), argues that individuals do not in fact make risk assessments on a case-by-case basis. As anthropologist Mary Douglas and sociologist Aaron Wildavsky in particular argued in the early 1980s, any social community is affected by a wide range of risks, but only some of these are selected for conscious awareness and given particular significance. This significance is best explained in terms of what it accomplishes for the values and ultimately the perpetuation of the social structure that defines it. On the basis of their association with certain types of social structures, the risk assessments of individuals can then be predicted in broad terms.[15] A third line of research has focused on technological controversies and on the interaction of stakeholders and their values in a particular technology.

One central issue informing research on risk across these paradigms is the difference between expert and lay perceptions. To give one notorious example, experts tend to rank the risk associated with nuclear power plants much lower than nonexperts, based on the limited number of actual accidents and deaths; nonexperts, regardless of the low statistics, assess them as much more hazardous than, say, coal mines or highways, which cause a much larger number of fatalities annually. Psychometric research in particular has focused on the variables that shape such perceptions. Some of the most important ones include the distinction between voluntary and involuntary risk (people tend to be much more tolerant of voluntarily selected risks than those imposed by others, as we already saw in *White Noise*), the scale and controllability of adverse effects, the presence or absence of a particular kind of "dread," and the level of public trust in the authorities that manage a particular risk.[16]

Closely associated with the difference between lay and expert assessments is the question of the objective or subjective nature of risk. In the 1970s, the prevailing assumption was that technical risk assessments by experts in science, statistics, and engineering represented the "objective" degree of risk; divergent risk perceptions by lay people were considered less objective, less rational, and in need of explanation as well as, ultimately, correction. In the course of the 1980s, this sharp distinction was increasingly questioned, and some parts of the field moved toward analyses of the social and cultural construction of risk. To begin with, it was pointed out that technical definitions of risk, which are mostly based on probability and magnitude of adverse effects, leave out crucial dimensions that a more comprehensive but perfectly rational assessment might want to take into account: for example, the unequal distribution of risks and benefits among different social and geographical groups or the emergence of indirect costs. Even judgments that are not based on these more broadly understood rational terms, however, might make sense when the social and cultural contexts are considered. In the mid-1980s, the concept of the "social amplification of risk" was proposed to describe the mediating processes and institutions that shape the social experience of risk and magnify or minimize it.[17] This concept has remained extremely important to the field today, and it points to precisely the problems of distinguishing realism from hyperbole that I mentioned in the discussion of *White Noise* earlier: in both analytical and literary contexts, the question is not only whose risk assessments are the most realistic but also what criteria should be used to gauge degrees of realism in the first place.

In a more radical perspective, though, it has been argued that even those elements of lay assessments that are not rationally founded cannot be used to mark an unequivocal boundary between objective and subjective judgments about risk. In this view, the assessments of experts are not exempt from bias, specific interests, and underlying value structures, and the concept of objective risk really makes no sense. Any debate about risk includes participants who have widely varying values and priorities, and their definitions of risk, as well as their assessments of what constitutes acceptable risk or of the size of a particular risk, will depend on these values; being an expert or nonexpert is only one variable in this priority structure. Any decision about risks is therefore at bottom political. This argument comes in several different versions, with some theorists willing to accept some distinction between different degrees of objectivity (if not between absolute objectivity and subjectivity), while others dismiss the notion of objectivity completely and associate their rejection with a more general critique of science as a privileged mode of knowledge.[18]

Needless to say, these controversies are far from mere academic quibbles. Risk assessment is a large, practical field in industry and government today, and sometimes comes loaded with political charges. In the area of risk communication—the study of how particular types of risks should be brought to the attention of the public—the assumption in the 1970s was that lay people's judgments needed to be aligned with those of experts. Much more sophisticated strategies of risk communication tend to be adopted today, but struggles over risk assessment often remain deeply embedded in conflicts over cultural values and the question of who has the right to make decisions over how technologies are implemented.

As even this extremely brief overview shows, risk theory deals not just with technological and other dangers in a narrow technical sense but defines its object of study within cultural contexts and social systems without which the notion of risk itself cannot be conceived. It is this constitution of risk from within specific sociocultural fields that establishes an interdisciplinary bridge to the concerns of literary critics. Cultural variables in risk analysis have so far been understood rather broadly, with relatively little attention to the impact that particular metaphors, plot patterns, or visual representations might have in the formation of risk judgments. The emergence of the oil-covered sea bird as an international symbol of environmental disaster or the impact of the Frankenstein story (in both its book and film versions) on current perceptions of genetic engineering, for example, call for close investigation.[19]

More generally, reasoning about risk, with its foregrounding of causal connections that are not immediately obvious and with its postulation of possible future sequences of events, calls for at least a rudimentary, and often quite elaborate, narrative articulation. Concepts of narrative analysis might therefore play an important role in examining the ways in which risk perceptions manifest themselves in both literary and nonliterary writings. Implicitly or explicitly, accounts of risk can invoke different genre models: the detective story, in the evaluation of clues and eyewitness accounts and in the discovery and exposure of the criminal; pastoral, in the portrayal of rural, unspoiled landscapes violated by the advent of technology; the gothic, in the evocation of hellish landscapes or grotesquely deformed bodies as a consequence of pollution; the bildungsroman, in the victim's gradually deepening realization of the danger to which he or she is exposed; tragedy, through the fateful occurrence of evil in spite of the participants' best intentions; or epic, in the attempt to grasp the planetary implications of some risks.[20] Along with the selection of such templates that make risk scenarios intelligible to the reader or viewer in a particular way, narrators have to make choices about which individuals or institutions are cast as protagonists or antagonists in technological controversies, about where and how to conclude their story, and about how to characterize their own relationship to the narrative material (for example, as eyewitness, victim, scientific expert, or journalist). Given such strategies, literary and cultural critics have a potentially important contribution to make to a finer-grained analysis of risk perceptions as they manifest themselves across a range of cultural artifacts.[21]

Inversely, risk analysis also has an important role to play in some parts of literary and cultural criticism. The question of what prompts individuals and groups to view certain technological and ecological risks as significant and to consider others as minor or nonexistent is itself a matter of crucial importance for an ecocritical perspective. Beyond that, the emergence of ecological and technological risk scenarios as a thematic component of various artistic practices warrants investigation for the pressures it brings to bear on existing aesthetic forms: Do writers and artists approach such risks mainly by way of established templates such as those I've mentioned, or do they modify them or invent new, experimental ones? How are particular representations of risk generated, reflected, worked through, or resisted by means of such formal choices? What might be their cultural and ideological implications? Through questions such as these, the analysis ultimately moves beyond the study of individual artifacts to the broader issue of how they participate in social and cultural processes of risk communication.

In an attempt to bring such an analysis to bear on a widely known novel, I have shown in the first section how *White Noise* examines the working of risk perceptions and communication at a mostly local level. The novel focuses on the confrontation between lay and expert approaches to risk (evident in the conversation I quoted at the beginning), voluntary and involuntary risk exposure, and the ways in which risk transforms individuals' experience of the public and domestic spheres. A novel that foregrounds somewhat different aspects of risk is Richard Powers's *Gain*, which elaborates on the theme of chemical exposure in terms that are comparable to DeLillo's and yet quite different in that they situate the problem much more explicitly in social and economic systems that span the globe.

Toxic Systems: *Gain*

Powers's *Gain* (1998) consists of two strands of plot that are narrated in alternating sections. The first outlines approximately 150 years in the development of a company that starts out as J. Clare & Sons, a family soap- and candle-making business in 1830s Boston. In the course of its long history of technological invention, shrewd business maneuvers, repeated near-failures, mergers, cutbacks, and expansions, this company evolves by the 1990s into Clare International, a multinational chemical and pharmaceutical corporation manufacturing everything from detergents, cosmetics, and drugs to pesticides, fertilizers, and synthetic construction materials. Clare's agricultural division is headquartered in the midwestern town of Lacewood, where it has for decades been the community's major employer and principal financial source. The other plot strand revolves around Laura Bodey, a middle-aged, divorced real-estate agent with two children who lives in Lacewood. During a routine medical examination, she is diagnosed with ovarian cancer, and the novel follows her through surgery and periods of chemotherapy to her final decline and death. In her last months, Bodey discovers not only that some of the chemicals Clare produces have been associated with cancer but also that a class action lawsuit is in progress against the company, which her divorced husband Don urges her to join. She does, after some resistance, and although the settlement money comes too late to benefit her, it is passed on to her children. A third narrative element is set apart from these two plots: descriptions and quotations of legal documents and, above all, advertising materials referring to the Clare corporation and its products, which often form an ironic counterpoint to the evolving story of Bodey's cancer.[22]

Gain has some obvious similarities with *White Noise* in its portrayal of technological risk. Both novels focus on chemical exposure; both describe it as befalling a dysfunctional but only too normal family in a midwestern small town.[23] In both cases, the choice of location and type of family signal risk scenarios affecting a social class that had formerly believed itself exempt from such environmental dangers. Most importantly, both novels attempt to capture the dual nature of chemical substances as killers and cures: the antithesis between poison and drug structures the juxtaposition of Nyodene D. and Dylar just as it does that of the herbicide that may have triggered Laura Bodey's cancer and the drugs she is given during chemotherapy. In both cases, the antithesis is an uneasy one, as the therapies fail and their side effects turn out to be potentially as serious as the symptoms they were designed to cure. But the play on toxins and drugs, on involuntary risk from chemical exposure and voluntary risk from substances that might bring benefit, is ultimately developed into a quite different conceptualization of risk in *Gain*.

White Noise puts considerable emphasis on the substances themselves, the way in which they enter human bodies and the time intervals and circumstances under which they take effect. This emphasis is not only obvious in the conversations Gladney has with doctors and technicians about his toxic gas exposure but also in the episode in which a neurochemist explains to him the sophisticated physical and chemical mechanisms of Dylar (*WN* 187-89). Powers displays similar attention to detail in the description of Laura Bodey's chemotherapy, in which the names, quantities, ingestion times, and effects of all the medications are presented in excruciating detail. But the same is not true of the substance that might have caused Bodey's cancer, the herbicide she used in her gardening. The most obvious reason for this elision seems to be that there is no way of being sure. As Bodey discovers, once her awareness of environmental chemicals has been kindled, she is surrounded by them, to the point that it is impossible to get rid of them:

> No longer her home, this place they have given her to inhabit. She cannot hike from the living room to the kitchen without passing an exhibit. Floor by Germ-Guard. Windows by Cleer-Thru. Table by Colonial-Cote. The Bodey mansion, that B-ticket, one-star museum of trade. But where else can she live?
>
> She vows a consumer boycott, a full spring cleaning. But the house is full of them. . . . They paper her cabinets. They perch on her microwave, camp out on her stove, hang from her shower head. Clare hiding under the sink, swarming in her medicine chest, lining the shelves in the basement, parked out in the garage, piled up in the shed.
>
> Her vow is hopeless. Too many to purge them all. Every hour of her life depends on more corporations than she can count. (*G* 303-4)

This profusion of potentially dangerous products eerily echoes Heinrich's remark in *White Noise*: "'It's the things around you in your own house that'll get you sooner or later'" (*WN* 175). One is tempted to pick out the herbicide from this line-up because it is the chemical that Bodey most obviously recognizes: when Don, in a whole list of Clare products suspected of being carcinogenic, mentions only the first two syllables of its name, "Atra-," Bodey immediately thinks of the garden she loves and agrees without further ado to join the lawsuit. In part, what is at work here is unquestionably the rhetoric of "disrupted pastoral" that Buell has diagnosed as one of the elements of discourse about toxic waste: the garden, Bodey's own plot of unspoiled nature, turns out to be what may be slowly killing her (Buell 36-38). May be killing her: the novel never confirms that this is so, never even completes the name of the guilty product (though Powers most likely had the controversial herbicide Atrazine in mind). This uncertainty is deliberate and points to a structure of causality quite different from the one that informs *White Noise*. If Jack Gladney declares somewhat melodramatically after his toxic exposure, "Death has entered. It is inside you" (*WN* 141-42), no such concrete moment of poisoning can be identified in *Gain*. For Powers, the real poison lies not in any concrete substance but in the complex technoeconomic system that has evolved over more than a century to deliver chemical products to the individual.

It is, above all, the novel's narrative structure, with its stark juxtaposition of the rise of a company and the decline of an individual, that makes this point. From the outset, the inverted plot lines of these stories suggest that Clare is causally related to Bodey's illness, though the concrete circumstances only emerge later.[24] The causal link is reinforced through the play on words related to the body. The female protagonist's name, of course, is merely a misspelling of the word body, and her antagonist turns out to be an "incorporated" company:[25] "The law now declared the Clare Soap and Chemical Company one composite body: a single, whole, and statutorily enabled person. . . . an artificial being, invisible, intangible, and existing only in contemplation of law" (*G* 158). In the historical narrative, Powers spends considerable time describing the rise of the incorporated enterprise as a legal concept in the late nineteenth century, which he characterizes as the transfer of individual rights to the business company. Part of the point in juxtaposing the two narrative strands, then, is to show how the corporate body and the individual body depend upon each other, and how the corporate organism can become a lethal threat to the individual one. More than any single substance and more even than the whole array of products it delivers, it is the corporation as a social form that kills Laura Bodey.

But the play on incorporated and embodied beings already reveals that the relationship between the two narrative strands is not one of pure antagonism. If the metaphor of the body connects them, so does the metaphor of cancerous growth. Just as Bodey's cancer returns and spreads after surgery and chemotherapy, so the Clare Company keeps growing in spite of economic recessions, adverse legislation, and internal crises that sometimes take it to the brink of failure.[26] Through this continued expansion, the family business of the early nineteenth century evolves into a multinational corporation by the end of the twentieth. And even money that Clare disburses to its opponents seems inevitably destined to further corporate growth, as is made clear by the settlement money that Bodey's children receive from the class-action lawsuit after her death. Years later, Bodey's son Tim starts working in the computer industry; he helps to develop software that predicts and even manipulates the behavior of certain protein sequences, producing a "chemical assembly plant at the level of the human cell" that will be able, it is hoped, to cure cancer (*G* 355). In order to put this software to use, he and his friends decide that with the help of his savings, they will incorporate: indirectly and with considerable time delay, corporate money generates yet another corporate body. This new corporation may be able to cure the cancer the old one caused, but in that very process it can only worsen the other cancer that is incorporated business itself. The novel's ending, then, is curiously optimistic and pessimistic at the same time.

Because he portrays the multinational corporation as a lethal risk both in its products and by virtue of its structure, Powers has been accused by some reviewers of mounting an "assault on corporate America" (Caldwell C4).[27] Others have pointed out a good deal of admiration and optimism in his portrayal of capitalist enterprise.[28] These diverging assessments are due to the fact that Powers, especially in the first half of the novel, considers risk in both its negative and positive dimensions: not only as danger or hazard but also as opportunity, as the voluntary acceptance of uncertainty or danger in the expectation of profit. One of the Clare founding fathers, for example, is described as "handl[ing] cotton and indigo and potash. But above all else, he dealt in risk. Profit equaled uncertainty times distance. The harder it was to haul a thing to where it humanly belonged, the more one made" (*G* 10). There is indeed a good deal of admiration in Powers's descriptions of how the first few generations of Clares deal with economic risk and the frequent setbacks it imposes, and how they manage it with perseverance, ingenuity, and skill. But the breaking point seems to come with the rise of the incorporated enterprise, precisely because at that moment the company is allowed to continue making a profit without incurring all the risks it formerly had to confront. Powers places great emphasis on the concept of "limited liability" in this context:

> If the Fifth and Fourteenth Amendments combined to extend due process to all individuals, and if the incorporated business had become a single person under the law, then the Clare Soap and Chemical Company now enjoyed all the legal protections afforded any individual by the spirit of the Constitution. And for the actions of that protected person, for its debts and indiscretions, no single shareholder could be held liable,

he points out, and quotes the definition of a corporation from Bierce's *Devil's Dictionary*: "'An ingenious device for obtaining individual profit without individual responsibility'" (*G* 159).[29] Business that faces risk and engages it creatively is described approvingly, while business that is shielded from risk becomes a hazard to those in its environment.

In *Gain*, then, the risk of chemical exposure is represented not so much in terms of the mysterious and dangerous substances that occupy center stage in *White Noise*; beyond such specific materials, it is a complex system of the kind described by Thomas Hughes that comes to embody risk in *Gain*. While DeLillo focuses on the hazardous substances whose origins and effects are difficult for average individuals to discover and understand, Powers shifts the emphasis to the complex technoeconomic systems that deliver such substances, and whose workings are even more impenetrable to the ordinary citizen. In fact, they are nearly impossible to control even by those who do understand them: toward the end, the novel gives a brief glimpse of Franklin Kennibar, CEO of Clare International, reflecting on his own powerlessness in crucial decisions about the company. These systems beyond comprehension and control really are the overarching risk that *Gain* seeks to address, a risk of which household toxins are only the most minor, if still potentially lethal, manifestations.

Resistance to these complex systems is as futile in *Gain* as it is unimaginable in *White Noise*. Bodey's daughter and her friends publicly burn their Clare cosmetics in a televised protest against the company, but such temporary outbursts and the more protracted lawsuits against Clare in the end produce merely a shifting of the problem, with no solution.[30] With lower ratings on the Stock Exchange, Clare sells its Agricultural Division to Monsanto some time after Laura Bodey's death, and Monsanto two years later relocates the agricultural products plant to a *maquiladora*, precipitating Lacewood into economic ruin. Corporate deals and global expansion thereby cancel any possibility of resistance. Ironically enough, the character that comes closest to offering some hope for opposition is Bodey's former husband Don, whom she had divorced because, among other things, she could not stand his habit of seeing connections, conspiracies, and cover-ups everywhere. Don is the one who, as she herself notes, knows how to ask all the right questions about her cancer diagnosis and therapy, who studies the medical background, finds out about the Clare connection, and makes her join the lawsuit. Indefatigable in his search for accurate and comprehensive information, Don is the only one who achieves some measure of knowledge and success in the struggle with Clare.[31] But nothing he does approaches any serious challenge to the underlying system, and Powers's novel as a whole does not offer any prospects of change. Against the complex system of Clare's global body, the local bodies of individuals or small communities are powerless.

But while *Gain* portrays with astonishing conceptual sophistication individuals' inability to resist or even comprehend the worldwide networks that entangle them, its narrative structure does not in the end offer a persuasive formal correlative for this approach to the global. Indeed, Powers's narrative strategies suggest that whatever difficulties the characters may encounter in their attempts to grapple with the global corporate world, the readers can rely on the comprehensive map that the self-assured omniscient narrator unfolds before them. It is precisely the novel's split into two narrative strands that creates this schism: the historical narrative acquaints the reader with a wealth of detail regarding the development and functioning of multinational corporations and their relation to risk scenarios, while such insight is not available to Laura Bodey and other characters, even though they may occasionally glimpse a fragment of this information. Mostly, the characters perceive the corporation through the kinds of language exemplified in the novel's third narrative component—snippets of advertising, corporate self-promotion, and legal documents gleaned from Clare's discursive archive. As noted earlier, these rhetorical samples often stand in ironic contrast to the actual evolution of Clare International, and even more so to its effects on the environment and public health as they are spelled out in the two narrative strands.

Powers here deploys a narrative technique that is derived from the modernist urban novels of John Dos Passos, James Joyce, and Alfred Döblin: the insertion of fragments of "authentic" discourse from a variety of modern institutions and media into a fictional story.[32] This transfer of a technique that originally served to illustrate the bewildering diversity and fragmentation of languages in the modernist metropolis to the portrayal of a multinational corporation is not unproblematic, since Powers ultimately aims to capture not heterogeneity at all but precisely the dangerous singularity of purpose that lurks behind the apparent diversity of consumer products. But whatever effect these high-modernist fragments might have is, at any rate, neutralized by their insertion into an omniscient narration that provides the reader with just the kind of overarching and authoritative information that is usually not available in *Manhattan Transfer*, *Ulysses*, or *Berlin Alexanderplatz*. The shock, surprise, and disorientation that such fragments cause in the high-modernist novel are absorbed, in *Gain*, through a mode of narration that consistently restores context, control, and orientation to the reader; narrative collage is reabsorbed into orderly progression.

In the last third of the novel, Powers resorts to a somewhat different technique to portray the workings of Clare International. In some sections, he juxtaposes snapshots of individuals in some way involved with the company and its products across the globe; in one, he focuses on a specific consumer product, a disposable camera, and traces back the processes and materials that went into its making to their places of origin around the planet. This stylistically intriguing and innovative passage centers on the insight that "[p]lastic happens; that is all we need to know on earth. History heads steadily for a place where things need not be grasped to be used" (*G* 347); it counteracts this reification of consumer objects by showing one of them gradually emerging out of a network of globally dispersed raw materials, production, and distribution processes:

The camera jacket says: "Made In China With Film From Italy Or Germany." The film itself accretes from more places on the map than emulsion can cover. Silver halide, metal salts, dye couplers, bleach fixatives, ingredients gathered from Russia, Arizona, Brazil, and underwater seabeds, before being decanted in the former DDR. Camera in a pouch, the true multinational: trees from the Pacific Northwest and the southeastern coastal plain. Straw and recovered wood scrap from Canada. Synthetic adhesive from Korea. Bauxite from Australia, Jamaica, Guinea. Oil from the Gulf of Mexico or North Sea Brent Blend, turned to plastic in the Republic of China before being shipped to its mortal enemies on the Mainland for molding. Cinnabar from Spain. Nickel and titanium from South Africa. Flash elements stamped in Malaysia, electronics in Singapore. Design and color transfers drawn up in New York. Assembled and shipped from that address in California by a merchant fleet beyond description, completing the most heavily choreographed conference in existence. (*G* 347-48)

From what follows, it is clear that this globally assembled object was once in the possession of Laura Bodey, who forgot it in a drawer next to one of her hospital beds. It is, in fact, a memento mori of sorts, following as it does the last scene in which the reader sees Bodey alive. But even if she were not yet dead by the time the narrator draws up the camera's map of global origins, it is clear that Bodey had no access to this kind of detailed information while the camera was in her possession. What presents itself to the character as a finished product that provides little information about itself—except, significantly, the manufacturer's warnings and disclaimers of liability—is portrayed for the reader as a shape that gradually emerges from the planetary dispersion of its raw materials. Interestingly, however, the human design, work, and organization that go into this emergence are downplayed in the passage above, whose lack of inflected verbs and passive constructions foreground its elision of agency: the object seems to be assembling itself before the reader's eyes. The critique implicit in this description clearly aims less at capitalism's exploitation of human beings than at its waste of global resources: "[T]he entire engineering magnificence was designed to be pitched. Labor, materials, assembly, shipping, sales markups and overheads, insurance, international tariffs— the whole prodigious creation costs less than ten dollars. The world sells to us at a loss, until we learn to afford it" (G 348).

Tracing a trajectory from photosynthesis to photography—from the trees that are felled for the camera's cardboard packaging ("[a] thing that once lived for light" [G 345]) to the pictures on its forgotten film—this section stands out by its conceptual sweep and its industrial lyricism. But considered as part of the overall narrative structure, it presents a problem similar to the alternation of the two narrative strands with their punctuation by fragments of corporate discourse or, for that matter, the occasional allegorization of Clare International as the protagonist of an unfolding bildungsroman.[33] All these strategies present to the reader a fictional world in which the individual is shaped by, dependent on, and intermittently threatened by networks of global capitalism but has few resources to recognize and comprehend, let alone resist, them. Yet the fundamental challenges to ordinary conceptions of individuality, privacy, and freedom that this vision articulates are not translated into any disturbance in the reading process. While the novel shows in detail how individuals and local communities cannot know or control the corporate forces that shape their existence, this panorama is drawn up by a narrator who knows the corporation in both its historical and its geographical extension down to the most minute details, and who delivers them in an idiom that never questions the reader's ability to grasp and connect these details. This narrative strategy is, in the end, far removed from DeLillo's, whose subtle deployment of satire defies the readers' sense of realism and reality in their encounter with a fictional world whose risk scenarios challenge the characters in a similar way. It is even more fundamentally opposed to the narrative techniques of Burroughs or Pynchon, as whose literary successor Powers has often been designated. But Burroughs, Pynchon, or Kathy Acker, all of whom similarly place their protagonists in worlds that are shaped by forces and institutions they are ill-equipped to understand or combat, persistently refuse to reassure their readers that they, after all, can grasp this world with the help of omniscient narrators and realist narration. On the contrary, these authors constantly challenge their readers to reflect on the kinds of cognitive strategies and language that might be able to map global connections, strategies at which their own novels can only hint. In Powers's *Gain*, by contrast, the self-assurance of the narrator's command of the global and his transparent (though complex) language remain in tension with the scenario of individual powerlessness vis-à-vis the global power networks that the novel portrays. In this respect, the novel's formal accomplishment lags behind its conceptual sophistication.

These differences notwithstanding, both Powers and DeLillo place their protagonists in environments fraught with multiple risks of the most varied kinds, and one of the central challenges for the characters is to gain awareness of these riskscapes and find ways of living and dying within them. In both novels, chemical toxins become the most crucial of these risks as agents that effectively blur the boundaries between body and environment, the domestic and the public spheres, and beneficial and harmful technologies. It is in the territory between these realms that the uncertainties of risk perception and risk assessment play themselves out. Aesthetically, *White Noise* remains the more interesting novel as it translates these uncertainties into the uneasy satire, the "unreliable menace" I analyzed earlier. But it is able to do so because it limits the conceptual horizon of risk perception to the individual and the local, while Powers precisely attempts to move beyond these limitations. Representing complex and global techno-economic systems as a source of risk is one of the challenges that faces contemporary narrative, and no canonical form has yet emerged in response. It may well be that such a narrative architecture will have to rely on more experimental forms of storytelling, and perhaps even on the resources of new narrative media such as the multiple links of hypertext. What shape narrative innovation will take in the risk society is the uncertainty that literary critics face at the turn of the millennium.

I would like to thank the National Humanities Center, the John D. and Catherine T. MacArthur Foundation, and the American Council of Learned Societies for institutional and financial support during a fellowship year that allowed me to write most of this essay.

NOTES

[1] See Mark Osteen's introduction to Don DeLillo, *White Noise: Text and Criticism*, vii; this edition also contains materials documenting the novel's parallels with the Bhopal accident (353-62). Further references to *White Noise* will be to this edition and will be cited parenthetically in the text as *WN*.

[2] See, for example, Michael Valdez Moses's Heideggerian interpretation of this scene in his "Lust Removed from Nature."

[3] For discussions of spectacle, simulation, and the role of media in shaping reality in *White Noise*, see the essays by Duvall, Reeve and Kerridge, and Kerridge. A different interpretation is proposed by Paul Maltby, who argues that a romantic sense of transcendence emerges in some crucial scenes of the novel, so that the postmodern scene of the simulacrum does ultimately lead to some experience of authenticity.

[4] Interestingly, this remark occurs in a book review of Richard Powers's *Gain*, which I will discuss later (see A. O. Scott, "A Matter of Life and Death"). In *Gain*, unlike *White Noise*, Scott contends, chemical risk is not symbolic (41). But simply rephrasing "ambient dread" as "environmental dread" in Scott's claim would restore full materiality to the toxic event.

[5] The term *riskscape* is Susan Cutter's; quoted in Deitering, 200.

[6] See Ulrich Beck, *Risk Society: Towards a New Modernity*, originally published as *Risikogesellschaft: Auf dem Weg in eine andere Moderne* (Frankfurt: Suhrkamp, 1986), which I will discuss presently in more detail. I've explored elsewhere the temporal perspective that arises from this focus on the risk society in *White Noise*. See Heise.

[7] Bianca Theisen, for example, accounts for DeLillo's narrative strategy by arguing that it is aimed at "the paradoxical enterprise . . . of dissolving plot by means of plot" (132). The translation to English is mine.

[8] It is tempting to relate Beck's concept of "second-hand non-experience" to Baudrillard's notion of the hyperreal, the copy without an original. But the context and import of the two concepts is ultimately different. Beck's argument is not so much about imitation as anticipation, and his aim is to explore the ways in which new types of risk overturn modes of common-sense reasoning rather than to suggest the broader scepticism vis-à-vis the authenticity of contemporary culture that Baudrillard proposes.

[9] Reeve and Kerridge argue similarly that "[f]or all the satirical pressure it applies to so many aspects of the contemporary world, *White Noise* recognises that the positions from which any such overview can proceed are themselves continually at risk of undermining" (305).

[10] See Starr. By tracing the field back to Starr, I follow the account presented in Ragnar E. Löfstedt and Lynn Frewer's introduction to *The Earthscan Reader in Risk and Modern Society* (3); Löfstedt and Frewer also outline a different account according to which the roots of risk theory can be traced back to the Chicago School of geography.

[11] For a well-articulated critique of this kind, see Goldblatt, 154-87.

[12] See Hughes, *American Genesis: A Century of Invention and Technological Enthusiasm, 1870-1970*.

[13] See Perrow, *Normal Accidents: Living with High-Risk Technologies*.

[14] My summary of approaches to risk perception in this paragraph and the following is indebted to Löfstedt and Frewer's introduction to *The Earthscan Reader*.

[15] See Douglas and Wildavsky, *Risk and Culture: An Essay on the Selection of Technological and Environmen-*

tal Dangers, and Wildavsky and Dake, "Theories of Risk Perception: Who Fears What and Why?" Steve Rayner gives an overview of cultural theory in risk analysis and offers a critique of the way in which Douglas and Wildavsky deploy it ("Cultural Theory and Risk Analysis").

[16] See Fischhoff, Lichtenstein, Slovic, Derby, and Keeney, 61-133; Slovic, 280-85; Fischhoff, Slovic, and Lichtenstein, 161-202.

[17] See Kasperson, et al., 177-87; Kasperson, 153-78; and Flynn, Slovic, and Kunreuther.

[18] See Otway, 215-28, and Wynne, 127-43.

[19] See Ross, 159-201 (especially 166, 171-72), and Turney.

[20] In his discussion of the pastoral and the gothic in descriptions of toxicity, Buell has begun this kind of analysis (see 36-38, 42-45). Leo Marx's *The Machine in the Garden: Technology and the Pastoral Ideal in America,* to which Buell alludes, is one of the most important sources for a study of how the pastoral genre in particular mediates the encounter of nature and technology.

[21] The question of whether risk theory itself is susceptible to an analysis in literary or rhetorical terms is much more complex and would require a detailed discussion of different types of risk theory that cannot be carried out here.

[22] The juxtaposition of two storylines, which is also featured in Powers's other novels, has been widely commented upon by his reviewers (see Kirn, Quinn, and Scott). For a perceptive discussion of how the relation between the two strands of plot in *Gain* differs from that in the earlier novels due to the absence of a mediating figure, see Harris, especially 98-99.

[23] These two similarities are noted by Scott (who otherwise dismisses *White Noise* as a serious engagement with chemically induced illness) as well as by Kakutani.

[24] This inversion is discussed by Jeffrey Williams, "Issue of Corporations"(par. 9); and by Bawer, 11.

[25] This play on words is also discussed in Scott, 38.

[26] See Caldwell, C4; Williams, "Issue of Corporations."

[27] See also Kakutani, "Company Town's Prosperity," E6.

[28] See Kirn, "Commercial Fiction," 103; and Williams, "Issue of Corporations."

[29] Williams comments on this reversal in Powers's portrayal of business companies and his emphasis on "limited liability" in "Issue of Corporations."

[30] Williams notes the absence of a "utopian prospect" and describes Powers's political program as "modest" but praises him for avoiding "rote political judgment" ("Issue of Corporations"). Buell also points to the "never-had-a-chance quixoticism of the resistance effort" in the novel (290, n. 5) but argues that corporate hegemony can at least be questioned through an examination of its impacts in the realm of the local and the individual body (56).

[31] My interpretation of Don differs from Tom LeClair's, which claims that the novel rejects Don's "paranoid style." That Don is cast as a much more positive figure than LeClair lets on is also indicated by the fact that Powers puts into his mouth one of the most crucial insights in the novel, namely, that human activities have subdued the earth to the point that it can bear no more (*G* 353). See Powers's own comment on this scene in his interview with Jeffrey Williams: "This insight, on the part of a character who shouldn't have been able to reach it, is for me the emotional core of the book" ("The Last Generalist: An Interview with Richard Powers," n.p.).

[32] The echoes of Dos Passos's and Joyce's techniques are mentioned briefly in Williams ("Issue of Corporations") and those of Dos Passos also in Buell (55).

[33] Scott notes that Powers's "chronicle of Clare, Inc. . . . [is] less the company's history than its life story" (38).

WORKS CITED

Bawer, Bruce. "Bad Company." *New York Times Book Review* 21 June 1998: 11.

Beck, Ulrich. *Risikogesellschaft: Auf dem Weg in eine andere Moderne.* Frankfurt: Suhrkamp, 1986.

———. *Risk Society: Towards a New Modernity.* Trans. Mark Ritter. London: Sage, 1992.

———, Anthony Giddens, and Scott Lash. *Reflexive Modernization: Politics, Tradition, and Aesthetics in the Modern Social Order.* Cambridge, Eng.: Polity Press, 1994.

Buell, Lawrence. *Writing for an Endangered World: Literature, Culture and Environment in the U.S. and Beyond.* Cambridge: Harvard UP, 2001.

Caldwell, Gail. "On the Soapbox." *Boston Sunday Globe* 7 June 1998: C4.

DeLillo, Don. *White Noise: Text and Criticism.* Ed. Mark Osteen. New York: Penguin, 1998.

Deitering, Cynthia. "The Postnatural Novel: Toxic Consciousness in Fiction of the 1980s." *The Ecocriticism Reader: Landmarks in Literary Ecology.* Ed. Cheryll Glotfelty and Harold Fromm. Athens: U of Georgia P, 1996.

Douglas, Mary and Aaron Wildavsky. *Risk and Culture: An Essay on the Selection of Technological and Environmental Dangers.* Berkeley and Los Angeles: U of California P, 1982.

Duvall, John N. "The (Super)Marketplace of Images: Television as Unmediated Mediation in DeLillo's *White Noise.*" In *White Noise: Text and Criticism.* 432-55.

Fischhoff, Baruch, Paul Slovic, and Sarah Lichtenstein. "Lay Foibles and Expert Fables in Judgments about Risks." *Progress in Resource Management and Environmental Planning.* Ed. Timothy O'Riordan and R. Kerry Turner. 4 vols. Chichester, Eng.: John Wiley, 1981.

———, Stephen L. Derby, and Ralph L. Keeney. *Acceptable Risk.* Cambridge, Eng.: Cambridge UP, 1981.

Flynn, James, Paul Slovic, and Howard Kunreuther, eds. *Risk, Media, and Stigma: Understanding Public Challenges to Modern Science and Technology.* London: Earthscan, 2001.

Goldblatt, David. *Social Theory and the Environment.* Cambridge, Eng.: Polity Press, 1996.

Harris, Charles B. "'The Stereo View': Politics and the Role of the Reader in *Gain.*" *Review of Contemporary Fiction* 18 (fall 1998): 97-109.

Heise, Ursula. "Die Zeitlichkeit des Risikos im amerikanischen Roman der Postmoderne." *Zeit und Roman: Zeiterfahrung im historischen Wandel und ästhetischen Paradigmenwechsel vom achtzehnten Jahrhundert bis zur Postmoderne.* Ed. Martin Middeke. Würzburg: Königshausen & Neumann, 2002. 373-394.

Hughes, Thomas P. *American Genesis: A Century of Invention and Technological Enthusiasm, 1870-1970.* New York: Viking, 1989.

Kakutani, Michiko. "Company Town's Prosperity and Pain." *New York Times* 11 August 1998: E6.

Kasperson, Roger E. "The Social Amplification of Risk: Progress in Developing an Integrative Framework." In Krimsky and Golding. 153-78.

———, et al. "The Social Amplification of Risk: A Conceptual Framework." *Risk Analysis* 8 (April 1988): 177-87.

Kerridge, Richard. "Small Rooms and the Ecosystem: Environmentalism and Don DeLillo's *White Noise.*" *Writing the Environment: Ecocriticism and Literature.* Ed. Kerridge and Neil Sammells. London: Zed Books, 1998. 182-95.

Kirn, Walter. "Commercial Fiction." *New York* 15 June 1998:103.

Krimsky, Sheldon, and Dominic Golding, eds. *Social Theories of Risk.* Westport: Praeger, 1992.

LeClair, Tom. "Powers of Invention." *Nation* 27 July-3 August 1998: 35.

Lentricchia, Frank, ed. *New Essays on "White Noise."* Cambridge: Cambridge UP, 1991.

———. "Tales of the Electronic Tribe." In Lentricchia, 87-113.

Löfstedt, Ragnar E. and Lynn Frewer, eds. *The Earthscan Reader in Risk and Modern Society.* London:

Earthscan, 1998.

Maltby, Paul. "The Romantic Metaphysics of Don DeLillo." In *White Noise: Text and Criticism*. 498-516.

Marx, Leo. *The Machine in the Garden: Technology and the Pastoral Ideal in America*. London: Oxford UP, 1964.

McHale, Brian. *Postmodernist Fiction*. New York: Methuen, 1987.

Moses, Michael Valdez. "Lust Removed from Nature." In Lentricchia. 63-86.

Otway, Harry. "Public Wisdom, Expert Fallibility: Toward a Contextual Theory of Risk." In Krimsky and Golding. 215-28.

Powers, Richard. *Gain*. New York: Farrar, Straus & Giroux, 1998.

Quinn, Paul. "On the Tracks of the Rhino." *Times Literary Supplement* 17 March 2000: 22.

Perrow, Charles. *Normal Accidents: Living with High-Risk Technologies*. Princeton, N.J.: Princeton UP, 1999.

Rayner, Steve. "Cultural Theory and Risk Analysis." In Krimsky and Golding. 83-115.

Reeve, N. H. and Richard Kerridge. "Toxic Events: Postmodernism and Don DeLillo's *White Noise*." *Cambridge Quarterly* 23.4 (1994): 303-23.

Ross, Andrew. *The Chicago Gangster Theory of Life: Nature's Debt to Society*. London: Verso, 1994.

Scott, A. O. "A Matter of Life and Death." *New York Review of Books* 17 December 1998: 38-42.

Slovic, Paul. "Perception of Risk." *Science* 236 (17 April 1987): 280-85.

Starr, Chauncey. "Social Benefit versus Technological Risk." *Science* 165 (19 September 1969): 1232-238.

Theisen, Bianca. "White Noise." *Im Bann der Zeichen: Die Angst vor Verantwortung in Literatur und Literaturwissenschaft*. Ed. Markus Heilmann and Thomas Wägenbaur. Würzburg: Königshausen & Neumann, 1998.

Turney, Jon. *Frankenstein's Footsteps: Science, Genetics, and Popular Culture*. New Haven: Yale UP, 1998.

Wildavsky, Aaron and Karl Dake. "Theories of Risk Perception: Who Fears What and Why?" *Daedalus* 119 (fall 1990): 41-60.

Williams, Jeffrey. "The Issue of Corporations: Richard Powers' *Gain*." *Cultural Logic* 2.2 (1999). <http://eserver.-org/clogic/2Ð2/williamsrev.html>.

——. "The Last Generalist: An Interview with Richard Powers." *Cultural Logic* 2.2 (1999). <http://eserver.org/clogic/ 2Ð2/williams.html>).

Wynne, Brian. "Institutional Mythologies and Dual Societies in the Management of Risk." *The Risk Analysis Controversy: An Institutional Perspective*. Ed. Howard C. Kunreuther and Eryl V. Ley. Berlin: Springer, 1982. 127-43.

JOSEPH TABBI
WILLIAM GADDIS AND THE AUTOPOIESIS
OF AMERICAN LITERATURE

Epic and System

Gaddis's last fiction, which is also in some ways a final accounting, brings the author's own work deliberately into conversation with the work of the dead. The book presents itself in one solid block of text without paragraphs or section breaks, in sentences whose infrequent commas seem only to indicate pauses, or gasps, for breath. A deathbed monologue, the work is nonetheless dialogical. Gaddis knew that the book would appear posthumously, and this knowledge, that for once his absence would be given, not guarded, seems to have allowed him an intimacy and a personal mode of address rarely found in his previous work—although it is not the reader who is addressed so much as authors no longer living. Pursuing his own theme of mechanization in the arts, Gaddis has Walter Benjamin trade observations with Johan Huizinga, for example, while the narrator himself enters into discourse with other characters in fiction: John Kennedy Toole's narrator Jones in *The Confederacy of Dunces*, Svengali in George De Maurier's *Trilby*, Tolstoy's Pozdnyshev and Levochka in *The Kreutzer Sonata*, and Gogol's Golyadkin in *The Double*. Creations of other imaginations, these figures become, in *Agapē Agape*, both a block and a stimulus to a living author's own creation: the Other, as Gaddis writes, "thinking your thoughts so you could have them" (79).

Gaddis has his narrator cite Homer's "dangerous demons," automata who appear in *The Iliad* like repressed elements of a human psyche "with lives and energies of their own that aren't really part of you since you can't control them" (89). The purpose of such citations from the classics is ambivalent. At times Gaddis seems attracted to the Flaubertian model of intertextual conversation as the refined province of "a small group of minds, ever the same, which pass on the torch" (Flaubert in a letter to Georges Sand cited in *Agapē Agape*, 50). More often, however, and more productively, Gaddis treats the "demonic" energies of epic literature, larger than consciousness and outside any one author's control, as the automata that they are; fixed in the primordial past of pre-history, identifiable with no single self, uncontrollable, but nonetheless available to anyone at any time, for unexpected purposes (beyond the primarily religious and communal purposes for which epic images were intended). A piano keyboard once programmed (by punchcard or computer technology) makes music available for selection and remixing rather than interpretation by a master; and a thought, once had, becomes citable and so fit for recirculation and mass distribution. As Gaddis's frequent Platonic references indicate, writing was always, in the first instance, a *technology*; and like all technologies, writing marks an absence. Not only does writing permit the withdrawal of the author, it also makes possible the articulation of differences that belong solely to the work—

the distinction between author and narrator, for example, or (more fundamentally) the distinction between perception and communication, human thought and its circulation among characters and between readers and authors. "We are not accustomed to the idea that communication is unable to perceive" (15), writes Niklas Luhmann. But this distinction between cognitive operations helps make sense of Gaddis's insistence that, in literary realms, others might think our thoughts *so we can have them*, or his claim elsewhere that another author can have "plagiarized" his ideas "in advance." Once distinguished from thought or perception, "communication" is given a life of its own, independent of whatever goes on in specific human minds engaged in reading, conversation, or composition. The technological, in such an account, consists in the preservation, archiving, and dissemination of past works through a medium independent of readability or interpretation;[1] whereas the aesthetic, for Gaddis, consists not in the interpretation of past works but in their *recognition*—literally, the re-cognizing of one author's creation in the mind of another. Through citations, implied or explicit, that link a thought to past works and thoughts, one's own thought is able to constitute itself as *literary*.

Any invocation of Luhmann and systems theory takes us immediately away from the mainstream of theory, even that branch represented by Mikhail Bakhtin which insists on placing art in a social context. For Bakhtin, the "dialogic imagination" was famously humanizing, capable of bringing to life not only the many languages of populations held together by the modern nation state, but also the more recent proliferation of "socio-ideological" languages, those "belonging to professions, to genres, languages peculiar to particular generations, etc." (*xix*). No American author has been more attentive than Gaddis to the polyphony and immense plurality of language as it is actually spoken, transmitted, written down, and marked up, every day in ordinary contexts. But the stratification of languages and the creation of hybrid identities in corporate America do not produce, in Gaddis, the "living mix of varied and opposing voices" that Bakhtin found in Pushkin, for example (Bakhtin *xxviii*). Although Gaddis's major novel of American capitalism, *J R*, is written predominantly in dialogue, the speech Gaddis records in print is not reducible to utterance; the novel's languages do not of themselves rise above their circumstances, or combine together into a "higher unity" (Bakhtin 263). No conflicts get resolved; no one language sheds light on any other, differing language; and the only metalanguage in the novel is the literary tradition itself, a tradition that persists in citations known to the author, but rarely known to the fictional speakers themselves (and most likely only sensed even by a reader of wide experience, unless this reader has consulted the exhaustive online annotations compiled by Steven Moore).

In Gaddis, dialogue with the Other is often more demonic than human; recorded speech produces narrative energies that I find more epical than novelistic, though not in the way that Bakhtin distinguishes epic and novel. Where the "epic," according to Bakhtin, was fixed and settled in the past, in the primordial time of pre-history, the novel was to be of the present. Written most often as "a discourse of a contemporary about a contemporary addressed to contemporaries," the novel for Bakhtin was more profoundly contemporary still in its ability to comprehend *change*. The novel might do this because it was itself a young genre, and "only that which is itself developing can comprehend development as a process" (7). *J R*, to be sure, is a narrative written in an unremitting, continual present; its form remains as fresh, as innovative, and as greedily accretive as its 12-year-old narrator, whose wheeling and dealing and self-positioning at the levers of capitalist systems affects numerous lives and localities. Much is destroyed, much talent and much time is used up in the material world depicted in *J R*. Yet change, deep, systemic change, is precisely what escapes the novel's otherwise considerable inventiveness. The corporate systems it depicts are devoted to sustaining themselves through feedback, not forward motion; reflexivity, not reflection; and an expansiveness in the realm of communications distinct from, and unhindered by, thought. There is no question of staging ideological conflicts or religious crises in the conversations among characters—no Grand Inquisitors, no direct authorial voicing of political themes that mix with the network of lives, the catalogue of objects, the encyclopedia of voices. Although Gaddis's narrative operates continuously on an open terrain and in constant renewal, and while it may, like earlier epics, sacrifice formal and finished architecture so as to include a multiplicity of non-literary languages, the narrative remains *organizationally closed*: languages from the social environment, from the "outside," can get in, but they will be recognized as meaningful only in terms that the novel itself creates, in what Luhmann would call "a systems-specific play with forms" (Luhmann, *Art* 17). The epic at the end of history has folded into to itself, as an autopoietic system.

"A gaping hole in humanity"

By way of introduction, and to give a precedent for Gaddis's perennial neglect at the hands of reviewers and most critics, I want to develop one parallel in particular, with a Russian author who, like Gaddis, has remained highly regarded but slightly to the side of the mainstream, a generation ahead of Tolstoy and Dostoevsky (as Gaddis was ahead of Pynchon, DeLillo, and the brief flourishing of the postmodern epic in the United States), but not himself assimilable to the aesthetic he engendered. Bakhtin himself regarded Gogol's *Dead Souls* as a "failure." Modeled on the *Divine Comedy*, its "tragedy" was to have become not a modern epic but a Mennipean satire because (writes Bakhtin), "Once having entered the zone of familiar contact [Gogol] was unable to leave it, and he was unable to transfer into this sphere distanced and positive images" (28). It was among Tolstoy and Dostoevsky, not Gogol, that George Steiner meted out the epic tendencies that he felt still lived in the modern novel, but Steiner never mentions that Tolstoy and Dostoevsky achieve epic magnitude only by largely neglecting the day-to-day operations of business and capital, and the slow, steady, and never-ending work of making contacts, cutting a figure, and managing the gossip generated when doing business—activities Gogol excelled at representing. In contrast to Tolstoy's epic of the upper classes and Dostoevsky's excavations of the lower, Gogol in *Dead Souls* had attempted the impossible: an epic of the *middle*. His main character Chichikov, a bachelor of uncertain standing who must invest his assets, who will rise or fall in society as his capital grows or depreciates, is too familiar, too bound up in contemporaneity, to be carried into the "distanced images of the epic" (27). "Gogol lost Russia," Bakhtin concludes; "he lost his blueprint for perceiving and representing her" (27). The book's presentness, and the new positioning of the author on a level with his characters, may represent a new start for the novel as a genre; but the loss of distance, the immersion of novelistic discourse in the "now," is precisely what keeps *Dead Souls* from attaining the poetic force of epic.

I am not in a position to judge whether or not *Dead Souls* fails or succeeds on its own terms, although I can say that the "distancing" features that Bakhtin finds in pre-modern epic might describe a difference not in literary quality, but in the kind of society and power structures that epic takes from society into itself, into its own genre-specific forms of communication. Russian literature, it is said, emerged out of Gogol's *Cloak*; the Americans have been "less fortunate" in that Poe, Hawthorne, Melville, and Gaddis remain obscure and idiosyncratic, bequeathing not a recognized national literature but a model for what "talent is capable of producing in relative isolation" (Steiner 33). So writes George Steiner, forgetting that the retention of singularity, the constitutive resistance of the individual to absorption by a collective, may be precisely what distinguishes American society and pushes American power toward its own, particular development. Steiner was able to find epic qualities in the Russia of Gogol, Tolstoy, and Dostoevsky because the country was almost a world to itself, the source of greatest resistance to the Napoleonic reconstruction of Europe, and a nation-empire unfolding unpredictably and uniquely. America, too, is a geo-political reality distinct from the European nation state. So when it comes to defining an American epic, singularity and "relative isolation" may well prove representative, not iconoclastic. And this singularity may also be representative not only of one national character: in the current condition of Global expansiveness, the operative concepts of inclusiveness, hybridity, and borderlessness are no longer limited to circumstances in the United States *per se*. The faithful preservation of singularity could well be precisely what outfits American fiction, in its more expansive modes, as the epic for an emergent empire "on the model of networked power" rather than national, monarchical, or otherwise transcendental sovereignty (Hardt and Negri 167). Steiner, however, is correct in regarding both the American and the Russian novel as distinct from the European because, excepting pre-revolutionary Russia's relatively small and Eurocentric aristocracy, neither Russia nor America could reference clear "intellectual standards" or touchstones of manner. (Steiner is here citing Henry James on Hawthorne, although the comment is applied to American Literature generally.) When a standard is drawn not from fixed society, but from antiquity, the work (in Gogol, in Joyce, in T. S. Eliot) may be monumental, but it is epical only if the term is recast, as in the "Modern Epic" described by Franco Morretti, or the "Novel Epics" considered by S. J. Rabinowitz.[2] The epic is made "new" precisely by incorporating elements of the novel, by existing in its present or, in the case of Thomas Pynchon's *Mason & Dixon*, in a colonial past that is however presented in the subjunctive, containing a future that might have been possible *then*, but is only realized in some future, which is to say, *our now*, when we and Pynchon are living. Epic does not realize itself in the modern world until the work *gives up* its modern*ist* reliance on mythic parallels or other aspirations toward transcending the present. The novel, to achieve epic magnitude (rather than ironical distance and an inevitable sense of belatedness), needs to take seriously its own potential on the plane of immanence, as a field where a singular, irreducible subjectivity can play itself out. Yet the novel-epic is one hybrid that Bakhtin himself never recognized; on the contrary, he regarded *Dead Souls* as a failure precisely because it compromised novelistic and epical modes. A multiplicity of language systems gives the novelist a way of refracting identity, of dispersing aspects of the author's self and language among the characters and their languages. Dialogism brings the author *into* the fiction, but as someone or something *other*. The relativity of literary and non-literary language, Bakhtin argues in "Discourse in the Novel," and the mixing of forms in the novel,

> open up the possibility of never having to define oneself in language, the possibility of translating one's own intentions from one linguistic system to another, of fusing "the language of truth" with "the language of everyday," of saying "I am me" in someone else's language, and in my own language, "I am other." (315)

Unlike novelistic languages, which can co-exist on a single field of representation, the "distanced images" of epic (what Bakhtin found lacking in Gogol), remain on a separate plane, outside and distinct from familiar language. The novelist, too, distances him or herself from the work, but this is more of an *internal* distancing, one that establishes itself on the same plane as the characters and events in the novel. The former, image-based, epical distance preserves the idea of an *outside*; a sphere of the gods, or a nature that is unchanging, cyclical, capable of renewing itself with each rosy-fingered dawn despite the shifting fortunes of love and war. By contrast, the latter, language-based, internalized distance of the novel opens out from a plane of immanence. One can appreciate why a secular humanist criticism would want to retain the immanent, open-ended sphere as an exclusive site, and the novel as a privileged genre-without-genre where all that is uniquely human is capable of finding expression in language. But there is no reason why systems, too, cannot occupy the same field of immanence—so that nature, animals, and machines have as much to do with what is "human" as does language itself. And it is in this "fluid terrain of the new communicative, biological, and mechanical technologies" that the epic today is most likely to take its form and definition (Hardt and Negri 218).

In networks, not in bounded nations; in circulation and redistribution, not in conquest: this is how Empire's distanced images find contemporary form. Money, for example, has enormous distancing powers not recognized by Bakhtin, or perhaps by Gogol himself as he engaged a society only partially removed from feudal arrangements. And money, like poetry and religion, demands a certain faith that, once recognized, offers a kind of demonic equivalent to "spirit" in the epic. To participate imaginatively in Gogol's "poem of Russia" and to enter into Chichikov's world, a reader must maintain faith in the newness, in the "novelty," of the literary project, even as business can be conducted only so long as the businessman maintains credit in the eyes of others, and society as a whole maintains faith in a system set up to create value. In Russia of the nineteenth century, and in America then as now, the lack of strong bourgeois values (and the absence of a middle class "in the European sense of the word," as Marx noted in his later years), made faith in systems potentially that much stronger (cited in Steiner 37). The value of an estate, in Tsarist times, depended partly on the number of peasants, or souls, working the land, the number established by a national census. Chichikov's scheme is to buy up the listed peasants who have died in the interval between censuses, and so establish himself as a man of means and property fit to marry and move in society. Of course his only movement, in his signature "smallish spring brezka" (Gogol 3), is from one inn to another around one of those towns so familiar in Russian literature, "the provincial town of N," until the time when he is run out. But this movement is enough to create from within an image of society in all its classes, professions, and languages. One landowner, living with his wife in rural isolation, is only too happy to avoid paying the quitrent on the dead souls, and so he makes each one over to Chichikov at a fraction of the cost of a healthy laborer. At the house of another, a gambler and dissolute, Chichikov barely escapes with his life. A third, suspecting treachery, wants from him *more* than the price of a living laborer. But it is the fourth landowner, Plyushkin, who best completes Gogol's "blueprint" for Russia (Bakhtin 28). This old man has lived for years in miserliness and isolation, hoarding grain, collecting tithes, storing rags until they turn to dust, and refusing to throw away even a used toothpick. Without his realizing it, the estate itself has fallen to ruin and the items themselves have all "turned to rot and gape." Indeed, the landowner has himself "finally turned into a sort of gape in mankind" (*Dead Souls* 120).

A hitherto unnoticed source for Gaddis's title, this line in Gogol (which Gaddis would have read in translation), is worth noting because it presents the old man not so much as a Dickensian caricature, but as a representative "soul"; and this not because the old man represents any actual person or allegorizes the dehumanizing effects of capital. Rather, in the dusty figure of the hoarder and the miser we find expressed the overall strategy of internal distancing; the presence, at the boundary of the capitalist system, of a subjectivity that is neither good nor evil, is known only as a "gape in mankind." Within the world but not a part of it; existing more as its boundary or limit, the old man has become the system's subjectivity, a once vital power whose spirit over time (and unnoticed by himself) has been stripped away. In place of "virtue" and "rare qualities of soul" (courtesies which even Chichikov, a practiced flatterer, cannot bring himself to utter), Chichikov gives as a reason for visiting his desire to meet a man reputed for his "economy" and "order" (121). The social bonds of *Agapē*, the early Christian ideal of fellowship, in this novel are torn apart (rendered "Agape") because exchange has separated out from value; economics and organization, in turn, have supplanted the material world they are supposed to organize, while nature, so long neglected, overtakes the social order and the human body itself through processes of decomposition. And it is not only the old miser who is made unrecognizable by his blind devotion to the forms of capital, rather than the substance of production; Chichikov, too, when he comes to the attention of the town, is revealed as oddly substanceless: "The whole search carried out by the officials revealed to them only that they did not know for certain what Chichikov was, and that all the same Chichikov must certainly be something" (199).

Failures of recognition abound in Gogol's novel. On first sight, Chichikov takes the decrepit landowner for a housekeeper; only on a second appearance does he take this housekeeper for a man, not a woman, and he realizes his mistake only after asking the old man, in some perplexity,

> "About the master? Is he in, or what?"
> "The master's here," said the housekeeper.
> "But where?" Chichikov reiterated.
> "What, my dear, are you blind or something?" said the housekeeper. "Egad! But I am the master!" (116)

The same mis-recognition is rendered in Gogol's short novel, *The Double*, and recounted twice by Gaddis in *Agapē Agape*. Early in the narrative, Gaddis's narrator cites Huizinga on the identification of tribal humans with animals, when the savage "in his magic dance . . . is the other" (Huizinga 25). The narrator in his extremity, uninclined to symbolic distancing or literary doubling, identifies himself fully and finally with the dying animal other:

> Got to stop it's got to end right here can't breathe the other can't speak can't cross the room can't breathe can't, can't go on and I'm, I am the other. I am the other. Not the two of us living side by side like the, like some Golyadkin he invented in a bad moment no, no not those Zwei Seelen wohnen, ach! In meiner Brust one wants to leave its brother, one clings to the earth and the other in derber Leibeslust no, no no no, can't breath can't walk can't stand I am the other. (20)

A few pages later, thinking of the work he is trying to finish (a social history of the player piano), Gaddis's narrator recounts the scene of misrecognition in *The Double* (Chapter 8), so close to the one in *Dead Souls*:

this work of mine trying to explain this other it's not Golyadkin no, it's not this doppelgänger who's gone with his bed in the morning when Petrushka brings in tea and complains that
his master is not home, shouting You idiot! I'm your master, Petrushka! And the "other one,"
Petrushka finally blurts out, the "other one" left hours ago it's not like that, this doppelgänger of Golyadkin's I've never even seen my, seen this plagiarist because I am the other one it's
exactly the opposite, I am the other I just said that didn't I . . . ? we're not these Golyadkins
we're not doppelgängers, it's either/or, it's all-or-none, it's this whole binary digitized pattern of holes punched in those millions of dusty piano rolls. . . . (22-3)

The dying man will return once more to Gogol before the narrative comes to an end:

Ought to go out and get some fresh air, get out of this dim suffocating airless lightless little
no no wait not yet no, these demons of Homer's and Golyadkin's doppelgänger who's gone
with his bed in the morning when Petrushka brings in tea and explains that his master's not
at home shouting You idiot Petrushka! I'm your master! (79)

The refusal here of a doubling strategy can be understood more generally as a refusal
of the novelist's own separate existence as a speaking presence within novelistic discourse. "I am the other," a major refrain in a narrative that is nothing but last words, is a
lament, obviously, that expression must cease. But the phrase also indicates a condition
that has influenced all of Gaddis's writing, not just this final fiction. Identification with
the other, particularly the "either/or, . . . all-or-none" alterity of digital technology
and network communications, is the condition of novelistic epic today, where distances
are eliminated, consciousness becomes the distinctions it creates, and the human subject, rather than trying to transcend either nature or the world system, occupies their
boundaries.

One of the key innovations of systems theory is to allow us to conceive of a boundary actively, as a subjectivity that joins even as it separates: "there are no systems independent of environments, only systems/environment couples" (Clarke, elucidating
Luhmann, n.p.). And subjectivity itself is conceivable as a way of bringing forth that
coupling - whether through human or non-human agencies. Hence, in systems theory, a society can be conscious even as an individual is capable of embodying social
forces of generation and corruption. What happens when "*Agapē*" becomes "Agape" is
that an isolated, human-made system decomposes, ceases to differentiate itself from
the non-human environment. Entropic disintegration, turning productive difference
into sameness, rot—Gogol's "gape"—might appear as an inevitability, the collapse of
consciousness with the organic dissolution of the dying body. Death cannot of course
be recognized *by* consciousness: it is aware only of its own operations and selections,
able to process only those aspects of the environment that it is set up to process ("eit-
her/or, . . . all-or-none," replications and duplications rather than recognitions). But
if the system boundary is conceived as something two-sided, a systems/environment
coupling that may work at various levels (including both the psyche that perceives and

the society that communicates), then it is possible to imagine a way out of the mirror-like doubling that (literally) bedevils Gaddis's narrator. By shifting the focalization, from the dying man to the admixture of living systems and communicative networks that give form to the work, Gaddis in *Agapē Agape* stages a crossing-over. The autonomous, dying consciousness, an entity incapable of experiencing its own end, can however combine with the non-human, with Homer's demons and all their equivalents in the current world system. This is not a crossing over into the spirit worlds familiar in traditional epic, but rather a way for one, authorial consciousness, to pass his observations on to another, readerly consciousness. The author thus completes a transition from a single, dying system to many systems, to a combination of psyches that perceive and societies that communicate. And that transition out of the author's private observing system is what allows others—readers—to think an author's thoughts so he can "have" them (in circulation and communication, not in consciousness).

In *Dead Souls*, incidentally, Chichikov's fall has very little to do with the transactions themselves, their lack of substance and their vaguely disreputable—though entirely legal—character. Rather, his worldly fall results from an uncharacteristically spontaneous attempt, near the completion of his project, to court the governor's daughter. The businessman's awkwardness is noted in society, but the trouble really begins the next day, with a conversation among two woman of the town, one "simply agreeable," the other "agreeable in all respects" (*Dead Souls*, chapter 9). The ladies are no more distinguishable than are Anne and Julia Bast, the aunts who are the first to speak in *J R*. More than anywhere else, the dialogue between the old ladies is where Gaddis introduces details of his own biography and family history in Long Island. The aunts, whose memories (in all fairness) are actually quite precise with regard to essentials and whose talk is not nearly so addled as readers might think, are also capable of becoming more than just vehicles, more than disembodied voices who set the plot in motion. They may start out that way, but it is evidence of Gaddis's breadth and compassion that the most incidental character, over time and in unexpected circumstances, will be revealed as an individual, as one in possession of a singular, irreproducible life. Anne (or is it Julia?), while trying to help with a pressing legal matter, suggests making a phone call to the "family lawyer," who (if he is still alive) is probably long retired from practice and living thousands of miles away in the Indiana town where the family was established generations in the past. The aunt remembers passing by "the old Lemp home" in Indiana (14), and (much later in the book) she recalls how as a girl she imagined getting married and living there one day. The brief memory is all the more moving for being scarcely noticeable, within the mundane and instrumental talk that surrounds it.

Another character, the lawyer Beaton, is figuratively "beat on" by the Governor whose orders he is expected to carry out. This he does up to the very end of the book—when he quietly and unexpectedly ignores the Governor's barked instruction ("–Hear me. . . !") and refuses to declare a dividend, something he's been reminded of at least three times before (*J R* 712). The entire plot, affecting both Amy Joubert's guardianship of her only son and the fate of an entire corporation, may depend on this single, deliberate inaction, which is given magnitude only through Gaddis's attention to *the inhuman*, the slowly accreting and detailed processes of corporate power and legal languages. Small as it is, Beaton's inaction shows how much the system depends on obedience, and how vulnerable it is to even a singular refusal of work and authority. Refusal, as Melville's "Bartleby" shows, is the beginning of a liberatory politics; but (as Hardt and Negri point out) "refusal in itself is empty" (204). One must also know one's place, literally, in the corporate system, where even to identify a class enemy is something of a challenge. Character in Gaddis, though far from conventional and certainly not rounded or psychological, takes epic dimensions that would be impossible to achieve without this detailed immersion in systems. The "recognitions" that began, in Gaddis, as largely aesthetic judgments, have become more literal acts of cognition in *J R* and his later narratives. As the purpose of art is to create a bridge between perception and communication; character in Gaddis becomes less an end in itself than a means of locating the self and its desires within networks of power.

"If you could have seen what I saw there": Second-Order Observation

Before going ahead with my reading of *J R*, a novel that I think is especially yielding to the terms and methods of systems theory, I want to distinguish some aspects of Luhmann's theory that are available for literary criticism, and some that are not. My main point of reference will be the most recently translated volume from Luhmann's series for a theory of society, *Art as a Social System*.

In that volume, Luhmann sees criticism in our time as no longer "the perfection of art, as the production of its history, even as its 'medium of reflection'"—the approach favored by Walter Benjamin (53). Certainly in the modern era, criticism's function is not "to assist in judging or creating works of art" (3)—although Luhmann would not have objected to critics assuming a more active role in deciding what is acceptable *as* art. Selection, not interpretation, is the critic's first obligation. At a time when the demand for novelty by a mass audience has displaced the cultivated judgment of a few, there remains the need to determine "criteria for rejecting some innovations as failures" (Luhmann, *Art* 201). Indeed, Luhmann implies, we should look to systems theory not for a method of reading literary texts, viewing works of art, or creating music out of sound and noise, but rather for principles that are of use in the drawing of boundaries. The shift is from interpretation to observation, from a concern with an individual author's subjectivity to what is public and intersubjective. Only then, when a space is re-opened for "the mere perception" of a literary work in its material reality, might critics think of constructing literature as an object of institutional recognition within the otherwise unbounded environment of mass entertainment (Luhmann, *Art* 10).

The work of criticism is relational, paratactic, so that rather than "applying" theory to a specific work, critics should try observing *how* it works *as art*; also, by recognizing that a complex composition will sometimes work *against* the artist, critics might use theory to generate perceptions at times contrary to the artist's purpose in the work and in society. By definition, neither social reality nor a literary tradition can be unique to an individual; what is unique, however, is the position from which an artist observes and, especially in an artist who assigns vantages to characters in fiction, the particular mix of differently located and differently embodied individuals, each with a particular history of structural coupling within a complex environment: "Look! If you could have seen what I saw there," the exclamation of the visual artist, Schramm, spoken near the end of his life and cited near the end of *J R* (he is paraphrasing Broch's *Sleepwalker*), is every artist's implicit plea to every viewer, and every author's plea to a reader (724). Of course it is impossible to see through another person's eyes or to think another person's thoughts. But to observe what an author has been able to hold in thought is to begin to know one's own mind and to locate oneself within the field of operations, quotations, blind spots, and occasional correlated perceptions that can be said to produce a living tradition or evolving art system. There should be no question of studying either the work or its tradition for direct insights into the working of society: both the work and society are self-constituting, or autopoietic, systems. But the work can function as a *stage* for "second-order observations," inviting readers to look again at the world, to observe their own observations, and "to discover previously unacknowledged idiosyncrasies, prejudices, and limitations" (Luhmann, *Art* 87).

Criticism according to Luhmann participates in this process of observing the work and then reintegrating what one has learned into the work's form—advancing to a second-order observation where it is possible to *think with* the work, to converse through it and to explore social forms and possibilities at the level of the work's autopoiesis, its self-creation out of multiple perspectives (out of the multiple systems with the work's environment). But what might autopoiesis look like in a work of art—particularly in a literary work made not of plastic materials or sound and not of formal relations alone but of language? Autopoiesis means that the decisions made by the artist do not follow an external set of rules or strive toward a specific end; rather they emerge from relationships within the work whose endpoint is unforeseen in the making and recognized only in retrospect. Different readers will view these relations differently and construct out of them different meanings, for good or for ill. But it is not clear to me—and I'm not sure whether Luhmann himself really believed—that this readerly construction of a literary text is itself a system. Indeed, in places Luhmann does distinguish art as a developing social system from "other, more rigidly programmed functional systems" because in art

one cannot assume the existence of selection criteria in the way one can assume a profit motive in the economy, a criterion of methodological correctness in science, or the distinction equality/inequality in current legal practice. If artworks constitute their own programs, then they can convince only after the fact. (*Art* 230)

But such noted differences between the work of art and social systems are not incidental but essential, and they suggest to me that what is really describable as a system is not the artwork or literary text itself but its *context*. A system—a literary tradition, for example, or a society—does not exist in the same way that a work of art exists. A printed novel, for example, is available for me to experience, and to do so in communication with you, another reader, because the novel as a potential for experience has an objective existence. You and I can agree on the text, in a consensus, and we can return to that novel, later, for more. It won't have changed. By contrast, a tradition or genre cannot be gone back to because it will have changed in its contents and their relationships. Instead of evolving systems, what we have instead, as objects of study, are particular texts, and unless we as critics account for individuality in language, fixed in a specific, unchanging textual object, there will be little to distinguish aesthetic observations from more strictly—and necessarily more transient and abstract—sociological observations. This abstraction is a shortcoming that at least one critic, Florian Cramer, has noticed in applications of Luhmann's theory: "While Luhmann was a sociologist indeed," observes Cramer,

> It appears to me that also the non-Luhmannian attempts to employ systems theory as a literary theory always boiled down to sociology. Systems theory helps to analyze how "art" and "literature" work as social systems, but in my view hasn't proven yet to be usable for analyzing texts and artworks themselves. There might be, however, an exception: namely those artworks which are autopoietic systems themselves. (n.p.)

I am, to an extent, reading *J R* and perhaps the postmodern epic in general as just such an exception, but with one caveat: even a literary work that (like *J R*) is autopoietic in its form or systemicity exists, as art, only insofar as it is experienced in a consciousness. The work is intelligible only as an elaboration of another consciousness in language, always invincibly personal. Thomas Pynchon is as confessional as Anne Sexton; Gaddis as much a narrative presence as Fielding. That presence is refracted and distributed among characters in the fiction and expressed through language other than the author's own—in citations, in instances of extra-literary language, in allusions direct and implied, and so forth. In none of these writers is language a system, however.

To account for the fact of literary art, one needs to account for its individuality—but individuals, as Luhmann of course recognizes, "are not and cannot be 'parts' of society"; language is never a system; and "communication cannot receive or produce perceptions" in or from another mind (10). Our "autopoietic closure as minds and as living bodies" keeps us outside the social system, much as our language and our consciousness emerge out of, but evidently remain separate from, cognition. So for Luhmann to treat the arts (including literature) as a social *system*, he needs to distinguish language in art from its usual function in communication. This is why, in the opening chapter of *Art as a Social System*, Luhmann insists on the primacy of perception in consciousness when experiencing works of art. Only by "participating in communication via perception" can an individual psyche "generate intensities of experience that remain incommunicable as such" (48). And only by keeping perception distinct from communication can art have an effect on society that is indirect and non-destructive. Art's purpose, Luhmann recognizes, is not to represent the social but to "irritate" and provoke it; to define the work's own difference and to mark off a space in which readers can observe the emergence of order and disorder. I'll come back to the question of how literature can be rooted in perception—it is the aspect of Luhmann's theory that speaks most pointedly to what is unique about Gaddis's aesthetic. For the moment I would simply note that, unless we keep this fundamentally *in*communicable aspect of literary art clearly in view, we are likely to fall into the trap Florian Cramer observes in Luhmann's followers, of treating works of literature as documents of sociology.

One obvious field of application for Luhmann's theories has been the modernist poem—the autotelic poem of Warren and Brooks cited approvingly by Luhmann, which becomes "a unity only at the level of connotation, by exploring the liberties that come with using words exclusively as a medium." The words and repeated motifs give meaning to one another not through their outward or informational content so much as their self-referential combination of "sound, rhythm, and meaning" (Luhmann, *Art* 26). Cramer, however, has more recent models in mind, along the lines of John Barth's "Frame Tale," which uses words themselves as the codes for a self-enclosing unity: "Once Upon a Time there was a Story that Began"—and that's it, the story in its entirety, arranged vertically along two sides of a page, so as to produce (with the reader's help and a pair of scissors) a Moebius strip in which the words themselves are the self-encircling code, enclosing instructions for the story's own assembly. When Cramer delivered his comments in the year 2001 at the Tate Modern, he was speaking on a panel with Robert Coover, in whose work "autopoiesis, recursion, self-reference and self-reflexivity have frequently been observed." These qualities can also be observed in the work of William Gaddis, credited by Tony Tanner for having bridged American modernism and postmodernism in the art of fiction (400) and identified, by Tom LeClair, specifically as a "systems novelist" (87-105). More consistently even than literary heirs such as Barth, Coover, Pynchon, Didion, Caponegro, and DeLillo, Gaddis would let the language of systems—office talk, depositions, press releases, legal judgments, etc.—act as a medium through which his own work, as fiction, achieves its form.

But before Gaddis reached this level of self-consciousness expressed *through* the non-literary language of the "other," he had to get past the more direct self-consciousness in his first novel, *The Recognitions*, which, for example, presented several characters at parties and on the streets of Greenwich Village discussing a long talkative book that very much resembles *The Recognitions*: "You're not reading that are you?" asks one character. "No, I'm just reviewing it." At two points in *The Recognitions* Gaddis appears in cameo, as a character named "Willie." He also gives his initials to the book's main character, Wyatt Gwyon, a forger of sixteenth-century Flemish masterworks. In *J R*, one of Gaddis's many distinct personae is named "Eigen," from the German word indicating "of one's own," what belongs to the self. An eigenvalue is also a term cited by Luhmann to describe the self-referential basis of the brain's perceptual processes:

> Today we know that the external world is the brain's own construction, treated by consciousness as if it were a reality 'out there.' The extent to which perception is prestructured by language is equally well known. The perceived world is nothing but the sum total of the 'eigenvalues' of neurophysiological operations. (Luhmann, *Art* 6)

That we see the world as separate and independent of observation is a result of the mind's filtering out, or repressing, its own operations. And Gaddis, the author of cognitive fictions, creates a similar effect in *J R* by repressing his own organizing presence, and presenting the narrative as a "recording" of multiple voices (LeClair). Instead of putting himself "in" the fictional world—as authorial will and the world-engendering Willy of *The Recognitions*—in his later novels Gaddis avoids any objective presentation of his individuality and distributes his agency as a sum of eigenvalues, with each persona indicating aspects of his own engagement in society, and his various locations within its networks of technoscientific relations.

Observing Complexity, or: the Primacy of Perception Over Communication in Narrative

What Gaddis accomplishes in *J R* might be described as formally similar to Barth's "Frame Tale," but carried out over the length of a 726-page novel, not just a ten-word phrase. For Gaddis had undertaken in *J R* a thoroughgoing critique of corporate America that hardly ever strays from the programs and languages generated by an increasingly mediated environment. By exploring at encyclopedic length the entire social order and composing largely with found language, the language of headlines, talk, box carton labels, advertisements, and innumerable social others, *J R* realizes an order and form of its own; and by imagining the rise of a corporation run by an "unkempt 11 year old whose penny stock and defaulted bond operations [blossom] into a vast and perilous financial empire," Gaddis is able to focus his critique, demonstrating how much of society and the economy is pre-ideological and available to the mind of a pre-adolescent ("J R Up to Date," *Rush* 62). The boy, J R Van Sant, speaks only what is spoken by the society, knowing nothing of the sociality within which adults are expected to conduct themselves, and using grown-up language but with a literal-mindedness that reveals tacit expectations not covered by the corporate program: "through his simple creed of 'get all you can' by obeying the letter of the law and evading its spirit at every turn" ("*J R* Up to Date," *Rush* 62), young J R tests the limits of the economic system and participates in its systematicity, its continued growth for the sake of growth without regard for consequences or costs on human lives and the environment—indeed, without ever recognizing the *existence* of an environment: "wait a second," J R tells his lawyer (whom he hired by dialing a number on a matchbook). The boy is speaking from the school payphone in Long Island, where he conducts most of his business:

> look did they do that mineral essay of that water they're using in this here beer. . . ? No I did see if . . . No but see if it's got any of these minerals in it we should get to take this here percentage depletion allowance off the whole . . . What do you mean we're depleting them aren't we? I mean if we get some tax benefit off depleting something why shouldn't we de . . . okay so go ahead and get a ruling on it look, the next thing . . . where? That says mineral assets mineralclaims we've got how does anybody know there's not these mineral and gas deposits worth twen . . . Look okay look that's the whole thing then look, if there's any crap about that we just go ahead and drill or whatever you . . . What does it matter for what! for whatever they give out these deductions for these here intangible drilling costs for I mean what do they expect us to. . . . (*J R* 469-70)

J R might not understand the difference between a mineral "assay" and a school essay (in class, maybe he missed that day). Often as not he will misplace the decimal point when practicing sixth-grade math on the billions of dollars that flow through his business (though neither he nor his employees ever pause to enjoy the profits). He might mistake "amphibious" for "anphibious" ("J R Up to Date," *Rush* 67), and maybe he does not exactly distinguish an Indian reservation from a preservation; but he knows environmental and tax law. If the system allows a deduction for "depletion," the J R corp will go ahead, drill, and deplete. All the boy can see, and all the system expects him to see, is the deduction on a balance sheet that a paid accountant can sort out for him. The corresponding environmental depletion is invisible to him, and so unreal (even as the "stuffed Alaskans" he assumes are placed on display in the Museum of Natural History might as well be human bodies to a boy of twelve with no experience of mortality).

"Postmodernism," writes Fredric Jameson, "is what you have when the modernization process is complete and nature is gone for good" (*ix*). By "Nature," neither Jameson nor Gaddis is primarily addressing such things as the depletion of natural resources or the loss of habitats and wildlife, real as these losses are. Nor would either the novelist or the theorist deny the continued existence of drives and passions, however vacant and affectless the presentation of character in such fiction and its theorization might be. What is being dramatized rather, in both the literature and the theory, is a new, because truly global, *incorporation* of the drives and senses. "We have no nature," Hardt and Negri comment, "in the sense that these forces and phenomena are no longer understood as outside, that is, they are not seen as original and independent of the artifice of the civil order" (187). No longer available as an eternal, unchanging environment or setting against which human wars and artifice can be measured, nature is itself now a participant in human wars, a force that remains invisible to a system until the system breaks down or nature breaks in, in the form of disease, climate change, floods, hurricanes, and other disasters no longer regarded as accidental or insurable as "acts of God." Nature has become, "as some might say, a part of history" (187).

There can be no epic effect, of course, in the cited dialogue of a boy, however recognizable the consequences of his sorcerer's apprentice-like decisions and instructions. Yet J R's blindness to nature does not change the fact of its presence, as a part of history and on the same plane of immanence through which the dialogue unfolds. A presence more perceived by the reader than communicated among characters, the natural world is given in small phrases interspersed through the dialogue, and in longer, transitional passages. Indeed, what is most remarkable about the self-consciousness of *J R* is Gaddis's decision (despite a number of authorial winks, such as a publisher's list of books under review whose titles are all anagrams of THE RECOGNITIONS) to impart an authorial perspective not to any one character or group of characters but to these wholly impersonal, at times technological, at times natural, passages of transition—instances of prose poetry without comparison in the body of American literature:

> . . . and they entered the [train] car out of sight behind its filthy windows as its lights too receded and became mere punctuations in this aimless spread of evening past the firehouse and the crumbling Marine Memorial, the blooded barberry and woodbine's silent siege and the desirable property For Sale, up weeded ruts and Queen Anne's laces to finally mount the sky itself where another blue day brought even more the shock of fall in its brilliance, spread loss like shipwreck on high winds tossing those oaks back in waves blown over with white-caps where their leaves showed light undersides and dead branches cast brown sprays to the surface, straining at the height of the pepperidge tree and blowing down the open highway to find voice in the screams of the electric saws prospering through Burgoyne Street. . . . (*J R* 74-5)

Although the book has no chapter breaks, the predominant dialogue in *J R* is continuously marked off by such passages. Time's passing is quietly registered (here with an allusion to Thomas Carlisle, "another blue day"), while scenes are demarcated by passage through a sensible *environment*. Each time the narrative returns to Burgoyne Street, one of maybe a dozen stable settings in the novel, we have variations on the same foliage and the same set of markers—the Marine Memorial, the For Sale sign, a church memorial to "Our Dear Departed Member"—all of which may or may not be perceived by the characters, who may or may not be present at each transition. Violence is done not only by the ever-present electric saws, but by nature itself, where woodbine is said to renew "its attack on the locusts in the next lot, penetrating to the mangled saplings and torn trunks at the forward edge of the battleline . . . " (*J R* 235). Trees are said to "[ride] high losing sight of each other as though readying to hurl their fruit in all directions and make a real night of it, one to emerge from with old wounds reopened and new ones inviting attention" (*J R* 143). No human presence is needed for subjectivity to exist; no armies need to battle for war to carry on. Something unprecedented is taking place in such prose—not an animism so much as a re-situation of subjectivity and human violence. The human in Gaddis, as in systems theory, is never a part of nature; rather it is a material operation sensed at nature's boundaries that connects us, body and psyche, to the environment whether or not we know it.

Call it a cognitive ecology. A consciousness at once authorial and impersonal carries the narrative from voice to voice, and from scene to scene, through television monitors, phone lines, cars and trains, or through a static landscape where time passes in the absence of any observer. The "sunlight, pocketed in a cloud" on the first page of *J R*, is a small-scale use of the device, at once establishing the "setting" and setting off the dialogue of the two elder sisters:

> —Money. . . ? in a voice that rustled.
> —Paper, yes.
> —And we'd never seen it. Paper money.
> —We never saw paper money till we came east.
> —It looked so strange the first time we saw it. Lifeless.
> —You couldn't believe it was worth a thing.
> —Not after Father jingling his change.
> —Those were silver dollars. And silver halves, yes and quarters, Julia. The ones from his pupils. I can hear them now . . .
> Sunlight, pocketed in a cloud, spilled suddenly broken across the floor through the leaves of the trees outside. (*J R* 3)

We have now reached a point where we can observe how *J R* fulfills the particular aesthetic demand identified by Luhmann—that a work of art should create a bridge between perception and communication. The very first voice that we hear rustles, like money itself, and like the rustling pages of the book we are reading. At the same time the word, "rustled," works as a reference to the voice of an elderly woman. The sunlight, "pocketed in a cloud," is as much a medium as the money jingling in the pocket of the elder Bast; nature is thus appropriated as a commodity, although it's a careless, wasteful, and destructive appropriation because the pocketed bounty spills "suddenly broken across the floor." The first of many spills in the novel (scarcely a page will go by without an accident), this line signals the constant but scarcely noticeable intrusion of the environment into a society concerned with its own, more loquacious, activities. (Not until the trees are cut down one day, by those very buzzsaws "prospering" on Burgoyne Street, do either Anne or Julia notice their former presence.) But we, the readers, are meant to notice, and we're also meant to pick up on meanings unavailable to the characters or miscommunicated among them. *We* can know, if we are listening and paying attention, that the lawyer Coen's name is spelled "without the h," as Coen tries to explain. But the aunts, Anne and Julia, don't know it, and Coen himself does not know that the ladies don't know. He's a restless communicator, unable to "come and sit down" (3), and unable to *listen* for meanings outside the coded meanings he busily cites as legal precedents. When Gaddis at the end of the novel indirectly (through the boy J R, himself heard through a dangling telephone receiver) asks the reader, "hey you listening?" the author himself is asking whether we have learned to keep still and listen to what's being said, not because we're expected to respond or act (as to a direct judicial *order*) but rather to participate in a second-order communication with the author, a kind of co-writing or collaboration that produces the narrative out of voices and materials provided by the culture and selected by the author.

This opening passage reveals how it is that Gaddis gives "primacy to perception in consciousness" rather than reflection or representation: pocketed sunlight is a shadow, a vacancy; it is followed, in the very next transitional passage, by "the graveled vacancy of a parking lot" (*J R* 18); and then, when the sunlight gets in a character's eyes, "It caught him flat across the lenses, erasing any life behind them in a flash of inner vacancy" (18). A word, "vacancy," is not a concept already "out there"; it is a humming with "sound, rhythm, and meaning" (Luhmann, *Art* 26). By building poetic connections out of repeated words and everyday (mis)communications, and by utilizing "media such as space and time," Gaddis makes his narrative appear more world-like, consistent in its own internal relations but remaining dependent on "triggering perceptions (not least, the reading of texts)" (Luhmann, *Art* 7). Gaddis's radical empiricism, with his unmatched attention to the environmental blindnesses and evacuated subjectivities generated by self-regulating professions such as business and law, does not make *J R* an *imitation* of the society it depicts; nor is the novel itself a social system in microcosm. On the contrary—Gaddis critiques the system, but to understand how requires that we enter the "spirit" within or behind the "letter" of the law (and Gaddis's text), that we as readers complete the cognitive circuit between perception and communication. The difference between a literary and a social experience, already anticipated in the title of Gaddis's first novel (*The Recognitions*), depends on the author's cognitive activity in putting the work together, and the reader's *re-*cognition of this activity. Gaddis has said that his intention in *J R*, and in his third novel, *Carpenter's Gothic*, was for "the characters to create themselves," something that is true of the stage and movies but requires verbal mediation in a novel and requires, again, the imaginative participation of a reader:

> It is the notion that the reader is brought in almost as a collaborator in creating the picture that emerges of the characters, the situation, what they look like, everything. So this authorial absence which everyone from Flaubert to Barthes talks about, is the sense that the book is a collaboration between the reader and what is on the page. ("Art of Fiction" 79-80)

Gaddis, as a composer of narrative elements, remains always at the level of the speech he cites in this book; even the transitional passages that comment on actions and set the stage for spoken discourse remain fixed in the here and now. There is also a certain distance between the narrative voice and the numerous voices of characters, but—again—rather than rising above the characters, Gaddis creates a narrative presence to the side of them, observing their actions and indirectly commenting on what the characters say or do. "Educationwise it isn't hurting us PRwise, I'll say that, Miss Flesch said it. . . . " "Me? Paid to me? No, it was paid for consultation, representation, and what? No, say legal services, rendered by Ganganelli during this legislative session in conjunction with . . .no conjunction, conjunk, junk . . ." (*J R* 28). Next to the first-order (mis)communication among characters, the narrator in *J R* achieves a kind of second-order communication unavailable to the characters—but available to the attentive reader who is willing to enter into this second-order conversation, and able to put together significant connections within the environment of junk language and junk bonds.

The inflection Gaddis gives to so many utterances, however empty they may be in themselves, also bespeaks a generosity of attention reminiscent of, but rather different from, the practice that Steiner notes in Tolstoy of "giving even minor characters proper names and of saying something about the lives they lead outside their brief appearance in the novel," a technique that is simple but "far-reaching" in its effects (101). The practice in Tolstoy reveals a mind incapable of thinking of a character as lifeless; in Gaddis, having a character (Miss Flesch, for example) constantly speak "through bread," might reveal a colder humor in an author's observations, and even a *disbelief* in the character's reality: "Mister Urquhart creeping around picking up napkin wads like something out of Dickens . . . ," is an observation made by one of the novel's main characters, Jack Gibbs (*J R* 118). But nowhere does Gaddis allow himself the direct presentation of a character's subjectivity in language. Authorial commentary in Gaddis, though equally present and pervasive, is always of a *second order*; for this is how an author today, while differing from a Tolstoy or Dickens, can still open up a space within the narrative, on the same plane of immanence inhabited by the characters, for the broad-based social commentary and naturalistic dimensions of a possible epic.

Autopoiesis

In some ways, Luhmann and Gaddis make for an odd pairing. They do share a certain independence of thought and a craggy separation from the discursive communities their work helped to establish (the German social constructivists, the metafictionists in post-World War two America). There is also an intriguing biographical and professional similarity: after the commercial failure of *The Recognitions* and before settling down to work on *J R*, Gaddis worked as a corporate speechwriter. Luhmann also had substantial extra-academic experience: he "was a public administration consultant before he became a sociology professor, and his experience with complex bureaucracies seems to have profoundly shaped his individual offshoot of General Systems Theory [as originally elaborated by the Austrian biologist, Ludwig von Bertalanffy]" (Cramer n.p.). Any order achieved through bureaucratic organization is recognized, by Luhmann and Gaddis, as exceptional rather than normal, a "temporary and contingent crystallization" (Luhmann, "Globalization" n.p.) or "a thin, perilous condition we try to impose on the basic reality of chaos" (*J R* 21). Both the American novelist and the German social theorist experienced chaos, incompetence, corruption, and the apparent bureaucratization of everything at first hand. But whether one responds with Luhmann's equanimity or Gaddis's Protestant resistance is beside the point: what these two unique figures more deeply share is an understanding of the self-exemplifying nature of any imposed order, its autopoietic circularity, which is so fundamental to each writer's thought that—for all their obvious stylistic differences—it shows up in the way they shape their actual sentences and prose structures.

This circularity in phrasing is designed, in Luhmann, to short-circuit paradox and take philosophical discourse past one blind spot to another point of observation (in turn generating new blind spots). Circularity is most noticeable, in Gaddis, as the ordinary mark of a bureaucratic mind: "As a former president of our great nation once observed," says a congressman out of *J R*, "when many people are out of work, unemployment results" ("*J R* Up To Date," *Rush* 63). Oscar, the main character in *A Frolic of His Own*, is both plaintiff and defendant in a lawsuit: he had been run over while trying to start his car, but since liability falls on the owner, not the manufacturer, he is obliged to sue himself. (The car he drives is a Sosumi; his insurance advisor happens to drive an Isuyu.) The examples proliferate, in satirical indictment not of the legal profession alone, but of the more general autopoietic functioning of society's "self-regulating" and functionally differentiated systems: "Legal language," Christina complains to her lawyer husband in *Frolic*,

> I mean who can understand legal language but another lawyer, it's like a, I mean it's all a conspiracy, think about it Harry. It's a conspiracy.
> —Of course it is, I don't have to think about it. Every profession is a conspiracy against the public, every profession protects itself with a language of its own, look at that psychiatrist they're sending me to, ever try to read a balance sheet? Those plumes of the giant bird like the dog cornering his prey till it all evaporates into language confronted by language turning language itself into theory till it's not about what it's about it's only about itself turned into a mere plaything . . . . (251)

Neither conspiracy theory nor postmodern simulation is needed to explain the function of social systems. An awareness of their functional differentiation and their self-regulation is enough to distinguish Gaddis and Luhmann from their novelistic and sociological peers.

The economic roots of this circularity, Luhmann has suggested, are (like legal language) produced by a shift from first-order credit to a second-order system of derivatives that make "speculation" itself the primary object: "The economic system," Luhmann writes in his late essay on "globalization or world society," has shifted its bases of security from property and reliable debtors (such as states or large corporations) to speculation itself: "He who tries to maintain his property will lose his fortune, and he who tries to maintain and increase his wealth will have to change his investments one day to the next" (n.p.). The boy J R, who owns no property and sends in daily change orders from the school pay-phone and, later, through agents working out of rented rooms at the Waldorf Astoria, is thus a much better economic and legal player than Oscar, who remains immobilized in bed and in a wheelchair after his accident, and then at his family property through most of *A Frolic of His Own*. J R, fatherless and never seen at home (where his mother, a nurse, is said to keep irregular hours), is a great example of Zigmunt Bauman's "vagabond" class, striving through economic speculation to become not (like Oscar) a landed and settled owner but a "tourist," imagining himself and his hapless business partner—it is the only fantasy the boy harbors— "you and, and me riding in this here big limousine down, down this, this here big street . . ." (*J R* 637).

Unlike most intellectuals who have developed "their own derivative instruments. . . , describing what others are describing under the common denominator of 'postmodernity,'" Gaddis and Luhmann understand reflexivity as something active, a way of crossing from one side of the system/environment boundary to another, and back. This understanding is unabashedly textualist: their work facilitates second-order observations of a textual object created out of first-order observations of society and direct or indirect citations from other literary texts. Instead of using leftover progressivist vocabularies whose ambition was to define an ideal social order or literary tradition, their work clears discursive and narrative "space in which we can observe the emergence of order and disorder" under conditions that actually exist, through selections and possibilities observed in speech and perceptions (as these have been recorded in the media of our time) (Luhmann, "Globalization" n.p.).

Regarding media not as engines of simulation but as a first-order archive, a living material record of what is being said here, and now, Gaddis and Luhmann underwrite a social aesthetic that is pragmatic, though not necessarily static or conservative. It would be wrong to regard this work's radical realism as an apology for what exists (for example, the current system of global capitalism). "Emergence" is a key term in Luhmann's thought that implies a collaboration or conflict, not always conscious, among various nodes in the networked society. Emergence also comes out of differences between what an author chooses to narrate at the level of text, what the characters do at the level of story, and what the reader makes of these differences. To read a self-reflexive novelist such as Gaddis is not only to follow a text, but at the same time, and in parallel, to follow a story told *by* the text. This is how language can be, in art, not a means of communication; it is rather a "bridge between perception and communication" (Luhmann, *Art* 18). What emerges out of that interpenetration is an understanding that belongs to neither the work nor society, neither to the author nor the reader alone, but to a circulating literary consciousness newly aware of its primary perceptions. For this perceptual consciousness to be communicated, the work itself does not have to be a closed system, operating within a perpetual present from which history, time, and change have been excluded. Insofar as the work is a printed textual object that does not change over time, it may be a closed *structure*. But such a structure only provides materials for a more open readerly system, out of which we create a narrative (in the context of other narratives within a tradition that itself changes: tradition, indeed, could well be the environment that a structurally closed narrative opens onto, where the reader may find resonances, allusions, and repetitions that both join and separate the new work from works in the past). Only at this level of second-order observation, when the reader observes a structure of prior decisions put in place by an author, does the work achieve autopoiesis—that is, structural closure (at the level of perception) and environmental openness (in communication, in textual citation and circulation). And, like the experience of listening to music ("for as long as the music lasts," in a line from T. S. Eliot Gaddis liked to cite), the work is sufficient to itself only so long as we hold the book in hand and its structures in mind.

NOTES

[1] The recent decision of the Library of Congress—a fortunate decision, in my view—to preserve digital texts not in the platform of their first appearance but in "unreadable" zeros and ones so as to be accessible at any time in any format, testifies to the need to separate inscription, what enables the perception of material text, from communication.

[2] See Franco Morretti, *Modern Epic,* and S.J. Rabionowitz, *Novel Epics.*

WORKS CITED

Bakhtin, M.M. *The Dialogic Imagination* [1975]. Austin: U of Texas P, 1981.

Bauman, Zygmunt. *Globalization.* New York: Columbia U P , 2000.

Cramer, Florian. "Niklas Luhmann." <http://www.metamute.com>.

Clarke, Bruce. "Narrative, Systems, and Time." Paper given at the Society for Literature and Science conference, October 2003.

Gaddis, William. *Agapē Agape.* New York: Penguin, 2002.

——. "The Art of Fiction." *The Paris Review* Winter 1997: 55-89.

——. *J R* [1975]. New York: Penguin, 1985.

——. *The Rush for Second Place: Occasional Writings.* New York: Penguin, 2000

——. *A Frolic of His Own.* New York: Scribner, 1994.

Gogol, Nikolai. *Dead Souls* [1842]. New York: Vintage, 1996.

Hardt, Michael, and Antonio Negri. *Empire.* Cambridge: Harvard U P , 2000.

Huizinga, Johan. *Homo Ludens: A Study of the Play Element in Culture* [1938]. English trans. (anonymous) 1949. Boston: Beacon, 1955.

LeClair, Tom. *The Art of Excess: Mastery in Contemporary American Fiction.* Urbana: U of Illinois P, 1989.

Luhmann, Niklas. *Art as a Social System* [1995]. Trans. Eva M. Knodt. Stanford: Stanford U P, 2000.

——."Globalization or World Society." *International Review of Sociology* 7.1, issue 1 (1997): 67-80. Web version at <http://www.libfl.ru/Luhmann/Luhmann2.html>.

Moore, Steven. "[Annotations to] *Agap_ Agape.*" The Gaddis Annotations. <http://www.williamgaddis.org/agape/aanotes.shtml>

Morretti, Franco. *Modern Epic: The World Epic fromGoethe to García Márquez.* London: Verso, 1996.

Rabinowitz, S. J. *Novel Epics.* Evanston: Northwestern U P, 1990.

Steiner, George. *Tolstoy or Dostoevsky* [1959]. New Haven: Yale U P, 1996. <http://www.libfl.ru/Luhmann/Luhmann2.html>

Tanner, Tony. *City of Words: American Fiction, 1950-1970.* London: Jonathan Cape, 1971.

Walter Grünzweig

Science-in-Fiction: Science as Tribal Culture in the Novels of Carl Djerassi

I.

In 2002, the Innsbruck based Haymon Publishing House re-issued the German translations of the first two novels of Carl Djerassi's Science-in-Fiction tetralogy under a new title, *Stammesgeheimnisse* ("Tribal Secrets"). This title was designed to generate new interest in Djerassi's two most successful novels, *Cantor's Dilemma* (1989; German translation 1991) and *Bourbaki's Gambit* (1994; German 1993, one year before the original version in English), which had previously been published in German by another publisher.[1] But the title *Stammesgeheimnisse* also provides an interpretive insight into Carl Djerassi's fictional inquiry into the cultures of modern science, which he deals with in both his novels and his plays. In the preface to this new edition, he refers to scientists, especially those "at the harder edges of chemistry and physics," as "members of a tribal culture, whose idiosyncratic ways of behavior are not only foreign to outsiders but frequently not even recognized by the members of the tribes themselves" (7, my translation). This knowledge is transmitted from teacher to student in the course of a long, traditional relationship likened by Djerassi to an "osmotic process."

Like the many anthropologists who have dealt with tribal cultures in the past two centuries, Djerassi attempts an exploration of the "cultural practices" of this tribe which he terms esoteric. The anthropological approach implied in his fictional proceedings are rather traditional. To describe contemporary Western society, French sociologist Michel Maffesoli has defined a new kind of postmodern tribalism of small, very temporary communities, very unstable tribes, which human beings constantly enter and leave again (Shields *ix-xii*). Djerassi's scientific tribe has little that is postmodern in this sense. At least at the outset it is hermetically sealed off and rather static, thereby resembling traditional tribal definitions. In contradistinction to anthropological methods, however, his method of exploration is fictional, and it is easy to see why. Djerassi was—and in many ways still is—a member of that tribe. Thus, given his own experience in this little known culture, he promises not only an analysis of tribal behavior, but also a revelation of its "secrets." Unlike most anthropologists and ethnographers, for whom a radical distance between their own biographical, social, familial, and educational contexts and their target cultures is a methodological must, Djerassi requires a medium which makes possible a heightened degree of self-reflexivity. Science-in-fiction, Djerassi claims, is autobiography,[2] and it is precisely the lack of self-reflexivity which he criticizes in natural scientists and which led him, in his early sixties, to exchange his laboratory coat for the writer's pen.

What the reader of Djerassi's novels gets is a kind of fictional cultural anthropology, a novelistic, and later drama-based, environment where Djerassi fictionally constructs the very worlds which are at the same time the objects of his literary scrutiny— and all this in one and the same fictional discourse without any formal differentiation between one and the other. From the point of view of modern science, this is not as paradoxical as it may seem, as it acknowledges the fact that researchers are always in some ways not only directly implicated in their research, but that their very scientific intervention actually co-determines the outcome of their investigations. Anthropology, especially, would seem to be amenable to such an approach. We have not only experienced a pervasive "anthropological turn" in literary studies, but also a maybe less vehement "literary turn" in anthropology that acknowledges the narrative and narratological qualities of its research.

It seems justified, therefore, to use the occasion of Carl Djerassi's prominently placed anthropological reference to evaluate his science-in-fiction, and in particular the first of the novels subsumed under the title *Stammesgeheimnisse,* in the context of tribal discourses. I will argue that in this way, he both critiques the culture of the "hard" sciences and opens up a dialogue between the natural sciences and literature (the humanities) as part of his pedagogical attempt to raise the scientific literacy of our society to higher levels.

II.

In Routledge's *Encyclopedia of Social and Cultural Anthropology,* published in 1996, one will not find "tribe," "tribal," or "tribalism" as a main entry. However, the term does appear in the fine-print glossary at the end of the book where it says: "The terms 'tribe' and 'tribal' [. . .] have a variety of meanings, some of which are taboo in modern anthropology" (626).[3] Apart from the fact that I find it amusing, and maybe also an indication of post-modern self-reflexive humor, that an anthropological reference work uses the term "taboo" for the description of its own disciplinary developments, this indication of a forbidden subject strongly points to the significance this category will have for the analysis of Djerassi's works.

Whereas according to the *Encyclopedia,* the category *is* acceptable for the designation of a "political unit larger than a clan and smaller than a nation or people, especially when indigenous populations themselves use the term"—something that clearly has *not* been the case among natural scientists *before* Djerassi—it is "less politically correct in some quarters," and indeed is "generally discouraged" when referring to "aspects of culture other than politics."

It is precisely this taboo territory that Djerassi's science-in-fiction addresses. The lack of political correctness has to do with the evolutionist approaches in anthropology and the attendant value judgments, which would define some forms of social and cultural organization as superior to others, with "tribal" cultures of course occupying a position pretty much at the bottom of the list. Such a value judgment is a result of our white, male, eurocentric, and in any case self-proclaimed position of superiority which must be abolished both for reasons of scientific objectivity and—political correctness.

Djerassi's tribe, however, represents, with some exceptions, a white, predominantly male, and eurocentric group—at least in terms of its rationalist, efficiency-oriented direction which is under scrutiny in his novels. Whereas Marxist anthropologists have described the conception of the "tribe" as a colonialist construct provided by anthropologists to validate and vindicate colonialist exploitation (Ahmed 329), in the case of the tribe called "Natural Science," this critique is turned against itself. The paradoxical situation is that, evolutionarily speaking, the "Natural Sciences" tribe is one of the youngest, and in some way, the most developed. Yet, in spite of this, members of that tribe retain many qualities of the tribes located at the other end of the evolutionary spectrum, in the "infancy" of humanity.

The critical—and ironic, often delightfully comical—potential of Djerassi's novels is located precisely in that seeming paradox. *Cantor's Dilemma,* published in 1989, is still Djerassi's single most famous literary work, and it will be my primary focus in this essay. In the afterword, the author explains that "Science is both a disinterested pursuit of truth and a community, with its own customs, its own social contract" (229). Characterized by rationalism and an emphasis on thinking and logic, scientists should not be expected to display the naiveté of tribal cultures. Yet, in spite of this, and possibly because of it, scientists behave in the "primitive manner" of tribal societies.

But how exactly is the tribal conception used in Djerassi's works and which insight does it provide? In an Americanist context, is it an American tribe? Functionally, how does the interpretation of the culture of the natural sciences as tribal reflect on that area of scientific inquiry? And, finally, can the tribal model, as a sort of annex to the widely branched-out field of literary anthropology, contribute to our understanding of the construction of the sciences in fiction?

III.

There are as many characterizations of what tribal cultures are and represent as there are studies of tribes and cultural anthropologists or ethnographers investigating them. Still, there are *some* constants which recur in most studies no matter in which part of the world they have been undertaken. In addition to summary expositions of the subject, my conceptional sources are "traditional" studies such as those of African and Australasian cultures.[4] Also, I have consulted a very helpful recent investigation of the patriarchal family of the Balkans, especially Albania, the Kosovo, Macedonia, and various regions of Serbia (Kaser).[5]

As an overall conception, the comparison seems faulty at first, because tribes lived or live in relatively self-sufficient isolation. Scientists, on the other hand, are part of a society with an extremely high division of labor and thus closely interlock with all other parts of the social system. Given their central position for society, one would expect their location in it to be similarly in the middle. However, it is not. In Djerassi's novels, especially in *Cantor's Dilemma*, natural scientists live far away from the "real world," with which they have an uneasy relationship. When central protagonist Professor Isidore Cantor, in short I.C., wants to have something of a private life every few weeks, he drives hours from his large midwestern university to Chicago, where he owns a fancy condominium with a magnificent view. There, the internationally famous organic chemist turned cell biologist meets up with three friends and they engage in something like *Hausmusik*. But neither his graduate students nor his colleagues know anything about his private life—it took years until his favorite graduate student finally set foot into the door of Cantor's private home—and such a private life barely exists for this workaholic, at least until he meets the sophisticated woman of his dreams.

Another basic question which would have to be asked at the outset is whether scientists all belong to one tribe or whether there are different tribes competing with each other. The answer to this question is uncertain, in part because of the different definitions of tribes, in part because of the uncertainties written into Djerassi's texts. To the extent that they share similar myths, also myths of origin, which are central to anthropological definitions of tribes, they are members of one and the same tribe. To the degree that a tribe is defined territorially, they would, given their different disciplines and their different geographical locations, be members of different, competing, albeit also in some ways related, tribes.

Because these are fictional works playing with these concepts, it is advisable not to be overly narrow in the comparison between tribal existence and scientists' lives, nor to place too much emphasis on anthropological consistency. It is not critical that the "Natural Science" tribe meet all characteristics traditionally ascribed to tribes by anthropologists. It is much more important to explore the different, at times contradictory, models of tribal behavior among Djerassi's scientists. The brutal competition among scientists, for example, could be either interpreted as intratribal feuds or intertribal warfare. In their rites, certainly, they seem all very similar, thus appearing to be members of one tribe, or at least of several closely related tribes.

Territoriality, a central concept in the definition of tribes, is in two ways an important aspect also of the tribal quality of Djerassi's scientists. It is, of course, not the territoriality of modern statehood, but, rather, territory directly connected to the working environment. Although Harvard is referred to as an Empire in *Cantor's Dilemma*, it is really much more a tribal territory with a chief, the "big man," in Cantor's line of research. The novel mentions quite a few other tribal territories, located mostly on the East or the West Coast, but also, like Cantor's, in the Midwest. Loyalty is clearly owed, though by no means always paid, to one's territorially defined tribe. When Jeremy Stafford, Cantor's student, decides to change sides and moves from the Midwest to Harvard, his boss considers this treason and lack of solidarity, which are unacceptable in any tribal society. Among Djerassi's tribes, one can be accused of tribal infidelity for much smaller infractions. Earlier in the novel, even a visit to Jeremy's supposedly sick grandfather has Cantor complain: "'Where's the man's loyalty,' he grumbled, to his grandfather or to the lab?" (86).

The second, and more important, version of territoriality, is the field itself, which is defined, measured, defended, and contested. More than even geographical territoriality and in many ways interlocked with it, it defines tribal limits. Interdisciplinarity, then, can be either viewed as large-scale tribal feuding or as inter-tribal alliances designed to bring about something new— such as the cooperation between four elder scientists from different fields in *The Bourbaki Gambit,* which brings about PCR (polymerase chain reaction), a collaboration which ends in great difficulties because of disciplinary differences and an overly competitive spirit.

The territoriality principle in tribal life is counteracted by another principle central to tribal organization, namely the taboo of inbreeding. In traditional tribal society, this obviously does not apply to the tribe as a whole, but to smaller segments such as families. There are very complex systems designed to avoid incest, and in some ways, scientists, especially in their formative years, follow that pattern. The move from one institution to the next results in a productive intellectual mix, which helps to avoid the negative effects of an inbred research community. That, in *Cantor's Dilemma,* seems to be the main task of the large state universities and other second-rank institutions—namely to provide new blood for the institutions of, as it says several times in that book, the academic superstars. Tribal researchers have pointed to exogamy as a strategy to enlarge one's network of relatives, and thus one's power. In *Cantor's Dilemma*, it says explicitly that one reason for moving from one territory to the next is to establish an "old boy's network" of mentors who will be supportive in one's career.

Tribal research consistently points to the question of lineage in tribal society, i.e., a generally believed myth of descendance from a particular mythical forefather. Natural scientists form such a lineage, which is important for their identity. Carl Djerassi's novels and plays are replete with references to the history of science(s). Even in his own autobiographies, Djerassi always explains his most important achievements in terms of the tradition in which they stand.[6] In his play *Oxygen* (2001), he introduces the idea of a "retro" Nobel prize in order to celebrate scientists' past achievement. In *Cantor's Dilemma*, problems or questions are frequently solved by consulting predecessors: "[. . .] in preparation for their trip to Stockholm, many Nobel laureates have studied the records of their predecessors: what words they voiced here; what their experiences were in subsequent years" (189).

In most cases, lineage implies a patriarchical system of society, with the present chief claiming identity with, or at least proximity to, the mythical forefather. Patriarchal, Djerassi's scientific tribe certainly is, though increasingly challenged by energetic young females, who, however, are forced to adapt to the prevalent models of behavior and relationship. The novel speaks of "scientific machismo" (86), and this manifests itself nowhere more clearly than in the relationship between mentor and young researcher. The "picking of a Ph.D. mentor is probably the single most important decision they [graduate students] make when they start their graduate work. It's really like an orphan picking a new father" (24). However, the *mentor* resembles more a godfather, whose function, according to tribal researchers, is to enter into a mental, or even intellectual, relationship with his godchild.

Trust and cooperation between mentor and Ph.D. student are a central characteristic of Djerassi's scientific tribes. The favorite—often said to be the most intelligent or advanced—student carries an especially large burden. If that relationship, as in the case of Cantor and Stafford, is uneasy or even disturbed, the life of the tribe is in danger. The man on top is then unable to operate effectively; scientific development comes to a standstill.

Djerassi's fiction is justly famous for a number of female researchers and scientists who are true role models for their peers in the extrafictional terrain. In volume four of the trilogy, *NO* (1998), a woman from India is introduced who makes it in the American corporate as well as scientific world. Yet, these advances are only successful if women are willing to become members of the tribe on its terms. Ethnographic research has shown that under certain conditions it is possible to *join* tribes, but the requirements for acceptance are often complex and intense.

In *Cantor's Dilemma*, the best example is one Celestine Price, who seems to have almost been born a control freak. When she decides that it is time to lose her virginity, she throws a towel at her swimming team trainer and commands him to lay her. Whether she is conscious of it or not, she picks her males according to her academic and career needs, getting, as her housemate, a deconstructionist graduate student of English, observes, "access to [a man's] knowledge through [her] sexuality" (119).

Just as among her successful male counterparts, the sciences determine Celestine's behavior; in fact, it can hardly be separated from them. For her, sex is at times "an experiment rather than a romantic interlude," and it is maybe not surprising, that, as a record of that experiment, she has learned to become a verbal lover who insists on an oral protocol of the act. Her rigidity in choosing sex life and partners is astounding. She is not alone: many characters in Djerassi's books find that the combination of sex and the lab, sex in science, is irresistible, and the connection of work and sexuality is often made explicit.

Sex is not restricted by many taboos in this tribe, although the central character of *Cantor's Dilemma*, Isidore Cantor, has been sexually abstinent for over a decade. Another professor's habit of not pursuing his female students until he has handed in their grades and not before they have turned 21 has a legalistic connotation, though it reminds one of initiation ceremonies. But the real rituals take place in the lab, in the lecture hall, and at conferences. A pervasively oral culture rules life in these territories. Even though one would think that in the natural sciences it is not important *how* a message is delivered but *what* is said, the results, the polished rhetoric, and the etiquette-ridden way of asking and answering questions are obviously of prime importance for success or failure. In Kurt Krauss's famed noon seminars at Harvard, successful presenting is at least as important as the scientific argument. Other examples of oral communication also abound: there are "rumors" (5) emerging from the lab, and, altogether, a "lore" (10) develops which goes far beyond the individual members of research groups of graduate students and attaches itself to a particular chairholder or even the chair itself.

In *Cantor's Dilemma,* this hierarchy is prominently reflected in the question of the order of the authors. Should all authors of a research group be listed alphabetically, or should the tribal chief always receive first place? One clever female professor, realizing that she will not have much of a chance with a name like Yardley, starting with a "Y," goes to the court house, pays a small fee, and becomes "Ardley," thus putting herself into academic pole position. It is the Ph.D. student in English literature, an ardent Bakhtinian and deconstructionist and obviously member of a *very* different tribe of scientists, who gets to ask Prof. Ardley why a professor, not having done any of the lab work, should be listed on the publications of their staff at all? Whereas the deconstructionist argues in political terms, the natural science establishment defends itself in tribal language, namely that it is a group effort and that all members of a team deserve to be on it. Implicitly, of course, the point is that the head of the tribe is responsible for what is going on in his group and, logically, shares in all its achievements.

Djerassi's natural scientists are a very American tribe, but it seems as though their American tribal origins have been expanded to all members of that tribe globally or that they exist independently of their American existence. Thus, the pervasive competitiveness rules not only the lives of American scientists but of scientists world-wide. One of Djerassi's most important conceptions, discussed in virtually all of his novels and plays, is *priority.* By this is meant scientists' peculiar preoccupation with making a particular discovery first. If one researcher makes a discovery but is only one day later in the publication of his results than his colleague who has happened to have the same insight, years of work will be useless. Even simultaneous discovery, should it occur and be established as such, will take away much of the researcher's triumph. This explains the aura of secrecy which surrounds the labs in Djerassi's novels and the long discussions over how, where, and when to publish particular findings. Whereas this competitiveness may strike us as very American, it is, of course, also part of the tradition of tribal feuds. It is interesting that in spite of the intensity of these feuds, also in Djerassi's novels, there is a sense of egalitarianism between the different segments of the one tribe or between the different tribes, however one wants to interpret Djerassi's scientists. The various groups around the country, which are very similarly structured, accept each other. It is a kind of competitive collegiality with an awareness that all parts of the system need each other. Paradoxically, the striving for hegemony does not invalidate this egalitarianism.

Although success manifests itself in original discoveries and publications, the ultimate dream of any natural scientist in Djerassi's tribal world is the Nobel Prize. *Nobel lust* is the main subject of *Cantor's Dilemma,* and no scientist is immune to it. The recognition *it* provides, nationally and internationally, the rites one goes through when receiving it in Stockholm, are the supreme fantasies in the life of a scientist. It is not the considerable sum of money connected with the prize that these scientists are after. It is the distinction—and the Nobel lecture the prize winner gets to give—which is important, because it will make a scientist immortal. It is easy to see that through the Nobel distinction, scientists are able to partake in the defining myth of their tribe and are raised to the status of those who give meaning and significance to it.

A prerequisite for a smooth functioning of tribal life as I have described it so far is trust. It is a concept which goes beyond the solidarity and loyalty often reported as characteristic of tribal life, and yet it is the central characteristic of Djerassi's tribe. In order for scientists to succeed, they must be able to trust each others' results and research methods. However, this ability to depend on the results of a scientist colleague is threatened by the very human qualities of the researcher. Cantor himself points to a "dissociative" personality of scientists:

> [. . .] on one side, the rigorous believer in the experimental method, with its set of rules and its ultimate objective of advancing knowledge; on the other, the fallible human being with all the accompanying emotional foibles. [. . .] A scientist's drive, his self-esteem, are really based on a very simple desire: recognition by one's peers, the Krausses of this world. (113)

Cantor here points to a basic incompatibility, which is potentially destructive for the whole life of the tribe. Cantor's grand design for a model explaining the formation of tumors, an "intellectual tour de force," as the novel repeatedly says, is threatened by the sloppiness of his favorite student, Stafford, in executing the experiment that would prove the theory. His own credibility is threatened, exposing himself to *Schadenfreude*, as it says in the English text, the gloating over the failure of other less successful scientists. Instead of breaking the vicious circle and talking to Stafford about his failings, Cantor now starts hiding things from him, thereby expressing his own distrust in his collaborator—who, in turn, hurt by this lack of trust and recognition of his mentor, takes his leave and starts to work for the competition.

Even though the novel goes further than that—Harvard chief Kurt Krauss, the villain of the book, even dares to blackmail Cantor—the novel basically deals with such "gray issues" (229) of science. In the afterword, Djerassi asks what "harm is caused to its [the natural scientists'] culture when the elite displays such occupational deviance" (229). Even though he does not provide an explicit answer there, I believe the text itself, as well as his other texts, provides it.

Finally, to this list of tribal characteristics with predominantly negative implications, a positive dimension of the metaphor should be added. For certain schools of postcolonial thinking, tribes have positive connotations because they are largely or even completely independent from the centralized state and its government and live a self-sufficient, self-sustainable life style. Both of these aspects form a positive counterargument to the charge of isolationism. When scientists link up politically in a peace organization in order to bring about disarmament and global peace, as presented in volume 3 of the series, *Menachem's Seed* (1997), or when they collaborate clandestinely against senseless bureaucratic rules, such as the age limits for professors, there is a positive sense of networking against centralist administrative coercion, which is rather hopeful.

IV.

More importantly even than an understanding of the specific ritual, mythical, or sexual characteristics of the Scientists' tribe, Djerassi's anthropological fiction presents the world of natural scientists as constituting a specific culture of its own. Thus, the project of the natural sciences, which is often said to be constituted by objectivity and rationality and thus set into opposition with the humanities, is rendered as relative, preliminary, ritualistic. The rhetoric of necessity, of *Sachlogik* and *Sachzwang,* is subverted and replaced by a relativistic perspective, where different discourses compete with each other.

This does not mean that the "pursuit of truth," the ideal of objectivity in the natural sciences, is destroyed. We do not get a characterization of science as a version of magic in the sense of Lévi-Strauss, who has pointed to the role magic has played in the progress of science. We also do not get the feminist, "deep-ecologist" criticism of science as a version of an unacknowledged, repressive myth.[7] Instead of setting the natural sciences *against* a world of "soft" cultural relativity, it dissolves the false dichotomy of culture and (natural) science by showing the latter's *own* cultural quality. By integrating, or rather re-integrating, scientists into the scientific project, rather than abstracting from them, the sciences can be evaluated on a new cultural level.

Of course there have been many novels and plays about the ethical responsibility of scientists for what they are doing. They, too, have included the scientist into the context of his work. In *Menachem's Seed*, a number of scientists, including nuclear scientists, are shown as participating in what amounts to the fictional version of a Pugwash meeting, and they display precisely that spirit of responsibility and concern.

However, what we get through Djerassi's anthropological perspective on natural scientists is something else; namely, a look at the individuals in their own working environment and *together with* their working environment. It is, after all, science-in-fiction and not only scientists in fiction, and that permits us to view the interaction between the two.

The point is not so much that the scientists in Djerassi's novels are less than pleasant. Of course, they are oftentimes disgusting. Their sexist, authoritarian, often slave driver-like behavior, their clumsy ways, their success-driven obsessions, their inability to talk to each other, and their tendency to hide behind ritualistic forms—all of that makes them frequently very unpleasant characters. But then, so are most other characters, in a variety of similar, but also different, ways. What is remarkable is that

Djerassi's fiction places the scientists, who are oftentimes considered to exist outside of society, squarely in it. They, just like everybody else, have a specific culture, a specific way of relating, specific modes of behavior, which can be compared to those of everybody else. Paradoxically, by pointing to lovable or less lovable cultural specifics, Djerassi is destroying the myth of the exotic otherness of scientists and also the isolation his characters find themselves in.

The breakthrough which some of his scientists make towards members of other tribes—such as artists, historians, or business people and, the male ones among them, towards smart and sexy women—suggests that. But even if they do not connect to the outside world, the anthropological look at scientists as tribal establishes a communicative avenue between scientists and non-scientists. In this way, his promise of a dialogue (dialogue for Djerassi being central to literature as opposed to the monological sciences)[8] between the two cultures is fulfilled, at least incipiently. Unlike C.P. Snow's two cultures, which remain strangely separate and isolated from each other and whose breach can only be bridged by knowledge, Djerassi's science-in-fiction *has* opened up a dialogue between the cultures and between the texts and their readers. In view of the prominence of that dialogue, which we find repeated in his other novels in many different ways, it is not surprising that Djerassi has switched to theater as an even more congenial genre for communication.

Unlike Carl Djerassi, who insists on the critical significance of the scientific knowledge imparted by his novels, I believe strongly that one can understand and appreciate his work also without a profound knowledge of the scientific principles involved. This does not belittle his pedagogical abilities in explaining processes in the natural science, but they may, unfortunately, be lost on some readers. A strong focus should be placed on the qualities in his fiction which facilitate communication and which go beyond the pedagogical impetus. It is there, where Djerassi's greatness lies.

Carl Djerassi's literary works have opened up an avenue towards an understanding of the cultural basis, and thus also relativity, of the natural sciences and, in part, also of the technical sciences. The existence of such a specific culture is often not recognized or acknowledged by scientists themselves. One next step might be to investigate more closely whether these cultures are diversified nationally and ethnically. In many ways, the members of Djerassi's science tribe are international and universalized, part, not of a *Gelehrtenrepublik*, but of a *Gelehrtenstamm*. But could it not be that these cultures are different according to national and ethnic origin? This might explode the tribal metaphor—but certainly not Carl Djerassi's achievement of having formulated these questions.

NOTES

[1] Carl Djerassi, *Stammesgeheimnisse: Zwei Romane aus der Welt der Wissenschaft* (Innsbruck: Haymon, 2002).

[2] See Carl Djerassi, *"Science-in-Fiction ist nicht Science Fiction: Ist sie Autobiographie?"*

[3] For a summary of the anthropological discussion of the tribal concept, see also Morton H. Fried, *The Notion of Tribe*.

[4] See, for example, Gluckman.

[5] For an example of making metaphorical use of the tribal model, see Brandes, et al, the edited proceedings of a conference highlighting the parallels between business/entrepreneurial/company cultures and tribal culture.

[6] Especially in *This Man's Pill: Reflections on the 50th Birthday of the Pill*.

[7] See Ruether, especially the first two chapters.

[8] See Djerassi, *The Pill, Pygmy Chimps, and Degas' Horse*, 107.

WORKS CITED

Ahmed, Abdel Ghaffar M. "'Tribal' Elite: A Base for Social Stratification in the Sudan." *Toward a Marxist Anthropology: Problems and Perspectives*. Ed. Stanley Diamond. The Hague, Paris, New York: Mouton, 1979.

Brandes, Uta. Richard Bachinger, Michael Erdhoff, eds. *Unternehmenskultur und Stammeskultur. Metaphysische Aspekte des Kalküls*. Frankfurt/M.: Georg Büchner, 1988.

Djerassi, Carl. *Cantor's Dilemma: A Novel*. New York: Penguin, 1991.

——. *The Pill, Pygmy Chimps, and Degas' Horse: The Autobiography of Carl Djerassi*. New York: BasicBooks, 1992.

——. *"Science-in-Fiction ist nicht Science Fiction: Ist sie Autobiographie?"* *Science in Fiction: Zum Gespräch zwischen Literatur und Kunst*. Ed. Wendelin Schmidt-Dengler. Wien: Hölder–Pichler–Tempsky, 1998. 71-104.

——. *This Man's Pill: Reflections on the 50th Birthday of the Pill*. Oxford & New York: Oxford UP, 2001.

——. *Stammesgeheimnisse: Zwei Romane aus der Welt der Wissenschaft*. Innsbruck: Haymon, 2002.

Fried, Morton H. *The Notion of Tribe*. Menlo Park: Cummings, 1975.

Gluckman, Max. *Politics, Law and Ritual in Tribal Societies*. Chicago: Aldine, 1965.

Kaser, Karl. *Familie und Verwandtschaft auf dem Balkan: Analyse einer untergehenden Kultur*. Wien, Köln, Weimar: Böhlau, 1995.

Ruether, Rosemary Radford. *Gaia and God: An Ecofeminist Theology of Earth Healing*. New York City: HarperCollins, 1992.

Shields, Rob. "Foreword: Masses or Tribes." Michel Maffesoli. *The Time of the Tribes: The Decline of Individualism in Mass Spcieties*. Trans. Don Smith. London, Thousand Oaks, New Delhi: Sage, 1996.

"Tribe, tribal." *Encyclopedia of Social and Cultural Anthropology*. London & New York: Routledge, 1996. 626.

Carl Djerassi
Science-in-Fiction: Literary Contraband?

As the only working scientist as well as one of the few novelists at this conference on "Science, Technology, and the Humanities in recent American Fiction"—surrounded by speakers from literary academe, some of whose discourse and even titles I find barely comprehensible—I shall allow myself some liberties. In contrast to most of the other speakers, who critique, admire, re-interpret, or just deconstruct *other* author's works, I shall shamelessly discuss only my own and do so in non-academic prose. I can indulge in that luxury, because I am about to have the unusual experience to be followed by a speaker[1] who will discuss my own literary work from a professional academic standpoint. And since he will dwell mostly on my "science-in-fiction" tetralogy and autobiographical writing, I shall focus on my use of "science-in-theatre" plays where I illuminate important aspects of science or scientific behavior. But is "science-in-theatre" literature in the *literal* sense? To be *read* rather than just *seen* on the stage? Much of what follows will illustrate my belief that this is so.

But first what was the reason why I decided at age 63 to write fiction and now plays? Because I wanted to contribute beyond PUS ("public understanding of science") and PEST ("public engagement in science and technology") to PUSH ("public understanding of science and humanities") by using the tools of the humanist rather than the scientist to illuminate the latter's culture for a broader audience. If one actually wants to use fiction to smuggle scientific facts into the consciousness of a scientifically illiterate public—and I do think that such smuggling is intellectually and societally beneficial—then it is crucial that the facts behind that science be described correctly. But I am more ambitious than just wanting to describe in an entertaining but obsessively accurate way *what* scientific research we scientists perform. Good science journalists can also play that role and frequently perform it very well. But to even attempt bridging C.P. Snow's two-culture gap, which has widened enormously since he first raised that contentious issue, it is also necessary to illustrate *how* scientists behave. And it is here that a scientist-turned-author can play a particularly important role—a point that I expect will be made in the next talk by Walter Grünzweig. So let me immediately jump to "science-in-theatre."

By "science-in-theatre" I refer to plays in which science and scientists do not fulfill primarily a metaphoric function—praiseworthy and attractive as such efforts have been in major plays like Brecht's *Life of Galileo*, Stoppard's *Arcadia* and *Hapgood,* or Dürrenmatt's *The Physicists*—but rather constitute the central focus of the play, as for instance in Frayn's *Copenhagen*. My personal definition of "science-in-theatre" is even more restricted in requiring also that the science depicted is real or at least plausible, and that the behavior of my scientific characters is authentic in the sense of documenting their tribal behavior and not just picture them as Frankensteins, Strangeloves, or nerds. Indeed, these same self-imposed restrictions pertain also to the form of literary prose writing in which I have indulged during the past 15 years in a tetralogy of novels[2] that I have categorized generically as "science-in-fiction" to differentiate it from the much more widely practiced genre of science fiction. For me, a novel can only be anointed as "science-in-fiction" if all the science or idiosyncratic behavior of scientists described in it is plausible, if not actually factual. None of these restrictions apply to science fiction, which is not meant as criticism, but simply as a statement of fact.

So is "science-in-theatre" simply "science-in-fiction" presented on the stage rather than within the covers of a book? I prefer to claim that there is more to it. Since the beginning of the Age of Enlightenment, dialog has essentially disappeared from the *written* discourse of scientists. Yet dialog humanizes discourse in an important sense, and since my objective as a scientist-author is to depict the human foibles and virtues of my tribe's culture, I have turned in my recent writing to the most dialogic form of literature, namely drama.

And while I clearly wish my plays to be seen on the stage, even the most popular plays are only performed occasionally and only in a few locations at any one time. But I believe that my type of "science-in-theatre" can also be read on its own merits as a tale of science and scientists, which just happens to be presented entirely in dialogic form. My first two "science-in-theatre" plays, *An Immaculate Misconception* and *Oxygen* (the latter written jointly with Roald Hoffmann), have each been translated into eight languages and published in book form in six of them. Clearly, they are widely read—be it for pleasure or for instruction—and I hope that the same fate will also apply to my third one, *Calculus*, which has been published in English and German within months of its theatrical premiere in April 2003.

An Immaculate Misconception—as the subtitle "sex in an age of mechanical reproduction" implies—deals with a scientific discovery that is revolutionizing the nature of human reproduction. It does so through the use of a new and contentious technique of assisted reproduction (ICSI = intracytoplasmic sperm injection) that promises to push to the limits the consequences of the impending separation of sex ("in bed") and fertilization ("under the microscope")—easily one of the most momentous prospects for the twenty-first century. In the process of reading or observing my play, a person is bound to appreciate both the societal and technical aspects of this new IVF technique as illustrated by the following abbreviated excerpts from Scenes 2 and 5.

Excerpt from Scene 2:
> *MELANIE: If your patients knew what I was up to in here . . . they'd be breaking down my door. Men with low sperm counts that can never become biological fathers in the usual way.*
> *FELIX: My patients just want to fertilize an egg. They won't care if it's under a microscope or in bed . . . as long as it's their own sperm.*
> *MELANIE: You're focusing on male infertility . . . that's your business. But do you realize what this will mean for women?*
> *FELIX: Of course! I treat male infertility to get women pregnant.*
> *MELANIE: Felix, you haven't changed. You're a first-class doctor . . . but I see further than you. ICSI*

could become an answer to overcoming the biological clock. And if that works, it will affect many more women than there are infertile men. (Grins). I'll even become famous.

FELIX: *Sure . . . you'll be famous . . . world-famous . . . if that first ICSI fertilization is successful . . . and if a normal baby is born. But what's that got to do with (slightly sarcastic) "the biological clock?"*

MELANIE: *Felix, in your IVF practice, it's not uncommon to freeze embryos for months and years before implanting them into a woman. Now take frozen eggs.*

FELIX: *I know all about frozen eggs. . . . When you rethaw them, artificial insemination hardly ever works. . . . Do you want to hear the reasons for those failures?*

MELANIE: *Who cares? What I'm doing isn't ordinary artificial insemination . . . exposing the egg to lots of sperm and then letting them struggle on their own through the egg's natural barrier. We inject right into the egg. . . . Now, if ICSI works in humans . . . think of those women – right now, mostly professional ones—who postpone childbearing to their late thirties or even early forties. By then, the quality of their eggs . . . their own eggs . . . is not what it was when they were ten years younger. But with ICSI, such women could draw on a bank account of their frozen young eggs and have a much better chance of having a normal pregnancy later on in life. I'm not talking about surrogate eggs—*

FELIX: *Later in life? Near or even past the menopause?*

MELANIE: *You convert men in their fifties into successful donors—*

FELIX: *Then why not women? Are you serious?*

MELANIE: *I see no reason why women shouldn't have that option . . . at least under some circumstances.*

FELIX: *Well—If that works . . . you won't just become famous . . . you'll be notorious.*

MELANIE: *Think beyond that . . . to a wider vision of ICSI. I'm sure the day will come – maybe in another thirty years or even earlier—when sex and fertilization will be separate. Sex will be for love or lust—*

FELIX: *And reproduction under the microscope?*

MELANIE: *And why not?*

FELIX: *Reducing men to providers of a single sperm?*

MELANIE: *What's wrong with that . . . emphasizing quality rather than quantity? I'm not talking of test tube babies or genetic manipulation. And I'm certainly not promoting ovarian promiscuity, trying different men's sperm for each egg.*

FELIX: *"Ovarian promiscuity!" That's a new one. But then what?*

MELANIE: *Each embryo will be screened genetically before the best one is transferred back into the woman's uterus. All we'll be doing is improving the odds over Nature's roll of the dice. Before you know it, the 21st century will be called "The Century of Art."*

FELIX: *Not science? Or technology?*

MELANIE: *The science of . . . A . . . R . . . T (Pause): assisted reproductive technologies. Young men and women will open reproductive bank accounts full of frozen sperm and eggs. And when they want a baby, they'll go to the bank to check out what they need.*

FELIX: *And once they have such a bank account . . . get sterilized?*

MELANIE: *Exactly. If my prediction is on target, contraception will become superfluous.*

FELIX (Ironic): *I see. And the pill will end up in a museum . . . of 20th century ART?*

MELANIE: *Of course it won't happen overnight. . . . But A . . . R . . . T is pushing us that way . . . and I'm not saying it's all for the good. It will first happen among the most affluent people . . . and certainly not all over the world. At the outset, I suspect it will be right here . . . in the States . . . and especially in California.*

FELIX (Shakes head): *The Laidlaw Brave New World. Before you know it, single women in that world may well be tempted to use ICSI to become the Amazons of the 21st century.*

MELANIE: *Forget about the Amazons! Instead, think of women who haven't found the right part-*

ner . . . or had been stuck with a lousy guy . . . or women who just want a child before it's too late . . . in other words, Felix, think of women like me.

Excerpt from Scene 5:

MELANIE (Puts on rubber gloves): Would you start the VCR?

FELIX: Sure. (Pushes the button and turns toward the monitor so that only part of his face is seen. Both are completely silent as the screen lights up. MELANIE is hunched over the microscope, both hands manipulating the joysticks on each side of the microscope. She sits so as to be able to coordinate her words to action on the screen). Ah . . . here we are.

MELANIE (As a single active sperm appears at bottom of image, excitedly interrupts): Okay . . . let's see whether I can catch it with this capillary, one-tenth as thick as a human hair. But first I've got to crush its tail so the sperm can't get away. . . . (Quickly moves pipette toward sperm and sounds jubilant as the injection pipette crushes the sperm's tail) Gotcha!

FELIX: Not bad. Not bad at all.

MELANIE: Now comes the tricky part. I've got to aspirate it tail first. . . . As soon as I get close enough, just a little suction will do the trick. . . . Hah! Gotcha! (Screen image displays the sperm, tail first, being sucked into the pipette. Image now shows MELANIE "playing" the sperm's head by moving it back and forward to demonstrate that she can manipulate it easily).

FELIX: Quit playing with him!

MELANIE: I'm not playing with it. I just want to be sure that I can manipulate it at will. And why do you always call sperm "him"? Is it because the sex of a baby is always determined by the sperm? (Silence for a few seconds.) Here we are. (Image of egg appears). Isn't she a beauty? Just look at her . . . here you are my precious baby . . . now stay still while I arrange you a bit . . . while I clasp you on my suction pipette . . . polar body on top. . . . like a little head. I want it in the 12 o'clock position. (Egg on screen is now immobilized in precisely the desired position for the penetration). Felix, now cross your fingers. (He leans forward, clearly fascinated. Injection pipette containing sperm appears on image but pipette remains immobile.)

FELIX (Points to pipette on extreme right of image): What's the problem? It isn't usually that difficult.

MELANIE: No . . . but to do it with this sperm into . . . this . . . (does not finish the sentence as pipette penetrates the egg. MELANIE lets out audible gasp of relief).

FELIX (Makes sudden start, as if he had been pricked): My God! You did it! Beautiful penetration! (Image shows pipette resting within egg). Now shoot him out! (Points to sperm head in pipette)

MELANIE: Here we go. (Image shows sperm head at the very end of the injection pipette. She aspirates it back and gives it a second push). Ah, that's a good boy. (Carefully withdraws pipette without apparent damage to the egg).

FELIX: You did it! Look at him, just look at him! Sitting in there. (Approaches image and points to sperm head on screen. Calmer voice). It's amazing. That egg looks . . . what shall I say? . . . inviolate, almost virginal.

MELANIE (Looks up for first time from microscope): It better not be . . . (Mimics his voice with a slightly sarcastic edge) "inviolate", to use your precious term . . . I violated it very consciously and tomorrow, I want to see cell division . . . Felix (points to VCR), press the pause button, will you? (He does and image of fertilized egg remains frozen on screen in full view).

FELIX: So who is the father?

MELANIE: There isn't any father in the usual sense of the word.

FELIX (Ironic): An immaculate conception?

MELANIE: You know, in a way that's true. There was no penetration of the woman, no sexual contact. In fact, at that moment, there was no woman, no vagina . . . nor a man (pause). . . . The only prick (pause) . . . was the gentle one by a tiny needle entering an egg in a dish, delivering a single sperm. (Laughs).

Even that prick was provided by a woman. That process means nothing until the egg is implanted into the woman.
FELIX: And who is this woman? Whose eggs were you injecting?
MELANIE: Mine!

In the play, the entire procedure is also shown visually on a screen, but even the words without image make the technical aspects of ICSI clear as was demonstrated by a radio version of this play broadcast by the BBC on the World Service.

Just as I tried in my first play to hide my didactic motivations behind the scrim of sex, in the second play, *Oxygen,* Hoffmann and I did this by taking up a theme—the Nobel Prize—that, at least to scientists, is potentially also sexy. The year 2001 was the centenary of the Nobel Prize. In *Oxygen*, the Nobel Foundation decides to celebrate the centenary by establishing a new Nobel Prize, a "retro-Nobel," to honor discoveries made before 1901, the year when the first Nobel Prize was awarded. For a change, why not pay attention to the dead?

Our play attempts to deal with two fundamental questions: what is discovery in science and why is it so important for a scientist to be first? In *Oxygen*, we approach these questions as our imaginary retro-Nobel Committee meets in 2001 to select, first, the discovery that should be so honored (they settle on the discovery of oxygen, which led to the chemical revolution), and then—as it turns out, not a straightforward question—which scientist to credit for it. Throughout the play, as the retro-Nobel Committee debates its selection, the audience learns about the three leading candidates through their wives in a trialogue that occurs in a Swedish sauna in 1777 just prior to a royal adjudication concerning the respective claims of their husbands: the Swedish apothecary Carl Wilhelm Scheele, who made oxygen first; the English minister-turned-chemist, Joseph Priestley, who published first; and the French chemist, tax collector, economist, and public servant, Antoine Laurent Lavoisier, who understood first the revolutionary implications of this gas's existence. In switching back and forth between 2001 and 1777, not unlike the time shifts in Stoppard's *Arcadia*, we present the historical and personal record that leads the Nobel Committee to its final conclusion. Here is an excerpt from a 1777 scene in which the three scientists confront each other at the royal adjudication convened by King Gustav III.

SCHEELE: "Resolve the question: Who made fire air first?" That was His Majesty's command.
LAVOISIER: Is that the real question?
PRIESTLEY: Of course. And you, Monsieur . . . did not make that air first . . . as you yourself in effect conceded yesterday.
LAVOISIER: I understood it first . . .
SCHEELE: Understanding only comes after existence!
PRIESTLEY: But proof of such existence must be shared!
SCHEELE: I shared it! Here is the letter . . . dispatched to you almost three years ago. Describing work done earlier still.
LAVOISIER: I never heard about that letter until today . . .

SCHEELE: *It describes the preparation of fire air . . .*

LAVOISIER: *No such letter ever reached me.*

SCHEELE: *A recipe you reproduced in front of all of us today.*

LAVOISIER: *But certainly not years ago as you now claim. (Impatient). What is the real purpose of this meeting?*

PRIESTLEY: *Priority! In August 1774 I made dephlogisticated air . . . your (exaggerated French pronunciation) oxygène . . . at Bowood House . . . my patron's estate!*

LAVOISIER: *Then you thought you had nitrous air, sir.*

PRIESTLEY: *The first steps of discovery are often tentative.*

LAVOISIER: *Some of us are more careful than others.*

PRIESTLEY: *In October of that year, I met the leading chemists of France (Pause) . . . including you, Sir.*

LAVOISIER: *Indeed, you dined in my house in Paris.*

PRIESTLEY: *I told the gathering . . .*

LAVOISIER: *in your imperfect French . . .*

PRIESTLEY: *. . . which Madame Lavoisier comprehended fully . . . of my discovery.*

LAVOISIER: *Your report lacked clarity. Your methods were imprecise . . .*

PRIESTLEY: *Sir, your words are unworthy.*

LAVOISIER: *At best, you, Dr. Priestley, supplied us with the smallest of clues . . .*

PRIESTLEY: *I thought details mattered to you, sir.*

LAVOISIER: *Only if they are relevant.*

PRIESTLEY: *More than once, my experiments in pneumatic chemistry were cited by you—*

LAVOISIER: *Is that a reason to complain?*

PRIESTLEY: *Only to be then diluted . . . if not evaporated.*

LAVOISIER: *How did I do so?*

PRIESTLEY: *You write (heavy sarcasm) "We did this . . . and we found that." Your royal "we", sir, makes my contributions disappear . . . poof . . . into thin air! (Pause). When I publish, I say, "I did . . . I found . . . I observed." I do not hide behind a "we."*

LAVOISIER: *Enough of generalities . . . (Aside) . . . or platitudes. (Louder). What now?*

PRIESTLEY: *The question, sir! The question! Who made that air first?*

SCHEELE (Much more insistent than before, to audience): *I did. And future generations will affirm it.*

PRIESTLEY (To audience): *But by the grace of God, I made it too . . . and published first!*

LAVOISIER (To audience): *They knew not what they'd done . . . where oxygen would lead us.*

(The three men start arguing simultaneously in loud tones so that the words cannot be understood)
        OFFSTAGE

COURT HERALD'S VOICE (Tapping of staff): *Order! Order! Order! Three savants? Yet you cannot agree? So be it. (Pause). The king will not reward you!*

Like *Oxygen*, my third play, *Calculus*, deals less with science (in this instance mathematics) than with the morals of scientists in terms of the vicious priority struggle between two of the greatest European intellectual giants, Newton and Leibniz, which persisted for three decades. Like *Oxygen*, it is meant to illustrate one aspect of the scientific culture – the drive for priority – that is both the nourishment and the poison of research scientists. But in the Newton-Leibniz brawl, the fight is hardly conducted *mano a mano* but rather through surrogates—a committee of eleven fellows of the Royal Society appointed by its President, Isaac Newton, to adjudicate his priority argument with Leibniz. *Calculus* deals with these surrogates, some of whom are barely known even to historians of science. The following excerpt involves a London salonière, Lady Brasenose, and two historically documented Committee members, Dr. John Arbuthnot (physician to Queen Anne) and Louis Frederick Bonet (Minister of the King of Prussia in London).

LADY BRASENOSE: Now tell me: did he do it?

ARBUTHNOT: Why ask us?

LADY BRASENOSE: Because you were there!

ARBUTHNOT: But so were nine others.

LADY BRASENOSE: I had more confidence in you . . . both of you.

BONET: My Lady uses the past tense. You have no confidence now?

LADY BRASENOSE (Sharp, yet smiling): You listen to nuances . . . is that another reason why your King sent you to London?

BONET: In diplomacy, precision in language leads to imprecision in meaning.

LADY BRASENOSE (Laughs outright): I am tempted to pursue this line of conversation . . . it does suit a salon. But I shall resist the temptation. (Turns to Arbuthnot). My dear doctor. I presume you took your wife into your confidence.

ARBUTHNOT: Reluctantly.

LADY BRASENOSE: Reluctance is no virtue in my eyes——

ARBUTHNOT: Nor did I claim it so.

LADY BRASENOSE: So out with it! The report is at the printers. Was your Committee's decision unanimous?

BONET: It was.

LADY BRASENOSE: Without giving notice to Leibniz? Without inviting him to offer documents in his defense?

ARBUTHNOT: Without such actions.

LADY BRASENOSE: Yet you all signed? Shame on you!

BONET: You're overlooking the nuances, Lady Brasenose! I said the decision was unanimous——

ARBUTHNOT: But we did not sign.

LADY BRASENOSE (Taken aback): How did you two accomplish that?

BONET: None signed!

LADY BRASENOSE: Sir Isaac is more malleable than I thought. He never compromises as Master of the Mint.

ARBUTHNOT: Not more malleable . . . just more subtle as President of the Royal Society. It goes with that office . . . controlling minds rather than coinage.

LADY BRASENOSE: More subtle or more devious? (Makes dismissive gesture). No matter. What caused his change of mind?

BONET (Points to Arbuthnot): Our doctor's diplomacy.

LADY BRASENOSE: If our physicians now turn into diplomats, what happens to our diplomats?

ARBUTHNOT: I'm afraid my Lady's question is not applicable to the case at hand. Both the physician (points to himself) and the diplomat (points to Bonet) chose prevarication.

BONET: Dr. Arbuthnot . . . you're too severe.

ARBUTHNOT (Turns to Bonet): Am I? What is a prevaricator in your eyes?

BONET: A quibbler . . . or equivocator.

LADY BRASENOSE: In other words . . . a diplomat.

ARBUTHNOT (Quietly): We were cowards . . . but hardly diplomats.

LADY BRASENOSE: Cowardice and diplomacy are not mutually exclusive! But Dr. Arbuthnot! I've never before seen you wear a hair-shirt . . . at least not in my house. It's time you discarded it. Enlighten me . . . both of you!

ARBUTHNOT: It was clear to me . . . already when I met the President alone . . . that not a word would be changed in the report . . . and that it would be published even if some of us protested.

LADY BRASENOSE: And you were unwilling to be such a protester?

ARBUTHNOT: I have never had an appetite for disputes. This time, even my wife advised against it. For Sir Isaac, such a protester would be an apostate . . . in his eyes unforgivable in the Church and in the Royal Society. Think of John Flamsteed or Robert Hooke. He destroyed them. (Tired voice). So why even attempt it?

LADY BRASENOSE: For principle's sake?

BONET: Principles exist to be broken . . . at least at times.

LADY BRASENOSE: The diplomat is speaking.

BONET: Or the churchman. "Thou shalt not kill" has never prevented religious wars.

LADY BRASENOSE (Impatient): I want to hear about the prevarication . . . not its rationalization.

BONET: Dr. Arbuthnot's proposal was adroit. What was needed was a published unanimous report . . . but for that the identity of the Committee could remain undisclosed. (Assumes precious, ironic tone). A "Numerous Committee of Gentlemen of several Nations" was surely adequate—

LADY BRASENOSE: Using Sir Isaac's own words?

BONET: Precisely. And once granted that, how could the President deny the logic of Dr. Arbuthnot's request that unanimity by vote of an anonymous Committee surely need not be confirmed by signature? Publication is enough.

LADY BRASENOSE: Like the death warrant for Charles I?

ARBUTHNOT: An apt comparison. Killing a scholar's reputation is also murder.

BONET: Be that as it may. (Pause). Dr. Arbuthnot's proposal was carried unanimously.

LADY BRASENOSE (Admiringly): I never thought prevarication could be so effectual. I stand enlightened. (Turns to Bonet). But you could have been the honorable exception to unanimity. You have the least to fear of Newton. His wrath will not follow you to Geneva.

ARBUTHNOT: Lady Brasenose . . . and Mr. Bonet. Forgive me, but I must take my leave. A royal patient waits who must not be kept waiting.

>   *(Exits)*

LADY BRASENOSE (Turning to Bonet): Now that we are alone, I trust you will answer honestly.

BONET: I did not vote for Newton . . . I voted against Leibniz.

LADY BRASENOSE: You judged Leibniz a plagiarizer?

BONET: I am not qualified to pass judgment in mathematics.

LADY BRASENOSE: But that was the issue!

Having demonstrated—at least to my personal satisfaction— that doses of pedagogy in "science-in-theatre" are not necessarily the kiss of death in terms of securing theatrical performances and an engaged audience as well as readers for book versions of these plays, I have now gone one step further by shifting "science-in-theatre" from the stage to the place where new pedagogy is best suited: the classroom. In an attempt to move at least occasionally away from the all-pervasive monologist lecture format in science, I have started on a series of "pedagogic wordplays" for classroom use in lieu of a conventional 50-minute lecture. And rather than expect these to be performed, i.e. learned by heart by actors, students are simply asked to "read" these plays in front of the class with the aid of audiovisuals that are contained in a CD ROM that is included in the paperback book version of the wordplay. I shall end with an excerpt from the second of these pedagogic wordplays, *NO* (written with Pierre Laszlo). The ease, with which such wordplays can be performed was illustrated by the actual "performance" at the Paderborn Conference of the beginning of scene 1 of *NO*, where the woman's role (simply named **B**) was assumed by a student volunteer who had only received the text a few hours earlier.

Two biochemists—**A** (male) and **B** (female)—sit in a café facing each other on two sides of a table covered with a paper table-cloth and a paper napkin holder. They are drinking coffee and are dressed informally, possibly even in jeans.

A: First . . . we need money. Otherwise, it's no go!

B: "The love of money is the root of all evil." (Pause). 1 Timothy 6.10. (Laughs). The Bible says so!

A (Dismissive): I'm talking about the need *for money . . . not* love. *Timothy was no scientist. Or he would've said, "Grant applications are the root of all evil."*

B: I hate begging for money . . . for research!

A: Welcome to the 21st century! (Takes sip of coffee). So let's start on NO.

B: Just a few years ago, this would've been crazy. Fund a collaboration between a chemist and a biologist . . . on nitric oxide?

A: Especially when most people still confuse nitric with nitrous oxide . . . and assume we're interested in laughing gas.

B: And roll their eyes when they learn that nitric oxide . . . as an industrial gas and environmental pollutant . . . is toxic! Now we've come full circle . . . with NO a panacea for God knows how many medical problems. (Pause). Which biological function of NO should we pick?

A: Penile erection.

B: Typical male response.

A: That's hitting below the belt.

B (Jocular): You'll recover.

A: I was thinking of grantsmanship. Penile erection in the title is bound to stand out.

B: Many other catchy applications would also do that.

A: Such as?

B: Migraine, for instance, where NO plays a role. Just thinking of writing our grant application gives me one! (Pause). But let's pretend we're sitting here with another couple . . . non-scientists . . . who innocently joined us for coffee.

A: What's that got to do with our research proposal?

B: Assume one of them asks us what we're working on—

A: And we give him or her a tutorial on nitric oxide? (Ostentatiously looks at watch): We're wasting time.

B (Sharply): We're not! It's good discipline . . . explaining it to the taxpayer . . . and then putting it into language for a grants committee. Let's give it a try.

A (Reluctantly): Okay . . . but let's make it snappy. Where do we start?

B: I'd suggest with simple chemistry.

A: Even that will require pencil and paper . . . or slides . . . or a blackboard.

B: The eternal plight of chemists unable to explain what they do in simple words! Let's pretend we've only got those napkins.

A: How about the tablecloth? It's also paper.

B: Too large! I'm hooked on napkins . . . they force you to be concise.

A: What about conciseness for you biologists?

B: First, we've got to start with chemistry. Explain why one of the very simplest known molecules . . . made of just one nitrogen and one oxygen atom . . . fulfills so many functions.

(Pretends to draw NO on napkin. Image of slide No. 2 appears on screen).

And then proceed to tell them all the awful things automobile emissions cause: acid rain . . . destruction of the ozone layer—

(Projects slide No. 3)

A: And thus feed the public's chemophobia? At least show them that NO is a bit more complicated than you drew it here.

B: Okay . . . okay! It can exist as a neutral, positively or negatively charged species.

(Reproduces neutral, negatively charged and positively charged forms on the same napkin, which is displayed on screen in slide No. 4).

A: First, how would you explain the environmental damage caused by NO?

B: In a few words . . . in a café?

A: On one napkin!

B: Go ahead, you do it.

A: We could tell them how NO is made now . . . not deliberately, but inadvertently . . . on a scale of tens of millions of tons from the burning of fossil fuels. How it is released into the environment by automobiles and diesel engines.

B: I know . . . the main cause of acid rains as well as a major health hazard. (Pause). But we're wasting time!

A: It's not a waste. How many people realize that while NO has been known for a couple of centuries, its real role was only discovered less than two decades ago? Give me one minute . . . maximum two!

B: Even after a couple of minutes, your coffee buddy would be yawning. In fact, even chemists would yawn . . . they aren't interested in history.

A: In that case, let me overcome those yawns by teasing them a bit. Mentioning that NO is produced by an extraordinary range of species . . . from fruit flies . . . chickens . . . trout . . .

B: Stop! First we should point out that humans also produce NO continually in the body . . . yet this wasn't discovered until the late 1980s. The obvious questions are . . . how come we didn't know that before . . . and why are we making the stuff in the first place?

A: In that case start by saying that the half-life of NO in the body is only a few seconds . . . and for that, ever more sophisticated sensors had to be devised first.

B: But how will you explain detection of minute amounts of nitric oxide within a cell?

A: I'll just list the methods currently used. Otherwise, we'll need a dozen napkins.

I suspect that the overwhelming portion of this Paderborn Conference audience does not know the difference between nitric oxide (NO)—the causative agent for penile erection and a myriad of other biological functions—and nitrous oxide (N_2O)—generally known as laughing gas. Nor that the recent discovery of the biological functions of NO is so important that it was honored by the award of a Nobel Prize in 1998. So why not learn such facts in dialogic form—be it from watching such a wordplay or reading the text?

Of course, it remains to be seen whether such a pedagogic application of "science-in-theatre" will catch on. At least in Germany, the prognosis seems promising, since a publisher specializing in plays for schools, DEUTSCHER THEATERVERLAG, has already published for distribution to German gymnasiums a paperback of the text (the first in both German and English, and the second in German, English and French) together with a CD containing all the audiovisuals. Feedback since the autumn of 2002 from students (and the press) during the first performances in Münster, Vienna, Dortmund, Bielefeld, and Giessen indicate that such wordplays may become a useful pedagogic tool and thus stimulate the creation of more plays of this sort. Who knows? Science-in-theatre might even become infectious.

NOTES

[1] See Walter Grünzweig, "Science-in-Fiction: Science as Tribal Culture in the Novels of Carl Djerassi," in this volume.

[2] *Cantor's Dilemma (1989), The Bourbaki Gambit* (1994), *Menachem's Seed* (1997) and *NO* (1998), all published in paperback by Penguin-USA.

WORKS CITED

Brecht, Berthold. *Life of Galileo.* Trans. John Willett. London: Methuen, 1980.

Djerassi, Carl. *Cantor's Dilemma.* New York: Penguin, 1989.

——. *The Bourbaki Gambit.* New York: Penguin, 1994.

——. *Menachem's Seed.* New York: Penguin, 1997.

——. *No.* New York: Penguin, 1998.

——. *An Immaculate Misconception.* London: Imperial College P, 2000.

——. *ICSI-Sex im Zeitalter der technischen Reproduzierbarkeit / ICSI-Sex in the Age of Mechanical Reproduction.* Paperback containing both German and English versions, plus compact disc. German trans. Bettina Arlt. Weinheim: Deutscher Theaterverlag, 2002.

—— and Roald Hoffmann. *Oxygen.* Weinheim: Wiley-VCH, 2001.

—— and Pierre Laszlo. *NO.* Paperback containing German, French and English versions, plus compact disc. German trans. Bettina Arlt. Weinheim: Deutscher Theaterverlag, 2003.

—— and David Pinner. *Newton's Darkness: Two dramatic views.* Paperback, containing inter al. the text of *CALCULUS.* London: Imperial College P, 2003.

Dürenmatt, Friedrich. *The Physicists.* Trans. James Kirkup. New York: Grove, 1964.

Frayn, Michael. *Copenhagen.* London: Methuen, 1998.

Stoppard, Tom. *Arcadia.* London: Faber and Faber, 1993.

Stoppard, Tom. *Hapgood.* London: Faber and Faber, 1988.

PETER FREESE

FROM THE APOCALYPTIC TO THE ENTROPIC END:
FROM HOPE TO DESPAIR TO NEW HOPE?

> "About one hundred years ago there lived a British physicist named James Clerk Maxwell. Entropy fascinated him also. As a physicist he had great affection for the wonders of our physical universe, and it seemed to him too cruel that all the moving things of our world, all the marvelous, spinning, humming, ticking, breathing things, should be doomed to run down and die. Was there no remedy to this unfair fate?"
> —Ken Kesey, "Demon Box"

> "She did gather that there were two distinct kinds of this entropy. One having to do with heat-engines, the other to do with communication."
> —Thomas Pynchon, *The Crying of Lot 49*

For two millennia, Western literature has envisioned the end of the world with recourse to St. John's scenario of a final reckoning, which has provided Christian writers with an inventory of arcane similes and mysterious prophecies, that range from the seven seals and the four horsemen of the Apocalypse to the final battle of Armageddon and the beast with the number 666 and that have become deeply inscribed in our cultural matrix.[1] John's vision of the end is named after its first word—Greek απokαλυπτω = 'I reveal something hitherto hidden'—and it is anything but "apocalyptic" in the sense which the much abused term has assumed in the faddish endtime visions of Hollywood disaster films, where it has become a mere synonym of "catastrophic." Predicting not only the terror of an end but also the glory of a new beginning, the Biblical apocalypse is revelatory, and pious believers await it not only with fear and trembling but also with hope and exultation. This binary notion of the end engendered the periodical oscillations between millennial and cataclysmic expectations in the rich strain of American endtime literature from the detailed description of the Last Judgment in its very first bestseller, Michael Wigglesworth's *The Day of Doom* (1662), to the disturbing visions conjured up in such recent novels as Stanley Elkin's savagely funny *The Living End* (1979) or Paul Auster's harsh *In the Country of Last Things* (1987). Usually these fire-and-brimstone scenarios are hortatory extrapolations of alarming developments in the venerable tradition of the Jeremiad, and Frank Kermode has shown that "the paradigms of apocalypse continue to lie under our ways of making sense of the world" (28) and that therefore the envisioned end is often more immanent than imminent.

In the mid-nineteenth century, however, a competing paradigm of the end came into being, which conceived of human life no longer as what John Bunyan had once defined as *The Pilgrim's Progress from this World to that which is to come* (1678), but saw human existence as an irreversible movement through a world which is to end. Being the irrefutable consequence of the newly discovered Second Law of Thermodynamics, this paradigm was incomparably more frightful than the Biblical one, because even agnostics could no longer dismiss it as religious speculation, but had to accept it as scientific fact. When, in his recent short story "Desert Island Discs" (1992), George Steiner envisioned the scene in which Rudolf Clausius penned the equation for the property which he would then christen *entropy*, he made the frightened scientist ponder the momentous implications of his newly found formula as follows:

> The equation stood. Against reason. Against the long-drawn breath of life. In uncaring defiance of the future tense. Formally, the algebra was nothing but the proof, at once abstract and statistical, of the unrecuperability of caloric energy when turned to heat, of the degree of loss in all thermal and thermodynamic processes. [. . .] what he was staring at [. . .] was the determination, irrefutable, of the heat-death of the universe. The *n* minus *x* function would not be bought off. Entropy meant run-down and the transmutation of spent energy into cold stasis. A stillness, a cold past all imagining. Compared to which our own deaths and the decomposition of the warm flesh are a trivial carnival. In that equation, the cosmos had its epitaph. In the beginning was the Word; at the close was the algebraic function. A pen-nib, bought in a scrolled cardboard box at Kreutzner's, university stationer, hat put *finis* to the sum and total of being. After the downward right-hand stroke of that *n* came not infinite blackness, which *is* still, but a nothingness, an unfathomable zero. (82ff.)

Steiner was wrong in crediting Clausius with inventing the notion of the *heat-death*, since as early as 1852 William Thomson, the later Lord Kelvin, had speculated that "within a finite period of time past the earth must have been, and within a finite period of time to come the earth must again be, unfit for the habitation of man as at present constituted, unless operations have been, or are to be performed, which are impossible under the laws to which the known operations going on at present in the material world are subject" (306). And it was Wilhelm von Helmholtz who first announced the inevitable heat-death of the universe in February 1854 in a Königsberg lecture by stating

> that, in the course of every natural process, the first part of the supply of power, namely, the unchanging heat, increases continually, whereas the second part, namely, the mechanical, electrical, and chemical powers, decrease continually. And if the cosmos is left, without interference, to the course of its physical processes, finally all its supply of power will be converted into heat, and all heat will reach an equilibrium of temperature. Then every possibility will be exhausted, then a complete standstill of all natural processes of every possible kind must be reached. Naturally, also the life of plants, humans and animals cannot continue when the sun has lost its higher temperature and, with it, its light, and when all the components of the surface of the earth have entered into the chemical compounds which their degrees of relationship demand. In short, from then on the cosmos will be condemned to eternal rest. (116ff, trans. P. Freese)[2]

But Steiner was right in picking Clausius, since it was he who coined the term *entropy*, succinctly defined the First and the Second Law of Thermodynamics, and famously stated them in the two laconic sentences "The energy of the world is constant" and "The entropy of the world tends towards a maximum" (400).[3] These two sentences were frequently, and often creatively, misunderstood, and one of these misunderstandings is still haunting many contemporary writers.

Von Helmholtz's notion of the ultimate *Wärmetod* of the universe, which was soon translated into English as *heat-death*, refers to the "death *of* heat" and not to a "death *by* heat," since the ongoing conversion of free into bound energy will eventually leave no available heat. H. G. Wells, whose novel *The Time Machine* (1895) is among the first fictional enactments of the workings of the Second Law, knew full well that the misnamed *heat-death* is really a *cold-death* reached at minus 273 centigrade on the Kelvin Scale, and thus he made his hero time-travel into an icy future in which a cooling "sun grow[s] larger and duller in the westward sky, and the life of the old earth ebb[s] away," and soon "all [will be] over" (77, 78). And Kurt Vonnegut was equally correct when he had Dr. Hoenikker's ice-nine freeze the globe into a shimmering glacier in his cult-novel *Cat's Cradle* (Chapter 116, "The Grand Ah-whoom"). But many other science-fiction writers violate the Second Law by unthinkingly envisioning a creatively misunderstood *heat-death* as a fiery cataclysm in the apocalyptic tradition. Thus, in Pamela Zoline's story "The Heat Death of the Universe" (1967), a California housewife ruminates on both her domestic duties and the end of the world and muses about

> the Heat Death of the Universe. A logarithmic of those late summer days, endless as the Irish serpent twisting through jeweled manuscripts forever, tail in mouth, the heat pressing, bloating, doing violence. The Los Angeles sky becomes so filled and bleached with detritus that it loses all colour and silvers like a mirror, reflecting back the fricasseeing earth. Everything becomes warmer and warmer, each particle of matter becomes more agitated, more excited until the bonds shatter, the glues fail, the deodorants lose their seals. She imagines the whole of New York City melting like a Dali into a great chocolate mass, a great soup, the Great Soup of New York. (94)[4]

And in *Less Than Zero* (1985), Bret Easton Ellis' bestselling apprentice novel, bored rich youths in heat-drenched LA are haunted by the scientifically unfeasible concept of an all-encompassing death by heat, and the girl Ronette has "this dream, see, where I saw the whole world melt" (103).[5] This widespread metamorphosis of the *Wärmetod*, however, is not the only misunderstanding to which the Second Law fell prey in its transfer from the realm of scientific denotations to that of cultural connotations, since its reception was multiply disturbed by the misleading name given to the entropy-concept, by its inaccessibility to any kind of sensory perception, and by its discovery at a most untimely historical moment.

When Clausius coined the term *entropy*, he did so because he was convinced that the names of scientific concepts should be taken from Greek or Latin in order to be available in all languages. Since he wrongly thought that *energy* was a compound of *en+ergon*, meaning "work-content," he formed a parallel compound of *en+trope* to mean "transformation-content."[6] Three years later Peter Guthrie Tait imported Clausius's neologism into English, and since then science has been stuck with a puzzling misnomer, which Felix Auerbach tried unsuccessfully to replace by *ectropy*[7] and of which Heinz von Foerster only recently complained that it should have been *utropy* to indicate that the longer transformation processes go on, the less heat can be turned into work.[8]

In contrast to such concepts as *gravity* or *energy*, *entropy* cannot be perceived, and that is why puzzled lay persons have difficulties imagining its effects. It is understandable that a heat-engine, which converts thermal energy into mechanical energy by making heat flow from a hot to a cold body, can do no more work when the two bodies have reached the same temperature, and that the two now lukewarm bodies cannot unmix themselves into hot and cold again in order to repeat the process. It might also be comprehensible that, due to the First Law, no energy has been lost in this process, but that, due to the Second Law, the initial energy is no longer available for work because it has changed from free into bound energy. But things become forbiddingly abstract when it is said that the entropy of the system has increased in proportion to the decrease of available energy. The basic mathematical equation, commonly written as $dS=dQ/T$, with dS being the increase in entropy, dQ the increment of the heat transferred from a hotter to a colder body, and T the temperature of the former, states that when a colder body absorbs an amount of heat Q from a hotter body at temperature T, an amount of entropy $S=Q/T$ is gained by the former and lost by the latter. All this is rationally comprehensible, but difficult if not impossible to imagine, and that is even truer of the crucial consequence of this equation, namely, that since $S=Q/T$ becomes larger when T becomes smaller, the colder body gains more entropy than the hotter loses, and that therefore entropy must increase in all closed systems which are not in equilibrium.

However, not only its name and its repulsive abstractness have kept the entropy-notion from becoming common knowledge, but also the fact that at the time of its discovery its frightful workings stood in stark contrast to the dominant *Zeitgeist*. Even the pious and God-fearing scientists who formulated the Second Law did not want to believe that the Almighty had built an irredeemable flaw into his creation, and James Prescott Joule spoke for all of them when he flatly denied the possibility of the decrease of what he called "living force" and said, with the certitude of a theologian rather than the skepticism of a scientist, that "it is manifestly absurd to suppose that the powers with which God has endowed matter can be destroyed any more than they can be created by man's agency" (268ff.). Moreover, the spirit of the time was that of a boundless belief in growth and progress, with the Industrial Revolution giving birth to ever new mechanical wonders, the proud European nation states busily building their colonial empires, and Darwin's theory of evolution promising the very opposite of entropic dissipation. Consequently, for a long time the difficult and untimely notion of entropy not only remained confined to the narrow realm of specialists, but its early history was also punctuated by fervent attempts at refuting its validity. Such attempts seemed all the more promising when, soon after the formulation of the Second Law, Ludwig Boltzmann initiated the major step from macroscopic thermodynamics to statistical mechanics by replacing the measurement of the vaguely defined property called "heat" by a statistical computation of molecular movement as dependent upon changing temperatures,[9] and thereby made, in Max Planck's words, "the hypothesis of elementary disorder [. . .] the real kernel of the principle of increase of entropy and, therefore, the preliminary condition for the existence of entropy" (50).

With Boltzmann's findings the Second Law became what Eddington famously called a secondary instead of a primary law, dealing not with things that are impossible but with things that are just too improbable to happen (75). Many stubborn scientists like Josef Loschmidt, who wanted to destroy what he called "the terroristic nimbus of the second law, which has made it appear to be an annihilating principle for all living beings of the universe" (Brush 605),[10] invented ever more complex schemes for the sole purpose of explaining away the unacceptable dissymmetry of nature, and the most famous construction of these Doubting Thomases is certainly James Clerk Maxwell's "intelligent doorkeeper,"[11] whom William Thomson ironically dubbed a "demon" ("Sorting Demon" 137-41)[12] and whose later mutation, as the immortal "Maxwell's Demon," from a being intent upon creating new free energy into a being concerned with the collection of random information, has since not only personified the paradigm change from energy to information, but also greatly annoyed scientists from Leo Szilard ("Über die Entropieverminderung")[13] to Charles H. Bennett ("Demons") and deeply pleased writers from Thomas Pynchon[14] to Stanislaw Lem[15] as the metaphorical carrier of metaphysical insights.

In the cultural realm, resistance against the Second Law was even more pronounced. Whereas Herbert Spencer, in his *First Principles* (1862), strove for a reconciliation of the hopeful teachings of evolution with the pessimistic message of thermodynamics (228, 413), Henri Bergson, who in his *L'Evolution créatrice* (1907) characterized the Second Law as "la plus métaphysique des lois de la physique" (701), invented his *èlan vital* as a psychological and extraspatial energy exempt from the workings of entropy. Friedrich Nietzsche, who could not stomach the idea of a "final state," apodictically refuted this hateful notion in *Der Wille zur Macht* (1906) with his concept of eternal return (167ff.). Friedrich Engels, for whom the idea of man's unavoidable doom ran counter to the eventual triumph of the proletariat, emphatically rejected the Second Law in his *Dialektik der Natur* (278) and thereby established an axiom of dialectical materialism, which Soviet philosophy would long uphold by dubbing the heat-death theory the aberration of bourgeois scholars.[16] And as late as 1951, in an address to the Papal Academy of Science, Pope Pius XII took care to state that, contrary to common assumptions, the entropy notion does not invalidate the belief in a creator, but demands the existence of a necessary being.[17]

The first major American contributor to thermodynamics was the Yale physicist Josiah Willard Gibbs, whose seminal papers on the entropy of non-homogeneous bodies were so forbiddingly difficult that he remained a figure known to insiders only, until William Gaddis resurrected him as the inspiring shadow behind the failed writer Jack Gibbs in his novel *JR* (1975). And the first US author to introduce the Second Law into cultural discourse was Henry Adams, the cranky intellectual who in his *Education* (1907) ruefully contrasted an enviable medieval universe under the sign of the Virgin with the hateful twentieth-century multiverse as ruled by the dynamo, and who caustically observed that "Chaos was the law of nature; Order was the dream of man" (451). Influenced by the German *Energetik* of Wilhelm Ostwald and haunted by his metaphysics of doom, he later used, or better abused, in "A Letter to American Teachers of History" (1910) and in *The Degradation of the Democratic Dogma* (1919), the Second Law as the major instrument for his new historiography, which is based upon the laws of physics and posits that human history does not proceed in terms of progress and ascent, but of degradation and descent.

Aware that human individuals could not be understood as closed systems, Adams was nevertheless convinced that "vital Energy obeys the laws of thermal energy" ("A Letter to American Teachers of History," *Degradation* 146) and thus took great pains to show that the laws which govern thermodynamic systems also apply to social configurations. He even borrowed an equation from Gibbs' "Equilibrium of Heterogeneous Substances" in order to compute, in "The Rule of Phase Applied to History" (1909), that thought would come "to the limits of its possibilities in the year 1921" (*Degradation* 302). It is all too obvious that Adams misconstrued the Second Law, which he faultily translated from a scientific concept into a cultural metaphor, and none less than William James ironically refuted his friend's unfounded theories when he reminded him that "though the *ultimate* state of the universe may be its vital and psychical extinction, there is nothing in physics to interfere with the hypothesis that the penultimate state might be the millennium" (James 344ff.). But in spite of his glaring errors, Adams' gloomy predictions about the inevitable entropic doom influenced such writers as Nathanael West and F. Scott Fitzgerald.

Often unaware of the meaning, if not the existence of the Second Law, literary critics have usually missed this context, but contemporary writers have not, and when William Gaddis was asked whether Thomas Pynchon had influenced the entropic concerns of his *JR*, he answered "Well, going back a bit further, Nathanael West had sketched entropy nicely in *Miss Lonelyhearts* in the early thirties" (Abády-Nagy 66). In his application for a Guggenheim fellowship, West referred not only to *The Education of Henry Adams* but also to Oswald Spengler's *Der Untergang des Abendlandes* (1918-22)[18] in which one reads: "*The end of the world as the perfection of an internally necessary development* – that is the twilight of the gods; that is what, as a last and irreligious version of the myth, is meant by the doctrine of entropy" (547, trans. P. Freese). These connections justify a reading of West's novels as dealing with the irresistible movement of the world towards disorder and inertia, and such a reading is confirmed by the fact that the earliest reference to entropy which I could find in US fiction occurs in *Miss Lonelyhearts* (1933). There, in a nightmarish vision, the protagonist sits in the window of a pawnshop and thinks:

> Man has a tropism for order. Keys in one pocket, change in another. Mandolins are tuned G D A E. The physical world has a tropism for disorder, entropy. Man against nature . . . the battle of the centuries. Keys yearn to mix with change. Mandolins strive to get out of tune. Every order has within it the germ of destruction. All order is doomed, yet the battle is worth while. (*Novels* 93)

Whereas Miss Lonelyhearts is haunted by his sensitivity to order in an ever more disorderly world, a similar threat of a sneaking movement towards decay and inertia informs *A Cool Million* (1934), where Lemuel Pitkin loses limb after limb in his quest for the American Dream and finally consists of almost as many artificial as natural members. His gradual movement from an animate to an inanimate state, by the way, anticipates Victoria Wren's deterioration from a good-looking young girl into a reified robot in Thomas Pynchon's *V.* (1963), which is just another drastic illustration of growing entropy. And in *The Day of the Locust* (1939), it is the Hollywood "dream dump" (*Novels* 326), that burial place of human hopes and aspirations in a world of surrogates and impersonations, which serves as a felicitous concretization of the entropic process.

The famous "valley of ashes" in F. Scott Fitzgerald's *The Great Gatsby* (1925) is usually related to Eliot's *Waste Land*. But since Fitzgerald, who opened *The Crack-Up* (1936) with a laconic restatement of the Second Law in human terms by observing that "of course all life is a process of breaking down" (39), not only knew Henry Adams, but initially wanted to call his novel *Among Ash Heaps and Millionaires,* there are good reasons for contextualizing it differently. The novel depicts the magnificent country which the early Dutch sailors had experienced as "a fresh, green breast of the new world," as having gradually deteriorated into a desolate "valley of ashes," whose bleak "ashheaps" (29, 30, 187; see also 142, 166), are strongly reminiscent of Adams' claim "that the ashheap was constantly increasing in size" (*Degradation* 138). In this context, Tom Buchanan's statement that he had "read somewhere that the sun's getting hotter every year. It seems that pretty soon the earth's going to fall into the sun—or wait a minute—it's just the opposite—the sun's getting colder every year" (124) can be seen as another tongue-in-cheek reference to the entropy-concept, and thus *The Great Gatsby* can be understood as an early fictional comment on the relentless workings of the Second Law.

Generally speaking, however, in the first half of the twentieth century the scientific notion of entropy remained a poor competitor to the Biblical tradition of apocalypse and, to use Eliot's terms, "the whimper" was as yet no match for "the bang" (86). Besides Flammarion's *La Fin du Monde* (1894), Wells's *The Time Machine* (1895), Sack's *Ein Namenloser* (1913), and Zamyatin's *We* (1924), there are only few examples and in most of them, as in West's novels, entropic ideas are conflated with apocalyptic images. But after World War II this situation changed drastically, and this is not only due to the fact that the Second Law assumed a central role in the new discipline of cybernetics, but in many other disciplines as well. One is economics, in which Nicholas Georgescu-Roegen's seminal monograph *The Entropy Law and the Economic Process* (1971) has initiated a radically divergent school, which is based on the assumption that "the Entropy Law is the taproot of economic scarcity" (353), which makes all its calculations subject to time's arrow, and which demands an environmentally beneficial behavior because "mankind's dowry is finite" (363) and both the energy and the matter available on our planet are subject to irreversible dissipation. Georgescu-Roegen's ideas were later popularized in Jeremy Rifkin's bestseller *Entropy: A New World View* (1980), which postulates that "the Entropy Law will preside as the ruling paradigm over the next period of history" and has helped to initiate our growing concern for "sustainability" (16).

It is against such a background that Claude Lévi-Straus could observe that anthropology as the study of civilization's process of disintegration should be renamed "entropology"[19] and that the Second Law has become an attractive paradigm for ever more writers who defiantly pit their sense-making and order-creating fictions against the proliferation of both thermodynamic and linguistic detritus in a universe running-down. Since replacing a religious prophecy with a scientific prediction implies a loss of transcendental aspects, supplanting the binary meaning of apocalypse, with both its cataclysmic threat and its millennial promise, with the single meaning of entropic dissipation and death effects a painful abandonment of hope. But on the other hand such a change also grants humans better chances of and greater responsibilities for delaying the end. Whereas the coming of the Last Judgment is exclusively determined by God's gratuitous providence, the occurrence of the cosmic heat-death can be postponed by thoughtful and environmentally beneficial behavior, and instead of emotional strategies like fervent prayer it calls for rational ones like careful husbandry. This is exactly what the writers who employ the entropy-concept as a cautionary *memento mori* plead for when they measure man's subjective experience of temporal flux against the thermodynamic arrow of time as the only objective yardstick, depict the human condition as a defiant attempt at creating islands of order in an increasingly disorderly universe, and wrestle with the epistemological quandary of whether the world's tendency towards randomness is really an objective fact or only the product of human ignorance.

The American novelist who most persistently represents this position is John Updike. In his first novel, *The Poorhouse Fair* (1958), Updike evokes a dystopian world that has replaced religious conviction with a concern for physical well-being, and treats the theme of individual versus institution as that of anti-entropic and homeostatic organism versus entropic and deadly organization by pitting a benevolently disciplinarian superintendent, who believes in the "physical theory of entropia" (46) and tries to convert his poorhouse into an island of systematic order, against the resentful inmates, who struggle for a rest of human dignity and defy his regulations by all sorts of infringements upon his closed system. This novel ends with the hovering "cold of the void" (75) remaining unalloyed. A similar skepticism dominates Updike's convoluted Rabbit-tetralogy, which depicts a world pervaded by the irreversible process of what Rabbit calls "life's constant depreciation" (*Rabbit at Rest* 420) as brought about on both the individual and the cosmic scale by the workings of the Second Law. But Updike's well-informed use of the entropy-notion is most obvious in one of his lesser known works, *The Coup* (1978), in which the US-educated president of a newly independent African desert state sees the world in terms of a battle between life-giving energy and death-dealing entropy, and muses:

> It may be [. . .] that in the attenuation, desiccation, and death of religions the world over, a new religion is being formed, in the indistinct hearts of men, a religion without a God, without prohibitions and compensatory assurances, a religion whose antipodes are motion and stasis, whose one rite is the exercise of energy, and in which exhausted forms like the quest, the vow, the expiation, and the attainment of suffering through wisdom are, emptied of content, put in the service of a pervasive expenditure whose ultimate purpose is entropy, whose immediate reward is fatigue, a blameless confusion, and sleep. Millions now enact the trials of this religion, without giving it a name, or attributing to themselves any virtue. (103)

Here, too, for the knowledgeable reader, the mysteriously disappeared US-AID officer Gibes, whose correct name, the protagonist insists, must be Gibbs, turns out to be a hidden allusion to Josiah Willard Gibbs and, through him, to the country that eats up the planet's energy and exports its wasteful ways to the newly formed states of the Third World.

Stanley Elkin employs similar strategies in his second novel, *A Bad Man* (1967), which depicts the losing battle between individual and institution as that between the desperate energy of a driven salesman and the inexorably increasing entropy of a wasteful consumer-society and in which the protagonist rejects the offers of a developer by saying, "We're in the homestretch of a race: your energy against my entropy. The universe is running down, Mr. Developer" (260). In *Continental Drift* (1985), a tale of hopeful dreams and dirty realities in the mendacious world of Florida, Russell Banks pursues an analogous course by charging the interplay between a white Christian man's obsessions with race and sex and an oppressed Haitian woman's painful journey to the promised shores of America with recurring references to the movement of the aging earth, that is, the continental drift of the title, and by thus revealing both the slow "metabolic rate of geology" and the fast "metabolic rate of history" (36) as nothing but variations upon the all-embracing entropic process:

> [. . .] just keep on moving, keep breeding and pissing and shitting, keep on eating the planet we live on, keep on moving, alone and in families and tribes, in nations and even in whole species; it's the only argument we have against entropy. And it's not truly an argument; it's a vision. (39)

And in the unduly neglected title story of his *Demon Box* (1986), Ken Kesey has Dr. Klaus Woofner, a mad psychoanalyst from the barely disguised Esalen Institute, deliver a brilliant lecture on the history of entropy, which he dubs "Izzy Newton's Nameless Famine" (301), and on the earliest attempt to stall it, namely, Maxwell's Demon, whom he elevates, in a daring metaphorical leap, into a model of what he calls "the cognitive process of Modern civilization" (309), significantly doing all this at the precise moment of the American oil crisis.

In the able hands of these and many other writers, the workings of the Second Law are dramatized as a sort of Manichean survival contest, with decreasing energy being the good and increasing entropy, which Felix Auerbach, in *Die Weltherrin und ihr Schatten* (1902), had personified as a dark goddess, being the bad force, and with the former fighting a losing battle against the latter (2).[20] But for others writers, entropy has assumed yet another, and even more intriguing, meaning, and that has to do with the momentous discovery of Claude Shannon, an engineer from the Bell Telephone Laboratories, who was the first to measure "information" in physical terms and who published, in "The Mathematical Theory of Communication" (1948), what has become the accepted function for "information, choice and uncertainty" (50). Finding that it was identical with that of entropy in statistical mechanics, he adopted that term, and tradition has it that he did so because John von Neumann advised him as follows:

> You should call it 'entropy' and for two reasons: first, the function is already in use in thermodynamics under that name; second, and more importantly, most people don't know what entropy really is, and if you use the word 'entropy' in an argument you will win every time! (qtd in Tribus, 2ff.)

Thus the entropy-concept entered the nascent discipline of information theory, where it assumed a crucial role when Norbert Wiener published his demanding monograph *Cybernetics, or Control and Communication in the Animal and the Machine* (1948). But it was only when Wiener addressed a lay audience and dealt with the social consequences of the new discipline in his extremely popular book *The Human Use of Human Beings: Cybernetics and Society* (1950) that the notion of informational entropy entered public discourse and soon became widely known.

Wiener's book was a warning against the repercussions of growing entropy in man's habitat—the world—and man's means of communication—language—; and it greatly relativized the cosmic *memento mori* of the Second Law. Although conceding, in a famous phrase, that "we are shipwrecked passengers on a doomed planet" (26), Wiener insisted that the world is full of islands of decreasing entropy and that therefore "the theory of entropy, and the considerations of the ultimate heat-death of the universe, need not have such profoundly depressing moral consequences as they seem to possess at first sight" (26). But what made his book so influential was not his qualified optimism, but his shift of interest from thermodynamic to informational entropy, through which he effected what might be called the "linguistic turn" of the Second Law from energy to information as the essential property. Starting from the insight that speech is man's most distinctive achievement, what he managed to convey to a large audience of non-specialists was this: As in thermodynamics the amount of energy available for work, so in cybernetics the amount of information conveyed depends on the complementary amount of entropy. And as in statistical mechanics an increase of entropy is understood as a molecular movement from the least to the most probable state, from organization and differentiation to chaos and sameness, so in information theory it is understood as a movement from more to less information, from unexpected and thus informative to predictable and thus empty messages. Therefore the physical world's "tropism for disorder, entropy" (*Novels* 93) as deplored by West's Miss Lonelyhearts, finds its linguistic analogue in Meatball Mulligan's quip in Pynchon's story "Entropy" that "most of the things we say, I guess, are mostly noise" (77).

By demonstrating that the information content of speech as the distinctive human characteristic can be measured by the same order-disorder ratio as the state of the material world, Wiener not only opened up intriguing possibilities of relating a given state of language to the concomitant state of the world, but also a more important possibility for which Zamyatin had so emphatically pleaded thirty years earlier,[21] namely that of arresting or at least slowing down the entropic decay of a part of the world by means of the most significant anti-entropic activity human beings are capable of, namely, the construction of meaningful messages. This re-accentuation of the Second Law explains why from the fifties onward ever more writers began to employ it as an appropriate paradigm of the human condition, because now their very craft assumed the additional dignity of being the most effective antidote against the running down of the universe.

But such adoption was beset with new difficulties, since it was not only Shannon who related thermodynamic to informational entropy, but also Leon Brillouin, another founding father of cybernetics, in his book *Science and Information Theory* (1956). Shannon was concerned with *potential* information as with what one could but does not yet know, and so he focused on the uncertainty present *before* a message is sent, whereas Brillouin was concerned with *actual* information as the knowledge already available or what he called negative entropy or *negentropy*, and so he focused on the uncertainty left *after* a message had been received. Consequently, for Shannon information and entropy were directly, whereas for Brillouin they were inversely, proportional. Mathematically this poses no problem whatsoever, but for literary critics who employ "entropy" and "information" not as numerical quantities but as evaluative categories, the choice of the one or the other of these definitions without understanding their implications results in diametrically opposed judgments. Following Shannon, they use "entropy" as synonymous with information and thus as a positive concept, as Porush does when he speaks of the "ideal of maximum entropy" (58) in the sense of an unlimited potential not yet domesticated by social and technological forces. But following Brillouin, they use "entropy" as a negative concept, as Abernethy does when he speaks of entropy as "a failure to communicate" (23). And the fact that many critics are ignorant of this difference and make do with simplified dictionary definitions explains the bewildering amount of contradictory and highly entropic comments on Pynchon and Gaddis.

Apart from this bewildering ambiguity and from the fact that the adoption of the entropy concept by cultural criticism has burdened the notions of "order" and "disorder," which in physics and cybernetics are value-free descriptions of molecular or informational aggregates, with aesthetic implications that are all too often unwarranted,[22] this adoption has also imported further contradictions, which result from two hotly contested issues. The first derives from Boltzmann's macrostate-microstate distinction, which turned the macroscopic entropy-notion of earlier thermodynamics into a stochastic concept and, by relating entropy to uncertainty, raised the vexing question as to whether this uncertainty refers to the state of the system observed or only to the observer's lack of knowledge about it. Today, there are the two camps of the materialists and the mentalists who conceive of "entropy" as either the immanent property of a given system or the measurement of an observer's lack of information about this system. The second issue arises from the unanswered question as to whether "entropy" in information theory and "entropy" in statistical mechanics are identical or only analogous. Both issues are closely related, since someone who conceives of a gain in entropy as a loss in information and vice versa will more easily concede the identity of the two entropy concepts than someone who insists on the "objective" quality of thermodynamic entropy and thus sees informational entropy as nothing but a heuristic analogy. Today, there are many scientists who claim that the Boltzmann and the Shannon equations are only symbolically isomorphic but otherwise have little in common.

Among the challenges which these unsettled issues pose for writers and the difficulties they create for critics, the most intriguing one is this: The fact that the amount of information necessary to describe a closed system undergoing irreversible processes grows proportionally to its increase in entropy bears the frightening message that the more one knows about the world, the more one needs to know about it, or, in other words, that one's knowledge about the universe cannot keep pace with the latter's irreversible development towards increasing disorder. This is another way of saying that the Second Law has changed a world of being, which for Newtonian physics appeared fully comprehensible in terms of the timeless laws that governed it, into a world of becoming that is ultimately incomprehensible, since now entropy is not only a quality of the observed object but also of the observing subject, and every answer inadvertently leads to a set of new questions. There is no "immaculate perception," as scientists like to quip—an insight which Gregory Bateson sees at the bottom of self-destructive "runaway systems" (328, 447, 490), which Lyotard considers an essential aspect of the "postmodern condition,"[23] and which might be said to provide the scientific *raison d'être* for the postmodern strategy of the narrative *regressus in infinitum*. This insight is most succinctly expressed in one of Jorge Luis Borges' *ficciones* en-

titled "Del rigor en laciencia," in which an emperor, who wishes to have a perfectly accurate map of his empire, leads his country into ruin because now the entire population
have to devote their energy to cartography (129). And it is laconically summed up in the
two mottos of Douglas Adams' *The Restaurant at the End of the Universe*, which read:

> There is a theory which states that if ever anyone discovers exactly what the Universe is for
> and why it is here, it will instantly disappear and be replaced by something even more bi-
> zarre and inexplicable. [. . .] There is another theory which states that this has already hap-
> pened. (153-54)

It is of course Thomas Pynchon's story "Entropy" (1960) that offers the seminal fictionalization of the Second Law in its newly acquired double meaning. This fugue-like story,
which was inspired by *The Education of Henry Adams* and Wiener's *The Human Use of Human
Beings*, artfully contrasts Meatball Mulligan's disorderly and totally random lease-breaking
party as an open system with Callisto's "hermetically sealed" (68) hothouse as a closed system and has Saul, the fugitive from a violent conjugal fight about "communication theory"
(75), add the aspect of informational noise. Through this constellation Pynchon brilliantly
thematizes the threat of both thermodynamic and informational entropy, and the crypti-
cally shortened epigraph from Henry Miller's *Tropic of Cancer* and other clues show that he
does not share Callisto's pseudo-intellectual view of an imminent heat-death, but achieves
the very opposite by relativizing the traditional understanding of the Second Law and by
upholding the possibility that its relentless workings can be at least temporarily stalled, not
only through pragmatic means—Meatball's decision to take action—but also through the
most negentropic gesture of all, the ordering work of the imaginative writer. This defiant
message is then unfolded in much greater depth in Pynchon's second and most tightly organized novel, *The Crying of Lot 49* (1966), which unfolds the entropy conundrum in all its
ramifications. Here the mysterious underground system of the Tristero offers a potentially
negentropic means of rescue from the growing entropy of a society on the verge of suffocating under its material and informational detritus. Here the mad inventor John Nefastis
develops Maxwell's Demon Box into a new—and significantly dysfunctional—machine,
which combines, in his words, "two distinct kinds of this entropy. One having to do with
heat-engines, the other to do with communication" (77). And here the puzzled heroine's
abortive quest for "a hieroglyphic sense of concealed meaning" (13) confirms the Second
Law's message of the world's ultimate incomprehensibility by reversing the traditional detective plot from a movement towards growing certainty, which culminates in a final denouement, into one of increasing uncertainty, which ends in a denial of closure.

In Donald Barthelme's minimalistic fictions, the Second Law also figures prominently, but instead of providing, as with Pynchon, a referential horizon for an all-embracing
view of a random world, it is conjured up through passing allusions, which are sprinkled
over the texts and illustrate their author's confession that "for me it's more attempting
to deal with parts instead of attempting to deal with the whole" (qtd. in Kakutani 20).

Thus, in "Down the Line with the Annual," it is observed that "we are adrift in a tense and joyless world that is falling apart at an accelerated rate" (*Guilty Pleasures* 4); in "The Rise of Capitalism," it is ironically stated that "the imminent heat-death of the universe is not a bad thing, because it is a long way off" (*Sadness* 146); and in "The Police Band," the orchestra is asked to "play 'Entropy'" (*Unspeakable Practices* 70). In the hilarious pop novel *Snow White* (1967), Dan defines his age as a "trash age" with regard to both material and informational waste, and when his cigar is described as "stretch[ing] from Mont St. Michel and Chartres, to under the volcano" (137), once more the shadow of Henry Adams is conjured up in the typical oblique manner. In Barthelme's fictional universe, linguistic exhaustion has far progressed, and chaos and inertia beckon on the horizon. But once again the imaginative writer can stall a development, in which the "stuff" of sense-making communication has turned into the "stuffing" of mere noise, by putting his polished negentropic tales against the entropic disorder of the world he describes and by insisting, as in "Sentence," that "the sentence itself is a man-made object, not the one we wanted of course, but still a construction of man, a structure to be treasured for its weakness, as opposed to the strength of stones" (*City Life* 121).

Whereas Barthelme deals in polished anti-entropic vignettes, Don DeLillo's major thematic concern is the betrayal of the once promising American Dream by an increasingly homogenized consumer culture. In his award-winning novel *White Noise* (1984), for example, he employs the entropy-concept as a yardstick for measuring the sickness of a world which not only produces ever-growing quantities of garbage, but also relies on "white noise," that is, the meaningless "information" incessantly disseminated by the contemporary mediascape, for the construction of its social reality. Since what the protagonist experiences as an "incessant bombardment of information" has long replaced what once was a shared reality by endlessly reproducible Baudrillardian *simulacra*, it is small wonder that one of the novel's characters can say that "the eventual heat death of the universe that scientists love to talk about is already well underway and you can feel it happening all around you in any large or medium-sized city" (24).

But the most comprehensive fictionalization of the Second Law and its cultural repercussions is provided by the elephantine novels of William Gaddis, whose art of excess recycles the detritus of an entropic society into negentropic art. Of his first novel, *The Recognitions* (1955), he said himself that "the concept of entropy—as removed from physics and the second law of thermodynamics to communications"[24]—plays an important part in it. But it is especially in the second, the immensely demanding *JR* (1975), that, to quote him again, "entropy rears as a central occupation of our time" ("Rush" 35). This novel is what Gaddis's fellow writer William Gass called an "acoustical collage" (Gass 102), which consists of a convoluted pattern of linguistic exchanges executed by disembodied voices and completely lacking the control of an ordering narrator. For the persevering readers who manage to creatively reconstruct this text, *JR* turns out to deal with both the destructive role of corporate capitalism and the failure of art in a money-mad America, and it fulfills John Barth's contention that "not just the *form* of the story but the *fact* of the story is symbolic; the medium is (part of) the message" (71). *JR* revolves around the Second Law from the opening scene—in which the failed writer Jack Gibbs, who not accidentally bears the name of Josiah Willard Gibbs, befuddles his school class with an erratic talk on order and chaos, mysteriously remarking that the world "can't be understood without a grasp of the second law of, yes?" and writing "ENTROPY" on the board (21)—to the scene in which he drunkenly explains to the failed composer Edward Bast why he cannot finish his book:

> [. . .] whole God damned problem listen whole God damned problem read Wiener on communication, more complicated the message more God damned chance for errors, take a few years of marriage such a God damned complex of messages going both ways can't get a God damned thing across, God damned much entropy going on [. . .]. (403)

And from the mad project of a machine that disposes of informational surplus by freezing noise to the hilarious experiment in teleportation, the text abounds with knowledgeable references to the history of entropy, with the latter experiment collating Thoreau's skeptical observation, "We are in great haste to construct a magnetic telegraph from Maine to Texas; but Maine and Texas, it may be, have nothing important to communicate" (52), with Norbert Wiener's contention that, since an organism is not defined by the tissue of its cells but by its informational pattern, "the idea that one might conceivably travel by telegraph, in addition to traveling by train or airplane, is not intrinsically absurd, far as it may be from realization" (139). This unique novel, which exposes an endtime civilization with an intimate knowledge of physics and cybernetics, is not, as uncomprehending critics would have it, an "entropic narrative" (Sawyer 122), but, on the contrary, a triumphantly negentropic investigation of the workings of both thermodynamic and informational entropy, and thus it sounds, in the author's own words, "a *real* note of hope" (Abády-Nagy 72).

Whereas the qualified hope which some contemporary authors have wrestled from the gloomy entropy-notion reminds one of earlier gestures of defiance from Horace's *exegi monumentum* to the adversative "but" in Shakespeare's Sonnets, the Second Law has recently developed—unbelievable as this may seem—new and objectively hopeful implications and thus belatedly achieved the very binary character of its competitor, apocalypse. As early as in the thirties, the Austrian biologist Ludwig von Bertalanffy developed his "General Systems Theory" in order to solve what he defined as "the violent contradiction between Lord Kelvin's degradation and Darwin's evolution, between the law of dissipation in physics and the law of evolution in biology" (39ff.), a puzzling contradiction that has kept the scientific community on their toes since Clausius's memoir. Meanwhile the systemic approach has been greatly refined by Ervin Laszlo and Erich Jantsch, fertilized by Walter B. Cannon's influential concept of the "homeostasis" of living beings, popularized by Fritjof Capra's bestseller *The Turning Point* (1982), and specified in James E. Lovelock's *Gaia* (1979), whose title, by the way, was suggested by the novelist William Golding and is shorthand for the daring notion that "the Earth's living matter, air, oceans, and land surface form a complex system which can be seen as a single organism and which has the capacity to keep our planet a fit place for life" (x).

All these writers have attempted to bridge the gulf between the natural sciences and the humanities, a gulf which C. P. Snow diagnosed as an abyss between "The Two Cultures" (1959) and, significantly, found illustrated by the culture critics' ignorance of the Second Law of Thermodynamics.[25] And all of them have done their very best to prove that the entropy-concept does not apply to open systems, which, as Bertalanffy postulated, maintain "themselves in a steady state, can avoid the increase of entropy, and may even develop towards states of increased order and organization" (40), and which, as Jantsch maintained, make things "much more complicated than suggested by the image of the general decay of structures in a 'heat death' as has been concluded from equilibrium thermodynamics" (59).

More often than not, such assertions were, to use the phrase from Banks' *Continental Drift* quoted above, "not truly an argument; [but] a vision." It was the Nobel Prize-winning chemist Ilya Prigogine's work in the new field of nonequilibrium thermodynamics which made them feasible by showing, as the *New York Times* phrased it, "How Life Could Defy Physics Laws" (Browne D19). Prigogine demonstrated that what he had named "dissipative structures," that is, open systems fluctuating in a non-linear way far from equilibrium, can under certain conditions spontaneously organize themselves at a more complex level by making deterministic but unpredictable leaps from what appears to be a state of chaos into what proves to be a state of new order. His programmatically entitled book, *Order Out of Chaos: Man's New Dialogue with Nature* (1984), bears the welcome message that the Second Law can be defied by processes in which order and organization arise spontaneously out of disorder and chaos through acts of self-organization, and thereby it changes the entropy-notion from an all-embracing *memento mori* into what he calls "a selection principle" (260). Prigogine's controversial insights, which have meanwhile been triumphantly corroborated by chaos theory and applied in numerous fields from population dynamics to traffic patterns, introduce time into physics and change it from a science of being into one of becoming, thus opening, as the title of the French original, *La Nouvelle Alliance*, suggests, chances for a new and promising cooperation between the natural sciences and the humanities.

Whereas it took a long time for literature to take note of the pessimistic entropy-concept, Prigogine's more optimistic variant almost immediately found its way into fiction, and it plays a central role for a school of science-fiction writers closely associated with Austin and the University of Texas, where the master teaches. These writers, especially Lewis Shiner and Bruce Sterling, employ Prigogine's idea of dissipative structures and the insights of chaos theory about the order hidden within apparent chaos for the purpose of projecting alternative worlds in which entropy has turned from a messenger of death into a harbinger of rebirth. Thus, at the end of Sterling's extremely complex novel *Schisma-*

trix (1985), whose beings pit their ordering *matrices* against the *schisms* dividing a universe drifting towards entropic decay, and whose history is measured in ascending "Prigoginic Levels of Complexity" (183), as defined in the thematically related story "Cicada Queen" by "the ancient Terran philosopher Ilya Prigogine" (64), a highly developed "presence" calmly states: "I'll wait out the heat-death of the Universe to see what happens next!" (287). Thereby it implies that the heat-death will not be the ultimate end but just another transitory stage from which a leap into a new beginning is possible.

It should be obvious by now that an adequate understanding of an ever more important segment of contemporary American fiction presupposes a thorough knowledge of the major variants of the Second Law, which, however, is deplorably absent from much fashionable criticism. Peter Koslowski's sweeping argument, for example, that whereas modernity owed its belief in progress, its conviction of growing complexity, and its evolutionary theories of biology and cosmology to the First Law of Thermodynamics, postmodernity owes its conviction of inevitable regress, its awareness of the limitations of energy and raw materials, and its replacement of belief in economic growth by a concern for ecological conservation to the Second Law,[26] can be easily shown as untenable. What one needs to realize instead is this: among those writers who mourn thermodynamic entropy as the gloomy messenger of an unavoidable end and see in it what Charles Bowden called "the ultimate nightmare of industrial culture" (102), those who fight informational entropy by means of the negentropic activity of meaningful storification and insist with Thomas Pynchon's Nefastis that "communication is the key" (*Crying* 77), and those who celebrate non-equilibrium entropy as a harbinger of new and spontaneous order out of chaos and believe with Bruce Sterling's character that the heat-death is not only the end of this but also the beginning of another world, the constantly evolving Second Law has assumed the ambiguously binary value system of its Biblical competitor.

In the apocalyptic paradigm, a tension between annihilation and rebirth results from the interplay of human sin and divine redemption. In the competing paradigm of the Second Law, tension between ultimate chaos and stasis, on the one hand, and new order and movement, on the other, results from an opposition between the gloomy insight that Boltzmann's logarithm of probability announces an irreversible movement towards randomness and disorder and the consoling message that the iterations of nonlinear dynamics promise the unexpected generation of new order or what is, more precisely, called "orderly disorder." Thus, instead of only threatening us with dire affliction, as seemed to be the case for over a century, the Second Law now also promises us hopeful transition. And since both its threat and its promise are not based on sin but on science, it allows for what might be called a modest millennialism for grateful agnostics.

NOTES

[1] See, e.g., the books by Robinson, Zamora, and, as the most recent contribution to the theme, Gysin.

[2] An English translation of the complete article is available as "On the Interaction of Natural Forces," in *Popular Scientific Lectures by Hermann von Helmholtz*, sel. and intr. by Morris Kline (New York: Dover, 1962).

[3] The original statements read "Die Energie der Welt ist constant" and "Die Entropie der Welt strebt einem Maximum zu."

[4] For the generic implications of Zoline's story, see Hewitt.

[5] For details, see my *Apocalypse to Entropy and Beyond: The Second Law of Thermodynamics in Post-War American Fiction*.

[6] In "Über verschiedene für die Anwendung bequeme Formen. . . ," Clausius said: "If one searches for a characteristic name for S, one could—parallel to saying about the quantity U that it is the warmth— and work-content of a body—say that it is the conversion-content of a body. Since I find it appropriate to take the names for such scientifically important quantities from the classical languages, so that they can be used in all modern languages without having to be changed, I suggest that the quantity S be named the *entropy* of a body after the Greek word ἡ τροπη, the conversion. I have purposively made the term *entropy* as similar as possible to the term *energy*, for both quantities which are to be named by these terms are so closely related with regard to their physical meanings that I find a certain similarity in their naming suitable" (390, trans. P. Freese).

[7] "It would have been better to have given a name to the extensity factor instead of the intensity factor of energy, for which the appropriate term 'ectropy' would have suggested itself, and then to formulate the principle: The ectropy of the world tends towards a maximum. In this way, the unfavorable tendency of the cosmic process would have found a direct and positive expression" (Auerbach 38ff., trans. P. Freese).

[8] See Heinz von Foerster: "[Clausius] realized what is going on here: with the decrease in the difference between the two temperatures, the convertibility, the change, the turning of heat energy into work, becomes less and less possible. Therefore he wanted to give this possibility of being able to turn or to change heat into work a good and catchy name. At that time it was very popular to use Greek for neologisms. So he went to his dictionary and looked up the Greek for 'change' and 'turn.' He found the word *trope*. 'Aha,' he said, 'but I would like to talk about *not change*, because, you see, the longer these processes go on, the less heat can be turned into work.' Now unfortunately, either he had a lousy dictionary, or he could not speak Greek very well, or he had friends who did not understand what he was talking about. Instead of calling it *utropy*, because *ou* is the Greek word for *non*, as in 'Utopia' (no place)—and *utropy* is what he should have called his new concept—for some reason he called it 'entropy,' because he thought that *en* is the same as the Latin *in* and therefore means 'no.' That is why we are stuck with the wrong terminology. And what is worse, nobody checked it! An incredible state of affairs!" (180ff.). The quotation from Clausius shows that von Foerster's charge is unfounded, since Clausius did not think that Greek *en* means *no*, but used it to mean *in*.

[9] Ludwig Boltzmann, who upheld the position of atomistics against the competing school of energetics, formulated the new understanding of entropy by arguing that the probability (W) of two independent configurations is represented by the product of the individual probabilities ($W = W_1 \times W_2$), while the entropy (S) is represented by the sum of the individual entropies ($S = S_1 + S_2$). Concluding that therefore the entropy must be proportional to the logarithm of the probability, he arrived at his famous equation $S = k \log W + c$, with k being the so-called Boltzmann constant and c being an arbitrary constant, the value of which depends on the particular circumstance of the problem under discussion.

[10] For a description of his experiment, see Loschmidt.

[11] James Clerk Maxwell first outlined his consequential thought experiment in a letter of 11 December 1867 to Peter Guthrie Tait, then described it in more detail in a letter of 6 December 1870 to Lord

Raleigh, and later incorporated yet another version into his *Theory of Heat* (1871), which is usually, and wrongly, cited as the first mentioning of the "Demon."

[12] Maxwell heartily disliked this designation and suggested in a letter to Tait that his "finite being" should be called "no more a demon but a valve" (quoted in P. M. Heimann, 204). And Clausius, when confronted by Peter Guthrie Tait with Maxwell's Demon as proof against his formulation of the Second Law, enragedly replied, in *Die Mechanische Wärmetheorie*, "My sentence is not concerned with what heat can do with the help of demons, but with what it can do on its own" (316, trans. P. Freese)

[13] An English version of Szilard's influential paper, which the University of Berlin accepted as *Habilitationsschrift*, was published posthumously as "On the Decrease of Entropy in a Thermodynamic System by the Intervention of Intelligent Beings," *Behavioral Science*, 9.4 (October 1964): 301-310.

[14] The Demon plays a central role in *The Crying of Lot 49*, and it also reappears in *Gravity's Rainbow*.

[15] In his *Cyberiada* (1965), the Polish science-fiction writer has a tale which, in the German translation (*Robotermärchen*, trans. I. Zimmermann-Göllheim and Caesar Rymarowicz [Frankfurt: Suhrkamp, rpt. 1978], pp. 200-219), is entitled "Wie Trurl und Klapaucius einen Dämon Zweiter Ordnung schufen, um Mäuler den Mäuler zu besiegen."

[16] See, e.g, the chapter on the "Wärmetodtheorie" as advanced by Clausius and still upheld by "einige bürgerliche Gelehrte" in Basarow, *Thermodynamik*.

[17] See the relevant quotations in Karl-Heinz Kannegiesser, 852.

[18] See his "Proposal to the Guggenheim Foundation," in *Novels and Other Writings*, 465f.

[19] "Plutot qu'anthropologie, il faudrait écrire 'entropologie' le nome d'une discipline vouée à étudier dans ses manifestations les plus hautes ce processus de désintégration" (Levi-Staus 478ff.).

[20] "What can be the use of energy in the long run, if its shadow, in correspondence with the progress of the world, will grow longer and longer the more evening falls upon the earth, and will finally envelop everything in dark night?" (trans. P. Freese).

[21] See Zamyatin's important essay, "On Literature, Revolution, Entropy, and Other Matters," and his attempt at fulfilling his own demand for a revolutionary and anti-entropic literature, his science-fiction novel *We*, which was first published in an English translation in 1924, whereas the Russian original appeared belatedly in 1952 in New York.

[22] For an attempt to sort out these misunderstandings see Rudolf Arnheim, *Entropy and Art: An Essay on Disorder and Order*.

[23] Lyotard, *The Postmodern Condition: A Report on Knowledge*, postulates that the price one has to pay for information constitutes an essential aspect of the "postmodern condition," and observes that "a complete definition of the initial state of a system (or all the independent variables) would require an expenditure of energy at least equivalent to that consumed by the system to be defined" (55).

[24] In an unpublished interview quoted in Tom LeClair, *In The Loop: Don DeLillo and the Systems Novel* (12).

[25] In *The Two Cultures: And a Second Look*, Snow argues that the scientific ignorance of literary intellectuals can be easily exposed by asking them to "describe the Second Law of Thermodynamics," that is, by having them perform an elementary task which according to him is "the scientific equivalent of: *Have you read a work of Shakespeare's?*"

[26] See Peter Koslowski,13.

WORKS CITED

Abády-Nagy, Zoltán. "The Art of Fiction CI: William Gaddis" [interview]. *Paris Review* 29.105 (1987): 56-89.

Abernethy, Peter L. "Entropy in Pynchon's *The Crying of Lot 49.*" *Critique, Studies in Modern Fiction* 14.2 (1972): 18-33.

Adams, Douglas. *The Hitch Hiker's Guide to the Galaxy: A Trilogy in Four Parts.* London: Book Club Associates, 1986.

Adams, Henry. *The Education of Henry Adams* [1907]. Intr. by James Truslow Adams. New York: Modern Library, 1931.

——. *The Degradation of the Democratic Dogma* [1919]. New York: Capricorn Books, 1947.

Arnheim, Rudolf. *Entropy and Art: An Essay on Disorder and Order.* Berkeley, Los Angeles, and London: U of California P, 1971.

Auerbach, Felix. *Die Weltherrin und ihr Schatten: Ein Vortrag über Energie und Entropie.* Jena: Gustav Fischer, 1902.

——. *Ektropismus oder die physikalische Theorie des Lebens.* Leipzig: Wilhelm Engelmann, 1910.

Banks, Russell. *Continental Drift* [1985]. Harmondsworth: Penguin, 1986.

Barth, John. "The Literature of Exhaustion." *The Friday Book: Essays and Other Nonfiction.* New York: Perigee, 1984. 62-76.

Barthelme, Donald. *Snow White* [1967]. Toronto: Bantam, 1968.

——. *Unspeakable Practices, Unnatural Acts* [1968]. Toronto: Bantam, 1969.

——. *City Life* [1970]. Toronto: Bantam, 1971.

——. *Sadness* [1972]. Toronto: Bantam, 1974.

——. *Guilty Pleasures* [1974]. New York: Delta, 1976

Basarow, I.P. *Thermodynamik.* 2nd ed. Berlin: VEB Deutscher Verlag der Wissenschaften, 1972.

Bateson, Gregory. *Steps to an Ecology of Mind: Collected Essays in Anthropology, Psychiatry, Evolution, and Epistemology.* London: Intertext Books, 1972.

Bennett, Charles H. "Demons, Engines and the Second Law." *Scientific American* 257 (November 1987): 88-96.

Bergson, Henri. *L'Evolution créatrice* [1907]. In his *Œuvres.* Paris: Presses Universitaires de France, 1970.

Bertalanffy, Ludwig von. *General Systems Theory: Foundations, Development, Applications.* London: Allan Lane the Penguin Press, 1971.

Borges, Jorge Luis. *Narraciones.* Edición de Marcos Ricardo Barnatán. Catedra: Letras Hispanicas, 1986.

Bowden, Charles. *Blood Orchid: An Unnatural History of America.* New York: Random House, 1995.

Browne, Malcolm W. "A Chemist Told How Life Could Defy Physics Laws." *New York Times* 12 October 1977: D19.

Brush, Stephen G. *The Kind of Motion We Call Heat: A History of the Kinetic Theory of Gases in the 19th Century.* Amsterdam, New York, and Oxford: North-Holland, 1976.

Clausius, Rudolf. "Über verschiedene für die Anwendung bequeme Formen der Hauptgleichungen der mechanischen Wärmetheorie." *Annalen der Physik und Chemie* 125 (1865): 353-400.

——. *Die Mechanische Wärmetheorie.* Vol. 2. *Die Mechanische Behandlung der Electricität* Braunschweig: Friedrich Vieweg, 1879.

DeLillo, Don. *White Noise* [1984]. New York: Viking Penguin, 1985.

Eddington, Sir Arthur. *The Nature of the Physical World.* 2nd ed. Ann Arbor: U of Michigan P, 1963.

Eliot, T.S. *The Complete Poems and Plays of T. S. Eliot.* London: Faber and Faber,. 1981.

Elkin, Stanley. *A Bad Man* [1967]. New York: E. P. Dutton, 1984.

Ellis, Bret Easton. *Less Than Zero* [1985]. New York: Viking Penguin, 1986.

Engels, Friedrich. *Dialektik der Natur* [1875]. Berlin: Dietz Verlag, 1973.

Fitzgerald, F. Scott. *The Great Gatsby* [1925]. Harmondsworth: Penguin, 1962.

——. *The Crack-up with Other Pieces and Stories* [1945]. Harmondsworth: Penguin, 1965.

Foerster, Heinz von. "Disorder/Order: Discovery or Invention?" *Disorder and Order: Proceedings of the Stanford International Symposium (Sept. 14-16, 1981)*. Ed. Paisley Livingston. Saratoga: Anma Libri, 1984. 177-89.

Freese, Peter. "Bret Easton Ellis, *Less Than Zero*: Entropy in the 'MTV Novel'?" *Modes of Narrative: Approaches to American, Canadian and British Fiction*. Ed. Reingard M. Nischik and Barbara Korte. Würzburg: Könighausen & Neumann, 1990: 68-87.

——. *From Apocalypse to Entropy and Beyond: The Second Law of Thermodynamics in Post-War American Fiction*. Essen: Die Blaue Eule, 1997.

Gaddis, William. *J R*. New York: Alfred A. Knopf, 1975.

——. "The Rush for Second Place." *Harper's* April 1981: 31-39.

Gass, William. "Authors' Authors." *The New York Times Book Review* 5 December 1976: 102.

Georgescu-Roegen, Nicholas. "Energy and Economic Myths." *Southern Economic Journal* 41 (1975): 347-81.

Gysin, Fritz, ed. *Apocalyps*. Tübingen: Narr, 2000.

Heimann, P. M. "Molecular Forces, Statistical Representation and Maxwell's Demon." *Studies in History and Philosophy of Science* 1 (1970): 189-211.

Helmholtz, Hermann von. "Über die Wechselwirkung der Naturkräfte und die darauf bezüglichen neuesten Ermittelungen der Physik." In his *Populäre wissenschaftliche Vorträge*. 2nd ed. Braunschweig: Friedrich Vieweg und Sohn, 1876. 101-133.

Hewitt, Elizabeth. "Generic Exhaustion and the 'Heat Death' of Science Fiction." *Science Fiction Studies* 21.3 (1994): 289-301.

James, Henry, ed. *The Letters of William James*. Vol. 2. New York: Kraus Reprint Co., 1969.

Jantsch, Erich. *The Self-Organizing Universe: Scientific and Human Implications of the Emerging Paradigm of Evolution*. Oxford: Pergamon, 1980.

Koslowski, Peter. *Die postmoderne Kultur: Gesellschaftlich-kulturelle Konsequenzen der technischen Entwicklung*. München: C. H. Beck, 1987.

Joule, James Prescott. "On Matter, Living Force, and Heat [1887]." In *The Scientific Papers*. Vol. I. London: Dawsons of Pall Mall, 1963. 265-276.

Kakutani, Michiko. "Donald Barthelme." *International Herald Tribune* 25 September 1981: 20.

Kannegiesser, Karl-Heinz. "Zum zweiten Hauptsatz der Thermodynamik." *Deutsche Zeitschrift für Philosophie* 9 (1961): 841-859.

Kermode, Frank. *The Sense of an Ending: Studies in the Theory of Fiction*. New York: Oxford U P, 1967.

Kesey, Ken. *Demon Box* [1986]. London: Methuen Paperbacks, 1987.

LeClair, Tom. *In The Loop: Don DeLillo and the Systems Novel*. Urbana and Chicago: U of Illinois P, 1987.

Lévi-Strauss, Claude. *Tristes Tropiques*. Paris: Librairie Plon, 1955.

Loschmidt, Josef. "Der zweite Satz der mechanischen Wärmetheorie." *Sitzungsberichte der Mathematisch-Naturwissenschaftlichen Classe der Kaiserlichen Akademie der Wissenschaften* 59.2. Abteilung, Heft I-V (1869): 395-418.

Lovelock, James E. *Gaia: A New Look at Life on Earth*. Oxford: Oxford UP, 1989.

Lyotard, Jean-Francois. *The Postmodern Condition: A Report on Knowledge*. Minneapolis: U of Minnesota P, 1984.

Nietzsche, Friedrich. *Der Wille zur Macht: Versuch einer Umwertung aller Werte* [1906]. In his *Werke*. sec. VIII, vol. III. Ed. Kritische Gesamtausgabe, Giorgio Colli, and Mazzino Montinari. Berlin and New York: de Gruyter, 1970.

Planck, Max. *Eight Lectures on Theoretical Physics Delivered at Columbia University in 1909*. New York: Columbia UP, 1915.

Porush, David. *The Soft Machine: Cybernetic Fiction*. New York and London: Methuen, 1985.

Prigogine, Ilya and Isebelle Stengers. *Order Out of Chaos: Man's New Dialogue with Nature*. Toronto: Bantam, 1984.

Pynchon, Thomas. *The Crying of Lot 49* [1966]. Toronto: Bantam Books, 1967.

——. "Entropy [1960]" In his *Slow Learner*. Toronto: Bantam, 1985.

Rifkin, Jeremy, with Ted Howard. *Entropy: A New World View*. London: Paladin, 1985.

Robinson, Douglas. *American Apocalypses: The Image of the End of the World in American Literature*. Baltimore and London: Johns Hopkins U P, 1985.

Sawyer, Thomas M. "JR: The Narrative of Entropy." *International Fiction Review* 10 (1983): 117-122.

Shannon, Claude, and Warren Weaver. *The Mathematical Theory of Communication*. Urbana, Chicago and London: U of Illinois P, 1972.

Snow, C. P. *The Two Cultures: And a Second Look*. Cambridge: Cambridge UP, 1965.

Spengler, Oswald. *Der Untergang des Abendlandes: Umrisse einer Morphologie der Weltgeschichte*. München: C. H. Beck, 1963.

Spenser, Herbert. *First Principles*. Vol. 1. *The Works of Herbert Spenser*. Osnabrück: Otto Zeller, 1904.

Steiner, George. *Proofs and Three Parables*. London: Faber and Faber, 1992.

Sterling, Bruce. *Schismatrix*. Harmondsworth: Penguin, 1986.

——. "Cicada Queen." In his *Crystal Express*. London: Legend, 1990.

Szilard, Leo. "Über die Entropieverminderung in einem thermodynamischen System bei Eingriffen intelligenter Wesen." *Zeitschrift für Physik* 53 (1929): 840-856.

——. "On the Decrease of Entropy in a Thermodynamic System by the Intervention of Intelligent Beings." *Behavioral Science* 9.4 (October 1964): 301-310.

Thomson, William, Lord Kelvin. "On a Universal Tendency in Nature to the Dissipation of Universal Energy." *Philosophical Magazine* 4 (1852): 304-06.

——. "The Sorting Demon of Maxwell" [1879]. Rpt. in Thomson. *Constitution of Matter*. Vol. 1 (of 3 vols). *Popular Lectures and Addresses*. London and New York: Macmillan, 1889. 137-141.

Thoreau, Henry David. *Walden*. Ed J. Lyndon Shanley, with an intr. by Joyce Carol Oates. Princeton: Princeton UP, 1989.

Tribus, Myron. "Thirty Years of Information Theory." *The Maximum Entropy Formalism: A Conference Held at the Massachusetts Institute of Technology on May 2-4, 1978*. Ed. Raphael D. Levine and Myron Tribus. Cambridge: MIT P, 1979. 1-14.

Updike, John. *The Poorhouse Fair* [1959]. Greenwich, Conn.: Fawcett, 1964.

——.*Rabbit at Rest* [1992]. Harmondsworth: Penguin, 1991.

——. *The Coup* [1978]. New York: Fawcett Crest, n.d.

Vonnegut, Kurt, Jr. *Cat's Cradle* [1963]. New York: Dell, 1970.

Wiener, Norbert. *The Human Use of Human Beings: Cybernetics and Society*. Boston: Houghton Mifflin, 1950.

Wells, H. G. *Selected Short Stories*. Harmondsworth: Penguin, 1965.

West, Nathanael. *Novels and Other Writings*. New York: Library of America, 1997.

Zamyatin, Yevgeny. "On Literature, Revolution, Entropy, and Other Matters." *A Soviet Heretic: Essays by Yevgeny Zamyatin*. Ed. and trans. Mirra Ginzburg. Chicago and London: U of Chicago P, 1970.

——. *We*. Trans. Bernard Guilbert Buerney. London: Jonathan Cape, 1970.

Zamora, Lois Parkinson. *Writing the Apocalypse: Historical Vision in Contemporary U.S. and Latin American Fiction*. Cambridge: Cambridge U P, 1989.

Zoline, Pamela. "The Heat Death of the Universe." *Best Science Fiction Studies from New Worlds 3*. Ed. Michael Moorcock. London: Panther, 1968. 89-103.

≈ Contributors ≈

KLAUS BENESCH is Professor of English and Chair of American Studies at the University of Bayreuth. His publications include *The Sea and the American Imagination* (editor/2003); *African Diasporas in the Old and the New World* (editor/2003); *Romantic Cyborgs: Authorship and Technology in the American Renaissance* (U of Mass P, 2002); *Technology and American Culture* (editor/1996); and *The Threat of History: Geschichte und Erzählung im afroamerikanischen Roman der Gegenwart* (1990). He has also contributed to numerous anthologies, journals, critical handbooks, and encyclopaedias.

CHRISTIAN BERKEMEIER is Assistant Professor of American Literature and Culture at the University of Paderborn. Since his dissertation on strategies of parody in Donald Barthelme, his research has been concerned with media in comparative contemporary literature and recent approaches to literary theory. His current project deals with reflections of fin de siecle aesthetics and aestheticism in contemporary fiction. He is the editor of a collection of essays on Paul Auster, a forthcoming essay collection on intermedia in American fiction, and a volume on travel narratives past and present.

HANJO BERRESSEM is Professor and Chair of American Literature and Culture at the University of Cologne. He has published books on Thomas Pynchon (*Pynchon's Poetics: Interfacing Theory and Text,* U of Illinois P) and on Witold Gombrowicz (*Lines of Desire: Reading Gombrowicz's Fiction with Lacan,* Northwestern UP). He is the editor, together with D. Buchwald und H. Volkening, of the collection *Grenzüberschreibungen: Feminismus und Cultural Studies* (Bielefeld: Aisthesis, 2001), and, together with D. Buchwald, of *Chaos-Control/Complexity: Chaos Theory and the Human Sciences* (special issue of *American Studies*, 2000).

MICHAEL BERÚBÉ is the Paterno Family Professor in Literature at Penn State University. He is the author of four books, including *Public Access: Literary Theory and American Cultural Politics* (1994) and *Life As We Know It: A Father, a Family and an Exceptional Child* (1996). He has written for a wide variety of academic and general journals, such as *PMLA, Modern Fiction Studies, American Literary History, American Quarterly, Social Text,* the *New Yorker, Dissent,* the *Nation,* the *Village Voice,* and the *New York Times.*

JOSEPH CONTE is Professor and Chair of English at the University at Buffalo. In addition to numerous articles, he is the author of *Design and Debris: A Chaotics of Postmodern American Fiction* (U of Alabama P, 2002), which won the press's Elizabeth Agee Prize for Best Manuscript in American Literary Studies for 2000; *Unending Design: The Forms of Postmodern Poetry* (Cornell UP, 1991); and a three-volume series of the *Dictionary of Literary Biography* devoted to American Poets Since World War II (Gale Research P, 1998).

DAVID COWART, Louise Fry Scudder Professor of English at the University of South Carolina, is the author of five books and numerous articles. His most recent book, *Don*

DeLillo: The Physics of Language (University of Georgia Press, 2002), won the $1000 SAMLA Studies Award (for best book published by a SAMLA member the previous year). An updated, paperback edition of this book was published by the University of Georgia Press in October 2003. He is completing a study of the contemporary literature of immigration.

CARL DJERASSI, Professor of Chemistry Emeritus at Stanford University, is one of the few American scientists to have been awarded both the National Medal of Science (for the first synthesis of a steroid oral contraceptive) and the National Medal of Technology. His literary writing (short stories, poems, 5 novels, 4 plays as well as an autobiography and a memoir) focuses on themes related to science. His newest book, *Newton's Darkness: Two Dramatic Views,* appeared in October 2003.

PETER FREESE is Professor and Chair of American Studies at the University of Paderborn and past president of the German Association for American Studies. His 40 books include *Die Initiationsreise* (1971; rpt. 1998), *Die amerikanische Kurzgeschichte nach 1945* (1974), *"America": Dream or Nightmare? Reflections on a Composite Image* (1990; 1994), *The Ethnic Detective* (1992), *From Apocalypse to Entropy and Beyond: The Second Law of Thermodynamics in Post-War American Fiction* (1997), and *Teaching "America": Selected Essays* (2002). He has published more than 150 articles on literature, popular culture, and EFL-methodology.

WALTER GRÜNZWEIG is Professor and Chair of American Literature and Culture at the University of Dortmund and Adjunct Professor at the University of Pennsylvania, State University of New York at Binghamton and Canisius College. He has published and edited books on 19th and 20th century American literature (Charles Sealsfield, Walt Whitman, and Upton Sinclair), on the Austrian author Peter Henisch, and on international educational exchange. Whereas most of his research focuses on transatlantic cultural dialogues, he also heads the interdisciplinary research group "Culture/Technology" at Dortmund.

CHARLES B. HARRIS directs the Unit for Contemporary Literature at Illinois State University. His books include *Contemporary American Novelists of the Absurd* (1971) and *Passionate Virtuosity: The Fiction of John Barth* (1983), his articles on recent American fiction and the profession of English studies have appeared in numerous scholarly journals and essay collections, and he is publisher of *American Book Review*. In 1997 the Modern Language Association honored him with the Francis Andrew March Award for Exceptional Service to the Profession of English.

N. KATHERINE HAYLES, John Charles Hillis Professor of Literature at the University of California, Los Angeles, teaches and writes on the relations of literature, science, and technology in the twentieth and twenty-first centuries. Her recent book, *How We Became Posthuman: Virtual Bodies in Cybernetics, Literature, and Informatics*, won the Rene Wellek Prize for the Best Book in Literary Theory for 1998-99. Her latest book, *Writing Machines* (2002), won the Susanne Langer Award for Outstanding Scholarship. She is currently at work on a book entitled "Coding the Signifier: Rethinking Semiosis from the Telegraph to the Computer."

UDO J. HEBEL is Professor and Chair of American Studies at the University of Regensburg. He was Distinguished Max Kade Visiting Professor at Colorado College, Colorado Springs, and a Visiting Scholar at the University of Michigan and Harvard University. He published *Romaninterpretation als Textarchäologie* (1989), *Intertextuality, Allusion, Quotation* (1989), *Transatlantic Encounters* (ed., 1995), *"Those Images of Jealuosie"* (1997); *The Construction and Contestation of American Cultures and Identities in the Early National Period* (ed., 1999), and *Sites of Memory in American Literatures and Cultures* (ed., 2003).

URSULA HEISE is Associate Professor of English and Comparative Literature at Columbia University, where she teaches contemporary literature and literary theory. She is the author of *Chronoschisms: Time, Narrative, and Postmodernism* (1997), and is currently completing a book entitled "World Wide Webs: Global Ecology and the Cultural Imagination." She has co-edited the twentieth-century volume of the *Longman Anthology of World Literature*. Her articles on late twentieth-century fiction, science and literature, and ecocriticism have been published in a variety of journals and essay anthologies.

JOHN J. JOHNSTON, Professor of English and Comparative Literature at Emory University, is the author of two books, *Carnival of Repetition: Gaddis's The Recognitions and Postmodern Theory* (1990) and *Information Multiplicity: American Fiction in the Age of Media Saturation* (1998). His edited book, *Literature, Media, Information Systems* (1997), contains an introduction to the German media theorist Friedrich Kittler and a selection of Kittler's essays. His recently completed book *The Lure of Machinic Life* discusses how new information machines and computational assemblages are transforming conceptual oppositions and opening new spaces of non-organic "life."

BRIAN McHALE is Distinguished Humanities Professor in English at the Ohio State University. Besides many articles on modernist and postmodernist fiction, contemporary poetry, and narratology, he is the author of *Postmodernist Fiction* (1987, twice reprinted) and *Constructing Postmodernism* (1992), and most recently of *The Obligation toward the Difficult Whole: Postmodernist Long Poems*, forthcoming early in 2004, which has been awarded the University of Alabama Press's Elizabeth Agee Award for the best book of the year in American Studies. He is co-editor of the journal *Poetics Today*.

MICHAEL PORSCHE is Professor of American Studies at the University of Paderborn. He has also taught at the universities of Bielefeld, Chemnitz, and Jena. In 1994 he received an ACLS-Fulbright research grant and spent the academic year at the University of New Mexico in Albuquerque. His books include *Der Meta-Western* (1992) and *Geographie der Hoffnung? Landschaft in der zeitgenössischen Erzählliteratur des amerikanischen Südwestens*. His articles on recent American fiction and popular culture have appeared in numerous scholarly journals and essay collections.

JOSEF RAAB is Associate Professor of American Studies at the University of Bielefeld. Raab is the author of *Elizabeth Bishop's Hemisphere* (1993) and he is currently completing a monograph entitled *The Borderlands of Identity in Mexican American Literature* as well as editing a collection of essays on *Hybrid Americas: Contacts, Contrasts, and Confluences in New World Literatures and Cultures*. Previously he (co-)edited *Das 20. Jahrhundert—Nachkriegszeit* (1998), *Negotiations of America's National Identity* (2000), and *American Vistas and Beyond* (2002).

JOSEPH TABBI is the author of *Cognitive Fictions* (Minnesota 2002) and *Postmodern Sublime* (Cornell 1995). He edits the *electronic book review* (www.altx.com/ebr), teaches at the University of Illinois at Chicago (www.uic.edu/depts/engl/-index.html), and has edited and introduced the last fiction and collected non-fiction of William Gaddis (Viking/Penguin). His essay on Mark Amerika appeared at the Walker Art Center's phon:e:me site, a 2000 Webby Award nominee. Also online (at the Iowa Review Web) is an essay-narrative, titled "Overwriting," an interview, and a review of his recent work.

CURTIS WHITE is a novelist and essayist. His novels include *Requiem* (2001) and *Memories of My Father Watching TV* (1998), both published by Dalkey Archive Press. His nonfiction work, *The Middle Mind: Why Americans Don't Think for Themselves*, appeared in 2003 with Harper San Francisco. He teaches at Illinois State University.

≈INDEX≈

SELECTED DALKEY ARCHIVE PAPERBACKS

PIERRE ALBERT-BIROT, *Grabinoulor.*
YUZ ALESHKOVSKY, *Kangaroo.*
FELIPE ALFAU, *Chromos.*
  Locos.
  Sentimental Songs.
IVAN ÂNGELO, *The Celebration.*
  The Tower of Glass.
ALAN ANSEN, *Contact Highs: Selected Poems 1957-1987.*
DAVID ANTIN, *Talking.*
DJUNA BARNES, *Ladies Almanack.*
  Ryder.
JOHN BARTH, *LETTERS.*
  Sabbatical.
ANDREI BITOV, *Pushkin House.*
LOUIS PAUL BOON, *Chapel Road.*
ROGER BOYLAN, *Killoyle.*
IGNÁCIO DE LOYOLA BRANDÃO, *Zero.*
CHRISTINE BROOKE-ROSE, *Amalgamemnon.*
BRIGID BROPHY, *In Transit.*
MEREDITH BROSNAN, *Mr. Dynamite.*
GERALD L. BRUNS,
  Modern Poetry and the Idea of Language.
GABRIELLE BURTON, *Heartbreak Hotel.*
MICHEL BUTOR, *Mobile.*
  Portrait of the Artist as a Young Ape.
JULIETA CAMPOS, *The Fear of Losing Eurydice.*
ANNE CARSON, *Eros the Bittersweet.*
CAMILO JOSÉ CELA, *The Family of Pascual Duarte.*
  The Hive.
LOUIS-FERDINAND CÉLINE, *Castle to Castle.*
  London Bridge.
  North.
  Rigadoon.
HUGO CHARTERIS, *The Tide Is Right.*
JEROME CHARYN, *The Tar Baby.*
MARC CHOLODENKO, *Mordechai Schamz.*
EMILY HOLMES COLEMAN, *The Shutter of Snow.*
ROBERT COOVER, *A Night at the Movies.*
STANLEY CRAWFORD, *Some Instructions to My Wife.*
ROBERT CREELEY, *Collected Prose.*
RENÉ CREVEL, *Putting My Foot in It.*
RALPH CUSACK, *Cadenza.*
SUSAN DAITCH, *L.C.*
  Storytown.
NIGEL DENNIS, *Cards of Identity.*
PETER DIMOCK,
  A Short Rhetoric for Leaving the Family.
ARIEL DORFMAN, *Konfidenz.*
COLEMAN DOWELL, *The Houses of Children.*
  Island People.
  Too Much Flesh and Jabez.
RIKKI DUCORNET, *The Complete Butcher's Tales.*
  The Fountains of Neptune.
  The Jade Cabinet.
  Phosphor in Dreamland.
  The Stain.
WILLIAM EASTLAKE, *The Bamboo Bed.*
  Castle Keep.
  Lyric of the Circle Heart.
JEAN ECHENOZ, *Chopin's Move.*
STANLEY ELKIN, *A Bad Man.*
  Boswell: A Modern Comedy.
  Criers and Kibitzers, Kibitzers and Criers.
  The Dick Gibson Show.
  The Franchiser.

  George Mills.
  The Living End.
  The MacGuffin.
  The Magic Kingdom.
  Mrs. Ted Bliss.
  The Rabbi of Lud.
  Van Gogh's Room at Arles.
ANNIE ERNAUX, *Cleaned Out.*
LAUREN FAIRBANKS, *Muzzle Thyself.*
  Sister Carrie.
LESLIE A. FIEDLER,
  Love and Death in the American Novel.
FORD MADOX FORD, *The March of Literature.*
CARLOS FUENTES, *Terra Nostra.*
  Where the Air Is Clear.
JANICE GALLOWAY, *Foreign Parts.*
  The Trick Is to Keep Breathing.
WILLIAM H. GASS, *The Tunnel.*
  Willie Masters' Lonesome Wife.
ETIENNE GILSON, *The Arts of the Beautiful.*
  Forms and Substances in the Arts.
C. S. GISCOMBE, *Giscome Road.*
  Here.
DOUGLAS GLOVER, *Bad News of the Heart.*
KAREN ELIZABETH GORDON, *The Red Shoes.*
PATRICK GRAINVILLE, *The Cave of Heaven.*
HENRY GREEN, *Blindness.*
  Concluding.
  Doting.
  Nothing.
JIŘÍ GRUŠA, *The Questionnaire.*
JOHN HAWKES, *Whistlejacket.*
AIDAN HIGGINS, *A Bestiary.*
  Flotsam and Jetsam.
  Langrishe, Go Down.
ALDOUS HUXLEY, *Antic Hay.*
  Crome Yellow.
  Point Counter Point.
  Those Barren Leaves.
  Time Must Have a Stop.
MIKHAIL IOSSEL AND JEFF PARKER, EDS.,
  *Amerika: Contemporary Russians View the
  United States.*
GERT JONKE, *Geometric Regional Novel.*
JACQUES JOUET, *Mountain R.*
DANILO KIŠ, *Garden, Ashes.*
  A Tomb for Boris Davidovich.
TADEUSZ KONWICKI, *A Minor Apocalypse.*
  The Polish Complex.
ELAINE KRAF, *The Princess of 72nd Street.*
JIM KRUSOE, *Iceland.*
EWA KURYLUK, *Century 21.*
VIOLETTE LEDUC, *La Bâtarde.*
DEBORAH LEVY, *Billy and Girl.*
  Pillow Talk in Europe and Other Places.
JOSÉ LEZAMA LIMA, *Paradiso.*
OSMAN LINS, *Avalovara.*
  The Queen of the Prisons of Greece.
ALF MAC LOCHLAINN, *The Corpus in the Library.*
  Out of Focus.
RON LOEWINSOHN, *Magnetic Field(s).*
D. KEITH MANO, *Take Five.*
BEN MARCUS, *The Age of Wire and String.*
WALLACE MARKFIELD, *Teitlebaum's Window.*
  To an Early Grave.

FOR A FULL LIST OF PUBLICATIONS, VISIT:
www.dalkeyarchive.com

SELECTED DALKEY ARCHIVE PAPERBACKS

FOR A FULL LIST OF PUBLICATIONS, VISIT:
www.dalkeyarchive.com

CPSIA information can be obtained
at www.ICGtesting.com
Printed in the USA
BVHW080356050820
585523BV00001B/116